Clear The Track

Clear The Track

A History of the Eighty-ninth Illinois
Volunteer Infantry,
The Railroad Regiment

PHILIP J. REYBURN

authorHOUSE®

AuthorHouse™
1663 Liberty Drive
Bloomington, IN 47403
www.authorhouse.com
Phone: 1-800-839-8640

Published by AuthorHouse   08/14/2012

ISBN: 978-1-4772-5415-8 (sc)
ISBN: 978-1-4772-5414-1 (e)

Library of Congress Control Number: 2012913586

DEDICATION

To my wife Pat for the occasional nudge to finish this project and to my grandmother, "Dollie" Reyburn, whose story about Uncle Theodore Rabourn, a soldier in Sherman's army, sparked a lifelong interest in the Civil War.

CONTENTS

INTRODUCTION

Twenty years ago, while searching for prairie remnants, my wife and I came across the Old Scot's Cemetery. Located west of Victoria, in Copley Township, Knox County, Illinois, is the site of the former John Knox Church with its 78-grave adjacent burial ground. The sacred ground, with its scattered headstones, some dating to the 1840s, has over the years been reclaimed by native grasses and wildflowers. In the back, and enclosed by an aged iron fence, are two graves, the final resting place of two Civil War soldiers—brothers who died on far-off battlefields to return home and lay side by side for eternity. The weathered markers, with their inscriptions barely legible, read as follows: *JOHN TAIT, PRIVATE IN CO G 89 REGT ILL VOL, DIED FROM THE EFFECT OF A WOUND REC'VD AT THE BATTLE OF DALLAS, GEO'A, MAY 27, 1864, AE 29 Y. 10 M. 27.; P G TAIT, LIEUT IN CO G 89 REGT ILL VOL, KILLED AT THE BATTLE OF NASHVILLE, DEC. 16, 1864, 26 YRS, 3 MO, 29 DAYS.*

It was the summer of 1992, when we came across the graves, and my wife jotted down the information carved on the stones. Months passed before I retrieved the note from the car's glove box. But after re-reading the words from the headstones, I was curious about these long-dead soldiers. Who were they? Why had their bodies been brought home? With these questions in mind, I spent a wintry Sunday afternoon at the local public library digging through local history. The initial effort was followed by many evenings and weekends there and at the Knox College Library. Those first months brought renewed interest in the Civil War and began two decades of historical research, culminating in a regimental history of the

Eighty-ninth Illinois Volunteer Infantry, better known as the Railroad Regiment.

From the beginning the goal was to write the history of the Eighty-ninth Illinois Infantry in the War of the Rebellion, but more importantly, the work would be in the voice and words of the men who served in the regiment. Accumulating letters, diaries, and memoirs from sources throughout the country turned into a labor of love. As the years passed, the material gradually came together, allowing for a detailed and in depth manuscript to be composed. But bear in mind, this book belongs to the men of the regiment, for it is their story.

Chapters are introduced with minimal background, providing the reader with an understanding of the period and/or the event covered. The basis of narrative is what regiment's soldiers saw and recorded, and in no measure is it a complete and objective history or analysis of the battles and engagements in which they participated. There is no assertion that the actions of the Railroad Regiment were pivotal in any battle or changed the course of the war. But, William F. Fox listed the Eighty-ninth Illinois Volunteer Infantry among the "Three hundred Fighting Regiments" of the war. In his *Regimental Losses in the American Civil War, 1861-1865*, he noted that 133 men or 10 percent of the regiment was either killed in action or died of wounds, with another 173 dying of disease, by accident, or in prison. Fifty men perished at Andersonville.

Other than a higher number of skilled laborers, the Eighty-ninth Infantry differed little from the other regiments which answered Lincoln's call to preserve the Union and put down the rebellion. These men in blue suffered privation, maiming and death, and saw it as a duty to their nation. One Eighty-ninth soldier, William James Tomlinson, spoke for most when he responded to his mother's urging that he find a way to be discharged wrote: "The cause in which I am engaged is the same today that it was the day I enlisted. I enlisted for three years unless sooner discharged and I expect to serve them if they see fit to keep me that long. If they do I shall not murmur at it. I had rather fall in battle than to be called a Copperhead. I will remain true to my county if I die by it."

*   *   *

For readability some minor changes were made in punctuation and spelling. On the whole this is a history written and told by the soldiers. The reader will find a wide range in education, and thus, writing ability. But no matter whether the soldier was a college graduate or barely literate, the hard marching, battles, foraging expeditions, sickness, camp life, and death was the same for all. As they engaged in the great adventure of their lives, these citizen soldiers recorded their thoughts and observations. By using their words, and therefore, making it their story, the author chronicled the war that the men, who made up the Eighty-ninth Illinois Infantry, saw and lived.

The effort would have been impossible without the assistance of a number of institutions and individuals. Carley Robison, Knox College archivist, and her staff, Bonnie Niehus, Kay VanderMeulen, and Maryjo McAndrew, were instrumental in locating material from the college's Ray D. Smith Civil War Collection. Bob Conklin, Marcia Heise, and Patty Mosher of the Galesburg Public Library assisted with interlibrary loan requests and with material from the library's Illinois Room. The staffs at the Abraham Lincoln Presidential Library in Springfield; the Illinois State Archives; Cambridge Public Library, Chicago Historical Society; Historical Society of Quincy and Adams County; Kendall County Historical Society; Navarro College, Pearce Collections Museum; University of Tennessee, Hoskins Library; Yale University, the Beinecke Rare Book and Manuscript Library; Stones River National Battlefield; Old Court House Museum (Vicksburg, Mississippi); and the U. S. Army Military History Institute, all provided research assistance. I wish to thank the following for the use of diaries, letters, photographs, or other material without which this history would not have come together: Gerard Buckman; Roddy A. Burwell; Ray Glasgow; Don Hamerstrand; Sally Hutchroft; Les Lipshutz; Thomas A. Pearson; Barbara Schenck; George Shuman; Karl Stark; Steve Stewart; and Sally Ryan Tomlinson. If I omitted anyone who assisted in this project, I herewith apologize.

I wish to thank both Lynn McKeown and Terry Wilson for reading the manuscript, recommending corrections, and offering suggestions that added materially to the final product. Needless to say, any errors within are entirely my own.

I, also, would be remiss if I did not thank my long-time friend, Steve Watts, for the open use of his law office photocopy machine.

Last but not least, I thank my wife, Pat, for her patience and willingness to visit Civil War battlefields/visitor centers, museums, and libraries across the country as I went about researching this project. And, it was Pat who firmly pointed out that my love of research was impeding my goal of writing a regimental history of the Eighty-ninth Illinois Volunteer Infantry. She further emphasized that I needed to produce a written work or my time and effort would have come to nothing. With that, not so gentle nudge, I began putting words to paper, while still keeping my eyes open for additional sources. At this point, I wish to state that this effort is in no way a complete or definitive history of the Railroad Regiment, but a base on which another researcher/historian can build.

CHAPTER 1

"WHAT ARE THE RAILROADS DOING?"

From the moment of his election, Abraham Lincoln faced one crisis after another. By late June 1862, the difficulty before the President was a manpower shortage. When the killed and wounded were combined with those lost from disease and desertion, the Union armies had been seriously reduced in size. The heaviest losses were suffered by Grant at Shiloh and by McClellan during the Peninsula campaign. For the Federal Government to put down the rebellion and to restore the Union additional men would be needed and they would have to be induced somehow to come forward.

The matter of raising troops was further complicated by the fact that Secretary of War Edwin M. Stanton, in a cost cutting measure, abolished the established recruiting-replacement system. He had concluded and decreed on April 3 that the Union Army was large enough to do the job. Lincoln would shortly realize this was a mistake. To hide the Administration's embarrassment and to keep the blunder from the public, Secretary of State Seward was dispatched to meet with the northern governors, who were at a conference in New York. Here it was agreed the governors would urge the President to call upon the states for new volunteers. A letter was dutifully written and signed by all. On July 1, Lincoln responded to the governors' request, accepted their offer, and called "into the service an additional force of 300,000 men."[1]

Following Lincoln's call for volunteers, Illinois Governor Richard Yates wrote the Chief Executive an advisory letter that was published throughout the state. Yates concluded Lincoln's cautious policy toward the rebels had failed and that "the time has come for the adoption of more decisive measures. Greater animus and earnestness must be infused into our military movements. Blows must be struck at the vital parts of the rebellion." He continued: "Mr. Lincoln, the crisis demands greater efforts and sterner measures. Proclaim anew the good old motto of the Republic, 'Liberty and Union, now and forever, one and inseparable . . . . '"He informed the President that "Illinois, already alive with the beat of the drum, and resounding with the tread of new recruits, will respond to your call. Adopt this policy, and she will leap like a flaming giant into the fight."[2]

Not as confident as Governor Yates, the *Chicago Tribune* feared that not enough young men could be found to fill the Illinois quota. In a column entitled, "Shall We Draft?" the editor wrote that "the labor markets of the North, caused by the rush of young men to the field, has given profitable employment to those who remained at home; and at this stage of the contest it is hard to persuade the man who is in the receipt of good pay . . . that there is an exigency which demands of him the sacrifice that he is called upon to make." He added however: "We trust we are mistaken and that the result will prove that we have underrated the patriotism of the class to which the Government has sent out its appeal." But in the same breath he concluded: "In this emergency, we may say it would be the extreme of folly to [a]wait the voluntary gathering of the forces that the Government has the undoubted power to compel."[3]

To ignite the fire of patriotism, Union defense committees sprang up, organizing rallies in cities and villages throughout the

---

[1]   Marvin A. Kreidberg and Merton G. Henry, *History of Military Mobilization in the United States Army 1775-1945* (Washington, D. C.: U. S. Government Printing Office, 1955), 102-103; Chicago *Tribune*, July 4, 1862. *Chicago Tribune*, July 12, 1862.

[2]   *Chicago Tribune*, July 12, 1862.

[3]   *Chicago Tribune*, July 9, 1862.

North. Politicians of all stripes and importance came forward to make speeches calling for volunteers to come to the defense of the flag and to the aid of the government, so it could maintain "its dignity and power, by sustaining its Constitution and executing the laws in every portion of our country . . . ."[4]

In the new call for 300,000 volunteers, the Illinois quota was set at 28,000 men. To spur enlistment the State offered every man who signed up for three years his first month's pay of $13 in advance. Twenty-five dollars of the $100 bounty would also be paid immediately upon muster and a $2 premium to each accepted recruit or a total of $40 up front. Chicago and Cook County offered another $60.[5]

Governor Yates immediately commissioned recruiting officers whose duties were spelled out in General Order No. 42 released by Illinois Adjutant General Allen C. Fuller on July 14. It was the duty of these men to raise a company a full company consisting, on paper at least, of 101 men. If an enlisting officer failed to get enough signatures, lists would be consolidated until the required number was attained. Once a company was organized, the men were transferred to temporary rendezvous camps located throughout the state.[6]

With a war meeting called for the evening of July 19 at 8:00 P.M., the *Tribune* encouraged: "All patriotic citizens of Chicago, without distinction of party, who are disposed to lend their aid and support to the best Government known to mankind, are earnestly requested to attend a Mass Meeting . . . ." The purpose of the gathering was to express "our undiminished confidence in the justice of the Federal Union cause, and our inflexible determination to put down armed rebellion at all hazards, and to maintain the supremacy of the Constitution and Laws . . . ."[7]

Robert Tarrant, an employee of the Chicago and Milwaukee Railroad, confided in his diary on Saturday, July 19, 1862: "There is a large war meeting called to night at Bryan Hall." He added,

---

4   *Chicago Tribune*, July 18, 1862.
5   *Chicago Tribune*, July 16 and 19, 1862.
6   *Chicago Tribune*, July 16, 1862.
7   *Chicago Tribune*, July 19, 1862.

"There will also be speaking at the Metropolitan Hall and in the Court House Square." The next day, Tarrant wrote: "The meeting last night was very large and enthusiastic. I stayed until it was out [at] 11 ½ o'clock."[8]

The doors of Bryan Hall were opened to the sound of bells ringing and cannon firing. As the crowd poured in, Barnard's Light Guard Band entertained by playing "Hail Columbia," "The Star Spangled Banner," and "Yankee Doodle." Those assembled that evening heard the speakers express "one common sentiment—the salvation of our common country...." The *Tribune* reported: "A prevailing characteristic of all the meetings was the unanimous and hearty approval of every sentiment favorable to the confiscation of rebel property, foraging upon the enemy, and the employment of blacks in the fighting against the rebels." Some speakers went as far as calling for arming the blacks to fight and "if necessary . . . giving him his freedom for it." *The Tribune* concluded: "There was no dissent from the proposition that we should use every means that Providence has given us to put down the rebellion."[9]

When all the venues were totaled, the *Tribune* writer estimated the crowd at about 15,000. It was, he wrote, "an imposing gathering in enthusiasm, in spirit, in numbers." Money had been pledged and enlistment encouraged. The case for preserving the Union at any cost, using any means was made. Now the men needed to carry out this task had to be found, equipped, and sent to the field.[10]

On Tuesday, July 22, the Chicago Board of Trade held a war meeting of its own, and members pledged $11,500 to the war effort. The following day the subscriptions jumped to $17,000, with 172 men enlisting in the Board of Trade Regiment, while the Board of Trade Battery was reported "full, to overflowing."[11]

---

8   Robert Tarrant, diary entries for July 19 and 20, 1862, original diary at the Chicago Historical Society, hereafter cited as Tarrant diary.

9   *Chicago Tribune*, July 21, 1862.

10   *Ibid.*

11   *Chicago Tribune*, July 23 and 24, 1862. The Chicago Board of Trade sponsored two regiments the 72nd and the 88th Illinois Infantry and were known respectively as the First and Second Chicago Board of Trade Regiments.

Efforts were now in full swing to gin up patriotism and enthusiasm for the war. A second mass meeting was called for Saturday afternoon, July 26. At 2:00 P.M. all the city bells were rung for a half-hour. While the bells tolled, minute guns fired for an hour. Once more the *Chicago Tribune* asked the citizenry to "rally and gather every patriot, to kindle anew the fires of our zeal . . . and from to-day as never before let the stern duty of the war begin." Robert Tarrant noted: "There was a gigantic War Mass Meeting this P.M. at [the] Court House square. All the shops, Banks & places of business in the City were closed." The *Tribune* expressed the hope that "this vast uprising of the people . . . will give a material impetus to recruiting . . . ." The speakers told the crowd, estimated at twenty thousand, that the authority of the Constitution had to be restored and the Union preserved at any sacrifice. As freedom loving people, they were asked "to act and fight for liberty." [12]

However, it was soon apparent that the patriotic rallies filled with fiery speech were not generating the needed volunteers. With enlistment slow, the *Tribune* on July 26 wrote that a date must be set, "say August 15th," after which *"drafting will commence."* The writer concluded "this would bring activity to the work of recruiting. Men would come forward eagerly, unwilling to lose at once the bounty to volunteers and the opportunity for choice in their company and regiment." Three days later the *Tribune* editorial resumed, stating "that in spite of the rub-a-dubbing and spouting, and in spite of the extraordinary inducements offered in the way of bounties, the men are not enlisting." The paper's headline was "WHY NOT DRAFT?"[13]

While the *Tribune* fretted, individual and collective efforts continued. The Chicago Mercantile Association formed a committee and met Tuesday morning, July 28. They resolved to sponsor a battery and regiment. Observing the effort of the Mercantile Association and the Board of Trade, the *Tribune* took the railroads to task in a piece the editor headlined, "What Are the Railroads Doing?" Based on an informed source, the *Tribune* could report: " . . . that a company is about to be organized for the Board of Trade regiment to be styled the 'W. R. Arthur Guards,' in [a] compliment to the superintendent

[12]   *Chicago Tribune*, July 26 and 28, 1862; Tarrant, diary, July 26, 1862.
[13]   *Chicago Tribune*. July 26 and 29, 1862.

of the Illinois Central Railroad. Mr. Arthur, in furtherance of the plan, is using his influence to have every station upon the road furnish a man." "Now this is a good example," the writer noted." "What are the rest of the railroad corporations doing? The Board of Trade have raised a battery and are organizing a regiment to support it. The Mercantile Association are working in the same direction. Why do not the railroads put into the field a railroad regiment? They can do it quickly and easlly [sic]."[14]

The writer proceeded to put forth a plan. "Let each company agree to pay a bonus of $50 per man for a full company of 101 men. Every man upon the company pay roll would most cheerfully assent to an assessment of three per cent per month to create a fund for the support of families or care of sick and wounded. Will not Chicago furnish a railroad regiment? Let this set the example and every railroad in the State will send forth a company. What say the railroads? Will they respond?"[15]

Two days later, July 30, the Board of Directors of the Pittsburgh, Fort Wayne and Chicago Railroad, while holding a scheduled meeting in Chicago, voted a sum of $12,800 to be used in paying bounties to volunteers. The money would go to counties through which their road ran. Fifteen hundred dollars were earmarked for Cook County, with the money being paid into the Board of Trade Fund. It appears the directors' action was more in line with the patriotic atmosphere of the country than the request of the *Chicago Tribune*. In complimenting the Pittsburgh, Fort Wayne and Chicago Railroad, the *Tribune* chided the industry as a whole. "The generosity of the road is praiseworthy and should stimulate contributions from other railroad companies abundantly able to subscribe liberally."[16]

A month had passed since Lincoln's call for 300,000 more men, and volunteers were slowly responding. The city of Chicago on August 1 held its third war meeting, with ten thousand gathering

---

[14] *Chicago Tribune*, July 29, 1862. The Mercantile Association was an organization of prominent Chicago merchants. While the Chicago Board of Trade established in 1848 to help set agricultural product prices, dealt in trading commodities futures and options contracts (e.g. corn, wheat, etc.).

[15] *Ibid.*

[16] *Chicago Tribune*, July 31, 1862.

in the Courthouse Square. Once more, Robert Tarrant joined the crowd and in a few words summed up the event in his diary. "Went down to a war meeting this evening & heard Gov. Yates, the Hon. Mr. Sherman of Ohio & Lovejoy of Ill. The speaking was excellent." The *Tribune* summed up Yates' speech. "Fight, confiscate and emancipate are now the three articles of every patriot's creed . . . ." However, patriotic speeches and rallies could only do so much. The Lincoln Administration would wait no longer, men were needed now, and they would have to be made to come forward.[17]

The War Department notified the northern governors that if any state failed to meet its quota of three-year volunteers by August 18 a special draft from the militia would be held to make up the difference. All men between 18 and 45 were considered part of the militia, and therefore, subject to the draft. The order listed a number of exceptions. Men employed as telegraph operators, railroad engineers, arsenal and armory workers, pilots, and the merchant marine would not be drafted. The Vice President, members of Congress, judges, certain Federal appointees, custom officials, and postal workers were also exempt. August 15 was the final day volunteers would be accepted for new regiments. All men volunteering or drafted after that date would be used to fill up the old regiments.[18]

Writing from Augusta, Illinois, William James Tomlinson told his brothers, Uriah and Joel, that "ther is a call for 300,000 men. It is thought they will have a draft to get them. If they draft heare, I shall enlist." Tomlinson stated that he would enlist before he would let himself "be drafted and be put in front of battle like sheep." Tomlinson then turned to the current Confederate offensive. "The Rebels are marching on Nashville with 15,000 strong. They are

---

[17] *Chicago Tribune*, August 4, 1862. John Sherman, brother of William Tecumseh Sherman, in 1861 had been elected to fill Salmon O. Chase's vacant Ohio Senate seat. Owen Lovejoy, brother to Elijah Lovejoy, the abolitionist martyr slain by an Alton, Illinois mob, resided in Princeton, Illinois where he was elected a Republican member of Congress in 1856.

[18] *Annual Report of the Adjutant General of the State of Illinois* (Springfield: Baker and Phillips, Printers, 1863), 32-34; Kreidberg and Henry, *History of Military Mobilization in the United States Army*, 104.

raising in Kentucky again. Ther is excitement in Louisville for feare of an attack."[19]

Tarrant entered in his diary for August 5: "The President yesterday issued orders for a draft of 300,000 men." He then wrote: "Hank Rowell commenced recruiting a company on our road today." A carpenter for the Chicago and Milwaukee line, Henry L. Rowell was thirty-one and single. In appearance he stood six feet with blue-eyes and sandy hair. He must have been a natural leader for Tarrant writes on August 7: "Hank Rowell is getting his company pretty well filled up. He has got 37 names." The following afternoon thirty-six men from the Milwaukee Company were sworn in. Tarrant noted: "Recruiting goes on very briskly this week."[20]

At Aurora, forty miles west of Chicago on the Chicago, Burlington, and Quincy line, thirty-two-year-old John Watkins, a railroad agent, and thirty-four-year-old machinist Bruce Kidder, were already busy enrolling a company of railroad men. On Thursday, July 24, the *Aurora Beacon* pronounced Watkins' company would be full by the week's end.[21]

Out at Amboy, Lee County, Illinois, a passenger train conductor for the Illinois Central Railroad, twenty-seven-year-old Samuel C. Comstock, acquired the necessary documents to become a recruiting officer. On August 8, he commenced signing up men, and by the 15, he had eighty-eight enrolled.[22]

Seven days had passed since the *Chicago Tribune* challenged the railroads to action. Their August 6 issue revealed the managers had heard the newspaper's call. The *Tribune* reported: "There is now a practical movement on foot whereby the various companies being recruited on the several trunk lines leading into Chicago will be consolidated into a regiment; and although the plan has

---

[19] Sally Ryan Tomlinson, *In Good Courage: The Civil War Letters of William James Tomlinson* (San Francisco: 1982, Revised 1995), 1.

[20] Tarrant, diary, August 5, 7, and 8, 1862; "Muster and Descriptive Roll of Co. C," 89 Infantry Regiment, Record Group 301, Illinois State Archives.

[21] *Aurora Beacon*, July 24, 1862; "Muster and Descriptive Roll of Co. E," 89 Infantry Regiment, Record Group 301, Illinois State Archives.

[22] "Muster and Descriptive Roll of Co. I," 89 Infantry Regiment, Record Group 301, Illinois State Archives.

not assumed such a tangible and official form as will warrant our publication of the details, we are satisfied that to-day the full arrangements will be made whereby a new regiment, and that right speedily raised, will be put in the field from this district. The plan, to our mind, promises better than, any yet proposed, and we heartily wish it the best success." They even went as far as to brag that "one regiment of railroad men and mechanics is worth two of the best infantry put into the field under any auspices."[23]

That same edition of the *Tribune* carried a story with the headline, "Patriotic Action of the Galena & Chicago Union Railroad Employees." On Saturday evening, August 2, the men working in the road's machinery department met at the shop to discuss the current crisis. They readily agreed that "the time has come, and now is, when every man ought to prove his loyalty and his patriotism . . . ." These employees concurred that "many men would gladly volunteer their services to fight the enemies of their government, could they be assured that their families would be assisted and cared for . . . ." And finally the workers concluded: "It is the bounden duty of every loyal man, if he cannot drop his tools and leave his family, and go to the defense of country, to contribute to the best of his ability towards protecting and assisting the dependent ones of those who can and will exchange the peace [of] professional labors for the danger of the battle field . . . ." To back up their words, the men formed a Soldiers' Relief Society "for the benefit of soldiers and the families of soldiers who have gone or may go into the army from this department . . . ." They then unanimously agreed to a three percent assessment on each member's monthly earnings.[24]

On July 29, four days before the machinery shop men met, Herbert M Blake, a twenty-nine-year-old painter with the Galena and Chicago Union Railroad began a recruiting campaign on the line. Eighty-one men had signed Blake's muster roll by August 8. Of this number, sixty-five joined after the Soldiers' Relief Society was formed.[25]

---

[23] *Chicago Tribune*, August 6, 1862.

[24] *Ibid.*, August 6, 1862.

[25] "Muster and Descriptive Roll of Co. K," 89 Illinois Regiment. Record Group 301, Illinois State Archives.

For all intents and purposes the organization of a Railroad Regiment can be seen as a case of the tail wagging the dog. While companies of railroad men were being raised and support groups organized to aid their families, newspapers across Chicago reported on Thursday, August 7, that the superintendents and managers of the railroads headquartered in the city would meet that day to initiate the organization of a Railroad Regiment. The *Tribune* reported: "We give elsewhere the details of the Railroad Regiment now being rapidly enrolled, the joint product of the patriotism and enterprise of the several lines centering here. It will prove of the best kind of stock, and will be excellently officered. Col. Forsyth, long and widely known as general freight agent of the Illinois Central Railroad, will make an admirable officer, and the whole regiment, throughout, will reflect high credit upon our city and State."[26]

With both the *Tribune* and the *Evening Journal* posting nearly identical pieces in their August 7 editions, someone associated with the railroads must have released a statement to the press. Even though railroad titans were still unorganized and the Railroad Regiment was only talk, they showed no lack of confidence. The articles began: "The Board of Trade Regiment must look to their laurels, for although first organized, and receiving names two weeks in advance of the Railroad Regiment, the latter bids fair to be the first full regiment in camp. Already ten companies are nearly full; the number of names on the several muster rolls at dark yesterday was by actual count six hundred and twenty-three! To the proposed regiment the Illinois Central Railroad contributes two companies; the Chicago, Burlington and Quincy, one company; the Galena and Chicago, two; the St. Louis, one; the Pittsburg [sic], Fort Wayne and Chicago, one; the Rock Island, one; the Milwaukee and Northwestern, each one—in all ten companies. These companies will be full, and the regiment will number *a thousand men by Saturday night.*" Having never met to formally adopt a plan, the railroad leaders audaciously proclaimed that in forty-eight hours they would assemble enough men for a full regiment.

That same day the railroad executives planned to meet and hammer-out the final arrangements for the regiment's organization.

---

[26]   *Chicago Tribune*, August 7, 1862.

It was hinted that the Illinois Adjutant General might be present. While behind the scenes, it was said, the railroad brass had settled on Robert Forsyth, General Freight Agent of the Illinois Central road, to be the regiment's colonel. Both papers agreed that this selection could not have fallen "upon a worthier man, nor one better calculated for the position." The release concluded with a statement from the Illinois Central Railroad. Hearing of the Galena and Chicago's effort, the road's employees notified Superintendent William R. Arthur of their intent to donate five percent of their annual wages to a fund supporting the families of those fellow workers who enlisted.[27]

That same day the Democratic *Chicago Times* carried a complementary story on the formation of a regiment comprised of Chicago railroad men. The paper either failed to receive or chose not to publish the press release. The *Times* reported: "For several days past there has been a movement on foot, looking towards the organization and raising of ten companies to be known as the Chicago Railroad Regiment. The project was well received from the start by superintendents and managers of all the principal railroad lines leading from this city, who have given it their earnest and unanimous support. The Galena and Chicago Union, the Chicago Burlington and Quincy, the Illinois Central, and the Pittsburg, Fort Wayne and Chicago Railroads have all lent their aid to the enterprise, and now present over six companies of men ready to enter camp on Friday." The reporter added: "And they will be no mean fighting material either, they will comprise the sturdy engineer, and machine-shop men, and brakemen, and the cautious conductor, who leave their lucrative positions and for the country's service. The regiment will be officered by picked men, while the ranks will consist of such fighting men as never entered regiments before. The scheme is not a pet one to be created to-day and abandoned to-morrow, but is already a fixed fact."

The *Times* went on to note that the superintendents and managers of the railroads would meet at 9:00 A.M.. to put together the final organization. Robert Forsyth, the General Freight Agent of the Illinois Central Railroad, the *Times* added, has led the enterprise

---

[27] *Chicago Tribune*, August 7, 1862; *Chicago Evening Journal*, August 7, 1862.

and is to be in charge of the regiment when it is completed. The newspaper endorsed Forsyth stating that he was a man "of marked administrative ability, and all the requisite qualifications that combine to make a fighting man and an excellent general manager. Under his lead and under the auspices of the principal railroad men in the city the organization will not lack, and will be pushed on to a complete and speedy success."[28]

The highly publicized meeting finally took place that evening at 8:00 P.M. in the McCormick Building on Dearborn Street. The railroad leaders gathered at the law office of Robert Hervey and Elliot Anthony for a short session. Colonel Charles G. Hammond, General Superintendent of the Chicago, Burlington, and Quincy Railroad, was chosen to chair the committee, while A. Bigelow of the Michigan Central Railroad was elected secretary. After those details were completed, Robert Forsyth took the floor and said "as one of those who had been instrumental in calling the meeting, he felt called upon to explain their intended action." In plain words a number of men "wanted to raise a regiment of railroad men, and he had no doubt it could be done speedily, if permission were granted to do so." Forsyth informed the group that "he had called upon the Governor, but had been unable to see him."[29]

Colonel Hammond then interjected that "commissions had been given only for the formation of companies, not regiment or brigades. It was contrary to the well known rule to give any man or men the authority to raise a regiment, still he had no doubt that if the Governor was satisfied that a sufficient number of companies could be raised from the employees of the roads, he would be quite willing to have them consolidated into one regiment."[30]

Forsyth then proposed that a committee be appointed to present the issue of a Railroad Regiment before the Governor. Elliot Anthony spoke up telling the committee that he "had seen the Governor already, and had ascertained that, if the men of the various railroads could get up a regiment, Governor Yates would be happy to further the project." Continuing, he informed his colleagues that "a letter was

---

[28]   *Chicago Times*, August 7, 1862.

[29]   *Chicago Times*, August 8, 1862; *Chicago Tribune*, August 8, 1862.

[30]   *Chicago Times*, August 8, 1862.

received from the Governor . . . in which he stated that the rule was to raise men by companies, but this need not prejudice such action as was contemplated, for companies could be consolidated."[31]

Colonel Hammond rose to say that it should be their "very first consideration . . . to find persons to lead who would take care of their men." He emphasized that "many of their men had been in the employ of the company for years, and were regarded by him almost as members of his own family. While men could not—and he felt confident the railroad volunteers would not—shrink from necessary hardships, it was due to them as to the country that all proper care should be taken of them."[32]

Taking the floor again, Forsyth proclaimed "that the discipline to which railroad men were subjected was akin to that of the army." It was his opinion that: "They would make the very best, the most obedient of soldiers, and he thought that it would not be well to throw open the rolls to any but railroad employees, unless men enough could not be found without it, and he apprehended no difficulty on that head." He then told the committee that the Illinois Central was good for at least two companies. Recruiting on the Illinois Central line was in full swing, and the *Tribune* announced that day that J. A. Bunce, the recruiting officer for the Forsyth Guards, muster roll was nearing the minimum number.[33]

Anthony announced the Galena and Chicago Union was "good for two companies." Joseph Moore of the Pittsburgh, Fort Wayne and Chicago said they could put together one company. Seth C. Baldwin told the committee the Chicago and Milwaukee had one company two-thirds full, while C. C. Wheeler of the Chicago, Alton and St. Louis said they had 120 men already recruited. Charles Tappan, speaking for the Chicago and Northwestern, told the group his road had already raised one company, but it was to be part of a Wisconsin regiment. He felt they could raise another company.[34]

The muster rolls of several recruiting officers were reviewed, and it was determined "that already more than half an entire regiment

---

[31] *Ibid.*

[32] *Ibid.*

[33] *Chicago Times*, August 8, 1862; *Chicago Tribune*, August 8, 1862.

[34] *Chicago Times*, August 8, 1862.

had enlisted . . . ." After further discussion a committee was appointed: to procure authority from the Governor to raise a Railroad Regiment; to ensure that men belonging to the different railroads had commissions to recruit companies to form a regiment; to make sure that their meetings were publicized; to appoint a temporary Quartermaster and Adjutant, who would see to the organization of the regiment; and to obtain necessary workspace.[35]

At the committee's request, Forsyth took over organizing the regiment. His acceptance was conditioned on the understanding that he would not be considered as a candidate for any regimental position. Forsyth wanted to do all he could for the cause, and he wanted it clear that he was not angling to be an officer, nor would he accept any appointment as one. The next day Forsyth penned a note to Adjutant General Fuller explaining that "our Rail Road men are anxious to get up a regiment . . ." and that he been delegated "the duty of organizing & supporting same." To start the ball rolling, Forsyth sought Fuller's "authority and sanction," assuring the adjutant general that he could "place in the field a superior body of men."[36]

"The railroad men of our city are taking hold of the war in earnest, and have determined upon raising a regiment, to be composed chiefly or entirely of employees upon the various roads centering in Chicago," the Saturday, August 9 edition of the *Times* reported. Unfortunately, the *Times* wrote, the railroad committee was "unable to obtain an interview with Governor Yates," but, more important, they did received a telegram from Adjutant General Fuller granting authorization to organize the regiment. Fuller also informed the committee that he would be in Chicago next week and would personally attend the mustering in of the regiment.[37]

When it came to accolades for the railroad managers, the *Chicago Evening Journal* was not to be outdone. That same day they wrote "that almost enough companies had been already offered to make up a brigade. It was determined, however, to raise but one regiment, and to have that composed as nearly as could be of Simon Pure

---

[35]   *Chicago Tribune*, August 8, 1862; *Chicago Times*, August 8, 1862.
[36]   *Chicago Times*, August 8, 1862; Forsyth letter to Fuller, August 8, 1862, Record Group 301, Illinois State Archives.
[37]   *Chicago Times*, August 9, 1862.

railroad men. The men who compose this regiment have never been equaled, and we predict that when they get started towards the enemy, that everybody must 'clear the track.'"[38]

Saturday morning found the committee of railroad managers meeting to complete the regimental organization. The muster rolls were further perused, and the volunteer number stood close to six hundred men. The committee was notified that Captain John Christopher, the mustering officer for Chicago, had yesterday sworn in the company recruited from the Chicago and Galena Union Railroad. The members were updated on the status of the Illinois Central Railroad's other company, the "W. R. Arthur Guards," named after the line's superintendent. The company recruited by George W. Smith and George F. Bigelow was reported to be "full to overflowing" and with sixty men mustered in. Based on this, the *Times* printed: "This crack regiment is rapidly filling up" and, without having seen a single recruit, proclaimed: "The men are all above the average, able-bodied, hale and hearty, and appear able to stand the hardship of war without flinching."[39]

*   *   *

Among those presenting muster rolls to the railroad committee was John McCreath Farquhar, president of the International Typographical Union. Born near Ayr, Scotland on April 17, 1832, Farquhar immigrated to the United States and settled in Buffalo, New York, where he took up the printing trade. He eventually moved west to Chicago, and in July 1862 was working for the *Evening Journal.* At some point he joined a local militia unit, the "Chicago Light Guard," and "learned his rudiments of soldiery . . . ."[40]

Granted a commission by Governor Yates, Farquhar set up shop in *The Evening Journal* building at 50 Dearborn Street. He signed his name to the muster roll, making him the first employee of the

---

[38] *Chicago Evening Journal,* August 9, 1862.

[39] *Chicago Times,* August 11, 1862.

[40] *Biographical Directory of the American Congress 1774-1971* (Washington, D.C.: U. S. Government Printing Office, 1971), 929; *Chicago Evening Journal,* August 22, 1862.

Journal to enlist under the new call for volunteers. The *Journal* said of him: "Mr. Farquhar is himself a military man of experience, and as good and true and staunch a man and patriot as can be found among the young men of the West. His whole heart is in the Union cause, and he has taken hold of the matter with us in right-down earnest."[41]

The *Journal* explained that Farquhar was getting together a company to be called 'The Chicago Journal Guards" and that newspaper would do its share in helping the Board of Trade fill up regiment. The writer appealed "to the friends of THE CHICAGO EVENING JOURNAL, to the friends of the Union, the Constitution and the Government, to come up and help us in the speedy filling up of this company." The paper pledged to "stand by them with a fatherly fidelity—watch them when in the field, help them when in need, encourage them and cheer them under all circumstances." The paper's next issue reported: "The first day's recruiting (yesterday) brought quite a number of names to the muster-rolls, one of which may be found in the JOURNAL counting-room."[42]

The editors of Chicago's four newspapers and two men representing the job printers got together and on July 30 sent an open letter to the "Printers of the Northwest." They wrote: "The undersigned . . . in order to advance enlistments, and at the same time aid the craft in giving Typos in the West a favorable position in the Grand Union Army, agree to give all aid within our power for the formation of a Union Typo Battalion . . . ." The letter requested the volunteers to enlist in Chicago where they could take advantage of the generous bounty offered by Cook county. For the effort to succeed, the informal committee appointed John M. Farquhar, President of the National Typographical Union, as the battalion's chief recruiter.[43]

Neither "The Chicago Journal Guards" nor the "Typo Battalion" materialized. Farquhar ran a short note in the August 7 edition of the *Evening Journal* requesting all parties recruiting for the Typo Battalion to contact him before August 9. He stated this was the "last

41 *Chicago Evening Journal*, July 24, 1862.
42 *Chicago Evening Journal*, July 24 and 25, 1862.
43 *Chicago Tribune*, July 31, 1862.

call." In a letter to Adjutant General Fuller dated August 19, Farquhar explained that he had attended the Railroad Regiment Committee organization meeting on August 7 and that after that date he had devoted his time to the formation of the Railroad Regiment. He added that he had made no use of his commission as Recruiting Captain, but that he had aided in the raising two companies of men. And he concluded by stating: "The honor you were pleased to confer upon me I fully appreciate, and I hope my services, gratuitously rendered, in bringing together the Railroad men, may entitle me, in time, to a better position then a private in the ranks of the Spencer's (Duquoin) Company."[44]

Twenty-four-year-old Chicago attorney Duncan J. Hall also gained Governor Yates' authorization to raise a company. For the past year Hall, like Farquhar, was a member of a Chicago militia unit, holding the rank of first lieutenant in the "Scammon Light Infantry." And he too, set about to recruit a company for the Board of Trade Regiment, getting started on July 23. By August 6, the *Tribune* reported that Hall's company was fast filling up with some of the best men that had come forward. The writer, probably Hall, added: "To those who are [thinking] about enlisting, and are looking for a good company and good officers, go and see for yourselves." He deftly finished with the carrot and stick argument by stating: "Enlist at once and save the bounty offered by Cook county and the government. Remember being drafted cuts off your bounty of $162." The *Tribune* reported on August 8 that D. J. Hall "has forty-two men sworn in, and has a number more promised."[45]

Hall, though, had the embarrassment of finding out that one of his recruits was a Rebel escapee. Captured at Island No.10 and imprisoned at Camp Douglas, the man had managed to slip away on July 3. When discovered, he told the authorities that he was a northerner by birth and still had family in Pennsylvania. To keep from being exchanged and returned to the Rebel army, he chose to escape.

---

[44] *Chicago Evening Journal*, August 7, 1862; Farquhar letter to Fuller, August 19, 1862, Record Group 301, Illinois State Archives.

[45] Muster and Descriptive Roll of co. A, Record Group 301, Illinois State Archives; *Chicago Evening Journal*, July 26, 1862; *Chicago Tribune*, August 6 and 8, 1862.

For the past month he had lived in La Salle, returning to Chicago three days before enlisting in Hall's company. Obviously, he was "looking for a good company with good officers" and maybe a $162 bounty! He "was delivered to the commandant at Camp Douglas . . . ."[46]

Captain Hall, as he was now called, switched his effort from the Board of Trade to the newly established "Railroad Regiment." With his father, Amos T. Hall, the treasurer for the Burlington Road, the younger Hall probably saw his prospects with the "Railroad Regiment" would be much better than with the Board of Trade. The *Evening Journal* carried a paragraph on Hall's company with the leader, "THE RAILROAD REGIMENT." Under the pretense of selectivity, Hall announced: "A few more good men are wanted for this crack company. If you want to find a company where good officers and men are what you are looking for, here is the place." Still holding out the carrot, he softens the stick by gently stating: "Remember the bounty of $162, and save the money by enlisting at once." Hall concludes by subtlety alluding to the company's railroad connection. "This will be the best regiment from Illinois. Last call. All board."[47]

On August 14, *The Evening Journal* reported that Captain Hall had arrived back in Chicago with "forty-five fine looking men" recruited along the line of the Chicago, Burlington & Quincy Railroad. These men, the *Journal* figured, would bring Hall's company up to the maximum. The paper commented that "He has done much better than others who made more noise."[48]

Twenty-five year-old William James Tomlinson from Augusta, Illinois, an off and on section hand for Chicago, Burlington & Quincy Railroad, was part of the group Captain Hall returned to Chicago with. Acknowledging that he was one of the 300,000 men Lincoln looking for, Tomlinson informed his two brothers that locally "it is thought they will have to draft to get them." As for himself, he confided: "If they draft heare I shall enlist, [even] if I have to go to Springfield, before I will be drafted and be put in front of battle like sheep."[49]

[46] *Chicago Tribune*, August 9, 1862.
[47] *Chicago Evening Journal*, August 12, 1862.
[48] *Chicago Evening Journal*, August 14, 1862.
[49] Sally Ryan Tomlinson, *In Good Courage: The Civil War Letters of William James Tomlinson, ix*, 1.

With the draft deadline looming, enlistment numbers rapidly increased. On August 11, Hank Rowell's company counted 64 men. While in Aurora the local *Beacon* informed its readers that Watkins' and Kidder's company, made up principally of railroad men, now had 120 men and was full. On Wednesday, August 13, these men met and elected officers. Bruce Kidder was voted captain, John B. Watkins first lieutenant, and George White as second lieutenant. The *Beacon* concluded: "All things considered, we are inclined to the opinion that this is, if not the best, it comes mighty near being the best company ever raised in this city. The good name achieved by our boys in the field will never be dimned [sic] by the gallant men and officers composing our railroad company."[50]

News items began appearing daily in the Chicago papers posting the status of the Railroad Regiment's formation. The *Evening Journal* for August 12 ran a notification that "all persons who have joined the Railroad regiment . . . must report themselves forthwith to the committee, preparatory to going into camp." The *Journal* added that transportation to Camp Douglas would be provided to all recruits on request. This was to be a temporary arrangement while the men awaited the arrival of the remaining companies. Once mustered in, the regiment would move to Wright's Grove located at the corner of North Clark and Diversey streets. By Thursday, August 14, the *Evening Journal* announced the regiment was nearly full, and will most likely be to be mustered in tomorrow. The following day the *Times* reported that yesterday the "Railroad Committee" received a telegram from Adjutant General Fuller stating that Captain Spencer's Company, composed principally of railroad men from DuQuoin, and Captain Comstock's Company of railroad men from Amboy were immediately ordered to Chicago to be part of the Railroad Regiment." As of last evening, the *Times* printed on August 16 the regiment was nearly full and seven full companies were at headquarters, while four others in various stages of completion were on the grounds, and one or two of these were nearly at the minimum number. The

---

[50] Tarrant, diary, August 11, 1862; Aurora *Beacon*, August 5, 1862.

full companies belonged to Captains Hall, Blake, Spencer, Wickam, Rowell, Gorham, and Comstock.[51]

*   *   *

The newspaper articles detailing the organization of the "Railroad Regiment" tend to all be very similar. It is obvious that written press releases were distributed because many of the same ideas and phrases appear in all the stories, no matter which paper you read. It is evident that the reporters and editors of Chicago's three major newspapers, with no distinction by political persuasion, were in lockstep and taking their cue from the same source, the Railroad Committee.

The proposition that the railroad executives were men of action who could accomplish most anything was pushed in the Chicago newspapers and was probably how the men saw themselves. The Republican *Evening Journal* wrote: "The success which has attended it ["The Railroad Regiment"] so far is quite remarkable; when it is considered that the first initiatory steps were not taken until last Friday evening." Not to be outdone, the Democratic *Times* echoed: "The work of organizing it [Railroad Regiment] has been no ordinary enterprise. The initiatory steps were taken on Friday night last, and in the space of a week there has been enrolled and organized a regiment of as hale, active men as can be found anywhere. Much of the success is due to the energy and influence of the men who began and fostered the enterprise." Under the headline, *"THE RAILROAD REGIMENT OF ILLINOIS, Their Motto—'Clear the Track,'"* the *Chicago Tribune* reported in a similar vein that "so practical and popular were these early measures for accomplishment framed, that to-day we find pleasure in chronicling the fact that the regiment is an actual success, and one that the State of Illinois, and even the whole loyal Northwest, may feel high pride in."[52]

---

[51] *Chicago Evening Journal*, August 12 and 14, 1862; *Chicago Times*, August 15 and 16, 1862.

[52] *Chicago Evening Journal*, August 14, 1862; *Chicago Times*, August 14, 1862; *Chicago Tribune*, August 15, 1862.

Nothing captured personality of the railroad magnates more than their adopted motto of "clear the track." When these titans of the rail got up a head of steam, it paid to get out of their way. Any and everything was possible, even raising a regiment in record time. The *Journal* saw the volunteers as a reflection of this philosophy and wrote: "Their motto is already 'clear the track,' and rest assured that they will do it." The *Tribune* looked beyond the present into the future when it likewise printed: "With 'clear the track' as its motto, the Railroad Regiment will win substantial fame for itself and its projectors . . . ."[53]

Articles in Chicago's newspapers were filled with accolades for the organizers and praise for the men making up the Railroad Regiment. The *Journal* declared: "The high standing of the men who have been instrumental in organizing the regiment is more a sure guaranty that nothing will be lacking to make it the best regiment which ever took the field." The reporter noted: "The Governor of the State and Adjutant General have expressed their gratification at the patriotism exhibited by the various railroad and express companies, and are doing all in their power to facilitate the movement." The *Tribune* pointed out that the organizers were a "Committee of Management, composed of well-known and energetic representative men from the various trunk lines entering into this city . . . ."[54]

To the Chicago scribes, the "Railroad Regiment" volunteers were the epitome of American manhood. For instance, the *Times* observed the "Railroad Regiment" is "composed of no mean material. Everyone knows what type of physical and manly perfection the American railroad man is from the common brakeman, through all the grades to the Superintendent and his subordinates." The *Tribune* portrayed the railroad recruits as "healthy and skillful young men inured to all weather changes, hardened and toughened in bone and muscle through their kind of employment, and courageous because ever alert to the dangers which would seem to lurk around them in the hazardous avocation they follow."[55]

To induce the man with a wife and family into enlisting, the Railroad Committee let it be known that measures were underway

---

[53] *Chicago Evening Journal,* August 14, 1862; *Chicago Tribune,* August 15, 1862.

[54] *Ibid.,* August 14, 1862 and August 15, 1862.

[55] *Chicago Times,* August 15, 1862; *Chicago Tribune,* August 15, 1862.

ensuring dependents would be cared for. The *Evening Journal* reported that the railroads were contemplating a plan where the family of every man who enlisted in the regiment would be provided for and taken care of. While the *Tribune's* readers read that the railroad executives "planned to create a general fund raised by an equitable deduction from the pay-rolls of the various roads, which, placed in the hands of a finance committee of responsible gentlemen, will give to all enlisted a sure faith that their parents, wives and little ones left at home will be permanently and certainly cared for in their absence." The *Tribune* brought up the fact that "already several of the roads have hundreds of signatures to the articles of agreement which will yield monthly the means for creating the bounty fund, and we have yet to hear of one objection among the employees to signing." The writer estimated that the payroll deduction would both bring in "thousands of dollars every month," and added, that he and his colleagues at the paper were confident "it will be given ungrudgingly as it will be received thankfully."[56]

The newspapers continued reporting that the "Railroad Regiment" was nearly full with seven companies numbering about 730 men sworn in and at camp. The reality was much different. Companies raised and earmarked for the "Railroad Regiment" were ending up elsewhere. For instance, the "W. R. Arthur Guards," named after the superintendent of the Illinois Central Railroad, opted to go with the "Board of Trade Regiment." "Gorham's Bloomington Company," promised to the committee and reported to have 82 men sworn in, never materialized. When would the final companies arrive, bringing the regiment up to the maximum, was unknown and now up in the air. The *Chicago Times* wrote: "We can affirm nothing, however, for, although our reporter has made repeated application for information, he has received nothing each time but indefinite replies." For all the promises made by the roads two weeks earlier, the committee's effort now appeared stalled. The enlistment deadline was up, and the pledged companies needed to form a regiment of railroad men were not forthcoming.[57]

[56] *Chicago Evening Journal*, August 14, 1862; *Chicago Tribune*, August 15, 1862.
[57] *Chicago Times*, August 16 and 18, 1862.

William D. Manchester of the Michigan Southern and Northern Indiana Railroad Company assumed the job of secretary for the Railroad Committee. On August 21, he wrote Adjutant General Fuller a letter apprising him of the problem the committee faced. He began by acknowledging Fuller's telegram of August 18 which informed the committee that the companies raised at Aurora and Bristol would join the regiment. Manchester then explained to Fuller that Bruce Kidder, tiring of the rendezvous camp and seeking better quarters for his men, brought the Aurora company in that morning. The acting "Boss," as Manchester saw himself; let Fuller know that he questioned Captain Kidder as to why he came in without orders. Manchester then reported to the Adjutant General that: "Mr. Haige of [the] Am[erican] Ex[press] Co[mpany] to whom you gave permission to raise a co[mpany] has taken considerable interest in our Regt & now reports a company full & ready to come in as soon as you will give [the] necessary orders. It is Captn. Whiting & co. of Altona on the C. B. & Q. RR.—They will be ready to come on Monday next." He then asked, "Will you please give the necessary order in reference to this co. & the Bristol Co.[?][58]

Manchester now laid the situation out. At Camp E. H. Williams he had 551 men, with fifty-five more expected to arrive in five days, bringing the total to 606. The men were formed into seven companies. One company, John W. Spink's, numbered fifty-eight men. With the men from Bristol and Altona, the "Railroad Regiment" would have nine companies. He asked Fuller: "Where shall we get the other co.[?]" Almost answering his own question, he added: "We will do our best to fix it before tomorrow night."[59]

For the Railroad Committee it was a matter of numbers. The maximum size of a Civil War infantry regiment was 1,025 men, with the minimum being 845. A regiment was made up ten companies, each having eighty-two privates, a wagoner, two musicians, four sergeants, a first sergeant, a second lieutenant, a first lieutenant, and a captain. The field staff had two principal musicians, a hospital steward, a commissary sergeant, a quartermaster sergeant, a

---

[58] William D. Manchester, letter to Adjutant General Fuller, August 21,1862, Record Group 301, Illinois State Archives.
[59] *Ibid.*

sergeant major, a chaplain, two assistant surgeons, a surgeon, a quartermaster, an adjutant, a major, a lieutenant colonel, and a colonel. The two companies had 101 men each; the staff added fifteen, for a total of 1,025. When a regiment dropped to the minimum acceptable number of 845, each company was reduced to sixty-four privates.[60]

Men who came up short in recruiting a full company set about combining with others who were in the same fix. Part of the committee's problem was solved when the companies recruited by Mr. Wickham on the Fort Wayne Railroad and Mr. Spink on the Rock Island Railroad were consolidated under the title of "Robert Forsyth Guards"—named in honor of Major Forsyth, acting colonel of the regiment.[61]

Orders soon followed for the Bristol men of Captain Willett, known as the "Kendall County Guards", and the Altona company, under Captain Thomas Whiting, to come to Chicago. Nineteen year-old Fredrick W. Goddard's diary entry for Monday, August 25 stated the Kendall County men "left the station for Chicago at 3; arrived safe & sound; at 6 marched from the State street [station] to our camp ground at cottage grove; found the tents all pitched; slept on hay with blankets over us."[62]

Once at Camp E. H. Williams, Joseph Buckley, another of Willett's men, penned a short letter to his wife, Mary. "We arrived safe in camp about sundown. We had to march about 5 and ½ miles from the depot to the camp; instead of being north, we are south of Chicago, a very little South of Camp Douglas." Buckley went on: "We saw some of the Rebel prisoners as we marched past their camp. Our tents were all ready when we arrived, and we received blankets as our names were called from the muster roll. We had plenty of good dry hay to lay on the ground under out blankets."[63]

---

60 Clyde C. Walton, *Illinois and the Civil War* (Springfield, Illinois, 1961), 17.

61 *Chicago Evening Journal*, August 21, 1862; *Chicago Times*, August 22, 1862.

62 Fredrick W. Goddard, diary entry for August 25, 1862, original diary in possession of Karl Stark, Charlottesville, Virginia, hereafter cited as the Goddard diary.

63 Joseph Buckley, letter to Mary Buckley, August [27], 1862, original letters in possession of Les Lipshutz, Flossmoor, Illinois, hereafter cited as Buckley letter.

Goddard and Buckley were familiar with hay since both were farmers. The three latest companies assigned to the "Railroad Regiment"—those commanded by Travis O. Spencer, a Methodist minister, Henry S. Willet, a lumber merchant, and Thomas Whiting, a farmer—were composed chiefly of farmers. Spencer's and Whiting's companies were represented by eighty-five and eighty-two men who respectively stated their occupation was farming. Seventy-seven of Willet's men listed their livelihood as farmer. The initial muster-in rolls for the Railroad Regiment totaled 922 men of whom 440 or approximately forty-five percent made their living from agriculture. The regiment would be organized and sponsored by the railroads in Chicago. A substantial number of railroad employees would be in the ranks, but it would not be a regiment made up entirely of railroad workers.[64]

For whatever reason, the Railroad Committee failed to raise a regiment of pure railroad men. Robert Forsyth's words that "it would not be well to throw open the rolls to any but railroad employees, unless enough men could not be found without it, and he apprehended no difficulty on that head" now sounded like bravado. Truth was, not enough railroad men had come forward, leaving the committee scrambling to save face. All effort now focused on finding men, no matter their occupation, getting them in camp and fielding a regiment as soon as possible. The *Chicago Times* was able to report on August 28 that "the organization of the railroad regiment is progressing rapidly. There are now nine companies in camp, seven of which are full and have elected officers. It was announced yesterday that the regiment was full, and that all the field officers had been elected. Such is not the case. The regimental roster stands much the same as before . . . ."[65]

*   *   *

From the moment the idea of a Railroad Regiment was bandied about until the men started arriving in camp, the Chicago press

---

[64]   Muster and Descriptive Roll of Cos. B, G, and H, Record Group 301, Illinois State Archives.

[65]   *Chicago Times*, August 8 and 28, 1862.

floated a number of candidates for the unit's prospective colonel. The first name to surface was that of Robert Forsyth, who the *Tribune* pronounced as "an admirable officer" while *Evening Journal* concluded this selection "could not fall upon a worthier man . . . ." But just as quickly, it was reported that General John Wilson, the land Commissioner of the Illinois Central road would be made the colonel. And, not long afterward the *Times* speculated that Elliot Anthony would probably be the colonel. The paper added that his appointment would "insure [sic] energy and capacity to the regiment." The last name to crop up was that of Captain John Christopher, the United States mustering officer for Chicago.[66]

A native of Pennsylvania, John Christopher became a first lieutenant when the 16 Regular U. S. Infantry was organized in May 1861. On February 21, 1862, he was promoted to captain and later that year was ordered to Chicago as the U. S. mustering officer. As a regular army officer in a prominent position, Captain Christopher gained the attention of the Railroad Committee. Impressed with this young officer, the Committee held a special meeting on August 18 and "unanimously Resolved 'That Capt. J. Christopher be recommended to the Officers of the several Companies forming the Regiment as Colonel of said Regiment.'" As secretary, William D. Manchester notified Captain Christopher of the Committee recommendation.[67]

The following day Captain Christopher penned a reply to the Railroad Committee. "I have the honor to return my sincere thanks for the complement you have conferred upon me by selecting me as the Regimental Commander of the Battalion organized under the auspices of the Union Rail-Way corporations of this City and State." Accepting the position tendered, Captain Christopher noted it was subject to the approval of the Governor of Illinois and the Secretary of War. He continued: "Should those in authority permit me to accept, I shall spare no pains to make this Regiment in

---

[66] *Chicago Evening Journal*, August 7, 1862; *Chicago Tribune*, August 7, 1862; *Chicago Times*, August 11 and 12, 1862.

[67] Francis B. Heitman, *Historical Register and Dictionary of United States Army (1789-1903)*, 2 vols. (1903; rep., Urbana, Illinois: University of Illinois Press, 1965) 1:300; William D. Manchester, letter to Captain John Christopher, August 18, 1862, Record Group 301, Illinois State Archives.

discipline &c second to none in the service, and to accomplish this end will [devote] the best energies of my life. As far as myself and the Regiment is concerned I propose the future shall speak for itself, but while I am its engineer the Rail-Road Regiment shall never be allowed to switch off, but from the moment of its departure for the field, and until its return brakes and steam shall always be up, and the Regiment on time."[68]

The Committee immediately released news of Christopher's acceptance to the press. The *Tribune* and the *Evening Journal* printed the announcement in their August 19 editions. Both newspapers published the two paragraphs exactly as given. Unfortunately, whoever wrote the statement committed a minor blunder, and it was not buried in the article but up front and glaring. The article began: "The officers of the Railroad Regiment held a meeting last evening and unanimously elected Capt. Christopher, U. S. mustering officer in this city, to the colonelcy of the regiment."

Fait accompli was not how newly organized Civil War regiments determined their colonel. For better or worse, officers in Civil War volunteer regiments were elected. Captains and lieutenants were chosen from the men within each company. The company officers then met and elected, normally from amongst themselves, the regiment's field officers. The state governor then certified the results and forwarded the commissions. Once in the field, the men soon found out whether their leadership choices were good or not. Resignations, illness, and death, followed by new appointments, rid the regiments of those unfit for command.

After informing the public and the regiment who would be colonel, the papers proceeded to explain how the Committee planned to skirt current government policy, which prevented volunteer regiments from "cherry picking" regular army officers away from their units. Being used to having things their way, the railroad barons felt no need to worry about Secretary Stanton's order barring regular army officers from accepting positions in volunteer regiments. The newspapers reported that the prominent railroad men of the city and State were determined

---

[68] Captain John Christopher, letter to William D. Manchester, August 19, 1862, Record Group 301, Illinois State Archives.

that Christopher should be the colonel of their regiment; and consequently, they would bring to bear their influence to have the war department waive the regulation. Both papers backed the railroads and hoped they would be successful in securing Christopher's appointment.

The article went on to defend the Committee's selection of Captain Christopher to lead the Railroad Regiment. "Of the qualifications of Capt. Christopher for the position it is hardly necessary to speak. He is a thorough, practical military man, and would bring to his post the valuable experience of long years in the service. As an executive officer he has few equals, and to his individual efforts is largely due the prompt manner in which our regiments hitherto have reported themselves ready for duty. Indefatigable in the discharge of his duties, well versed in military tactics, an excellent gentleman and gallant soldier, we trust no obstacle will prevent his attaining the colonelcy of this regiment."[69]

The *Chicago Times* on August 20, 1862 pointed out the controversy stirred by the previous day's *Tribune* and *Journal* articles. The *Times* let it be known that "the announcement that has been extensively made of the election of Captain Christopher to the colonelcy of this regiment is premature.

Christopher to the colonelcy of this regiment is premature. No such election has been made." The *Times* piece is evidence that the leaders of the Railroad Committee may have suffered a bit embarrassment by the articles. They, therefore, attempted to clarify the earlier release by making the previous stories appear to be a mistake in reporting. They wanted it to be known that "the Railroad Committee simply discussed the availability of recommending that gentleman to the line officers for election to the colonelcy." The *Times* article pointed out: "The election can scarcely be made till the regiment is full." And, the *Times* reported: "From present appearance that selection of the field officers will probably be a strongly contested point. A strong current is sought to be set in motion towards certain family distinctions which may be accepted or may not. The matter has even attracted so much attention that the name of the regiment has been proposed to be changed, and the

---

[69] *Chicago Tribune*, August 19, 1862; *Chicago Evening Journal*, August 19, 1862.

name of one of our leading lines of railroad substituted for the more general family title." The last tidbit suggests there was dissension between the railroads on the subject of regimental officers.[70]

The modest controversy, however, did not deter William Manchester in his effort to have Captain Christopher made colonel of the regiment. In a letter to Adjutant General Fuller dated August 21, he enclosed copies of the correspondence passed between he and Christopher and stated: "Please note contents & I will consider it a special favor if you will assist us in having Capt. C. transferred or relieved to take charge of this regiment. Any information you can give me on the subject will be duly appreciated."[71]

While the Railroad Committee dealt with numbers and finding a colonel, the work of making soldiers out of civilians was going ahead. Captain Herbert M. Blake, the painter for the Galena and Chicago Union Railroad, took charge of the men at Camp E. H. Williams. Assisting him were acting Adjutant Edward F. Bishop, nineteen-year-old first Sergeant for Captain Duncan J. Hall's "Scammon Light Infantry," and temporary Quartermaster Frederick L. Fake. Twenty-seven-year-old, Fake came to Chicago from New York in 1855 to work in the Land Department of the Illinois Central Railroad. Interestingly, Fred Fake was married to Hall's sister, Lucy.[72]

* * *

The *Times* sent a reporter out to the regimental camp to look over the men and their situation. What he saw was a "fine looking body of men, nearly all having been employed on the railroad. They have all got their uniforms, and present a fine appearance." Robert Tarrant noted the men from the Milwaukee Road found camp life "first rate." Another soldier wrote his wife: "We are all very cheerful

---

[70]   *Chicago Times*, August 20, 1862.

[71]   William D. Manchester to Adjutant General Fuller, August 21, 1862, Record Group 301, Illinois State Archives.

[72]   *Chicago Times*, August 20, 1862; Muster and Descriptive Roll of Co. A, Record Group 301, Illinois State Archives; Frederick L. Fake, manuscript, "Concerning Abraham Lincoln and Containing Captain Frederick L. Fake's Reminiscence," Chicago Historical Society, hereafter cited as Fake manuscript.

and comfortable, under the circumstances. We have a very good place for a camp."[73]

Beginning Wednesday, August 27, Fred Goddard wrote the men were examined by the U. S. Surgeon and five from his company were rejected. He "was pronounced sound." The next day the regiment line up and drew their "overcoats, blouse coats, pants, shirts, drawers, stocking, shoes, knapsacks, & were sworn into [the] service." Joe Buckley explained to his wife that "we took the oath to serve in the United States Army for the term of three years, if not sooner discharged. And I may as well say that we are not required to serve, [but] during the war, unless the War is over before three years is out." Friday dress coats were issued. The men now had all their clothing except the caps, which had not been made yet. Since they now looked like soldiers, the men commenced the drill process necessary to make them soldiers. Goddard commented: "We have got a nice level drill ground."[74]

From August 20, 1862 through November 13, 1862, the State of Illinois transported, received, quartered, fed, clothed, equipped, and armed fifty-nine three-year regiments. The volunteers initially settled in rendezvous camps. Serving the purpose in many counties was the local fair ground. At these locations the companies and regiments were organized. With field staff, company and non-commissioned officers in place, the regiments moved to a mustering-in camp. Camp Douglas and the adjacent area served both as a rendezvous and a mustering-in site. The flood of men turned these camps into a beehive of chaotic activity. Delays and shortages were a natural result, and the Railroad Regiment was not immune.

When acting Quartermaster Fake arrived in camp on August 27, a disgruntled crowd of men confronted "him and assailed his ears with that peculiar sound emitted by sheep who have been led astray." The leaders "complained loudly of their rations, mouldy [sic] bread and no bread at all, and some of the articles mentioned as being included in the rations have not yet been seen upon the ground." Coming to his own defense, Fake told the rowdies that "it

---

[73]   *Chicago Times*, August 23, 1862; Tarrant, diary, August 24, 1862; Buckley, letter, August [27], 1862.

[74]   Goddard, diary, August 27, 28, and 29, 1862; Buckley, letter, August 31, 1862.

was not his fault, and explained the matter to some of them while others kept up their expressive 'bah,' 'bah.'" The men finally quieted down when Fake promised "that no cause of complaint should be permitted in the future."[75]

Coming into camp, mustering into the service, and drawing uniforms were the first steps in the evolution from civilian to soldier. Officially in the army, these citizen soldiers had to adjust to a daily routine of roll call, drill, and guard duty. Being unused to a structured and restricted environment, some men soon became acquainted with military discipline and the guardhouse. As green soldiers, many away from home for the first time, military life was new and different, and it was the foremost topic in their letters home and in their diaries.

Joe Buckley wrote to his wife, Mary: "We have to appear at Roll Call at sun rise, at sun down, and at nine o'clock in the evening. If we miss answering to our names three times, then we shall have to do extra duty. I have not missed a call yet." In the midst of the letter, Joe commented that "we have had to leave writing since we commenced our letters this afternoon. The Captain came and gave us orders to put on our Dress Coats and attend Divine service . . . ." Back to his letter, Joe wrote: "I had to leave my writing again. We had to go out and drill in a review. There were five regiments besides one Regiment of Artillery. Our Captain told us after review that our Regiment was highly complemented."[76]

On Saturday, August 30, Fred Goddard's noted in his diary: "Stood guard today for the first time. We read a chapter in the testament every morning and evening. Went into Mr. [Thomas C.] Morley's tent to prayers today." Civil War pocket diaries gave little room for extended entries. Brevity was the standard for most writers. Goddard's comments are more like notes or reminders to himself. A good example is his entry for August 31: "Review in the afternoon. There were Co., reg[iment,] and 1 Batt[ery] of 6 guns. It don't seem much like Sunday."[77]

---

[75] *Chicago Times*, August 28, 1862.

[76] Buckley, letter, August 31, 1862.

[77] Goddard, diary, August 30 and 31, 1862.

Guard duty was at the top of the many daily details the new soldiers were assigned. In a letter home George Berry explained a typical rotation. "I stood on duty eight hours, two hours on and four hours off. It comes around once in ten days." Rules and regulations, like forbidding men to leave camp without a pass, seemed silly to some young men. Buckley relates one episode that took place shortly after arrival at Camp E. H. Williams. "There were three or four of our company that ran past the guard and went out of the camp towards Camp Douglas, when the guard there took them up and kept them there all night, besides which they get two days extra duty in our camp."[78]

It was not all drill and drudgery as Buckley describes an afternoon off in a letter to his wife. "I got a pass last Thursday which let me out at one o'clock until six in the evening. I went into the city and bought what things I wanted. The street cars came clear up to the Southeast corner of our camp. We can ride clear down to Lake Street for five cents. It is about 5 ½ miles from here. There are so many wanting passes that it makes it difficult to get out, because the acting Colonel won't let out more than four at once, that is every half day." Granted one of the coveted passes, George H. Berry, a Knox County farmer took in the sights. He touched on his visit to downtown Chicago in a letter to his wife, Harriet. "Sunday, I went up to the City and I went to the first M E Church and heard Bishop Janey preach. I whent [and] seen the princi[p]al part of the City. I went up in the top of the Court house. It was splended view. It was about two hundred feet high."[79]

Whether they voted for him or not, the soldiers recognized Douglas as one of the most influential politicians of their time. As a Senator from Illinois from 1847 to 1861, Douglas had represented the Prairie State for most of their lives. During this time, he stood at the center of the political debate on slavery and its expansion. In 1860, with his party splintered, he was the Northern Democratic presidential candidate. But the fracture assured Lincoln's election.

---

[78] George H. Berry, letter to Harriet Berry, September 1, 1862, original letters in possession of Steve Stewart, Chicago, Illinois, hereafter cited as Berry letter; Buckley, letter, August 31, 1862..

[79] Buckley, letter, August 31, 1862; Berry, letter, September 1, 1862.

Political defeat did not silence Douglas, for he continued working to preserve the Union. He returned to Springfield at the urging of Illinois Democrats and addressed a special secession of state legislature. Arriving early in the morning on April 25, he spoke to the legislators that evening in the statehouse. Douglas told those gathered that "'the first duty of an American citizen is obedience to the constitution and the laws of the country.'" In Douglas' opinion the current crisis required that "party creeds and platforms must be set aside, party organizations and partisanship must be dispensed with." Having struggled the past months for a peaceful solution, Douglas was physically worn down by the effort and contracted typhoid, dying June 3, 1861.[80]

With Camp E. H. Williams located near the home and grave of Stephen A. Douglas, many men in the Railroad Regiment stopped and paid their respects to the late Senator from Illinois. Joe Buckley too wrote his family of the camp's location in relation to Douglas' home and grave. "We are camped in Cottage Grove. Senator Douglas' grave is about 20 rods east of our camp, and the house he lived in is about 20 rods south of his grave. We visited it this morning. We go past the house every other morning when we go to the Lake to bathe. We bathe about 12 rods east of his house." He further explained to Mary: "You will recollect the breakwater on the lake shore. When we go to bathe, we dive right off the Breakwater and when we get on our feet, we are about up to our shoulders in the water. We have a fine time of it. I shall soon learn to swim if I stay here, but there is some talk of us going away next week, but I do not credit it."[81]

Between rumors and actual events, Camp E. H. Williams was the center of non-stop activity. One of the more ceremonial activities was mentioned by Robert Tarrant in a diary entry for August 29. in a diary entry for August 29. "The Galena men had a grand time at the Round House this P.M. They presented each of the commissioned officers of their military Co. with a full outfit." The affair grabbed the attention of the *Chicago Tribune*, who sent a reporter to the

---

[80]   Robert W. Johannsen, *Stephen A. Douglas* (New York: Oxford University Press, 1973), 862-868.

[81]   Buckley, letter, August 31, 1862.

presentation. The resulting story was one of the longer pieces the paper devoted to the Railroad Regiment.[82]

At 2:00 P.M., Herbert M. Blake's "Galena Railroad Guards" formed up at the corner of State and Randolph Streets and began marching to the company's roundhouse located at West Kinzie and Halsted Streets. In front of the City Railway office, Barnard's Old Light Guard Band and a crowd of citizens met the men and joined the procession to the ceremony. On arriving at the yard, the men found "the spacious engine house was handsomely decorated with shrubbery, flowers, flags, banners, devices, &c. A commodious stand was erected for the band, reporters, and speakers, and seats provided for the soldiers and ladies."[83]

Packing the roundhouse were the company's fellow employees. After a number of speeches, Elliot Anthony addressed a few pertinent remarks to Captain Blake, first Lieutenant Sampson and second Lieutenant Jackson and afterward presented each with a full uniform, sword, and revolver. The scabbards were engraved with each officer's name and the words, "Presented by the employees of the Galena Railroad, August 29, 1862." After the presentations, the company formed, with the band leading, marched through the principal streets, halted opposite the office of the *Times* office, and saluted the newspaper with three rousing cheers.[84]

At 7:00 P.M. on Monday evening, September 1, the doors of Bryan Hall opened on the Railroad Festival. Three weeks earlier two young girls took upon themselves to get up a "grand fair and festival" whereby "a full set of regimental of colors" would be presented to the Railroad Regiment. In a paragraph filed under "INDEX," the young women's idea found itself in the August 12 edition of the *Evening Journal*. The writer waxed politics as he commented on the motivations behind the gala. "The boys of the Railroad regiment are a glorious set of fellows, and these young ladies are determined they shall not leave for the battlefield without some emblem to rally around and fight under. We know they will protect those flags, and while they are defending them and their

---

[82]   Tarrant, diary, August 29, 1862.

[83]   *Chicago Tribune*, August 30, 1862.

[84]   *Chicago Tribune*, August 30, 1862; *Chicago Times*, August 30, 1862.

country, they will also remember those two young girls, by whose labors they are to be presented to them." The heart of the piece was a request that "merchants and hotels give them a helping hand by contributing such things as will be suitable in carrying out this affair." He concluded by observing: "We are happy to say that we know these young ladies and know they are all right, and we trust and hope their enterprise will be attended with success, and that the Railroad boys will have such a set of colors given to them as they will be proud to look upon."[85]

The girls' inspiration took hold, and they were soon joined by a "number of patriotic ladies." Bryan Hall was rented for the fair and festival, while well-known artist, Charles L. Dubois was commissioned to design the flags. The funds raised at the event would be used to pay for the stand of colors presented to the regiment. The Light Guard Band provided the music for the evening.[86]

A *Tribune* reporter described the setting: "The hall was adorned by many American flags, from the smallest to the largest size. On one side the tables were covered with articles of fancy needle-work. On another were tables of fruits and refreshments, interspersed with boquets [sic]. A table filled with the greatest profusion of magnificent boquets [sic] stood upon the front of the platform. At the left of these hung a splendid banner bearing the American eagle. Over his head were the Stars of the Union as it shall be, and beneath his talons the time-honored motto of our nation. At the opposite end of the wall the national flag hung; on its centre stripe the number and name of the regiment were beautiful executed in gold. Its stars encompassed the railroad man's most expressive phrase, 'Clear the Track.'"

On observing the regimental flag, he wrote: "Resting against the wall back of all these was the finest banner and most expressive design of all, corresponding in size with the first. Its center displays a magnificent engine, 'The Union.' The engineer is at his post, throttle bar in hand, and all steams on. At the opposite end of the device is a brakeman, at his post."

The *Tribune's* reporter spotted a squad of the boys "down from camp—'on pass' of course," viewing and admiring the regiment's new

---

85 *Chicago Evening Journal,* August 12, 1862.

86 *Chicago Tribune,* September 1 and 2, 1862.

colors. Overhearing their banter, he made note of their conversation. "'Take off that brakeman,' said one, 'we want no such officer on our train.' Another looking thoughtfully at the splendid stand of colors remarked, 'Well, I hope they will give us drill to fit us for this new work, and then give us a chance to show what we can do—we mean fight, earnest, real war.' Just then an officer came up, and said to the boys: 'We are ordered to report to camp immediately—we are under marching orders.'"[87]

As for the festival, it was a success with the *Evening Journal* reporting that a large number of visitors stayed throughout the entire evening. Spotted among the crowd were three railroad superintendents, William R. Arthur of the Illinois Central, Charles G. Hammond of the Chicago, Burlington, and Quincy, and John F. Tracy of the Chicago and Rock Island. Impressed by the affair, the *Evening Journal* wanted all to know that the women who "originated the plan and carried it to a successful consummation are deserving of all praise."[88]

*   *   *

When September arrived, the men of the Railroad Regiment were in the midst of transitioning from civilian to military life. Two companies, Willett's and Whiting's, were finishing the first week in camp and still adjusting to being away from home. "Camp life," George Berry wrote his wife, "Is a wicked Place . . . swearing [and] hollering all of the time or very near it."[89]

The issue of obtaining a furlough and going home was on the mind of many. They wanted to see their loved ones and to tie up loose ends on their farms or with businesses before leaving for the field. Joe Buckley was in camp twenty-four hours when he wrote: "I do not know whether I shall be able to get a furlough or not yet, but I shall if I can." Four days later he was still waiting for an answer: "I have just been speaking to the captain to find out if I can get a few days furlough, he says he cannot promise me, but he says he will do

---

[87] *Chicago Tribune*, September 2, 1862.

[88] *Chicago Evening Journal*, September 2, 1862; *Chicago Tribune*, September 2, 1862.

[89] Berry, letter, September 3, 1862.

so if he can. There is another company coming here tomorrow to fill up our Regiment, and if it does I think we shall leave probably this week. If we leave this week, I will come home if I can, but if I cannot, I will write to you to come. For if I get my pay, I would rather give it to you than send it by mail, as I think it would be safer. We expect to receive our Arms tomorrow."[90]

George Berry found himself in a similar predicament. "I have not received my furlow as yet," he wrote Harriet on September 1, "and I don't know as I shall. They think of going on Thursday but it is uncertain. I told Thomas Whiting that I must have a furlow if it was not but twenty four hours at home but if I cant all wright." Berry followed-up with a letter on the third informing Harriet that he would not be home as "the company has marching orders to go some place. I do not know what place we shal go to. I should of liked to seen you and the children fo I went down into Dixey, but I calculate to make the best of it." Since he will not get back to the farm, George tells Harriet: "You must hier somebody this fall to feed the hogs and pigs." With that thought off his mind, Berry then explained to Harriet that: "I received twenty seven dollars of bounty money. I am going to send you home twenty dollars by Express. Thomas is going to send his home. We will send it all in one letter to Mr. Waldo the Railroad agent. Thomas will Direct it to Estell Berry. You can go there for it. It will save cost by sending it all in one letter."[91]

On August 31 Joe Buckley wrote in passing to Mary: "We expect to receive our Arms tomorrow." Buckley and the camp rumor that the regiment would receive their weapons on September 1 were correct. Nine hundred stands of arms were delivered on Monday. In spite of all the hubbub and disorder, the Railroad Regiment was coming together. Roster numbers increased daily. But the tenth and final company still had not arrived, and until then, the field officers could not be elected. Acting Colonel W. D. Manchester, with the assistance of Bishop and Fake, continued to be in charge. As it stood, the regiment was not nearly ready to take the field. But all that changed late

[90]   Buckley, letters, August 27 and 31, 1862.
[91]   Berry, letters, September 1 and 3, 1862.

Tuesday, September 2. Robert Tarrant confided to his diary on September 2: "News to day is rather unfavorable. The Rebels are threatening Louisville and Cincinnati & they are under martial law & all business is suspended." Late that evening that the Railroad Regiment got its marching orders.[92]

Wednesday afternoon, September 3, a committee of attractive young women made their way to Camp E. H. Williams where they presented the regiment with an elegant stand of colors. The flags were purchased from the proceeds of the festival held at Bryan Hall. Dr. Brock McVickar, post surgeon at Camp Douglas, made a presentation speech and was followed by acting Colonel W. D. Manchester and Colonel Rosell M. Hough of the 67 Illinois Infantry, who each made brief remarks on acceptance of the colors. Observing from the ranks, Private Joe Buckley opined: "We had our Flags presented to us . . . beautiful flags they are . . . ."

When the ceremony concluded, the line officers gathered aside to elect the regiment's field officers. For colonel, the men unanimously selected Captain John R. Christopher, while C. T. Hotchkiss and John L. Newel were respectively chosen lieutenant-colonel and major. Ed Bishop and Fred Fake had the term "acting" removed from their positions of adjutant and quartermaster. On the choice for colonel, Joe Buckley told Mary: "Our Colonel's name is John Christopher. I like his looks first rate."[93]

Men who were attempting to make arrangements to see loved ones suddenly found they were writing hurried letters filled with good-byes and last minute instructions. The camp literally awoke to find out that a message arrived overnight ordering the Railroad Regiment, now known as the Eighty-ninth Illinois Infantry, to leave. But as expected, before the men were officially notified, word of the pending departure flew about the camp. Berry jotted a short letter to Harriet with the news. "I heard that we hafter start tomorrow knight Thursday evening. There is some talk of going in to Kentucky

---

[92] *Chicago Evening Journal*, September 2, 1862; *Chicago Times*, August 30, 1862; Tarrant, diary, September 2 and 3, 1862.

[93] *Chicago Tribune*, September 4, 1862; *Chicago Times*, September 4, 1862; Buckley, letter, September 3, 1862.

and some sayes we are going to Cincinnati. Thay the rebels are thirty thousand strong on the other side." Joe Buckley wrote Mary: "We are under marching orders. We have received our arms but they have not distributed them yet, but they will do so this forenoon. The order was for us to be ready by noon today, but I do not think we shall move from here today, and I doubt whether tomorrow . . . ." Buckley was either immune to rumor or privy to the facts for he told his wife: "We do not know where we are going to yet." He does know that: "Our arms are the Springfield Rifled Musket. They are light and handy, and our Colonel says they are the best . . . in the United States."[94]

With the issuance of their military clothing completed, orders came to send their civilian apparel home or as George Berry put it: "The armey have come to say we shall send all our clothes home in one box to Altona." Aware that he would have no need for most of his personal clothes, Buckley forewarned his wife: "There will be a satchel full of things to send home." By September 3, George wrote Mary that he had sent his belongings to home by railroad freight. However, to be safe, the key to the satchel was hidden in newspaper which George mailed separately.[95]

"I am going to get my portrait taken this afternoon as soon as I get this letter written," Joe Buckley wrote Mary. That afternoon found a number of guards looking the other way so fellow soldiers could escape camp and visit Chicago. Buckley described his experience: "Charles Chancer and me slipped past the guards this afternoon and went to the City to get our portraits taken. It is well that we did so for it was our only chance of getting them. We got in camp again safe. I had my Dress Coat on when I got it taken. I was not fixed up as I wanted to be, but it was the best I could do. I have sent mine and Chancey Talmadge's by the Express to Morris." That same day George Berry made his way to a photographer. He wrote his wife

---

[94] Berry, letter, September 3, 1862; Buckley, letter, September 3, 1862; Ken Bauman, *Arming The Suckers, 1861-1865, A Compilation of Illinois Civil War Weapons*, (Columbus, Ohio, 1989) 175. The 89th received 471 Springfield rifled muskets.

[95] Berry, letter, September 3, 1862; Buckley, letters, August 31, 1862 and September 3, 1862.

that he had his "likeness taken to Day. I will send it home in my clothes. I tide it up in one of my <u>coat</u> sleaves."[96]

In their absence, men like Buckley and Berry counted on bounty money to help provide for their families. With the regiment on alert for movement to the front, officials arrived with the payments. Buckley demonstrates one man's struggle to get the money to his wife. He wrote: "We received 27 Dollars of our Government Bounty last night and should have received the balance of what is coming to us from the Government if they had got the blanks to fill up in time. I expect we shall get it to day. They say we shall get our County Bounty today. They are expecting Cole here today to hand them over to us, but if he should not come, we can get an order on the County to the amount that is due to us, and if I get an order, I can send it to you. If it so happens that you can't come, I would rather you would come if possible. Furloughs are out of the question now."

The following morning he apprises Mary that "I saw John Hargreaves and he told me he had seen you and what you said to him. I think I will send 15 dollars by him. He will not leave here before Saturday as he is going to stay to see the horse fair. You can drive over there Monday or Tuesday and get the money from him. It is United States Treasury notes. It is as gold so that if you keep money on hand, you had better keep it."

"I have had to leave off writing while I eat breakfast, and I saw Thomas Britton's wife. I have sent 15 dollars by her and an order for you to get my County Bounty Order. She will leave it with John Litsey, and if she forgets to leave it with him, you can see her. She goes home on the nine o'clock train this morning. I want you to go as soon as you get this letter and get the 15 Dollars in treasury notes and the order, and then the first opportunity, I want you to go to Oswego and get the County order. All you will have to do will be for you to present the order that I send to you unto him, and he will give you an order on the County for 70 dollars. I shall not send any money by Hargreaves now.

Before posting his letter, Buckley's bounty situation takes another twist. "Since writing the above Mr. J. J. Cole has arrived and paid us our County Bounty Orders of 70 dollars each, so the order I sent you

---

[96] Buckley, letter, September 3 and 4, 1862; Berry, letter, September 4, 1862.

this morning by Thomas Britton's wife will be of no account, and of course you will destroy it as soon as you get it. I am sending my order by Mr. J. J. Cole to Oswego, and he will send it down to you by Sherrill Bushnell next week. If Bushnell does not call with it, it will not be very far for you to go to get it. It may be Thursday or Friday before he (Bushnell) gets back to Oswego with it."[97]

Pending orders gave way to fact when the men were ordered to break camp and pack equipment. Fred Goddard wrote that the regiment "got marching orders at one PM. In half an hour the tents were all down [and] we received our caps, canteens & just previous to starting a number of friends were here from Bristol to see us off." Writing his wife, Co. C Private George Gresham Sinclair, now a former engineer on the Milwaukee Road, said: "We struck tents on Thursday afternoon and started for Cincinnati about six o'clock . . . ." Robert Tarrant missed bidding farewell to his colleagues and friends that evening. Knowing they were leaving he headed out after work, but remarked in his diary: "The 89 Railroad Regiment left for Kentucky this afternoon at 6 o'clock. I went down to camp to see them . . . but they had already left." Thirty-six hours had passed since the Railroad Regiment first received word of pending departure. When the final order arrived Thursday, September 4, the men marched out Camp E. H. Williams and were soon enveloped in a cloud of dust. It was a hot afternoon and unused to the load they were carrying, sweat poured off men, who "growled pretty hard and some swore considerable . . . ." Buckley commented that "it was most certainly hard work," making the boys glad to see the Michigan Central depot where they boarded a train which took them south.[98]

---

[97] Buckley, letter, September 3 and 4, 1862. To induce enlistment, bounties were paid by Federal, state, and local authorities. Congress voted a $100 bounty, which was paid over a period of time rather than in one lump sum. Once sworn into the service, each enlistee received $27. Twenty-five dollars was advance bounty money and an additional $2 premium. During most of the conflict, a Union private was paid $13 a month.

[98] Goddard diary, September 4, 1862; Buckley, letter, September 7, 1862; George G. Sinclair, letter to Francis Sinclair, September 6, 1862, (Transcriptions are at the Abraham Lincoln Presidential Library in Springfield, Illinois. Originals are in possession of Nancy Kersey, New Madison, Ohio. Hereafter cited as Sinclair

Each man had arrived at this point in life for a variety of reasons. Without question a majority came out of patriotism and a desire to preserve the Union. Many others volunteered only when threatened with the draft. Enlisting preserved the bounties being offered and the right to pick the men and officers with whom the soldier would serve. And, a few enlisted strictly for the adventure of going to war.

The minds of some of these departing soldiers may have reflected back to the mass war rally held in Chicago on July 26. That afternoon, performed for the first time on the courthouse square was the latest composition of noted song writer, George F. Root, "The Battle Cry of Freedom." It and Stephen Foster's "We Are Coming, Father Abraham, Three Hundred Thousand More," became the anthems of the regiments leaving for the field that fall. As the cars carrying the Railroad Regiment left the city, someone amongst the 900 men probably began and others soon joined in singing these words:

Yes, we'll rally round the flag, boys,
We'll rally once again,
Shouting the battle cry of Freedom,
We will rally from the hillside,
We'll gather from the plain,
Shouting the battle cry of Freedom.

The Union forever, Hurrah! boys, hurrah!
Down with the traitors,
Up with the stars;
While we rally round the flag, boys,
Rally once again, Shouting the battle cry of Freedom.[99]

---

letter.) Tarrant, diary, September 4, 1862; *Chicago Evening Journal*, September 4, 1862; *Chicago Tribune*, September 6, 1862.

[99] Theodore J. Karamanski, *Rally 'Round the Flag: Chicago and the Civil War* (Chicago: Nelson-Hall Publishers, 1993), 109-110.

CHAPTER 2

"BOUND FOR DIXIE LAND"

During the first six months of 1862, Federal forces were on the move in the Western and Trans-Mississippi theaters. Battlefield victories followed at Forts Henry and Donelson, Pea Ridge, Shiloh, and Corinth, giving Union troops control of Kentucky, middle and western Tennessee, northern Mississippi, and most of Missouri. On the Mississippi River, operations by the Union army and navy successfully opened all but 200 miles of the waterway. The closed section lay between the guns at Vicksburg and the Rebel bastion at Port Hudson.

Despite their losses and setbacks, the rebels in the West were far from beaten. As Union troops advanced deep into rebel territory, guerilla operations and cavalry raids cut and damaged Federal communication and supply lines. Limited as these successes may have been, the actions buoyed Confederate morale while taking a toll on the Union advantage. The rebel ever-confident rebel leaders were determined to reverse their fortunes. They could take heart in the fact that their armies were still intact and their officers were full of fight. On July 31, 1862, Generals E. Kirby Smith and Braxton Bragg met in Chattanooga, Tennessee and agreed to launch a counteroffensive and invade Kentucky. The objective was to drive Don Carlos Buell's Army of Ohio out of middle Tennessee, and if possible, draw the Yankees into a fight and destroy them.

The victory would regain both Tennessee and Kentucky and force the Federals along the Mississippi River to retreat. With Bragg and Smith heading north, Earl Van Dorn and Sterling Price were ordered to move on the Federals at Corinth, Mississippi, retake the city with its vital railroads, and clear the Yankees from northern Mississippi. In the East, the defeat of Federal General John Pope at the Battle of Second Manassas afforded Robert E. Lee the opportunity to cross the Potomac and bring the war to the North.

While Bragg massed his troops around Chattanooga for the offensive against Buell, plans were laid for Smith to force the Federals from the Cumberland Gap. Bragg intended that Smith eventually join him in defeating Buell. As drawn up, his plan for the invasion of Kentucky may have been sound, but its weakness lay in that it lacked overall coordination and control. Otherwise, Smith and Bragg operated separately.

With 9,000 men, Smith departed Knoxville, Tennessee on August 14 and bypassed the Union troops of George Morgan holding Cumberland Gap. The movement forced the Federals to hastily dispatched two brigades of "green" recruits, numbering 6,500 men, from Louisville to Morgan's aid. On August 30, the Confederates routed these troops at Richmond, Kentucky, taking over 4,300 prisoners. Cutoff, Morgan's Yankees finally abandoned the Gap on September 17 and eventually fled across the Ohio River to safety.

Preceding the main body of the Army of the Mississippi was a brigade of cavalry. They left Kingston, Tennessee also on August 14 and captured London, Kentucky three days latter. Bragg's main body marched from Chattanooga on August 28 for the Blue Grass State. By September 13, he was in Glasgow, Kentucky. The next day his leading brigade struck the Federals at Munfordville where they were repulsed with heavy losses. By September 16, Bragg's entire army was on the scene, surrounding the Union troops of Colonel John T. Wilder. Seeing the situation as hopelessness, Wilder surrendered his command of 4,133 men the following day.

Buell initially miscalculated Bragg's intentions and moved to protect Nashville. He soon realized that Nashville was not the target, and set out after Bragg and toward Louisville, staying on a parallel track to the Confederates. By capturing Munfordville, Bragg's army was able to rest across the Louisville & Nashville Railroad and

Buell's line of communication. Buell came up, and the armies faced each other for three days, with both generals avoiding battle. On September 21 Bragg headed northeast toward Bardstown, and Buell marched directly for Louisville. When Buell's leading elements arrived on September 25, they found the city's defenses manned by 40,000 raw troops.

Bragg's move north into Kentucky frightened the governors of Illinois, Indiana, and Ohio into forwarding every available regiment to Louisville and Cincinnati. The *Chicago Tribune* reported August 17: "The news from Kentucky creates the most intense excitement here. Troops are being rushed forward with all possible speed. Gov. Morton has ordered Major Gen. Lew Wallace and Gen. Dumont, who are here on leave of absence, to take command temporarily of the new regiments." The units sent, however, were the recently organized and partially trained regiments formed from the recent call for volunteers. The Railroad Regiment, now the Eighty-ninth Illinois Volunteer Infantry, was among the troops ordered south.[1]

As the train loaded with the Railroad Regiment pulled out of Chicago, Fred Goddard quietly entered into his diary for Thursday, September 4, 1862: "To day has been one of great note and importance. We are on the cars bound for Dixie Land." When the regiment arrived at Michigan City, Indiana, however, a teletype message with amended orders awaited. George Sinclair wrote his wife that the regiment was rerouted to Louisville "as the secesh were threatening the city and were within six miles of it." The following evening the Railroaders arrived at Jeffersonville, Indiana opposite Louisville.[2]

Goddard's small pocket diary, with its short but cryptic daily entries, summarized the three-day trip Louisville. Friday, September 5 the men enjoyed the day rolling through the Indiana countryside, and when the train slowed or stopped the local population handed the soldiers apples and peaches, supplementing their crackers and meat. Saturday found Goddard tiring of the trip, but commenting that "the folks along the road treat us very well." Sunday, September 7, the engine and cars crept slowing along

---

[1] *Chicago Tribune*, August 18, 1862.

[2] Goddard, diary, September 4, 1862; Sinclair, letter September 6, 1862.

and finally arrived at Jeffersonville after dark. From the depot, the regiment moved to the landing, boarded a ferry, and crossed the Ohio River to Louisville. Formed up, the regiment marched 5 miles before stopping for the night. The men fell out and "laid down on the ground" to sleep.[3]

On leaving Camp Williams and Chicago the train carrying the Railroaders passed through Michigan City, Lafayette, Indianapolis, and halted at Jeffersonville across from Louisville where the regiment disembarked. The Knox County farmer, George Berry noted the men "had firstrate cars to ride in all the way throu" while "the Board of Trade Regiment from the same place had to ride in cattle cars and had to stand up at that." As the train rolled through the Hoosier State, crowds gathered along the track to wish the soldiers well. "Lots of little girls and boys' wave there white handkerchief as we past a long the road," Berry wrote his family. Once in Louisville, he reported that "fresh troops ar pouring in evry Day."[4]

Joe Buckley and George Sinclair provide similar observations about the trip to Louisville. "We were cheered very much at every station, and were treated to apples and peaches in abundance," Buckley wrote his wife. While Sinclair's letter home said the men were met "with the warmest of receptions from the inhabitants of all the places along the line, being waited upon with water and fruits in great plenty [and] with plenty of kisses and waving of handkerchiefs, which of course were appreciated by us."[5]

After two days the men disembarked from the cars and pulled on their knapsacks. It was around 9:00 P.M. The regiment, however, did not move out, but waited for several hours before eventually marching for the ferry that took them across the Ohio River to Louisville. When the Eighty-ninth arrived at Jeffersonville, Indiana, George Sinclair wrote that "we were caused to stop there until midnight so as to blind the secession sympathizers as to our strength and our effectiveness. But as it was many people were up. Some waved banners to us while others said nothing and some

---

[3] Goddard, diary, September 5 through 7, 1862.
[4] Berry, letter, September 6, 1862.
[5] Buckley, letter, September 7, 1862; Sinclair, letter, September 6, 1862.

devils threw a lot of rubbish and a bottle from a five story building intending no doubt to quiet some good Union soldier. But the Lord did not will it so, for it did no harm, only just reminded us of what we might expect at any time from some disinterested Kentuckian."[6]

At 1:00 A.M., the regiment halted and made camp for the first time in the field. "We did not have our tents along . . . so we rolled ourselves in our blankets and slept on the ground until morning, and we all slept as sound as though we were in a bed of feathers," Joe Buckley wrote. They awoke on Sunday to no breakfast, but at noon received "a few crackers and a little salt ham." Buckley complained: "That has been our fare since we left Camp Williams." With or without rations, the new soldiers found quickly that military life goes on. The tents arrived and the men set about putting them up and organizing a formal camp. On completion the place was christened Camp Manchester. With this chore out of the way, Buckley and part of Company H hiked four miles to the Ohio River where they bathed and washed their clothes. The men had a "fine time of it" at the river."[7]

Having set up camp, George Berry penned in a letter home that "we have good tents to sleep under but we hafter sleep on the ground with little hay under us." Now in the field George confided that he began "to under stand [a] soldier's life," which included the daily routine of details like guard and picket duty. The Railroaders found this part of Kentucky in the grip of a severe drought. "It has not rains hear for foure months. It is very dusty and worme," George Berry pointed out in the same letter. He added that water was so scarce that "we hafture guard wells." Berry further commented that the regiment would not allow the local citizenry "to come nigh ower watering places."[8]

The rebel offensive and the Midwestern governors' reaction brought a flood of bluecoated troops to defend Louisville and Cincinnati. Being part of this effort, the men of the Eighty-ninth Illinois quickly realized that they were part of an extensive build up of men and material. Buckley estimated: "There are about 20 or 30

6   Sinclair, letter, September 6, 1862.
7   Buckley, letters, September 7 and 8, 1862.
8   Berry, letter, September 9, 1862.

thousand soldiers encamped in the neighborhood. A great many of the men are not drilled."[9]

When the men of the Eighty-ninth embarked for the seat of war, their newly elected colonel, John Christopher, was not with them. An order from the War Department mandated "that he could not be released from his present duties till after the new levies are mustered in." The *Chicago Times* reported that "this will probably occupy four weeks yet, after which it is expected Colonel Christopher will be able to join his regiment."[10]

Assuming command of the regiment was thirty-year-old Lieutenant Colonel Charles Truman Hotchkiss. Born in Virgil, Cortland County, New York, Hotchkiss grew up on a farm in Calhoun County, Michigan. He attended the Albion Seminary, but at age sixteen set out on his own for Wisconsin to become a teletype operator. In 1850, he came to Chicago where he continued in that occupation. By 1853, he had moved to Rockford, Illinois and was working for the Galena and Chicago Union Railroad. Here, he became the line's freight agent, resigning in 1857 to enter business as a contractor. Hotchkiss' company constructed bridges and docks, while also doing dredging and harbor work. He also partnered with his father in a lumber business known as S. W. Hotchkiss & Son. With the outbreak of the Rebellion, Hotchkiss closed his construction operation and enlisted on April 23, 1861 as a private in the Eleventh Illinois Volunteer Infantry, a three-month regiment. On mustering in, he was appointed regimental adjutant with the rank of first lieutenant.[11]

Most of the regimental paperwork, from issuing orders to handling routine correspondence, fell to the adjutant. Hotchkiss' background fit the job. He soon became an invaluable assistant

[9]   Buckley, letter, September 8. 1862.

[10]   *Chicago Times*, September 6, 1862.

[11]   *Hand-Book of Chicago Biography (Chicago:* John J. Flinn, *1893), 204-205; Memorials of Deceased Companions of the Commanderey of the State of Illinois, Military Order of the Loyal Legion of the United States From January 1, 1912 to December 31, 1922* (Wilmington, NC: Broadfoot Publishing Company, 1993), 184-186; Charles George, *Forty Years on the Rail: Reminiscences of a Veteran Conductor* (Chicago: R. R. Donnelly & Sons, Publisher, 1887), 107.

to Colonel W. H. L. Wallace, a Mexican War veteran and La Salle County attorney. When the Eleventh's term of service expired on July 30, 1861, the regiment re-enlisted for three years. Hotchkiss was re-mustered as captain of Company F but never actually held command. Instead, he became an assistant adjutant general when Wallace took charge of a brigade. While serving as one of Wallace's aides, Hotchkiss was at the battle of Belmont, Mo., the capture of Fort Henry, and the battle and capture of Fort Donelson.[12]

In his diary, Private George D. Carrington of Company B, described Adjutant Hotchkiss as a "'fleshy little man' always 'puffing and perspiring,' scurrying up and down the ranks babbling on about the regiment like a worried housewife dusting the settee prior to the pastors visit.'" What the men in the ranks considered fussy and nitpicking, a superior saw as conscientious and efficient.[13]

On March 21, 1862, Wallace was promoted to brigadier general and given command of U. S. Grant's second division which he led at Pittsburg Landing, Tennessee. Hotchkiss continued on Wallace's staff and was with him when he was mortally wounded at Shiloh. Captain Hotchkiss along with the general's brother-in-law, Lieutenant Cyrus E. Dickey, accompanied the remains back to Illinois for burial.[14]

After Wallace's death, Captain Hotchkiss was transferred to Major General John A. McClernand's staff, where he served during the campaign for Corinth, Mississippi. In late August, the *Tribune* while reporting that Captain Hotchkiss was back in Chicago said the following: "Major Hotchkiss, who was formerly a Lieutenant in the National Guards of this city, was one of the first to respond to the call of the President, and has ever since been actively engaged among the fighting portion of our forces, having held the position of

---

[12] Ezera J. Warner, *Generals in Blue: Lives of the Union Commanders* (Baton Rouge, LA: Louisiana State University Press, 1992), 536-537; *Hand-Book of Chicago Biography*, 203.

[13] Jim Huffstodt, *Hard Dying Men: The story of General W.H.L. Wallace, General T.E.G. Ransom, and their "Old Eleventh" Illinois Infantry in the American Civil War* (Bowie, Maryland: Heritage Books, Inc., 1991), 15.

[14] Warner, *Generals in Blue: Lives of the Union Commanders*, 537; H. M. Parker, *Proceedings of the First Reunion of the Eleventh Regiment Illinois Volunteer Infantry* (Ottawa, Illinois: Osman and Hareman, 1875), 65-66.

Captain in the famous Eleventh Illinois Volunteers, Adjutant General of the late Gen. Wallace and for time past Adjutant General of Maj. Gen. McClellan [McClernand]. In all these responsible positions, Maj. Hotchkiss has won the highest commendations."[15]

Hotchkiss fit the template the railroad committee set for a leader. He was a self-made man, an entrepreneur, who had left a secure job to engage in the construction business. Much of his company's work came from the railroads for which he built bridges. These railroad men looked upon Captain Hotchkiss as a respected equal, but with military experience; therefore, he was the type of officer they could entrust with their regiment. The selection soon became more significant with Captain Christopher left behind in Chicago.

Further complicating matters, and probably more of an embarrassment to the railroad committee than anything, was the resignation of the regiment's newly elected major, John L. Newell. The *Tribune* reported that Newell, the Chief Engineer of the northern branch of the Illinois Central Railroad, had "found it impracticable to go at this time." Captain Duncan J. Hall was quickly appointed his successor. Born in Detroit, Michigan on September 15, 1838, Hall was educated at Urbana University in Ohio. In 1855, the Hall family came to Chicago where Duncan read law with a prominent firm and was admitted to the bar in 1861. He had also joined the Chicago National Guard to gain military experience. For his twenty-third birthday, Captain (now Major) Hall was given a Model 1850 foot officer's sword with the inscription "'Duncan J. Hall, from his Parents, Chicago, 15th Septr. 1861.'"[16]

Also staying behind in Chicago to tie up any remaining loose ends was John M. Farquhar, now the regiment's sergeant major. One of his duties was to round up those men who were either on one last fling or having second thoughts about military service. On Tuesday, September 9, the *Evening Journal* printed the following: "THE

---

[15]   *Chicago Tribune*, August 28.

[16]   *Chicago Tribune*, September 4 and 6, 1862; Alfred T. Andreas, *History of Chicago From the Earliest Period to the Present Time*, 3 vols. (Chicago: The A. T. Andreas Company, Publishers, 1885), II: 249; Don Troiani, [Internet website] *Don Troiani-The Collection*, (Accessed February 23, 2003), http://www.dontroiana. com/collectionducansword.htl., 1862.

RAILROAD REGIMENT.—It is ordered by Colonel Christopher that all absentees from the 89 Illinois Regiment report for duty immediately or they will be published and treated as deserters. Stragglers in the city will report to me at the Warren House, Randolph [S]treet. This is the last call." On a positive note the sergeant major offered to receive and deliver any "letters and parcels for the Regiment, if left at the Michigan Southern Railroad office, 56 Clark [S]treet, previous to Wednesday noon . . . ."[17]

Once in the field the men soon found Lieutenant-Colonel Hotchkiss was just as determined to turn the Eighty-ninth into a trained and functional regiment, as he was in his days with the Eleventh Illinois. The business of regimental drill began immediately. On Monday, September 8, Private Fred Goddard wrote that "we drill eight hours a day. It is quite warm and drill is hard." The thirty-one-year-old Joseph Buckley held a more realistic view of the current situation. He explained to his wife, Mary that "we are commencing to drill this morning in good earnest. We will have to drill from 8 to 10 hours a day. We do not know how soon we may be called on to fight. I don't care how much they drill us for the more we practice, the better it be for us." Born in Lancashire, England, Joseph Buckley immigrated to the United States in 1849. When his father died in 1851, he returned to England to settle the estate, and was gone for four months. When he returned to Illinois, he took up farming in Kendall County. In August 1862, even though he was married with two children and not "a full-fledged citizen," Buckley answered Lincoln's call for more men.[18]

The Eighty-ninth was barely settled into their encampment when they received marching orders. Federal regiments were needed to defend the Queen City of the Ohio since Kirby Smith's rebels were reported "only seven miles from Cincinnati, threatening the invasion of Ohio and Indiana." It was near sundown on Wednesday, September 7, and the Railroaders had finished with battalion drill and dress parade when an order came to get knapsacks packed and

---

[17] *Chicago Evening Journal,* September 6 and 9, 1862.

[18] Goddard, diary, September 8, 1862; Buckley, letter, September 7, 1862; *History of Grundy County, Illinois Illustrated* (Chicago: O. L. Baskin and Company, 1882), 42.

haversacks filled. The men were given 30 minutes to be squared away and ready to march. With each man carrying four days of rations and 50 rounds of cartridges, the regiment fell in and set off for the Ohio River to board a transport to Cincinnati. "After trudging three or four hours, with a knapsack on my back," George Sinclair wrote, "we laid down on the river bank for the night with the starry heavens for a canopy and a lot of broken bricks for a bed. They were those soft red brick or we should have fared hard." He continued: "Well the transport that was to take us did not come during the night, so we crossed [on] the ferry to Jeffersonville to take the cars for Cincinnati. But we had as good luck as on the Kentucky side for we were packed onto open flat cars and old stinking cattle cars . . . ." After creaking along for about 15 miles, the train slowed to a halt as track was out ahead. "We staid in the open cars most of the day," Joe Buckley added, "and while we sat there, we had one of the heaviest rains I ever saw. We got one good soaking, and finally we received orders to move back and finally we moved back to Camp Holt that night and slept on the ground in a field of stubble, about as rough ground as I ever saw." During the night another storm brought heavy rain which wrapped in there blankets the men endured. Nothing took place the next day, "till three oclock and then had marching orders to go back to ower ould camping ground," George Berry wrote. And afterward, he concluded: "It all did not amount to nothing."[19]

After completing its first "hurry up and wait" operation, the Eighty-ninth was right back where it started, about a mile outside of Louisville. Sunday, September 14, Goddard noted: "We are back at our old camp (Camp Manchester) and have got our tents all pitched and are writing letters. We expect to leave again tomorrow." Uncertainty and confusion is the enlisted soldier's lot as George Sinclair revealed to his wife. "We are going to move tomorrow morning for where I can't tell as we are not let into the secrets of their movements . . . . Well, thank the Lord [that] I have not much curiosity on that score. Only I want them to end this war as soon as possible so as I can get Home." With that out of the way, Sinclair was proud to speak of his recent promotion. "By the way I got the second

---

[19]   Andreas, *History of Chicago*, II: 244; Buckley, letter, September 18, 1862; Sinclair, letter, September 13, 1862; Berry, letter, September 13, 1862.

sergeant both by the captain's appointment and the approval of the men. I am proud of it for it is certainly great an honor to hold such in this regiment as a lieutenancy would be in some regiments . . . ."[20]

The recent mix up and exposure left a number of men ill. Corporal John Browning of Camp Point, Adams County, wrote his wife, Eliza, that he was sick and unable to do his duty. He said that John Miller, also of Camp Point, was "falling off every day. The doctor told him he could not do him any good or had no medicine that would do him any good." Miller died in New Albany, Indiana on November 21.[21]

* * *

When the Eighty-ninth Illinois arrived in Louisville, the regiment was attached to the Army of Kentucky and was temporarily assigned to Woodruff's brigade and Cruft's division. In defending Louisville, the Railroaders mainly served on outpost duty, but at times the regiment marched out to meet reported Rebel threats. Monday, September 15 was one of those instances. Sunday's rumor was confirmed with the Eighty-ninth being ordered into line with some other regiments to form a makeshift brigade." As the inexperienced and overloaded soldiers fell in, Joseph Buckley's observed that "it was about the hottest day I ever saw,"—a comment that proved to a prophetic.[22]

The column commenced a marching about 8:00 A.M.. The pace was such that Buckley judged the regiment covered five miles in a little over an hour before halting. Making matters worse it was "a hot sultry day." Buckley wrote that it was "the hottest sun pouring down on us that I ever experienced." On the back of each green soldier was a knapsacks filled with clothes, rations, and blankets.

---

20 Goddard, diary, September 14, 1862; Sinclair, letter, September 13, 1862.

21 John Browning, letter to Eliza Browning, September 13, 1862, original letters at the Historical Society of Quincy and Adams County (Illinois), hereafter cited as Browning letter

22 Thomas M. Eddy, 2 vols. *The Patriotism of Illinois: A Record of the Civil War and Military History of the State*, (Chicago: Clarke, 1866) II: 336; Buckley, letter, September 18, 1862

Add a water-filled canteen, fifty rounds of cartridges, a slung rifle, and each "strapped and loaded" man had "upward of 80 pounds" on his person. Sinclair likened it to carrying "the load of a mule on our back and body." Consequently, a number of men "fell out of the ranks from sun stroke and sheer exhaustion . . . ." Buckley related "that about half of the Regiment gave out when we had traveled that distance." He went so far as to claim that "several men in the Regiment died right off from the effects of the sun and the march together." Buckley's letter detailed how the neighborhood men faired. "Morgan Skinner fainted. We all thought he would not live, but he is gaining strength now. Charles Litsey, Will Litsey, Chauncy Talmadge and [Henman] Bresee all gave out. Talmadge was very bad for a while. They all got over it. Next day we marched 8 or 10 miles. After that there was only about 30 of us that stood it through that is in our company."[23]

Not overly literate, but having his own way with words, was George Berry. He wrote: We had marching orders on last Monday morning. We marched about Eight miles. It was hot and dusty and in going that distance there was ten men in ower Regiment that fell down in the road over come with the heat." When the regiment made camp that night, Berry conjectured that over hundred men were not yet in." He told his wife that "all of the Victoria Boys stood it well. In ower Company there was some ten or twelve fell by the wayside and come in after Dark. We traveled to fast and we had ower dress "coat on. The Colonel was to blame for not restin us ofner. I was some sore the next day."[24]

Chaplain, James H. Dill, disclosed in a letter to the *Chicago Tribune* that one soldier, eighteen-year-old Magloire Ponton of Company A, had died of "congestive chills" on the September 15 and "was buried in the northeast corner of a lot opposite the toll gate, two miles out on [the] Bardstown Pike." Joseph Buckley, still fuming when he wrote Mary on the September 18, painted another picture of the event. "We had a funeral last Tuesday for one of the men that died on the march the day before. It is impossible for me to convey the idea of indignation that was felt by the officers

---

[23]   Buckley, letter, September 18, 1862; Sinclair, letter, September 23, 1862.

[24]   Berry, letter, September 18, 1862.

and soldiers. They threatened to shoot the Brigadier General for marching us so unreasonable, and they would have done it, if he had shown himself."[25]

Tuesday, September 16, began with intelligence that the enemy was heading for Bardstown. The Eighty-ninth and the brigade quickly broke camp and set off in that direction. "We marched 10 miles on that [Bardstown] road and encamped for the night, Sergeant Sinclair wrote. The next orders came "to march back to Louisville as that place was expected to be attacked." The trip back was "a forced march through . . . dust ankle deep." After the hardships and complaints of the first few days in the field, Sinclair stated that "we received quite a compliment on our march back to camp by saying that our regiment marched like veterans . . . ."[26]

Once in Louisville, the Eighty-ninth joined the rest of the army outside the city in "digen intrenchments" and making battery emplacements. Manning picks and shovels along side the soldiers were "about five hundred negroes." And after another day of digging, Joe Buckley told his wife: "I expect we have done our share of trenching now." To protect Louisville everybody had been set to work on the defenses. In looking back, one Railroader, Private Alfred French of Company A remembered that "here we got a taste of army life; we had to go on picket, dig trenches, work on the fortification, &c."[27]

With the rebels threatening Louisville, the city was in a state of panic and constant turmoil. The Federal defenders were no better off. Orders were flying about the Railroaders' camp to either prepare to march or to man the works. By September 18 the Railroaders were alerted that something was up. "We are going some place this afternoon. I do not know whear," wrote George Berry. While Joe Buckley ended his letter home with the following: "We have just received orders to be ready to march at a moments notice . . . ." The

---

25 *Chicago Tribune*, September 27, 1862; Buckley, letter, September 18, 1862.

26 Sinclair, letter, September 23, 1862.

27 Berry, letter, September 18, 1862; Buckley, letter, September 18, 1862; Illinois in the Civil War, [Internet website] *Civil War Scrapbook-Alfred D. French Memoirs*, (Accessed January 6, 2006), http://www.rootsweb.com/~ilcivilw/scrapbk/frenchmemoirs.html, hereafter cited as French Memoir.

turmoil persisted and five days later George Sinclair told his wife that "this is the second time that I have been . . . called to arms. We expect to be attacked every minute. The regiment is in good spirits some dancing, playing cards to amuse themselves, just aching for a fight."[28]

"For two weeks past, our regiment has been constantly marching and countermarching in the vicinity of this city until we have become almost afraid to unpack our baggage, lest at the next moment should come an order to march," wrote Chaplain Dill. He informed the Chicago readers that "it is exceedingly gratifying to see what unwillingness there is among the railroad boys to shirk or to report themselves on the sick list. Many a man I've seen marching along with his musket and knapsack who if at home would have been on his bed . . . ." Reverend Dill continued his observation with the following: "Yet this and every other hardship our soldiers have met with cheerfulness, knowing it to be a necessary part of that good discipline which shall fit them to serve their country. In fact, the harder our boys are worked, and the more unseasonable the hour at which they are roused by revielle [sic], the more jovial and songful [sic] they seem to be."[29]

Named the regiment's chaplain, James H. Dill took it upon himself to keep the Railroaders' families updated on their welfare and travels. Flattering the *Tribune* editor, he made this offer: "Since the CHICAGO TRIBUNE has so wide a circulation in those parts of Illinois where are the homes of our boys, I propose, through your columns, to keep their friends advised of what transpires in this and neighboring regiments." Dill arrived in Chicago in May 1859 when he was appointed the pastor of Chicago's South Congregational Church. The Reverend Dill was born at Plymouth, Massachusetts and educated at Yale College where he also went to the Seminary. Before coming to Illinois, he had served churches in Connecticut and New York. Age forty-one, married, and with children, the Reverend Dill could easily have assisted the war effort on the home front. However, he commented to a friend

---

[28]   Berry, letter, September 18, 1862; Buckley, letter, September 18, 1862; Sinclair, letter, September 23, 1862.

[29]   *Chicago Tribune*, September 27, 1862.

that "he could not bear to have the war close without having had a hand in it." In his last sermon he told those assembled that it was "serious business to go" and seeing that his future was uncertain, he remarked, "I leave my family with you and with God." [30]

*   *   *

With new troops arriving daily, Major General William "Bull" Nelson's force now totaled about 36,000. Unfortunately, most of the regiments were, like the Eighty-ninth Illinois, part of the new levies sent to defend Kentucky and at this juncture, Louisville, its largest city and the major supply depot for the Federal war effort aimed at the heart of the Confederacy. With this in mind and with Buell falling back in retreat, Nelson prepared to defend the city against an attack from Bragg and Smith. Consequently by September 22, he placed Louisville under martial law and ordered women and children to evacuate. Sergeant Sinclair noted that "the streets look desolate enough, no business doing at all," while Chaplain Dill reported that "the city seemed almost deserted except by soldiers and negroes, since in accordance with Gen. Nelson's proclamation a large portion of the women and children had left for safer quarters." Word in the ranks was that Nelson "would burn the City before he would let the Rebels have it."[31]

By September 28 the fear of a rebel attack on Louisville had subsided. Back in camp after a night on picket duty, George Berry wrote a quick note to Harriet saying as much. From the rumors circulating among the ranks, he concluded, "I don't think Louisville will be atacked by the Rebels. I dont think that we shall have a fight

[30]   *Chicago Tribune*, September 27, 1862 and January 24, 1863; Franklin Woodbury Fisk, *The Chaplain's Memorial: A Sermon, Preached in Chicago, January 31, 1863, at the Funeral of Rev. James H. Dill, Chaplain of the Eighty-Ninth Regiment Illinois Volunteers, Called the "Railroad Regiment,"* (New York: John A. Gray and Green, 1863), 14-15.

[31]   Kenneth A. Hafendorfer, *Perryville: Battle for Kentucky*, (Louisville, Kentucky: K H Press, 1991), 58-59; Sinclair, letter, September 23, 1862; *Chicago Tribune*, September 27,1862; Berry, letter, October 1, 1862.

heare. They say that the Rebels haz turned in another Direction. They say that there is ten thousand troops arrived heare to Day."[32]

Chaplain Dill wrote to the *Tribune* "of the grand scare, which this place has for some days suffered from the threatened approach of Bragg with his vandal hordes." He then turned to laying out his reason for Bragg's failure to attack. Dill drew a written picture of the Federal buildup to protect the city. "It was a noble sight to see every where, as far as eye could reach, regiments on the hills, in trenches, in the streets and rays of the sun glancing and glittering from innumerable bayonets, sabres [sic] and cannon. All seemed eager for the fray, and were disappointed as night drew on and proved Bragg's threat to be only brag."[33]

"Major General Buell and his advance guard entered the city to day," Goddard noted in his diary on Thursday, September 25. That same day, as the Eighty-ninth was taking its turn in the trenches, Private Goddard recorded that "our regiment were (sic) reviewed by Major General Nelson . . ." He then added: "We have orders to be ready to move in a minute's warning. Have got our canteens filled with water. Will probably leave tonight and commenced mess cooking today." Even as his men constructed and manned trenches to defend Louisville, Nelson probed for Bragg's army. When not on picket duty or manning the trenches, the Railroaders were sent on forced marches, searching for the rebels. So, rather than a period of drill and training, the Railroad Regiment, like many other newly formed units, were learning the ropes of military life through on the job training.[34]

Bragg veered away for now, but Major General Nelson kept the army on alert to prevent a surprise attack. His attention was focused on protecting both Louisville and his troops. The letters home and diary entries not only reflect Nelson's orders but they also reveal the day to day life and the hardships the soldiers endured during these hectic days. Shiloh was fresh in Nelson's mind, and he made every effort to keep from being caught unawares. Private George Berry detailed one of measures Nelson undertook at Louisville. "We

---

[32] Berry, letters, September 24 and 28, 1862.

[33] *Chicago Tribune*, September 27, 1862.

[34] Goddard, diary, September 25, 1862.

hafture get up every morning by half Past three o clock and stand in Battle line till daybreak so we should not be taken by surprise if they happen to be around and then we ar marched to ower tents." Sergeant Sinclair described one typical day. "We laid in the trenches all day . . . or near them expecting an attack from Bragg's army. At night at about 11 o'clock, we were roused out at a moment's warning to go on a reconnoitering expedition. Well, we marched out about three miles and laid in the cornfields and woods taking turn about a[t] watching for the enemy. No enemy appeared for some reason or other not known to us. The next day we marched back to Louisville near where we laid the day before and pitched our tents." This routine began to ware on the men. Berry wrote: "Dread the Marching. If I don't hafture carry the knapsack I shall get along firsrate. We have bin traveling about twenty miles in and around Louisville." Between the loss of sleep and forced marches, the men had to come to grips with the elements. With tongue-in-cheek Sinclair penned: "We had a slight taste of the inconvenience of camp life yesterday. After marching all day in a heavy rain and pitching our tents in the night, laying on the ground, which was as wet as it could be after such heavy rain, our blankets wet. We found a little straw, which was also wet but [it] took the curse off from the ground. It will do very well as long as it is warm weather, but we expect to have to take it cold and wet shortly." Speaking of the same evening, Goddard wrote: "We were relieved about 8 Oclock last night and marched for home, but when we got there there was no home. Our tents were all pulled down and we were ordered to march on. We marched about 4 miles [and] found our tents. We pitched them and by the time it was done the mud was shoe deep. For it had rained all the time we were on the march and while we pitched our tents. We were wet to our hides and passed a very uncomfortable night."[35]

The effect of exposure, over exertion, poor diet, and cramped quarters began showing up at morning sick call and on the death roll. Private John W. Harper died on September 19 from a "violent inflammation of the throat." Chaplain Dill told the Chicago public that Harper "was happy in his sickness and death, and was anxious

---

[35]   Berry, letter, September 29, 1862; Sinclair, letter, September 28, 1862; Goddard, diary, September 27, 1862.

only for his wife and children . . . ." Joseph Buckley who was on guard duty near the hospital saw it differently. "There was a man died this morning from the effects of the march last Monday. My beat was close to the hospital last night and I think I never heard anyone cry out with pain as he did. He must have been in great agony. I offered up a prayer to God that he might be release from his suffering, and if he should die that God would receive his soul into heaven where suffering is no more."[36]

The regimental spokesperson, Chaplain Dill informed the *Chicago Tribune* that the "prevailing diseases, besides those brought with them into camp, are bowel complaints and intermittent fever." In his letters, George Berry kept Harriet current with the health of the Walnut Grove boys'. "Mr. Copley has bin sick ever since he left Chicago. I am afraid he cant stand it. Mr. Whales (sic) is quite sicke. I think he has the ague. He is in the hospital." On the whole, he explained "there is some sickening hear in camp. Them that are able to walk haftur go up to the hospital every morning and get theare Medicines. I counted in ower Regiment sixty person(s) one morning." Many of "the soldiers don't take care of there health," Berry concluded and added that they are "drinking Whiskey [and] eating all kind of stuff." Illness knew no bounds. Sergeant Sinclair told his wife that he was "acting orderly sergeant in place of the 1st sergeant, who is sick as is also both of our lieutenants which duties of all I have to attend to just now . . . ."[37]

Joseph Buckley related a tragic incident to Mary which occurred at this time. "They are very strict with us now when we are on guard. If a man does not stop when we have called out to him to halt, our orders are to shoot him. There was one of our regiment shot yesterday by one of the guards. They took him to the post hospital . . . as our surgeon is away on business." Years later, Captain George Robinson recalled the tragic incident. Private Fronville was "suffering from diarrhea or dysentery and obeying the wants of nature was going towards the common privy for soldiers" located "a small distance outside the lines . . . ." On the way "the intensity

---

[36] *Chicago Tribune*, September 27, 1862; Buckley, letter, September 19, 1862.

[37] *Chicago Tribune*, September 27, 1862; Berry, letters, September 9 and 28, 1862.

of his disease forced him to stop and he stooped. He was noticed by a guard who tried to make him get up." Whether he "could not understand the English language or could not get up," his lack of response caused the nervous picket to panic and fire." Fronville had come to the United States in May 1856 with his parents and two siblings, and the family settled near Clifton in Iroquois County. The twenty-two-year-old Belgian immigrant enlisted on August 14 in Chicago. Chaplain Dill reported a guard accidentally shot Louis Fronville on September 18, and the ball struck Fronville in the thigh near the femoral artery. Taken to Hospital No. 3 in Louisville, he lingered until his death on November 14.[38]

Chaplain Dill's correspondence to the *Tribune* dated October 3 stated, "The health of the regiment is improving. We have only about seventy-five men on the sick list, and most of them will recover and rejoin the regiment. All the officers, I believe, are well enough to be on duty, except Lieutenants Copley, Rice and Jackson." He also reported that Dr. Samuel F. Hance, the regimental surgeon, had arrived in Louisville, bringing "with him a great box of nice things sent to the boys by their friends in Aurora." A graduate of Albany Medical College, the thirty-seven-year-old Hance was a practicing physician in Aurora, where one of his patients was Captain Bruce Kidder of Company E.[39]

Dr. Hance had remained behind in Aurora closing out his practice and attending to other business matters. This was not an indulgence granted to the enlisted men. The common soldier used the mail to get his affairs in order. The letters home from the men, in the ranks contained specific instructions for the management of their farms. In answering Lincoln's call, these fellows literally left crops in

---

[38] *Chicago Tribune*, September 27, 1862; *Belgians in the American Civil War*, [Internet website] *Belgian Civil War Soldiers in Illinois*, (Accessed September 26, 2002), http://users.swing.be/sw032310/Illinois/Illinois.htp; Buckley, letter, September 19, 1862.

[39] *Chicago Tribune*, October 8, 1862; Thomas P. Lowry, M.D. and Jack D. Welsh, M.D., *Tarnished Scalpels, The Court Martials of Fifty Union Surgeons* (Mechanicsburg, PA: Stackpole Books, 2000), 127; J. Fletcher Williams, *History of Hennepin County and the City of Minneapolis* (Minneapolis: North Star Publishing Co., 1881), 557.

the field and livestock to be marketed. With the harvest now in the hands of their wives, all they could do was ask questions and give directions. "Have you got the wheat thrashed, and if you have, how did it turn out?" Buckley asked. He then told Mary, "I should advise you to get the corn picked as soon as you can if it is ready." As farm issues crossed George Berry's mind, he explicitly stated his wishes to Harriet. "Tell [the] Giddings Boy that he must be careful not to give them horses green corn when he is husking corn for the hogs. I was glad to hear them hogs aur doing well. When they git fat I gess you had better sell them on foot if you can. Git Thomas Melung to [—] the thrashing. You must git Mr Smith to help the one that I helped. You may sell them heifers [at] ten or twelve Dollars a piece."[40]

Still a problem for a number of men was the receipt of the county bounty. They found payments were being withheld pending the completion of the proper paperwork. For some families these funds were necessary to get by, and as a consequence, letters from the soldiers reflect the effort made to resolve the matter. "Did you get the County Bounty Order that I sent by J. J. Cole for the amount of Seventy Dollars?" queried Buckley. He then added that, "The one I sent by Thomas Britton's wife you will have to destroy, if you have not done so." The semi-literate George Berry explained, "They say that [the] Bounty order is not ritten right that I sent you. Let Joseph Copley see it. If it is not right, let me know." In the following letter, Berry begins, "I have sent two Bounty orders to you and they say they ar not right. This order was sent from Knox County and I copied from it. This order is dated the 29th. This is right they say."[41]

With September drawing to a close, the Railroad boys found themselves in camp for a change. Their first order of business, one man noted, was "to clean our guns [as] they were very rusty . . . ." The job took the entire forenoon. That afternoon, being Sunday, church services were held in a grove about a quarter of a mile from camp. The correspondent attended and was pleased with Chaplain Dill's sermon.[42]

---

[40] Buckley, letters, September 18 and 19 and October 16, 1862; Berry, letters, September 20 and 29, 1862.

[41] Buckley, letter, October 16, 1862; Berry, letters, September 24 and 29, 1862.

[42] Goddard, diary, September 28, 1862.

*   *   *

On the morning of September 27 the last of the Army of the Ohio filed into Louisville. The new levies watched a ragged group of veterans, many shoeless, move into camp. While quartermasters issued new clothes, shoes, and equipment, Major General Buell quickly reorganized the army. To bolster the depleted brigades, a new regiment was added to each. He divided the now 81,000-man Army of the Ohio into three corps. On September 29 Goddard noted the Eighty-ninth Illinois was "under a different Brigadier." The Railroad Regiment had been transferred to Brigadier General Willich's sixth brigade of Brigadier General Joshua W. Sill's Second Division which was part of the First Army Corps, commanded by Major General Alexander McCook.[43]

Monday, September 29, the morning was spent in drill. Private Goddard noted that "we can drill much better than we could a month ago." He then jotted down the news buzzing through the Union camps that "Major General Nelson was shot today by Brigad. General Davis." The facts of the shooting are this. General Nelson, known for a gruff and overbearing manner, had six days earlier argued with Brigadier General Jefferson C. Davis, an Indiana native, and ordered him out of the department to Cincinnati. Davis returned to Louisville with Oliver P. Morton, the Indiana Governor, to settle the issue. He confronted Nelson at the Galt House where they exchanged words. Nelson struck Davis twice in the face with the back of his hand. Davis retreated; borrowed a pistol; returned and shot Nelson in the heart. Although arrested, Davis was never tried for murder. Regarding Nelson's death, Private Berry told his wife "We have lost a grate man." And in his down home manner George Berry explained what he had heard. "General Nelson was shot . . . by a brigadiere oficere. His name was Davise. Nelson insulted him. He made a grate mistake insulting a hier ofecer. Thay say that Daviese was not to blame."[44]

---

[43]   *War of the Rebellion: The Official Records of the Union and Confederate Armies,* 128 vols. (Washington, D. C., 1890-1901), Series I, Volume 16, Part 1, 1024 and Part 2, 591, hereafter cited as *OR.* All references are to Series I unless otherwise states. Goddard, diary, September 29, 1862; *Chicago Tribune,* October 8, 1862.

[44]   Goddard, diary, September 28, 1862; Berry, letter, October 1, 1862; Haffendorfer, *Perryville: Battle for Kentucky,* 67-68; Warner, *Generals in Blue: Lives of the*

Shocked by the shooting that morning, senior officers were further stunned in the afternoon when word spread that General Buell had been dismissed and replaced by Major General George H. Thomas. Upset with Buell for some time, the Lincoln administration placed blame squarely on his shoulders for the current situation in Kentucky. At Lincoln's direction the War Department issued an order dismissing Buell. However, Thomas wired Washington refusing command, stating preparations were in place to move against the enemy and no change need be made. Boxed in, Halleck rescinded the earlier order.[45]

Word circulated through camp on September 28 that the army was moving. Sarcastically, Sergeant George Sinclair wrote his wife, Frances. "We have got to pull up stakes and leave again today. I don't know for what purpose that they are agoing to move, but our officers of the division don't consult the will, pleasure or comfort even of the soldiers, they are nothing but machines to go when told to without asking questions." If there was any movement on the 28th, it was for the Eighty-ninth to align with the veteran regiments in their new brigade. Tuesday, September 30, the regiment received orders to march at 8:00 A.M.., and immediately a few companies struck their tents only find the order was countermanded and had to pitch their tents again. No one got the opportunity to laze about, as the afternoon was spent on the parade ground with Captain Hobbs of the Thirty-sixth Illinois drilling the regiment.[46]

Whether the men in the ranks were aware or not, movement was afoot. Chaplain Dill reported that "our officers have been very busy lately repacking their baggage and reducing it to the dimensions of a carpet bag, which is all they are allowed to carry." This effort, he said, "furnished work for express companies, whose depots are crammed with trunks to be sent home." The command to reduce personal property touched even the lowly privates, who were ordered to lighten their load and were restricted from carrying side arms.[47]

Union Commanders, 343-344.

[45] Haffendorfer, Perryville: Battle for Kentucky, 68-70.

[46] Sinclair, letter, September 28, 1862; Goddard, diary, September 30, 1862.

[47] Chicago Tribune, October 8, 1862.

The Chaplain neatly summarized for readers at home the experiences the men of the Eighty-ninth had recently endured. "In fact for a month past," Dill wrote, "we have been seeing the inside of camp life, and learning the difference between the amateur soldier in Chicago camps and the working soldier in the field." He then pointedly tells those at home that "if anybody comes into the army from any other motive than patriotism, he is, to my mind, either a fool or a great lover of adventure." Continuing, he explained: "We know nothing of what is going on in the outside world, and do not know half as much about the army as those who are not in it. We eat, sleep, dress and move under command, and know no reasons but the command for anything we do. And yet these things we bear with joy, knowing that the[y] are sacrifices necessary for our country."[48]

---

[48] *Ibid.*

CHAPTER 3

"IN FULL BLAST AFTER THE REBELS"

On October 1, two days after the last hungry, ragged, and dust covered division dragged into Louisville, General Don Carlos Buell's refitted and reorganized Army of the Ohio marched out of the city to fight the invading rebels. Knowing that Kirby Smith held Frankfort and that Braxton Bragg's army remained near Bardstown, Buell advanced with about 77,000 men in four columns. Taking different roads, Buell's three corps, totaling 58,000 men, advanced so as to converge on Bragg's army at Bardstown. Two divisions, Sill's, of McCook's corps, and Dumont's, an unassigned unit, moved east on the Shelbyville Road toward Frankfort and General Edmund Kirby Smith's army. Fielding 19,000 men, Sill and Dumont were assigned the task of holding Smith in check and keeping him from reinforcing Bragg.[1]

By Sergeant George Sinclair's watch, it was going on 10:00 A.M.. when the Eighty-ninth took to the road, and already "the sun [was]

---

[1] William S. Dodge, *History of the Old Second Division, Army of the Cumberland* (Chicago: Church & Goodman, 1864), 335-336; Thomas B. Van Horne, *History of the Army of the Cumberland, Its Organization, Campaigns, and Battles*, 2 vols. (1875; rep., Wilmington, NC: Broadfoot Publishing Co., 1988), I: 184-185; Hafendorfer, *Perryville: Battle for Kentucky*, 71-72.

hot enough to scorch the hair off a man's head." Sinclair estimated the column the Eighty-ninth funneled into to number around "20,000 men with artillery, cavalry and all . . . ." Chaplain Dill noted that when the Railroaders departed after the enemy, they did so "without tents or knapsacks . . . ." Sinclair further observed that "another detachment started on another road running south and still another of the same number started on the Bardstown Pike to drive the rebels from Kentucky . . . . We took the right direction for we started [running] them about 12 miles from Louisville. It proved to be part of Kirby Smith's horde, who started [running] on the first sight of our advance and we saw nothing more of them. Now and then we picked up a stray gun cartridge box that some poor devil that was hard pushed had to throw away to save himself. We shoved on after them [as] fast as possible . . . ." That evening the diarist, Fred Goddard, penned a summary of the day. "This morning we received orders to get into line. We were in line by nine and off, as we supposed [we were] to do picket duty, but tonight shows us our mistake as we have marched all day. We are very tired. We have suffered some for want of water and from the heat. We have marched 15 miles." The next morning Goddard arose to find his body "stiff and sore," but, before starting on the day's march, he found energy enough to down a quick "breakfast of hard bread and tea." The weather he noted continued to be "very warm in the forenoon but rained in the afternoon," bringing a needed respite from the heat and dust. The Eighty-ninth covered 17 miles, reaching Shelbyville at sundown. Sergeant Sinclair reported only 12 men from C Company, including the captain and one lieutenant, were still marching when the regimented halted to make camp.[2]

Two days out, the men were given a rest at Shelbyville. Without tents, Goddard explained the men slept on the ground with only their blankets as shelter from the elements. Buell's order reducing baggage eliminated company kettles and pans and replaced them with individual tin cooking utensils. This quickly proved unwieldy, and as a consequence, the men soon divided into small "messes of 6 in a mess" and received some pans to do their cooking. Goddard noted

2   *Chicago Tribune*, October 8, 1862; Sinclair, letter, October 4, 1862; Goddard, diary, October 1 and 2, 1862.

in his diary that "our food is hard bread, coffee, and bacon." Long marches, short rations, and a wandering hog will make enterprising soldiers. This combination and a night on guard duty gave Goddard and another Railroader the opportunity to kill a hog, providing their messes with "plenty of fresh meat." But, shooting a hog was not all that he was up to. Private Goddard was also responsible for bringing some other Southern property into camp. He reported that while out with the ammunition train he had "coaxed a couple of negro boys to run away and they are now in camp and are going along with us." He made a point to pen that "they were owned by a couple of secesh."[3]

The men of the regiment continued to make the best of their new-found environment. "I am the hero of about a thousand men," wrote Sergeant George Sinclair to his wife. "I climbed a tree and knocked a coon off the limb when fifteen or twenty men had tried to get up but dare[d] not." The coon was sacrificed for a good cause. The old bandit was field dressed on the spot, and Sinclair added, "I had a good feed of coon meat . . . ." His good fortune had not ended. Whether on midnight requisition or by pure accident, Sinclair told Frances that he had "stumbled on a fine pig and confiscated him for our mess and it did not go bad . . . ." He and his messmates also acquired help with their daily chores, for Sinclair informed his wife: "I'm a going to have a nigger to work for us and then I shall be satisfied as far as camp life is concerned."[4]

When the regiment moved out, the sick were left behind—some still hospitalized while others remained in camp. George Berry was unable to leave with the regiment, and he explained to his wife the reason. "Ower Regiment had orders to go [on a] three days martch on a [s]couting Expedition. They started to day. I had the diarhea very bade on Monday [and] I did not go with them. I stay[ed] Back in camp guarden the tents. There is ten of us here. I took some pain Killer and it cured me right up. I am well only [a] little weak." He then reflected on the last few weeks and his current state. "The soldiers

3 Larry J. Daniel, *Days of Glory, The Army of the Cumberland, 1861-1865* (Baton Rouge, LA: Louisiana State University Press, 2004), 127; Goddard, diary, October 3-5, 1862.
4 Sinclair, letter, October 4, 1862.

don't have a very ease time of it. They hafture be a marching around so much. We have moved five difern times since we have bin in Louisville. But wen a person is well he can get along firstrate. Wen he is sick it is a harde Place."[5]

While Berry lingered behind in camp recovering from his intestinal ailment, he observed that "there is a general movement to day. Ther is some thing up. Troops ar a leaving as fast as they can." In his note to Harriet, George says that his detail will stay behind "till the tents goes." Whether or not the tents had been struck, Berry was well enough on October 3 to head out with the provision train, catching up with the regiment on the following day at Shelbyville. When he reached the regiment it became clear to him that when the "regiment hade started out it was a forward movement of Buell['s] army," not another reconnaissance mission as was first rumored.[6]

When George rejoined Company G, he was informed of the new mess arrangement and told he would share rations with his brother, Thomas, Theodore and Wilford Whitney, Rob Wilson, and William Dayton. The change pleased him, and he wrote: "We have [a] firstrate time now. The boys goes out and brings in potatoes and pig meat, apples and sweet potatoes. We are living fine." Around the campfire Berry's messmates brought him up to date on their march from Louisville. Taking up his pen and paper, he interpreted the news to for his wife. "In coming this fere the advance arme drove four hundred Rebels back in to the country. In Shelbyville they had the Rebels bage[d] up but wen the Arme came in cite, they all left." His comrades also explained that the Eighty-ninth, as the new regiment in the brigade, marched at the rear of the column. The boys further pointed out to him that "half of McCook['s] troops are olde soldiers," and George wrote that he had heard, "when we come in battle, we are heald as reserve."[7]

Second Lieutenant William Harkness of Company H wrote his parents: "Such vast armies passing through the country back and forth makes provisions very scarce. In fact, every thing eatable is either bought at enormous prices or stolen by the soldiers. It is

5   Berry, letter, October 1, 1862.
6   Berry, letter, October 1 and 5, 1862.
7   Berry, letter, October 5, 1862

Clear The Track

entirely against orders for any soldier to leave the ranks while on a march." But he added "they do it by the hundreds and scour the country for miles around in quest of chickens, potatoes, honey, bread, anything in fact. Thus they can eat. They all draw their regular rations, but it is rather tiresome living on hard crackers and coffee which is about all they get while on a march. While in camp they get plenty. Beef, pork, salt, etc." The diminutive Harkness, who stood 5'4", possessed an affable demeanor and became a favorite of the enlisted men. Born December 13, 1835 in Bowden, Scotland, he came to the United States as a small child with his family. Like so many others, he left a wife and farm in response to Lincoln's call "to save the Union."[8]

* * *

The veterans or "olde soldiers" of the Sixth Brigade of the Second Division of the Army of the Ohio were the Thirty-second and Thirty-ninth Indiana and the Fifteenth and Forty-ninth Ohio regiments. The Thirty-second Indiana, also known as the First German regiment, was organized through the efforts of August Willich, a former Prussian Army officer and political refugee from the Revolution of 1848. Willich mustered in as colonel of the Thirty-second Indiana and now commanded the Sixth Brigade. His Hoosiers gained acclaim on December 17, 1861 when part of the regiment held off an estimated 1,300 rebel infantry and cavalry near Rowlett's Station, Kentucky. As the skirmish progressed, Confederate General Thomas C. Hindman ordered a cavalry charge by Colonel Benjamin Franklin Terry's Texas Rangers (Eighth Texas Cavalry). The cut-off Germans formed a hollow square to meet the charging Texans. The tactic succeeded as the Thirty-second repulsed the Rangers, killing Terry. A determined Hindman followed with an infantry charge against the Hoosiers, which was also thrown back. The rebels then withdrew, leaving the victorious Thirty-second in possession of the field. Starved for victories, northern newspapers trumpeted the German's

---

[8]   [Internet website] *Letters Written By Captain William Harkness*, (Accessed April 30, 2004), http://www.rootsweb.com/~ilkendal/Military/CivilWar/INF089th/ WmHarknessLtrs.htm.

70

stand. The *Chicago Tribune* announced: "The Indiana German Troops Whip Ten Times their Number . . . ." The reporter began the article by writing: "The recent . . . engagement, considering the disproportion of numbers, proves the most brilliant Federal victory yet achieved."[9]

The Fifteenth Ohio began as a three-month regiment but reorganized and entered the service in September 1861 as three-year volunteers. The regiment first saw action in Western Virginia in the summer of 1861. The entire Sixth Brigade was engaged on the second day at Shiloh and again in the operations leading up to and at the siege of Corinth. With over a year of service, these men were not bandbox soldiers, but a veteran outfit that had "seen the elephant." To be on equal footing, the new fellows from Illinois would have to show their mettle and earn their respect. Until then, the Eighty-ninth would march at the rear of the column. And from this position, the Railroaders only heard army rumors and the distant rumble of musketry and cannon. Sinclair's following lines are an example of the exaggerations that made their way to the back echelon. "There was quite heavy continued firing heard yesterday [October 3] and day before [October 2]. The upshot of it was that a part of my division captured four thousand prisoners, rebel cavalry."[10]

General Kirby Smith's rebel column halted its advance about thirty miles from Louisville at Shelbyville, Kentucky. When the Confederates neared Shelbyville, Union men, like Henri F. Middleton, fearing the worst, fled with their families to Louisville for protection. Middleton, a loyal citizen, was both the owner and editor of the *Shelby News*. In that capacity he had demonstrated that he was "an uncompromising Union man, and one who, in the sight of God and with a full knowledge of the right, fears not to speak his mind, and that in the face of enemies." The publisher's actions and words

---

9   OR, Vol. 16, Pt. 2, 591; Ann Turner, *Guide to Indiana Civil War Manuscripts* (Indianapolis: Indiana Civil War Centennial Commission, 1965), 106-107; *Indiana at Chickamauga, 1863-1900. A Report of the Indiana Commissioners, Chickamauga National Military Park.* (Indianapolis: Sentinel Printing Company, 1900), 160; *Chicago Tribune*, December 19, 1861.

10   Whitelow Reid, 2 vols. *Ohio in the War: Her Statesmen, Her Generals, and Soldiers* (Cincinnati: Moore, Wilstach, and Baldwin, 1868), I: 111; Sinclair, letter, October 4, 1862.

were well known to the rebels, and when they took possession of Shelbyville they "searched his house and threatened to burn his office . . . ."[11]

With the advance of Federal forces to Shelbyville, Middleton returned expecting to find his home and business in ashes, but to his surprise everything was in place and unharmed. Relieved that the rebels had not exacted revenge for his Union stance, Middleton was more than willing to give the men in blue full use of his office, supplies, and equipment. The Eighty-ninth, a regiment with several printers and the former president of the National Printers' Union, put their talents to work and printed probably the only edition of *"The Headlight*, the official organ of the 89th Illinois (Railroad) Regiment." It was a single sheet printed on both sides and distributed on October 4. *The Headlight* was conceived "from a scarcity of writing paper and three-cent stamps . . ." as a method to pass news of the Eighty-ninth to family and friends in the North. By exchanging *The Headlight* with established newspapers, the boys figured that parts of the paper would be picked up and reprinted. The *Chicago Tribune* acknowledged that "the Railroad Regiment, the 89th Illinois Infantry, have commenced the publication . . . of a spicy little sheet . . . ." The short-lived newspaper says much about the material that made up the Eighty-ninth, for they were a resourceful lot who constantly looked for ways to put their talents and skills to use.[12]

While the Eighty-ninth rested in Shelbyville on Saturday, October 4, a hard day's march away in Frankfort, Confederate officials and military officers gathered at the state capital for Richard Hawes inauguration as Governor of Kentucky. Both Kirby Smith and Braxton Bragg attended the ceremony. They had come to the Bluegrass State counting on thousands of Kentuckians joining their ranks and the state entering the Confederacy. To date, their 15,000 stand of arms had gone begging. Kentuckians had not flocked to the rebel colors, and now cannon could be heard in the distance as the Confederates left the Kentucky Capitol. Couriers arrived reporting the Federal advance from Shelbyville. Kirk's Brigade of Sill's Division had left

[11] *The Headlight*, October 4, 1862, photocopy of original in possession of the author.
[12] *The Headlight*, October 4, 1862; *The Chicago Tribune*, October 29, 1862.

Shelbyville earlier that morning, and they were now in contact with rebel cavalry. General Bragg rode out of Frankfort about 4:00 P.M., and Hawes soon followed. The Confederate government of Kentucky was gone as quickly as it had appeared.[13]

After a two-day rest, the Eighty-ninth shouldered rifles and moved out on Monday, October 6. Private Goddard jotted in his diary that we "started on our march toward Frankfort this morning. Halted about 2 and started on toward Frankfort. We marched until near dark and halted and got supper [about] 9 miles from Frankfort. We started and got to Frankfort in the night." The next day Goddard quipped that "we are lying in Camp at Frankfort. We do not have any thing to do except cook and eat."[14]

The blue-clad troops who had fallen back from Nashville and who had not been expected to resume the offensive for weeks or even months advanced and were now converging on Bragg's Army of the Mississippi. Caught off guard by the unexpected and rapid Federal movement, Bragg took steps to quickly unite his army. Orders to concentrate at Harrodsburg, however, did not work out, leaving Bragg's formations to come together at Perryville. By October 7, Union troops also were drawn up north of Perryville. Couriers were dispatched with orders to consolidate, and Sill's Second Division left Frankfort at 1:00 A.M.. on October 8, heading south to rejoin McCook's Corps and Buell's army near Perryville, where a fight was now expected.[15]

"Started on our march toward Lawrenceburg at one; got there at 11; and found the enemy in some force," Goddard noted in his diary. "Our Cavalry [Ninth Kentucky] made a dash at them but were refused with some loss. Our Artillery opened on them and drove them off. The 89th were drawn up in line of battle to support the artillery." George Berry gave his pithy version of Eighty-ninth's first smell of powder. "We have traveled seven days [and] we was hindred one day by the Rebels. Ower cavalry come in contact

13 Hafendorfer, *Perryville: Battle for Kentucky*, 88-91.
14 Berry, letter, October 5, 1862; Goddard, diary, October 6 and 7, 1862.
15 Hafendorfer, *Perryville: Battle for Kentucky*, 90-106; Alexis Cope, *The 15th Ohio Volunteers and Its Campaigns, 1861-1865* (Columbus, OH: Edward T. Miller Company, 1916), 205.

with the Rebels cavalry. The Rebels had two hundred cavalry [and] we had seventy-five. Ower artillery came up in time and run them off. Ower Regiment come up wen the artillery was firing. We came in line on the right of the artillery and [were] ordered to set down. The shell busted in the ranks of the Rebels Cavalry and way they went." As the Eighty-ninth lay in support of the guns, Sergeant Sinclair watched the wounded being brought back and wrote: "It was a nasty sight to see human beings cut up in the way they were." Observing his comrades, Sinclair concluded the sight of the wounded "only made the men more eager to get at them. Not a man flinched." But the fact was, Sinclair wrote: "We did not get a shot at them . . . ." For those that did, it was the reality of war. After the cavalry clash, Goddard detailed that "the 32nd were thrown out as skirmisher but could not find the enemy." With the rebels gone, he wrote: "We then continued our march toward Salt River and reached there at dark. We have marched 33 miles today."[16]

Marching orders for October 9 were set for 7:00 A.M.. The men were up, had eaten their breakfast, and were preparing to move out when they heard cannonading in the rear of the regiment. The Fifteenth and Nineteenth Regulars went out as skirmishers while the Thirty-second Indiana and First Ohio formed in a line of battle to meet the rebel attack. All the Railroad boys could do was form up, wait, and listen. After the firing ended, they recorded what little they heard and observed. "We have had quite a heavy skirmish the entire forenoon and have drove the rebels back," reported Fred Goddard. While George Berry briefly touched on the episode writing that "there infantry stoped us a few howers. They killed six of ower men out of ower brigade." But it was Sergeant Sinclair who spelled out what actually took place. "We had an attack in the rear by part of Kirby Smith's detachment, who had come onto us by mistake . . . and did not discover our force so we deployed around as skirmishers running over hill and valley trying to bag them. They smelt a mouse and left after killing eight men and wounding some others. Our regiment lost none. We fooled around until ten o'clock

16   Goddard, diary, October 8, 1862; Berry, letter, October 13, 1862; Sinclair, letter, October 13, 1862; OR, vol. 16, pt. 1, 1028.

and then started off full tilt . . . ." Officially five were killed and eight wounded.[17]

With the rebels driven off, the division got underway, heading toward Perryville. Having marched in hot dry weather for weeks, the men found relief when rain began to fall and the temperature cooled. A few soldiers like George Berry had figured the unseasonable weather would eventually change. Counting on it, Berry spent the last of his money on "an oil cloath blanket" and noted happily that "it [has] come in good use wen it is raining." As the men neared the site of the recent conflict, the effects of the battle became evident. Fred Goddard entered in his pocket diary on October 11 that "we are drawing near to the battle field of Perryville. Every house and barn for miles around here is one complete Hospital. The houses are all filled with wounded soldiers."[18]

The Eighty-ninth linked up with the Buell's army that evening, Saturday, October 11. Arriving after dark, the men camped on the battlefield, which was only partially cleared. Darkness temporarily hid the sight, but the odor of the carnage hung over the ground. "The smell from dead men and horses is awful," wrote Goddard. Scratching a hurried letter to his wife, Private George Berry described the carnage at Perryville. "Wen we came up, the dead rebels was laing on top of the ground [while] ower men was all bured. We sleeped on the Battle ground. The rebels had no time to beary there Dead. It [was] harde to see dead horses and dead men all to gether." For a new regiment to bivouac with the dead was indeed troubling. Whether he came to calm or rally the shocked men that evening, General McCook rode over to the Eighty-ninth's camp and made a speech to the boys.[19]

When reveille sounded on October 12, it could not have seemed like Sunday. With daylight the men gazed upon the death and destruction the battle of the 8th had wrought. "I have walked over the battle field and have seen sights that I do hope I will never see again," wrote Fred Goddard of Company H. "The ground is covered

---

[17]   Cope, *The 15th Ohio Volunteers*, 206-207; Goddard, diary, October 9, 1862; Berry, letter, October 13, 1862; Sinclair, letter, October 13, 1862.

[18]   Berry, letter, October 13, 1862; Goddard, diary, October 10 and 11, 1862.

[19]   Goddard, diary, October 11, 1862; Berry, letter, October 13, 1862.

with dead rebels and with the graves of our own brave boys." Another man described the image he awoke to. "I'll tell you it was hard to walk over the field and see the fresh graves and dead secesh laying on the ground. They were a perfect specimen of those that were in Camp Douglas. And as I have heard General Rousseau say that as they did not care to bury their dead that we would not, and they were so mean the hogs would not eat them. We or I have gotten used to such sights now." The Eighty-ninth stayed on the Perryville battlefield long enough for the effect to sink in and were once again back on the road, "in full blast after the rebels." Passing through Perryville about mid-morning, one Railroader recorded the town was "one complete hospital [and] the houses are full of bullet holes."[20]

Out of writing paper, Joseph Buckley had not written his wife, Mary, since the regiment left Louisville. Two weeks passed until he scrounged a few sheets and penned a short letter. The Eighty-ninth was at Crab Orchard, which Buckley estimated was "about 125 miles from Louisville." The regiment, Buckley pointed out, had "traveled a great deal further" in chasing the Rebels, leaving the men "tired of marching" and eager "to meet the enemy." The "expected a battle with Bragg" never developed as he kept retreating. And, it was generally concluded that Bragg would not make a stand until he arrived at Cumberland Gap. "The calculations are to surround him," Private Buckley wrote, "but I think we have no faith in Buell. We think he will leave some place for him to crall (sic) out of." Sergeant Sinclair had a somewhat different take on the situation. He told Frances that "since I wrote you last I have been tumbling about considerably not knowing any time our next day's destination. At last writing we were full blast after General Bragg. But that all buggered out for we were stopped at Crabb Orchard about 50 miles from Cumberland Gap." He continued: "We are using up his army faster by keeping his men a running than by a battle for they were hard up for the necessaries of life and were pretty well tired of this war and were coming over to us every day in numbers saying that they had enough. But Old Buell did not see fit to let us use his, Bragg's army, up in that manner, for that would help end the war . . . ."[21]

---

[20] Goddard, letter, October 12, 1862; Sinclair, letter, October 13, 1862.

[21] Buckley, letter, October 16, 1862; Sinclair, letter, October [25], 1862.

Chaplain Dill addressed the question of General Buell's competence in his regular letter to the *Chicago Tribune*. "I do not pretend to be a judge in military tactics or strategy, and do not know but that our government has a bloodless policy which our Gen. Buell is carrying out in Kentucky; but this I do know, that this policy is sacrificing lives of thousands of our soldiers, without shedding their blood or that of the rebels; and that every soldier and officer of the army whom I have heard expressing his sentiments, most heartily deprecates and curses this policy. The universal outcry is, that Bragg might many a time and ought to have been bagged, and his army destroyed." Ironically, Dill's letter was written two days after Buell's dismissal. None the less, the comments reflect the mind and mood of the officers and men who had yet to hear about Buell's being sacked in favor of Rosecrans. Back in Washington the Administration was as disillusioned with General Buell's performance after Perryville as were the men in the ranks. When it finally became evident that Bragg's army had escaped unmolested, Lincoln instructed General-in-Chief Halleck to draft an order replacing Buell. General William Starke Rosecrans was notified on October 24, 1862 that he was directed to Louisville to relieve Buell of command.[22]

* * *

Unbeknownst to the pursuing men in blue, the halt near Crab Orchard on the evening of October 15 meant the chase after the retreating rebels was over. "I don't know what is going to happen we did not receive the usual orders to prepare for a march," Fred Goddard recorded that morning. Afterward, he wrote: "We have washed our clothes and I have written 5 letters. It seems quite odd to not be on the move. We are in camp in an old potato field [and] we had potatoes and beef soup for dinner." No movement again on October 17. "Today we have been lying in camp," wrote Goddard. "Our time has been spent writing letters and in cooking. Richard Field and I went and got some corn and made a grater out of an old tine plate and had mush for supper. It was a nice

---

[22]   *Chicago Tribune*, November 5, 1862; Daniel, *Days of Glory: Army of the Cumberland, 1861-1865*, 173-181.

change." With the regimented given a rest, Company A Private Jim Tomlinson found a drum for a desk and wrote his mother. He began by stating that "58 rebel prisoner[s] passed here just now" and that the southerners told the inquiring Railroaders that "Braggs army is cut up."[23]

"We have laid in camp two days," George Berry began in a letter home, and "it gives us time to clean up. I went to the creek and wash[ed] my stocking[s] and shirte. I have not had my shirte washed for two weeks." He added that "I have not but one Paire of stocking[s] and one shirte with me. The rest of my clothes are at Louisville [and] I don't know wen I shall git them." Berry's lines point out that Buell's army was traveling with only the bare essentials. Since October 1, camp had been no more than a fire and spot nearby to lie down. With summer giving way to fall, Berry remarked that "we had a heavey frost last knight [and] wen I weaked up this morning my blanket was all frosted over. So far we have plenty of hay to lay on." But not mincing words, Berry summed it all up in a few words: "Camp life is a harde place to live." Joseph Buckley had much the same thing to say when he wrote Mary from Crab Orchard. "A soldier's life is a hard life to live. We live well one day and starve the next." In regard to joining the army, he made it clear that "nobody ought to enlist unless they are as tough as a boiled owl."[24]

"We have suffered much for want of water, especially such as was fit to drink," wrote Chaplain Dill. "The most we have had, has been dipped from green or muddy pools left in the dried up river beds—water which, in Illinois, we would not give to horses—and yet, such as it is, it is drank with the greatest eagerness." As for the food distributed by the army, Dill writes: "The hard bread we have is of the hardest and toughest sort, and would make tolerable sole leather. I am sorry, for the fame of our city, to say that this sort comes from Chicago, and that it is a great treat when we receive some from Cincinnati."[25]

---

[23] Goddard diary, October 16 and 17, 1862; Tomlinson, *In Good Courage: The Civil War Letters of William James Tomlinson, 3.*

[24] Goddard, diary, October 16 and 17, 1862; Tomlinson, *In Good Courage: The Civil War Letters of William James Tomlinson, 3.* Berry, letter, October 18, 1862; Buckley, letter, October 16, 1862.

[25] *Chicago Tribune*, November 5, 1862.

In response to the rank and file's complaints about the hard bread, *The Headlight* reported Lieutenant Colonel Hotchkiss told the men "that a chunk of pilot bread was better than a thump on the head with a sharp stone." Obviously, Hotckiss felt bad rations were better than no rations and complaining did no good. The writer noted that "he's 'Old Regulation' himself, and more too; but we take notice that none of the Field Officers of the 89th hanker after 'pilot.'"[26]

"This camp life is harde Place for the sick [as] they are neglected," observed plain spoken George Berry. "This marching about the country [and] laying out in all weather exposed in every manner kills more men than all the battles fought," commented Sergeant Sinclair, the former railroad engineer and California gold miner—a man well acquainted with the elements. As for the local fellows, he informs Frances how they were holding up. "Billy Del has gone home insane . . . Charlie Foster is well but has been sent to Lebanon with a lot of sick men. Mr. Fonda is sick and in [the] hospital at Bardstown. Our first lieutenant is also there . . . . Our regiment has in it now about 500 men in the ranks for duty, the balance have given out and are in the hospital." Despite the loss in manpower, Sinclair said that the Eighty-ninth was still one of the largest regiment's he had come across and that "the old troops say that's a bully regiment as we pass them by on the march."[27]

Chaplain Dill wrote at length to the *Tribune* on the health of the Railroad Regiment. His words are more upbeat and pragmatic than those found in the letters of some of the enlisted men. Dill stated that "the health of the regiment is good, considering the seasoning process which all raw troops have to pass through (for soldiers as well as children have to cut their teeth), and considering the forced marches and exposures to which so raw a regiment has been put." He informed the Chicago readers that "so far as known, there have been but four deaths. The sick at Louisville are, with few exceptions, not seriously sick; and the same may be said of those left near Frankfort and of those sick with measles left in Lebanon. From these hospitals our men are returning as fast as they become

---

[26] *The Headlight*, October 4, 1862. Pilot bread is a sailor's term for hardtack.
[27] Berry, letter, October 18, 1862; Sinclair, letter, October [25], 1862.

sufficiently strong." Some of the men, though only "half recovered," Dill noted, "will trudge on foot fifty miles to rejoin us again." He further reported that the army's medical corps had shown itself to be able, efficient and devoted to their work. While on the march, though short on equipment and medicine, the Eighty-ninth's Dr. Hance had done all he could for the sick and disabled."[28]

For married men the bounty money and the financial assistance it was suppose to provide their families continued to be a worry. "We don't draw no Bounty money from the railroad Regiment as they Promised. We [only] get ower county money and government mony," explained George Berry to his wife. Once more, he tells her that he has "sent three county orders. The last one is right, and it is "dated, I think, the 26 Sept." Sergeant George Sinclair told his wife that "I want you to see Mr.?, the man who pays the Cook County relief fund and find out when they are going to pay anything. You can find him at the County Clerk's Office at the Court House. Attend to it, will you Franky? You can also draw something for [the] baby."[29]

The regiment remained at Crab Orchard. Orders to march came and went with no movement. Meanwhile on Saturday, October 18, the Eighty-ninth drew fresh rations, consisting of hard bread, sugar, coffee, and beef. To add a bit to their fare, Goddard and another soldier ventured "out into the country and got some Sorgum (sic) molasses." He commented that "it is first rate on hard bread." The following morning he "went down and washed at the creek and got ready for Church." The thought of Saturday's ration draw must have been on Chaplain Dill's mind when he selected the text for his sermon. He preached that autumn morning from Luke chapter 15, verse 17, "'How many of my father's hired servants have bread enough to spare, but I perish here with hunger!'" Camped in a potato patch with no shelter and meager rations must have left all the men, not just the good chaplain, feeling a little like the prodigal son.[30]

Before that Sunday, George Berry had informed his wife that "we don't have much Preaching. I have not heard but one sermon since I left Victoria." For Private Fred Goddard there was not only

---

28 *Chicago Tribune*, November 5, 1862.
29 Berry, letter, October 1, 1862; Sinclair, letter, October [25], 1862.
30 Goddard, diary, October 18 and 19, 1862.

a lack of religious services but there was also "no respect for the Sabbath in the army. Our sutler arrived to day from Louisville with a new supply of goods. He set up his tent and gone to selling just as if it were not the Sabbath."[31]

The next morning, Monday, October 20, the Eighty-ninth filed out on the road at 7:30 A.M.. and marched twenty-one miles, "going back on the same road that we came out on. What we are going back for I don't know but the Camp rumor is that we are going into winter quarters at Lebanon Junction," jotted Fred Goddard. Sitting by campfire and writing in his diary, Goddard noted the regiment was in a wood six miles from Danville. A dozing Goddard wrote, his messmates were "pounding coffee and cooking bacon for supper." So the men could have something between the damp earth and their tired bodies, the officers, that evening "let the boys take a couple of haystacks for beds." For looking the other way at the theft, Hotchkiss was put under arrest and ordered to give up his sword. Goddard spoke for all the Railroaders when he put this line in his diary: "Oh that guarding secesh property would cease." After the fuss, the column moved out at 8:00 A.M.. on Tuesday, halting at Danville for two hours. Underway again, the men covered six more miles and made camp for the night. Supper consisted of the usual bacon, hard bread, and coffee. With no hay for a bed, Goddard noted that he "laid down on the ground and slept well."[32]

Reveille sounded 4:00 A.M.., and Private Goddard was immediately up and after fence rails and water. Soon he was warming himself by the fire while he "cooked some coffee." Eating quick breakfast, the men fell in and the regiment took to the road "with the sun only half an hour high." Having been continually on the move since arriving in Kentucky, the Railroaders' had lightened their individual load. Goddard explained: "We carry a haversack with two days rations, cartridge box with 40 rounds of cartridges, blanket, canteen, and gun." Unencumbered and moving like veterans, the Eighty-nine passed through Perryville by midmorning and headed southwest toward Lebanon. Overcome by darkness, the regiment halted for the day about ten miles from town. Supper was quickly prepared, and afterward provisions were issued

31 Berry, letter, October 18, 1862; Goddard, diary, October 19, 1862.
32 Goddard, diary, October 20 and 21, 1862.

for tomorrow. Goddard recorded the rations "consisted this time in coffee and 5 hard crackers" for each man. The men attempted to sleep, but "the night was very cold and frosty" so to keep warm they "set up around the fires." They were up and off by sunrise, covering 20 miles. Another cold night spent without shelter, leaving Goddard to comment that "we miss our tents very much." Food was down to coffee and crackers. The men were informed that they were "on half rations, only four crackers being allowed for two days."[33]

Friday, October 24, the men assembled later than usual and started out at 10:00 A.M.. The regiment had gone about a mile when seven men on horseback came up and stopped the column. The leader informed the officers that they were out looking for a fugitive slave. Fred Goddard watched as their eyes searched the column of Railroaders. When they spotted "the boy in the ranks," they "swore at him and ordered him to come and go back to his master." But the Negro "did not choose to go and the boys did choose to let him go. The men tried hard to get him but the boys threatened to shoot them if they did not leave and after a good many hard words the negro drivers were bluffed off and sent home minus the nigger." Goddard wrote that the ruckus left the fugitive "well scared but [he] is in camp with us tonight." With the whip-carrying slave catchers driven off, the Eighty-ninth resumed the march covering 12 miles and went into camp at dusk. After the men bedded down for the night, the regimental wagons arrived with their tents and knapsacks. With no movement on Saturday, the boys spent the morning pitching tents and retrieving their belongings. In a newsy letter to his parents, Company H Lieutenant Harkness explained that the regiment's tents were "round, about 12 feet across the bottom, running to a point at the top where there is a small opening. We built a fire in the center, which makes it quite warm only rather smoky." Unfortunately, as Chaplain Dill and some of the men discovered, their knapsacks "cases were more or less plundered of their contents." By afternoon it began to rain, which eventually changed to snow, leaving Goddard to write that "our tents feel quite comfortable. We have got a fine fire . . . and are enjoying ourselves finely."[34]

---

[33] Goddard, diary, October 22-24, 1862.

[34] Goddard, diary, October 24 and 25, 1862; *Chicago Tribune*, November 5, 1862; Harkness, letter, October 26, 1862.

"We have had some rather cold weather the last two weeks [and] laying out when it froze hard enough to cover the ponds with ice," Sergeant Sinclair complained to his wife. "Last night our tents came from Louisville and it was mighty lucky too," he added, "for we just barely got them pitched when it came on a heavy snowstorm; and on turning out in the morning, [we] found six inches of snow on the level, bully for Kentucky, and the sunny south." Since leaving Crab Orchard, the Eighty-ninth had been on short rations. "We marched all last week," Sinclair wrote his wife, "without any meat at all and only four small crackers a day about the size of soda crackers. I eat mine every morn before starting and then marched all day from four or five o'clock in the morn until seven and sometimes nine o'clock at night on an empty stomach. Talk about serving one's country and suffering all that . . . ." Unclear to where the regiment was heading, Sinclair gave Francis his best guess. "We are supposed to be enroute to Nashville to go into winter quarters there, but nothing definite is known of our destination or what we are to do." Lieutenant Harkness spelled out in a letter to his parents dated October 26 that the Eighty-ninth was on its "way to Nashville, Tenn., something over a hundred miles from here. What the objective is [in] going there, I cannot tell as all our movements are kept very still. I am getting so that I never care where we are going but make up my mind to obey orders whenever they are given and ask no questions."[35]

Chaplain Dill pointed out in his latest correspondence to the *Chicago Tribune* that the Eighty-ninth was "in Taylor county, near Saloma, about fifteen miles from Lebanon, in the direction of Nashville, whither it is said, we are going." He noted in his letter that conditions were trying and he was writing "under the greatest of difficulties . . . ." But tough as things were, Dill took time to shed light on his own abolitionist leanings and alluded to the regiment's giving refuge for runaways. "We suffer and fight for God, for right, for liberty and for our country; we face the lion of slavery in his den, curse him to his face, and have torn several black lambs out of his mouth, which we expect to bring home with us to a land of light and liberty." He then noted that not all the boys of the Eighty-ninth hold this view. And, he explained: "However, little some of our regiment

---

[35]   Sinclair, letter, October [25], 1862; Harkness, letter, October 26, 1862.

care for the rights of the black man, yet all are compelled to despise a civilization where the leading characteristic is the oppression of the negro, in which there is little beside law which renders the white man his superior."[36]

---

[36] *Chicago Tribune*, November 5, 1862.

CHAPTER 4

"WE ARE GOING IN TO TENESSEE"

Passing through the Cumberland Gap on October 23, Bragg and the Army of the Mississippi safely escaped into Tennessee, retiring to Knoxville. The 27,000 rebel soldiers who made it to safety were ragged, hungry, and ill. Over half the army would soon be hospitalized. The demoralizing defeat at Perryville, followed by the ensuing retreat, and the deteriorating condition of the army brought a call from both the Southern public and from fellow Confederate generals for Bragg's dismissal. Amidst this uproar, Bragg traveled to Richmond to confer with Jefferson Davis. Returning from the conference, and with Davis' approval, Bragg set out to move the Confederate army to Middle Tennessee. Once there, Chattanooga and its railroad network would be protected, while positioning his army to threaten Nashville.

To Buell's way of thinking, any advance by Union forces into East Tennessee would be a supply and logistics nightmare, and consequently a military mistake. He therefore abandoned his pursuit of Bragg and turned the Army of the Ohio about and headed for Nashville, preferring Middle Tennessee as his base of operations. Buell's defiance of the Lincoln administration's preferred course of action resulted in his dismissal on October 24. Six days later, October 30, Major General William S. Rosecrans caught up with the Union column at Bowling Green, Kentucky and assumed command of the

Department of the Cumberland. The order changing commanders also eliminated the Army of the Ohio. It temporarily became the Fourteenth Army Corps and eventually, on January 9, 1863, the Army of the Cumberland. To the tired and hungry Federal troops slogging their way southward, the changes meant little. All they learned was there would be no change in Buell's orders. For on October 28, a Confederate division arrived at Murfreesboro, jeopardizing the Nashville garrison 32 miles to the north. Middle Tennessee would be reinforced and protected from the rebels.

The second division left camp near Saloma on October 27, crossing the Green River several miles above Munfordville at the "Burnt Bridge," and on the 31 October arrived at Bowling Green. Private Fred Goddard of Company H jotted in his diary on October 27 that "we were called in from picket at an early hour this morning and were ordered to get ready to move. The tents were struck and packed into the wagons. The knapsacks were first into the wagons and we were ordered to get into line. When we were drawing up into line the Colonel rode along the line with his sword hanging by his side. The men cheered him and he returned the compliment by a wave of the hat." Continuing Goddard wrote the regiment marched 18 miles that day, crossing the Green River at 2:00 P.M. Taking up his pen again, Goddard's journal entry for October 28 began: "slept in our tents last night. The night was cold and frosty. Arose and cooked a breakfast of salt pork and coffee; marched at 8 O'clock; crossed the Little Barren river at 11 o'clock; halted at 12 and made coffee; marched until near sundown and halted in a meadow near a nice spring for the night." He noted that "the land belonged to an old secesh and the way we confiscated the rail fence and hay was not very slow. General Gibson told the boys to take any thing they wanted." Wednesday, October 29 brought more of the same. Up again at 5:00 A.M.., Goddard's mess "cooked breakfast of beef soup" to go along with their "hard crackers." The column "started at 7 and marched until 12 and halted half an hour for dinner and then marched until dark and halted for the night within a few rods of a rail road." The steel track was a welcome sight for the Railroaders. Goddard noted that this was "the first rail road I have seen since we left Louisville. It done the boys good to see a train of cars go along and they cheered lustily.

The first train that went along was loaded with troops." October 31, Goddard penned that the regiment "crossed the Green river at Bowling Green at 2 O'clock on a Pontoon bridge. The old bridge was burned by the rebels some time ago." The Eighty-ninth picked up their step and marched "through the town to the tunes of Dixie and Yankee Doodle."[1]

Watching the Union column march through the city was the Bowling Green correspondent for the *Louisville Journal*. Overjoyed at the arrival of Federal troops, he wrote: "This has been a stirring day in our town." He recounted that "this morning about nine o'clock General Sill's Division of Gen. McCook's corps began to pass through the town en route for Nashville." He told the readers "that this division is composed for the most part of veteran troops. Their valor has illustrated almost every battle-field during the war." He described the soldiers for the readers: "They are a fine looking body of men—stalwart and hardy—and, notwithstanding their recent long marches . . . they exhibited no evidence of fatigue. They are sun-burnt and covered with dust, but their tread is elastic and firm. The colors of many of these regiments are soiled by smoke of gunpowder and tattered by bullets."

"There are two tunnels on this side of Gallatin, on the Louisville and Nashville Railroad. Only one of these had been destroyed by the rebels," the reporter explained. "It is reported here to-day that they have now destroyed the other and torn up a long stretch of the rails. I trust Uncle Sam will soon clear the track and open up free communication by the might of his strong right arm."[2]

* * *

In his correspondence to the *Tribune*, Chaplain Dill noted that "at Bowling Green we were joined by company F, seventy-four men, Capt. Williams [in command]. The long marches, after almost sleepless nights, were hard upon them, but were borne in such a way as to show that they were men of grit and stamina." In a letter

1   Dodge, *History of the Old Second Division, Army of the Cumberland*, 368; Goddard, diary October 27-29, 31, 1862.

2   *Nashville Dispatch*, November 8, 1862.

home George Berry laconically remarked that "we have another company atached to ower Regiment. It come from Chicago."[3]

For nearly two months, the Railroad Regiment had been short one company. When it left Chicago on September 4, the Railroad Committee was frantically trying to obtain a tenth company to complete the regiment. On September 8 William D. Manchester, the Committee secretary, wrote a blistering letter to Adjutant General Fuller regarding the situation. "When I was in Springfield a week or so ago," he began, "I supposed we should have our 10th company in a very few days, as two or three different companies had made application to go into our Regiment but I find that for some reason they have not been allowed to come." Manchester continued to hammer the state's top military official. "Our Regt. Has been orderd into the Field & has only 9 Companies & I understand from Christopher that inquiry has been made by the department as to why the 89th was allowed to go into the field with only 9 cos." He begged: "Cannot you give us some assistance? There must be detached companies somewhere & you are the only person I know of that knows where they are." And finally the letter reveals his complete frustration with the adjutant general when he wrote: "If buying companies is the order of the day, we are ready to try our hand with the rest and if you will let me know where any one or more of these companies are, I will fill the 89th." Manchester concluded with a bit of enticement. "Our Quartermaster has drawn clothing & equipment in full for an entire regiment & I have them in charge awaiting to get the men to put into them, & I have to request that you will give me such assistance as you have at hand that the organization of the 89th may be perfected at as early day as possible."[4]

That day had finally come. Joining the regiment on October 31 was Captain William D. Williams' company from Rock Island County, Illinois. When President Lincoln called for three-month volunteers in April 1861, Williams, a Rock Island attorney, was the first man in the county to enlist and was chosen captain of the first company raised there. The company was assigned to the Twelfth Illinois Infantry,

[3]   Berry, letter, November 10, 1862; *Chicago Tribune*, November 18, 1862.
[4]   William D. Manchester to Adjutant General Fuller, September 8, 1862, Record Group 301, Illinois State Archives.

and Williams was elected major at the regiment's organization. At the end of three months' service, the Twelfth volunteered for the duration of the war. Not slated by the "Chicago clique" for major at the regiment's reorganization, Williams resigned October 2, 1861 and returned to his law practice.[5]

In reaction to the president's call for more troops, a reader sent a note to the *Rock Island Argus*, suggesting "that Major Williams take hold of the matter and set the ball rolling. His well known patriotism and experience in military matters points him out as the man to lead off in the matter. Should he open a recruiting office the boys will flock to his standard . . . ." Major Williams' replied in the following issue: "I have to say that I am ready and willing to go in for the war. In this emergency, sacrifices of feelings and interest must be made, if we would preserve unimpaired the constitution as it is and the union as it was." Williams let it be known that "a company ought to be raised in Rock Island . . . and the sooner the work is commenced the better." Not waiting for someone else to take the lead, he initiated the movement by attaching his signature to a muster roll and asking for the cooperation of local patriots. The *Argus'* editor reminded the paper's subscribers that "Maj. Williams, in April 1861 was the first man in this county to volunteer in defense of the union." He then added, "We are glad to see him again in the field, at the call of his country."[6]

From the day he placed his name at the top of the muster roll, the forty-year-old Williams, along with Jerrie Prescott, Laertes Dimick, and E. T. Wells, devoted all their time and attention to raising a company. On August 15, the day they boarded a train for the rendezvous camp at Dixon in Lee County, Illinois, the company numbered 107 men. The night before, by a vote of acclamation, the recruits rewarded the organizers for their effort and devotion by making Williams captain, Wells and Dimick respectively first and second lieutenants.[7]

---

5   A. T. Andreas, *History of Chicago*, II: 245; Eddy, *The Patriotism of Illinois*, II: 336; *Report of the Adjutant General of the State of Illinois*, I: 336, 341, 551; *Rock Island Argus*, July 14, 1862.

6   *Rock Island Argus*, July 9 and 10, 1862.

7   *Rock Island Register*, August 13, 1862; *Rock Island Argus*, August 15, 1862; *Rock Island Weekly Argus*, August 20, 1862.

Probably as a result of his experience with the Chicago faction, Williams set out to organize a purely Rock Island County regiment, where hopefully he would not be the odd man out. When he began raising another company for the war, he had the support of J. B. Danforth, Jr., the editor of the *Argus*, and a number of others who wanted to put together a regiment made up of area men. In July, Williams met with Governor Yates in Springfield. He reported back to the *Argus* that "the governor gives no authority for raising regiments; he only authorizes men to raise companies . . . and when companies enough are raised for a regiment, he commissions the regimental officers." In the August 7 issue of the *Argus*, Danforth presented his case for a Rock Island County regiment. He stated that "a full regiment of volunteers can be raised and ready to march, from this county within two weeks." Currently eight muster rolls were being circulated. Danforth reasoned: "If an arrangement could be made by which these companies could go into camp at Dixon as fast as they organize, and there organize as a Rock Island county regiment, and be officered exclusively by Rock Island county men, enough men would immediately follow to make an entire regiment from this county." Major Williams returned to Springfield and once more met with Governor Yates to make his case. Afterwards he notified Danforth in a message sent August 9 that "the Governor will accept the Rock Island Regiment *if raised by the sixteenth.*" The *Argus* reported on August 15 that the county had three companies at Dixon and six more at home with two of these already full and organized. Editor Danforth pleaded: "Let us all work together now, and fill up these companies and all go in the same regiment. It can be done . . . ." Eventually, Rock Island County would have seven companies at Camp Fuller in Dixon.[8]

The *Argus* continued to promote Major Williams for colonel even if the regiment was not made up totally of Rock Island County men. Danforth wrote: "We hope and believe that the line officers of the regiment now forming at Camp Fuller at Dixon, will agree upon and elect Maj. Williams of this city as colonel of that regiment." He then presented to the public why Williams should lead a regiment. First, "his experience, as major of the old Twelfth, and his known energy

---

[8]   *Rock Island Argus*, July 22, August 7, 9 and 15, 1862.

and excellent business qualities render him peculiarly fit for the place." Second, "there can be no man among the officers attached to that regiment whose knowledge of military matters or experience in the service, can compare with that of Major Williams." And third, "we have four companies in the regiment . . . and we think our county is justly entitled to the colonel of the regiment—especially when we present a man as well fitted for the place as Wm. D. Williams."[9]

Two regiments were organized at Dixon on September 2. The Seventy-fifth was made up of men from Lee and Whiteside Counties, while the One Hundred Fifth was mainly from DeKalb County. On receiving this news the *Argus* complained that "our seven companies are in camp, not organized." With a tad of bitterness, the writer quipped that if "the adjutant general will send three companies to the Rock Island county regiment . . . then it will be organized at once." When Adjutant General Fuller made an appearance in Dixon and inspected the Rock Island companies, the *Argus* editor was informed that he "was greatly pleased with the perfect drill and fine appearance of Capt. Williams' company, and he publicly declared, before the regiment, that he had never seen its equal in the state."[10]

After two weeks in camp, a local recruit, using the pseudonym "High Private," mailed a letter to Danforth. An insightful fellow, he presented a detailed account of the problem facing the organization of a Rock Island regiment. The young man told the editor: "I suppose that before this we should have been organized into a regiment, and have our money and clothes, both of which we very much need, but thus far we are doomed to disappointment." He explained that "the One Hundred Fifth regiment has been organized since we have been here and left. The Seventy-fifth has been also organized, and I believe is under marching orders—leaving seven Rock Island companies here by themselves, like a pack of Kilkenny cats, to eat one another up, and in my opinion their prospects for an organization are poor: and why? Because outsiders will not leave us alone." High Private now spelled out the problem. "There are men in camp nearly every day, principally from Rock Island, seeking for office, and of all the logrolling and wire-pulling, this beats me. Most of them profess

9   *Rock Island Argus*, August 30, 1862.
10 *Rock Island Argus*, September 4 and 5, 1862.

to be good union men, and love their country . . . but instead of enlisting as honest patriots and taking their chances for office, they refuse to enlist, but go sneaking about camp button-holing the company officers, and unless they can secure a good paying office, they are not in . . ." He also professed that "we have men here in camp who are just as capable of filling all the offices as they are, and men who have proved themselves better patriots by enlisting in the service of their country, without demanding high office and big pay." To those Republicans who claimed to have carried torches and been prominent "wideawakes," he asks: "We want some present proof of your patriotism, and a little less of your office seeking."[11]

For the reason outlined by "High Private," a Rock Island County regiment was never formed. The seven companies were soon transferred to Camp Douglas in Chicago. By mid-October the adjutant general assigned these companies to three regiments. The Eighty-ninth and Ninety-third each received a company, while the remaining five companies went to the One Hundred Twenty-sixth.[12]

*   *   *

Williams' company, lettered F, joined the Railroaders as they halted for a rest. On November 1, Private Goddard happily recorded in his diary that there would be no movement. For the first time in the last six days, he slept past sunrise. Following a leisurely breakfast, he gave his rifle a thorough cleaning, and then "went to writing letters." George Berry, the Knox Country farmer, also took advantage of the break from marching and wrote home, explaining to his wife: "Them that thought it was apretty thing to go to the ware has found it diferent now. We have more traveling than I thorte I should have. As long as I have my health I can stand it. We are agoing in to tenessee." Life for the men had been made somewhat better with the arrival of each company's "baggage wagon," Berry told Harriet that "the last five days we have sleep in ower tents." Finding that runaways further eased the daily routine of camp life, the Eighty-ninth continued to welcome Negroes into their lines. Private Berry informed his wife

---

[11] *Rock Island Argus*, September 6 and 15, 1862.
[12] *Rock Island Argus*, October 18, 1862.

that "we have 3 Darkeys in ower company. Capt. Whiting has one and [so does] Howell and John Smith. They like them firstrate. We finde the negroes quite inteligent. They are all glad to see us."[13]

The men made the most of the unexpected but welcomed break. Goddard wrote: "there is a nice stream close to camp where we can get our water. It is called the lost river. It comes out of the hill and runs perhaps 100 yds and then disappears into a cave. It is a great curiosity." George Berry took advantage of the time off and clean water to wash his "shirts and stockings." He noted there were "some four or five hundred was[h]ing to day. The nicest spring I ever saw it runs like a river." After weeks on the move, the officers used the halt to catch up with their paper work. Berry wrote his wife that "they are makin out the pay roll to day. I think I shall have some money befolong. I was agoing to tell you to send me a few Dollars but I shall have some in a few days." That afternoon the regiment "mustered in for our pay."[14]

Sunday, November 2, was another day of rest. By Monday, the period of leisure was over as the men had squad drill first thing in the morning, with company drill in the forenoon, followed by battalion drill in the afternoon. Not feeling well, Goddard wrote that he had "a touch of the ague." Going about his duties, he observed men "cutting and drawing wood" and noted that "it looks as if we were going to stay here for a spell." Rations of sugar, coffee, hard bread, and bacon were drawn. The next morning Goddard wrote that the regiment was "called up very early . . . and ordered to get ready to march by 6 O'clock. Before sunrise we were on the march toward Nashville." The Railroaders covered 23 miles.[15]

Private Goddard, the youthful Kendall County farmer, began his diary entry for November 5 by stating the regiment once again "started before daylight this morning." Still not feeling well, he and a friend, Silas Page, who was also ill, were given permission to go ahead of the regiment. Before heading out, they lightened their load by placing their blankets and cartridge boxes on the company wagon. Goddard recorded the two "crossed the State line at 8" that

13 Goddard, diary, November 1, 1862; Berry, letter, November 1, 1862.
14 Goddard, diary, November 1, 1862; Berry, letter, November 1, 1862.
15 Goddard, diary, November 1, 3, and 4, 1862.

morning. At noon they stopped to rest. While Silas and he sat by the side of the road, gathering strength to continue, the whole brigade passed by. They finally got up and "went to a union man's house and got some dinner." He recorded the regiment made 22 miles.[16]

"At daylight, we left Bowling Green on our march towards Nashville," reported the forty-two year old Reverend Dill. The next morning with the "sun an hour and a half high," the chaplain continued, "we reached the line which separates Kentucky from Tennessee, and as each regiment passed under the great tree and over the square stone which mark the boundaries of these States, a shout went up and a cheer which bade defiance to rebeldom, and showed how heartily our troops are engaged in this war."[17]

The turnpike from Bowling Green to Nashville parallels the Louisville and Nashville Railroad. Fortunately, for the Eighty-ninth, the railroad became operational about the time the regiment crossed into Tennessee. With the railroad bridge at Munfordville repaired, the trains ran through as far as Mitchellville, Tennessee. Here the regiment "got supplies and winter clothing . . . ."[18]

On November 6, Goddard confided to his diary that "we were told by the Colonel that we would not move to day except to just change camp. We are going to stay here for the present to guard the hospital and pike." Before the war the hospital had been a spa and a summer resort. The area was known as Tyree Springs, and the regiment moved a short distance to be nearer the water. No sooner had Goddard's Company H pitched their tents then they were ordered out on a foraging expedition. "We went about 2 miles and came to a grist mill. We entered it and confiscated a big wagon load of meal and flour. I made out to get some shorts potatoes, turnips, and a few onions," Goddard wrote. He added that "General McCook told us we might take anything [with]in 15 miles of here. This is a strong secession county."[19]

"We are detached from our brigade," wrote George Sinclair, "and put on duty at this post to guard the springs from the rebels as this

---

16 Goddard, diary, November 5, 1862.
17 *Chicago Tribune*, November 18, 1862.
18 Sinclair, letter, November 15, 1862.
19 Goddard, diary, November 6, 1862.

is a regular watering place for trains running to and fro between Nashville and Mitchellville." Sinclair noted that Tyree Springs "had been a regular sporting place in time gone by for the bloods of the south to rusticate, drink good water and bad liquor in plenty . . . ." Sinclair added: "The hotel is used now for our officers' headquarters and a hospital for the sick of our regiment." [20]

Thirty-four-year Elijah Youlin, a private in newly arrived Company F, wrote his wife, Phebe, of the regiment's current location on November 15. "We are in camp here in Tenisee to gard the provision tranes on thare road to Nashvill[e] to the troops that are thare. We have to be on picket every other day & night. When we go out we take our sow bely, as the boys cale it, . . . & bacon & hard bread & coffe & shuga & blanket & then we are ready to stay out in the woods 24 hours and then we are reli[e]ved by an other companey and so on day after day.[21]

From Tyree Springs Chaplain Dill informed the *Tribune's* readers that "Colonel, Hotchkiss, was appointed commandant of this post, and our regiment, with a section of artillery, and some cavalry, was left behind to guard the place, and keep the road open for the passage of trains to and from Nashville." Alfred D. French, a private in Company A, recounted in his memoirs the regiment's stay here. He recalled: "The Confederates in their retreat from Ky. Had torn up the rail road from Bowling Green to Nashville, Tenn. So that all the supplies for the army had to be taken through by mule teams." He explained that "stations were located on the line about 25 miles a part, and there the teams would stop for the night. We had to go on picket every other night, half of the regiment on duty one night and the other half, the next night. No rations were issued to us while here. We had to forage for our living."[22]

"I am in tennesee now," George Berry penned his wife. We ar about twenty mile from Nashville. Ower Regiment was left behind

---

[20] Sinclair, letter, November 15, 1862.

[21] Youlin, letter to wife, November 15, 1862, [Internet website] *Family History-Post, Master, and Youlin Ancestors*, (Accessed January 15, 2007), http://dkwilde. com/Genealogy/Post/Histories/EYoulinWar2Trans.jpg, hereafter cited as Youlin letter.

[22] French Memoirs.

to guard a tavern . . . [It is] a very important place. We have a good deale of Picketing to do. We hafture watch [for] Morgan's gurillia band. Each company takes turn in goin out foargin. Ower company went out one day in the country with six mule teams. We got three loads of corn and 3 loads of hay and fifty chickens. I ketch three chickens and fetch[ed] them home to camp." Private George Berry observed that "it looks harde to go take every thing a poore man has and see three or foure children bare footed and rag[g]ed. The men that ar at home if they will come up to head quarters and take the oath they will git there pay. [A] good ma[n]y has don so."[23]

Private Youlin gave a graphic description to Phebe of one such foraging detail. "We went for something to eat for ourselves and the horses and we got it. We took the man of the house and his nigers first & then we took a pig he just drest for his table and then we went to his still house but found nothing but hogs & then went at them. They kilt 23 of them & then we went back to the house and thare we found some honey, we ate that pretty sone. Then we got some sweat potatoss & hens & geas & wheat & corne & five head of horses & while all this was going on some more of the boys took four more white men & too nigers & fore horses & three mules." When the company was called to formation, Youlin said "it was a laughable sean . . ." With order somewhat restored, he wrote, "we started for camp & on the way we got three more rebels & while they wer taking them I went in the tobackco house and helped myself to the best it aforded. It was a treat to me you can bet for the sutler had sold out & we could not get eny in that way." As for his role when out foraging, Elijah minced no words, "I have bin . . . one of the acters in seans that makes the rebels think that we have no mercy on them. I have sean a good deal more than I can rite. When I get home, I will be more mynute in what I have done."[24]

Fred Goddard woke up Wednesday, November 12 and found it raining. After having breakfast with his mess, he was ordered out on picket duty. He recorded in his diary that "it has rained incessantly all day [and] we are pretty well wet." Either out of curiosity, boredom, or hunger, Goddard left his post and headed for a house about a

---

[23]   Berry, letter, November 10, 1862

[24]   Youlin, letter, November 15, 1862.

quarter of a mile away. From the residents he took two haversacks filled with apples. Afterward he wrote the following about the family: "The owner of the property was a private in John Morgan's guerilla band. The woman and two daughters were all secesh and said they would rather die on the gallows than ever come under the government of the U S of A again.[25]

Organized details were sent out to forage for the regiment, but freelance acquisition of property was frowned upon and punished. Goddard described the fate of two brothers caught returning to camp with appropriated items. "Joseph and Ben Haigh brought in a quarter of veal and some dried apples this morning. The Colonel saw them bringing it in and had them arrested and sentenced to carry the meat for 4 hours on their shoulders in front of his headquarters. He relieved them in one hour." The story of the Haigh brothers' crime and punishment was the talk of the camp, and Rock Island County farmer, Elijah Youlin, reiterated a version to his wife. "Thare was two boys got a quarter of beaf last night when they wer on gard & brought it in this morning but the Cornel saw them and he made them carey it around in front of the headquarters for 4 hours then let them have it." Hotchkiss' disciplining of the Haighs failed to serve as a deterrent to the rest of the regiment. Private Youlin words depict reality. "We had but little meat in camp so we got a pas to go & get some Chesnuts which . . . are plenty [here]. We got whare the Chesnuts were thick & had got our packets prety well fild when who should come a long, [but] some nise hogs. We derst not shoot so we fixt bygonet & charged on them. We got one of them & then we [took] out . . . our nives & skinned mister hog in [no] . . . time and sholder[d] it, fealing that we are lerning to be soldgers fast."[26]

When not on picket duty or out foraging, the Eighty-ninth was on the drill field. Colonel Hotchkiss soon gained the reputation as "the ablest drill master and shrewdest disciplinarian in the division . . . ." His effort on the parade ground made the Railroaders "the pride of several commanding generals." It was important to maintain good military bearing, especially at Tyree Springs, as the former resort was a draw for all those traveling to Nashville. One guest of the

---

[25]   Goddard, diary, November 12, 1862.

[26]   Goddard, diary, November 15, 1862; Youlin, letter, November 15, 1862.

regiment was General Rosecrans, and from that time on, "Old Rosie" was held in high esteem by the boys of the Eighty-ninth.[27]

In his *History of the Old Second Division* William Sumner Dodge explained that commands were left "at Bowling Green, Mitchellville, Tyree Springs, Gallatin, and other sites along both the railroad and turnpike. It was essential, he wrote, to protect the Louisville and Nashville Railroad, the only line of communication between our army and the Ohio River. When the Army of the Ohio withdrew to Louisville, the railroad was attacked and badly damaged by rebel raiders. With the Confederate defeat and withdrawal from Kentucky, the railroad was quickly repaired from Louisville to Mitchellville. However from Mitchellville to Nashville, about forty miles, all supplies had to be hauled in wagons until the railroad could be returned to running order, a feat which took nearly a month. The last segment to be repaired ran through a rugged and guerrilla infested terrain. Therefore, Dodge noted that the Eighty-ninth Illinois Infantry was left at Tyree Springs, to help protect the line of communication, remaining here some two weeks before being ordered to rejoin the division.[28]

*   *   *

Chaplain Dill reported that the halt was "very opportune for our sick, of whom we have now about twenty-five in this building [the former hotel]; and they are by no means insensible to the comforts of a bed and a blazing fire, home comforts rare to soldier life." Dill unfortunately was obligated to list the Eighty-ninth's recent losses. "D.L. Martin of company B, died to-night of typhoid fever—and since my last report, Jas. Morris, W. N. Hunt, James Plasters, James, Perry, and Louis Bodett have died."[29]

Summing up the health of Company G, George Berry wrote his wife that the "the last time I heard from Mr. Copley, he was at Luisville [and] not mutch better. I think he will go home on a furlow. Mr. Wales he has bin in the hospital pretty mutch all of the time. We

---

[27]   Eddy, *Patriotism of Illinois*, II: 336 and 337.

[28]   Dodge, *History of the Old Second Division, Army of the Cumberland*, 372.

[29]   *Chicago Tribune*, November 18, 1862.

have eight or ten sick in ower Company. One person has dide out of ower Company. I did not learn his name."[30]

Berry often referred to Mr. Copley in his letters to his wife, showing a concern for both his health and his ability to stand up to the rigors of military life. At the time of his enlistment Isaac Copley was forty-five, married, and the father of nine children. Born and reared in New York, he was the first of five brothers to settle in Knox County, Illinois, arriving in 1844. Copley farmed and ran a general merchandise business in the village of Victoria. When the township where he lived was organized, it bore his name. He was also elected the township's first justice of the peace. Prominent in the community, Copley "took an active part in arousing public opinion and enlisting volunteers; some of whom went into the 17th Regiment of Illinois infantry early in 1861 and part into the 9th Illinois cavalry." In August 1862, despite his advanced age and large family, Isaac and his son-in-law, Thomas Whiting, enlisted. The popular Copley was chosen first lieutenant. Copley would resign for health reasons on May 8, 1863."[31]

Like Copley, neither age nor family kept Massachusetts born Harrison G. O. Wales from leaving his farm and answering Lincoln's call for more volunteers. Wales, who was fifty and who still had four children under eighteen at home, freely signed the enlistment roll. No one could say he was unaware of the dangers and hazards of military life, even for a younger man, since his two older sons, Edwin M. and Otis A., had enlisted in Company D, Seventeenth Illinois Infantry in 1861. Edwin had been wounded at Shiloh. Sergeant Wales' health would recover, and he would serve throughout the war, mustering out with the regiment."[32]

By the time the Eighty-ninth reached Tyree Springs most of the men were either broke or down to change. Many were now writing their family for money. George Berry acknowledged that he was glad to receive the stamps and the dollar Harriet enclosed in her last letter. He explained to her that "ower pay role is maid out and

---

[30]   Berry, letter, November 10, 1862.

[31]   *Galesburg Register-Mail*, February 2, 1933.

[32]   A. W. Bowen, *Progressive Men of Western Colorado* (Chicago: A. W. Bowen & Co., 1905), 580-582.

the pay man has got it. I don't know when I shall receive the money. We may have it rite a way or we may hafture wate till January." He informed her that a "little change come [in] handy [for] bying little peace of cheese or butter, and little molasses. Ower grub is harde crackers, fat porke and fresh beefe and sugar and coffee and rice ... But when we are marching dry crackers and pork and coffee is what we have. When I don't have a very good appetite, [a] little change come handy in bying some thing that I can relish."[33]

Outraged by the news from home that the politicians and railroad executives were failing to keep their word in caring for the wives and children of those who enlisted, George Sinclair wrote his wife on November 15 with specific instructions to obtain what was due her and their daughter from both Cook County and the railroad. He explained that he mailed the needed certificate for a monthly payment from the Cook County War Fund to Mr. Downs, the treasurer of the Milwaukee Road. All she had to do was pick it up from a Mr. Huntley at the Chicago yard. "I don't want you to beg of the county, but this is your right. Mrs. Loomis went to Colonel Christopher and got her certificate and draws $2.00 per week. You can draw $1.50 for yourself and 25 cents for Gertie, making $1.75 a week which would be quite a help and to be had for going after it for it is rightfully yours."

After completing the letter, Sinclair decided he had the time and paper to return again to the issue of funds for his family. "I want you to go right to Mr. Huntley at the Shops and have a talk with him. He will see you righted, if it is a possible thing to do. You must tell him that you need it, that what little money that I left has been spent and you need more to live on. He will also see about the war fund for you. Now don't fail to attend to all of this for I find out that some of the old troops in our brigade has not been paid off for six or eight months. They are paid according as the paymaster comes across them . . . ."

Concern for his wife and infant daughter turned to anger when word circulated among the men in Company C that their former employer was reneging on its promise to assist their families. Sinclair wrote: "I tell you I was blue last week for one of the men

---

[33]   Berry, letter, November 12, 1862

received a letter from his wife saying that Baldwin [Seth C. Baldwin, Superintendent of the Chicago and Milwaukee Railroad] had denied ever promising to pay $10.00 per month to their families, but by last night's mail I found out that some of them had gotten it. I am in hopes that you may be one of the lucky ones." Frustrated with the whole situation, he let his feelings be known. "As for the $10.00 from the railroad folks . . . I shall not stop here for I don't believe in letting them bamboozle me into this cursed business and then laugh to their selves at my foolishness in taking their promises."[34]

On Sunday morning, November 16, a well-armed supply train of several hundred wagons came along the turnpike enroute to Nashville. Sizing up the passing column, Chaplain Dill and the regimental surgeon saw an opportunity to travel to Nashville where they could take care of some needed business. "As the doctors are getting out of medicine, and the theological department (as well as the rest of the regiment) was getting out of letters," Dill explained, "these two departments took possession of an ambulance, and, providing ourselves with a driver and sundry revolvers, we passed twenty-one miles through a complete hornet's next of guerillas to Nashville." He confessed to the *Tribune* readers that tagging along with the train "somewhat diminished the peril of the journey, and the demand on our courage."

That night Dill's party located the brigade headquarters. Welcomed by the general and his staff, they settled in by the campfire to a cup of coffee and some hard bread. With the horses fed and tied to the ambulance, they bedded down for the night. "In the morning, after loading in about three bushels of mail," they proceeded over the pontoon bridge into Nashville.

While regimental surgeon went about procuring medical supplies, Dill happened upon the U. S. Sanitary Commission building and stepped in. Passing through "a pile of dry goods' boxes of all sizes and shapes," Dill found a back office and set up shop "for interchange of news." While writing his current article, the chaplain-turned-correspondent commented that "judging from the notices of my communications which the soldiers read me from their letters, our friends at home have learned to look to your columns

---

[34]   Sinclair, letter, November 15, 1862.

for the whereabouts and condition of the Railroad Regiment." It was probably well that Chaplain Dill wore a number of hats. For George Berry told his wife that the chaplain "is a good man but no preacher. When he preaches, he has about fifty to here him."[35]

It was Sunday morning and Private Goddard arose and ate a quick breakfast before washing up and dressing for church, only to be ordered out on battalion drill. The men were first drilled in the manual of arms, and then had a sham fight, followed by a bayonet charge on a double quick. During the maneuver, Goddard's Company H deployed as skirmishers, and he noted the men had a great time. While the Railroaders were finishing up, Major General Lovell Rousseau and his staff rode up. Colonel Hotchkiss ordered the regiment into formation and the men to present arms. Some companies turned their backs to the general. This display may have been a reaction to Rousseau's bringing orders returning the Eighty-ninth to their parent brigade.[36]

An upset George Sinclair sounded off to his wife on the regiment's move. "Old General Rousseau with his division came to take his quarters at the springs, keeping a whole brigade to do the same duty that our regiment had been doing alone. We were not much please as we had just got fixed up comfortable for cold weather and there was plenty to confiscate around that point," Sinclair wrote. However, orders are orders, and at daylight on Monday, November 17, the Railroaders struck their tents and started for Nashville.[37]

---

[35] *Chicago Tribune*, November 21, 1862; Berry, letter, December 13, 1862.

[36] Goddard, diary, November 16, 1862.

[37] Sinclair, letter, November 24, 1862.

CHAPTER 5

"WE CAN NOW HEAR THE REPEATED ROARING OF MUSKETRY"

When the Army of the Ohio fell back toward Louisville, Buell left two divisions behind to hold Nashville. For most of the autumn, the city and the isolated Yankee garrison had been under a limited siege. Totally cutoff from the North, the Federals survived by purchasing food from area farmers, who had no compunction with feeding the Yankees as long as they got a good price and prompt payment. Pressure by the Administration to move into East Tennessee subsided when additional rebel units began appearing outside of Nashville. Fearing the Union troops would be compelled to surrender, Rosecrans dispatched Major General Alexander McCook on November 4 to the relief of the beleaguered force. McCook's command reached Nashville on November 9, lifting the siege. As he advanced toward the city, McCook secured a line of communication and provided protection for supply trains by leaving regiments at key locations.

While McCook headed to Nashville, Rosecrans issued another order on November 7 dividing the Fourteenth Army Corps into three wings. Major General George H. Thomas would command the center, with Major Generals Alexander McCook and Thomas

Crittenden commanding respectively the right and left wings. Crittenden's wing followed McCook's to Nashville, as Rosecrans began gathering the army together in preparation to confront the enemy. However, of utmost priority was the repair and protection of the rail link with Louisville, without which the army could not be supplied. The mission was assigned to Thomas. He had the railroad repaired and reopened by November 26. For many a lowly soldier, subjected to long marches on scanty rations, little seemed to have changed in his daily routine or life. But unbeknownst to the rank and file, Rosecrans' orders of the November 4 and November 7 were the first steps in his advance on the rebel army.

On his arrival in Nashville, Rosecrans focused his attention on disciplining and equipping the army. Immediately, inspections, from division down, were ordered by the commanding general. And when possible, he personally reviewed the troops talking with the men as he passed down the line; establishing rapport while showing a true concern for those in the ranks. Rosecrans further assured the troops that they would be properly armed, clothed, and fed. His personal touch boosted the army's morale and confidence. When the railroad was opened from Louisville to Nashville, the promised supplies began arriving, filling the empty warehouses. Quartermasters lined up to draw everything from hardtack to uniforms, while ordnance wagons picked up loads of small-arms ammunition and artillery shells.

Rosecrans' army formed up south of Nashville with the rebels remaining close by. In fact, by early November, Bragg's Army of Tennessee had concentrated about thirty-five miles away at Murfreesboro. Rebel cavalry controlled the front and patrolled right to the Federal lines, where they frequently exchanged fire with pickets and foraging parties. Rosecrans too was active, ordering brigade-size reconnaissance to probe the enemy's strength and location. For the men of the Railroad Regiment, all that separated them from the relative quiet of guarding Tyree Springs and the sounds of war was a two-day march.[1]

[1]   Henry M. Cist, The Army of The Cumberland (New York: Charles Scribner's Sons, 1882), 80-81; Daniel, Days of Glory: The Army of the Cumberland 1861-1865, 186-187; Dodge, History of the Old Second Division, Army of the Cumberland,

After Rousseau's review of November 16 the men of the Eighty-ninth drifted back to camp in pairs and small groups, grumbling amongst themselves about their bad luck. Having spent over a month constantly marching here and there; sleeping on the ground with little or no shelter from the elements; and eating a steady diet of hardtack, fatty pork, and coffee, the Railroaders had quickly adjusted to their surroundings at the abandoned spa. The officers and men of the Eighty-ninth found Tyree Springs to be as close to a permanent camp as they had seen since leaving Chicago. And, in no time, the men had settled into a routine of picket duty, drill, and foraging. The long hours standing at a picket post, even in inclement weather, could be tolerated. Consequently, the order to pull up stakes was hard to swallow. If their spirits were not low enough, it began to rain. Still they went about making preparations to break camp.

Private Goddard jotted in his journal for Monday, November 17: "We struck tents this morning at day-light and started on our march toward Nashville. It rained all of yesterday afternoon and all of last night and this morning[.] [I]t is very muddy[.]" George Sinclair commented on the mud and the march in a letter to his wife, telling her "it having rained two days before hand and anyone can imagine what fine footing it was . . . ." Sleeping for some of the men proved as troublesome as the march had been. Goddard recorded that "it rained all of last night and drowned some of the boys out of their beds, and they had to dig around their tents in the middle of the night and in the mud to keep the rain from running under their tents. Our tents happened to be on a noll [sic] and the water did not trouble us." Sinclair continued reporting that "we weathered the two days march, finally passing through the best looking part of the south that we had seen yet." However, he may have been speaking sarcastically since his next words detailed the destruction that had occurred. "We cannot give a very correct idea of the country as everything is torn and ransacked to pieces. Nearly every farm that we pass has nothing but ruins to mark the place where once stood some fine mansions. Their owners leaving everything behind and

371-375; Van Horne, *History of the Army of the Cumberland Its Organization, Campaigns, and Battles*, I: 207-211.

scooting for the land of Dixie. You might look in almost any direction and see tall old fashioned chimneys standing, a sad monument of this cursed rebellion . . . ."[2]

Chaplain Dill depicted the scene in his correspondence. "Through the whole extent of this road scarcely a fence was left on either side; most of the houses were deserted, some burned, and from but few chimneys was the smoke rising, which betokened a family within." Trampled fields, strewn with straw, tent stakes, and earth blackened by campfire indicated the recent camps of rebel or federal soldiers. Smoldering fires along the route showed where stragglers, convalescents, cavalry guards, or wagon trains, had halted to cook their meals.[3]

"We crossed the Cumberland river at half past 10 on a pontoon bridge and marched through Nashville . . . at 11 o'clock," Private Goddard noted in his diary on November 18. Sinclair, who had written of the destruction of farms and plantations, informed his wife that "as we entered Nashville, we could see more of the effects of war, bridges and everything that could be destroyed has . . . ." Chaplain Dill gave a graphic account of what the soldiers of the Eighty-ninth viewed as they passed through the city. "There stands the abutments of that magnificent suspension bridge, destroyed by rebel hands; there also, spanning the river, that lofty railroad bridge, whose sides are pierced with holes for rifle shooting, and its ends surmounted with sentinel boxes; there, on the top of the river bank, is a breastwork of cotton bales; and everywhere in the suburbs of the city are rifle pits, embankments, barricades of roads, prostrate trees, and all manner of military arrangements for the defense of the place." He continued: "In and around this once beautiful city war has done its desolating work. The courthouse and other important buildings are occupied as barracks and hospitals, and groves and gardens have gone to destruction under the hard necessities of war."[4]

"It is awful muddy," complained Private Goddard, as the regiment continued southward, where six miles beyond Nashville

2   Goddard, diary, November 17and 18, 1862; Sinclair, letter, November 24, 1862.
3   *Chicago Tribune*, November 21, 1862.
4   Goddard, diary, November 18, 1862; Sinclair, letter, November 24, 1862; *Chicago Tribune*, November 21, 1862.

they hooked up with their brigade. From a cozy situation in the rear of the army, the Eighty-ninth found itself after two days on the road in the extreme advance. That evening, as the regiment settled in, a buzz went through the camp that "a private in Co. G shot his hand off . . . ." George Berry explained the incident: "We had an accident happen in Company G. Isac Berry['s] gun went off and the ball went rite threw his hand. His fingers had to be taken of[f.] His thumb was left on." For his wife's benefit, he noted: "I have traveled about five hundred miles [and] I have not shot my gun of yet, but I have come pretty near some of the time. I have loaded my gun about ten times. I am not alowed to shoot it off in camp, and when I was on duty, there was no Rebels came neare. When we come of[f] Duty we draw ower load from ower gun."[5]

The Eighty-ninth's new encampment was on the grounds of the Tennessee Asylum for the Insane. The Railroaders must have wondered at the strange turn of events after being unceremoniously removed from relatively safe duty in the rear of the army and deposited on the front lines. On the first morning back, the brigade inspector appeared and checked each man's weapon and cartridge box. While the regiment stood in formation and each man's equipment was inspected, Goddard noted the distinct rumble of cannon fire from the front could be heard. George Sinclair reported on the regiment's changed circumstances in a letter to his wife. "We are now in a country where it is nothing new to hear them skirmishing every day. They have been at it today since three o'clock this morning. We can now hear the repeated roaring of musketry and now and then mixed by a field piece or two." Writing his wife, Private Berry pointed out "the rebel Pickets are one mile from ower Pickets[.]"[6]

*   *   *

At this juncture in the war, battlefield tactics were much the same as those used in Napoleon's time. Compact units of men

---

5   Goddard, diary, November 18, 1862; Berry, letter, November 20, 1862.

6   Chicago Tribune, December 8, 1862; Goddard, diary, November19, 1862; Sinclair, letter, November 24, 1862; Berry, letter, November 20, 1862.

marched in line and fired volleys at each other. If the enemy did not flee after trading volleys, commanders ordered charges or flanking maneuvers to break their line. Having fought at Belmont, Forts Henry and Donelson, and Shiloh, Colonel Hotchkiss believed that drill and more drill was the only method to prepare his green regiment for combat. To deliver fire and parry enemy moves, the Eighty-ninth would have to respond automatically to commands and act as a unit. Fred Goddard's diary entries reflect his feelings concerning, and undoubtedly the feelings of most others, on the tried and true method of preparation for "seeing the elephant." "Had to drill this afternoon. Had Co. drill at 9 this morning. I have not drilled any to day. The rest have drilled as usual. Had Battalion drill from 2 until sun down[.] The boys had just came in from drill . . . We are lying in Camp and do nothing but have Co drill and cook and eat our rations."[7]

Throughout the army the new commander's order to hold inspections was being carried out. Fred Goddard entered in his diary for Sunday, November 23, that we "had orders to prepare to go out on Division review at half past 9. We were reviewed by Gen. Sill and Brig. Gen. Gibson and Staff and then we were marched in review in line of Battle. After this we were drawn up in line and Gen. Gibson made an address to each of the regiments sepperately)." These spit and polish reviews were one of Rosecrans methods to instill discipline and *esprit de corps* in the army. He also began weeding out incompetent officers, which further endeared him to the enlisted soldier. However, not all of Rosecrans' changes were readily accepted. "The substitution of shelter for Sibley and Bell tents" was met by "a storm of indignation" by the army.[8]

"I have just come in from batallion drill, which is a whole regiment's drill. It is now five o'clock and I will try and finish out this sheet before supper or crackers and coffee, I should say," George Sinclair wrote his wife, before turning to his family's welfare. The former engineer was unable to contain his anger with the Chicago and Milwaukee Railroad and angrily wrote: "I hope you receive that

---

7   Goddard, diary, November 19, 20, 22, 24, 27, 1862 and December 2, 1862.

8   Goddard, diary, November 23, 1862; Dodge, *History of the Old Second Division, Army of the Cumberland*, 383.

money from the company and myself imparticular, for if I do not receive what they promised, I shall do everything by compulsion and I would even desert rather than see you suffer or be dependent on anyone." He continued: "I would leave and go to some other part of the states and let them whistle for me and be damned with their country to save, for when there is not public opinion and patriotism enough in the wealthy at home to take care of the families of volunteers which they solemnly swear to do on getting us to go and fight their battles. And after we are gone, repudiate all they have said and leave the dependent ones to suffer or become outcasts of society to procure the necessities of life . . . ."[9]

Chaplain Dill had a conversation with two emissaries of Illinois Governor Richard Yates. The pair had been dispatched to visit with and check on the Illinois troops in the field. The fact-finders found some troops "poorly clad and cared for," along with some "general grumbling and desire to get home." Dill wrote to his readers back home: "I urged upon them the importance of hurrying up the paymaster, since the families of the soldiers were now in the beginning of winter, suffering for want of money." Rosecrans, too, recognized that the government's failure to pay the men was a serious problem and incited desertions. He wrote Stanton asking for a million dollars and additional paymasters to pay the army up to September.[10]

Alfred French, a twenty-one-year-old farmer from Amboy, remembered that while outside of Nashville the Eighty-ninth spent most of the time "picketing, scouting, and foraging for feed, for the horses & mules." Seventy-eight years later, he recalled one of the foraging expeditions. "We learned of a large farm seven or eight mile out, where the corn had not been gathered; the owner was a Colonel in the Confederate Army. As he could not well attend to the harvesting, our regiment was sent out to do the work, and we did it. We cleaned the field of corn, but I think they must have forgotten to tell us where the cribs were."[11]

---

[9]   Sinclair, letter, November 24, 1862.

[10]   *Chicago Tribune*, December 8, 1862; Daniel, *Days of Glory: The Army of the Cumberland, 1861-1865*, 185.

[11]   French Memoirs.

To keep an eye on Rosecrans Yankees, General Bragg kept a cavalry force close to the Union lines. Consequently, the daily foraging parties and scouting patrols came into frequent contact with the rebel horsemen. Ill and confined to camp, Fred Goddard faithfully made his daily diary entries. For Thursday, November 27, he wrote: "The boys had just came in from drill and stacked their guns and gone to getting dinner when they were ordered to fall in and went off on a double quick [at the] report of a fight." The following day he reported that "the boys came back without seeing the secesh. The alarm was on account of our advance having a skirmish with the enemy. They were ordered out to be in supporting distance in case they were needed, but the secesh 'skedaddled.'"[12]

Joe Buckley was looking forward to having Thanksgiving afternoon off and re-reading his wife's letter which had arrived in the morning's mail. But, he described to her how he actually spent the day. "We were reviewed by General Willick (sic) in the forenoon, and after the review, I went down to the Division Suttler to buy me a[n] apple pie for I thought I would have a treat as it was Thanksgiving, but I had only just got there when I heard our drums beating for us to fall in, so I had to go back in a hurry and get on my shooting tackle. We marched out about two miles to be in readiness to support the 5th Brigade which was having a skirmish with the Rebels about 3 miles ahead of where we were ordered to be in readiness in case the Rebels were stronger than our men." Buckley summed up the day. "I should have said that our Brigade was all ordered out and the Battery too. It commenced raining and rained most all day which made it very uncomfortable, but we did not mind that, as we were sure of having a fight with the Rebels. We are in good fighting trim for we all think we have followed them far enough without giving them a taste of our lead. About 4 o'clock the news came that our men had driven the Rebels so we were ordered back to camp." Back at camp Buckley concluded that his "Thanksgiving dinner was spoiled for that day" and had to content himself "with a little raw pork and a few broken crackers."[13]

---

[12]   *Chicago Tribune*, December 8, 1862; Goddard, diary, November 27 and 28, 1862.

[13]   Buckley, letter, November 29, 1862.

The fracas also upset Private Berry's plan to respond to his wife's most recent letter. "I had not time to answer . . . untill now," he explained to her: "We have hade some stere in camp. The fifth Brigade went out a skirmishing and they got into a fight and we was called out to reinforce them. By the time we got out there, they had whiped them out, so we return[ed] to ower camp." He went on: "Yesterday we went out a foraging five miles from camp. Two Regiments of us and two Peaces of Artillery. Company G exchanged some shots with the rebel cavalry. No person hurt."[14]

"We moved camp to-day, and are about seven or eight miles south-east of Nashville. The enemy are in force only eight or nine miles off. We may see fun any day," Lieutenant E. T. Wells of Company F wrote the editor of the *Rock Island Union* on November 29. He added that we "had an alarm day before yesterday and heavy skirmishing in front. Our regiment was in line in less than ten minutes, our company *first.*" Sergeant Sinclair addressed the latest move in his December 3 letter to his wife. "We have moved our camping ground since I wrote you. I do not know of their reasons for changing only to get in another part of the army." With uncanny foresight he wrote: "We expect to be in the advance of Rosecran's Grand Army, which is only waiting for supplies and . . . plenty of subsistence for his men. Then we go on, the devil knows where, for we don't pretend to ask. All we have to do is to march onward when ordered and ask no questions."[15]

Monday evening, December 1, Joseph Buckley completed a lengthy letter to Mary. He began: "On Saturday evening I thought I would finish this letter in the morning but instead of doing that our Regiment and the 32nd Indiana Regiment were ordered out to get along with the Division Train of Wagons on a foraging expedition right among the Rebels. We went along to protect the wagons. They had got most all the way out, filled with corn and other things which that they wanted, when the Rebels fired at some of our men." The Kendall County farmer continued: "We were immediately ordered forward which I assure you did not take us long to do, but the Rebels

---

14   Berry, letter, December 1, 1862.

15   *Rock Island Weekly Union*, December 10, 1862; Sinclair, letter, December 3, 1862.

were on horseback and of course we could not overtake them. So we took our position and waited for them to come back again as it would not be safe to leave the wagons any further because we did not know how much of a force they had." Buckley then explained that "we had several pieces of artillery along with us, six pounders." In an attempt to send the rebels on their way, "our artillery boys sent some shells out to them which made them skidaddle."

The rebels scattered, but quickly regrouped for another charge. Sheltered by timber, Buckley's Company H seemed to have a secure position for the coming fight. However, when the attack came, the rebels bypassed them and hit further down the line. Out of the immediate fight, Buckley described the action. "Captain Spencer and his company had been ordered a distance to our right. I think the Rebels discovered our position as they charged around to the right of us and more in front of Captain Spencer's company. When Captain Spencer's men commenced firing on them, and the Rebels returned the fire, Captain Spencer took a gun from one of his men and took aim at one of the Rebels and sure enough one man fell from his saddle, and the horse shot out as fast as he could go." He noted that "Captain Spencer is a Preacher and I believe a Methodist. This is different business from going to [a] meeting, but you know a soldier has no Sunday."

Taking no part in the firefight, all Buckley could say was that "if the Rebels advanced in front of us, we should no doubt [have] killed or captured them for we had a very good position." He wrote that at the height of the action "we were in the woods and the bullets came over our heads and struck a rail just about 2 inches from one man's foot. You would have laughed to see some of the boys lower their heads when the bullets came over." In the end, the rebels withdrew; while Union troops, with their wagons filled by that time, started back. It was nearly sundown when the two regiments along with the loaded wagons completed the 7 mile trek to camp.[16]

In a letter home George Sinclair wrote a few lines summarizing the recent fight. "We had our maiden battle three days ago. We were sent out on a foraging expedition and were assailed by some of Breckenridge's cavalry, but we laid six or seven of them

---

[16]   Buckley, letter, December 1, 1862.

[dead], they not doing us any damage in return," he noted. "We are gaining quite a reputation as a crack regiment," George penned, "and I tell you, we earn[ed] it too, for finer [men] never turned into the field." With food always on the Railroaders' minds, some men literally took cover in a garden. Sinclair explained: "Well on that day we were thrown out as skirmishers and we skirmished right on a bed of sweet potatoes and cabbage which were buried for winter use. We appropriated all that the whole company could carry."

Sinclair's wife's latest letter relieved George of his mounting anxiety over the family's financial straits. He responded to her news that the issue was resolved. "I am very glad that you got that money from the company for I had worried considerable on your account, but now as long as you receive that amount monthly, there is no danger of your suffering. I do not like the idea of your being dependent on your father or anyone else. We shall probably be paid off in a month or two and I can then send you what I get."

Aware of George's need for money, Franky enclosed a small sum in her letter. Her kind act brought a summary rebuke. "I don't want you to keep sending me money and stamps for I do not need them, and it's only a mistaken kindness in your sending it for I do not need anything here that I have not. We are in a country that if you pretend to pay for what you get, it would take a young fortune to live decently and pay the prices that we consume." For example, the price of cheese, Sinclair noted, was a dollar a pound, "butter is a dollar and half a pound, potatoes and apples a dollar a peck . . . and everything else [is] selling at the same proportions." He added: "So I am content to take what Uncle Sam furnishes us and jayhawk all that we can from the country. So my dear, I would rather you would save or use the same money for your own benefit . . . You need not worry on my account for I will not go without as long as there is anything to eat in the country around."

Darkness brought an end to Sinclair's letter writing for the day. He finished the page by stating: "As we are out on picket, we shall try to replenish our stock of vegetables before tomorrow night." When he got back to the letter, Sinclair jokingly wrote that "you see by this that I have passed another night in succession on picket, the most dangerous of all military duty, and come off with a whole head and a half bushel of potatoes besides which I went outside of the lines this morn early and confiscated. And the owner extended his hospitality by presenting me with a warm breakfast of sweet potatoes, corn bread and buttermilk, which I appreciated a great deal but not enough to refund the potatoes that I had got." He further commented that he "was kind enough to stop a lot of other soldiers from robbing . . ." the poor farmer. But he let it be known that "it is our maxim here to let everyone take care of himself and the devil take the hindmost."[17]

* * *

August Willich, the sixth brigade commander, returned on November 28 after a period of convalescence. Goddard noted that "General Willich joined us yesterday and reviewed our Regiment." The young private wrote as if he had been surprised about the general's nationality. "He is German." The general certainly was German and spoke with a heavy accent that gave the Railroaders a chuckle or two. They got such a kick out of his speech that they took to quoting him in their letters. The day after Willich's return Lieutenant E. T. Wells, the former Rock Island attorney, wrote: "We had a fine compliment from Gen. Willich . . . the other day on inspection. 'Ha!' said the old fellow 'dare is meeletary movements in dis companee!'" Wells then added that "our's is considered to be the best drilled company in the regiment, and the Eighty-ninth has no mean reputation."[18]

Even for Civil War officers, August Willich was an old man. So much so, that the men in the Ninth Ohio and Thirty-second Indiana regiments, where he served before taking over a brigade, referred to him as "Papa Willich." Willich was fifty-two years of age, having been born November 19, 1810 in Braumsberg, Prussia. In order to be able to serve in the Union army, Willich altered his year of birth to 1820. The change enabled him to circumvent the Ohio governor's declaration that no one over age forty-five would be commissioned

---

[17]   Sinclair, letter, December 3, 1862.

[18]   Goddard, diary, November 29, 1962; *Rock Island Weekly Union*, December 10, 1862.

an officer. If anyone knew differently, they said nothing, for he was too valuable a soldier, no matter what his age.[19]

Willich was born into an old noble family. His father was a Hussar captain, and fought in the Napoleonic Wars and the Polish insurrection where he was wounded and rendered unfit for service. When he died in 1813, he was working as a civil servant. August and an elder brother were raised by a distant relative. At age 12, young August entered the cadet house at Potsdam. In 1825, he was admitted to the military academy in Berlin. Completing his education in 1828, he was commissioned a Second Lieutenant of the Royal Artillery. By 1841 he was a captain.[20]

Despite his noble heritage and military training, August Willich readily accepted the liberal call for reform sweeping through Germany. He espoused such republican ideas as universal suffrage, freely elected parliaments, freedom of press and religion, public education, just taxation, and trial by jury. These beliefs were strongly opposed by the Prussian monarchy. Holding views in conflict with his class and superiors, Willich attempted to resign in 1846 but instead was assigned to a new post in Pomerania. He refused the transfer and reapplied for discharge, sending an open letter to the King. This impudent action resulted in a court-martial, but his comrades were unwilling to punish him and his resignation was accepted.[21]

Planning for this day, Willich had prepared himself to be a carpenter, a solid proletarian occupation for an eventual member of the Communist League. A man willing to put his beliefs into action, he led a mob that marched on and forced its way into the Cologne city council chamber, demanding the municipal leaders

[19] James Barnett, "August Willich, Soldier Extraordinary," *Historical and Philosophical Society of Ohio Bulletin* XX (January 1962), 62; Charles D. Stewart, "A Bachelor General," *Wisconsin Magazine of History* XVII (1933), 131.

[20] Ella Lonn, *Foreigners in the Union Army and Navy*, (Baton Rouge: Louisiana State University Press, 1951), 190; Reid, *Ohio in the War: Her Statesmen, Her Generals, and Soldiers*, II: 868.

[21] William L. Burton, *Melting Pot Soldiers: The Union's Ethnic Regiments*, (Ames, Iowa: Iowa State University Press, 1988), 5; Lonn, *Foreigners in the Union Army and Navy*, 190-91; Reid, *Ohio in War: Her statesmen, Her Generals, and Soldiers*, 868.

present their reforms to the king. The takeover collapsed when the military arrived, scattering the mob and arresting the leaders. Willich miraculously escaped punishment. [22]

Frustrated with the monarchy's refusal to address the "basic rights" of the German people, a committed radical Fredrick Hecker attempted to overthrow the government of the German State of Baden. To support the provisional republic, Willich turned to his former calling, and raised a ragtag force of armed workers that was known as "Willich's Free Corps". Joining him in the fight and serving as his adjutant was Friedrich Engels, the co-author of *The Communist Manifesto*. Royalist troops soundly defeated Willich's fighters at Kandern, on April 20, 1848 and again in 1849, suppressing the rebellion. Following the failed uprising, Willich fled to Switzerland and later settled in London.[23]

Here the reunited members of the Communist League immediately began quarrelling and soon fractured over philosophical issues. Willich and his supporters stood for immediate revolution, while Marx and Engels were content to bide their time. The formal split took place on September 15, 1850, when Willich lost a vote on the future direction of the Communist movement to Marx. Willich's faction never gained any steam and eventually dissolved. Without purpose or funds, Willich immigrated to the United States in 1853, where he initially toyed with the idea of gathering an army and returning to Germany. In the meantime, to make ends meet he worked as a carpenter at the Brooklyn Navy Yard. His mathematical skills did not go unnoticed and led to work with the United States Coastal Survey. Judge Johann Berhnard Stallo, a leader in the German-American community at Cincinnati, met Willich on a visit to the East in 1858 and convinced him to come to the "Queen City of

[22] Lonn, Foreigners in the Union Army and Navy, 190-91; Carl Schurz, *The Reminiscences of Carl Schurz, 1829-1852*, 2 vols. (New York: The McClure Company, 1907), I: 115.

[23] Stewart, "A Bachelor General," 146; Lonn, *Foreigners in the Union Army and Navy*, 191; James Barnett, "The Vilification of August Willich," *Cincinnati Historical Society Bulletin* XXIV (January 1966), 29; Eden and Cedar Paul, trans., Otto Ruhle, *Karl Marx: His Life and Work*, (Garden City, New York: Garden City Publishing Co., Inc., 1928), 167.

the West" and edit the German language newspaper, *Der Deutscher Republikaner.* Willich readily agreed.[24]

Willich's editorials promoted socialism, denounced Catholicism, and criticized all religion and earned him the nickname "Reddest of the Red." Judge Stallo, who helped found the Ohio Republican Party, was unsuccessful in weaning Willich away from Marxism. The *Republikaner,* despite Willich's leftist leanings, backed the fledgling Republican Party and its policies. In 1861, the newspaper was a strong supporter of Abraham Lincoln, drawing the German community to the Republican candidate.[25]

After the firing on Fort Sumter, the Germans of Cincinnati held a mass meeting at the Turner Hall, affirming their allegiance to their adopted country. To demonstrate their willingness to protect the Union, over one thousand men volunteered within twenty-four hours, enough to form an all-German regiment. August Willich signed on like many others, as a private. When the men assembled at Camp Harrison to begin training, there were plenty of experienced German officers, and Willich was a proven military leader. But when it came time to select the regiment's colonel, Judge Stallo's law partner, Robert L. McCook, was elected over Willich. It was felt the politically connected McCook would get "the regiment armed and equipped sooner than it could be done with a German in command." And the "immediate objective of the regiment was to get into service as quickly as possible."[26]

---

24   Stewart, "A Bachelor General," 146-48; Barnett, "The Vilification of August Willich," 31-32; Burton, *Melting Pot Soldiers: The Union's Ethnic Regiments,* 5; Lonn, *Foreigners in the Union Army and Navy,* 191; Robert Payne, *Marx,* (New York: Simon and Schuster, 1968), 245; Edward H. Carr, *Karl Marx: A Study in Fanaticism,* (London: J. M. Dent and Sons, Ltd., 1938), 104; Franz Mehring, *Karl Marx: The Story of His Life,* (London: George Allen & Unwin, 1951), 190.

25   Stewart Sifokis, ed., *Who Was Who in the Civil War,* (New York: Facts on File Publications, 1988), 720; Lonn, *Melting Pot Soldiers: The Union's Ethnic Regiments,* 5-6.

26   James, Barnett, "Willich's Thirty-Second Indiana Volunteers," *Cincinnati Historical Society Bulletin* XXXVII (Spring 1979), 49; Barnett, *August Willich, Soldier Extraordinary,* 60-61; Burton, *Melting Pot Soldiers: The Unions' Ethnic Regiments,* 81.

By acclamation Willich was named the "'military father of the regiment' and given the rank of adjutant." It was "Papa Willich" who drilled the regiment, while McCook handled the required paperwork. With Willich the *de facto* colonel, "McCook remarked that he was 'just a clerk for a thousand Dutchmen.'" Willich on the other hand saw himself as the boys' father while they were away from home and treated them that way. The men responded and quickly became a well-drilled and disciplined regiment.[27]

The McCook/Willich German regiment was designated the Ninth Ohio, but the Germans called it, "Die Neuner." The Willich-trained Ninth was sent to West Virginia and saw action at the Battle of Rich Mountain on July 11, 1861. Having been offered a commission by Indiana governor, Oliver P. Morton, Willich, on August 10, announced that he was leaving "Die Neuner." The Hoosier Governor banked on Willich's fame being magic, and hoped Germans from Ohio and Illinois would flock to join Indiana's all German Indiana regiment. A recruiting office was opened in downtown Indianapolis and business was brisk for a few days. By August 24, it was reported the regiment was completely organized and mustered into Federal service as the Thirty-second Indiana Infantry. But the truth was the Thirty-second was having trouble filling its ranks. It took until September 21 for the final company to be mustered in and the regiment had its complete compliment of men and officers. Ordered to Kentucky the Thirty-second departed on September 28. On the way to the railroad station, the regiment paraded though downtown Indianapolis. In parades colonels usually led the way on horseback, but Willich marched on foot, unable to afford $150 for a horse.[28]

---

[27] Barnett, "Willich's Thirty-Second Indiana Volunteers," 49-50; Barnett, "August Willich, Soldier Extraordinary," 62; Burton, *Melting Pot Soldiers: The Union's Ethnic Regiments*, 81.

[28] Barnett, "Willich's Thirty-Second Indiana Volunteers," 50-51; Barnett, "August Willich, Soldier Extraordinary," 64; Burton, *Melting Pot Soldiers: The Union's Ethnic Regiments*, 80-81; Reid, *Ohio in the War, Her Statesmen, Her Generals, and Soldiers*, 868-69; Joseph R. Reinhart, trans. and ed., August *Willich's Gallant Dutchman: Civil War Letters from the 32nd Indiana Infantry* (Kent, Ohio: The Kent State University Press, 2006), 22-28.

On December 17, 1861, four companies of the Thirty-second Indiana, numbering 418 men, were guarding a civilian work crew repairing a railroad bridge across the Green River at Rowlett's Station, when they were attacked by 250 cavalrymen of Terry's Texas Rangers. The Rangers were supported by two infantry regiments and a four-gun battery, bringing the total rebel force to around 1,300. Quick thinking Lieutenant Colonel Henry von Treba ordered his detachment to form a hollow square whereby the German infantry held off the rebels, repulsing several attacks. The spectacle of four companies of infantry without cavalry or artillery support holding off rebel cavalry supported by both infantry and artillery was unthinkable. But with Willich's training and discipline, the Thirty-second stood their ground, winning the fight and gaining national recognition.[29]

Willich further understood that morale was as important as drill and discipline. While the rest of the army ate hardtack, Willich had brick ovens built, and the Thirty-second had freshly baked bread each day and a beer ration when available. No wading streams or waiting for pontoons for the Thirty-second. Willich ordered special wagons built. "The wagons carried planking, and when a river needed crossing, they removed the wheels and the wagon beds became boats over which the planking was laid to form a pontoon bridge."[30]

* * *

Twenty miles from Savannah, Tennessee on April 6, 1862, the men thought they heard thunder. Not sure, Willich made a small hole in the ground with his sword and then laid down with his ear over it. When back on his feet, he announced the distant rumble was the sound of battle. Orders soon followed, and Buell's army

[29] Barnett, "Willich's Thirty-Second Indiana Volunteers," 51; Barnett, "August Willich, Soldier Extraordinary," 65; Stewart, "A Bachelor General (August Willich)," 145; Reinhart, *August Willich's Gallant Dutchmen: Civil War Letters from the 32nd Indiana Infantry*, 42-43.

[30] Barnett, "Willich's Thirty-Second Indiana Volunteers," 52; Burton, *Melting Pot Soldiers: The Union's Ethnic Regiments*, 83.

hurriedly set off on a forced march to link up with Grant, arriving at Savannah an hour before midnight. The following day Willich's reputation not only as an innovator but also as an eccentric would attain a new height.[31]

Nine miles above Pittsburg Landing at Savannah, the German Thirty-second Indiana, along with the Thirty-ninth Indiana and the Fifteenth and Forty-ninth Ohio, boarded the steamer *John J. Roe* to the strains of the *"Marsellaise."* An hour later at 10:00 A.M.. the brigade arrived and the Thirty-second disembarked first. Willich marched his men through the mob at the landing and up the hill "where he received orders from General Grant to start immediately for the field of action." Grant elected to detach the far more experienced Willich from his brigade and let him act independently. Willich reported: "The regiment marched as fast as possible, and having received no special direction, took its course to the heaviest firing." Coming across General McCook, the Thirty-second was ordered to form as the reserve behind his division and wait for action. In the back and forth of the fighting an opening appeared in the line where McCook's and Crittenden's divisions joined. The rebels, seeing an opportunity, quickly attempted to flank McCook's position. The Thirty-second was ordered to plug the hole and drive off the rebel force. An eyewitness to the charge, General Lew Wallace recalled: "I was watching the up-coming of the strangers. They were but a regiment; yet at sight of them the enemy halted, about-faced, and returned to his position in the woods. There he struck out with a fire so lively that the new-comers halted and showed signs of distress." As he watched the regiment, Wallace said that he saw an officer ride "swiftly round their left flank and stopped when in front of them, his back to the enemy. What he said I could not hear, but from the motions of the men he was putting them through the manual of arms—this notwithstanding some of them were dropping in the ranks." Willich recognized his men were losing their composure and were firing too hastily and too high. Thus, the halt to drill brought the men under control, and once "responding sharply and precisely to command," Willich "ordered them back to work again." "Taken all in all," Wallace wrote, *"that* I think was the most audacious thing that

---

[31] Barnett, "Willich's Thirty-Second Indiana Volunteers," 57.

came under my observation during the war. The effect was magical. The colonel returned to his post in the rear, and the regiment, steadied as if on parade, advanced in face of the fire pouring upon them and actually entered the wood."[32]

The Federal line took up the advance and pressed the rebels steadily back until resistance turned to retreat. After pursuing the enemy for a mile, Willich halted his exhausted men for a rest. The attack cost the Thirty-second six killed, ninety-three wounded, and four missing. On July 17, 1862, for his gallantry and courage under fire, August Willich was promoted to brigadier general.[33]

While he had his back to the enemy at Shiloh, Willich was a conspicuous target, and the rebel infantry did not ignore the opportunity. Several bullet holes were counted in his coat and one spent ball broke a rib. When Buell's army arrived at Louisville, General Willich, after months of pain, was forced to seek treatment and was hospitalized until the rib healed. On November 27, 1862, Willich returned from sick leave and made it a point to meet and review the newest regiment in the brigade, the Eighty-ninth Illinois Infantry. The Railroaders saw a confident man with military bearing. He was six-feet-tall, solidly built with broad shoulders, a long thin aristocratic nose, flashing teeth, and blond hair. He was the epitome of a Prussian officer.[34]

The men of the Eighty-ninth found that General Willich was not only a consummate professional soldier but also an untiring

---

[32] Henry Villard, *Memoirs of Henry Villard, Journalist and Financier, 1835-1900*, 2 vols. (New York: Houghton, Mifflin and Company, 1904), I: 248; Lew Wallace, *An Autobiography Illustrated*, 2 vols. (New York: Harper & Brothers Publishers, 1906), II: 561-63; OR, Vol. 10, Pt. 22, 315-18; Stewart, "A Bachelor General (August Willich), 136-38; Barnett, "August Willich, Soldier Extraordinary," 66-67; Barnett, "Willich's Thirty-Second Indiana Volunteers," 57-62; Burton, *Melting Pot Soldiers: The Union's Ethnic Regiments*, 81-82.

[33] Ann Turner, *Guide to Indiana Civil War Manuscripts* (Indianapolis: Indiana Civil War Centennial Commission, 1965), 107; *Indiana at Chickamauga 1863-1900, Report of Indiana Commissioners: Chickamauga National Military Park*, (Indianapolis: William B. Buford Contractor for State Printing and Binding, 1901), 160; Barnett, "August Willich, Soldier Extraordinary," 67;

[34] Barnett, "Willich's Thirty-Second Indiana Volunteers," 62.

hands-on officer. "Had Brigade drill to day," wrote Fred Goddard in his diary, "[and] General Willich commanded in person. We had 2 sham battles. We drilled 4 hrs. and done first rate so the General said." In another entry he recorded that the men "went out on Brigade drill at eight and drilled until noon. We had a number of battles (Sham ones of course). Willich drilled us." On December 9, he wrote: "We were ordered to be ready to march at day light, but we are now out on picket. We are stationed on the reserve. General Willich came out here and said he was afraid we would be attacked and told us we must hold our position." The General demonstrated to the Railroaders that he was not a tent commander. Goddard cites an example of Willich's penchant for being with his men no matter what they were doing. In his journal for December 11, Goddard noted: "We were ordered last night to be ready to march at daylight. We were off before daylight this morning. We went after forage and collected 100 wagons loads and brought it off without firing a gun. We went in sight of the rebels picket lines. General Willich was with us. The rebels sent in a flag of truce to our General on business."[35]

General Willich's ever-present quirkiness showed up in many ways. For some unknown reason, he requested the men in his brigade refrain from shaving. Joe Buckley speaks of this when informing Mary that "I should have to shave before I could kiss you. General Willick (sic) tells us not to shave."[36]

*   *   *

Feelings of homesickness along with the bitter reality of war began appearing in the letters home. George Berry told Harriet that "I want to see the children so much. They hean't a day pases but I think of home." George Sinclair wrote: "Oh how I should like to pick up and start for home. I could foot it all the way barefoot at that and thank God for the chance to do it . . . ." A distraught Joe Buckley confided to Mary his weariness when he wrote: "may God relieve me from this wicked war so that I can come home and take care of you." In the same letter he asked her: "How do you get

---

[35] Goddard, diary, December 9, 11, 20, and 23, 1862.
[36] Buckley, letter, November 29, 1862.

along without anyone to sleep with? Do you not wish sometimes that your husband was laid by your side with his arms around you, or do you have no desire to have any dealings with regard to copulation?"[37]

While some longed for their wives or sweethearts, others found comfort in the wrong place. Private William Stanley and other enlisted men in Company F sought treatment for gonorrhea from Dr. Samuel Hance, the regimental surgeon. Hance refused to furnish the men medication for the disease, telling them that the government did not supply such items when indeed he had the medicine. His indifference to their health and well-being resulted in his court-martial. Inexplicably, he was acquitted. Fortunately for the regiment, he resigned March 26, 1863.[38]

Letters from loved ones and friends, even newspapers, helped alleviate the loneliness suffered by the soldiers. Some men relied on their faith to see them through. When he was able, George Berry read the Bible for solace. He wrote that "last Sunday I read six chapters in the olde and new testament. My minde is fine. I don't calcolate to turn to the right nor to the left but keep in that straight and narrow path that leads to heaven." Commenting on the spirituality of his fellow soldiers, Berry told Harriet: "All the reding I have now is the bible. That book is not reade much in camp.[39]

Her concern for his character prompted Joseph Buckley to write his wife, Mary: "You wanted to know how I got along with my morals. I will tell you in a few words as I can . . . I do not smoke tobacco or cigars. I have not swore since I left home. I do not drink whiskey, and to tell truth, my morals are better than they were when I left home. I feel fully prepared to die at any moment, so you see that you have done some good by the help of God." In another letter Joseph once again reassured Mary of his fidelity and wrote: "I have kept faithful to you both in body and mind. I have

---

37 Berry, letter, December 13, 1862; Sinclair, letter, December 3, 1862; Buckley, December 1, 1862.

38 Thomas P. Lowry, M.D. and Jack D. Welsh, M.D., *Tarnished Scalpels: The Court-Martials of Fifty Union Surgeons* (Mechanicsburg, Pennsylvania: Stackpole Books, 2000), 124-128.

39 Berry, letter, December 13 and 16, 1862.

not had a desire to have dealings with any female but yourself since I left home. If I cannot return as pure as when I left, I shall not return at all."[40]

Illinois held statewide elections in the fall of 1862, and the Union party, an alliance of Republicans and War Democrats, went down to defeat with the Democrats replacing the Republicans in the statehouse. Nationally, nine of Illinois' fourteen seats in the House of Representatives went to Democrats. Even Springfield and Sangamon County went Democratic. The Republican politicians paid a heavy price for military failure and Lincoln's preliminary emancipation decree. Talk soon spread of a possible compromise to end the conflict. On hearing this, George Berry made it clear where he stood on the subject. "I don't go in for no Compromise. If Illinois has gorn Democratic, we will shoe them when we get home how to vote." His political fervor fueled by his wife's forwarding of a newspaper, George acknowledged that he "was glade to get it. Seme like olde time." The news seemed to suit him, as he told Harriet that "the president['s] message was firstrate."[41]

Maybe it was his New England rearing. But New Hampshire-born Berry seemed more sympathetic to the plight of the slaves than many Midwestern soldiers. While out foraging he often came into contact with both Southerners and Negroes. "The men have left and gorn south," he wrote. "A grate many bilding[s] are burnt down. Olde men is about all is left here. The people seem to be clever and nice. What I have conversed with the negores, they understand them self. They know what this ware is fore. I ask them if they are fore the union. They would say yes all of the time. I finde them inteligent." He continued: "About all of the corn that is raised here is don by slave laber. I would asked them if his master union man. He would say not much but he hasture be so now when we are here." Berry related one instance. His company "went to a house and we took all of the corn that the slavehoulder had. The negroes they was lookin on. They said that they did not care ware it wen to. They said

---

[40]   Buckley, letter, December 1 and 21, 1862.

[41]   Paul M. Angle, *"Here I Have Lived" A History of Lincoln's Springfield 1821-1865*, (New Brunswick, New Jersey: Rutgers University Press, 1935), 274; Berry, letter, December 8 and 16, 1862.

its ben so all there life time. Received nothing for there worke. It come harder on ther master then it did on them."[42]

With winter's approach, letters home were suddenly filled with requests for mittens or gloves. Joe Buckley asked Mary to knit him a pair, telling her that "it is pretty cold nights handling our guns with bare hands . . . ." Two weeks later he again mentioned the need. "I want you to send me a pair of gloves or mittens with one finger in them . . . ." Fred Goddard noted on December 8 that "we each had a pair of mittens presented to us by the ladies of Chicago they are knit with one finger in them so we can handle the gun as well as though we were barehanded and much better on a cold morning." Tennessee winters may not be as severe as those in Illinois, but Private Berry testified that the hardest thing he "hafture do is standin on pickit these colde knights." Berry welcomed his mittens and said they "came in good time. It is cold down hear (sic). We have some snow. The ground is frose harde." Mary Buckley's package with mittens for her husband arrived on December 21.[43]

While out on authorize parties gathering fodder for the draft stock and riding horses, the Railroaders took upon themselves to supplement their dull army fare of hardtack, salt pork, and coffee. "I received your ever welcome letter last night after we came in from a foraging expedition, which though the day was very stormy, [it] provide[d] a good one to us, that is our mess, for I secured a fine pig of a hundred pounds, a lot of potatoes, turnips, chickens, geese, and I guess that we can live for a few days as well as any of the officers can afford to," wrote Sergeant Sinclair to his wife. In the same letter, he explained that "the boys are busy cleaning up their guns, some cooking, some cleaning what they stole or jayhawked . . . ." "I would say," he added, "for I consider anything that we can lay hands on, confiscated to a good cause [and] that is to keep us in good condition."[44]

Chaplain Dill reported that "there is nothing very new with our (Railroad) regiment. William Scott is dead. Berry shot off his hand,

---

42 Berry, letter, December 21, 1862.
43 Buckley, letter, November 15 and 29, 1862; Goddard, diary, December 8, 1862;Berry, letter, December 8, 1862.
44 Sinclair, letter, December 16, 1862.

and with a number of others will be discharged. Several others, who have proved themselves unable to march, will be sent to hospitals or to permanent camp, and before we march again there will be quite a sifting in our ranks." George Berry informed Harriet that "Isaac Berry left for home to day. He lives in Galva. Some think that he shot his hand off [on] purpose. He has a wife and three children." As for Harrison Wales, George wrote that he "has bin in the hospital pretty much all of the time. He has got his health now. He stays to take care of the sick."[45]

Left unchecked, the rebel cavalry continued to harass the Union pickets, disrupting the daily routine and the sleep of all. "I had just commenced reading your letter last night", wrote Joseph Buckley to his wife "when the sound of cannons surprised us a little, and then word for us to fall into line of battle was given, so I had to put it in my pocket. We stood there about an hour to be in readiness in case we were attacked. I heard today that the Rebels had fixed a battery and fired on our pickets." George Berry was in a similar position. He told Harriet that "I had just reade the letter little over half through when bang went some rebel artilery. I had to drop my letter and take my gun and we was ordered in to line to wate for further orders. The rebels fired three or foure rounds. That is the last we heard of them. No person was hurt. We stack[ed] ower guns in line and went back to ower tents and then I finished reading you[r] letter." As long as the two armies remained in close proximity, reconnoitering and probing continued.[46]

---

[45] *Chicago Tribune*, December 8, 1862; Berry, letter, December 16, 1862.
[46] Buckley, letter, December 21, 1862; Berry, letter, December 21, 1862.

CHAPTER 6

"WE HAVE HADE A HARDE TIME IN THIS FIGHT."

By mid-December the Army of the Cumberland numbered nearly 82,000 men. Enough rations had been shipped and stored at Nashville to feed the troops through January. Therefore, as far as Washington was concerned, everything was in place for Rosecrans to move after Bragg and Chattanooga. For weeks both Halleck and Lincoln had urged, prodded, and threatened Rosecrans—all to no avail. When the Administration had run out of patience and Old Rosy was out of excuses, the rebels weakened their force at Murfreesboro. Rosecrans saw this as his opportunity to advance and destroy Bragg's army.

Bragg concluded the Federal army was not preparing to advance, and that Rosecrans would be content to go into winter quarters at Nashville. Confident in his judgement, he released Morgan and Forrest to raid behind the Union lines. The former headed for Kentucky to destroy Rosecrans' communications with Louisville while the latter struck for West Tennessee to harass Grant. The departure of a large part of Bragg's cavalry, and his confirmation of President Davis' order for Bragg to send reinforcements to Pemberton was the opening Rosecrans sought. The transfer of 7,500 infantrymen and the absence of a good portion of the cavalry left the Army of Tennessee with about 38,000 men. On paper Rosecrans' army doubled that of Bragg's, but in reality he could barely field 44,000 troops—the rest were needed to guard the railroad and garrison Nashville. With the troop numbers still in his favor, Rosecrans saw it was time to act.

As 1862 drew to a close, the Federal armies had suffered a string of defeats. In the East, Burnside was repulsed with a staggering loss of life at Fredericksburg. On the Mississippi River, Grant and Sherman were both checked in their separate advances on Vicksburg and forced to fall back. The eyes and the hopes of the North now focused on the Army of the Cumberland. Rosecrans felt the pressure, as a Northern victory was sorely needed. When he called his commanders together, he understood, unlike his predecessor Buell that his military career was on the line. With his subordinates gathered around his maps, Rosecrans laid out the plan that he and Thomas had drawn up. After the details were covered, he gave the order for the army to break camp at dawn on December 26.

For two weeks the weather remained mild with clear skies and warm winds. But when the bluecoated soldiers marched out on their assigned routes, the wind was cold and a steady rain fell. McCook's wing was in the center, marching on the Nolensville Pike toward Triune, where it would turn east and head for Murfreesboro. Crittenden was on the left advancing on the Nashville Pike while Thomas moved on the Franklin Pike. From the beginning every mile was contested and every hill defended as Wheeler's remaining rebel cavalry put up a stout resistance, giving Bragg time to concentrate his force.[1]

---

[1] Peter Cozzens, *No Better Place to Die: The Battle of Stones River* (Chicago: University of Illinois Press, 1991), 44-46; Dodge, *History of the Old Second Division, Army of the Cumberland*, 391-392; Shelby Foote, *The Civil War: A Narrative, Fredericksburg to Meridian* 3 vols. (New York: Vintage Books, 1986), II: 79-85; James M. McPherson, *Battle Cry of Freedom: The Civil War Era* (New York: Oxford University Press, 1988), 579-80; Jim Miles, *Paths to Victory: A History and Tour Guide of the Stone's River, Chickamauga, Chattanooga, Knoxville, and Nashville Campaigns* (Nashville, Tennessee: Rutledge Hill Press, 1991), 13-15.

Christmas Eve found the Eighty-ninth formed in a line of battle when the regimental adjutant, First Lieutenant Edward F. Bishop, came along and told the men to prepare three days cooked rations and be ready to march at daylight. "We struck tents soon after daylight, packed them on the waggons, and sent them back to Nashville. We took up our line of march toward Nolansville [and] went about 1 mile when [the] orders were countermanded," explained Private Goddard. Consequently, "the waggons came back and so did we. In about an hour the waggons started again and again they came back." Being a tad sarcastic, Sergeant George Sinclair gave this description of that morning. "The day before Christmas we pulled up stakes and took a start forward on our grand forward movement that has been talked about so much, but marched out two or three miles than back again to pitch our tents until further orders, holding ourselves in readiness to move at a minute's notice."[2]

Christmas Day saw the Railroaders out on a forage detail once more. With General Willich leading, the entire brigade went along to guard the wagons. Contact was made with the rebel pickets about 10:00 A.M.. "We drove in their pickets . . . and skirmished with them . . . constantly until four in the afternoon," Sinclair wrote. "The loss being trifling on both sides, perhaps a half a dozen killed or wounded on either [side]." But in a serious tone, noted that "the loss seems light to speak of and a constant skirmish kept up half a day, but light as it was it will make many a once cheerful family desolate." Godard added: "We went about 10 miles to collect our forage. We did considerable fighting with the Texan rangers. The firing lasted all day." By the time the brigade returned to camp darkness had overtaken the column.[3]

A man's stomach sometimes can overrule all else. So, in the midst of the fight Godard "made out to capture an old hen and about a peck of Irish potatoes." He philosophized that "we are agoing to have our Christmas dinner to morrow instead of having it to day." When the brigade returned, they again received marching orders. They would leave at dawn on the twenty-sixth. Godard confided in his diary: "I set up last night and cooked my Chicken and we had it

2   Godard, diary, December 24, 1862; Sinclair, letter, January 6, 1863.
3   Sinclair, letter, January 6, 1863; Godard, diary, December 25, 1862.

for our breakfast. We had Irish potatoes also." After completing his delayed holiday meal, Godard stated that "we struck tents at daylight this morning and took up our line of march towards Nolansville."[4]

"The morn[ing] of the 26th Dec., bright and early we started out again," wrote Sergeant Sinclair. "We being on the right, that means in military parlance that our division was ahead, we taking the Nolensville pike, also one on the Franklin and Murfreesboro Pikes towards the latter place where we expected the enemy to make a stand." The advance immediately made contact with Wheeler's cavalry. The rebel horsemen screening Bragg's army fought a delaying action, giving up ground grudgingly. "We have had to fight our way; the cannons have been booming nearly all of the time," Godard noted. Twenty-year-old Alfred D. French of Company A recalled that "before noon we met with heavy opposition. Our reg[iment] was ordered to support a battery of light artillery (six cannon) which was planted on a high ridge. Then they opened on the enemy with grape and canister, and as they fell back, we followed them up, through fields and woods until night, and how it did rain." Goddard lamented: "It has rained constantly all day and is very muddy."[5]

Observing from the ranks, George Sinclair gave this perspective of the first day of Rosecrans' campaign. "We made nine miles, it taking us until dark to accomplish that on account of the bridges being either burnt or blown up so as to delay us as much as possible, it taking some time to repair, so as to get the artillery across." He pointed out that "this day's march was a very disagreeable one. It raining all day, a cold winter rain completely saturating us and you can imagine how comfortable we were to lay down without any shelter at all on the cold wet ground, though we laid more comfortable than could be expected, for we did not go to bed any too early." Private Godard ended his entry for the day by stating that "we passed through Nolansville soon after dark and pitched our shelter tents the other side of town."[6]

---

4   Godard, diary, December 25 and 26, 1862.

5   Sinclair, letter, January 6, 1863; Godard, diary, December 26, 1862; French Memoir.

6   Sinclair, letter, January 6, 1863; Godard, diary, December 26, 1862.

With the Federal advance, the population fled southward, abandoning their homes and businesses. Curious blue-clad soldiers began entering the buildings. Curiosity soon gave way to vandalism and looting, slowing the forward movement. Sinclair wrote that the men concluded "that everyone down here are secesh, out and out. So we did not hesitate to help ourselves to anything that we wanted. So the boys just pitched in and opened the stores in the town and dwellings in the vicinity, completely sacking everything." He confessed that "as badly as I hate the secesh, I had not the heart to destroy what I did not want as some did, but took only what I wanted to eat." Sinclair knew his wife "would think it hard sight to see, the fine large mirrors broken, carpets torn up, pianos turned [over] by soldiers . . . ." He may have taken no part in the destruction, but summed up his feelings when he wrote: "I will say in our defense the people deserved all that was put upon them."[7]

Rosecrans expected Bragg to make a stand south of La Vergne where Stewart's Creek crossed the Murfreesboro Pike. But, Bragg had not anticipated a Federal movement; and as a consequence, his army was in no position to respond. While Polk and Kirby Smith's divisions were near Murfreesboro, Hardee's corps was to the west somewhere between Triune and Eagleville on the Nolensville Pike. While Bragg may have been caught off guard by the advance of the Army of the Cumberland, Wheeler's cavalry kept him abreast of the Federals' progress. With Wheeler's delaying action slowing the Union columns, Bragg set about bringing his scattered divisions together. Rosecrans on the other hand, without a strong cavalry presence, moved slowly and somewhat blindly in search of the enemy.[8]

Saturday, December 27, Hardee's rear guard skirmished with McCook's advancing troops. By 4:00 P.M. the Federals were on the outskirts of Triune, where they were temporarily halted by a six-gun battery supported by cavalry. A Union battery was brought forward. The guns let out a roar, which was followed by an infantry charge

7   Sinclair, letter, January 6, 1863.

8   Dodge, *History of the Old Second Division, Army of the Cumberland*, 392; Van Horne, *History of the Army of Cumberland Its Organization, Campaigns, and Battles*, I: 220.

that scattered the rebels, but not before the withdrawing enemy burned the bridge over Wilson's Creek. With the bridge repaired, Johnson's division crossed and bivouacked south of Triune.[9]

The Eighty-ninth had taken up the march that Saturday morning at 9:00 A.M.. Private Sinclair wrote: "Raining all day we moved very cautious, this day our advance driving the rebels before them. And at Triune we heard that the rebels intended making a death stand, and I should say that the place is admirably situated for a strong defense, being situated on the top of a high range of hills . . . and a stream running at the base of the hill. And the bridge was blown to[o], there was no crossing for artillery for miles. But with all these natural defenses in their favor, they were easily shelled out." The laconic Goddard summed things up when he wrote that we "have been fighting all day. We passed through Triune this evening and are in camp on the other side of town."[10]

Triune also suffered at the hands of the Railroaders. "The boys serving this place as we did Nolensville" is the way Sinclair put it. Company C did, however, managed to lose a man there. Sinclair explained that "a little accident happened to our company from the effects of the sacking, as they found some whiskey and abused it and one of our men fell into the opening for the bridge . . . ." The drunken soldier, John Blayney, died that night from his injuries. Sinclair commented that "we buried him at midnight. It seemed mighty hard to lay him here away from home or friends." The forty-year-old Blayney, an ironworker and native of Wales, left a widow in Chicago. The regimental record states he died December 28, 1862 of injuries on the march. [11]

It was still uncertain where Bragg's army was concentrating, but whatever direction Hardee had gone would answer the question. Until this issue was resolved, the Army of the Cumberland marked time. To determine whether Hardee's Corps had retired to Shelbyville or moved to Murfreesboro, Rosecrans ordered a brigade-size reconnaissance on the twenty-eighth. McCook was given the job, and he selected Willich's

[9] Cist, *The Army of the Cumberland*, 89; Dodge, *History of the Old Second Division, Army of the Cumberland*, 396-397.
[10] Sinclair, letter, January 6, 1863; Godard, diary, December 27, 1862.
[11] Sinclair, letter, January 6, 1863; Muster and Descriptive Roll.

brigade for the mission. Captain Horace Fisher, one of McCook's staff officers, and twenty orderlies and couriers accompanied Willich's assembled regiments. Bolstering the operation were a number of cavalry companies, acting as flankers and riding ahead of the column.[12]

To keep the formation from getting lost or falling into a trap, a dozen local farmers were rounded up and forced to go along as guides. Captain Fisher took charge of these men, assigning an orderly to each, with instructions to shoot his man if there was an ambush. If the expedition succeeded, they could go back to their homes safe and sound.[13]

With the cavalry out front, Willich's brigade headed south toward Shelbyville and pushed about seven miles down to Rigg's Crossroads. Following in the tracks of Hardee's withdrawal, the leading Yankee horsemen picked up forty-one rebel stragglers along the way. From the interrogated prisoners and through their own observation, Fisher and Willich concluded that Hardee had retired "down the Eaglesville road, then by a dirt road to the Salem turnpike," which led to Murfreesboro. [14]

After two days of cold rain, Sunday, December 28 began sunny and warm, making things a bit more comfortable for the troops. That morning Willich's brigade was ordered out on reconnaissance. It was thought "the rebs were drawn up to dispute the passage of a small stream with a big name called the Big Harper [Harpeth] . . . ." After having gone about 5 miles and not finding the enemy, the brigade returned to camp where the men drew rations of crackers and bean soup.[15]

---

[12] Cist, *The Army of the Cumberland*, 89; Daniel, *Days of Glory: The Army of the Cumberland 1861-1865*, 202-203; Van Horne, *History of the Army of the Cumberland Its Organization, Campaigns, and Battles*, I: 222.

[13] Horace C. Fisher, *A Staff Officer's Story: The Personal Experiences of Colonel Horace Newton Fisher in the Civil War* (Boston: Thomas Todd Company, 1960),51-52.

[14] Dodge, *History of the Old Second Division, Army of the Cumberland*, 397; John Fitch, *Annals of the Army of the Cumberland* (Philadelphia: J. B. Lippincott & Company, 1864), 387.

[15] Sinclair, January 6, 1863; Godard, diary, December 28, 1862; and *OR*, Vol. 20, Pt. 1 303.

"This morning [Monday, December 29] we countermarched back about three miles and took a short cut across to [the] Murfreesboro Pike over a high rolling country and rather bad roads for four or five miles," wrote Sinclair. McCook's wing went back through Triune and turned to the east on Bole Jack Road. The day's march continued well after dark. Godard summarized the day when he confided to his diary that we "have marched through a very rough country to day and through some cedar groves." Sinclair described the night's campsite. "We marched until seven o'clock and then camped on an old cornfield and as it had rained for two days heavily, the soft plowed ground was not very agreeable to lie on." He sarcastically commented that "to make things pleasant we were allowed no fire and it rained very hard during the night." Come morning, Sinclair found himself "laying right in a pool of water as each hollow between the corn ridges was full." As the men moved about shaking the cold and stiffness from their limbs, word circulated that the order forbidding fires was due to "the fear of being surprised by the enemy." The lead regiments had closed to within four miles of Bragg's rebel army.[16]

The morning of December 30, McCook's three divisions advanced down the Wilkinson Turnpike. Soon the head of the column was in contact with the rebel pickets, and it became obvious the enemy planned to make a stand at Murfreesboro. As rebel resistance stiffened and ground was stubbornly given up, Sheridan and Davis deployed their divisions in a line of battle with Johnson in reserve. The right wing proceeded to fight its way forward finally aligning itself with the rest of the army, but at a cost of 275 casualties.

A tiring day for McCook took a strange turn around 2:00 P.M., when a friendly farmer was brought to his headquarters with a piece of disturbing information. The man informed McCook that the center of the rebel army was opposite the general's extreme right. McCook responded by pulling Johnson's division from its reserve position and ordering it to form on the right of Davis' division. Johnson selected Kirk's and Willich's brigades to take over the end of the Union line.[17]

---

[16]   Sinclair, letter, January 6, 1863; Godard, diary, December 29, 1862.

[17]   Andreas, *History of Chicago*, II: 245; Cist, *Army of the Cumberland*, 90-91; Daniel, *Days of Glory: The Army of the Cumberland, 1861-1865*, 205; Dodge, *History*

For the Railroaders December 30 began early. It was cooler than the day before, resulting in thick fog settled while a light rain fell on the column of marching men. But after about a mile and a half, the sound of heavy firing could be heard ahead. Upfront Jefferson C. Davis' division had struck the Murfreesboro Pike which was held by the enemy, opening the ball. Skirmishing continued throughout the day, with Davis' attacking bluecoats slowly driving the rebels. When within three miles of Murfreesboro, the enemy, in considerable force, could be seen ahead in a piece of heavy timber. Closer inspection revealed the rebels "had thrown up rifle pits" and had clear view of the advancing Union troops. Sergeant Sinclair wrote the rebels could not be drawn out "so we shelled them until night. They answering for some time but were finally silenced." Sinclair noted the Railroaders ended the afternoon "in a piece of woods within a quarter of a mile of their batteries but received no damage . . . ." However, "just after dark," he further penned, "we were moved, that is our division, our brigade having the advance, up in the same piece of woods that the enemy were in all day. We encamped in a piece of under brush of cedars and briars."[18]

The last light of day was fast disappearing, as Sergeant Sinclair alluded, when Willich was ordered to move to the right of Kirk and to assume a refused position. The command further directed him to throw forward "a heavy line of skirmishers." When the maneuver was complete, Willich's brigade faced south with the Thirty-ninth and Thirty-second Indiana across the Franklin Road. Behind and to the right of the Hoosiers, in a wooded lot, were the Forty-ninth Ohio and Eighty-ninth Illinois. To the right and rear of the Forty-ninth Ohio and facing west was the Fifteenth Ohio. Goodspeed's Battery A, First Ohio Light Artillery held the angle between the two Ohio regiments. Colonel Gibson's after battle report provided a detailed description of the first brigade's position on the morning of December 31. He explained that five companies of the Thirty-ninth Indiana were camped in line of battle, fronting south of the Franklin Road and

---

of the Old Second Division Army of the Cumberland, 398; Van Horne, History of the Army of the Cumberland Its Organization, Campaigns, and Battles, I: 224-226.

[18] Sinclair, letter, January 6, 1863.

perpendicular to the right of Kirk's second brigade. To their right was part of the Thirty-second Indiana. Portions of each regiment were on picket duty with the Thirty-ninth's pickets out 700 yards in front in an open corn-field, while the pickets of the Thirty-second covered the brigade's flank and rear. On the north side of the road and slightly behind and to the right of the Thirty-second Indiana was the Forty-ninth Ohio. The Buckeyes were also formed in a line of battle, but inside a wooded field and within 30 yards of a fence fronting south. In their rear stood the Eighty-ninth Illinois in double column, closed in mass and fronting south. Perpendicular to the rear and to the right of the Forty-ninth, but facing west, was the Fifteenth Ohio. Its left wing rested within 60 yards of the Forty-ninth. And, in the southwest corner of this wooded field was parked Goodspeed's battery. To summarize, Willich's brigade formed a right angle at the end of Union line and was bent back toward the rear guarding against a flank movement.[19]

* * *

With McCook's arrival, the Federal army was all together and in a line facing the enemy. Rosecrans now called his three wing commanders to a meeting where he went over his plan of battle. He explained that the left, led by Crittenden and supported by Thomas, would attack Bragg's right at 7:00 A.M., while McCook held the Union right. If successful, Bragg's avenue of retreat to Murfreesboro would be cut off, and he would be trapped between the Federal pincers and destroyed. Concern about the army's right came up. The generals then discussed the possibility of a rebel attack on McCook. In the end, Rosecrans assured McCook that all his men had to do was to hold their position for three hours. The Federal commander was convinced that Bragg would have to break off any attack to reinforce his right. To deceive Bragg into thinking the Union thrust would open up on the rebel left; hundreds of campfires were built making it appear McCook's line extended further to the right. The ruse worked, as Bragg reacted by extending his line further to the left.

---

[19]   *OR*, Vol. 20, Pt. 1, 295, 303-304; Fitch, *Annals of the Army of the Cumberland*, 391.

General Bragg knew his army numbered fewer men than that of the approaching Federals. Accordingly, he assumed a defensive position and waited to be attacked. However, when it appeared that McCook's advancing wing would flank his left, Bragg's initial plan changed. First, he transferred Major General John P. McCown's division on the December 29 to shore up his left. Then, on the December 30, Cleburne's division was ordered to join McCown, and overall command of both divisions was given to Hardee. Finally, Bragg decided to deliver the first blow, hitting McCook with four divisions at first light on the December 31. The plan called for cutting Rosecrans' escape route to Nashville, and trapping the Federals against the river, where they would be hammered into submission.[20]

McCook shared his uneasiness about his position with General Richard W. Johnson, commander of the second division. Johnson claimed that McCook "told him that he would probably be attacked in the morning by the whole of the rebel army . . . ." Johnson in turn imparted McCook's fears to his brigade commanders, exhorting them to be extra vigilant. Under General Willich's orders, at 3:00 A.M.. Lt. Colonel Fielder Jones left with a company from the Thirty-ninth Indiana and patrolled 600 yards beyond the pickets. Jones returned, reporting that the patrol discovered no enemy presence or activity. Maybe the officers were relieved from their fear and anxiety of an attack since no order was given to wake the men and have them form a line of battle.[21]

Colonel Gibson reported that "at dawn of day orders were received to build fires and make coffee." While the camp was coming to life, General Willich came by and informed Gibson that he was going to General Johnson's headquarters. Gibson recalled Willich telling him that "in case anything occurred in front of our pickets," he was "to rally the Thirty-ninth and Thirty-second to their

[20] Cozzens, *No Better Place to Die: The Battle of Tones River,* 77; Daniel, *Days of Glory: The Army of the Cumberland, 1861-1865,* 206; Miles, *Paths to Victory: A History and Tour Guide of the Stone's River, Chickamauga, Chattanooga, Knoxville and Nashville Campaigns,* 16,20; Van Horne, *History of the Army of the Cumberland Its Organization, Campaigns, and Battles,* I: 227-229

[21] OR, Vol. 20, Pt. 1, 296, 304; Dodge, *History of Old Second Division, Army of the Cumberland,* 404, 406.

support." A sergeant with the Fifteenth Ohio noted the General's appearance that morning: "He wore a rubber cap, rubber overcoat, and rubber boots. He seemed changed in manner, for he was quiet and cool, where before he had been nervously and intensely active. Afterwards we learned that this quiet, cool, deliberate demeanor was his battle manner."[22]

Having taken their current position in the dark, most of the regiments in the brigade had little or no feel for the terrain or even their exact whereabouts. This, coupled with the fact the brigade was not roused hours before dawn and formed in a line of battle, was unusual. Colonel Hotchkiss harbored resentment for this omission after the battle. Years later he would write: "The situation of the Union Right Wing on the morning of December 31 was abnormal, for which I have now no criticism, but this excuse can be made, that the troops were put into position at an unseasonable hour of the night of the 30th . . . ."[23]

On December 31, Hotchkiss had the Eighty-ninth up by 5:30 A.M.. Corporal Nelson Burneson recalled that the night before they made "camp in a dense body of woods, and when the attack of the enemy was made, early in the morning, he at first supposed them to be his own men." In a letter to his parents, Private Theodore Whitney of Company G described what took place the evening before and the morning of the battle: "We were marched Tuesday knight after dark clear on the extreme right of the army & within 15 rods of the emenies line & thare we laid till daylight when we got up & was getting breakfast when the [next] I knew the balls began to fly around me like hail stone. Well, thare we was all in a hubbub." While in Sergeant George Sinclair's Milwaukee Railroad Company, "some of the men had just put on their coffee to boil, others [were] starting a fire and getting ready for breakfast when we heard light skirmishing on our flank and immediately the firing grew heavier and we were ordered into line." Likewise, Joe Buckley told his wife, Mary, that "[I] had just got my coffee ready, and was in the act of taking it off the fire when they came out of the woods—eight columns deep and fired on us, and charged our Batteries." Remembering that same

---

[22]   OR, Vol. 20, Pt. 1, 304; Cope, *The Fifteenth Ohio Volunteers*, 230.

[23]   U. S. Pension Office, John M. Farquhar file.

moment, Alfred French of Company A wrote that it was "a little past six [and] I was cooking my breakfast (bacon & coffee), the orderly sergeant sitting beside me. We heard a terrific yell right close. He said to me, 'That sounds like a charge.' We jumped up and here came the enemy, on the 'Double Quick.' We were surprised. I had my equipment on, and my gun by my side. So I got in a couple of quick shots, but all was confusion, and there was nothing to do but get back as fast as possible."[24]

Colonel Hotchkiss reported that "my men were building fires for cooking, [when] rapid firing was heard on Kirk's front, which was almost instantly followed by the men of his brigade rushing in confusion and indiscriminately through our ranks and over my men, closely followed by a heavy column of rebel infantry." The enemy attack came at us "without [an] alarm from our pickets or a bugle call from any regiment on our front." Panic stricken troops were followed by the charging Confederates, making "every second of time precious," remembered the colonel. Hotchkiss credits Sergeant-Major John M. Farquhar for grasping the gravity of the moment. He "was probably the first one in my regiment who took in the whole situation, and he darted from my side, gave the orders to take arms and deploy . . . ." To get a better idea of what was happening, Hotchkiss explained, Farquhar ran to and climbed up on "a fence bordering the stony field on our right, and from him I learned the strength and formation of the Confederate lines of infantry and cavalry." To provide as much protection as possible from enemy fire, Hotchkiss ordered the men to lie down. He stated "in that position they remained without confusion until my left wing was uncovered of fugitives and the enemy [was] within 50 yards of my position, when I ordered that wing to fire, which was done with good effect, the colors of the leading column of rebels falling."[25]

---

[24] OR, Vol. 20, Pt. 1, 310; *Soldiers' and Patriots' Biographical Album* (Chicago: Union Veteran Publishing Company, 1892), 617; Theodore F. Whitney to parents, letter, January, 8, 1863, original document in the Pearce Civil War Collection, Pearce Collections Museum, Navarro College, Corsicana, Texas, hereafter cited as T. Whitney letter; Sinclair, letter, January 6, 1863; French Memoirs.

[25] OR, Vol. 20, Pt. 1, 310; Farquhar pension file.

"The 89th at early morning light of December 31st, was saluted with a shower of bullets from the advancing regiment of Raines Tennessee Brigade," recalled Company K Private Jere M. Grosh, a former fireman on the Galena & Chicago Union Railroad. "The sudden attack stunned our field and staff officers," Grosh explained, "but a noncommissioned officer ordered the 'assembly' to be blown, and instantly followed it with 'take arms,' 'load,' 'deploy by right flank,' and in a jiffy a stake and rider fence on the right was smashed flat and the regiment took line as if on parade. Luckily the first volley of the Confederates went high, and was answered by the Railroaders with a stinging volley which brought down the colors of the advance regiment."[26]

Godard of Company H entered in his diary for that horrible Wednesday morning that "when they commenced firing in our front we were ordered into line. I took my place and was immediately shot in the side. I went and got behind a tree when I was struck by another ball in the left leg. I was soon after struck by a grape shot. It was spent and did me no harm except to bruise me slightly."[27]

George Sinclair revealed to Francis those horrible first moments of the battle: "The men were just forming when a little fellow from a company on our left . . . came running toward me and away from the firing. Thinking that he was getting scared rather early, I tried to stop him but says he 'I [am] shot in the bowels, I can't.' Just at that moment another [man] sings out, 'I've got one,' putting his hand to his head, and even then I would not believe that they were anything more than spent balls that were over shot . . . ." Sergeant Sinclair soon changed his opinion and wrote that "in a jiffy of time the balls were zipping past us from nearly all sides and the men were tumbling pretty fast. Then we began to realize that there was an enemy firing at us for just then our battery men, what there was left of them, gave four shots of grape and canister and left as there was no horses hitched up to the pieces." The stunned Sinclair came to his senses with the boom of Goodspeed's guns. Joe Buckley took a quick look in the direction

---

26   Jere M. Grosh, "His Last Contribution to Buffalo, Rochester & Pittsburgh Employees Magazine," *Railway Life: Employees Magazine, Buffalo, Rochester & Pittsburgh Railway Co.* vol. 2, no. 3 (February 1914), 12.

27   Godard, diary, December 31, 1862.

of the brigade battery and saw the yelling rebels come pouring after the guns. His words describe the scene: "The horses which belong to the Battery were gone to water so that there was no chance for them to get away. The Battery boys discharged their cannon on the Rebels which cut them up very much." He told his wife, Mary, that "we had not time to get into [a] line of battle as the Rebels were only 10 rods from us, and we had all our traps to pick up."[28]

"We then had the order to lay down and down we went, the balls whistling over our heads like mad," Sinclair wrote his wife. "Well we laid there for a few moments like good fellows. Our colonel looking for some command from our brigadier general, (Willich) who by the way was taken prisoner at the onset, but not getting any command, let us lay there, he sitting on his horse, our adjutant [Bishop] being wounded and unhorsed, the major [Hall] unhorsed and the bullets whistling like hail by him." Sinclair thought Hotchkiss "was a brick. I tell you . . . by his actions [that he] gave a great deal of confidence to his men. I thought as I saw him sitting there that my life was worth no more to me than his was to him. Just then the adjutant general rode up and said to the colonel who sat on this horse quite near our company. 'Order a retreat, colonel for God's sake, give your men a chance for their lives.'" With that exchange, Sinclair informed Francis that "the order was given and as we rose up the enemy was within twenty yards of us and they caught sight [of us] they fired a murderous fire into our ranks completely riddling the regiment." Theodore Whitney, the nineteen-year-old Knox County farmer, put it this way. "We was ordered to retreat. Well, we did. We got out of their way a little."[29]

Jere Grosh later wrote: "Although out-numbered four to one, the 89th stood its ground" and drew help from "about 400 hundred boys from the 15th and 49th Ohio regiments . . . . It was a warm time of 'give and take' for about fifteen minutes . . . but soon a brigade of cavalry covering the Confederate left flank began to move slowly inward, and our boys as slowly moved backward, but still holding in check the Confederate advance."[30]

---

28 Sinclair, letter, January 6, 1863; Buckley, letter, January 8, 1863.
29 Sinclair, letter, January 6, 1863; T. Whitney, letter, January 8, 1863.
30 Grosh, *Railway Life: Employees Magazine, Buffalo, Rochester, & Pittsburgh Railway Co.*, 12.

Colonel Hotchkiss' official version of the retreat order differs somewhat from Sinclair's observation. Hotchkiss wrote: "Having received no orders as yet, and seeing the other regiments of the brigade falling back, I gave the order to retire by the right flank, on the double quick, which was done (but with some confusion), to a lane 400 yards in a northwesterly direction, where I placed Captains Willett's, Whiting's and Comstock's, and lieutenant Wells' companies . . . ." The colonel had Companies F, G, H, and I intact. William Sumner Dodge, the Second Division historian, described what took place. "The enemy advanced in solid column and encountered a well-aimed volley from the Eighty-ninth, which riddled him with balls and lowered his colors. But this stand was momentary: the enemy was not halted, and the Eighty-ninth was obliged to retreat up the lane . . . ."[31]

"We had an open field to cross of about forty rods and it was impossible to keep a retreat in good order as all of the old regiments had left the field before us and was running in all directions. So we did the best we could to get to the first fence where there was a second growth of timber and underbrush," Sinclair wrote. He added that "here a part of us rallied . . . with our colonel . . . ." On reaching cover, Sinclair turned to see the rebels coming on "in a steady column, three brigades deep, their banners a flying." Shouldering his rifle, he told his wife that "here I took a good deliberate aim at the banner carrier. The banner was a triangle supported by a round frame. I believe it is the state seal of Arkansas. But that was the second time that I had covered him with my musket and failed to bring him down and at a good near shot at that, but I am satisfied that I could not shoot in that direction without hurting somebody."[32]

Private Buckley described the regiment's initial flight to his wife. "When our Colonel gave us the order to retreat . . . the bullets were falling very thick among us . . . ." At this juncture his friend, William Litsey, was hit. Buckley wrote that he "was wounded just after we commenced to retreat. I was about a rod away from him when he fell. Several of us stopped to help him, but he told us to

---

[31] *OR*, Vol. 20, Pt. 1, 310; Dodge, *History of the Old Second Division, Army of the Cumberland*, 429-30.

[32] Sinclair, letter, January 6, 1863.

take care of ourselves. Just at that moment, another man fell . . . on the other side of me." He continued: "We were about the last in the Regiment on the field when Will was shot, so we had either got to leave or be taken prisoner, so we left. Bullets were flying thick and fast, and how it was so many escaped without being killed is a mystery . . . ." The Railroaders ran about 400 yards across a cotton field until they came to a lane where Colonel Hotchkiss gave "the order to rally and give them a few of our bullets, we did so," wrote Buckley, "and ours was the only Regiment that made a stand there. We checked them some . . . ." The Knox County farmer, George Berry, also wrote his wife about the opening of the battle: "We had to retreat or be taken all prisoners. The hole brigade run for [their] life. In ower Regiment we lost [a] good many men the first fifty rods that we run. The bulets came past me like hale stone. I saw men shot down on my left and on my right and forward of me. I run aboute seventy rods and came to a fence. I went over pretty quick and then I turn[ed] around [and] rested my gun on a rail and fired at a Rebel that was picking one of our dead men's pockets."[33]

Hotchkiss peered at the advancing Confederates and observed that "but [a] few of our shots were wasted, the colors of the leading column of the enemy again falling under our fire . . . ." But the Eighty-ninth's stand was brief as the men were in danger of being cut off and gobbled up as prisoners. The Railroaders instituted a fighting retreat, moving 500 yards to the left. "We fought from fence to fence and tree to tree. Our men falling all around, some in front now one beside me then one would cry out from behind," wrote Sergeant Sinclair. He continued: "Well so we fought rallying a few men here and there. We waiting until they would come near enough for a good shot and they had to fire at random to clear the thickets ahead so by this means our loss was slight as we got shelter and theirs was heavy [and] at one field in particular, they laid in great number completely covering the ground."[34]

33 Buckley, letter, January 8 and 12, 1863; Berry, letter, January 12, 1863; *OR*, Vol. 20, Pt 1, 310.

34 *OR*, Vol. 20, Pt. 1, 310; Andreas, *History of Chicago*, II-245; Sinclair, letter, January 6, 1863.

"To take advantage of individual firing," Jere Grosh explained, "our boys gradually assumed open order, which neutralized the danger of volley fire from the enemy. The ground fought over was pasture and cotton fields, giving the crack shots of the 89th every chance to pick their victims." Grosh recalled: "At length we reached a corn field, the stocks still standing, and half way across it our boys took shelter in the furrows, facing the enemy, and delivered their fire at will. Here the Confederates received hard punishment, going down by the score . . . ."[35]

At a second rallying point, Colonel Hotchkiss discovered Captains Rowell's and Blake's companies located across a small creek and in a wood near the Wilkinson Turnpike. These companies provided covering fire for the retreating soldiers, who ran through the water and scrambled to find cover from the enemy. The colonel organized the regiment, which now numbered about 320 men, for another stand. The fire of the Railroaders temporarily checked the rebel onslaught. But not before a rebel bullet unhorsed Colonel Hotchkiss, killing his mount. Buckley confided to his wife that his captain, Henry Willett, was killed at this stage of the fight. The thirty-two-year-old, Bristol, Illinois lumber merchant was "shot in the head by a bullet just as he was turning around to face the enemy."[36]

"We fell back," Buckley explained, "until we got up to two more Regiments that did not Rally when we did." Sinclair said this about the Ninety-third Ohio which formed with the Eighty-ninth. "At this wood we made a stand with fifty or sixty of the Thirty-second Indiana with the Ninety-third Ohio to support us, but as the rebs came in sight through the cornfield, these bold Ohioians or Buckeyes run before they fired a shot at us, leaving the railroad boys to stand the charge and we did it, too, driving the rebs in turn across the woods and holding them in check for half an hour, until they got a battery to bear on us. Then as they advanced we were ordered to retreat . . . ." The rebel artillery was not the only problem the Eighty-ninth was

[35] Grosh, *Railway Life: Employees Magazine, Buffalo, Rochester, & Pittsburgh Railway Co.*, 12.

[36] Andreas, *History of Chicago*, II-245; Dodge, *History of the Old Second Division, Army of the Cumberland*, 430; Buckley, letter, January 8, 1863; Muster and Descriptive Roll, Record Group 301, Illinois State Archives.

facing at this juncture. The enemy "sent a large force to out flank us, and cut us off from the balance of our army and take us prisoners," wrote Joe Buckley. As a consequence, he explained: "Our Colonel gave us the order to retreat as we could do nothing with them alone, and at that time, the Rebels had got around us so as to throw a cross fire on us. I tell you the bullets came among us as thick as hail. This is where we had the most wounded."[37]

Having found his position untenable, Colonel Hotchkiss ordered the men to fall back once more. Retiring past the Second Division hospital, the Eighty-ninth came into an open field and there met up with a portion each of the Forty-ninth, and Fifteenth Ohio and Thirty-second Indiana Regiments. However, rebel pressure on the brigade did not let up. Hotchkiss reported his new dilemma: "The enemy's cavalry appearing on our right, and their infantry approaching on our left, threatening to cut us off, I moved by the left flank, the other regiments following . . . to a position in the woods on the south side of Wilikinson pike . . . ." Private Buckley later wrote: "We then got into the timber and all three Regiments formed into a line of Battle. We allowed them to get up pretty close to us when we were ordered to advance to the edge of the timber, and then give it to them which we did with a will and courage that did us credit. The Rebels lost a great many in that part of the fight." Hotchkiss recorded that the Eighty-ninth's "fire, at short range over an open field, thinned the ranks and partially checked the advance of the rebel's closely pressing columns." Stopped, the rebels brought up a battery to drive off the stubborn Yankees. "They threw their shells among us," recounted Buckley, "but we did not mind it much. We should have charged their Battery there, but they had a large force trying to out flank us." The brigade, however, was able to hold this position "for upwards of an hour with great spirit, repressing the rebel tide, while delivering and receiving a most withering fire."[38]

Caught up in the day's disaster, Alexis Cope of the Fifteenth Ohio observed that "there had been no attempt to reform our regiment and so far as one could see, the other regiments of the brigade with

[37] Sinclair, letter, January 6, 1863; Buckley, letter, January 8, 1863.

[38] OR, Vol. 20, Pt. 1, 310; Buckley, letter January 8, 1863; Dodge, History of the Old Second Division, Army of the Cumberland, 432.

one exception were in the same state of disorder. The exception was the Eighty-ninth Illinois. It appeared to be compact and in perfect order." He added: "its Colonel . . . was mounted and was coolly conducting its retreat."[39]

With the supporting regiments on both its right and left collapsing and falling back, the Eighty-ninth and what was left of the brigade retired once more. Jere Grosh remembered that it was about this juncture in the fight that the Eighty-ninth's cartridge boxes were almost empty when a staff officer "dashed up to the line and hurriedly shouted 'Whose command is this?' 'Part of Willich's brigade,' was the answer. 'Who is in command?' 'We're all in command,' was the saucy reply." He then ordered, "'Take direction by the right flank and you will find Gen. Rousseau's Division in the cedars . . . .'"[40]

Since dawn, Sergeant Sinclair noted that the Railroaders had fought and fallen back "in good order." "We retreated in good order through the woods and just as we got through," wrote Joe Buckley, "we got reinforced by General Rousseau's division." We then "made a stand right in front of one of Rousseau's batteries. It must have been pritty near noon by this time. We supported Rousseau's batteries for quite a while and I tell you the shells flew over our heads pretty thick, and some of them burst very near us but none of them did us serious injury." According to youthful Theodore Whitney this was a "scary place." He wrote his parents that the Eighty-ninth was hugging mother earth in support of a battery when "the Rebs got range on it" and "the shells made everything snap." Whitney noted "there was continual roar," and one of the Union guns was dismounted. The older Buckley added that "our batteries played the Rebels with great affect which turned the scale of the fight against them. Rousseau's infantry were fresh in the fight so they were ordered to advance on the enemy, and we were ordered to the rear to make way for them . . . and be in readiness to support them . . . ."[41]

---

[39] Cope, *The 15th Ohio Volunteers*, 237.

[40] Grosh, *Railway Life: Employees Magazine, Buffalo, Rochester, & Pittsburgh Railway Co.*, 12.

[41] Sinclair, letter, January 6, 1863; Buckley, letter, January 8, 1863; T. Whitney, letter, January 8, 1863.

"Receiving the brunt of the enemy's artillery and musketry fire, and my ammunition being exhausted, I retired my regiment by the flank, to the rear, there replenishing my ammunition and resting my men, who had up to this time taken and delivered an unceasing fire for nearly five hours," Lt. Colonel Hotchkiss officially reported. "About two o'clock, we were taken back on the reserve but it was not much [of a] reserve," quipped Sinclair, "for the firing was incessant from all directions, the booming of the cannons was tremendous and the clattering of musketry was awful to listen to, to say nothing about the damage that it must do."[42]

"We were ordered from one position to another wherever we should be most wanted," explained Joe Buckley, "but we were not called into action again that day." George Sinclair recounted one of the calls for help that the Eighty-ninth answered that afternoon. "We soon had enough to do again as the rebel cavalry had got in our rear and attacked our ammunition train, but were soon repulsed. Although they waved a large white flag . . . we paid no attention to that as it was an old story that white flag, for we could see them rush right in and capture the teams and hurry them off. But our cavalry soon overtook them and recaptured everything, punishing Mr. Rebs for their audacity." The day was still not finished for the Railroaders. "There was soon work found again[,] for as we expected an attack in considerable force on our extreme right. But when we got there it was so near night that there was nothing done excepting some pretty hard cavalry fighting out on an open field in our sight," Sinclair added. Late in the day Hotchkiss was informed of the location of the rest of the brigade and moved at once to rejoin them. That night the regiment bivouacked without fires, making back-to-back winter nights the Eighty-ninth spent without the warmth of a campfire. For men lying on their arms, it was another cold and frosty night. Making matters worse, Sergeant Sinclair noted in a letter to his wife was the fact that "our rations ran out the day before so you may imagine that we were rather hungry, fighting and running from here to there all day long."[43]

At the first crash of rebel musketry, Alfred French made a short stand before making a run for it. Finding himself separated from his

---

[42]   OR, Vol. 20, Pt. 1, 311; Sinclair, letter, January 6, 1863.

[43]   Buckley, letter, January 8, 1863; Sinclair, letter, January 6, 1863.

company and the regiment, he recalled that "after a while I saw a regiment that was in good order, and I asked one of their captains, if I might fall in with them, so I kept with them the rest of the day. About 5 o'clock I saw a member of my company, and went with him back to the regiment." French remember that when he rejoined his comrades "there were about 200 of them, out of the 500 of the day before." According to Theodore Whitney, Company G from Knox County "went in to the fight with 54 men & that knight we could muster 23. I tell you," Whitney told his parents, "[that] we was badly cut up." He also pointed out that he had "found out who the brave boys are. Some of them run five miles before they stopped. They throwed everything they had [away.]" He even named names but told his parents that "you musent say any thing . . . ."[44]

Darkness brought rain and gloom to the Eighty-ninth as they hunkered down to await dawn and the resumption of the fight. They were wet, cold, and hungry. Most had nothing but the clothes on their backs, having lost their knapsacks, blankets, and shelter tents when they fled their camp. Adding to the physical discomfort was the mental anxiety many were suffering. They had witnessed the death and maiming of friends, neighbors, and relatives. Now, as the firing died down, it was evident that a large number of men were absent. Throughout the evening a few filtered in, but most remained unaccounted for. Missing and presumed captured were Captain Whiting, Major Hall, and the wounded adjutant, Ed Bishop. Theodore Whitney said this about Thomas Whiting. "The cap was taken prisoner. The last time I saw the cap he and myself was retreating togather & he got behind a tree & told me to go on and I did so. I got out of their way." Aware throughout the day that he had been separated from his brother, Berry now realized that Thomas was not with the regiment. George recorded his thoughts and fears in a note to Harriet on January 4: "I have not seen Thomas. I don't know whether he is killed or taken prisner. We don't hold the ground that the dead is on. I think that he is a prisner." Theodore Whitney's brother also was among the missing. He, however, had an idea what happened to Will and wrote their parents that "poor Will was slightly wounded in the right neck & jaw. He went to the

---

44   French Memoirs; T. Whitney, letter, January 8, 1863.

hospital & had it dressed & by that time the rebels had them & I expect they took Will to Chatanuga."[45]

Sergeant Sinclair continued his description of the Eighty-ninth's predicament: "About midnight the provision train came in with supplies and about three thousand [additional] troops, a part of Thomas' division. I thought the night the longest Old Year out and New Year in that I ever watched for. Although I had not slept a wink in the past three nights, it was so cold and wet I could not sleep." He stated: "We laid in a cedar swamp or glade among big rocks and mud between them. And being allowed no fire, there was not much comfort to be taken in our position. Near morning they issued two crackers and a small piece of meat . . . with quarter rations of coffee and there was no water within a mile of us. But this was better than nothing and it proved lucky for us to get that . . . ."[46]

*   *   *

Hit three times when the Rebel attack swept the Eighty-ninth from their camp, Fred Goddard lay where he fell. On New Years' Day he painfully wrote two short sentences in his pocket diary. "I am still on the field and am suffering much from my wounds. The Lord is with me." Eighteen-year-old Curtis Knox of Company F suffered a similar fate. "Struck in the head, the bullet glancing off from a tree and tearing out a piece of his scalp," unconscious, Knox was abandoned by his fleeing comrades. When he "regained his senses [Knox] found himself in the hands of the enemy." Joseph Goyer, a physician turned soldier from Rock Island, suffered gunshot wounds to his left shoulder and right hip and was captured. Severely wounded, Corporal Emory Watson of Company K escaped death by a miracle. The former clerk for the Chicago and Northwestern Railroad was saved by a small testament he always carried in his vest pocket. The bullet pierced the pages of the little bible, but it was just thick enough to stop the deadly shot. Private John B. Hulich "is badly wounded," wrote Theodore Whitney, "the ball entered [his] mouth coming out breaking the jaw & going into the shoulder."

---

[45] Berry, letter, January 4, 1863; T. Whitney, letter, January 8, 1863.

[46] Sinclair, letter, January 6, 1863.

Private Alexander Patterson of Company H was "struck in the head by a minie-ball which destroyed the sight of his right eye."[47]

On the lighter side, Corporal Nelson Burneson, a brakeman for the Chicago, Burlington, & Quincy Railroad, recalled a humorous anecdote about himself. On one of the days before the fight, Burneson and a few of the Company G boys were looting a store where he pilfered "a white plug hat, which he wore during the battle, ignoring the fact that it made conspicuous mark for the enemy's bullets." The twenty-five-year-old Ostego, New York native survived the day unhurt much to everyone's surprise including Colonel Hotchkiss. The Colonel came over to him the evening after the first day and said: "'Hello! White plug; you here all safe? I never expected to see you get out of there alive.'"[48]

The afternoon of December 31, Curtis Knox was marched along with hundreds of captured Yankees to Murfreesboro and confined in the courthouse square. Knox's mind wandered back to the August day when he stopped shocking wheat and headed for Major Williams' recruiting office in Rock Island. He had naively commented to a fellow worker, "Let's join the boys on the battle field." His comrade had a change of heart about the venture and was now home by a warm fire. For his youthful enthusiasm, Curtis found himself imprisoned inside a stonewalled enclosure, relieved of his overcoat and all valuables, and being soaked by a cold and heavy rain. Piled nearby were "several thousand bushels of unhusked corn, into which the fortunate "boys' buried themselves for shelter against . . . the elements." When the rain subsided, a wet, cold, hungry, and suffering severely from his, still untreated, head wound, Curtis along with his fellow prisoners were each issued a "pint of crude, stale, and musty corn meal."[49]

---

[47]   Goddard, diary, December 31, 1862; *Soldiers' and Patriots' Biographical Album*, 631; *History of Crawford and Richland Counties, Wisconsin* (Springfield, Illinois: Union Publishing Company, 1884), 943; *The Elgin Daily News*, July 12, 1913; *The Elgin Advocate*, October 3, 1908; T. Whitney, letter, January 8, 1863; Newton Bateman and Paul Selby, editors, *Historical Encyclopedia of Illinois and History of Kendall County* 2 vols. (Chicago: Munsell Publishing Company, 1914), II-1031.

[48]   *Soldiers' and Patriots' Biographical Album*, 617.

[49]   *Soldiers' and Patriots' Biographical Album*, 631.

With the sound of musketry on his front, General Willich abandoned his trip to division headquarters and galloped back to join his command. But the rebel attack was so swift that the Prussian General rode head on into charging enemy. His horse was shot, and he was quickly pounced upon and captured. The proud old man ended up in the Murfreesboro courthouse yard with Private Knox and the other Union prisoners. He was seen overwhelmed with emotion, wringing his hand and repeatedly exclaiming: "Oh! My poor boys, my poor boys." The rebels had attempted to interrogate the Old General, but all they got out of him was an angry: "By tam I tell you nottin!"[50]

The Forty-ninth Ohio's colonel and the brigade's second-in-command, William H. Gibson, "was taken prisoner soon after the fight commenced," wrote Joe Buckley. For some reason Colonel Gibson "did not have his shoulder straps on when he was taken." The rebels confronted him about his rank, but all they got from Gibson was that "'he would tell them when he was ready.'" He was then ordered away with some other prisoners. First though, the "secesh" officer" in charge ordered the Yankees to drag their captured cannon to the rear of the Rebel lines. Buckley told his wife that "instead of dragging them to the Rebel line, Colonel Gibson ordered the boys to drag them to our lines. They were successful in getting 4 guns out of the six back again, besides escaping themselves." Gibson managed to escape when a Federal cavalry charge scattered his rebel captors. Once free he made his way back to the brigade where he assumed command.[51]

Throughout the long hours of darkness Sinclair, the former Milwaukee Railroad engineer, listened intently to the distant sounds from Murfreesboro, where he heard trains "running all night, the whistles blowing with as much consequence as if doing a heavy paying business." He thought all the noise could mean that the rebels were leaving the city and retreating. But, the truth was the rebels had not moved. Sinclair wrote that when dawn finally broke on January 1 "the ball opened after daylight, it being delayed a few moments . . .

---

50 Barnett, "August Willich, Soldier Extraordinary," 68; Buckley, letter, January 8, 1863.

51 Buckley, letter January 8, 1863; Cope, The 15th Ohio Volunteers, 238.

gave us the hope that the enemy had evacuated Murfreesboro. But our hopes turned [out] to be false, for in approaching their lines slowly, they opened upon us quite lively for a spell then it slacked up a little while, but was soon opened briskly for all day." Sinclair explained that our generals kept "us running about all day" while "each side tried to out do each other on the flanks, but most of the fighting was done on the front and centre." Around 2:00 P.M. the enemy was observed massing on the Union far right; however, the presence James S. Negley's division along with a portion of Lovell H. Rousseau's, and Gibson's brigade, with a battery, put an end to the rebel demonstration."[52]

Private Alfred French recalled that he was up early on New Year's Day 1863 and noted that "no time was wasted on cooking as we had nothing to cook. I found some nuts under a black walnut tree, which I cracked and ate as I got a chance; also in some way, our commissary got hold of a load of corn and each man was given one ear." After the battle George Sinclair put down on paper what he was thinking that first of January. "Today we have three ears of corn delivered to us as a days rations. Rather hard fare aint it for soldiers fighting to free the niggers, such a good cause . . . But I consider the feed as good as the cause and don't grumble." As the corn was distributed, Sinclair heard the officers tell the men "that was all we was to have until our [supply] trains get here or we whip the rebels out." Regarding whipping the enemy, the unhappy Sinclair expressed what he thought of the situation. "But I am afraid that is a larger job than Father Abraham anticipated and he has . . . gone and done it in issuing his emancipation proclamation, which only exasperates the rebs to fight harder . . . ."[53]

As the last rays of light faded from the first day of 1863, Sinclair reported that "our regiment had not much fighting to do, only one attack of cavalry and the shells to dodge that happened to fall near us." Private French remembered that the "fighting was not heavy . . . but [we] continued skirmishing . . . ." For others in the regiment, the day was a little more harrowing. Buckley wrote of a close call that he

---

[52]   Sinclair, letter, January 6, 1863; Fitch, *Annals of the Army of the Cumberland*, 402-403.

[53]   French Memoirs; Sinclair, letter, January 6, 1863.

and his comrades in Company H experienced. "The Rebels threw a great many shells among us beside some solid shot. One solid shot struck our company's guns as they stood in the stacks and broke six guns and bayonets all to smash, doubled some of them up. It also took the top of our Flagstaff off. We heard the ball coming, and we laid ourselves down just in time as we were standing close to the guns and some of them had their hands on the very guns that were struck." Theodore Whitney saw the same solid shot and the damage it did. Writing his parents of the incident, he said "that is what will try A mans steel." With darkness the shelling ended, and an orderly showed up with instructions for the Eighty-ninth to move "back two miles to stand picket." It was another cold night, and fortunately for the Railroaders, all was quiet.[54]

For those captured on the December 31 and being held in Murfreesboro the situation remained bleak. Rock Island native Private Curtis Knox recalled that "the next morning . . . the brave boys exchanged their 'Happy New Year' greetings amid these desolate and pitiful scenes of a rebel prison . . . ." The captors then ordered the prisoners into a makeshift formation and marched them "to a grist mill, where they each received another pint of musty corn meal." Using anything that they could grab and that was burnable; the hungry captives made fires and "cooked their meager rations." Knox remembered that shortly after their scanty meal the men "were crowded into cattle cars and transported to Huntsville, Ala . . . ." The train chugged away with its load of prisoners, including the wounded that had yet to receive any medical care. Knox could attest to the plight of the injured as he was "suffering severely" himself.[55]

*   *   *

When the fighting died down on New Year's Eve, Rosecrans' army was battered and bent, but not broken. The Union line resembled "a half-closed jackknife, most of it being at right angles to its original position." The Federal right had been dealt a devastating series

---

[54] Sinclair, letter, January 6, 1863; Buckley, letter, January 12, 1863; T. Whitney, letter, January 8, 1863.

[55] *Soldiers and Patriots' Biographical Album*, 631.

of blows, and with the exception of Sheridan's division, McCook's wing had been overrun and driven back three miles. The collapse was so thorough that by mid-morning the rebels had captured twenty-eight guns and close to 3,000 Union soldiers. Bragg's final assaults failed to shatter the Federal defenders, but in his mind Rosecrans was whipped, and facing annihilation, would retreat to Nashville. That night a gloomy set of Union generals gathered at Rosecrans' headquarters to assess the predicament and make recommendations as to what should be done. Most advised retreat, but Thomas would have none of it, and Rosecrans was undecided. When the conference broke up, the commanding general along with McCook rode out to inspect the front. Riding along the Union line, Rosecrans saw torches moving in the dark and concluded the enemy had the army cutoff from Nashville. Retreat appeared no longer to be a choice. In fact, it was only Union cavalry going about lighting fires for warmth, all against orders.

New Year's Day dawned with the Yankee army right where it was when the sun went down on the December 31. Convinced he had won a victory, Bragg wired Richmond the news. But much to Bragg's chagrin, Rosecrans had not cut and run for Nashville. Now neither general seemed to have a plan. While the lull in the fighting gave the Federal soldiers time to recover their resolve, Rosecrans used the opportunity to organize and consolidate the Union line. Part of his plan called for the occupation of a hill across Stones River. This decision marked the turning point of the battle.

After surveying the wreckage of the battlefield, Bragg spent the first day of 1863 waiting for Rosecrans to come to his senses, admit defeat, and retreat. When January 2 dawned with the Union line still in place, Bragg was left with two options, either to resume the offensive or abandon the battlefield. The latter was out of the question. However, before renewing the attack, the recently positioned Federal division, on the rebel side of Stones River, would have to be cleared out. Subordinates pointed out to Bragg that Union artillery had been positioned to enfilade any attacking Confederates. Bragg brushed off the information and assigned Breckinridge's division the task of driving the bluecoated troops back across Stones River. To increase the chance of success and to prevent a counterattack, the assault would not be launched until an hour before dark. Breckinridge again protested the order, emphasizing that the Federal cannons on the Union side of the river would shred his ranks and stop the attack. Bragg would not budge. The assault would take place as ordered.

By Friday, January 2 the Railroaders had a pretty good idea of the toll taken on the first day of the battle. Private Sinclair wrote his wife the following assessment of the casualties. "Our regiment lost on the battle of Wednesday one hundred and ninety killed, wounded and missing. A part of those will probably return; out of our company of forty though, fifteen are gone, one has since returned and we heard from another. But the balance are taken prisoner, wounded or killed." The regiment made adjustments, which Sinclair explained. "Today our captain is acting as lieutenant colonel, our second lieutenant commanding the company and your humble servant a lieutenant or two of them . . . ." Battle fatigue left Lieutenant Colonel Hotchkiss "unable to take active command," and he consequently turned the Eighty-ninth over to the senior captain, William D. Williams of Company F.[56]

Throughout Friday, the rebels continued to probe Union lines. George Sinclair wrote that "the enemy made several spirited attacks at several points today trying to find a weak one and to charge our batteries, but [they] were repulsed every time going off losers." Late in the day the regiment was ordered to the left. Arriving, the Eighty-ninth took up a position supporting Captain Stokes' (Chicago Board of Trade) battery that was helping guard the ford. From here Sergeant Sinclair and his fellow Railroaders watched Bragg's last effort unfold. "Just at sundown was the hardest and hottest charge that they had made during the battle. I have since found out that General Breckinridge led it himself and . . . they fairly acted like devils incarnate. But it was repulsed as spiritedly on our side . . . . We drove them nearly two miles, they fighting in their retreat gallantly, but we gained the day fairly," Sinclair wrote. As for the Eighty-ninth that afternoon, Sinclair explained: "Our brigade was [the] one that made the last charge, we being brought . . . to support the left as they were hard pressed." The plain spoken George Berry put it this way. "We made one Bayonet charge to wardes the rebels. But we did

---

56   Sinclair, letter, January 6, 1863; *OR*, Vol. 20, Pt., 1, 311.

not come in contack with them. They run soe fast that we could not ketch up with them." In a letter to his wife, Sinclair wrote: "I forgot to tell you what General Rosecrans said to us when he wanted us to make a charge on Friday night. He rode up in haste and said he, 'put the cold steel to them, the impudent devils,' but we did not get within pricking distance of them, as the sight of us advancing on a double quick in line yelling like mad men seemed almost enough to scare anyone."[57]

Joe Buckley recorded: "On Friday the 2nd of January, the fight did not commence so brisk as it did the two days before. We were held as reserve in the centre. About 2 o'clock the fighting commenced in real good earnest. The cannonading was terrific. The Musketry was very heavy too." Continuing on, he wrote: "About 4 o'clock, the Rebels tried very hard to force our left wing back, and I felt sure at one time that they would do it, if our men were not reinforced; and just at that critical moment General McCook came and gave us (that is our Brigade) the following orders to advance, and give them cold steel, for says he they cannot stand that." Buckley penned: "We fixed our bayonets on our guns and started off on double quick time, and advanced amidst a shower of balls and shells from the enemy, which, thank the Lord, did not hurt us much. They heard us give a Yell and saw us coming on them with fixed bayonets, and then they began to retreat. We followed them about a mile, and then some of our fresh troops were ordered to pursue them, which they did."[58]

In remembering the final action of the fight, Alfred French wrote "the forenoon was spent in getting the men in the best position for the final struggle. Our brigade was placed in front, and Col. Gibson, in command said to us, 'Boys, I expect we will be called on to make a charge, and if so, I want every man to feel that the result of this battle depends upon himself alone, and fight accordingly.' Scarcely were the words spoken when General McCook, bareheaded and swinging his sword shouted, 'Colonel, take your Brigade and meet them on the charge.'" Years later, French recalled that day. "The Confederates, 10 deep were charging on us. Then there was something doing. I

---

[57] Sinclair, letter, January 6, 1863; *OR*, Vol. 20, Pt., 1, 311; Berry, letters, January 4 and 12, 1863.

[58] Buckley, letter, January 18, 1863.

cannot describe it. But we broke the Confederate ranks, and won the Battle of Stone[s] River."[59]

An excited Joe Buckley told his wife that "our boys took nine guns from them that night, and several flags. When I speak of taking guns, I mean cannons—pieces of artillery." George Sinclair identified the capture artillery as belonging to "the famous Washington Battery of New Orleans" and that "these cannons were much heavier than any that we had on the field . . . . I tell you it was exciting to see the boys bring off the batteries and take in the prisoners, the heavens and earth fairly shaking with the dins."[60]

Initially, the 4,500 charging rebels swept away all that was in their front. But across the river, on the high ground, Rosecrans had positioned fifty-eight guns—lined up hub to hub. And, just as Breckinridge had forecast, the attackers were halted in their tracks by the Federal artillery and driven back by the ensuing counterattack, losing 1,500 men in an hour. Writing his parents, nineteen-year-old Theodore Whitney said that all "was quiet till one hour before sundown. Then they made a break . . . but they run against A Snag. Our Regt Made A Bayonet charge on them. Oh how they run. Our boys took 1500 prisoners & 4 pieces of artilery & By that time it was after dark. Our boys held the ground . . . ." The next day, Saturday, January 3, Bragg was astonished to see that Rosecrans, rather than having retreated, was actually being reinforced. He concluded the safety of his army now depended on withdrawal and gave the order. That night the Confederates slipped away.[61]

Having stopped Bragg, Old Rosey held his ground. "We laid on the battlefield that night, it commencing to rain at eight o'clock. Raining hard all night, nothing occurred of importance during the night until four o'clock in the morn, then we marched back to our position on the right." Saturday at 5:30 P.M. the Eighty-ninth was ordered "out on picket and . . . it was no pleasant duty for it was raining steadily with a cold raw northeast wind blowing." Private Buckley provided the following: "We were on picket that night and

---

[59] French Memoir.

[60] Buckley, letter, January 18, 1863; Sinclair, letter, January 6, 1863.

[61] Theodore Whitney, letter, January 8, 1863; Foote, The Civil War, A Narrative, II: 91-102; McPherson, Battle Cry of Freedom, 580-583

[in] the grand reserve. The Infantry commenced a heavy fire and drove the enemy out of their entrenchments. The firing continued until about twelve o'clock, when we did not hear any more." In actuality the enemy began pulling out at 10:00 P.M., and the last rebel passed out of Murfreesboro at dawn. The "next morning we went back to our old position," Buckley wrote his wife. "This was Sabbath morning, and we heard that the Rebels had left. And in the afternoon we were sure. For Colonel Gibson came and made a speech to us, and gave us the highest praise for our conduct." In a letter to his parents, Private Theodore Whitney said that Saturday and Sunday night the rebels "made tracks from Murfreesboro on A double quick. By the looks of things, they throwed tents, guns, haversacks, [and] blankets, & they did Skeedaddle for good."[62]

*   *   *

It was after dark on New Year's Day when Fred Goddard was taken off the field and carried to an old stable. He recorded in his journal: "I am in the hands of the rebels [and] my wounds have not been dressed." By Saturday he could write: "Had my wounds dressed by a rebel surgeon. It is quite cold and I suffer very much." The next day Goddard "was moved to Murfreesborough in an army wagon . . . ." The rutted roads made for very rough and uncomfortable trip, as the jolting pained his injured leg. In Murfreesboro he was placed in the care of a captured Union surgeon.[63]

Sunday the fourth, George Berry set down his thoughts on the battle and its aftermath. The effort was completed on the seventh, and he found a soldier going to Nashville to post it. In it, he reported that "we left Nashville on the 26 of Dec and arrived on the Battle field Tuesday knight and in the morning we was taken by surprise and was fired on by the Rebels and we had to retreat or be all taken prisoner. I got out safe but I have not seen Thomas." Continuing, he wrote: "We holde Murfreesboro but we hade to fight harde to gane it. I was in the hotes of the fight. Two Dayes after the fight I

---

62   Sinclair, letter, January 6, 1863; Cozzens, *No Better Place to Die*, 201; Buckley, letter, January 18, 1863; T. Whitney, letter, January 8, 1863..

63   Goddard, diary, January 2, 3, and 4, 1863.

was detail[ed] to go and burry the deade that was killed in ower company ware we was taken by surprise. I found three men in ower camp. One was George Murray and [David] Bestor, Dewitt Scudder." Regarding the wounded and captured, he said: "Wilford Whitney is slightly wounded in the neck. Robert Wilson is wounded some. 8 or 10 are missing. They think that John Hulich wont git well. The ball went in his mouth and came out by the side of his jaw bone. Thomas Whiting was taken prisoner. Charles Bainbridge is wounded. Great many is scaterd [and] coming in every day. I am in hopes that Thomas will come in yet. The last I heard from Thomas, he was going towards Nashville. He had no gun with him. I saw a man that knowed him. He might have bin taken prisner and paroled and sent to Nashville. They took [a] good many prisoner[s] from us and we took a goode many from them."[64]

George Berry concluded that "readin about the fight and being in it is quite [a] diferent thing. The wounded and the deade laying all round was awful. We had harde fighting here. 3 days [of] harde fighting. I have had bulets come all around me; one canon ball come within six feet of me and a good many within a roade of me. We haftros be up knight and day. In the two days all I hade was one cracker . . ." He made it clear that he hoped "we shant have another sutch a fight; [and] if we doe, I hope that we will not be taken by surprise. Wen we was in Louisville, we was up at three o'clock in the morning, but when we arrived on the battle ground we sleeped till day light. If they had come half of anougher sooner, they would have taken the hole [of us] prisoners."[65]

In his letter dated the twelfth, Berry told Harriet all he knew about his brother, which was mainly rumor and conjecture. "Thomas was seen Thursday afternoon. He was well and not wounded when one of ower boys saw him. I have not hearde from him sence. Something hiz happen[ed] to him or he would have bin in camp before this time. There was a bige fight that after noon ware he waz. [He] may have bin taken prisner or kille[d] or wounded or he may have bin taken prisner and paroled and sent to Nashville."[66]

---

64   Berry, letter, January 4, 1863.

65   Berry, letter, January 4, 1863.

66   Berry, letter, January 12, 1863.

"In the morning early when we found that the rebs had gone, there was a detail of men from each company of each regiment to go out and look up their dead and wounded, if they could be found." Sergeant Sinclair wrote that he volunteered for the job being "anxious to go over the field of our retreat and see the damage done to us," while checking out what had been inflicted upon the enemy. Since the rebels had had possession of that part of the field for three days, most of their dead had been buried. But looking over the field, he counted "three rebs for every Union soldier on that ground." As the burial party moved about, Sinclair noted they discovered "some awful sights." He added that "every one of our men was stripped of their clothing and shoes . . . ." Retracing the regiment's movement on the thirty-first, the squad came across a place where the Eighty-ninth made one of its rallies and found "the ground was literally covered in rows with dead men." Sinclair pointed out that "we never thought that we did such execution, but the work was inevitably ours as no other part of the army was near that spot, and to make it look far worse, the hogs of which there are a great number running about, had eat some of the bodies half up."[67]

"Our army is quiet to-day," wrote Lieutenant Laertes Dimick of Company F on Sunday, January 4. Unaware yet of the rebels' withdrawal, Dimick gave his assessment of the fight. "We have a great many prisoners. Our dead are all buried, and our wounded all taken good care of. I think this afternoon or to morrow will determine the battle. We will not leave here until we take the place. I will write again as soon as the battle is over."[68]

Monday, January 5, 1863, Fred Goddard pencilled in his diary that "our forces occupied the place at 9 this morning. The rebels skedaddled yesterday." But his ordeal was not close to being over. The following day Goddard entered that he had "lain all day on the floor." On January 8, he wrote: "They have been removing the wounded of other Divisions to more comfortable quarters. But there don't seem to be any provision made for ours and we are still on the hard floor." He could finally write that on Saturday, January 10: "Had my wounds dressed this morning. Slept very well last night.

---

67   Sinclair, letter, January 6, 1863.

68   *Rock Island Argus*, January 16, 1863

Had a good bed of straw to lay on. The Sanitary Commission from Chicago reached here today [and] one of them by the name of Moody visited us this evening."[69]

When Theodore Whitney sat down to write his family about the battle, the first words he penned were: "As my life has been spared . . . ." Acknowledging that the news of the recent fight had already reached her, Joseph Buckley began his letter to Mary dated January 8 by writing: "I am very anxious to let you know that I have, by the mercy of god, come safe through one of the greatest battles that was ever fought without a wound or scratch of any kind." On Sunday, January 4, Lieutenant Laertes Dimick sent word to his parents: "We fought them for five days, and for three days nothing could be heard but the deafening sound of cannon. I do not know how I escaped so well, I am not hurt yet, but the front of my hat was carried away by a musket ball." Writing the same day, George Berry informed Harriet that the regiment "arrived on the Battle field Tuesday knight and in the morning we was taken by surprise and was fired on by the Rebels; and we had to Retreat or be all taken prisoner. I got out safe." "Las Wensday morning we wer surprised by the enemy while eating breakfast. The balls came whisling around like so many bumblebees," Jim Tomlinson wrote his mother. With all the leaden missiles unleashed on the Railroaders, he explained "ther was but few killed, ther was several wounded, and some taken prisoner." And, he had been lucky. "A six-pound ball struck the flagstaff bye me and put a piece of brass through my coat collar . . . and it did not hurt me." Tomlinson, like most of the boys, had wanted to get in a big fight, but afterward he wrote that "I have seen all of it that I want to see." And, George Sinclair spoke for many of his comrades when he wrote that "the more I think of it the more I wonder how I ever got out of that field alive on Wednesday morning."[70]

The prevailing thought of those who survived the battle was that something had gone terribly wrong. In the days that followed the

[69]   Goddard, diary, January 5, 6, 8, and 10, 1863.

[70]   T. Whitney, letter, January 8, 1863; Buckley, letter, January 8, 1863; Berry, letter, January 4, 1863; Tomlinson, Sally Ryan, *In Good Courage: The Civil War Letters of William James Tomlinson*, 5; Sinclair, letter, January 6, 1863; *Rock Island Argus*, January 16, 1863.

battle the men searched for answers. Confiding to his wife, Mary, Joe Buckley wrote: "Most all the soldiers think that we were betrayed by our Division Commander Johnson. And his actions certainly gave it that complexion, for we have been drawn up in a line of battle every morning before and since except that morning that we were surprised." Except for the numbers, Buckley understood what actually happened on the December 31. "They attacked our division with 45 thousand men. They took three or four divisions off their right wing and put them on their left wing so as to surround our right wing and cut us off from the left. The maneuvers of the Rebels and the actions of Johnson correspond so well that I do not doubt that we were betrayed. That is what we don't like."[71]

Writing to his wife, George Sinclair addressed the same subject. "Our loss was severe owing to being the surprised party, for there was three whole brigades served just as we were. Now I blame our General [Richard W. Johnson] for his neglect of caution if not of duty in allowing us to be surprised . . . but before hand, I should say, he had no right to move his division right amongst the enemy without knowing their whereabouts . . . . He was so much more to blame for not cautioning his brigadiers to be on the lookout for a surprise, as we was the attacking party and should have caught them a napping . . . . He is held in very low esteem by . . . the whole army, for from his carelessness is owing our defeat on the right wing." Sinclair pointed out that "some of the men that have [lost] close friends or relatives, threatened him considerable and I don't blame them either." During the action on the December 31, "General Johnson was not seen by us but once," Sinclair noted, "and then he rode slowly by not taking any more notice . . . not even inquiring after the balance of the brigade which was the flower of the whole army, and we the only regiment that had come off in any sort of order. That cut us I can tell you, for when other Generals would ask what regiment it was and praise us for hanging together so well for new troops, and [then] have our own General pass us by and [he] not even recognize a salute from our colonel, it made many more hard feelings toward him."[72]

---

[71] Buckley, letter, January 18, 1863.

[72] Sinclair, letter, January 6, 1863.

In his official report Brigadier Richard W. Johnson stated that he had consulted with Major General McCook late in the afternoon of December 30. During this conversation, McCook informed Johnson that he had reliable information that the center of the rebel line of battle was opposite the Union's extreme right, "and that we would probably be attacked by the entire rebel army early on the following morning." Johnson said that McCook's "prediction proved true." Johnson further wrote that McCook "also informed me that he had communicated this information to the commanding general." He then added: "I expected a change in the programme for the following day, but none was made. My brigade commanders were called together, and the operations of the following day fully explained to them. Every arrangement was made for an attack. Two gallant and experienced officers commanded my two brigades, and every precaution was taken against surprise."

Johnson's report was a precise description of what took place early that day. He wrote: "At 6:22 on the morning of the December 31st the outposts in front of my division were driven in by an overwhelming force of infantry, outnumbering my forces greatly, and known to contain about 35,000 men. At the same time my extreme right was attacked by the enemy's cavalry."[73]

The *History of the Old Second Division* published in 1864 by William Sumner Dodge painted a much different picture then the one described by the men in the ranks, but very similar to Johnson's report. "At five o'clock in the morning," Dodge wrote, "the division was quietly called to arms, and thus awaited daylight. Just as day dawned, there being no indications of the enemy advancing, the order was issued to prepare breakfast. At precisely twenty-two minutes past six in the morning, and not ten minutes after dawn of day, a brisk firing was heard upon the extreme right of General Kirk's line. It was evident the rebels had commenced the movement against our right."[74]

Thirty-six years later Colonel Hotchkiss made a written statement summarizing that eventful day. "With my regiment intact and [with] the aid of disorganized portions of other regiments, we checked the

---

[73]   *OR*, Vol. 20, Pt. 1, 296.

[74]   Dodge, *History of the Old Second Division Army of the Cumberland*, 406.

Confederate advance, thus gaining time for the re-formation of the troops on our left . . . ." For "two hours we fought our way gradually back to the position of Rousseau's Division, which Gen. Rosecrans had placed on the extreme right of the new line." Hotchkiss noted: "Considering that Stone[s] River was the first heavy engagement in which my regiment participated, and that the honor belongs to it of being the rallying nucleus which repaired the disaster to the extreme Right Wing, I am always glad and proud to give deserved praise to the brave officers and men who fought every inch of that ground with gallantry and coolness of veterans."[75]

---

[75]   Farquhar pension file.

CHAPTER 7

"'EVERY MAN THAT DAY DID HIS DUTY.'"

On the night of January 3 and 4, the Army of Tennessee broke-off contact and withdrew through Murfreesboro toward Shelbyville. Rosecrans pursued the retreating rebels as far as Murfreesboro and halted. Bragg continued on for another 22 miles, crossing the Duck River at Shelbyville and stopped. Having suffered staggering losses and with Bragg's withdrawal, Rosecrans was satisfied to end the campaign and declare victory. The correspondents with the Army of the Cumberland eagerly wired news of a Union victory, and the northern press hailed Rosecrans and his soldiers as saviors. Without a doubt they were, for that fall the Lincoln Administration had been dealt a number of serious blows. Politically, November saw Democrats retake control of the state legislatures in Ohio, Indiana, and Illinois. Despite the general discontent over the initial announcement of the Emancipation Proclamation, the Republicans managed to retain a slight majority in Congress over the "Peace Democrats," who were willing to compromise on slavery. Militarily, the news could not have been worse. In the East, Burnside on December 13 attacked Lee's entrenched Army of Northern Virginia at Fredericksburg and was soundly defeated. In the West, Grant's overland campaign to capture Vicksburg collapsed when Confederate raiders destroyed his advance supply depot at Holly Springs, forcing an abrupt retreat. Civil War historian Peter Cozzens expressed the significance of the Battle of Stones River when he wrote: "Although what they had accomplished fell considerably short of a decisive victory, they at least had avoided defeat at a time when the Union could scarcely have borne another setback."

With the northern press treating Stones River as grand triumph of Federal arms, Rosecrans temporarily became a national hero. Tactically, however, Stones River was a victory for the Confederates, as the Union advance was stopped and did not resume until late June 1863. On the other hand, Rosecrans was satisfied for the time being to go into winter quarters and fortify his position. His army was in no shape to continue the offensive. The tenuous supply situation, which rebel cavalry and guerillas continued to attack and temporarily cut, was still a concern.

From individuals to company and regimental commanders, word of the battle and its casualties began appearing in newspapers. The numbers revealed that about one-third of those engaged on both sides were casualties. The Federals lost 12,906, of which 1,677 were killed, 7,543 were wounded, and 3,686 were missing. Confederate losses totaled 11,739, with 1,294 killed, 7,945 wounded, and 2,500 missing.[1]

On January 7, 1863, Lieutenant-Colonel Hotchkiss mailed the *Chicago Tribune* a copy of his after battle report and the Railroad Regiment's role in the "Murfreesboro Fight." With the report Hotchkiss attached a list, naming every man killed, wounded, or missing. Officially, the regiment's casualties numbered 149 of which 10 were killed outright on the field. The wounded totaled 45. Ten of these men would later die from their injuries. Ninety-four men were shown as missing. For families who had yet to hear the fate of

---

[1]   Mark M. Boatner III, *The Civil War Dictionary* (New York: David McKay Company, Inc., 1959), 807-808; Cozzens, *No Better Place to Die: The Battle of Stones River*, 204-207, 216; Doris Kearns Goodwin, *Team of Rivals: The Political Genius of Abraham Lincoln* (New York: Simon & Schuster Paperbacks, 2006), 485; E. B. Long, *The Civil War Day by Day: An Almanac 1861-1865*, (Garden City, New York: Doubleday & Company, Inc., 1971), 307.

a loved one, the Friday, January 16 issue of the *Tribune* bore the bad or good news they had been longing for.[2]

On January 9, Captain Williams wrote a letter to Colonel Danforth, his editor friend at the *Rock Island Argus*, summing up the outcome of the recent fight from his perspective. "I consider this battle a hard one, but the result indecisive. We must fight again to make it tell with effect." He added: "We captured nothing worth mentioning. My opinion is we lost more killed, wounded, and prisoners than the enemy. They captured the most artillery." As for the Rock Island Company, Williams provided a detailed list, which totaled "2 killed, 5 wounded, 13 missing." The captain minced no words regarding the character of one of his wayward soldiers, and Danforth made sure his readers knew Williams' sentiments when he chose to print them in full. "Wm. Golden has been heard from, in Nashville, unhurt,—a cowardly skedaddler." Williams continued: "The balance are undoubtedly prisoners. Our major, D. J. Hall, is a prisoner, and I am acting lieutenant colonel."[3]

Theodore Whitney notified his family that "we are 4 miles South of Murfreesboro [and] now in camp I don't know how long we will stay here." As for how he was holding up after the fight, Theodore told his parents, "I think I am good for them yet," and then changed the subject, writing about some of the men from back home. "George Berry come through all right. They was a round shot struck a stone & a piece of the stone struck Peter Tait in back & lamed him a little; otherwise, the Tait boys are all right, but they can run like Blood hounds."[4]

In his letters home after the battle, Private George Berry described the wounding and eventual death of John Hulick at Murfreesboro on January 16. Like Berry, the thirty-five-year-old Hulick was married and farmed in Copley Township. On January 4, Berry wrote: "They think that John Hulick wont git well. The ball went in his mouth and come out by the side of his jaw bone." Eight days later he updated the folks

2   *Chicago Tribune*, January 16, 1863; William F. Fox, *Regimental Losses in the American Civil War 1861-1865* (Albany, New York: Joseph McDonough, 1898), 373.

3   *Rock Island Argus*, January 17, 1863.

4   T. Whitney, letter, January 8, 1863.

at home on the wounded man's condition. "John Hulick was badley wounded. The ball went in his mouth and came out by the side of his face and went into his shoulder. He may live through it but it is harde telling." By the January 14, things were worse: "They think that he will not git well." But by January 24, "John Hulick he is Deade. He lived about fifteen Days after he was wounded. He was a splendid young man." Berry went on; saying that John "was a good soldier and was on hand to do his parte after he was wounded and bloode runing out of his mouth. He asked wheare the Captain was. He wanted to be with the boys to fight the Rebels. He must have bin firing on them on his retreate [as] the buckshot enterded his mouth."[5]

"Ther is seven of Company A wounded and some missing. Jone Working run to Nashville. Ther was ten of us from Augusta. Now there is three, Martin Booth, Ugene Austin and myself. We have not heard of Tom Sharpe since the battle," Jim Tomlinson informed his cousin, Joel Chambers, back in Hancock County.[6]

Corporal William Litsey, the soldier Joseph Buckley and his comrades had to leave or be captured, died later in a field hospital. The death caught Buckley by surprise as he had "heard a day or two before that he was improving." As for other local men, Buckley informed Mary that William Cooper, a fellow farmer and Lisbon Township resident, "was wounded in the left leg above the knee,' and he had seen "him a day or two after the fight." That afternoon Albert Cooper told Buckley that his brother "was a little feverish yesterday." Buckley gave his wife a more specific accounting of the company's casualties. "We had six or seven severely wounded, three killed as follows—Captain Willet, Willaim Litsey and Henry Huggins. There are about six that we have not heard from yet. There were three out of my mess that went into battle, and I was the only one that came out all right. One was wounded in the leg, and one was taken prisoner and paroled."[7]

Maybe Phebe Youlin refused to believe the *Rock Island Argus'* report of her husband's death as she wrote William Seaman asking

---

[5] Berry, letters, January 4, 12, 14, and 24, 1863; *Adjutant General's Report*, 279.

[6] Tomlinson, Sally R., *In Good Courage: The Civil War Letters of William James Tomlinson*, 5.

[7] Buckley, letter, January 8, 1863.

about Elijah. The twenty-eight-year-old Seaman, like Youlin, was married and hailed from Watertown in Rock Island County, where both men farmed. Seaman replied: "Mrs. Youlin, I received yours of the 17th and in compliance to your request to hear; [I now] answer your letter, but it pains me to have to inform you that Elijah was killed dead by a cannon ball shot in the head on the morning of the 31st of December . . . I know or imagine I know what your feelings are, but you must seek comfort from him that rules all things." William described how he found Elijah on the field after the battle. He consoled Phebe with the knowledge that her husband had not suffered, but died instantly. "With the help of Isaac Williams and others," he "carried him about half mile and buried him with Moses Beaver," another man from the same area. William located a board, carved his friend's name, placed it at the head of the grave, and "silently offered a prayer for him and his family." Seaman concluded by saying, "you may think I am a changed man and I can say thank God I am in many respects."[8]

The newspapers back in Illinois continued to report bits and pieces as information trickled in. Superintendent Williams of the Galena and Chicago Union Railroad provided a casualty list for Company K for publication in the *Chicago Tribune*. With little information the *Tribune* embellished that "at Murfreesboro they [Company K] played a conspicuous part in the long continued carnage. Luckily not one of their number was killed." The readers were further reminded that the company "was filled in an incredibly short space of time . . ." and was "composed entirely of Galena and Chicago Union railroad boys . . . ." Meanwhile the *Chicago Evening Journal* proudly reported that former employee and past President of the National Typographical Union, Sergeant Major John M. Farquhar, was cited by Lieutenant Colonel Hotchkiss in his official report for gallantry.[9]

"By a letter from Serg't James F. Copp," the *Rock Island Argus* reported, "we learn that he was wounded in the right arm, above the elbow, slightly fracturing the bone. He was taken prisoner, and

---

8 William E. Seaman, letter to Phebe Youlin, [January 1863], National Park Service, Stones River National Battlefield.

9 *Chicago Tribune*, January 16, 1863; *Chicago Evening Journal*, January 17, 1863.

paroled, and [is] expect[ed] to start for home as soon as his wound will permit." In the same issue the *Argus* reported that Sergeant Jerry Prescott, one of the organizers of Company F, was on "a list of wounded soldiers . . . in the hospital at Cincinnati." At the time of his enlistment, the twenty-seven-year-old Prescott had been an attorney in Moline, Illinois. On February 11, the *Rock Island Weekly Union* carried a paragraph, which began: "PROBABLE DEATH OF JERRIE S. PRESCOTT." The editor wrote that "the Chicago papers report among the deaths at Cincinnati hospitals, the name of Serg't Jesse L. Prescott, of the 89th Ill." He then added that "there is but little doubt that is intended for Sergeant Jerry S. Prescott, as he belonged to the 89th, and was wounded at the battle of Murfreesboro, after which he was taken to Cincinnati." Officially, the New Hampshire born Sergeant Prescott died January 28, 1863 of wounds received on December 31.[10]

The January 22 issue of the *Chicago Evening Journal* noted that "Adjutant E. F. Bishop, of the 89th Illinois (Railroad) regiment arrived home last night, on leave of absence." Giving more detail regarding his return home, the *Journal* reported: "He was wounded at Murfreesboro, during a severe attack upon the right wing . . . . He was struck by an Enfield rifle ball on the left cheek bone, from which it glanced downward, lodging in his neck, and was from there extracted." The writer added: "The young Adjutant is but 19 years of age, and is a son of Jas. E. Bishop, Esq. of this city, and a nephew of the publisher of THE EVENING JOURNAL. His conduct in the field, whether in action or in the less stirring events of camp life, is spoken highly of, and has been such as to win congratulations from his superior officers."[11]

The *Rock Island Argus* editor, J. B. Danforth, Jr., in the "Local Affairs" column for January 26 summarized a letter from Sergeant James F. Copp of Company F. "We learn that he was wounded in the right arm, above the elbow, slightly fracturing the bone. He was also taken prisoner, and paroled, and expects to start for home as soon as his wound will permit. He is in Murfreesboro,

---

10   *Rock Island Argus*, January 26, 1863; *Rock Island Weekly Union*, February 11, 1863; *Adjutant General's Report*, 277.
11   *Chicago Evening Journal*, January 22, 1863.

and says Dr. Bowman has called several times to see him." Four months later in a letter to Danforth, Captain Williams ironically explained that "Second Lieut. James Copp is still here. Gen. Rosecrans refuses to give him a furlough or leave of absence, and he cannot be mustered in on account of his wounded arm, and he cannot draw pay until mustered in." Williams then commented, "It is a hard case. He is still unable to use his arm. He ought to be at home, under Dr. Farrell's charge, where he would speedily recover."[12]

George Berry continued to make inquires regarding the whereabouts of his missing brother. He confided to his wife that "I have not hearde any thing from Thomas . . . ." However, he spelled out what he knew. "On New Year's Day in the after noon, he was seen on the Nashville Turnpike. He then was all alone. One of ower boys saw him. They did not say much to one [an]other. Thomas tolde him that the regiment [was] pretty well scattered. That was all they said and they left." In frustration George wrote that if "Thomas did not know where ower Regiment was . . . going towards Nashville was a poore place to finde it." With scant information, he considered the possibilities. "He might have bin taken prisoner and paroled and sent to Nashville, but he did not say any thing about it at that time. There was a big fight that after noon on the roade that he was on. He might have bin in the fight. I cant tell. Some thing has happened to him or he would have bin in." In his next letter, ten days later, George again took up the issue of his brother. "I have not hearde any thing from Thomas. If he was taken prisoner, he was taken south. If was killed, we shant know it untill they exchange [prisoners] or the ware is over. I am afraid that he is not living, but I hope fore the best."[13]

"I have not received any money from the government yet. My pocket book was not very good to holde money so I let Thomas have two dollars to keep till I call[ed] for it," George informed his wife. He then wrote optimistically about Thomas. "When he come up from Rebeldom, it [will] come in handy then." But still troubled over his brother's disappearance, George confessed: "I miss him very much. He and I allways sleeped to geather. On our march we had [a] shelby

---

12   *Rock Island Argus*, January 26 and May 15, 1863.
13   Berry, letters, January 14 and 24, 1863.

tent between us. He carried half of the tent and the other side [or] other half so [that] we have half [of] one between us."[14]

Benjamin Holdren and his older brother, William, enlisted in Samuel Comstock's company, known locally as the Amboy Guards. By trade Benjamin was a carpenter and a contractor, while William owned a buggy and wagon shop. At their enlistment the Holdren brothers were respectively age 42 and 39. There were only two men in the company older than the Holdrens. In fact William's twenty-year-old son, Dennis, had joined the Fifty-fifth Illinois in October 1861 and had seen action at Shiloh. Unfortunately, his war ended on December 31, when he was killed in action, joining eleven others from the regiment to die on the field. Unhurt, Benjamin and a burial party from Company I laid his brother to rest in the rocky Tennessee soil.

Sometime late in December 1862, the Railroad Committee's thoughts turned toward the New Year and the men in the field. The Committee thought it appropriate to draft a letter, have it printed, and forward it to all the soldiers of the regiment. Their words were high-minded, and at the time, probably seemed liked the right thing to say. But after what the regiment had seen and gone through at Stones River, the New Year's letter may have fallen a bit flat with the men. And even though the letter was dated Chicago, January 1, 1863, it is hard to imagine that it was received in timely fashion in the field. Furthermore, no existing evidence suggests Lieutenant Colonel Hotchkiss did anything with it. Putting all that aside, the letter from the Committee to the "Soldiers of the Rail Road Regiment" began:

The Railroad Companies with which you were formerly connected, and which you so nobly represent in the 89th, wish to express to you the interest they feel in your reputation, your welfare and your success.

The reports which have come to our ears from your Brigade and Regimental officers, of your large muster roll, of your courage, promptness, good order, harmony and discipline,

---

[14] Berry, letter, January 24, 1863. 15 Richard Duprel's Web Page [Internet website] Descendants of Matthias Holdren. (Accessed August 30, 2001) http://www.duprel/htmlnti000106htm. Hereafter cited as Holdren Family.

make us proud of you. The sacrifices which you have made of home and of home comforts, we thoroughly appreciate.

With a noble patriotism, you have exchanged the privileges of the citizen for the hardships of the soldier, and have rallied around our country's flag in the hour of its peril. You are engaged in a cause the most sacred and glorious—the cause of Freedom, Justice and Humanity. Our enemies are the enemies of the only successful Republic which the world has ever seen. In the eyes of all nations, the cause of Constitutional Liberty is trembling in the balance; and upon the fortunes of our arms is depending its success or failure . . . .

To have been a soldier in the Revolution, was glory. Equal glory is it to be a soldier in the army which fights for the vindication and perpetuity of that liberty, which our fathers sought to establish.

While fighting the battles of your country, you shall not be forgotten. We have already raised a fund of three thousand dollars, in aid for the sick and wounded of your regiment, and have requested your officers to appoint a committee who shall inquire into and minister to your wants.

We wish you to feel that you may look to us as your friends; and that when sick, wounded or otherwise in need, we are ready to help you. If you are in trouble, or if your interests at home are suffering, we wish to know it. Your cause is our cause, your honor our honor, and your interests are our interests.

After four months in the service, the regiment had yet to be paid. In letters from home these same soldiers heard complaints that the railroad companies were slow, bordering on reneging, in their pledge to assist those with families or dependents. And from the comforts of their homes and offices in Chicago, the railroad officials sent a letter to the soldiers in the field that concluded, "Wishing you all a Happy New Year, health, happiness and prosperity, we are Your Sincere Friends." The names and titles of the men making up the Committee for Disbursement of Fund and the Committee on Organization followed. Of the ten names making up the Committees, Amos T. Hall's topped the list. More than any other man involved with the two Committees, Hall had a personal interest and commitment to the Eighty-ninth since both his son and son-in-law were in the regiment. And now his son, Major Duncan Hall, was reported missing and probably a prisoner of war. The battle of Stones River changed things. Words such as "glory" and "sacrifice" held new meaning to the families and loved ones of all the soldiers of the Eighty-ninth and no more grandiose letters were forthcoming from the Railroad Committees.[15]

*   *   *

Sunday, January 18, Joseph Buckley wrote his wife, Mary: "I have just been to [a] meeting and heard one of the best of sermons. I do wish you could have heard it. It seemed like old times although it was in the open air . . . ." He pointed out, however, that Chaplain Dill "went home about two weeks before we left Nashville, on furlough" and that "Captain Spencer of Company B preached to us this afternoon."

Sent to Chicago on regimental business, Chaplain Dill arrived in the city on December 22 where he spoke at the New England Festival that evening. Shortly thereafter, he came down with a severe cold and a high fever. With his leave time nearly up, the ailing chaplain left on the night of December 26 to return to the regiment and his duties. Once in Louisville, and waiting for a boat to go on to Nashville, the fever which had never entirely left with him worsened to the point that a physician advised him to return home. Quite exhausted, he arrived back in Chicago late on December 30. But with the arrival of news of the recent battle and learning that Eighty-ninth had been severely engaged, he felt that it was his duty to be with the wounded and dying. Entirely unfit for travel, he once more set out to return to the Eighty-ninth. Knowing of the tremendous need, he brought supplies furnished by the Sanitary Commission and a generous monetary contribution donated by the Railroad Committee.

---

[15]   Committee for Disbursement of Fund and Committee on Organization to Soldiers of the Rail Road Regiment, letter, January 1, 1863, Charles T. Hotchkiss Collection, Chicago Historical Society.

Exceedingly sensitive to what the men thought that he, "like too many others, was unnecessarily absent." His condition was such that he was hardly able to rise from his bed. His wife endeavored to dissuade him, but he felt that he had to go. Once more arriving in Louisville, he caught the steamer "Lady Franklin" for Nashville rather than continuing by train. On Sunday evening the January 11, he was taken violently sick with high fever and subsequently died January 14 of what was diagnosed as typhoid fever. On notification of Dill's death, the *Tribune* reported that James F. Bishop, father of the wounded regimental adjutant, left the care of his son and was returning to Chicago with the deceased chaplain's remains.

Both Joseph Buckley and George Berry spoke of Chaplain Dill's death in letters to their wives. "Our Chaplain died on the boat as he was returning to the Regiment. He was a good man, and I have no doubt but he has gained a home in Glory," wrote Buckley. Berry matter-of-factly explained to Harriet that "ower Chaplin he is deade. He went on a visit to Chicago and on his return [was] taken sick and dide. We have a Captain that is [a] preacher and he preaches for us now. He is a Methodist. His name is Spencer. He is a smarte and a good man."[16]

In the Railroad Regiment there were a number of soldiers who held deep religious convictions. Berry, Buckley, and Goddard were among them. Their words revealed their faith. Throughout his ordeal Fred Goddard continued to make daily diary entries. After 10 days of lying either on the ground or floor, Goddard recorded that he "slept very well last night had a good bed of straw to lay on." More often than not his few words reflected his faith, as he wrote, "I feel the presence of the Lord constantly with me."[17]

The recent fight, however, demonstrated the hard truth about the odds and reality of surviving the war. In two letters after the battle, Berry broached the subject of his possible death. "I am in hopes that we shall see one [and] other agin," George first wrote Harriet. "I calcolate to look on the bright side of the picture and

---

[16] Buckley, letters, January 18 and February 14, 1863; Berry, letter, January 24, 1863; *Chicago Tribune*, January 24, 1863; Fisk, *The Chaplain's Memorial*, 16-17; *History of Chicago*, II: 245; Eddy, *Patriotism of Illinois*, II: 338.

[17] Goddard, diary, January 10, 1863.

put my trust in the Loarde and all things will worke out right." By the second letter he had adopted a more fatalistic attitude. "I hope that I shall see you and the children once more. Ther has bin a good many that has said so and have bin killed on the battle field. It may be my turn the next time. I hope fore the best and trust in the Lorde [that] all things will work[out] right."[18]

Buckley on the other hand wrote to Mary: "Oh the thought of going home to that Heavenly home where strife and bloodshed and war is no more is encouraging to those that love God, and if it was not for those I love on earth, I would pray to God to take me home to that Glory where trouble and trials are no more. But as it is I hope and pray that God will protect me and let me return home safe to you so that I can be of some use to you while you stay on this earth." Later in the same letter he confided to Mary, "I am still in hope that the war will not last long, but I will still put my trust in God and hope for the best. I have seen hard times and times that have tried men's souls. I have seen men that I thought were stronger in Faith than I am, that have fallen since they came in this war." He confessed: "I have been tried and tempted beyond endurance, but at such times you would come in my mind and thoughts would centre on you and whisper that I had still something to live for."[19]

Sergeant George Sinclair may have been like many men in the regiment. Not one to touch on faith in his letters to Francis, he took a moment after the battle and confided: "I am very thankful to my Maker for His protection toward me, so great a sinner." Unfortunately, Sinclair's cynical side showed itself too in his letters, and he never held back his emotions, especially when it came to abolitionism. Still angry over the Emancipation Proclamation, he told Francis: "I begin to hope that daylight may dawn toward the day of peace, for it is sincerely wished for by everyone except these nigger demons. I suppose . . . that the world should be put to the sword rather than one of their black pits should go without a white shirt or know how to read latin. Oh there's a hot place in <u>Hell</u> for the originators of this inhumane war . . . ."

---

[18]   Berry, letters, January 12 and 24, 1863.
[19]   Buckley, February 14, 1863.

Sergeant Sinclair followed this outburst with another on January 27. Still upset with the Republican Administration, he wrote Francis that he wanted to "find out what we are fighting for[,] whether it is altogether for the nigger or the Union and the Constitution as it was. If the nigger is the object and Abe Lincoln's Proclamation [is] still to be the main feature and guide for the prosecution of this unholy war against our own countrymen, then I am out of it forever and shall act conscientiously in leaving the army." [20]

*   *   *

By December, both the Eighty-ninth's officers and men expressed dissatisfaction with Colonel Christopher for his failure to take active command of the regiment. But the War Department never released Christopher from his duties as the mustering officer in Chicago. Consequently, discontent percolated until December 22 when a letter, calling for Christopher to join the regiment in the field or resign was circulated for the line officers' signatures. It began by stating the problem and concluded with a solution.

> We the undersigned Line Officers of the 89th Regt. desire most respectfully to call your immediate and earnest attention to the following facts and suggestions.
>
> Our regiment (as you are well aware) has been in the service over four months since leaving Chicago and during that time has endured and overcome difficulties such as are seldom presented to any troops (much less new ones) as we have been informed by our Generals, and these difficulties have been greatly enhanced by the fact of our being of necessity Commanded by a junior officer, who was always outranked by officers performing like duties surrounding him. Beside this there appears to be a restive and dissatisfied spirit daily gaining strength among both officers and men, which your long absence from the regiment has mainly and naturally caused.
>
> During these severe trials and disadvantages Lieut. Col. Hotchkiss has so deported himself as an officer as to win the

---

[20]   Sinclair, January 6 and 27, 1863.

love and admiration of our entire regiment and at the same time to win the reluctant tribute of commendation and respect from the experienced troops with whom we are brigaded.

Under these circumstances we feel that it is due to the regiment as an organization, to Col. Hotchkiss as an officer and to ourselves as honorable and responsible men that you immediately take some measures to provide for us a Colonel either by promptly assuming command in person or by taking the necessary steps to place Lieut. Col. Hotchkiss in the position which he has so honorably earned.

Twenty-five officers of the regiment endorsed the communication. Not signing were Lieutenant Colonel Hotchkiss, Major Hall, and Adjutant Bishop, giving the appearance that they were above the fray. These men had to be aware of what was taking place, since they would be the chief beneficiaries of Christopher's resignation. Even though he was still in Chicago, Colonel Christopher was aware of the rumblings against him taking place in Tennessee. Whether it was pure coincidence or via an open threat, the same day the petition was being circulated John Christopher resigned his commission as colonel of the Eighty-ninth.[21]

In his letter to Governor Yates, Colonel Christopher stated that "the best interests of the regiment demand that this resignation be tendered and the best interests of the service demand that it be accepted." Christopher then went to the heart of the matter. "I am confident . . . the squabbles brewing in the Regiment are in consequence of the delay of my joining it and believing it to be the wish of the regiment that I should join it and assume command or resign, it is with feeling therefore of deep regret that I tender herewith my resignation . . . ." He asked the Governor to forward the resignation to the Adjutant General of the Army with Yates' endorsement that it be promptly be accepted. Christopher graciously mentioned to Yates

---

[21] Line Officer 89th Illinois Volunteer Infantry, letter to Colonel John R. Christopher, December 22, 1862, Record Group 301, Illinois State Archives.

that the officers be notified of his resignation "in order that they may be permitted to proceed to the election of another commander."[22]

When Christopher notified him of his resignation, William Manchester, the Secretary of the Railroad Regiment Committee, fired off a letter to Governor Yates. He claimed that "until today I have never heard of any dissatisfaction in the Regt[.] although I have been in constant correspondence with it, and I am of the opinion that if there is any dissatisfaction it is through ignorance of the facts in the case that has caused the retention of Col[.] C for so long a time from his Regt." He ended his note by requesting "for myself & I think I express the desire of the majority of the Railroad Regt[.] Committee that you withhold your acceptance of his resignation until such time as a full explanation can be made to the Regt. Which I am confident will be entirely satisfactory to them." [23]

A month passed before the *Chicago Evening Journal* reported that "Lieutenant Colonel Charles T. Hotchkiss, of the 89th (Railroad) regiment, has been promoted to the Colonelcy." Obviously the *Journal* agreed with the promotion and commented, "It is a well deserved 'reward of merit' to a gallant, brave and true soldier." They further reminded the public that "Colonel Hotchkiss has been in the service from the beginning of the war."[24]

Reading in the *Chicago Journal* that Lieutenant Colonel Charles T. Hotchkiss had been promoted to the Colonelcy of the Railroad Regiment, Amos T. Hall, father of Major Duncan Hall, quickly sent a letter to Adjutant General Fuller. The elder Hall's correspondence was diplomatic but at the same time to the point. With the newspaper reporting only one promotion, Hall wanted to know from Fuller whether his son was also promoted or passed over. If the decision were still pending, he would plead the case. Deftly, Hall set out to ensure his son's imprisonment should not be held against him, by stating that he was captured with General Willich. He next

22 Colonel John R. Christopher, letter to Richard Yates, December 22, 1862, Record Group 301, Illinois State Archives.
23 William D. Manchester, letter to Richard Yates, December 22, 1862, Record Group 301, Illinois State Archives.
24 *Chicago Evening Journal*, January 21, 1863.

informed the Adjutant General that Major Hall had "performed the duties of Lieut. Col. ever since the Regiment took the field." He then requested: "If he has not been promoted[,] will you inform me if any reasons have been furnished why he should not be[?]" And if Fuller was unaware of Duncan's ability, Amos was quick to cite that his son was "reported to be an efficient officer & to have done his duty . . . & receive[d] the highest praise from his Regiment, Brigade, Division & Corps Commanders."[25]

Cognizant of a paperwork problem that could his nullify his effort, Hall addressed the issue in his letter to Adjutant General Fuller. "On the 4th of September, the day the regiment left for the seat of war an election was held at which Capt. Hall was elected Major . . . . Col. Tucker commanding at Camp Douglas presided at the election & is supposed to have reported the facts to your office, but as the commission have not been received by the officers, I have thought it is possible the report was not made out. As Col. Tucker is absent[,] I apply to you for information. If the report was made out[,] the commissions have not been issued. Will you cause them to be issued & sent to me?" The elder Hall went on to point out that when his son was elected the regiment's major, First Lieutenant Edward A. Smith became A Company's captain. William H. Rice jumped from Second Lieutenant to First Lieutenant, and Jacob N. Hopper went from Sergeant to Second Lieutenant. The point being that nullification of the election would result in a chain reaction of problems.

Hall was not just anyone's father. And if the Adjutant General needed reminding, Hall wrote after his signature, "Treas CB&Q RR & Chairman of the RR Committee for [the] 89th Regt Ill. Vol." When the *Chicago Evening Journal* reported Major Hall "among the missing and may possibly be taken prisoner," they made sure to inform the readers that he was the "son of our well-known fellow citizen, A. T. Hall, Esq., Treasurer of the Chicago, Burlington & Quincy railroad."[26]

---

25 Amos T. Hall, letter to Adjutant General Fuller, January 22, 1863, Record Group 301, Illinois State Archives.

26 Amos T. Hall, letter to Adjutant General Fuller, January 22, 1863, Record Group 301, Illinois State Archives; *Chicago Evening Journal*, January 15, 1863.

Aware that Duncan J. Hall's official commission as the regiment's major had never officially come through, Captain Williams made an effort to outflank the imprisoned officer and get the lieutenant colonelcy for himself. Lieutenant E. T. Wells penned a lengthy letter to Republican State Senator Thomas Pickett pleading Williams' case. While Wells, a graduate of Knox College and an attorney by trade, pointed out the flaws in Hall's claim for the lieutenant colonelcy, he was not above drawing on innuendo to sully him either. Regarding the latter, Wells wrote: "Just before leaving Chicago, Capt. D. J. Hall was with solicitation of influential friends and his father (who is Treas. Of the Quincy Road) (all under a misapprehension, as I am informed, on the part of the line officers) selected as Major." Lieutenant Wells continued: "By seniority Major Hall, ought perhaps be promoted to this vacancy. But he is now a prisoner in the hands of the enemy & may remain so for the Lord knows how long:—moreover candor compels me to say (in confidence of course) that he has not the confidence of either the officers or men of the command." Wells concluded by stating that "unless I am greatly mistaken Major H. never was commissioned; and I know that nearly all the line officers signed a paper requesting him to resign."

Wells wrote of his friend Williams to Senator Pickett: "Capt. W. behaved with great coolness & judgement, & with remarkable bravery in our late severe battle here; and not only in this, but in his connection with this company, and in the discharge of all his duties both as Capt. & Commander of the Regt., a duty which has fallen upon him on several occasions. I do not think a more competent man for either the Lt. Colonelcy or Majority, or one who would be more acceptable to the command, could be selected . . . ."[27]

The following day, February 1, Captain William D. Williams composed a lengthy letter to Pickett. "Friend Pickett[,] Having befriended me once. I naturally turned to you again when desirous of help." He got to the heart of the matter. "I am the senior Captain in this Regiment. The Lieut. Col. C. T. Hotchkiss will very likely be promoted to Colonel. This leaves the Lieut. Col. vacant. [O]ur Major D. J. Hall is now a prisoner in the hands of the enemy. He never

---

27   E. T. Wells, letter to Thomas Pickett, January 31, 1863, Record Group 301, Illinois State Archives.

received a commission for Major. My Commission as Captain seniors his by two days. (His only commission is that of Captain.)"

Captain Williams went on: "Now to be plain. I want promotion. I would like to be Lieut. Col. but would be thankful for Major. I want it on the ground of good conduct in the face of the enemy at Murfreesboro or Stones River." As a point of emphasis, Williams told Pickett that in both Hotchkiss' and Colonel Gibson's official reports he was "commended for good conduct." Williams requested: "I wish you would do me the favor to see the Gov. and Adjt. Gen. Fuller on this subject. I really think I ought to be Lieut. Col. of this Regt. And not unlikely, if the facts are brought home to the Gov. & Adjt. Gen. [T]hey will recognize the force of this claim."

Captain Williams turned to the real problem in the way of a promotion. "There is a sort of Committee of Rail Road men in Chicago that claim to run this Regt. [N]ow you know, they never by word or deed, done any thing to get up my company, but they are very anxious to put their friends in all the desirable positions. Never [will] I appeal to you to protect me from their intrigues." But Williams thought it necessary to remind Pickett: "You are my representative and the representative of my Company at Springfield. Again, Lieut. Wells and Dimick and Orderly Sergeant Copp behaved with great gallantry—judgement and coolness in the face of the enemy—they deserve promotion if any one does in this Regt. [T]hey are recognized as 3 of the very best officers in the Regt. Col. Hotchkiss . . . will bear willing testimony to this fact, but they cannot rise unless I am out of their way."

To ensure Pickett had as much leverage as he needed when making the rounds at the State Capitol, Williams noted that "Col. Hotchkiss will be at Springfield. I wish you would try and see him, and learn from him whether we deserve promotion or not. We are willing to abide by his judgement[,] believing him to be a straight forward—candid and honorable officer." And if somehow, he had failed to make himself clear, Williams concluded: "Now do us the personal favor [and] give your attention to this matter. You are 'inside the ring' and at 'court' and can see [to] fair play at least."[28]

---

[28] William D. Williams, letter to Thomas Pickett, February 1, 1863, Record Group 301 Illinois State Archives.

Wells and Williams had a powerful friend in Thomas J. Pickett, who was serving his second term as a State Senator from the Rock Island district. Within the Republican circle, the forty-two-year old Pickett was a man of some importance. He had owned newspapers in Peoria, Pekin, and Rock Island, dating back to 1840. However, in June 1862, he left the newspaper business to enter the army and was commissioned Lieutenant Colonel in the Sixty-ninth Illinois Infantry, a three-month regiment, which performed guard duty at Camp Douglas. Pickett had also served as the Illinois grandmaster of the Grand Lodge of Masons, as a regent of the Illinois State Normal University, and as president of the Illinois Editorial Association.

When the Illinois Republican Party formed in 1856, Pickett was a member of the State Central Committee. At the first Republican State Convention, he was selected as a delegate to the National Convention in Philadelphia, which nominated John C. Fremont for President. Two years later, in the 1858 election, Pickett campaigned in Tazewell County for Lincoln. Writing the candidate, Pickett asked Lincoln to provide "our friend Herndon" to speak locally and he would get out handbills. In closing his letter, he wrote: "Let me say that anything that I can do to 'vote you up' and Douglas 'down' will be done free, for in so doing I know I am serving the best interest of the country."

By March 1859, Pickett was behind an effort to promote Lincoln for President. In a letter to Lincoln dated April 13, Pickett wrote: "I would like to have a talk with you on political matters as to the policy of announcing your name for the Presidency . . . . My partner (C. W. Waite) and myself are about addressing the Republican editors of the State on the subject of a simultaneous announcement of your name for the Presidency." Lincoln quickly responded in a note dated April 16. "As to the other matter you kindly mention, I must, in candor say, I do not think myself fit for the Presidency. I certainly am flattered, and gratified, that some partial friends think of men in that connection; but I really think it best for our cause that no concerted effort, such as you suggest, should be made—Let this be considered confidential—"

Twenty months later Lincoln was elected President. Rewarded for both his loyalty and long-time support, Lincoln appointed Pickett Government Agent for the island of Rock Island, a military reservation. Williams turned to Pickett, a man he felt was connected to the Republican elite, to ensure he was dealt with fairly. But, it was all for naught.[29]

The *Journal's* report of January 21 was correct. Hotchkiss was promoted to colonel of the Eighty-ninth. The imprisoned Major Hall became the lieutenant colonel, while Williams took over as the regiment's major. The official promotion date was January 7, with muster being February 24. The *Journal* had only reported Hotchkiss' promotion, not the other two. Did letter writing campaign have an effect on the decision for lieutenant colonel? Were these promotions backdated? Or was this simply a case of seniority prevailing.[30]

Once the field officers were settled, other promotions followed. Now that Captain Williams was no longer the regiment's acting major, First Lieutenant Ebenezer T. Wells, the great-grandson of Revolutionary War General Artemus Ward, took command of Company F. Captain Travis O. Spencer, the sharpshooting Methodist parson, assumed the duties of chaplain, with Sergeant Major Farquhar taking Spencer's position as captain of Company B. Promoted for bravery, along with Farquhar, was Sergeant Erastus O. Young. He became a second lieutenant in Company

---

[29] Newton Bateman, David McCulloch, and Paul Selby, editors, *Historical Encyclopedia of Illinois and History of Peoria County*, 2 vols. (Chicago and Peoria: Munsell Publishing Company, 1901), I: 424-425; Charles A. Church, *History of the Republican Party in Illinois, 1854-1912*, (Rockford, Illinois: Press of Wilson Brothers Company Printers and Binders, 1912), 30-31; Robert S. Harper, *Lincoln and the Press*, (New York: McGraw-Hill Book Company, Inc., 1951), 28-29; *The Past and Present of Rock Island County, Illinois*, (Chicago: H. F. Kett and Company, 1877), 119; Ernest E. East and Thomas J. Pickett, "Reminiscences of Abraham Lincoln," *Lincoln Herald* XLV (December 1943), 3-4; T. J. Pickett, letter to Abraham Lincoln, August 3, 1858, R. T. Lincoln Collection, A. Lincoln, (microfilm), The Library of Congress; T. J. Pickett, letter to Abraham Lincoln, April 13, 1859, R. T. Lincoln Collection, A. Lincoln, (microfilm), The Library of Congress; Abraham Lincoln, letter to T. J. Pickett, April 16, 1859, R. T. Lincoln Collection, A. Lincoln, (microfilm), The Library of Congress.

[30] *Report of the Adjutant General of the State of Illinois, 1861-1865*, 9 vols. (Springfield, Illinois: Phillips Brothers, 1901), V: 261.

A. Former Galena and Chicago Union brakeman and Company K musician, Edwin J. Stivers, was appointed Sergeant Major. With Henry Willet's battlefield death, Company H saw First Lieutenant Franklin M. Hobbs elevated to captain and First Sergeant John A. Beeman commissioned first lieutenant. In a letter home Private Buckley wrote that Hobbs and Beeman "treated us to ten cans of oysters . . . on account of their promotion. The oysters were first rate."[31]

* * *

If the officer controversy was not enough, a long simmering dispute of a different sort surfaced in the "Local Correspondence" section of the *Chicago Evening Journal*. Two women, Helen W. H. LeBlanc and Farilla C. Hutchings, responded to a prior letter to the newspaper, while calling on the Railroad Committee to account for the funds raised. They began: "A call was made by 'A Friend of the Regiment,' last week, for a statement of the proceeds from the Fair held September 1st for the benefit of the regiment. As the parties who assumed the management of it have not done so, we (the originators of it) feel it incumbent on us to speak of it."

The ladies then explained: "The affair was first started for the purpose of raising a company flag for the 'Scripps Guard,' and for no other purpose. We subsequently decided to extend the enterprise, and also try to raise a full set of colors for the Railroad regiment, in addition to the 'Scripps Guard' flag." The "Scripps Guards," who were named in honor of John Scripps, a former *Chicago Tribune* employee, were composed of clerks and other workers at the post office. They became Company C of the Seventy-second Illinois Infantry, better known as the First Chicago Board of Trade Regiment. The pair continued by stating that "we consulted with the committee of gentleman who had

31 *Adjutant General's Report*, V: 263, 264, 275, 280, and 285; *Galesburg Republican-Register*, October 3, 1891; Heitman, *Historical Register and Dictionary of the United States Army*, I:927; Eddy, *The Patriotism of Illinois*, II: 337; Buckley, letter, March 7, 1863.

control of the regiment, and they promised to co-operate with us, which they did, most fully. It was understood by those gentlemen that we were to have the money for the "Scripps Guard," and we calculated on it. Had we been aware of the treatment we were destined to receive, we would have kept sufficient money, which was in our hands, to pay for it, but we paid *all* over to the Treasurer, who was appointed at our request." The women pointed out: "We discharged every liability that *we* incurred, viz., $230 for the colors, $40 for the hall, and $25 for music. Any further disbursements *we* know nothing of, all other bills being referred to Mr. W. G. Swan, the Treasurer." They let the initial complainant know of their frustrations with the Railroad Committee. "In answer to the request, we say, we do not know how much money was received. We requested Mr. Swan to publish a report some time after the Fair, but he thought it was '*premature*' to do so; if not considered too '*premature*' (by the public,) at this late day (nearly *five months* afterwards) we would call him, and the committee of ladies who assumed the arrangement of the whole thing, to make a statement in *full*."

LeBlanc and Hutchings felt the failure of the Railroad Committee to release a financial statement had damaged their reputations and said so. "We are interested in this, as it has been hinted more than once that we were benefited by the affair. These ladies decided that we should not have money to pay for the 'Scripps Guard flag' (when it rightfully belonged to us), saying that we had done nothing for the Fair any way, and that only railroad men patronized it. We most respectfully insist that these self-same ladies inform us and the public what disposition has been made of the balance of moneys paid to them. We understand that the receipts total were $810; of this amount we paid out, as before stated, $295." Returning to the issue of an accounting, they wrote that "if the Railroad regiment have been benefited by this money, it is right that the public should know it, as the funds were give by the public, and also what has been sent to the regiment for their comfort and convenience." Not finished, the two women again hammered home their point. "If our information was correct, there is $515 to be accounted for, which we know nothing of; and as we paid in considerably more than any one else toward this amount, we claim a right to demand a full report of the disbursement of the money so collected."[32]

Two days later William G. Swan, Treasurer for the Committee, gave an extremely formal and a very legally worded reply, and no accounting was forthcoming. His statement: "In reply, to the communication in your issue of Wednesday, under the head of 'Railroad Regiment Festival,' I will say that all disbursements of the fund have been made in conformity to the wishes of the Ladies' Committee having charge of the same, and the immediate authority of the President of that Committee, Mrs. Franklin, to whom I may refer the young writers and any others desiring information as to the disposition which has been made of their contributions." For daring to question him, Swan concluded his response to the young women with a statement full of condescension and smugness when he wrote: "To those acquainted with the names of the ladies composing the Committee or those immediately interested in the Railroad Regiment, this reference will be quite unnecessary." With that, the impudent girls were properly scolded and put in their place.[33]

* * *

While the officers politicked and maneuvered for promotion and the committees back in Chicago squabbled, the rank and file Railroaders at Murfreesboro soldiered on. In a letter to his mother dated January 31, Company A Private William J. Tomlinson of Augusta, Hancock County wrote, "we are fortifying the town, bin [to] worke there yesterday. We see nuthing but soldiers and negroes. Wher the people are I don't know . . . ." Tomlinson took the pick and shovel duty in stride, for the twenty-six-year-old was no stranger to manual labor and hard work. At his enlistment Tomlinson listed his occupation as a laborer. On the other hand Sergeant Sinclair complained to Francis: "I went on duty just after my last letter to you [January 27] and ever since it is picket one day and night and shoveling in the trenches the next . . . for our folks are building forts

---

[32] *Chicago Evening Journal,* January 28, 1863.
[33] *Chicago Evening Journal,* January 30, 1863.

at this place." Whether the common soldier men in blue recognized it or not, General Rosecrans viewed Murfreesboro as the military key to Middle Tennessee. It was here that the important turnpikes and roads of the area converged, and Rosecrans was determined to develop a strong defensive position. Consequently, each day part of the army worked on the project, and every hill was fortified. "North, south east and west these works present their fronts, some twenty in number, and from their strength and extent they seem to scorn the idea that they can ever be stormed or reduced," wrote William S. Dodge of the finished works.[34]

By January 24, George Berry had already written three letters home, but he had not heard from Harriet in almost a month. He attributed the lack of mail to the fact that "the Nashville and Louisville Railroad has bin stoped by Morgan and letters go slow." Berry was not only despondent over his missing brother and the lack word from home, but he was also ill. "I have bin sick with the Diarhea three days. It is the first harde sickness I have hade since I have bin in the Army. I reported to the Doctor and had it checked but I am week [sic] yet." He felt his illness came from "the hardship on the battle fielde and going out of my ration[s] helped it on." On February 5, he wrote in another letter to his wife. "I am giting some lonesome down hear. I have not received any letter frome you sence the twenty eight of December, but I am looking fore one everyday. We have a mail come in once a day."[35]

The northern army needed local subsistence to survive, and as a consequence the country for miles around was foraged. George felt well enough to go along with the regiment on one such an expedition outside the Union lines. He wrote Harriet that "I went out a fouraging yesterday [February 4]. The first time that I have bin on duty fore some time. We hade a lively time of it." He explained: "We had to shell the woods along time before we could loude ower

---

[34]   Judith L. Kammerer, "'Reflections' Hancock County, Illinois in the Civil War; includes accounts of Keokuk, Iowa, Adams Co., Ill. Northeast, Mo. Overview of war (Carthage, Illinois: Journal Printing Company, 1988), 77; Sinclair, letter, February 11, 1863; Dodge, History of the Old Second Division, Army of the Cumberland, 451.

[35]   Berry, letters, January 24 and February 5, 1863.

corn in the wagon. The rebels through [sic] shell right in the wagon traine. Fore a short time it made a regulare stampeade. One shell past within ten feet of me and [exploded] about fifteen rods off. They make awful noise. I don't like them first rate."[36]

"We have foraging to do about once a week," wrote Sergeant George Sinclair to his wife. "We went out [the] week before last and was attacked by Wheeler's Rebel Cavalry, and lost quite a number of men. Not any out of our regiment, but all out of our brigade. The rebs had what we call jackass artillery." "Jackass artillery," he explained was "a small cannon hauled by one mule and could be taken almost anywhere. While our artillery is confined to the pikes on account of the mud and soft ground." He continued: "Well, our men were standing around the fires that they had built for comfort as the enemy had stopped the train in front, when this jackass artillery let fly a solid shot right into a crowd and took the leg off one man and [the] foot of another. This was done within twenty rods of where our men were . . . ." The brigade "skirmished with them all day." Sinclair concluded: "I saw but one man that was hurt and his hand was shot away, and I heard of several that were killed."[37]

"The tennesson[s] are coming in to ower lines and giving them selves up most every day," remarked George Berry in a letter home. But, it was obvious to all, even the lowest private like George Berry, that a surrendering Rebel here and there was not enough to end the war. From observation and campfire discussion, Private Berry concluded, "If fighting has to settle this dispute, it will take a long time. As the army advance[s], we hafture leave a large army behind to guard places that we have taken. The rebels they have no guarding to do. They can concentrate all their forces at one place."[38]

Returning to a letter that he had begun on February 5, George Berry explained he had "bin sick about six days with a seaveare colde" and had "had [a] pretty harde time of it." He told Harriet that "if I had not went out a foragin I should not of had this sickeness." While confined to his tent, a neighbor from home and a fellow

---

36   Dodge, *History of the Old Second Division, Army of the Cumberland*, 451; Berry, letter, February 5, 1863.

37   Sinclair, letter, February 11, 1863.

38   Berry, letter, February 5, 1863.

member of Company G, Andrew Reynolds, checked on him. George wrote: "He hearde that I was sick and came to ower tent to give me three loaves of soft bread and it came in good time. I could not eat any things else. It revived me right up when I saw the breade." Berry tried to reimburse Reynolds for the bread, but "he would not take nothing." George instructed Harriet "the three loaves was worth sixty cents" and that "you may pay that amount to his wife." By the morning of February18, George was able to write that he was feeling better but still weak. On three different occasions he had attempted to finish the letter. He noted that he had "not written . . . since the last of January. I comenced this letter [a] long time ago. I think if nothing happens [that] I shall be stout in a few days. I keep up good courage. I think [that] I shall see home yet. I cant write very well [since] I am quite nervous." He managed to tell Harriet that he had "received a letter from Thomas Berry yesterday [February 17]." Too ill to write more, he reiterated nothing from the letter, saying only "he came around all right."[39]

"I wrote a letter to you only yesterday but I received yours of 21st January last eve and now hasten to answer it for in it I complained of not hearing from home thinking it high time for an answer and my letter might have not reached it's destination," explained an elated Sergeant Sinclair. "I was very impatient and glad to hear from you when it did come for I had almost given up of ever again getting a letter from the north district as Morgan's gang were continually pitching on the Louisville and Nashville Road making it unsafe to send mail by that route. And being then dependent on the height of the river for a chance of sending our mail that way." Sinclair as well as many others in the regiment had "come to the conclusion that a regular correspondence with our families and friends had about given out and that we would be lucky to get any word to and from out friends at all." After more than a month with no word from Harriet, George Berry could finally respond: "I received your letter dated Feb. 1 and one January the 11 letter was received Feb. 14."[40]

Many a letter from the army contained a line like the one penned by Private George Berry. "I have not rec[eived] any money

---

39   *Ibid.*

40   Sinclair, letter, January 28, 1863; Berry, letter, February 5, 1863.

from the government." Other than their enlistment bonuses, the Eighty-ninth had not received a cent in pay since their service began in September. They were not alone, as back payment was due all the Union forces. By mid-January the *Chicago Evening Journal* took up the soldier's cause with an editorial entitled, **"PAY THE SOLDIERS."** The writer spelled out "that measures are being taken by Congress to insure early payment of the soldiers, to whom several months of pay are now due, and which should never have been and never again so long delayed." The paper urged the "Representatives and Senators in Congress to push this matter forward with the utmost possible dispatch; even to the exclusion of other business." He also noted: "The complaints from the army are assuming a most serious character. We hear of them every day." More important, "the Government should be especially careful . . . to demonstrate to the soldiers its lively interest in their welfare and its appreciation of their self-sacrificing devotion to the cause of the country. Let them be paid without a day's delay." Two days later the *Evening Journal* could report that the soldiers were to be paid. It noted that a bill "introduced in Congress for the issue of sufficient legal tender Treasury notes to pay the soldiers and sailors . . . all that is due them, has become law, and that the payments will now be made as soon as possible." The *Journal* writer summarized: "Congress has very wisely declared that the officers and soldiers who are in the field, fighting the rebels, are the worthiest creditors of the Government, and must be paid in preference to all others."[41]

With Congressional legislation in place, the army paymasters were soon making rounds to the regiments. "They have bin paying them off all around us. The boys [are] saying that we was going to git ower pay to day but they have not come a round yet," George Berry wrote on February 20. The thought of actually being paid made Berry contemplate how best to send the money home to his family. "I was thinking of sending it in a letter ten dollars at a time. Five dollars at a time takes along time." George need not have given

---

[41] Berry, letter, January 24, 1863; *Chicago Evening Journal*, January 15 and 17, 1863.

any thought to sending the money home that day, as the paymaster failed to stop at the Railroaders' camp.[42]

On March 7, about every man in the Eighty-ninth put pen or pencil to paper and prepared a letter home. This is how Private Joseph Buckley expressed what had finally occurred. "And now I will tell you some good news. Yesterday forenoon we received our pay from Uncle Sam, at least all that was coming to us up to the first of January. They allowed us 13 dollars per month from the day we enlisted which amounted to 60 dollars and 66 cents. So you will see that Uncle Sam owes us a little over two month's pay yet." He pointed out that the pay "was all in greenbacks." Buckley informed his wife: "If I can keep this money with me safe, I should like to do so, but if you are wanting money, I shall send some home if you say so." Two days passed and Buckley changed his mind about keeping all his pay with him. "I have concluded to send thirty Dollars 30$ home to you as the Railroad Regiment has the privilege of sending it by Express free of all charges[;] and, I think it risky business keeping so much money by me as the Rebels would take it from me if they should happen to take me prisoner. So, upon the whole I thought [that] I would send some of it home for the present at least. I have just paid the money over so when you get this letter, you will have to go to Morris to the Express Office and get it."[43]

Private George Berry composed a quick note to his wife. He first apprised her that he was still under the weather but that his health was improving. He then wrote: "I Rec[eived] my money yesterday sixty one Dollars and half ($61.50). I want to send you forty Dollars. There is some talke that the soldiers can have a furlow in the coarse of the yeare. If that is so, I thought I would keep enough to go home on if it hapen to be my good luck to go." Before posting, George too had a change of heart and wrote an additional page to his correspondence. "I took this money out of this letter and sent forty Dollars by Express. I thought I would send it all together." As for the rest of his pay, George explained: "If I have any more than I want, I can send [it] home a Dollar at a time. I may have to buy a paire of boots. If I do, it will cost from five to eight Dollars." And

---

[42]   Berry, letter, February 20, 1863.
[43]   Buckley, letters, March 6 and 8, 1863.

finally, he added, "the money will be sent to Walnut Grove. I sent it in your name. It is a good deale of risk to send it by letter and it takes a long time. I hafture run the risk to send it by Express. The whole Company has sent [it that way]. Lieutenant Howell will send 3 hundred Dollars. If we lose, we lose alltogether."[44]

The unmarried Private William Tomlinson sent a short note to his mother back in Augusta, Illinois. "We got our pay last week. I got $60.25. The railroad committee sent Captain Smith here to take the money home for the regiment. It was sent to Amus Hall, Chicago, and he will send it to you. I sent you $50 . . . . You can use the money I sent you as you please."[45]

For all his past concern for his wife and child's welfare, Sergeant George Sinclair took a ho-hum attitude and penned most of his letter to Frances before he off-handedly mentioned that "the Boys got paid yesterday afternoon. By the way I was paid four months . . . and I will send you $50.00 by the first opportunity." He followed with an itemization of his expenditures. "I have paid debts for boots and sutler's stores to the amount of $14.00. The balance I shall keep by me for anything that I may need and [if I] get a chance to come home on a visit so I shall need a small amount." Sinclair's comment about a possible furlough was the result of a rumor circulating through the ranks. The word being passed about was that Congress had recently passed a measure allowing each company in the army to let a few men at a time go home. Keeping this in mind, many Railroaders kept back a few dollars travel money just in case the camp scuttlebutt proved to be true.[46]

*   *   *

To give credit to those men who had distinguished themselves in the recent battle, General Rosecrans issued General Order No. 19 on February 14. The Order called for a regimental Roll of Honor to be made up "of five privates from each company, and ten corporals and ten sergeants from the regiment." A brigade Roll of Honor

---

44   Berry, letter, March 7, 1863.
45   Kammerer, *"Reflections" Hancock County, Illinois in the Civil War*, 77.
46   Sinclair, letter, March 7, 1863.

would consist of "four lieutenants, four captains, and two field officers below the rank of colonel, most distinguished for gallantry in action, professional knowledge, skill, and zeal in the performance of duty." The Order officially proclaimed the Honor Roll would point out "to this army and the nation those officers and soldiers of this command who . . . distinguish themselves by bravery in battle, by courage, enterprise and soldierly conduct . . . ."

"I write this to request you to make known to their friends, through the columns of your widely circulated paper, the distinction which by the voice of their comrades, has been awarded to these brave men and most worthy soldiers," wrote Lieutenant E. T. Wells. He had forwarded a letter to the editor of the *Rock Island Argus* explaining the Roll of Honor and naming the selected men from Company F. Placed on the Regimental Roll of Honor were: Sergeant William McDaniels of Hampton; Corporal Isaac Meanor of Deanington; Henry Dreyer of Hampton; Michael O'Mara of Edgington; William E. Seaman of Watertown; George Smith of Hampton; and Isaac Williams of Pleasant Valley.

To form an elite arm of highly motivated, brave men, Rosecrans' Order further stipulated the organization of a Light Battalion, consisting of "three privates out of each company, and one commissioned officer, three sergeants and two corporals out of each regiment." Lieutenant Wells explained: "The Light Battalion are to be mounted, to carry the revolving rifle, to be relieved of picket and other guard duty, and, in the language of the order, 'will be looked upon as the *elite* of the army, and models for their profession.'"

In his letter to the *Argus* editor, Lieutenant Wells omitted the fact that Captain William D. Williams and he had been named to the Brigade Roll of Honor for their respective "gallant conduct at the battle of Stone[s] River . . . ." Once aware, J. B. Danforth wrote a stirring column acknowledging both men. He quickly pointed out that Williams and Wells *"were the only two officers selected from the 89th."* The editor then noted: "It was a splendid compliment, delicately conveyed, and from strangers, or at least those with whom they were little acquainted, and therefore could not be attributed to favoritism or regimental influence. Let our people remember that in the famous railroad regiment (the 89th) two of our citizens were the only persons in the whole regiment deemed worthy of going on the brigade roll of honor! They have a right to feel proud of it,—and we know our people will glory in their well-earned laurels, won on the field of battle, and awarded to them by strangers."[47]

"There were 5 men elected out of our company to go into the light infantry Battalion. I was away that day, so I did not get a chance," Joseph Buckley wrote in a letter to Mary. "Since then there was an order for five of the bravest men in the company and most faithful to obey orders, to be elected by the company to go into the Light Battalion of Infantry. John Buffham was elected by a clear vote. I was elected by a clear vote. The other three Tom Britton, Josiah Coleman and Alphonso Covell had [a] pretty tight running to get in, and then half the company were not satisfied with those three being elected as they said the three had been regular 'shirks' which was a fact as far as Covell and Coleman were concerned. Britton, I will not say anything about."

"Three out of the five were to go right off. They will have a horse each to ride, but I think they have not got their horses yet. These three out of the five had to be elected by the Captain in ten minutes after [the] five were elected," Buckley explained. He then added, "I knew which three had to go, for the Captain said that Buckley and Buffham had been too good [of] soldiers to go out of the company. Buffham and I were sorry that we were not allowed to go."

Unhappy with Captain Franklin Hobbs' decision, an angry Buckley expressed his resentment to Mary. "So you see the ones that do the most duty are not allowed to reap the benefit [and] that is the way it has been in our company all the time. We still stand a chance to go if any of the other three die or get killed. Then we have to take their place. It was the interest of the captain to keep the men in the Company that are always ready for duty. The rest of the boys were glad that the other three were the ones to go for they knew they would have more duty to do if Johnny and I did go." He advised Mary that he did "not care a snap" to become an officer. However, he would like to get out of Company H "for our first Lieutenant and Captain are always ready to assist the boys that lived in Bristol, but

---

47 Dodge, *History of the Old Second Division, Army of the Cumberland*, 454-455; *Rock Island Argus*, February 28, 1863 and March 7, 1863.

we from the prairie do not get any favors shown to us. Our second Lieutenant W. Harkness is a gentleman." [48]

"I am kept in the regiment," wrote Sergeant Sinclair to his wife, "instead of getting my horse office in the light battalion, as I am told, for something better. Although I am on the roll of honor still and thought as much as ever by my officers [and] to any and all . . . so I do not worry on that account, but for hope something still better when it may turn up."[49]

To acknowledge men for dedication to duty and valor on the battlefield was commendable and acceptable to all. But the removal of the most motivated enlisted men and officers from their companies and regiments faced opposition. Consequently, the idea of an elite, mounted battalion armed with repeating rifles was never realized.

Dodge explained: "The establishment of the Light Battalions, of which General Rosecrans hoped so much, proved to be of short duration. The authorities at Washington opposed the organization," and the War Department issued an order disbanding them. "The SECOND DIVISION had its full complement of names in these organization," he wrote, "and had the occasion ever presented itself, they would doubtless have justified the high expectation the commanding general entertained of them."

On April 24, General Rosecrans ordered that "those whose names appear on the rolls of honor remain on duty with their respective commands, and that they be distinguished, when on military duty, by wearing a red ribbon tied in the button hole or attached to the coat over the left breast."[50]

---

[48]   Buckley, letter, March 27, 1863.

[49]   Sinclair, letter, March 28, 1863.

[50]   Dodge, *History of the Old Second Division, Army of the Cumberland*, 455 and 458.

Eighty-ninth Illinois Volunteer Infantry National Flag.(Used with permission of the Adjutant General of the State of Illinois)

Photograph of Co. F probably taken near Murfreesboro, Tennessee in 1863.
(Laertes F. Dimick folder, Cambridge Public Library, Cambridge, Illinois)

George H. Berry, Co. G. The Knox County farmer was captured at Chickamauga and died at Andersonville, August 6, 1864. (Author's photograph)

Lieutenant John R. Darcy, Co. C, was a machinist on the Milwaukee Railroad at enlistment. (U.S. Army Military History Institute)

Chaplain James H. Dill. (Copy in possession of author)

Jerry M. Grosh, fireman on the Galena & Chicago Union Railroad on enlistment in Co. K, was promoted regimental sergeant major and later adjutant. (Courtesy of Leslie Lipschutz)

H. G. Bramble, Co. E, was living in Galesburg and a brakeman on the Chicago, Burlington, & Qunicy Railroad on enlistment. (Copy in possession of author)

William B. Holdren
I Co. 89th reg IL.

William B. Holdren, Co. I, killed at Stones River on December 31, 1862. (Copy in possession of author)

Brian O'Connor, fireman on the Galena & Chicago Union Railroad on enlistment in Co. K, was promoted regimental sergeant major and later first lieutenant in Co. A. (Copy in possession of the author)

Captain John W. Spink, Co. D, killed at Chickamauga. (Copy in possession of author)

George F. Robinson, a clerk with the Illinois Central Railroad on enlistment in Co. D. He moved up to captain when John W. Spink was killed at Chickamauga. (Courtesy of Leslie Lipschutz)

Surgeon Herman B. Tuttle. (Courtesy of Leslie Lipschutz)

E. C. Warner, Co. C. (Copy in possession of author)

Charles W. Mitchell, Co. G, was recruited as a replacement in September 1863. (U.S. Army Military History Institute)

Captain Ebenezer T. Wells, Co. F. (Library of Congress)

Chicagoan Charles T. Hotchkiss initially was the regiment's lieutenant colonel but was promoted when Captain Christopher never joined the regiment. He was brevetted brigadier general for gallant and meritorious service during the war.

(U. S. Army Military History Institute)

COL. MILLER.

1st MD. CALVARY.

J.H. Bufford Pub. Boston Mass.

Andrew Galbraith Miller, Jr. joined Co. B under the alias Frank Sumter. Miller, a West Point graduate and regular army captain, eventually promoted to second lieutenant. At the war's outbreak, he was appointed colonel of the First Maryland Cavalry.

(U.S. Army Military History Institute)

Captain Franklin M. Hobbs, Co. H.
(Abraham Lincoln Presidential Library & Museum)

Captain Henry L. Rowell, the Milwaukee Railroad carpenter, who
recruited Co. C. Rowell died of wounds received at Missionary Ridge.
(U.S. Army Military History Institute)

CHAPTER 8

"WE ARE KEPT BUSY AT SOMETHING NEARLY ALL THE TIME . . . ."

Life for the Army of the Cumberland at Murfreesboro settled into a routine in which regiments were regularly rotated between building earthwork forts, digging entrenchments, and foraging for provisions, while still performing the expected picket and scout duty. Through the remainder of the winter and spring, the Railroaders' letters home and personal diaries discussed and explained their numerous activities. As might be expected, their writings were also filled with homesickness, camp rumors, and general complaints. Chief among the gripes was the continual delays with the mail, which was caused by the incessant rebel cavalry and guerilla attacks on the army's line of communication. Frustrated by the failure of his letters to arrive in Chicago, an exasperated Sergeant George Sinclair pointed out: "I wrote again . . . but through some unseen fault it seems [it] did not reach you. I am really sorry that you were given cause to be so much worried but with [the] stealing of mail, guerilla raids[;] there is no certainty of getting or sending through safely what little correspondence a person does have."[1]

---

[1]   Sinclair, letter, May 22, 1863.

The receipt and answering of mail for some soldiers became the focus of their existence; with the time spent writing and reading letters occupied and offered a diversion from the dullness of camp life for many others. Mail was the link to the outside world of family and friends, making a letter from home foremost on the minds of all soldiers, and especially the ill. Still under the weather, George Berry wrote Harriet that he had "bin a pretty sick boy. It will be some time before I shall do duty. We have a good Doctor [and] that is a blessing to the sick. He seame to know what ale a man. We report to him every morning at the hospital tent and git ower medicen. He called on me three times [as] I was not able to go down." Concerned about George's health, Harriet Berry wrote, offering to come and care for him. He replied that her leaving home was "out of the question. I would like you[r] attention and your[r] help firstrate but that is impossible. You must give up all hope [of] coming here to take care of me. Theodore [Whitney] has been my nurse [and] he is first rate." By March 14, Berry could write that his health was improving. "I still take a little medicine from the Doctor." Regarding military service and his recent illness, George said this: "When I am well, it goes very well, but when a person is sick, it is awful place." Two weeks later George sent a letter stating, "I am quite smarte now. I am out on picket to day fore the first [time in] about two months."[2]

The Eighty-ninth, however, fared no better or worse than most Union regiments when it came to sickness. More men in the regiment died from illness and disease than from bullets or bayonets. Wherever the Eighty-ninth had marched, men were left behind in hospitals and graves. In a letter dated October 26, George Sinclair wrote that fellow sergeant "Mr. Fonda is sick and in [the] hospital in Bardstown. Our first lieutenant is also there with 30 men . . . all sick." Commissary Sergeant David B. Fonda never returned to Company C and was discharged June 8, 1863 due to disability. Likewise, nineteen-year-old Edward Cahill, a printer from Michigan recruited by Sergeant Major Farquhar, fell ill immediately after the regiment took the field and was discharged October 31, 1862. In November, Lieutenant Wells of Company F sent word to

---

2   Berry, letters, February 20 and 28, 1863 and March 14 and 27, 1863.

Rock Island that Sergeant William Dunlap had "died in the cars, on passage from Louisville, Ky., to Bowling Green . . . ."[3]

From August 30 through December 29, 1862, the Eighty-ninth saw twenty men die from either illness or accident. Eleven more men succumbed in March. "I am sorry to say that another of my friends is dead," Joe Buckley informed his wife on March 9. His friend, Thomas Holmes, was one of seventeen English immigrants on Company H's roster. Buckley pointed out that Holmes "was one of the stoutest men we had in our company." He quickly added, however, that "his lungs were affected" and that "those persons that appear to be the strongest are the ones that are taken sick the soonest." Death from sickness could come quickly, and Buckley observed, "It is not long since he was doing his duty along with the rest of us." Another who died of disease was thirty-eight-year-old Franklin County farmer and father of four, Isaac Gatlin of Company B, who succumbed March 15 at a Nashville army hospital.[4]

* * *

"Ower Regiment has received marching orders [and] five days rations in their haversack. I don't know wether it is a general movement or not. [If] Johnson's Division goes, they may go fore good or they may go out cupple [of] days travel and then come back agin," wrote Private George Berry on March 2. But before he finished, he scratched, "the order is countermanded . . . afture they hadde themselves in redeness." Four days later he wrote: "I have not done any duty for over three weeks. I have bin in camp all of that time. Ower company has a good deal [of] pickiting to do and foragin to do since we have bin here.[5]

3   Sinclair, letter, October 26, 1862; Muster and Descriptive Roll Co. A, Record Group 301, Illinois State Archives; *Adjutant General's Report*, 265, 269; *Rock Island Argus*, November 20, 1862.

4   Tom Pearson's Web Page [Internet website] The 89th Illinois Infantry Regiment: Roll of Honor-Chronological. (Accessed November 30, 2006) http://ilcivilwar. org/89_roll_chron.htm Hereafter cited as Roll of Honor; Buckley, letter, March 9, 1863; *Adjutant General's Report*, V: 266.

5   Berry, letter, March 2 and 6, 1863.

On March 7, a worn-out George Sinclair found time to write his wife. "I came in from a foraging jaunt at three o'clock in the morning having tramped all day and night with but a very little rest. In fact I never have been so near used up as I was on coming into camp." He added: "We had orders to go out on a reconnaissance, but nearly every man was so lame that it was impossible to drag them out of their quarters this morning. It is inhuman to use men so, but, we are awful busy just now for our forces are expected to attack Vicksburg about this time and we want to keep the Reb's in motion here too, on our front so that they cannot . . . reinforce Vicksburg."[6]

Sergeant Sinclair also wrote about the toll the war was taking on the local inhabitants as well as the Union soldiers. "I want to do something before long and help end this accursed war for we have to suffer as much here as the ones that live right here and shoulder the expenses." He explained to Francis that "wherever an army is quartered everything for twenty miles is laid waste and desolate, and as far as it is possible they live on the people of the surrounding country. You can barely imagine what [the] inhabitants have to suffer[.] For Union people or [Rebels] are used all alike and robbed of all they have[.]" To secure forage, Sinclair complained they were out "wading in the mud and fording streams at this season of the year, [and] let alone the chances of having [the] rebel cavalry dash in upon us, for they know every foot of ground here and how to take advantage of it and very often it proves fatal for some poor fellow."

"We came off picket this morning and had to pack up our knapsack and take the tents down and load everything on the wagons. And put three days rations in our haversacks, and be ready to march at a moments notice," wrote Joseph Buckley to Mary on March 9. When finished packing, some sat and talked, others slept, a few read or wrote letters, while they all waited for the command to move out. Two hours passed and no movement. The men were standing about and waiting when an officer announced the order was countermanded. It took about a half an hour and "all the tents were fixed just as they were before and everything put in order." Buckley noted: "We were very glad when the order came to unload the wagons and pitch tents, as we only slept a little more than

---

[6]   Sinclair, letter, March 7, 1863.

an hour last night as it was very cold standing on picket without fires."[7]

Returning to camp, Sergeant Sinclair found the tents struck and wagons being loaded. Soon after tossing his knapsack on a wagon, he was handed a letter from his wife. With the march on hold, Sinclair went off to himself with his mail. In his next letter home, he wrote: "I opened your letter, it entirely overcame me and I sat down and had a good crying spell to myself. It was the first tear that I had shed for years . . . ." As for the expected movement, Sinclair stated: "Our start the other day was a false one; we [ended up] camping the same night where we have been for nearly two months." But staying put was not so easy. "Forage is so scarce that we are run to death between it and scouting frequently making from twenty five to thirty five miles a day and part of the night and menaced and harassed by the enemy's cavalry, who are superior to ours and much more numerous," Sinclair pointed out.[8]

In a letter home George Berry also wrote of the regiment's ordeal during this period. "We have fighting most every day. One division [will] go out every day. We drive them back. Some time we git drove back. Ower division was called out once. Ower Regiment did not git into a fight. Ower company stood pickit. They come very near being all taken prisoner when they was out with the division." During most of this time, Berry was too ill to go out with the regiment, but remained back in camp. He wrote Harriet that he was "gaining strength every day. I shall be fit for duty in about two weeks. I think I shall hafture be careful not [to] go out to soone. Yesterday we took ower tents down and packed up every thing and laide around all day. Order came to pitch tents agin. We are still in camp yet. We did not go this time, [but] we may have hafture leave any moment." He informed Harriet that if a forward movement was called for, "the sick was to be sent to Murfreesboro. If we had left yesterday, I should [have] went to Murfreesboro and staid till I got stout."[9]

At noon on Sunday, March 22, the Railroaders were ordered to be ready to march in twenty minutes and have three days rations

---

7 Buckley, letter, March 9, 1863.

8 Sinclair, letter, March 11, 1863.

9 Berry, letter, March 10, 1863.

in their haversacks. And in twenty minutes the regiment was on its way toward Salem. "We halted when about half a mile from Salem where we found Davis's division on picket," wrote Joseph Buckley. "We relieved them, and we did not get relieved until last night. So we were on the picket four days and a half. This morning [March 27] we came on picket again at seven o'clock, but we are not more than one mile from camp. The other time we were four miles and a half from camp."

Buckley's letter home did take a personal turn as he responded to his wife's wish that she could have a chat with him. "I would like to have a chat with you, and that my Dear is not all I would like to have for those "oysters" operated most wonderfully, and if you had been very near me that night there would have been a prospect of there being an addition to the family in the course of time."[10]

George Sinclair received a welcomed letter from his wife when we came in from picket. The next day [March 28] he began a letter to Frances. He detailed that picket duty left the lonely soldier exposed to the elements with little or no cover. Recently, the regimental pickets suffered "one of the worst storms of the season, all day and night. But we came through all right with the exception of our ducking which was not very agreeable at even this season of the year, although it is warmer now than when we laid out last winter." Since he last wrote, George commented, "Frankly dear, I don't know of anything new or of interest to write, but that little piece of news of a probable close of this war before another winter that you sent me did much to cheer and encourage me on. But destiny is to be fulfilled, I claim at any rate, and the views of this one or that one on the subject, no matter what they may say, will not materially alter the end to be attained."[11]

The letters back to Illinois reflected the cat and mouse game the Railroaders continued to play with the rebels. Probing, foraging, and picketing took on a routine of its own while winter gave way to spring. A frazzled Joseph Buckley expressed his frustration to Frances. "We went on picket last Sunday, and did not get relieved until Friday. And when we were not on picket, they have us out

---

[10]   Buckley, letter, March 27, 1863.
[11]   Sinclair, letter, March 28, 1863.

drilling in company drill and Battalion drill in the forenoon, and company drill and dress parade in the afternoon. Then we have our own cooking besides, and [we have to] be in line to answer roll call four times per day. Then we have our washing . . . . They keep us very busy." George Berry wrote on May 2 that the regiment was "five miles from Murfreesboro on picket." He gave Harriet a quick explanation of the Eighty-ninth's current detail. "We hafture stay here five days. Ower brigade is out all at one time. We go out once in twelve days. We go on picket every other day. I like it better than I do in camp." Continuing on, Berry wrote: "They say that the Rebels are within thirty miles from us with a strong force. Rosecrans is reddy for them. We have three hundred acres fortified around Murfreesboro. If they come to us, we shant hafture go to them. I don't hardley think they will attack us." Sergeant Sinclair had quickly become an old soldier, and as a consequence, he held a more cynical view of what was being said around the campfires. He quipped: "There are several rumors as to our movements and also that of the enemy. But we can place no confidence in anything that we may hear nor believe that we are going anyplace until we find ourselves there."[12]

It had been a little over two weeks since George Sinclair penned his last letter to Frances and nothing had changed. Finally getting the opportunity to write, George spelled out why he had not written. "We are kept busy at something nearly all the time, on picket or a scout or drilling and the devil knows what not. I received your last letter [the] night before last on coming in from picket or scout, I should say, for we were out a week and I got one while out there, so I am indebted to you for two now but will answer both in this." If Frances was anxious or angry over not hearing from George, he attempted to soothe her feelings. "Frank, I will send you my picture in this letter, it's the best I can do just now, but no doubt you would rather have the original."[13]

"Our chaplain is preaching now and I suppose I ought to attend," wrote George Sinclair, "but I am doing as well for all the good I would obtain there." He added, "It is the first sermon that we have had for four months on account of the weather. They are singing

---

[12]   Buckley, letter, April 12, 1863; Berry, letter, May 2, 1863; May 22, 1863.
[13]   Sinclair, letter, April 12, 1863.

now and you know I love to hear that no matter what sort." Like any group of men some were more devout than others. Joseph Buckley missed the weekly religious services of home and informed his wife that "Captain Spencer of Co. B. is Chaplain of our Regiment now. He is a preacher, but it is seldom he gets a chance to preach to us as we are most always on duty on Sundays, which I regret very much." In a letter to Harriet, George Berry commented: "We have one Captain [who] is now ower Chaplin and postmaster. He is a smart and a good man. Quite a change over [our] other Chaplin [who] was a Congregationalist. The boys would not go out to heare him. He could not preach to satisfy them; otherwise, he was a fine man."[14]

Spring saw a religious revival take place at Murfreesboro, and it was attended by a number of men from the Eighty-ninth. "Lieutenant Harkness and about a dozen of us went to a meeting last night," Joseph Buckley wrote Mary on May 20. "There were about six hundred of us there, and there was about 300 more who could not get in. I tell you we had a first rate discourse. They have just organized an Army Church—that is a Church without regard to any particular denomination, but one for all denominations." He continued: "They are going to have a prayer meeting this evening at sundown, before the preaching commences. I shall go if I can get there. I enjoyed myself last night. It made me think of the good times we used to have at home." Buckley noted, "A great many joined the Church last night. They gave everyone a chance to put their name down whether they were members of the Church or not before they came in the Army. I think if I go tonight, I shall put my name down, but then I can hand my name in to our Chaplain." Speaking of the same service he told his young son, Charley, that "we had a meeting last night in one of the Forts, and I tell you we had a good time in serving the Lord. There were about 500 or 600 persons all singing at once."[15]

After Reverend James Dill's death, Captain, Travis O. Spencer of Company B was appointed the Eighty-ninth's chaplain. The thirty-two-year-old Methodist minister was a popular choice. To the

---

[14] Sinclair, letter, April 12, 1863; Buckley, letter April 12, 1863; Berry, letter, March 14, 1863.

[15] Buckley, letter, May 20, 1863; Joseph Buckley letter to Charley Buckley, May 20, 1863.

men of the regiment, Captain Spencer was not only a natural leader but also "a good preacher" and "a faithful pastor." Like many of them, he too, had left his wife and children to answer Lincoln's call to put down the rebellion. Back in August, he and attorney Henry W. Smith had recruited 95 men, mainly from Franklin County, of which 85 listed their occupation as farmer. When the company officially organized, Spencer and Smith were elected respectively captain and first lieutenant.[16]

While the regiment remained at Murfreesboro, Captain Spencer took advantage of the spring weather and began church services that were as regular as possible. Though not opposed to the open air, the men, however, thought that a meeting house would be more comfortable for all. Joe Buckley explained that we "built a very large shed and covered it with greenboughs to keep the sun off us . . . ." The Reverend Spencer put the makeshift church to good use, as Private Buckley explained to his wife. Captain Spencer, he said, "preached to us last Saturday night (May 16) as we were going out on picket at seven o'clock Sunday morning. He will preach to us tomorrow evening (May 21) if we are in camp. He is one of the best of the best preachers I ever heard. A great many from other regiments come to hear him preach. He is very well thought of."[17]

"I joined the Army Church a few days after I wrote to you last, if I recollect right," wrote Buckley. "We have formed a Bible Class and chosen Lieutenant Harkness as teacher. I also joined the Regimental Church. Quite a number joined that belong to our company, the other evening. So you can see we are going to try and serve the Lord all we can." On a personal note, he continued: "Dear Mary, All I ask for myself is that God will preserve my life for the special purpose of taking care of you and the boys and serving his cause while I live in this world, and I feel the assurance that he will do it. Yes, my faith is very strong in the Lord. I have not the slightest doubt but what the Lord is in this war and that he will bring things around all in his own good time."[18]

---

[16]   *Journal of Proceedings of the Methodist Episcopal Church of the Southern Illinois Conference, 1867* (General Minutes) 37-38; Muster and Descriptive Roll Co. B, Record Group 301, Illinois State Archives.

[17]   Buckley, letter, May 20, 1863.

[18]   Buckley, letter, June 12, 1863

"We hade preaching last knight," George Berry informed Harriet. He then matter-of-factly explained to her that "we are going to have a Regimental Church in ower Regiment. I Calculate to join it. I shall hafture tell ower Chaplen what Church I belong [to] and who is my preacher at home['s] name. When you write let me know your preacher's first name." Back in April, Berry wrote home. "We are going to have a bible class in our Regiment. I calculate to be one in the class. We have good methodist preaching now."[19]

*   *   *

Whether they were a Douglas Democrat or a Lincoln Republican, the Union soldier saw the northern peace and compromise movement as an act of disloyalty. Having volunteered to fight for the Union and save the Constitution, these men in uniform concluded that those who wanted peace at any price were not only stabbing them in the back but at the same time also encouraging the rebels. The Republican press soon labeled these Democrats as Copperheads after the poisonous snake that lies silently in wait before striking, unlike the rattlesnake, which gives a warning before attacking. Seen as conciliatory toward the South, the Peace Democrats and their allied newspapers were judged to be undermining the government's effort to suppress the rebellion. And as expected, those supporting the Administration viewed the Copperheads as traitors who gave the rebels hope, and thus prolonged the war. Among themselves and in their letters, the Railroaders sounded off on the treachery at home and the fire in the rear.

A passionate soldier from Company I penned a letter dated May 1 to the editors of the *Amboy Times*. The writer chose not to identify himself, but signed "89th REGT." He began: "I have never yet seen in your paper a letter from the Rail Road Regiment. This seems almost strange when more than a company was formed from Amboy and the adjacent country around it for the 89th. Over 9 months have passed away since we left our homes, and the loved associations that often come flitting across our memory while thinking of those left behind in Illinois." The writer told the newspaper that the company

---

[19]   Berry, letters, May 10 and April 12, 1863

had undergone many hardships "to sustain the Stars and Stripes and to transmit to future generations a government," which had stood as a model for the whole world.

"God forbid," he continued "that in *this* conflict which is now being waged between the North and South, or rather between those who uphold a free Government and the others who . . . enslave human beings, and thereby . . . do a grievous wrong . . . ." The writer informed the editor that the planter society cared little for the poor white population either. He wrote that southern aristocracy kept "those of their own race from the benefits of education, and all its inspiring influences."

The soldier pointed out that he had read a recent copy of the *Times* and regretted that "Amboy had been the scene of riotous attack from that class commonly known as copperheads." Enraged, he informed the editor that if there had been one company of seasoned soldiers about, the Copperheads "would have hunted their holes in 'short meter,' else there would have been a report [of gunfire] from those who have sacrificed much, rather than lose the Glory of our happy Union."

Like many of his comrades, the writer was not willing to return home "until this accursed rebellion is put down never more to show its hideous form, unless it be necessary for us to return and assist in giving some of those 'Peace men,' a nice 'cleaning out.' Can it be that they *love* the southern institutions? If so, we wish that they were in General Rose's hands, we would soon see them wending their way to the haunts of Jeff. Davis and his followers."

Turning to a brighter side, he confided that "upon the whole, we are not discouraged. We have confidence in our leaders, and believe that 'Rose is the man.' Without calling names we would say that the members of Co. I and the few left in Co. A from Amboy, are all in good health, and seemingly in good spirits. The influence of camp life over us, we trust, will not prove detrimental, and when the war is over we hope to return to meet loved friends and relations and enjoy the rest of life under a Government free and alike to all."[20]

The anti-abolitionist Sergeant George Sinclair also voiced disdain for the Copperheads. In June 20 letter to Francis, he said "there is

---

[20]   *Amboy Times*, May 14, 1863.

nothing new here at present, no prospect of a march or a fight. Our boys begin to pray for a fight rather than drill in this weather, as we have to do . . . ." He then added that "most of them want to be led back commencing at the Canada line and exterminate [both] 'Copperheads' and abolitionists together. Then we think that we would stand a chance of finishing this accursed war . . . ." Nevertheless, he concluded resignedly, "but let them keep on."[21]

Normally a man of few words, Private George Berry spelled out in length his thoughts on a compromise settlement to the rebellion. He told Harriet that "we are gaining on the Rebels. We shall fetch them to terms some time. Rosecrans may hafture fight another bige battle before it will be winde up. If one battle will settled it, let it come. If this could be settled with out another battle, it would suit me just as well."

Berry continued: "I go in for no Compromise. I have seen enough of slavery down here. It is a disgrace to any nation. One Rebel slaveholder close by ware we are in camp owns about five thousand acres of land." He observed that the "poore white men" renting and the landowner's "negroes is thought of as much as the other." Upset with what he had heard about a neighbor back home, he wrote to Harriet: "Tell Samuel that I don't Compromise with traters and Copperheads." He asked: "Is Sam so feint harted that he wants to Compromise with traters? Poore fellow! Tell him not to be afraid. The Bullets wont hit him up in Knox County. If he could only see these slave states. His mind would change how things are carried on."[22]

Harriet Berry wrote to George, an acknowledged strong Union and Lincoln man, that loyal forces were organizing to oppose the anti-Administration and pro-compromise element in Illinois. Not a long-winded fellow, Berry summed up his thoughts. "I think the union league is a first rate thing to keep down the Copperhead rebels. It keeps up union feeling and does a good deal of good I think." Still perturbed over his neighbor, Berry told Harriet, "Tell Samuel that I would rather fight beside a negro than to fight beside [a] Drafted Coperhead that don't believe in this ware. I

---

21   Sinclair, letter, June 20, 1863.

22   Berry, letter, May 20, 1863.

believe in arming the negrŏ. They are nobeter to be hit by a bullet than I be."[23]

Writing on March 27, Private Joseph Buckley commented that the Copperheads were doing "a great deal in making a Division in the North; but I hope to God the North will prove true to itself, and all will come out right. I hope Abe Lincoln will send every 'Copperhead' from the North to fight for the Union whether they are old or young."[24]

After receiving a letter each from his brother and sister, an anguished Joseph Buckley sat down and wrote his wife. "I can plainly see that Sister and Brother have no sympathy with the North, which has stunned me more than anything has for years. Although I have the facts before me, yet I cannot realize it as a fact." Disappointed and frustrated, he told Mary that "their judgement of the war has no foundation whatever. I think they do not understand it." And he, he added, "My conscience is clear as far as I am concerned. It is my honest and candid belief that I am doing my duty to the Country . . . ."

On the other hand, Joseph's brother and sister thought differently. He explained: "Brother speaks in a very disrespectful manner with regard to what I think is my duty. He seems to think that his 'ideas' are all right and mine all wrong. Sister seems to think the same. I shall judge from what he says in his letter that he considered it more my duty to be at home taking care of you and the things at home. For he says, 'In conclusion I would urge upon you to leave the service, if you can honorably, as I think other duties which you should fulfil are of more consequence than the duty you think calls you to the field of battle.'"

Buckley switched to his sister's correspondence. "Then Sister says 'She thinks there is more hope for the abolition of slavery by the South gaining its independence than by the North being victorious.' She says 'She thinks if the South succeeds there will be a chance of the gradual Emancipation by treaty with other Nations.'" He notes that "if she was here a short time all such foolish notions would vanish very quick. But come to think she married a Cotton Lord, and no wonder she can see nothing but cotton."

---

23 Berry, letter, June 19, 1863.
24 Buckley, letter, March 27, 1863.

Buckley now poured out his heart to his wife. "Dear Mary, I cannot help weeping as I write, but the tears of an honest soldier are nothing to be ashamed of. Now, I would ask you a question. Do you honestly think that I have willfully neglected my duty to you? I ask the question honestly and calmly and in all kindness, and if you think I have neglected my duty to you willfully, then I will give up all further claim to your affection, although it will break my heart in doing so. I never should have thought of asking you such a question if it was not for what Brother said in his letter."[25]

In corresponding with his mother in England, Joe Buckley had purposely withheld telling her that he had enlisted, knowing she would be upset and worry for his safety. Sometime in early 1863, probably from either his brother or sister, his mother became aware that he was serving in the Union Army. Mary must have passed the news to Joe, for he confided to her: "I am very much pained to learn that Mother takes it so hard. I hope she will be better . . . ." He then wrote his mother informing her of his enlistment. Her response only added to his woes. "I received your letter on the 30th of May," she wrote, "and oh! how thankful I was when I opened it, [and read] that you was alive and well . . . . And if my prayers and tears will avail, your life will be spared. My Dear Joseph: I pray night and day for your safety. I hope and trust the Lord will bring you safe[ly] through. My Dear Joseph: I am almost heart broken when I think of the dangers you are exposed to and what you must have gone through." Giving the same advice as his brother, Mrs. Buckley encouraged Joseph to leave the service. She told him: "I was disappointed that you did not state how long you volunteered for. I had been counting the days. I had got it in my head [that] you had gone for nine months. I want you to state how long you went for. If you did not fix a time, I want you to get a substitute. I beg and pray you will if it is possible. If it takes all the stock on the farm, I hope you try." And she too played the guilt card. "I am truly sorry for your dear wife. I cannot see what she can do without you on the farm. I hope she can keep up both in health and spirit." She continued. "My Dear Joseph: I shall be anxious until I hear from you again. I do nothing that I can leave undone for looking at the papers, and the accounts are dreadful

---

[25] Buckley, letter, May 4, 1863.

to think of. I hope the war will end soon and slavery with it. It is a disgrace to any nation and the sooner it is crushed the better. My sympathy is with the North, but then dear Joseph you have a duty to perform at home, you have a wife that requires protection, and may God protect her and the children in your absence." Returning to the subject of a replacement, she asked: "Could not Mary get a substitute for you? I am sure it would be the best thing she could do. As I said before, if it took all the stock on the farm, for what is money compared with life? But if it cannot be done, I must submit to the will of an allwise God and if I never see you again in this world, I hope we shall meet again in heaven."

*　*　*

In early March, George Berry got a letter from his brother. Still a prisoner, Thomas wrote that he was to be returned to Illinois and would have to stay there until exchanged. On March 27, George wrote Harriet that he was glad to hear that Thomas had made it home. Unfortunately, the news that his brother had been exchanged and back home turned out to be false. George next wrote on April 12 that he had received another letter from Thomas and that he was in St. Louis waiting to be exchanged. "I under stand to day that Thomas Whiting was Exchanged. If that is the case he will soon be with us," George penned. However, his brother's situation remained the same. George wrote Harriet that he had received another letter from Thomas. "He wants me to git Lt. Howell to send him his discriptive roll. Howell has to have orders from the major from st louis before he can send it." After receiving word from Harriet that Thomas had finally got his papers in order, Berry wrote: "I see by your letter that Thomas was at home. I understood that they are exchanged so he will be here soon. Thomas has bin pretty lucky to have the privelige to git home and see his family."[26]

In a letter to his mother back in Augusta, Illinois, Private William Tomlinson of Company A remarked that "our old captain [Duncan Hall] came back last week. He has been a prisoner since the battle." Writing home May 2, Private Buckley sent word that "Major Hall

26   Berry, letters, March 6, March 27, April 12, April 25, and June 2, 1863.

and Captain Whiting . . . arrived here yesterday." Both men were captured on the first morning of the fight at Stones River and had recently been exchanged. The two officers had reported that "they were badly treated while they were in 'Dixie.'" To bolster his family's spirits, Buckley reported the following: "They say from what they have seen that the war cannot last long. They say the Rebels can't hold out much longer."[27]

Private Curtis Knox was not among those returning to the regiment at this time. In fact he would not be back with his comrades until mid-September. Nearly forty years afterwards, Knox recalled his experience as a prisoner of war. He wrote that it was the middle of January when he reached Richmond and Libby Prison where he was confined for two months. Knox remembered that "he was treated fairly well, but received hardly enough food to hold soul and body together." He told of the time the weather was cold and to keep warm "the prisoners tore down several boards from an old bunk for fuel . . . ." For this offense the men were "cut off from food for two days." Sometime in March the captives were "loaded into dirty, filthy, roofless cars and transported to Petersburg, where they indulged in a little stealing of tobacco, for which offense they were to be killed." The "next day they were taken to City Point, on Chesapeake Bay, where for the first time in 2 months they got sight of their beloved stars and stripes . . . ." Several more months passed before he was shipped to Benton Barracks in St. Louis. Still on parole, Curtis had had enough of fatigue duty and "took up his heels and made his flight from custody . . . ." Making his way to Chicago, he reported to Colonel Hotchkiss, who provided him with transportation to the front.[28]

Sergeant Sinclair reported on May 28 that "our brigade general came back to us [the] day before yesterday. He had been for the past five months in the prison of Dixie being taken at Stone's River Battle. He was very glad to see us and we to have him back with us once more, for he is a fine gentleman and a splendid general." He mentioned that Willich told "some rather hard stories" of his

[27] Tomlinson, *In Good Courage: The Civil War Letters of William James Tomlinson*, 9; Buckley, letter, began April 30 and completed May 2, 1863.
[28] *Soldiers and Patriots Biographical Album*, 617.

treatment while imprisoned. Sinclair also repeated the often told camp story that Willich was "the illegitimate son of King Frederick of Prussia and consequently as he terms a Dutch Yankee General Willich."[29]

The *Chicago Tribune* correspondent reported on June 2 that "one of the most gratifying affairs of camp life came off yesterday evening, on the parade [ground] of the 1st brigade of Johnson's division. I refer to the resumption by the brave old fighting Gen. Willich of his old command." Willich's popularity with both the officers and men in the ranks made his return an occasion for general rejoicing. At the formal transfer of the command, the whole brigade turned out. "The troops were formed in squares, in the centre of which were grouped Col. Gibson and Gen. Willich, and Gen. Rosecrans and staff." Short speeches followed, resulting in "cheer upon cheer" being "given for the 'old Dutch fighter,' for Col. Gibson, and for Gen. Rosecrans. All in all, it was one of the happiest times imaginable, and gave the troops of the brigade a fine impetus for the splendid field maneuvering[,] which immediately followed."[30]

"Our brigade had a review yesterday," wrote Private George Berry. "It went off well. Rosecrans was out to see us. We have a German Dutchman to Comand ower brigade." Berry noted that "he was taken prisoner at Stone River," and "he is with us now. He is a splendid man." With the return of Willich and a review by Old Rosey, a sense of action was in the air. In a letter written on June 3, Sergeant George Sinclair spelled out that "we are in readiness to march at a moments warning." In an afterthought he commented: "There is some talk of making us mounted infantry. Will tell you more next time about it."[31]

While some men returned from captivity or the hospital, others left the service. Having been hospitalized and home on sick leave, First Lieutenant Isaac Copley, one of the organizers of Company G, returned to the regiment on March 15. He brought with him a pocket book and a number of letters for George Berry. Berry remarked that Copley didn't "look stout." On May 2, he wrote Harriet that "Mr.

---

29   Sinclair, letter, May 28, 1863.

30   *Chicago Tribune*, June 9, 1863.

31   Berry, letter, June 2, 1863; Sinclair, letter, June 3, 1863.

Copley I think will leave soon. He is waiting for his papers from headquarters and then he will leave for home." Unable to regain his health, Copley's resignation was accepted on May 8, and he left for home May 10. Berry wrote Harriet: "Mr. Copley leaves today for home. I have sent you twenty-five dollars by Mr. Copley I have sent home one dress coate and one over coate by Mr. Copley. I put three pounds of brown coffee in a coate sleave and three paire of mittens. You can pay Copley the freight on them coats. That coffee is for you [and] mother."[32]

Copley was the seventh company grade officer to resign since the regiment left Chicago. An eighth officer was cashiered on June 18. The only field grade officer to quit the service was Dr. Samuel F. Hance. He was court-martialed, tried, and acquitted for willfully failing to treat a number of enlisted men who had contracted gonorrhea when he had the medicine to do so. Unpopular, Dr. Hance thought it best to leave the Eighty-ninth and resigned March 26.[33]

Unable to resign and return to civilian life, the enlisted man needed a medical discharge to leave the army. A number of medical releases were granted to those either severely injured in battle or found unfit for the field. Suffering gunshot wounds to the left shoulder and right hip at Stones River, Private Joseph Goyer of Company F was discharged April 28. Also severely wounded at Stones River was Corporal George L. Richards of Company E. He was discharged May 19. Hit three times in the Rebel attack on the morning of December 31, Fred W. Godard survived to be medically discharged March 13. Discharged for disability on February 16 at Louisville was Private Robert M. Holt from Galesburg, Knox County. Along with his son, the 59-year-old blacksmith had enlisted in Duncan Hall's C. B. & Q. Railroad Company. While the elder Holt's health broke down, Sergeant James E. Holt served throughout the war and mustered out June 19, 1865, returning to work as a foreman for the "Q". Hospitalized for four months after the fight at Stones River, Private Houston P. Tait of Company G would be transferred to the Veteran Reserve Corps. Sent to Veteran Reserve

---

32   Berry, letter, May 10, 1863.

33   *Adjutant General's Report*, V: 263, 266, 271, and 273; Eddy, *The Patriotism of Illinois*, II: 338; Lowry and Welsh, *Tarnished Scalpels*, 124, 127-128.

Corps were soldiers, who either from wounds or hardships of service was no longer considered fit for field duty, but they were also not considered totally disabled. Here their duties were "to act as provost guards and garrisons for cities; guards for hospitals and other public buildings; and as clerks, orderlies, etc. If found necessary they may be assigned to forts, etc." After being hospitalized for 10 months, Corporal Levi C. Way of Company A was assigned to Camp Douglas in Chicago, where he guarded Rebel prisoners until discharged July 3, 1865.[34]

Still other men of merit or skill were pulled away from the regiment. A medical student before the war, William F. Tait was detailed for hospital service at Murfreesboro. He remained a hospital steward until discharged on June 4, 1865. Updating the editor of the Rock Island *Argus*, Major Williams explained that "First Lieut. E. T. Wells is now captain of Co. F. He has been appointed assistant commissary of musters for the 2d division, 20th army corps, which leaves 1st Lieut. Dimick in command of the company." The Knox College graduate and Rock Island attorney never returned to the regiment but continued to fill staff positions until mustered out of the service.[35]

*   *   *

Based on the courage and leadership Colonel Hotchkiss had shown the first day of the battle of Stones River, the men of the

---

[34]   *Adjutant General's Report*, V: 263, 264, 274, 276, 279, 281; *History of Crawford and Richland Counties, Wisconsin*, 943; *The History of Dubuque County, Iowa* (Chicago: Western Historical Company, 1880), 866; J. L. Dewey, *Dewey's County Directory* (Galesburg, Illinois: Liberal Book and Job Office, 1868), 43; *Portrait and Biographical Album of Knox County, Illinois* (Chicago: Biographical Publishing Company, 1886), 963; *Rock Island Argus*, July 22, 1863; R. I. Law, compiler, *Knox County Roll of Honor, Department of Illinois Grand Army of the Republic, Jas. T. Shields Post No. 45, Personal War Sketch* (Housed in the Knox County, Illinois Recorder's office), 31;

[35]   *Soldiers' and Patriots Biographical Album Containing Biographies and Portraits of Soldiers and Loyal Citizens in the American Conflict* (Chicago: Union Veteran Publishing Company, 1892), 358-359; *The Evening Argus*, May 16, 1863.

regiment thought some sort of token of their appreciation was appropriate. It was determined to honor him with a special sword. Private Buckley informed his wife that "we subscribed for a sword for our Colonel for his valuable services in bringing us through the Battle as safe as he did. They sent to Chicago for the Sword, but it is not come yet. I paid 50 cents." At the same time, Buckley wrote: "We have subscribed a Dollar each to buy Lieutenant Harkness a sword as a token of respect for the kindness and manly bearing he has shown to all of us." Sizing up Hotchkiss, Private Berry said this: "Ower Colernaul is giting to be firstrate."[36]

With the delay in pay and families to provide for, some soldiers felt they were put upon when asked to donate. The purchase and presentation of a sword for Company G's acting captain did not go over well with Private Berry. "Ower company made a present of a sworde to Lieutenant Howell. Some give from two to five Dollars. I gave one Dollar. I had rather sent it home. I did not want to be alone so I thought I would give something. That swoarde and the belt cost one hundred Dollars." Private Joseph Buckley painted a different picture of Company H. "At roll call tonight," he wrote, "Our Second Lieutenant was presented with the sword we bought him. John Sherwin made the presentation with a very appropriate address. When he finished, Lieutenant Harkness responded to it, but keep a look out for the Kendal County Press, and you will see the presentation speech and the response. They were very appropriate and true."[37]

Saturday evening, April 25, the Railroaders gathered while the Twenty-fourth Wisconsin Brass Band played in the background. "How the music did inspire me with pleasant sensations! It almost made me forget that I was in the war—how noble and elevating the music did sound," proclaimed Private Buckley. Once the regiment had congregated, a spokesman made a short speech and presented the sword the men had purchased to Colonel Hotchkiss. On acceptance, the colonel spoke a few words. Buckley remarked that Hotchkiss' "feelings almost overcame him when he made his reply. He felt happy and proud of us to know that we held such a good opinion of him. He said that was of more value to him than the sword."

---

[36]   Buckley, letter, April 20, 1863; Berry, letter, March 14, 1863.

[37]   Berry, letter, March 14, 1863; Buckley, letter, May 20, 1863.

Colonel Hotchkiss stepped aside giving way to General Gibson to address the Railroaders. Private Buckley stated the general "praised our Regiment very much. He said we always did our share of duty. All through Kentucky and on the Battlefield, he said, the Eighty-ninth never complained when they were on the march and were ordered to picket at night in a heavy rainstorm . . ." When all was said, Buckley concluded that "General Gibson gave us our due share of praise and we were satisfied."[38]

*　　*　　*

Homesickness and the hope of seeing family and friends were a recurring theme in the Railroaders' letters. The thought of a furlough was foremost on everyone's mind. When word spread among the men that the Government considered allowing a few men at a time from each company to return home, it caused a bit of a stir in camp. Sergeant Sinclair spoke to his wife about getting home. "Now it is a strife among the noncommissioned officers and privates to see who shall [receive] the first one to be given." A clever man and not wishing to seem too eager, Sinclair instructed his wife to lobby for him. "We don't know exactly when they are to commence, so if Captain Rowell should happen to come home before they conclude who shall go first, I want you and mother to put in a word for me. I rather think that I am all right but a word from a woman in asking for a favor is worth a days talking from a man. Then again I am too independent to ask any odd [favor] from anyone."

"If I could get a furlough for a month, I would not begrudge 50 Dollars," wrote Joseph Buckley. "It has been reported several times that we were going to have furloughs of 30 days for each man, two men for each company were to have 30 days furlough, and when the 30 days were up, two from each company would again leave for thirty days. And so it would go until all of us had been home or any place he wanted to go to," Buckley explained. "If such a thing should happen, I shall do my best to get home to see you all. I am very anxious to see you all, and if the Lord permits, I will do so. I will

---

[38] Buckley, letter, April 30, 1863.

leave all in his hands. He knows what is best for us, so let us have patience and put our whole trust in the Lord . . . ."[39]

At some point Mary Buckley may have alluded to visiting Joseph in Murfreesboro. He patiently responded why it was impossible by describing his current living arrangement. "Dear Mary this is no place for a woman to come to. I should have no place or tent to accommodate you with only a small canvas dog tent a little more than three feet high in the center and slopes down on each side . . . . There is no canvas on each end. They buttoned in the center so that we can take them apart and each of us carry half of it. So we carry our house, and bed, and board with us when we move." In the same letter Joseph metaphorically cautioned Mary that "returned Soldiers are very dangerous persons for Females to be very near, you see they learn to charge Bayonets."[40]

As days turned to weeks and weeks to months, Sergeant George Sinclair concluded: "There is no sign of a chance of getting a furlough that I can see. If I should get one at any future time before my time is out or the war ended, I shall be as much surprised as anyone. For no one here gets such a thing unless their nearest and dearest relatives die or something happens to them worse than death and even then a man must need be in considerable favor to get such a favor started. But never mind dear Franky, if the Lord spares me, I shall be at home in a little over two years. Just think, one of the three have nearly passed away."[41]

"I think of home, I was going to say, every half hour of the day," a melancholy George Berry confided to his wife Harriet. "I carry your Likeness all the time. When I look at it makes me [a] little home sick. You all look so much like olde times when I was at home." But he quickly changed the subject and wrote: "Thomas and I tent together. We have ower dog tent [with] ower bed [on] one side and table on the other side. After we got it all fix[ed], I told Thomas that I wish Harriet and Estell was here to see ower house. You would have a fine laugh over ower mansion." George concluded the letter by telling Harriet that "ower government, I think, is coming out all

---

39   Sinclair, letter, March 7, 1863.

40   Buckley, letter, April 30, 1863.

41   Sinclair, letter, June 3, 1863.

right. We must keep up good courage. We may see one [an]other yet." For George it was a matter of faith. "I still put my trust in the Lorde. I should feel Lonesome if the Lorde was to forsake me, but I know that he has not. I feel that the Lorde is [with] me on the march to the battle field and on [the] battle ground."[42]

[42]   Berry, letter, July 13, 1863.

CHAPTER 9

'LET ME ALONE AND HOLD THE FENCE!'

"The old date, the old town, the old encampment still," wrote the *Chicago Tribune's* reporter from Murfreesboro on June 2, 1863. For a man with nothing to say, his next words said it all. "Correspondents, editors and writers, and talkers have for days been tinkering at a movement, but—not yet. Have faith, O ye people! Have patience, the great heart of this army is with the struggling heroes at Vicksburg, and it's sturdy, supporting blows will be given in good time."[1]

For nearly six months Rosecrans busied his army fortifying Murfreesboro. While the earthworks progressed, the commanding general reorganized and re-equipped the troops in preparation for the summer campaign. Despite the lack of forward movement, Rosecrans' regiments and brigades were active with numerous reconnoissances and foraging expeditions. In a letter to his mother dated May 3, Private William J. Tomlinson of Company A explained: "Picket line near Salem, 4 miles from Murfreesboro . . . . The cannons are booming all around us. Ther is rebels coming in every Day and giving themselves up. Our men surprised the enemy the other morning. They run and left their tents standing and their

---

[1]   *Chicago Tribune*, June 9, 1863.

clothes on the line." As he perceived it, Tomlinson sized up the war on his front. "The rebs fight hard, but our men is driving them all the time. I think they will drive them out of Tennessee and give them one of the greatest thrashings they ever got . . . ." However, only one opinion counted and the commanding general was not convinced that driving the rebels would be so easy. For the time being, Rosecrans continued to inspect and review his brigades and divisions, while in the nation's capital, General Halleck along with the Lincoln Administration preferred General Rosecrans advance on Bragg's Army of Tennessee rather then building forts and holding parades at Murfreesboro. Voicing a similar opinion, the Eighty-ninth's Major W. D. Williams wrote his friend and editor of the Rock Island *Argus* the following on May 8: "The army is lying here, apparently 'on its oars.' It is, however, in a high state, of discipline, and eager for an opportunity to do something towards a restoration of the union. We estimate our strength (mere guess work) at about 75,000." He continued: "Of course we have any number of startling rumors, ever day, of the movements of the army, but they are not worth repeating. If anything important occurs you may rely on my giving you (if I live) early information." And so it went, the army was ready to go, but nothing moved. Rumors circulated, and sometimes, they were even followed by orders, but if so, they were cancelled. Lieutenant Dimick notified the *Argus* on June 4: "We are under marching orders, to move at a moment's notice. Will probably start tomorrow morning, to whip Bragg if possible."[2]

The ever observant Sergeant Sinclair had the situation pretty well figured out. Writing his wife on June 10, George explained that he delayed answering her last letter "a day or two to see if something different would be known," but he finally concluded that "the siege of Vicksburg will let us know soon whether we are to advance or to await and give the rebs battle here." He then switched to the other hot item currently being talked about in camp. "There is some hopes of our brigade being made mounted infantry. Some

---

[2]   Van Horne, *History of the Army of the Cumberland Its Organization, Campaigns, and Battles*, I: 287-300; Kammerer, *Hancock County, Illinois in the Civil War*, 77; *Rock Island Argus*, May 15 and June 13, 1863.

expect the horses as soon as July 1st, but I hardly think so," Sinclair penned.[3]

On May 1, Grant crossed the Mississippi and moved against Vicksburg. General Halleck and President Lincoln pressured Rosecrans to advance on Bragg, and thus, discouraging the Army of Tennessee from sending reinforcements to Vicksburg. However, throughout May and the better part of June, Rosecrans did nothing, leaving both Halleck and Lincoln extremely frustrated. To some, Rosecrans still seemed paralyzed by Bragg's attack at Stones River; he continued to find innumerable reasons for not advancing on the rebel foe. In truth, Rosecrans and the generals under his command concluded that they should and would do nothing until Vicksburg's fate had been sealed. And that is what they did, for it was not until June 23, ten days before Vicksburg's surrender, that the Army of the Cumberland finally swung into action.[4]

But, Bragg too had been busy the past six months. His army occupied a strong position; much of it on high ground and part of it strongly entrenched. Rosecrans, on the other hand, showed no inclination to recklessly throw his army against fortified field positions. He planned to use a number of feints to hold Bragg in place while turning his right flank. The maneuver would either result in a fight on Rosecrans' terms or Bragg's hurried withdrawal toward Chattanooga.[5]

Spread out on four roads and in five columns, the Army of the Cumberland set out to execute Rosecrans' long awaited plan. "On the 23d . . . I received an order from the major-general commanding the Twentieth Corps to hold my division in readiness to move on the following day at 5 A.M.., with twelve days' rations and at least six days' forage," wrote General Richard W. Johnson. General Willich reported that "my brigade was ordered to march from our old camp near Murfreesborough at 5 A.M.. on the 24th of June, at the head of the Second Division." But, as is the case more often than not, it turned into a hurry up and wait situation. Johnson explained in his report: "Some delay on the part of the troops which were to

---

3   Sinclair, letter, June 10, 1863.

4   Daniel, *Days of Glory, The Army of the Cumberland, 1861-1865*, 258, 261.

5   *Ibid.*, 266-267.

precede me delayed my movements until about 8 a. m., when I marched on the Shelbyville pike . . . preceded by five companies of the Thirty-ninth Indiana Volunteer Mounted Infantry, commanded by Col. T. J. Harrison." Willich confirmed: "By other commands with which our movements were combined, our march was delayed until 8 A. M., when the brigade followed the Shelbyville pike for some 6 or 8 miles, and then turned to the left on the road to Liberty Gap. Colonel Harrison being in advance with five companies of his mounted regiment (Thirty-ninth Indiana Volunteers), saved us a great deal of (for infantry) useless patrolling."[6]

In a letter to his father, a Company I soldier gave his account of the first day of the campaign. He wrote:

About 8 o'clock on the evening of June 23, we received orders to get ready to march at 11 o'clock the same evening. At the time designated we were ready and marched, but only went some three miles to the headquarters of Gen. Johnson, as companies A and C of the Pioneer Brigade were detailed to go with his division of the army (which suited me as the 89th regiment is in the front Brigade of his Division, and I would then be near my own company, which I think is about right,) to repair bridges, fix railroad tracks, or do any other thing that may require the services of the Pioneer Brigade. We reached his headquarters about 2 A.M.., and throwing ourselves down by the roadside slept until morning.

June 24—We started at 5 o'clock in the morning and marched some ten miles without seeing any rebels, but about 1 P.M., our advance gobbled up a rebel out-post of four men, and shortly after that fighting commenced and was kept up all the afternoon, until it was so dark neither party could see to shoot. We drove the rebels some two miles during the afternoon. It is a great wonder to me that we ever got them as far as we did, as they had the advantage both in numbers and ground. The rebels were posted on both sides of the road running between two steep hills which were heavily timbered, and this gave them a good chance to skulk around and take every advantage that could be taken, while our troops had to climb the hills, over stumps and stones, and through brush, all the time the rebels shooting at them from every convenient hiding

---

[6] OR, Vol. 23, Pt. 1, 483, 486.

place. But not withstanding they had two to one in number, and so much the advantage in position, our troops cleaned them out and got possession of what is called Liberty Gap. During all this time it rained continually, which made it very disagreeable. Our loss during the skirmish and engagement was some sixty or seventy killed and wounded.[7]

Willich described his brigade's deployment: "At about 2 P.M. Colonel Harrison informed me that he was skirmishing with some 800 infantry. I ordered him to halt, advanced with the brigade, and, reaching the skirmish line, I deployed" the 15th Ohio to the right of the road, the 49th Ohio to the left of the road, and pushed skirmishers with support companies to the front. Behind these regiments, the 89th Illinois went off to the right while the 32nd Indiana moved to the left. Goodspeed's 1st Ohio Battery was "in reserve, beyond the reach of the enemy's fire."

After all were in position, Willich ordered an advance that drove the enemy's skirmishers "back on their reserves, which were posted on the crest of the hills forming the northern entrance of Liberty Gap." His trained military eye saw that "the enemy had a very strong, and, in front, [an] easily defended position." Willich further observed that the hills were "steep, to half their heights[,] open, then rocky and covered with woods." He then ordered his troops to test the enemy's "front to ascertain whether he would make a decided resistance, and found him in force and determined." Realizing that a frontal "attack was out of the question," and concluding, if ordered, he "would have had to pay 10 for 1," the Old Prussian opted to push the Forty-ninth Ohio more to the left and the Fifteenth Ohio more to the right, in an effort to flank the enemy. The Forty-ninth and Fifteenth Ohio respectively had five and eight companies deployed. The completed maneuver failed to reach the end of the enemy's lines, and then out of the blue, Colonel Gibson (Forty-ninth Ohio) reported his left was being outflanked. Reacting instinctively, Willich sent two companies from the Thirty-second Indiana to Gibson's aid, while he simultaneously ordered Colonel Thomas J. Harrison's, with five companies of mounted infantry, to protect the left flank. Harrison "went there in full gallop, and arrived just in time to drive

---

[7] *Amboy Times*, July 23, 1863.

back 200 infantry, who were advancing" on the Forty-ninth Ohio's left flank. Undeterred by the threat, the Buckeyes along with the two Hoosier companies proceeded, even while "under a murderous fire," to advance straight up the hill, driving the enemy before them. While Colonel Harrison's and his horsemen now outflanked the enemy, forcing the fleeing rebels to run right through their own "camp, with tables set."

Reinforcing Willich's attack, Johnson sent forward the Twenty-ninth Indiana and the Seventy-seventh Pennsylvania. Willich posted these regiments to the right of the Fifteenth Ohio, giving orders to either find a weak point or the end of the enemy's line, and then to take the crest of the hill. Once at the top they were to swing to the left and advance in the direction of the gap. On seeing the task accomplished, Willich advanced the Eighty-ninth Illinois and the Thirty-second Indiana through the gap.[8]

The Eighty-ninth that day, Colonel Hotchkiss wrote, supported the Fifteenth Ohio, remaining in reserve until the Buckeyes crested the hill in their immediate front. Soon after, Hotchkiss ordered the Railroaders up the hill where they relieved the Fifteenth and deployed skirmishers. Hotchkiss continued: "Meantime, the enemy having fallen back . . . my skirmishers were called in, and I moved by the left flank to and along the main road to Liberty Meeting House . . . ." The third brigade now passed through the first and took up the front. After this, Willich's men went into bivouac. The day ended with the Eighty-ninth suffering two casualties.[9]

Private Alfred D. French of Company A recalled the march to Liberty Gap. "On the evening of June 23 1863 the order came: "Be ready to march at 7 o'clock tomorrow morning, with three days rations in your haversacks, and 40 rounds of cartridges in your cartridge boxes. So the next morning we again started on the march." He remembered that "a little before noon we came to a farm where eight or ten men were engaged in harvesting a field of grain. We captured them and found them to be Confederate soldiers who had been detailed to help the farmers harvest their grain. So we invited them to eat dinner with us before they were sent back as prisoners."

---

8   *OR*, Vol. 23, Pt. 1, 486-487.
9   *OR*, Vol. 23, Pt. 1, 490.

On reaching the gap, French recounted it was "about two o'clock in the afternoon [when] we came upon the enemy in force. Then the trouble began. The Confederates were on the crest of a high ridge which was covered with trees, while the sloping sides were cultivated." He continued: "Our brigade was ordered to take possession of that hill. Now you will understand that was no enviable undertaking, but we must obey orders, and we did. In about three hours we not only occupied the hill, but their tents and much of the camp equipage which we found very convenient that night."[10]

George Berry jotted a few lines in his diary summarizing the day. "Forward movement of the Army of the Cumberland, left Murfreesboro at 5 o'clock, marched about six miles on the Shelbyville pike, and turned off and went about four miles to Liberty Gap when heavy skirmishing commenced. Quite a number killed and wounded, the bullets whistled over our heads pretty thick." While Corporal John Browning wrote that the column "got about 10 miles" when it ran into a brigade of enemy cavalry "and comenst fighting." He noted that "the three old regiments" were "put in the front," and "we was ordered to lay down behind a fence where the bullets came round pretty thick." But the din of battle and the zip of a minnie ball seemed to not bother Browning. "I and Charley Anderson both went to sleep while laying behind the fence."[11] The *Chicago Tribune* correspondent wrote that the enemy had been routed from Liberty Gap "by Willich's brigade of Johnson's division, which had the advance upon the dirt road, leading south through Middleburg [Millersburg] to the gap." He reported: "The position was closely contested by the enemy, who used artillery and musketry at a cost to us of about seventy-five killed and wounded. But, after two hours stout resistance, they were forced, by the skill and bravery of Willich's brave men to retire." Blessed with a good source of information, he continued: "McCook and Johnson were each upon the ground, but I am told that the immediate direction of affairs was safely given to Gen. W., who planned the attack and fought the troops." The

[10] French Memoirs.
[11] George H. Berry, diary entry for June 24, 1863, photocopy of original in possession of the author, hereafter cited as Berry diary. John Browning, letter, July 9, 1863.

reporter said that Colonel Hotchkiss's Railroad Regiment "did not closely engage, and got off consequently, with two wound[ed]: Wm. Lewis, Company C, slightly; Corporal [Henry H.]Warner [Company C] shot in the arm and thigh."[12]

*　　*　　*

By nightfall on June 24, Johnson's Division had control of Liberty Gap. A strong picket line was established at the southern entrance of the gap to keep watch on the enemy. It had been a long march and a hard fight, and when the army left Murfreesboro, the sky opened. "The day had been one of incessant rain, and it continued as unremitting through the night." Undeterred by the elements "the men, exhausted by the weary march through deep mud and the excitement incident to battle, raised their shelter tents, rolled themselves in their blankets, and though lying on the soaked ground, were soon oblivious to all things earthly." However, their rest was short. By 3:00 A.M.. on June 25, the division was awake and to arms, followed by a few hours wait before an aid bringing orders arrived. The corps commander, Major-General McCook, sent word for Willich to relieve Colonel Philemon P. Baldwin's brigade, taking responsibility for the front. Baldwin's pickets reported observing a concentration of the enemy; and as a consequence, McCook warned Willich to "guard against surprise." In fact, "positive information had been received during the night that the division of General [Patrick] Cleburne had reinforced the enemy, and that a stout resistance would be made to our further progress."[13]

In relieving Baldwin's third brigade, the Old Prussian placed the Thirty-second Indiana on the left and the Eighty-ninth Illinois on the right and held the Fifteenth and Forty-ninth Ohio in reserve. The Thirty-second's line ran across a valley, over the road running through the gap, and up a wooded hill where it connected with the Eighty-ninth's line, which stretched on to another hill. "I did not form the picket line as a mere line of observation," Willich later

---

12   *Chicago Tribune*, July 2, 1863.

13   Andreas, *History of Chicago*, 245-246; Dodge, *History of the Old Second Division, Army of the Cumberland*, 483-484; *OR*, Vol. 23, Pt. 1, 487.

wrote, "but as a sound skirmish line, with support companies and reserves." Colonel Hotchkiss described his regiment's position that morning. "I was ordered on picket on the right of the main road," he wrote, "near Mr. Field's house . . . the right of my line resting on the crest of one hill . . . and extending along said hill, thence crossing a wheat-field, and to and along the crest of an adjoining hill, near the main road, and connecting with the pickets of the 32nd Indiana, on my left." To the Eighty-ninth's front were two fields, one in wheat and the other in corn.[14]

Shortly the rebels appeared, and at once began probing the Federals' position, only to be quickly repulsed by Willich's reinforced picket line. "The enemy advanced continually, on different points . . . with from 30 to 50 skirmishers, supported by cavalry, that kept out of reach of our guns," stated Willich. Hotchkiss later reported that "about 10 A.M.. the enemy's cavalry and infantry appeared in considerable force at different points" on the Eighty-ninth's front, but "more particularly on the midway slope of an open wooded hill," opposite the right, "and commenced firing at long range." As noon approached, a strong line of rebel skirmishers moved to the foot of the hill held by the Thirty-second Indiana and the left three companies of the Eighty-ninth. After a sharp, half hour firefight, the butternut-clad infantry were driven back. The rebel skirmishers, Colonel Hotchkiss wrote, "Were repulsed with a considerable loss," and fell back to a ditch "masked by a willow copse". The Eighty-ninth's three front companies were Captain Rowell's Company C; Company A with Lieutenant George F. Robinson in temporary command; and Captain Whiting's Company G. Available for support were companies K (Blake), E (Kidder), D (Spink), and F (Dimick).[15]

In less than an hour, the regrouped rebels came forward again with a reinforced skirmish line leading a heavy column of infantry and a supporting battery. When the enemy finally commenced firing, Hotchkiss stated they receive "a heavy fire from our men." The rebel attack rushed on, even though it was under continuous fire, and "temporally secured lodgment at the foot of the hill" below

---

[14]   Andreas, *History of* Chicago, 246; OR, Vol. 23, Pt. 1, 487.

[15]   Andreas, *History of* Chicago, 246; OR, Vol. 23, Pt. 1, 487, 491.

the Railroaders' position. Colonel Hotchkiss ordered companies K, D, and F forward to support Captain Rowell's Company C, which was holding the critical spot where the Eighty-ninth's line joined with the Thirty-second Indiana. No sooner had the three companies gotten to the critical juncture then they were "heavily engaged with a confident and largely superior force." The enemy advanced "within 20 yards of the position, but failed to press back the determined Railroaders . . . ."[16]

It was around 3:00 P.M. Hotchkiss reported, and after more reinforcements, the rebels let out another yell and "again attempted to advance, but, from behind each tree, stump, log, and fence, the rapid fire and almost unerring aim of my men sent him back down the hill, to again advance with a like result." During this assault, Hotchkiss called up the last of his reserve, Company E commanded by Bruce H. Kidder. While coming forward, Captain Kidder observed two companies of enemy infantry moving across the field and heading to the right of the Eighty-ninth's position. Seeing the threat to the Railroader's flank, Kidder immediately reacted, using a hill for cover, moved his company 200 yards forward and to the right of the Federal line. The men formed behind a fence and out of sight of advancing rebels. Holding their fire until the enemy advanced to within 40 yards of their ambush, Kidder's men let loose a lethal volley, killing eight outright, one a major, and wounding thirty of the rebels. Taken by surprise the rebels "immediately broke and ran, and did not stop until they had reached the woods on the opposite side of the open field." The enemy skedaddled so fast that the second volley had little effect.[17]

By 3:30 P.M., Hotchkiss sent word back that the Eighty-ninth's cartridge boxes were nearly empty. The truth was that both of Willich's forward regiments were running out of ammunition. The Old General ordered the Fifteenth Ohio to come up and join the front line, dividing their ammunition with the Thirty-second Indiana and the Railroaders. Orders were also issued to empty the cartridge boxes of the wounded and killed. Willich continued to hold the

16   OR, Vol. 23, Pt. 1, 487, 491.
17   Andreas, History of Chicago, 246; Dodge, History of the Old Second Division of the Army of the Cumberland, 488; OR, Vol. 23, Pt. 1, 491.

Forty-ninth Ohio in reserve, but moved the regiment up closer and behind the center of the line. Goodspeed's battery came forward too, taking a position on a hill in the rear of the Union line, and opened on the rebel guns.[18]

The fight continued and showed no sign of letting up; when Willich again realized that his men were running out of ammunition. He now called the fresh Forty-ninth Ohio forward to relieve the Thirty-second Indiana. Colonel Gibson immediately consulted with General Willich, and the two discussed the option of attacking. Willich had recently originated and introduced into the brigade a movement where a regiment continued firing while advancing, and directed Gibson to try it. It was about 5 P.M. when the Buckeyes stepped out "in splendid style, through the open woods, received with cheers by the rest of the brigade." The German Hoosiers with or without ammunition fell in with the Forty-ninth as the regiment went forward. Gibson soon spotted the enemy directly in front. The rebels were moving down the road under the cover of their artillery when they veered off behind an orchard and some outbuildings. Here they were gathering for another attack. Receiving a smattering of shots from the enemy, Gibson commanded, "'Advance firing.'" The Forty-ninth "formed in four ranks as promptly as if on drill, and opened a terrible fire . . . ." The first rank delivered a volley. Then, in succession, the fourth, third, and took to the front and fired. By the third volley the enemy did not answer. Colonel Gibson reported: "the enemy was driven from his concealment and compelled to retreat before our fire, which was delivered with regularity and rapidity that no veterans could withstand."[19]

The Eighty-ninth came up to the Forty-ninth Ohio and took a position to the right of the Buckeyes. It was at this time that Sergeant George C. Sinclair of Company C was hit. Colonel Hotchkiss cited Sinclair as "conspicuous for gallantry" and wrote the sergeant was out in front leading the regiment when felled "by a musket ball through the chest." Hotchkiss explained the severely wounded Sinclair "refused to be carried from the field or even from under fire, saying 'Let me alone, and hold that fence,' and

---

[18] *OR*, Vol. 23, Pt. 1, 487-488, 491.
[19] *OR*, Vol. 23, Pt. 1, 488, 496-497.

then cheered the men on." With men falling throughout the fight, Colonel Hotchkiss observed that Chaplain Travis O. Spencer "was invariably at just the right spot to be useful, and was unremitting in his efforts in removing the wounded from the field and caring for them."[20]

With the rebels driven off, Brigadier General William P. Carlin's brigade moved up and relieved Willich's regiments. The Twenty-first Indiana was assigned to replace the Railroaders, and, as soon as they arrived, Hotchkiss ordered his companies to fall back. No sooner had the Eighty-ninth started for the rear; than the enemy, thinking the Federals were pulling back, rushed forward to take the hill. Hotchkiss wrote: "My men, with only from two to four rounds of cartridges, turned and made a dash at them, driving them out of the woods and across the fields on a double quick." With the rebels sent flying one last time, the Eighty-ninth retired to replenish their ammunition and recover from the shock of battle. Colonel Hotchkiss duly noted: "All the officers and men engaged behaved like veterans, the officers acting with deliberation and using good judgment in their duties; the men steady, taking good aim, and shooting with good effect."[21]

"Willich's Brigade, holding a position in Liberty Gap, had heavy skirmishing with the enemy during the whole of the 25th," reported the Independence Day edition of the *Chicago Tribune*. "At length, in the evening," the correspondent continued, "the rebels made a general attack, rattling shot and shell upon our men like hail. The brigade stood its ground, however, fighting until exhausted of ammunition and reinforced by Johnson's 2d brigade . . . ." The *Tribune* reporter filed an annotated casualty list for the Eighty-ninth, showing two killed, ten wounded, none missing.[22]

The "Railroader" with the Pioneer Brigade either watched the engagement or more likely listened from a distance. He wrote his father what he knew; some of which failed to match other eyewitness accounts of the fight.

---

[20]   Andreas, *History of Chicago*, 246; *OR*, Vol. 23, Pt. 1, 491-492.

[21]   Dodge, *History of the Old Second Division, Army of the Army* Cumberland, 493; *OR*, 491-492.

[22]   *Chicago Tribune*, July 4, 1863.

June 25—Skirmishing commenced early in the morning and was kept up all day long. Our artillery did not do much, as they could not get a chance to without endangering our men. The principal [sic] part of the fighting was done by the Infantry. Our boys drove them about the same distance they did the day before. The 89th Ills. and 15th Ohio Regiments made a charge through a rebel camp, and the way—. They left everything, which our boys coolly appropriated to their own use. Our loss was about 130 killed and wounded. The rebel loss, during the two days engagement, as we have since learned from their papers, was 500 killed and wounded. It rained most of the night and nearly all day, which made the roads almost impassable. Our forces captured some 50 or 75 prisoners. Company I, 89th Ills. did not lose a man, although they were in the muss both days.[23]

"Out on picket, we have been under heavy fire most of the day," George Berry noted in his diary for June 25. "Quite a number of killed and wounded in our regiment. Captain Blake mortally wounded. Company G has come out all right so far. It has rained most of the time since we left Murfreesboro. Went into camp about sundown." Having been ill off and on since September, Corporal Browning was in his first fight. He wrote his wife saying, "I got a chance to try my hand but don't want to try it again. Since when I shoot a gun I'd like to have time to take a sight, but there we had to shoot as quick as we could, look[ing] out from behind a tree." That night, Browning "went over the ground and looked at the dead and wounded, and told his wife that "if I ever wanted home that was the time."[24]

The next day, June 26, remained quiet except for the occasional firing from the pickets. Our "Railroader," detailed to the Pioneer Brigade, wrote: "There is no fighting to day as the killed are being buried and the wounded are being sent to back to the hospital in Murfreesboro." Official causalities for Willich's brigade stood at 23 killed and 72 wounded. "The loss of the enemy in these actions is unknown," Dodge wrote in the division history, but he noted that "seventy-five of his dead were left inside of our lines. The citizens

---

[23]   *Amboy Times*, July 23, 1863

[24]   Berry, diary, June 25, 1863; Browning, letter, July 9, 1863.

in the neighborhood reported that his wounded were estimated at from four to five hundred."[25]

The fighting that took place on June 24 and 25 was over, but the picket line could still be a dangerous place; especially when the lines remained close enough for both sides to call out to the other. Hearing this story from his regimental colleagues, our Company I soldier wrote the following to his father: "The 89th Ills. were on picket, and so near the rebel pickets that they would blackguard each other, and then shoot at the first one that stuck his head from behind a tree." He gave this exchange between one of the Eighty-ninth's pickets and a rebel across from him: "'I say, Yank, how are you getting along at Vicksburg?' Federal picket replies, 'Tip top—Gen. Grant has superceded Gen. Pemberton.' Rebel—'It's a d—d lie—'and just as Mr. Rebel said this a bullet from the Federal picket whizzed very close to his head, which put an end to the conversation for the time being."[26]

* * *

Rosecrans never made it clear in his orders, but the main flanking column was probably Thomas' Fourteenth Corps, which headed down the Manchester Pike toward Hoover's Gap. Manchester lay 10 miles from the gap's southern end. And from Manchester it was a 12-mile march to Tullahoma, Bragg's main depot and the rear of the Confederate army. With Manchester as the initial objective, Thomas' column set off with Wilder's brigade of mounted infantry supported by Lilly's battery leading the way. Armed with Spencer repeating rifles Wilder's men literally blew through the gap, sending the lone rebel cavalry regiment flying back and out the other end. By 2:00 P.M. on June 24, Wilder reigned in and waited for Thomas' to come forward. The halted bluecoats were soon under attack by a brigade of Confederate infantry. The counterattack failed to dislodge the stubborn Wilder, who with his advantage in firepower and Lilly's guns stopped the rebels in their tracks.

[25] *Amboy Times*, July 23, 1863; *OR*, Vol. 23, Pt. 1, 422; Dodge, *History of the Old Second Division, Army of the Cumberland*, 499.

[26] *Amboy Times*, July 23, 1863.

With the way open to Bragg's rear, McCook received instructions to leave a division to hold Liberty Gap and shift his other two divisions east to Hoover's Gap. "Just at dark we had marching orders. We had orders to build large fires to deceive the enemy," George Berry noted in his diary. About 8:00 P.M. on the night of June 26, Johnson's Division of McCook's Corps marched back the way they came some four or five miles, and then took another road leading to Manchester. All told they marched bout eight miles before camping for the night in a corn field.[27]

Using the penname, "Railroader," solder described the march to Tullahoma.

At 6 o'clock A.M.. we started again, and after reaching the Manchester Pike found the road much better, but bad enough, I assure you. I thought that I had seen bad roads in Illinois, but now I [know] that I was mistaken, as the roads over which we passed since I started from Murfreesboro completely knock the sucker—orns off. If you imagine yourself traveling in a mud holewith the mud 1 to 9 feet deep on an average, you can form some idea of the roads in Tennessee, or a portion of them at least the ones we traveled—or rather waded—through.

June 28—To-day we marched about 14 miles and camped near Duck River. We did get into camp 4 in the morning. The reason was the artillery and baggage wagons got stuck in the mud about once—if not more—in every 40 rods, which detained us until near morning. Had not seen any rebels for the last two days; the reason was that a large force had driven them out of the Gap, (Hoover's Gap,) and they are now retreating. Nothing of importance has transpired during our march to-day.

June 29—Nothing doing to-day but drying blankets, cleaning guns, &c. We are about one mile and a half from Manchester, a small place now occupied by Federal troops, the rebels having evacuated the place, or rather was drove out of town. The weather [is] more pleasant to-day.

June 30—What are we waiting for I do not know unless it is to let to let the teams rest, and the men recruit up before we starting

---

27 Daniel, *Days of Glory, The Army of the Cumberland, 1861-1865*, 267-269; Van Horne, *History of the Army of the Cumberland Its Organization, Campaigns, and Battles*, I: 303-304; Berry, diary, June 26, 1863; *Amboy Times*, July 23, 1863.

up on a march. The sick and all unable to march are being sent back, and all baggage that is not actually needed is to be left behind, as so many teams are only a bother to the army, and now we have no forage for them. Rained hard to-day. Reports from the front say that Bragg has a force of from 35 to 50,000, and will make a stand at Tullahoma.[28]

Company H Second Lieutenant William Harkness had this to say: "The next day after the battle we lay still as the rebs had feel back and it was not our orders to follow them further in that direction. It was another very wet day. We spent it the best way we could trying to keep dry." Once it became dark, Harkness explained: "We built up good fires to make the rebels think we were going to stay all night but instead of staying we quietly left and marched nearly all night knee deep in mud and water having to wade cricks which were roaring like rivers owing to the heavy rains. Sometime after midnight, we stopped and rested and then started again." Digressing for a moment, Harkness wrote: "It would take me some time to write all the particulars of that hard march from the gap to Manchester." However, he continued: "The night before we reached the latter place we marched all night after marching all day and being on picket the night before. It was very hard, yet we lived through it. But a more tired and muddy set of men I don't think ever was seen than we were when we arrived near Manchester, about daylight and lay down on the wet ground for an hour's rest."

For some the exertion became too much, and the next day Lieutenant Harkness was put in charge "of about thirty men who had become unable to stand the marching" and were being sent back to Murfreesboro—a distance of thirty miles. Along with the men "a large train of wagons went back with all the extra baggage, knapsacks, etc." A disgusted Harkness commented: "It was all thrown away before we got half way, as the roads were almost impossible. Thousands of dollars worth of property was wasted on this trip."[29]

In his matter-of-fact manner George Berry told Harriet what was done with the poor enlisted man's baggage. He wrote that "it has rain[ed] pretty much all the time we have bin here." And, as a

28 *Amboy Times*, July 23, 1863.
29 Harkness, incomplete letter, probably July 5, 1863.

consequence of the rain and the ensuing mud, he expalined: "I have lost my knapsack in this trip. We hade ower knapsack[s] hauled. The teames all got stalled and they had to take them out and pile them up and burn them." He then explained: "In my knapsack I hade one shirte, one paire of stocking, one towell, one pillow, one bible, one paire of draw[er]s burnt up. I think that I shall have my shirt and stocking[s] and draw[er]s replace to me agin. The rest I shall lose," he concluded. Buckley also sent word home about this incident. "The roads got so bad that the teams could not haul all the rations and our knapsacks too, and as they thought we could not eat the knapsacks, and they had to lighten the wagons. They had better throw the knapsacks out, which they did and put them in a pile and burned them." He went on. "I am sorry they had to be burnt as all my clothing and blanket was in there. I have always carried your likeness and the boys likeness with me, but this time I left them in my knapsack for safety."[30]

Not all knapsacks were consumed by fire; Company A's met a different fate. "When we left Murfreesboro on our march we left our knapsacks to be brought on by wagons," Private Alfred French recalled. "But the roads were very bad, and one day coming to a bad mud hole they piled the contents of two of the wagons into it to make the road passable for the wagon train." However, his story did not end here. "Some time later, the 75th Ill. marching by, one of the men saw a Bible sticking in the mud. He got it out [and] found my name, company, [and] regiment in it, and brought it to me as they marched through Tullahoma. And I have it yet."[31]

In long a narrative letter to his father our Company I infantryman continued his daily account of the campaign.

On July 1, Much to his relief, Johnson's Division resumed their march.Our forces started from Duck River at 10 o'clock. Had went about six miles beyond the town of Manchester, when we heard the rebels evacuated Tullahoma, and our troops had taken possession of the place, and had also captured several siege guns.The roads are better from Manchester than they were before we came to that place.

---

[30] Berry, letter, July 13, 1863; Buckley, letter, July 21, 1863.

[31] French. Memoir.

July 2d.—To day we have been out foraging for meat and Corn, succeeding in bringing in some 4 or 5 cows and 3 hogs, together with some onions, corn &c. We arrived at Tullahoma, Tennessee last night at 11 o'clock, found that the rebels had certainly gone, and left some 7 large siege guns, and a large lot of shot and shell, together with some rice, beans . . . The rebels had the town very well fortified with a breast work of earth and logs all around the town, and two large forts nearer the town, where they had very large guns planted, but they were obliged to them, but before going they spiked the guns and burned the carriages, so that they are useless for the present, but they can be fixed very easily, and then they will do some tall shooting, two are 6 inch rifle cannon, and the others are smooth bore.—The rebels had to get out, in such a hurry that they left all their tents &c. standing, and some all done up ready to load on to their wagons. I think we must have taken at least a 1000 large tents that never cost them less than $100 each, Lieut. Hartsough and myself got a very good one which we are now a using, which comes in play, as our other one was sent back, and if we had not got it, we would have had to use our little "dog tents," which are a poor excuse in wet weather.[32]

Seventy years later Alfred French still had a vivid memory of the march to Tullahoma. "That night we gathered fuel and built large camp fires. Then about 9 o'clock we quietly started . . . and marched until one o'clock, when we camped for a few hours rest. Then we went on to Hoover's Gap. We hoped for a day of rest here but no we must go on picket. And when we came back the next morning, the order was 'We march at.'" French continued: "Now it is one thing to order a body of troops to start on a march at a certain hour, and, sometimes, quite another to get them started at that time. Anyway it was nearly noon when we really started on what turned out to be the hardest days march I ever made." Even as an elderly man the details of that march remained clear.

We marched very leisurely for two hours then they began to hurry us, and it was Hot. Hot. Hot. I was ready to stop at five o'clock, but no it was forward. Hurry up. Six, seven, eight, [and] no sign of stopping, nine and "Halt." And then the order was given 'One hour

---

32   *Amboy Times*, July 23, 1863.

for coffee, then four miles to camp.' At ten we started again, and at the same time it began to rain. I kept agoing until one o'clock. Then I said to Walker,'I cannot go another step.' 'That's just my fix,' said he. We stepped a few feet to the side of the road, and I spread my blanket on the ground. We laid down and he spread his blanket over us, and we lay there until eight in the morning.

I think there were only 16 in the regiment who [went] on until they reached the place where we were expected to camp, which proved to be ten miles from where we made our coffee, instead of four.[33]

Jotting in his pocket journal, George Berry briefly described the march to Tullahoma. "We have laid in camp today. Just at dark we had marching orders. We had orders to build large fires to deceive the enemy, and commenced marching. [We] went about five miles through mud and water. We had a hard march. Stopped about—o'clock," he penned for Friday, June 26. On Saturday he scrawled: "Started again at five. We struck the Manchester pike, Marched through Hoover's Gap, and went in camp about five o'clock. The rebels had a strong position here." Sunday he wrote: "Our regiment was out on picket last night. All was quiet. 12 o'clock marched about five miles. About twenty-five miles from Murfreesboro. Rained this forenoon." Monday, June 29, he noted that "we marched until three o'clock this morning, through rain and mud. We had a very hard time of it. Went in camp close to Duck Creek and about two miles from Manchester." For the first of July, he entered: "Left camp about 11 o'clock and arrived at Tullahoma about 11 o'clock this evening. The rebels evacuated this place so we did not have a chance to give them a—. Very warm first of July.[34]

After their arrival late on July 1, the Railroaders remained at Tullahoma until August 16. Once settled in, letters were sent back to Illinois detailing the two-day dustup at Liberty Gap. In a brief letter to his father Lieutenant Dimick described the engagement.

We left Murfreesboro, June 24th, and our brigade had a very hard fight. The rebels had a very strong position, but after three

---

[33] French Memoir.

[34] Berry, diary, June 26 through 29, 1863 and July 1, 1863.

hours' fighting, we succeeded in routing them. We had about 50 men wound[ed] and killed in the three hour's fight.

On the 25th our brigade stood the brunt of the fight and in so doing lost thirteen men and one officer during the afternoon. I had one man wounded and he is reported dead. His name is B. Cook, of Hampton. There were only four companies of our regiment that suffered any [causalities]. My boys fought nobly.[35]

The officer killed was twenty-nine-year-old Captain Herbert M. Blake of Company K. Shot in the abdomen and mortally wounded, the former painter for the Galena and Chicago Union Railroad died the following morning." Colonel Hotchkiss said of him: "In his death the service loses a gallant and excellent officer and society a Christian and accomplished gentleman." Three other Eighty-ninth soldiers died that day. Both Private I. N. Bayless of Company D and First Sergeant David H. Griggs of Company C were mortally wounded, while Company K Sergeant Sandford H. Stetson was killed in action.[36]

In a letter dated July 6, Captain E. T. Wells, formerly of Company F and now the Assistant Commissary of Musters for Johnson's Division, wrote to Lieutenant James F. Copp who was on medical leave in Rock Island. Lieutenant Copp in turn shared the letter with the *Argus*. The newspaper's editor noted that "Capt. Wells takes no credit to himself—says he was not in the line of battle but gives great credit to all his men." Wells said this about the fight on the June 25.

The 89th and 32d regiments had the front of the picket line and held against Liddell's brigade of 3,500 men, and never yielded an inch of ground. About 4 P.M. the 15th and 49th relieved the 32d, the 89th still bravely holding its ground until 6 P.M., when it was relieved by the 21st. The conduct of the 89th, and especially of our brave Rock Island county boys, elicits the highest praise. It was the hardest fighting the army had, to get into Tullahoma. The division lost 233 killed and wounded, out of 2,800 engaged. Not a man or musket was 'missing in action.' The loss of the 89th was comparatively light owing to the fact that they had better cover and were better instructed in skirmishing.

---

[35]   *Rock Island Weekly Union*, July 22 and August 5, 1863.

[36]   *OR*, Vol. 23, Pt. 1, 492; *Adjutant General's Report*, V: 269, 271, and 284.

Gen. Willich was extravagant in his praise of the 89th. He said: 'Poys, I wish you was all curls, den I would marry you everyone.'

Maj. Williams and Lieut. Dimick received honorable mention in the colonel's report, which they richly deserve.

Editor Danforth also included part of the Captain Wells' letter, updating Lieutenant Copp on the company's missing and wounded. "'All of the boys are now here, except for Cox, who I hear, is dead and Weaver of whom I have no certain information. Poor Burt Cook is badly hurt. He is one of my best boys.'"[37]

By July 21 the *Argus* could report: "Lieut. Copp telegraphed to Murfreesboro on Saturday, for Burt Cook's mother, to ascertain if he was living, and has received the gratifying news that he is living and is better." Copp found out that "his wound is a bad one, the ball entering his right side and coming out under his left arm—but hopes are entertained of his recovery."[38]

For reasons unknown, George Berry said little about the fight at Liberty Gap to his wife. In fact he may not have mentioned it at all to Harriet. It was not until his third letter after the battle that he touched on it, and this may have come about only because of a question by Harriet. He explained: "Johnson['s] Division did not go through Shelbyville. We went to Liberty Gap. There we had a fight. We hade four killed [and] eight wounded in our Regiment. Our Division lost killed and wounded was two hundred. We came through Hoovers Gap on to Manchester and then to Tullahoma. We are still at this place and I hope we shall stay here till cool weather." He said this about the march. "It comenced to rain the day we started from Murfreesboro. It rained five dayes rite along. We had deepe mud and water to wade through [and] some places it was foot deape. Take it all around it was the hardest time we have had since we have bin in the service. I came out safe, hartey, and well."[39]

Private Joseph Buckley's letter demonstrated how deep duty can be ingrained in some men. "I was attacked with a very severe

---

[37] *Argus*, July 17, 1863. [Washing ton R. Cox died March 6, 1863 at Annapolis, Maryland. Addison Weaver died on February 14, 1863 while a prisoner at Richmond, Virginia.]

[38] *Argus*, July 21, 1863.

[39] Berry, letter, July 25, 1863.

diarrhea which turned in a few days to bloody flux. I was just getting well when we left Murfreesboro, and I reported myself ready for duty," he told his wife. Taken ill three weeks before and still under Dr. Tuttle's care, Buckley was unfit to march when he left Murfreesboro. But as he explained, "I thought we were going to make a forward movement, and I was bound not to be left behind as long as I could set one foot after the other." It was about noon when he gave out and could not take another step. "I was so weak and the roads were heavy as it rained all day and they were badly cut up." When Buckley had fallen out of the column, the surgeon approached, told him he looked faint, and asked how he was. Buckley told him, and based on that, the surgeon allowed him to "ride for about two hours in the ambulance." Buckley informed Mary: "When we came up with the Rebs, I then got out and went to my company, where I have been ever since, for I felt new life come into me as there was a pretty good prospect for a fight." Buckley concluded: "You will have seen what I wrote James [his brother] about the fight at Liberty Gap. It was just before we got to Liberty Gap that I got out of the ambulance. I will tell you the particulars when I come home. I have not taken any medicine for more than a week."[40]

Twenty-five days had passed since Sergeant George Sinclair was seriously wounded while at the forefront of a charge on the June 25. Now a patient at one of the hospitals in Murfreesboro, Sinclair penned a short letter to his wife.

Today is Sunday [July 19] and I am sitting up in bed to write this to you to let you know that I am doing tip top that is I am gaining rapidly. I was dressed and downstairs this forenoon and what is better than all [that], the doctor told me yesterday that if nothing sets me back, that I would be able to start for Home in a week from tomorrow, Monday.

Oh how I long for the time to arrive and I wish that the journey was over with for I dread it. But I do so want to be with you. It seems as if I never should get there.

Mother is here with me most of the time. I am treated much differently since she came, being put into a room alone so that she can be with me. Then I am away from the stench of the ward, which

---

was enough to almost suffocate one where I was. Then they are very kind in the kitchen and allow mother to make anything she wishes for me. Then there is a host of women that come in to see her and always have something good for me. So you see my Dear Franky that I am very much favored all around.

My arm begins to ache so I shall have to knock off writing for this time sending much love to all with much more and many kisses for yourself and little Gertie . . . . [41]

Sergeant Sinclair, the former Milwaukee Railroad engineer who had come to regret his enlistment, was a hero. In January he had written his wife stating that he had "been deceived in the object of this war and swindled into enlisting to preserve the Union when in fact it was only a cloak to raise men to fight" the abolition battles. Only Sinclair knew why he was out in front and leading the counterattack that afternoon. For this meritorious act, he was promoted to First Sergeant of Company C. But in reality, his war was over. For on October 3, 1863, he was discharged as a result of the wounds he received at Liberty Gap.[42]

*　　*　　*

The first week of July 1863 brought hope that the war could soon be coming to an end. At least that is how many soldiers interpreted the recent events. "We have good news from ower armies," wrote George Berry. "Vicksburg is owers and Lee has bin drove back. We have Bragg to the Tennessee River. While we have bin here at Tullohoma there has bin a thousand five hundred that have deserted Bragg['s] army. They are pretty much all Tennessee men." He confided to Harriet, "Ower government, I think is coming out all right. We must keepe up good courage. We may see one [an]other yet." Expressing his steadfast faith, George told his wife, "I still put my trust in the Lorde. I should feel lonesom if the Lorde was to foresake me, but I know that he has not. I feel that the Lorde is [with] me on the march to the battle field and on the battle ground." Four days later George wrote that the "secesh is about played out in

---

41   Sinclair, letters, January 27 and July 19, 1863.
42   *Adjutant General's Report*, V: 268.

the south west." On July 25, he added, "I think the backbone of the Rebellion is broke."[43]

"What glorious news we have just received from Vicksburg. Vicksburg surrendered on the 4th of July," wrote a jubilant Joseph Buckley. "Our brigade was all called out under arms to receive the news, and there has been quite a number of blank cartridges fired from the cannon in honor of the occasion." That was not all the good news. There was even more reason for celebration. "They also gave us the intelligence that Meade has taken 20,000 prisoners from Lee's Army; and you need not fear for our army, for old Rosie is the man, and he has got just the right kind of men to go through fire and water."[44]

Two weeks passed and a still excited Joseph Buckley jotted his thoughts to Mary. "What do you think of the success of the Unions forces over the Southern forces?" He proceeded to answer his own question. "I expect to hear in a few days of the fall of Charleston. I think the Southern Confederacy is going to the "Dogs" pretty fast. We soldiers all feel first rate with regard to the future prospect of the war. Old Bragg is afraid of Rosecrans. I don't think he will ever give us Battle any more." He still had more to say. "We received good news here yesterday about John Morgan. It was telegraphed to Johnson's Head Quarters that Morgan and his forces, with the exception of about three hundred, were captured with all his artillery, and the three hundred are where they cannot get a way; so much for going north. I wish some more of them would go north." Before posting his letter, Buckley added the latest information. "There was another dispatch arrived today confirming the capture of John H. Morgan, the Guerilla Chief of the Rebel Confederacy. I hope they will keep him in a safe place, if they don't hang him.[45]

Morgan's Raid as it came to be known began July 8 when Brigadier General John Hunt Morgan's Confederate cavalry crossed the Ohio River into Indiana in an impetuous invasion of the North. Easily brushing aside hastily gathered Hoosier militia, the rebel raiders spread fear and panic as they rode through southeastern

---

[43]   Berry, letters, July 13, 17, and 25, 1863.

[44]   Buckley, letter, July 7, 1863.

[45]   Buckley, letter, July 21, 1863.

Indiana. Crossing into southwestern Ohio on July 13, Morgan was now pursued by organized Federal troops. The chase came to an end on July 26 when he and the remnant of command were surrounded and surrendered.[46]

When George Berry wrote these words in July 1863, they more-than-likely reflected what most men in his regiment thought. "I have seene harde times since [I] came in the army, but the way things are turning I don't regret the day that I enlisted."[47]

* * *

George Berry put forth the latest camp rumor in a letter to Harriet: "There is some talk that ower Brigade will be mounted on horses and be drill[ed] as same as cavalry. But when we go in to a fight we hafture dismount and fight till we drive them and then we mount ower horses [an] put after them. One man can holde foure horses when we dismount to go in to a fight." Ten days later he wrote again "ower brigade is going to be mounted on horses, so you see that the Rebels will hafture look out now."[48]

Sergeant George Sinclair had written his wife on June 10 that the Eighty-ninth might become mounted infantry. He also had heard that the army would "send one commissioned officer, one non-commissioned and one private home to see about fitting our regiment up with conscripts and select horses, etc." Sinclair added, "I don't want to raise any false hopes with you as to my coming home but if everything turns out as it is rumored, why I stand as good a chance as anyone for these three each are to be sent from each company, and I shall try my best to be one from this company . . . ."[49]

What had been rumored for weeks came true in mid-July when orders were issued for the rest of Willich's Brigade to be mounted. "I understand to day that five officers are going north to get new recruit[s] for ower Regiment," George Berry informed Harriet. "It

[46] Long, *The Civil War Day by Day*, 381-391.
[47] Berry, letter, July 17, 1863.
[48] Berry, letter, June 5, 1863, June 15, 1863.
[49] Sinclair, letter, June 10, 1863.

may be that Lieutenant Howell or Capt. Whiting may go. If they go, I want you to send by them some black threade and one hankerchief. I lost my hankerchief the other day. I hade a hole in my pocket." Four days passed and he wrote again telling his wife that "we shall git ower pay in a [few] dayes." He then interjected. "There was [an] order came around that five commissioned officers should go north and git new recruits to fill up the Regiment to twelve hundred. I understand that Lieut. Howell will go out of ower Company. If he does I shall send my money by him." [50]

The paymaster did indeed arrive at the camp of the Eighty-ninth, resulting in greenbacks being sent back to families in Illinois. The August 1, *Rock Island Argus* posted this note: "Lieut. James F. Copp, Co. F, 89th Ill. Vols. is in receipt of a sum of money for a number of families belonging to his company. They can get the money by calling on him in this city."

Five days later the *Argus* reported that Orderly Sergeant James Johnston also of "Co. F, 89th Ill. Vol., arrived home last evening, on detached service. He is in good health, and says our boys are well and in fine spirits." Major Williams preceded Sergeant Johnston by a week in getting back to Illinois and one of his visits while home was with Colonel Myron S. Barnes, the editor of the staunch Republican newspaper, *The Rock Island Union*. While conversing with Barnes on July 29, Williams gave the former colonel of the Thirty-seventh Illinois both an update on the war and a scoop on the Eighty-ninth. The *Union* editor reiterated much of the conversation with Williams to his readers. He could report that the Rock Island company was in good health, but somewhat depleted, numbering 40 men fit for duty. Barnes wrote that Major Williams is looked well, and gave encouraging news about the Army of the Cumberland. Williams updated the editor on the current military situation, informing him that "Rosecrans was at Tullahoma when he left, but was expecting to move up to Dechard Station on the railroad, and was only waiting the completion of the bridge over Elk river. Bragg and his forces were at Chattanooga and all the way along to Atlanta." The big news, however, for the Eighty-ninth, Major Williams told the editor was that their brigade was soon to be mounted and that the horses

---

[50]   Berry, letter, July 13, 1863.

were now on the way. Barnes injected: "We presume there are not many of the boys who will find fault with that arrangement."[51]

Special Order No. 193 had been issued July 27, 1863 and handed to Colonel Hotchkiss. Rosecrans' Chief of Staff, General James A. Garfield wrote that Hotchkiss was authorized to inform all parties that his "Regiment and Brigade will immediately be mounted, and as soon as practicable furnished with repeating rifles. Horses are now being purchased for that purpose." Rosecrans entrusted the project to Hotchkiss knowing that he "would push it forward with the utmost vigor," getting the job done as soon as possible. Hotchkiss was given specific instructions, ordering him to distribute his "force in such numbers and localities as may be deemed best for speedily procuring recruits, place each squad under a commissioned officer or non-comm. officer from whom you will require a report of his progress every third day." Garfield specified that Hotchkiss "proceed without delay to Springfield;" present his orders to the Governor; and seek his assistance in executing the order.[52]

On August 3, the *Rock Island Argus* ran an announcement that "Col. C. T. Hotchkiss, of the 89th Illinois, or railroad regiment, arrived in Chicago on Friday last [July 31]." The article confirmed what its rival, the *Union,* had published earlier and that was the regiment was to be mounted. The *Argus* stated: "Col. Hotchkiss, with a detail of officers and men, has been ordered to repair hither for the purpose of procuring horses and equipment. Our county has one company in the regiment—the one raised by Major Williams."[53]

The August 11 edition of the *Argus* ran a lengthy description of what heretofore had been only a news item of a few lines. More than likely editor Danforth, in an effort to keep pace with the rival *Union*, decided to write a longer and a very favorable article kicking off the local squad's recruitment effort.

The piece began by noting that Orderly Sergeant James Johnston now in Rock Island had received written notice from

51   *Rock Island Weekly Union*, July 29, 1863.
52   J. A. Garfield, order to Colonel C. T. Hotchkiss, July 27, 1863, Record Group 301, Illinois State Archives.
53   *Rock Island Argus*, August 3, 1863.

Colonel Hotchkiss directing him "to enlist a few good men as volunteers." Danforth pointed out that "this is the only regiment recruiting for mounted infantry in this state . . . and "is to be armed with the celebrated Spencer rifle." Just as important an enticement was the bounty offered—$100 and $25 that would be paid in advance. "Veteran volunteers—those who have been in the service nine months or more, and been honorably discharged, will receive a bounty of $400!" Twenty-five dollars of which would be payable in advance, and the balance in installments. The editor stated that these were the highest bounties being paid. And the attractions just kept coming. Volunteers would be "subsisted at the expense of the government from the day they enlist, and draw pay from that day, and will be furnished transportation to Chicago, where they will be examined, mustered in and draw their advance pay and clothing, and be sent forward to the regiment. They will enlist for the regiment and can, when they arrive there, join any company they please. The termis for three years unless sooner discharged, but they will undoubtedly be discharged with the balance of the regiment."

Danforth could not lay it on thick enough and wrote: "The 89th is one of the finest regiments in the service, and has the best name of any regiment in Rosecrans' department. Our fellow-citizen, W. D. Williams, is major of the regiment, and we have the finest company in this regiment—Capt. E. T. Wells' company, of which L. F. Dimick is 1st Lieut. and James Copp 2nd Lieut." He summarized by stating: "Here is a fine chance to join a splendid regiment, with fresh horses, new arms, and brave and accomplished officers, and we hope it will be embraced by all who wish to aid in putting down the rebellion."[54]

Two months later the *Chicago Evening Journal* carried a two-paragraph piece lending support to what appears to be Hotchkiss' stalled venture. The reporter had this to say: "Col. C. T. Hotchkiss, of the 89th Illinois (Railroad) regiment, who has been detailed on recruiting service by Gen. Rosecrans, and who opened his recruiting office in this city in August, has been remarkably successful thus far." Up to date he has enlisted and "sent forward to

---

[54] *Rock Island Argus*, August 11, 1863.

his regiment 200 men . . . ." The writer continued: "Col. Hotchkiss, in an advertisement in today's JOURNAL, offers bounties for recruits—$300 for new recruits and $400 for re-enlisting veterans. These are tempting inducements, and the Colonel will doubtless soon secure the additional 200 men he requires." And he concluded by stating that "the 89th is one of the best regiments in the noble Army of the Cumberland, and is soon to be mounted. Col. Hotchkiss' office is at 61 Clark street."[55]

The Eighty-ninth never became a mounted infantry outfit, and Hotchkiss' advertisement and the *Journal* article appeared to be a last ditch effort to revive a dying project. Rosecran's defeat at Chickamauga and eventual dismissal as the commander of the Army of the Cumberland may have also figured in the idea's demise. After spending five months marching about East Tennessee, Private Easton Weaver sent a letter to Adjutant General Fuller asking for a ruling on his situation. He spelled out that while considering enlisting in the cavalry, he eventually signed up in Rock Island on August 27 for the mounted infantry. The 29-year-old farmer sought assurances from the recruiting officer, and he received a written note from Colonel Hotchkiss explaining General Rosecrans' order that the Eighty-ninth regiment was to be immediately mounted. In his reply, an offended Hotchkiss wrote: "I question very much whether men who suppose that a Colonel would deliberately tell a lie for the purpose of getting recruits—would make good solgers. Every thing stated in our advertisement is true." Nevertheless Weaver proceeded to plead his case. "Now as a solger of Illinois I ask you to see that I get justice done acording to the regulations for Enlisting vol. I am an un Educated man but I know that to cary a musket & walk is not what I enlisted for."[56]

Private Weaver received a reply from Adjutant General Fuller. Whether he was satisfied or not is lost to time. And he probably was not, for if he was looking to be discharged or transferred to the cavalry, that did not happen. He continued to serve with Company F

[55] *Chicago Evening Journal*, October 7, 1863.
[56] Easton Weaver, letter to Adjutant General Fuller, April 11, 1864, Record Group 301, Illinois State Archives.

and walked many more miles. When the regiment was mustered out in June 1865, the spunky Private Weaver was among those recruits with time still to serve. These men were transferred to the Fifty-ninth Illinois and sent to Texas. He was discharged there on December 8, 1865.[57]

---

[57]   *Adjutant General's Report,* V: 277.

CHAPTER 10

"TELL MY PARENTS THAT I DIED FOR MY COUNTRY."

Despite Halleck's exhortations to continue pressing the enemy, General Rosecrans halted the Army of the Cumberland at Tullahoma. And true to nature, he informed Washington that the advance would resume when the railroad was up and running to the Tennessee River, corn was ripe in the fields, and his flanks supported. For the next six weeks Rosecrans set about repairing bridges, stockpiling supplies, and establishing forward supply depots. During the lull, Rosecrans and Halleck debated strategy. Rosecrans wholeheartedly agreed with Halleck's orders sending Burnside into East Tennessee to capture Knoxville. The move protected the Army of the Cumberland's left flank. However, Rosecrans argued that he should hold fast until Grant came over from Vicksburg to support him, bringing two Federal armies to bear on Bragg and increasing the odds of success. Tired of the back and forth debate and down to his last option, Halleck on August 5 used his rank as general-in-chief and issued orders to both Rosecrans and Burnside to advance against the enemy and secure Tennessee.

From Tullahoma, Bragg had fallen back to fortified Chattanooga and awaited Rosecrans' next move. The Confederate commanders briefly contemplated another offensive into Tennessee, but concluded that they lacked the manpower for an offensive. On the other hand, Rosecrans realized that Chattanooga was not an easy target. The terrain from the east and north could be easily defended. So, after studying the region's topography, Rosecrans opted for a feint to the east, holding Bragg in place, while marching the majority of the Army of the Cumberland to the southwest, crossing the Tennessee River, and coming back at Chattanooga from the south. If the strategy succeeded, Bragg would be forced to abandon Chattanooga or be trapped in the city with no line of retreat. With the plan settled on, Rosecrans issued orders on August 15 to initiate the move the following morning.[1]

* * *

"This army is perfectly quiet awaiting the completion of the railroad and the arrival of supplies. Our lines extend to the foot of the mountains, and reconnoitering cavalry daily push beyond, but no movement can be made until provisions have been brought forward," reported the *Chicago Tribune*, July 9, 1863. The correspondent noted that "many commands issued their last pounds to-day. The probability is that unless trains can be forced quickly up, the troops will have to march back to meet them . . . Trains, however, are likely to arrive to-day, when all will be well." At the last minute the writer added to his dispatch: "Information is just received that Bragg has retired beyond the Tennessee, burning the great railroad bridge at Bridgeport."[2]

On July 8, the Headquarters of the Department of the Cumberland put out a press release stating, "We have driven the rebels out of Middle Tennessee. Their retreat has been disastrous and demoralizing to them. It is generally believed they had lost

---

[1]   Boatner, *The Civil War Dictionary*, 149-150; Daniel, *Days of Glory, The Army of the Cumberland, 1861-1865*, 285-289; Victor Hicken, *Illinois in the Civil War* (Urbana: University of Illinois Press, 1991), 192-193; Miles, *Paths to Victory: A History and Tour Guide of the Stone's River, Chickamauga, Chattanooga, Knoxville, and Nashville Campaigns*, 41-41; Van Horne, *History of the Army of the Cumberland Its Organization, Campaigns, and Battles*, I: 310-313.

[2]   *Chicago Tribune*, July 9, 1863.

not less than five thousand prisoners in the mountains." A *Tribune* correspondent followed up with a dispatch dated July 10 that the "citizens of Franklin and Spring Hill report the country north of the Tennessee River filled with deserters from Bragg's army, mostly Tennesseeans. The number is estimated from 10,000 to 15,000." "Bragg's army is drove out of Tennessee," George Berry wrote in a letter home. He then added: "They are deserting from his Army every day. There has bin about two thousand come in [to] Tullahoma since we have been here and still they come." According to William Tomlinson of Company A, "ther was five Deserters come in yesterday [August 8] from Jackson, Mississippi. They belonged to Johnsons rebel army. They live not far from here. They say ther is plenty mor of them coming. These five walked 400 miles." He pointed out that "they have taken the oath to support the constitution and laws of the United States. This is the way to bring them back. Go hole hog or nun."[3]

"We are still at Tullahoma. I think that there will be another movement soon." When George Berry wrote his wife on August 10, he may have sensed the coming of a major battle and thought it necessary to remind Harriet of his exact unit designation. Knowing newspaper correspondents tended to omit individual regiments, but mentioned specific corps, divisions, and brigades in their dispatches. So that she could easily follow the Eighty-ninth in the coming campaign, he wanted her to remember that it was "in the first Brigade, second Division in the Twentieth Army Corps. We are in McCook's Corps. Johnson commands the Division and General Willich commands the Brigade," George explained. Back in June, he had written to Harriet about the brigade and division commanders. General Willich "is a German dutchman. He is a splendid man, [and] he looks after the welfare of the soldiers. Johnson is not liked so well." George explained to his wife that a regiment in the brigade, the Thirty-second Indiana, was an all German outfit. And in his words, "they make firstrate soldiers." Captain E. T. Wells said this: "For perfection in the manual of arms, and in all movements," the Thirty-second Indiana "had, I believe, no equal in our armies; in

---

3   *Chicago Tribune*, July 9 and 10, 1863; Berry, letter, July 17, 1863, Kammerer, *Hancock County, Illinois in the Civil War*, 77.

battle it had no superior." As for General Willich, Wells observed that his "disregard for tradition and precedent," and his reliance on experience made him unpopular with superior officers, especially those from the regular army. Consequently, Willich was the "object of unkind criticism." However, "among those who served under him," Wells wrote, "he was venerated, respected, and obeyed without question; and . . . uniformly the reports of the regimental commanders of his brigade speak of his courage, his devotion, and his intelligent fatherly care of his command and all its members."[4]

"When I started from home I did not think that this war would last so long, but once I came in to the armey I have found it different. It takes time to move sutch large armeys. Rosecrans Armey has to fight in the front and in the rear. We hafture move slow," George Berry explained in a letter home. He added: "We have given the south some telling blows that they will never git over untill they come in to the union. Them that lives to see twelve months from this time will see them entirely whip[p]ed out is my opinion." Torn between family and country, Berry confided to Harriet: "I feel so that I ought to be at home sometimes and tak[ing] care of my family. I know that I am doing grate work as a private soldier in sustaining my country." Twelve days earlier he had written her: "I would like to go home [and] see you and the children if it was not but fifteen days. If I was not in a good cause, I don't think [that] I could stand it to stay way from my Family so long. I am way down here protecting my home and to leave my Children a Republickan form of Government. The union now and Forever is my motto." He finished up by saying, "I cant begin to tell you what I have seen and what I have pass[ed] through in this war, but one thing is certain that I have seen the Elaphant. When I git home I can tell it to you better than I can write to you."[5]

Joseph Buckley told Mary that "if I was to consult my own wishes, I would like to stay here a month longer until most of the hot weather is over. But if, it is better for the Country's cause for us to move, then I say let us move along and put this Rebellion down for

---

4   Berry, letters, June 5 and August 10, 1863; E. T. Wells, "The Campaign and Battle of Chickamauga," *United Service* 16 (September 1896), 222.

5   Berry, letters, August 2 and August 15, 1863.

I am anxious to be home once more." George Berry also found the time at Tullahoma to be quite pleasant. "We have had [an] Easy time of it since we come here. Plenty to eat and not much to do." From the private soldier's view, the war even appeared to be turning in the Union's favor and might soon be over. Writing his wife, George Berry had this to say. "I went out on Picket line yesterday, and when I got there, there was ten ladies and Eight men at the line. The men wanted to come in and take the Oath. The officer of the day told the women that they could go in if they would take the oath. Five of them took the oath. The rest went back." Seeing the local inhabitants coming back to the fold led Berry to comment that "Tennessee is coming around all right for the union." In an earlier letter dated August 10, he observed: "The Union men of Tennessee have a harde time of it. They are leaving East Tennessee and coming in to ower army. Burnside or Rosecrans will be in East Tenn before long."[6]

In a letter home dated August 15, Berry foretold, "I think we shall leave here soon—that is the talk." The next day the Eighty-ninth Regiment received orders to march at 4:00 P.M. The regiment moved out an hour after the appointed time with Lieutenant Colonel Duncan J. Hall in command. Colonel Hotchkiss, five line officers, and 10 sergeants were still in Illinois on recruiting service. George Berry recorded in his pocket diary: "We Left Tullahoma [at] five o'clock. We continued to march until two o'clock this morning [and] went in Camp by Elk river [about] nine miles from Tullahoma." At age 90 former Company A Private Alfred D. French remembered the regiment "left Tullahoma at 5 P.M. [on] Aug 16 (Nice time to start on a march) and six days later we reached Bellefonte Alabama. It was not a long march in miles, but as it was in a mountainous region. We had much heavy work in moving our wagon train and artillery."[7]

On arriving at Bellefonte, Alabama, McCook's Twentieth Corps halted. George Berry took the opportunity to write Harriet. "Dear Wife, You see by . . . this letter that we are down in Olde Alabama. Ower Division tooke one Roade and went by themselve. We went through Winchester and Salem. We have crosed over the Cumberland Mountains. We are about two miles from the Tennessee River. The

---

6   Buckley, letter, August 7, 1863; Berry, letters, August 10 and August 15, 1863.
7   Berry, letter, August 15, 1863; *OR*, Vol. 30, Pt. 1, 542; French Memoir.

Rebel Pickets are on the other side of the River. We shall stay here a few days and then we shall go on." The rugged terrain, Berry pointed out, called for an all out effort to move wagons and artillery. "We hade to helpe the teames up the mountain. Some of the boyes hade to lifte at the wheels. I carried three guns up the mountains. That was just as much that I wanted to do. I took my time [and] went slow. I am stout and hearty and well and stood the trampe firstrate." During the six-day march, George ever the farmer observed closely the land and crops, and passed along his impression to Harriet. "The corn down here is firstrate [and] as good as I ever saw in Illinois. The land in the valley is splendid for corn. The folks have put in more corn and less cotton." Whether the men purchased from the local farmers or liberally foraged from their fields and orchards, George stated, "We hade plenty of green corn and peaches and apples and some potatoes."[8]

Three days after writing Harriet, George Berry penned a letter to an older brother, with an update on the current military situation. Providing more detail than he had to his wife. He stated the regiment traveled about 15 miles a day and crossed some of the roughest country he ever saw. After winding for three days through a valley, the road led up a mountain. George stated: "Ower Division was all day giting on top of the mountian. It was a one mile and half at the top. We hade to put ten mules to a wagaon. Ten men to each wagon to lift at the wheel[s] and block up some places. It was right straite up. He went on. "I think we shall move agin before longe. When we do the Rebels will hafture fight or have another foot race. The southern Confederacy is about playing out, I think." As for the latest news from Company G and the Eighty-ninth, Berry said: "Lieutenant Howell has went home to get recruits for ower company. He has about ten men." He then added, "I think we shall be mounted. I hope so. We have traveled one year [by] foot, and now I would like to ride horseback this year, and see how that will go."[9]

"On the morning of August 30 we broke up camp, and proceeded up the Tennessee River road to a point opposite Stevenson, Ala. On the 31st the brigade and regiment crossed the Tennessee River on

---

8   Berry, letter, August 23, 1863.
9   Berry, letter, August 26, 1863.

a pontoon bridge," wrote Major Williams. George Berry noted that the Tennessee River here was "about a quarter of a mile wide," and he counted sixty pontoons as he marched across. The pontoons he observed were put "crosway of the stream and then they lay plank[s] on them."[10]

"We left Tullahoma on the 16th of August and arrived at Bellefonte, Alabama on the 22nd and stayed there until the 30th, when we started on the march again," Joseph Buckley of Company H wrote his wife on September 6. He speculated, "I think we are going to Rome, Georgia." Not only had the troops dealt with a water barrier, like the Tennessee River, but Buckley explained the Railroaders had also "crossed one part of the Cumberland Mountains between Tullahoma and Bellefonte. Now we are crossing another part of the Cumberland Mountains."[11]

Taking-in everything of interest, George Berry included an anecdote for the folks at home. "I saw one Family in Alabama that had a son in ower Army. He has bin in ower Army fifteen montz without seeing or hearing from his folks. He has just came up as we came along. I saw his folks. We campe[d] by his house one knight." Captain E. T. Wells too found Union sentiment ran high among the mountain population and one of his letters found its way to the *Rock Island Union*. He wrote: "The people in the mountains are *all* Union, and have suffered horrible cruelties, as was the case on the march over the mountains from Winchester to Bellfont—the women and children cheer for the Yankees and the old flag." Wells pointed out that "these mountaineers, ignorant as they are, are well disposed, and as I said, have suffered intolerable persecutions. Almost all of them have at some time been in the Confederate army as conscripts and cleared [out], probably at the time of the Big Run, as they call Bragg's retreat from Tullahoma."[12]

George Berry's letter on the first of September reflected both the atmosphere and emotions of the Army of the Cumberland. There is little doubt the men were confident of success. The campaign seemed to be going the Federals way. "The union Armey is closing in

---

[10] *OR*, Vol. 30, Pt. 1, 542-543; Berry, letter, September 1, 1863.

[11] Buckley, letter, September 6, 1863.

[12] Berry, letter, August 23, 1863; *Rock Island Union*, September 23, 1863.

on them fast," George wrote. "I think that Rosecrance Armey will be to Atlanta before January. Burnside and Rosecrance are cooporating together." He took a moment to reflect on a thought his wife had written, and said. "I feel just as you do. I wish the war would close soon. I have bin in the war one yeare. We have bin in some harde Fighting and harde marching. The war may close soon and it may not. It is harde telling. If the war does close, I should git home. We can go around visiting and have a good time seeing the folks." He continued: "Time seem[s] to go fast in the armey. Soldiering is harde, being as a man must have [a] constitution to stand it. Rosecrance Armey has Accomplished a good deal. When I arived at Louisville last fall, Bragg's Armey was about thirty miles from Louisville and now it crosed the Tennessee River. He will soon hafter Retreat to Atlanta." He also realized that "horses and mules are goin to be high after this. They use up horses and mules fast down here."[13]

"Well Mary, I think we are going to give Old Bragg a pretty good thrashing this time. We are all in good health and good spirits and willing to give him what all Rebels deserve," an exuberant Joseph Buckley crowed. He did emphasize the difficulties the men faced in the mountains southwest of Chattanooga. "We have had a very rough march so far in Alabama. I was detailed twice to help the wagons over the mountains, but the worst of it is when we come to a large stream and have to take off our pants and wade through up to the middle in water while we are sweating hard."[14]

With the regiment camped at Sand Mountain, Berry too found time to scrawl a quick page with an update. "We are marching sloley. We have a Rough Country to travel over. We go some times three miles a day [and] sometimes ten miles a day. We are still in Alabama. We shall have [a] fight at Chattanooga. Burnside has drove Buckner from East Tennessee to Chattanooga. Burnside is on one side [and] Rosecrance on the other side of Chattanooga. We shall use up Bragg this time, I think, if he don't git out."[15]

From captured Yankee newspapers and his own intelligence, Bragg came to understand Rosecrans' plan and his own precarious

---

13 Berry, letter, September 1, 1863.

14 Buckley, September 6, 1863.

15 Berry, letter, September 6, 1863.

position. The day, September 6, Privates Buckley and Berry wrote their spouses, Rosecrans movement to force Bragg's retreat were in place. That same morning Bragg drafted orders to withdraw from Chattanooga and fall back toward Rome, Georgia. Bragg abandoned Chattanooga, but not the fight, for he intended to give battle to the Federals on his terms. Four days earlier, Burnside had occupied Knoxville, Tennessee, after the rebels withdrew. These troops, led by Confederate Major General Simon Bolivar Buckner, made their way to Chattanooga, reinforcing Bragg's army, while Burnside remained at Knoxville. By September 9, the last Confederate was gone from Chattanooga, and the primary objective of Rosecrans' campaign was in Yankee hands. That same day Longstreet's Corps was detached from the Army of Northern Virginia and started a journey by rail to Northern Georgia to reinforce Bragg.[16]

Like most of the regiment, Lieutenant William Harkness found time on September 6 to write home. To his parents, he wrote: "As no doubt you are aware, we are in Alabama, across the Tennessee River. We are now stopping in the above named valley [Lookout] which is about 20 or 25 miles southeast of where we crossed the river and within a few miles of the line between Alabama and Georgia. Our destination I think is Rome, which is about fifty miles from here. We are moving very slow, lying still more than half the time."[17]

September 9 found the Railroad Regiment near Lookout Mountain at a place the men called Camp Blake, Alabama. George Berry noted: "This camp is named after a captain killed at Liberty Gap. He belonged to ower Regiment. He was a fine man and a Christian." However, the Eighty-ninth's direction of march and current location was about 40 miles from the railhead and supply point at Stevenson, Alabama. Berry wrote that this resulted in having to "hall ower Provision[s] over the mountian to where we are in campe." He then spelled out his opinion for the near future. "We are in the

---

[16]   Boatner, *The Civil War Dictionary*; 149-150; Peter Cozzens, *This Terrible Sound: The Battle of Chickamauga* (Urbana and Chicago: University of Illinois Press, 1992), 53-56; Long, *The Civil War Day by Day: An Almanac 1861-1865*, 403-407; Van Horne, *History of the Army of the Cumberland Its Organization, Campaigns, and Battles*, I: 314-317.

[17]   Harkness, letter, September 6, 1863.

rear of Chattanooga about thirty miles. Rosecrans is going to cut off the Railroad that leads to Atlanta. We shall soon make a dash on Chattanooga or Atlanta. It is harde telling which. I think it will be Chattanooga. I think there will be some harde fighting in this move. When we git Chattanooga, Tennessee will be cleared of the Rebel Armey. When we git Chattanooga that will be all we shall do this fall. It may be decided before you git this letter." Regarding Eighty-ninth's current surroundings, Berry said this. "The southern country is harde country to fight in. Mountains and hilly and heavy timbered country. We are in camp on [a] Rebel Plantation. He is in the Rebel Armey. The Poore people that live here are all union pretty much. You git in to [a] neighborhood whare they are well off, they are all in the Rebel Armey."[18]

Before George Berry could mail the letter he had written on September 9, the Railroaders received orders to move out and covered fifteen miles on the tenth. By the eleventh George Berry scribbled a hurried addition to the original pages and made mail call. He noted that the rebels were falling "trees acrossed the roade" to slow the Union column. And to further retard the Yankees, the rebels fought delaying actions with the blue-coated cavalry out front of the advance. Berry was pleased to pass along the latest news circulating through the Eighty-ninth's ranks, which was that Bragg had evacuated Chattanooga. George thought, "If he has, we shall follow as fast as we can." A camp rumor, he added, was that "McCook['s] Corps is going to Rhome." The next day George wrote a few more lines. "We are still in camp. We are waiting for ower supply Traine to come up. The traine has come in to day." Arriving with supply train were 60 recruits sent by Colonel Hotchkiss.[19]

Charles Capron was one of the new men signed-up to fill the depleted ranks of the Eighty-ninth, enlisting on August 14 at Rock Island. Given a few days to settle his affairs, the eighteen-year-old Capron caught a train to Chicago and checked in at Camp Douglas. A few weeks went-by before the newly mustered men were ordered South to join the regiment. Capron wrote: "We left Chicago one cold morning and rode all day till we come to Indianapolis where

---

[18] Berry, letter, September 9, 1863.

[19] Berry, letter, September 11, 1863; Berry, diary, September 10, 1863.

we remained till 9 o'clock when we again took the train and went to Jeffersonville and then crossed the Ohio River to Louisville where we remained till the next morning and drawed rations and took the train and proceeded to Nashville." The men arrived in the Tennessee capital at dusk and were "conducted to the old Zollicoffer House" where they had "supper and then laid down to rest . . . ." Capron stated: "We was not destined to remain there long for at 3 o'clock in the morning we was arroused and told to pack up our traps and be ready to move. We then left the old building and threaded our way along the silent streets of Nashville to the depot where we was obliged to wait till 9 o'clock." Transportation arrived and the men "clambered on to the top of the train and slowly started on our way to Stephenson." It was twilight when train slowed to a halt. The recruits got off, formed up, and marched off to camp in a pleasant grove. Capron wrote that this was the end of the line, and "our riding was then done for the cars did not run any further." For the next week the men remained in Stephenson until orders finally came. He explained: "General Rosencrans supply train came back for supplies and we was to accompany it back to the grand army. This was received with a yell of delight for we was getting tired of laying around. We started that evening and crossed the Tennessee River and camped on its bank where we remained all the next day amusing ourselves as best we could." The following morning the supply train "started to the Cumberland Mountains which was no light task . . . and it would be all the mules could do to climb up them." To make the grade, Capron wrote that 12 mules were hitched "to one wagon and such cutting and slashing beggars description." Within 25 miles of their division and finding travel with the supply train too slow, Capron with nine other replacements headed off on their own. "We reached the picket just at dark. A dirty or tired set of fellows you never see. We went to Johnson's headquarters and reported." The ten were told to go into camp and make themselves comfortable for the night. The next morning, he recalled, "we joined our regiment that had already started on a forced march."[20]

---

[20]   Charles Capron to Mary S. Capron, January 23, 1865. Charles Capron Collection, Old Court House Museum (Vicksburg, MS). Hereafter, all letters will be cited as Capron Collection.

Word was passed through the ranks that mail needed to be in by 7:00 P.M. George Berry dated another sheet September 12 and quickly penned a few more lines to his wife. He let her know that "the mails will be irregular for some time, untill this fight is over." George wanted Harriet to know that the campaign was not coming to an end. "We may have a fight and we may not. It is hard telling. Harriet, I hope that I shall come out all wright. If I fall, it will be all wright. I shall put my trust in the Lord," he confided. "The mail is going out in a short time," so Joseph Buckley too hurriedly wrote Mary a few lines. "This is Lookout Mountain. The "Rebs" are going in camp about 14 miles to the left of us. The report is that our forces have surrounded them and they [the Rebels] are going to try and break through our lines . . . . I shall not be surprised if we have a fight in the course of a day or two, and I expect it will be a tough one for us, but time will show," he wrote. He then solemnly told her: "Do not wait for me to write again before you write for we may have no fight after all. I will now conclude . . . if I should fall in Battle, you may rest assured that my last thoughts were of my beloved wife, but my prayer is that the Lord will be merciful to me for your sake." Lieutenant Harkness commented in a quick note to his parents that "the mail is very uncertain from here and I can't get letters sent off very often." He speculated the army was still headed for Rome, Georgia, which he guessed was about 25 miles south of their present location. "We may have to fight them [the Rebels]," he added, "Before we go to much further." But, he opined: "I hardly think they will make much of a stand . . . as Bragg and his army has done nothing but run ever since we have been after him."[21]

Writing his mother from Camp Blake on September 9, Private William Tomlinson of Company A reported that "ther is deserters coming in every day and getting transportation north. Some of them take ther families with them . . . ." Deserters had been commonplace for weeks and most were men from Tennessee, who just wanting to go home. But all was not what it seemed to be. When Bragg pulled out of Chattanooga, he created a simple plan of deception. Selected

---

21   Berry, letter, September 11, 1863; Buckley, letter, September 12, 1863; Harkness, letter, September 12, 1863.

volunteers surrendered to the Federals and told interrogators, along with all who would listen, that Bragg's army was disintegrating and on the verge of collapse. The charade may have been successful; as some Yankees officers, as well as enlisted men, were confident the Confederate army was both running away and disintegrating. Those who were skeptical, deep down hoped it was true, and the war was nearing an end. In a letter to Mary dated September 6, an optimistic Joseph Buckley wrote: "I should not advise you to leave the place as I am certain I shall be home before spring's work commences, and I shall want a place to come to when I get back as I am tired of laying my head on forty rounds of cartridges for a pillow. Sometimes I have a stone for a pillow and sometimes a block of wood or an old tree root, and sometimes nothing at all."[22]

*   *   *

Convinced Bragg would evacuate Chattanooga and fallback toward Atlanta, Rosecrans prepared to cut off his retreat. The date was September 6, and Rosecrans' three army corps remained separated in Lookout Valley. Bragg, however, was not on the run but was consolidating his army at LaFayette, Georgia in preparation of defeating the Federals in detail once they emerged from the mountain passes. The situation was ripe for a Union disaster. No one, from the top brass to the lowest men in the ranks, entertained the thought of a Rebel attack. The Army of the Cumberland had been driving the rebels since they left Murfreesboro, and it appeared that there was little fight left in Bragg's army. The Union troops were fueled with optimism that the war on this front was about over. But in reality, even though Bragg had suffered setbacks in holding Tennessee, he was far from finished and had plenty of fight left in him. The demise of the Rebel army was an illusion. And by September 13, Rosecrans realized that Bragg's army had not fled in disarray to Rome but had been concentrated for a fight. Only the failure of Bragg's subordinate commanders to execute his plans had so far saved Rosecrans from catastrophe. Finally recognizing the

---

22 Kammerer, *Hancock County, Illinois in the Civil War*, 77; Cozzens, *This Terrible Sound: The Battle of Chickamauga*, 70; Buckley, letter, September 6, 1863.

peril, Rosecrans ordered the separate corps to come together at Lee and Gordon's Mill on Chickamauga Creek.[23]

Through a mix-up in orders between Rosecrans, Thomas, and McCook, a one-day forced march turned into "a three-and-a-half-day odyssey" for the Twentieth Corps. George Berry's hastily scribbled lines reflected the muddled situation. On Sunday, September 13, 1863, he wrote, "we Left Camp this morning. This place is called Lookout Mountain. Went up [a] steepe mountain hill. Went about 10 miles and then went in camp." Monday, September 14, Berry jotted, "we return[ed] Back to Lookout mountain to Campe Blake. Camp[ed] over knight." His note for the September 15 was simply, "M Cook Corps Laid over one days in the valley." For Wednesday, September 16, Berry wrote: "We Left Campe Lookout and went up the hill. We healped up the teams. Went twelve miles [and] went in campe. Ower regiment went on Picket." By Thursday, it was becoming critical that the Twentieth Corps link up with the rest of the Army of the Cumberland and George's diary revealed the effort made. "Ower Division went 25 miles. Went in campe [at] 9 o'clock Evening. The Rebels are close by. They say we shall have a fight here." Friday, September 18, Berry put down that "ower Regiment Picketing in front in Battle line. Artillery firing on ower left to day. We was Releaved by second Brigade in ower Division just before knight. Went in Camp."[24]

In his official report for the period prior to the Battle of Chickamauga, Major Williams summarized the Eight-ninth's travels this way. "The operations of the regiment from the crossing of the Tennessee River to striking the enemy's left, embraces a period of some sixteen days, which was employed in marching and counter-marching over mountains and through valleys." When the Railroaders came up with the rest of the army, "the regiment

---

23 Boatner, *The Civil War Dictionary*, 150; Patricia L. Faust, ed., *Historical Times Illustrated Encyclopedia of the Civil War* (New York: Harper & Row Publishers, 1986) 137-138; Hicken, *Illinois in the Civil War*, 195-197; Miles, *Paths to Victory: A History and Tour Guide of the Stone's River, Chickamauga, Chattanooga, Knoxville, and Nashville Campaigns*, 43-45.

24 Cozzens, *This Terrible Sound: The Battle of Chickamauga*, 87-88; Berry, diary, September 13 through 18, 1863.

stood picket (as Private George Berry noted) opposite the enemy's left and about 800 yards distant therefrom." Johnson's Division anchored Rosecrans' right. The following day Saturday, September 19, Berry wrote in his diary that "we had marching orders early in the morning."[25]

The cannonading the Railroaders heard was Bragg's initial move to turn Union left. If successful, Bragg would interpose the Rebel army between the Yankees and Chattanooga, cutting them off from their base of supply and leading to their defeat and surrender. This was the Confederate plan, and when the Rebels made contact with Union troops on September 18, Rosecrans understood the danger and immediately began shifting forces to strengthen his left. He detached Johnson's Division from McCook's Corps and sent it off to support Thomas' Fourteenth Corps. With Willich's brigade leading, the division marched across the army's rear. Major Williams described the movement. "At daylight on the morning of the nineteenth of September we marched with the brigade about 4 miles to a point opposite the left of General Thomas' corps, it being understood we were to re-enforce the left of our line of battle." Heading north up the Dry Valley Road, Willich halted at Crawfish Spring long enough for the men to fill their canteens. After the respite, the regiments hurried on and eventually veered to the right on Glenn-Kelly Road. Hearing musketry, the brigade left their train and struck out through the woods and fields until they came to the LaFayette Road. Alexis Cope of the Fifteenth Ohio recalled that here the brigade was given "a short rest, after which we were ordered forward at double quick." The time was a little after noon when Johnson's men arrived at Kelley's farm and maneuvered to fill a gap in Thomas' line. The second division formed in the following order: Colonel J. B. Dodge's second brigade was assigned the right; General Willich's first brigade was in the centre; while Colonel P. P. Baldwin's third brigade took up the left of the formation. When Willich's Brigade came to the Kelly farm, it turned off the road to the right and went into a line of battle and prepared for a fight." Twenty-three years later Sergeant I. K. Young of Company H wrote in *The National Tribune* that General Willich gave orders to drop their knapsacks

---

[25] Berry, diary, September 19, 1863.

and fix bayonets. With Lieutenant-Colonel Duncan Hall leading, the Railroaders plunged into and out of a wood, and then crossed a tobacco-field. Hall at once realized his men were beyond the Union battle line and promptly rectified the situation, and ordered the Railroaders to return to the edge of the open field. With everyone back across the field, Williams ordered the men to lie down. And, all at once, Young recalled: "Crash! Bang! Roar! The opening of the battle comes as suddenly as a thunder-clap." Heading for the same spot, were Cheatham's division of Tennesseans, who collided with the arriving Yankees of Johnson division.[26]

Captain John M. Farquhar wrote both a detailed and vivid description of Willich's brigade forming for battle. "The head of the column swung in to the right flank, and as each successive regiment came up it prolonged the line and went to work. Johnson's division maneuvered like clockwork . . . ." When the first brigade came on the field, the Thirty-second Indiana and the Forty-ninth Ohio formed the front line, while skirmishers went out ahead. The Eighty-ninth Illinois and the Fifteenth Ohio quickly took positions in the second line. The ground being wooded and hilly, making it difficult for his artillery to maneuver, Willich told Captain Goodspeed "to keep his battery out of musket-range and in the rear of the infantry until further orders." Shortly, the skirmishers found themselves outflanked and under heavy fire and fell back to the main line. In his after-battle report, General Willich detailed what took place when his brigade met the attacking Rebels. "My skirmishers soon engaged the enemy, who opened with shell and then with canister from a point right in front . . . ." He continued: "After having re-enforced the skirmish line, and having brought to bear two section of my battery, and having sufficiently shaken the enemy's infantry line, I ordered a bayonet charge, and took the Eighty-ninth Illinois into a

---

[26] Hicken, *Illinois in the Civil War*, 198; Rheihart, *August Willich's Gallant Dutchman, Civil War Letters from the 32nd Indiana Infantry*, 150; Cope, *The Fifteenth Ohio Volunteers*, 309; Dodge, *History of the Old Second Division, Army of the* Cumberland, 534; Van Horne, *History of the Army of the Cumberland Its Organization, Campaigns, and Battles*, I: 335; Daniel, *Days of Glory, The Army of the Cumberland, 1861-1865*, 318-319; *The National* Tribune, April 23, 1886; OR, Vol. 30, Pt. 1, 538, 543.

line with the Forty-ninth Ohio and Thirty-second Indiana, keeping the Fifteenth Ohio in reserve." As Captain Farquhar saw it, "our line had only been formed a few minutes when the enemy opened on us with six pieces of artillery and a crashing volley of musketry. Not a man within my view flinched." Orders were shouted to get down. More explicit are Major Williams' words. "We lay on the ground, without firing . . . subject . . . to the heavy musketry and artillery fire of the enemy, which wounded five of our men . . . ." For about forty minutes Willich's men hugged the ground until the brigade bugler sounded "Forward." Williams described the charge. "The officers and men obeyed with alacrity, starting forward on a double-quick, driving the enemy almost without stopping (at least not stopping more than five minutes) of a mile." The Old Dutchman proudly added that "the charge was executed in splendid order, and with such energy that everything was swept before it for about a mile."[27]

In a letter to Colonel Hotchkiss, Captain Farquhar said this about the charge. "'Willich's bugle sounded 'forward,'and the glorious old 'First' sent up one loud, lusty cheer and went in with a rush. The Eighty-ninth was on the right, and fought a portion of Claiborne's division; the left of the brigade fought Cheatham's men." He went on. "When we had fought our way about one hundred yards forward, the rebels made a determined stand to cover their artillery . . . . We worsted them in the grapple, and then cannon after cannon fell into our hands. The 'grapethrowers' being silenced the General gave orders for the 'four-rank formation,' and again sounding the 'forward,' we never halted until we had driven the enemy about a mile, and had gained a defensible position."[28]

In his after action report Major Williams spelled out what happened at the end of the attack. "About a mile from where we started to charge the enemy, the right and left companies . . . encountered two of the enemy's batteries; the left, Company C . . . captured one of the pieces opposite them (a 6-pounder Parrott and caisson), the enemy escaping with the balance." The three right companies were not as fortunate. Their zealous lunge to capture the rebel guns was "checked by murderous discharges of grape

---

[27]   *Chicago Evening Journal*, October 6, 1863; *OR*, Vol. 30, Pt. 1, 538-539, 543.
[28]   *Chicago Evening Journal*, October 6, 1863.

and canister . . . ." Among those who fell were Captain Spink and Lieutenants Warren and Ellis. Seeing the confusion with the right companies, Lieutenant-Colonel Hall ordered the entire regiment to halt and fall back 20 yards, while maintaining a fire on the enemy.[29]

Williams wrote that Hall's effort "restored order on the right." He also recognized the extraordinary effort of Private Alexander Beecher, who stepped up and took control of Company D when all of its commissioned and non-commissioned officers went down. Seeing the Railroaders had been rattled, Brigadier-General Willich came forward and temporarily assumed command. Standing in front of the regiment under a constant zip of Rebel bullets, Major Williams watched as the old battle-hardened German complimented the men of the Eighty-ninth "for its impetuous advance, calmed their excitement, instructed them how to advance firing and maintain their alignment with the advance of the brigade, and by his own inimitable calmness of manner restored order and confidence in the regiment, and after dressing them and drilling them in the manual of arms for a short time, ordered them to advance about 30 paces to the edge of an open space." Williams reported that the regiment "did so in good order; lay down and kept the enemy in check for the next two hours."[30]

William Sumner Dodge provided another account of this part of the fight. "The bugle sounded 'Forward!' and the men responded with a cheer and rushed upon the foe. It was quick work—short and decisive. On rushed the men, reckless of the death-shots falling thick and fast among them. The rebels retreated about one hundred yards, then faced about and made a most determined stand in defence [sic] of their artillery." Willich's line closed with the enemy, and "for the space of twenty minutes the deadly fray was waged" until the rebel line broke and retreated. "Our men, frantic with delight at their success, yelled like demons," Dodge wrote, "and at the point of the bayonet charged the rebel artillery." The Eighty-ninth Illinois captured one gun and a caisson; the Thirty-second Indiana took two guns, three caissons, and a number of prisoners; while the Forty-ninth Ohio grabbed two guns. The rebel artillerymen attached

---

[29]   *OR*, Vol. 30, Pt. 1, 543.

[30]   *OR*, Vol. 30, Pt. 1, 543, 546.

prolongs to their remaining gun and were in the process of drawing it off by hand. Seeing this, the Railroaders three right companies tore after the piece, only to have the Rebel gunners' discharge a load of grape into them. The death dealing blast threw the entire regiment into momentary confusion. Dodge stated that Lieutenant Colonel Hall immediately pulled back and reorganized his command. "But it was well to halt and reform the line," Dodge concluded, "for the foe, although driven back, was then partially reformed, and on the alert to take advantage of any break in our lines." Catching sight of a problem with the Eighty-ninth, "General Willich rode up amidst the shower of balls which the rebels still threw at a distance of not more than eighty paces, and complimented the gallantry of the regiment in its impetuous advance, calmed down its enthusiasm by his own cool conduct, formed a new alignment, and drilled it for a few minutes in the manual of arms." Willich then ordered the brigade forward "thirty yards, to the edge of an open [Winfrey] field, where it lay down, and for two hours, in common with the division, held the enemy at bay." In the meantime, Captain Goodspeed rolled up and using his caissons and teams hauled away the captured guns.[31]

For many Railroaders the charge that afternoon brought no glory. Private Alfred D. French of Company A spoke years later of his experience. "I went but a very little ways [when] a musket ball struck my left arm. I told my captain [W. H. Rice], who was not far from me, that I was hit, and he asked, 'can you get back alone,' and I said [that] I thought I could. He said in reply, 'All right if you can.' So I turned back and he went on with the company." French recalled that he nearly got back when he began to feel faint. He then "heard someone say 'there's a boy that ain't going to get back much farther; couple of you jump up and help him and two men came and helped me back to where I would not be under fire [and] laid me on the ground and left me." More wounded were arriving and French saw Captain Rice brought back. "He was laid near me. He only lived two hours."[32]

Editor J. B. Danforth of the *Rock Island Argus'* received a letter from Lieutenant Laertes Dimick of Company F summarizing the

---

[31]   Dodge, *History of the Old Second Division, Army of the Cumberland*, 541-542.
[32]   French Memoir.

bloody action that took place that first afternoon at Chickamauga. Dimick wrote: "About 1 o'clock we became heavily engaged—terrible fighting on both sides." A half an hour into the fight General Willich, ordered the brigade to make a charge, which Dimick reported that "we did in good order, capturing five pieces of artillery, and driving the enemy nearly three quarters of a mile." But, Dimick passed on the grim news that the Eighty-ninth suffered severely in the charge, with three company captains killed, while five lieutenants and a number of enlisted men were wounded. In a letter to Colonel Hotchkiss, who was still in Illinois, Captain Farquhar informed him of some of the first day's casualties. Right off, he wrote: "Capt. Spink was killed in our first charge . . . . The last I saw of him he had snatched up a musket and was firing alongside his men." He noted that "Capt. Rice was struck at the same time by a round shot. An arm and part of the shoulders were shot away. He just lived to reach the temporary hospital in our rear. His last words were: 'Send my love to mother.'" The former sergeant major, now captain of Company B, stated that in the same charge Lieutenants Darcy, Ellis and Warren were all seriously wounded. Farquhar stated that he had been hit in the "throat by a piece of shell and 'knocked out of time' for a few minutes, the stun being much worse than the wound." He passed along that Bugler Keeler, and the buglers of Companies F and K, were all seriously wounded. In a that-was-a-close-one incident, Isaac K. Young of Company H recalled many years later that a ball passed "through the hat of Capt. Frank M. Hobbs, of Co. H, cutting hair from the top of his cranium." Hobbs kept the "old white hat" as a reminder of his luck.[33]

The fog of war had not lifted when the post-battle letters and reports were written. These writings leave an incomplete and confused picture of what took place that first afternoon at Chickamauga. The writer of the Eighty-ninth's regimental history for Andreas' 1885 *History of Chicago* gave an overall account of the brigade's action that afternoon of September 19.

[Brigadier General John M.] Brannon, of Thomas's corps, had been driven back, and [Brigadier General Absalom] Baird,

---

33   *Rock Island Argus*, October 6, 1863; *Chicago Evening Journal*, October 6, 1863; *National Tribune*, April 23, 1886.

to his right, was giving way, when Johnson's division moved to his support. It formed on Baird's right, with Willich's brigade holding the center, Dodge's brigade the right, and Baldwin's the left. Willich's brigade formed in two lines, the 89th Illinois on the right of the second line, in support of the 32d Indiana. Baldwin's brigade, to the left, was first engaged, and then the center held by Willich. He had sent forward a line of skirmishers, who soon needed the reinforcement of their reserve companies in order to hold the advanced line. Willich moved his brigade in line-of—battle, and prepared to receive the onset of the advancing rebels. Their repeated charges were bravely and successfully repulsed, when they succeeded in planting a battery in front of the brigade, and, at close range, threw grape and canister into its ranks. A section of Goodspeed's battery, which was attached to the brigade, opened upon the enemy's guns, which the 89th Illinois and the 32d Indiana were ordered to charge.

Rushing forward at the call of the bugle, with a cheer, the regiments drove back the rebels about a hundred yards, who then faced about and rallied round around their battery, determined to hold it to the last extremity. Moving steadily forward until they could almost touch their foes, the two regiments stood there and fought until the rebels were forced to fall back. Then making a headlong bayonet charge they captured all of the battery except one gun, which the enemy succeeded in drawing off by hand. A portion of the 89th, in their zeal to capture this gun also, pressed forward to a dangerous distance in advance of the brigade; but the line being re-formed, the whole command advanced, about thirty yards, which position the division, held about two hours.[34]

*   *   *

With darkness closing in and the enemy creeping closer, Captain Farquhar was "ordered to reconnoiter the uncertain front with some good shots," but they advanced only a short distance before drawing

---

[34]   Andreas, *History of Chicago*, II: 246.

fire. "Luckily," for the patrol, "the first volleys are wild and high . . . the return fire lights up . . . a semi-circle of determined fighters, who, looking death square in the face, with shouts of defiance and occasional wild oaths, defy the hordes pressing the front and both flanks." Dodge's support on the right gives ground, and gradually the Eighty-ninth's "left flank is pressed inwardly, but Goodspeed . . . unleashed his 'brazen bull-dogs' there, and Gray's and Askew's boys [Forty-ninth and Fifteenth Ohio]" poured "in continuous volleys of lead." Realizing they were caught in crossfire, the words, "We are surrounded!" could be heard in the ranks. The enemy called out "Surrender!"—and the Railroaders answer back, "Never!" Forced to leave their dead and the wounded, the Eighty-ninth fought its way out of the trap.[35]

Corporal Nelson W. Burneson, a former fireman with the Chicago, Burlington, and Quincy Railroad, never forgot the enemy's attack that evening. After being in the line of fire all day and dark coming on, he and some companions took refuge behind a log. He recalled that it seemed the rebel charge centered on his position, and several men in his company, including Captain Whiting, were killed right away. In an instant, he remembered, the butternut-clad devils cleared the log and were in our midst, resulting in a "hand to hand fight with clubbed guns . . . ." Those remaining kept up the fight until the line had fallen back on either side. Realizing they were cut-off and with "bullets coming thick and fast," the survivors, most of whom were wounded, surrendered.[36]

Writing to Colonel Hotchkiss back in Chicago, Captain Farquhar revealed the regiment's predicament as the afternoon light faded away to night. "Here we waited patiently for troops to relieve us, or at least mend our connection on the right, but none came until darkness was closing around us. At last the 2nd brigade [Dodge's]

35 *Rock Island Argus*, October 19, 1863; *WILLICH AT CHICAMAUGA*, pamphlet, Charles T. Hotchkiss Collection, Chicago Historical Society, hereafter city as *Willich* pamphlet. [This pamphlet is the same as an article printed in the *Argus* under the penname "typo". Based on the style of writing and his past position as president of the International Typographical Union, I believe the author is John M. Farquhar.]

36 *Soldiers and Patriots' Biographical Album*, 617.

found our right, and then we learned, that our brigade had thrown itself so far forward as to become almost isolated." By this time, Farquhar explained, "Our situation was getting desperate; we were receiving rebel skirmish fire on both flanks and the front; and soon after they gave us volleys." Instinctively, the men hastily formed a semi-circle and commenced to return fire. "Luckily," Farquhar pointed out, "our boys carried over sixty rounds each into action, or it might have been ruin to us all." Next, we heard "during the lull which succeeds the heating of the guns, a loud voice from the rebel side called out: 'Surrender, and you're safe! Surrender!' A universal yell of 'Never!' intermingled, I am sorry to say, with considerable blasphemy, was the answer, and again the circle of fire lighted up the slaughter-pen." Farquhar wrote of the ensuing fire-fight. "Oh, Colonel, the scene was awfully grand, as well as terrible. Our boys fought like sullen demons; as men fell in the ranks, their comrades straddled over the wounded and dead bodies, careless about their own fate and apparently pitiless for the fallen." He continued: "During the forty minutes' struggle we received one shock which drove us gradually back about fifteen yards, forcing us from our poor wounded and dead boys. We tried to recover the ground, but what could a brigade do against a division? We did, however, manage, by occasionally running the gauntlet of fire, to drag in quite a number." Finally, after fighting for three-quarters of an hour, he wrote, "the rebels voluntarily withheld their fire and we moved back to the . . . grand line of battle."[37]

Farquhar's account may seem too lofty and downplay what in reality was a serious situation, bordering on disaster. William J. Tomlinson held a different view and succinctly summed up the situation. This is what he wrote in a letter to his mother. "We went in at 12 and drove the rebels a mile and helt them until Dark. They Threw us back a little. We got skattered. The officers got us together the best they could and gave the command Forward, and the rebels herd them and fired on us on one side and our men let us have it on the other side at the same time. Sutch churning of men I never herd. We went into the fight with 30 men and lost

---

[37] *Chicago Evening Journal*, October 6, 1863.

half of them." Sergeant Isaac K. Young gave a similar recollection in the *National Tribune*. "Later in the afternoon a terrible rush [by the rebels], and our brave boys are demoralized and stampeded." Once again General Willich came forward, seizes the Eighty-ninth's regimental flag, and bids the men to dress in line upon him, which they did. In a letter to his sister-in-law, Harriet, dated September 24, Thomas Berry described what took place at dusk. "The rebs made a desperate charge on us the evening of the 19th and I have not seen George since. George and me was close together before we fell back but it was so dark that the regiment was soon messed up. The rebels took a good many prisoners when they made the charge, and I live in hopes that he is taken prisoner and will come out all right." George was not alone, for Thomas mentioned that "Captain Whiting is amongst the missing, and it is supposed he is a prisoner. Some of the boys says that he was wounded in the leg." From his own knowledge, Thomas wrote out a list of Company G's missing men. They were: "Theodore Whitney, R[obert] Wilson, [John L.] Hall, [Henry] Goddard, Rosy [Hiram J.] Rosenleaf, [Jasper C.] Codding, [William] Stroyan, [Winslow B.] Newton, [Schuyler] Atherton."[38]

In the Eighty-ninth's official report, Major Williams stated that even though the rebels had been driven back, they never broke contact and "kept up a constant fire, which was vigorously returned by our men. About 5:30 P.M. the enemy, having been re-enforced and somewhat recovered from the severe fright and punishment we had inflicted upon him, advanced in heavy force and pressed our regiment and brigade back some 250 yards, where the brigade made a determined stand in an advantageous position, checked the advance of the enemy, but not without severe loss in killed and wounded." He wrote: "By this time it was pitch dark; prudence suggested a withdrawal to maintain connection with the brigades on our right and left." Williams discreetly omitted the panicked retreat.[39]

---

[38] Tomlinson, *In Good Courage: The Civil War Letters of William James Tomlinson*, 12; *National Tribune*, April 22, 1886; *Thomas* Berry, letter, September 24, 1863.

[39] *OR*, Vol. 30, Pt. 1, 543-544.

General Willich's after action report sugarcoated nothing. The Old General was straight to the point when he retold what took place. Soon after the advance ground to a halt, Willich realized that his brigade was beyond the Union line, and without support of any kind, other than from his own division. He pointed out, "It was, all I could do was to keep my position and be on the lookout for other attacks in the flank and rear." "With dusk the attack looked for took place. The enemy had succeeded in bringing his batteries and masses of infantry into position. A shower of canister and columns of infantry streamed at once into our front and both flanks," he wrote. The result, Willich explained, was that "my two front regiments were swept back to the second line. This line for a moment came into disorder. Then they received the command, 'Dress on your colors;' repeated by many men and officers; and in no time the four regiments formed one solid line, sending death into the enemy's masses, who immediately fell back from the front, and there, did not answer with a single round." It was now about 6:30 P.M., and Willich was handed a written order from General Johnson to fall back to the line held by Thomas' Corps. Unnerved, the Old Dutchman had the two lines fall slowly back until they merged with the general line of battle. Meeting with General Johnson, Willich acknowledged his brigade's heavy loss that day, but he was also proud of his men. Especially, for their blunting the final rebel attack before it rolled into the main Union line. Major Williams echoed the same thought when he wrote that the men were "exultant in our success, proud of our brigade and its incomparable commander, but saddened with the sight of our thinned ranks and the loss of personal friends. Thus ended the eventful 19th of September, 1863."[40]

When George Berry opened his pocket diary for September 19, he scrawled only a few short lines. "Our Brigade went in at one clock. Was under firer till darke. I was taken prisoner just at darke. The rebels come up on ower right and frount." George, as usual, penned no superlatives, just the facts.[41]

---

[40] *OR*, Vol. 30, Pt. 1, 539-540; Dodge, *History of the Old Second Division, Army of the Cumberland*, 536-537.

[41] Berry, diary, September 19, 1863.

* * *

With night fast approaching, General Thomas had selected better ground and ordered his divisions to form a more compact line. However, as we know, before Johnson could pullback his brigades, Cleburne's division, supported by Cheatham's men, attacked. Fighting in the dark for nearly an hour, with both sides taking heavy casualties, the rebels were finally repulsed, allowing Johnson's men to fallback to the safety of the main Union line. As the firing wound down, Rosecrans had, through the shifting of troops, managed to parry Bragg's blows, but not without heavy losses to both armies. Thomas Van Horne summarized the situation. "Neither army was willing to yield without further fighting, and yet to neither was there the assurance of ultimate victory; and as they lay on their arms in close proximity, there was to each the oppression of doubt with regard to the issue." During the night Rosecrans' troops continued preparing defensive positions, while Bragg planned to resume the offensive with daylight.[42]

"Early on the morning of the 20th," wrote Major Williams, "the brigade took a rendezvous position in a double column about the center of a large open [Kelly] field and about the center of the left of our entire line of battle, which, at this point, partook of the convex order of battle, around which the enemy was in heavy force." The Railroaders and the Thirty-second Indiana formed the first line with the Forty-ninth and Fifteenth Ohio in the second line. Farquhar's words describe what the survivors saw when they fell in and looked about. "The skeleton ranks that answer to the bugle call of 'attention,' seem like an assembly of mourners . . . whose duty henceforth should be to bury . . . the dead." Looking at a shell of a brigade, Farquhar thought to himself: "Surely the past day has been ill-spent, or the battle ill-planned, if Willich's shorn battalions have to fill the smallest breach." But, "in aide de camp parlance, Willich is in reserve." Farquhar added, "Practically speaking, he commands a body of light troops to be thrown at will into the first gap."[43]

---

[42] Boatner, *The Civil War Dictionary*, 151; Van Horne, *History of the Army of the Cumberland*, 339-340.

[43] *OR*, Vol. 30, Pt. 1, 544; *Rock Island Argus*, October 19, 1863; *Willich* pamphlet.

"On the 20th September the other two brigades of our division were ordered into temporary breastworks erected during the night in our front, my brigade in reserve," wrote General Willich. Now in an open field and in the rear of the breastworks, Willich assessed the lay of the land and positioned his regiments behind a slope. He thus allowed the first brigade to support both the front and the flanks, even the rear if needed. Not long afterward the Railroaders observed in the distance a "column of road-dust moving toward the left" of the center of the division's front. The officers estimated their division would be hit within half an hour. And when it came, the attacking rebels buckled Johnson's line. Willich instantly moved to the rescue, ordering the Eighty-ninth and the Thirty-second Indiana to double-quick to the pending breach and saving the line from caving in. A youthful Railroader described the action. "At 9.o.clock while we was laying on our arms [and] the ball opened in earnest with the rebels charging one of our batteries. The bugle sounded for us to fall in and in return we was ordered to charge the rebels which we did and drove them back and maintained our ground till noon when we was ordered to support the 6 Ohio battery." The timely reinforcements successfully drove back the rebel attackers with a little loss. But as a consequence, the attacking column shifted away from the Railroaders and fell "obliquely against the troops on" the left. The Eighty-ninth watched as the adjacent brigade gave way, and in Captain Farquhar's words, in poured "the gray-back stream of howlers." But, "as quick as thought," Willich ordered the Forty-ninth Ohio "to half-wheel to the left" and the Fifteenth Ohio "to half-wheel to the right, and advance, while half of Goodspeed's battery wheel into the new line and give the bold, steady advancing enemy rapid volleys of double-shotted grape and canister." With the Buckeyes closing on the flanks, and Beatty's brigade making "a hard push against the front" the rebels fall back into the woods.[44]

Month's later Charles Capron took time to write his mother about his role in the Battle of Chickamauga. The first day of the fight Capron spent with a detail guarding the baggage train. But,

---

[44]   OR, Vol. 30, Pt. 1, 540, 544; Rock Island Argus, October 19, 1863, Willich pamphlet; Chicago Evening Journal, October 6, 1863; Capron, letter, January 23, 1865.

overcome with the curiosity of youth, he stole away with nightfall and walked "over a part of the battlefield" that brave Railroaders had been over. Having never witnessed a battlefield, he found "the ground strewed with the dead" and heard the heartrending cries of the wounded. Rather than making his way back to the baggage train, the newly arrived recruit stayed at the front with the regiment. "The next morning," he wrote, "I took my place in the ranks resolved to see what they [had] done it on." He would soon find out, for it was not long before the noise of battle filled his ears, and the eighteen-year-old found the action he missed the day before.[45]

While the Union troops at Kelly Field repulsed the Rebel morning attacks, a fatal mistake brought the collapse of Rosecrans' right and center. He continued moving brigades to strengthen Thomas and the left, which finally led to confusion and eventually resulted in a blunder. A staff officer reported a gap between Reynolds' and Wood's Divisions, and accordingly Rosecrans ordered Thomas J. Wood to shift his division to plug the hole. Wood, however, could see what the staff officer and the commanding general could not, and that was, no gap existed. A few hours earlier, Wood had received a thorough chewing-out from Rosecrans for failing to timely obey orders. This time, Wood did promptly as he was told. It was 11:30 A.M.. when his division pulled out of the Federal line, leaving a quarter-mile long hole, which turned out to be an invitation for disaster. For at this very instant, and before Rosecrans' reserves could fill the vacancy, Longstreet's massed attack struck and poured through the space left by Wood's departure. The surging Confederates swept Rosecrans along with half the Army of the Cumberland from the field.

With the collapse of the Federal army's right wing and center, Thomas managed to form a defensive line on Snodgrass Hill and the adjacent Horsehoe Ridge. Throughout the afternoon, this makeshift force, and those still holding out on the left at Kelly Field, managed to beat back attack after attack. Able to hang on until dusk, Thomas withdrew, leaving the field to the Rebels. For this determined stand, Thomas earned the nickname, "Rock of Chickamauga."[46]

---

[45]   Capron, letter, January 23, 1865.

[46]   Faust, *Historical Times Illustrated Encyclopedia of the Civil War*, 137; Glenn Tucker, *The Battle of Chickamauga* (Harrisburg, Pennsylvania: Eastern Acorn

In his official report Major Williams' wrote that after the enemy was "handsomely repulsed" the brigade held their position for the next two hours until ordered to support Goodspeed's battery, which was located near a log-house at the southwest corner of the [Kelly] field. Captain Farquhar, however, observed General Willich appeared uneasy and was making "quick glances along the new front." Suddenly, Farquhar picked up Reynolds' Division coming out of the woods on the Railroaders left. Consequently, a large gap developed between Willich and Dodge. Reynolds' men were barely out of sight, Farquhar noted, when Goodspeed's guns received "a whizzing salute of rebel shell and round shot . . . ." Williams quickly realized that the Rebels had swung around and were in the rear of the Eighty-ninth's position. And as a consequence, Farquhar wrote that the Railroaders were subject to a half an hour of terrific shelling from the rebel batteries. Goodspeed's guns, however, vigorously fired on the enemy, and in turn they were "fiercely shelled and played upon . . . ." It was at this moment, Captain Farquhar wrote, while he was "intently surveying the range of the enemy's shells" that Lieutenant Colonel Duncan J. Hall "fell pierced through by the bullet of a sharpshooter." Also witnessing the event was Major Williams, who noted that it was about 3:00 P.M. when Hall was shot "through the bowels" by a rebel sharpshooter. Private Capron wrote his mother of the incident explaining the regiment was supporting the brigade battery when "our Lieutenant Colonel was killed by a sharp shooter." Capron noted: "I saw him when he fell. Several sprang to his aid and bore him off the field."[47]

One of the men sprinting to Hall's aid was Shepard Green of the Forty-ninth Ohio. About 75 yards away when the young lieutenant colonel fell, Green caught up with those carrying him from the line of fire. He wrote: "I saw it gave him pain to be carried so, and had them lay him down and get a blanket. I took his head in my lap and had his belt taken off. He said to me, 'Well Green, this is my last battle.' I answered, 'I hope not Colonel.' 'Yes,' said he, 'this

Press, 1919), 29-34.

[47] OR, Vol. 30, Pt. 1, 544; Chicago Evening Journal, October 6, 1863; Rock Island Argus, October 19, 1863, Willich pamphlet; Capron, letter, January 23, 1865.

wound is mortal—I feel it. Green, tell my parents that I died for my country. Tell my regiment that I have always done my duty toward them to the best of my ability, and that *I died like a soldier*. Tell my regiment to fight on; they are in a just cause—they are fighting for a nationality and a flag.'"

Suffering very much, Hall asked Lieutenant Green for water and was given a drink mixed with some opium for the pain. Green said that "he seemed to sink away for a few moments, but revived shortly and continued: 'Well, Green, I am dying; but I have nothing to regret—I am resigned to my fate.' I replied, 'Your death is enviable, and your reward a patriot's Heaven.' 'Yes, a patriot's grave,' was his answer, as a smile not earthly played over his countenance."

The men then carried him to the field hospital and placed him in a shady place. Hall "asked a surgeon for chloroform, but he had none," and Green "gave him more opium, which soon quieted him to an extent." Hall gave him his watch, sword and pocketbook, along with instructions to telegraph his parents and for Green to bury him and mark his grave. Green noted: "It seemed to give him much pain to talk. I asked him if I could do more, but he had become partially insensible for the time." Green was called to return to duty as the enemy was drawing near, and left his dying friend, not to see him again.

Three days after his friend's death, Shepherd Green of the Forty-ninth Ohio wrote Lieutenant Colonel Duncan J. Hall's father regarding the event. Amos Hall in turn gave Green's letter to the *Chicago Evening Journal* for publication. Attaching a short note, the elder Hall penned: "Believing that the friends of the late Lieut. Colonel Duncan Jackson Hall . . . desire some of the particulars relative to his death, I enclose a copy of a letter this morning received . . . ."

The letter dated Chattanooga, Tenn., September 23, 1863 began: "SIR—As a personal friend of Lieut. Col. D. J. Hall, and receiving from him, I fear, his last message to loved ones and brave comrades, it becomes my duty (how painful, a soldier's grief alone can tell) to transmit the message, which must be to you, his bereaved friends, precious indeed." Green provided the Halls with the preceding details of their son's mortal wound and final words before concluding his letter with the following: "In the death of your son the country has lost a valuable and faithful officer; his men a kind and efficient commander; myself a valued friend and brother. Gladly would I offer you consolation, but my own loss seems to entitle me rather to a place among the mourners—he was all to me that a brother could be.

Though strangers, together we mourn the loss of the noble dead, and become friends in bereavement. I ask only to be remembered among his friends, a humble place among the mourning ones. It is mine to strive on in the cause and for the country upon whose altar he has so gallantly, nobly, sacrificed his life—be it mine to *die his death* and receive his reward."[48]

*　　*　　*

Time is not always remembered by the exact hour but by the event. Captain Farquhar recalled that just as the dying Hall had been carried to the field hospital, the enemy's battery, having moved to a new position, furiously opened on us. The enfilading fire from a second rebel battery forced Goodspeed to abandon his position. Major Williams, now in command of the Eighty-ninth, put the time around 5:00 P.M. Looking about, Williams "observed that regiments and brigades on our right and left were giving away in extricable confusion; at the same time the enemy were shelling us furiously on our front, right, and rear, mingled with terrific musketry." To relieve the pressure on his brigade, General Willich ordered Goodspeed's battery to take a position about 100 yards to the left of its original position, which they did. With the battery in place, Williams explained that the Eighty-ninth "moved in good order by the left flank, fronted, and laid down," the Thirty-second Indiana, Forty-ninth and Fifteenth Ohio doing the same and formed on the Railroaders left. During this change of position, Williams watched a stream of bluecoated fugitives run through and over Willich's brigade. But he commended, our men "stood firm and undaunted," earning the sobriquet—"Iron Brigade of the Cumberland Army." In General Willich's words, "Here I assembled my whole brigade, and took a position in the northwest corner of the [Kelly] field, which

---

[48]   *Chicago Evening Journal*, October 5, 1863.

in my judgement, then was the most threatened point." The Old Dutchman recognized that the rebels were now between our wing of the army and General Thomas' position. As Willich's men held firm, all about them the Union line collapsed. General Willich described the situation. "One or two of our divisions on the right of our . . . portion of the battle-field under higher orders" left. "Then the storm broke loose; first in small squads, then in an unbroken stream, the defenders rushed without organization over the open [Kelly] field, partly over and through my brigade, which was formed in two lines." Adding to the crisis, Willich wrote: "At the same time the enemy's artillery in front of me and in the rear of our lines advanced within canister range, swept my position, and entered into a canister duel with Captain Goodspeed."[49]

When those fleeing the front reached the cover of the woods, General Willich ordered Goodspeed to retire. Then General Willich slowly withdrew his brigade in two lines. Though the brigade was still under heavy artillery fire, it was not pressed by any rebel infantry. Major Williams gave this account of Willich's withdrawal. "After the battery had withdrawn and the cloud of fugitives had passed to the rear, the First Brigade about-faced, and halting and fronting every 50 yards, presented a bold and defiant front, effectively checking the enemy." He went on. "The Eighty-ninth, with the other regiments of the brigade, halted about half a mile to the rear of [the] original position in the morning, confronting the enemy and holding him in check, while the balance of the Army of the Cumberland filed by our rear in full retreat to Chattanooga, some 10 or 12 miles distant."[50]

"The First Brigade formed the rear guard of the Army of the Cumberland; the Eighty-ninth Illinois formed the rear guard of the brigade," Major Williams proudly reported afterward. With darkness finally closing in and enveloping the Railroaders, Major Williams wrote: "We marched about three hours, picking up countless stragglers, and forcing them on to Chattanooga. The enemy did not molest us. We halted with the brigade about 8 miles from the battle-ground of Chickamauga." In a letter to his mother back in

---

49   *Rock Island Argus*, October 19, 1863, *Willich* pamphlet; *OR*, Vol. 30, Pt. 1, 540-541, 544-545.

50   *OR*, Vol. 30, Pt. 1, 541, 545.

Illinois, Private Capron gave this picture of the battle's end. "On our right and front we could hear the heavy roar of musketry and the deep tone of cannon [that] told us that they was dealing death and destruction elsewhere as well as in our front. But our battery had expended all but one round of ammunition and we received orders to fall back which we did while the battery gave them the last round they had and then pulled off the field." Continuing, he explained that "as soon as dark came we took up our line of retreat toward Chattanooga. We came to Rossville 6 miles from Chattanooga where we camped for the night and drew rations for we had had nothing to eat for 24 hours."[51]

"The next morning, September 21," Major Williams stated that the Eighty-ninth "took a position about 4 miles in front of Chattanooga, remaining there in line of battle until 1 A.M.., September 22 . . . ." Withdrawing to within a mile of Chattanooga, the Railroaders formed a line of battle, threw up a temporary breastwork, and awaited the enemy. The eighteen-year-old farm boy from Rock Island County, Charles Capron, wrote: "Early the next morning we went to work and built a strong line of works and waited for the Johnnies to attack us but [they] did not seem inclined to bite. And that night we retreated to Chattanooga where we arrived a short time before daylight." The young recruit further added: "I laid down and got a few minutes sleep when we was called and told that we had to go to work and fortify the place. So at it we went and by night we had a good line of works. Then the rebels got possession of Lookout Mountain and planted siege guns and we [were] subjected to more or less [a] shelling every day."[52]

*   *   *

Before the Rebel victory was complete, the Railroaders captured Saturday evening were shipped south. George Berry scrawled a few lines in his diary. It was 2:00 P.M. when the prisoners started for Atlanta. They "arrived at Ringold at dark. Went twelve miles [more and] went in camp at Dalton station." September 22, "We arrived at

---

51   *OR*, Vol. 30, Pt. 1, 545; Capron, letter, January 23, 1865.
52   *Ibid.*

Atlanta at dark," Berry jotted. As an after-thought, he put down the following: "One slice of breade to the man. In the morning we had two crackers to the man. That is all we had till the next morning." For the September 23, Berry recorded, "Laide over one day [and] we had two crackers for the day." He further penned that all "Blankets and Canteens[,] Jacknifes was taken away from the boys" by the Confederate authorities.[53]

"A little before noon on September 21," Private Alfred French remembered being removed "from the battle field, and taken in an ambulance train to Chattanooga." After, what he recalled to be a 7 or 8 mile trip, he was "laid on the floor of the old Confederate barracks." Two days later, he was "taken in an army wagon across the river and unloaded in the woods. "And that night about 9 P.M. for first time," a surgeon came around and dressed the wounds he had "received five days before." Two more days passed before the men were given a tent. The "bunks [were] made of fence rails and covered with straw. There was room in a tent for 16 men. Rations were scant. A cup of coffee and a cracker filled the bill, but not the stomach." French "remained here about a month" until one day he was placed in an ambulance and taken by steamboat to Bridgeport, Alabama. Two days passed and French was carried off the boat to the rail terminal. French's account of the next leg of his journey began when he and 19 others were loaded into a cattle car with straw spread on the floor. "We were give a box of army crackers, a half barrel of water, and a tin cup. The car was locked. Thirty-six hours later, it was unlocked and we were taken to Hospital No. 18 [in] Nashville. Here we got good care and plenty to eat."[54]

Messages from Chattanooga arrived in Chicago both during and after the battle of Chickamauga. News from the battlefield was passed to the city's newspapers to be given to the general public. On September 21, the *Chicago Evening Journal* ran a story based on a telegram from the front. The headline read, "Two Chicago Officers of the 89th Illinois (Railroad) Regiment Killed." The article stated: "Col. Hotchkiss, of the 89th Illinois, this morning received a dispatch from the Army of the Cumberland, announcing the sad fact that Captain

---

[53]   Berry, diary, September 20, 22, and 23, 1863.
[54]   French Memoir.

Wm. H. Price (sic), of Co. A, and Captain J. W. Spink, of Co. D, of that regiment, are among the killed in the great battle in Northern Georgia." The piece concluded by stating that "the dispatch to Col. Hotchkiss gives no further casualties of the regiment. By Wednesday, the September 23, the *Journal* had more news. "Telegrams received in the city from Chattanooga, by Amos T. Hall … announce the death, in the recent battle, of his son, Lieutenant Colonel Duncan J. Hall, and Captains J. W. Spink, William H. Rice, and Thomas Whiting—all of the 89th regiment Illinois volunteers." The editor noted that "a private dispatch says that 'the regiment is badly cut up.'" Officially, the Railroad Regiment suffered 132 casualties in the two-day fight. Fourteen men were killed, 88 wounded, and 30 captured. Four officers died in the battle while five were wounded and two were captured.[55]

In a letter to Colonel Danforth, editor of the *Rock Island Argus*, Lieutenant Dimick confided that the Eighty-ninth went into the battle with 294 men. "Out of that number," he wrote, "we lost, in killed, wounded and missing 134." He mentioned that "Lieut. Col. Hall, commanding the regiment was killed by a sharpshooter on the afternoon of the 20th, leaving the command to Maj. W. D. Williams, who led the regiment during the afternoon with great credit to himself. He is an able officer, and is admired by all who know him." For the men in the ranks, Dimick wanted the folks back in Rock Island County to know that their "boys fought nobly. No company of their number could have done better execution. I am proud of them, and I have the greatest confidence in them, wherever I am ordered." He concluded by stating: "We now hold a strong position near the foot of Lookout Mountain. I am confident we can hold our position against any force the enemy can bring to bear against us."[56]

A revised casualty list for Dimick's Company F was published in the October 14 issue of the *Argus*. Added to those killed was James S. Anderson of Hampton. Elsewhere in the newspaper the editor said this: "Mr. Anderson's age was 29, and he leaves a wife—Mrs. Laura Anderson, dress maker, who now resides over Warren's book store in this city. She has three small children." Colonel Danforth

---

[55] *Chicago Evening Journal*, September 21 and 23, 1863; *OR*, Vol. 30, Pt. 1, 174.

[56] *Rock Island Argus*, October 8, 1863.

wrote a final line reminding his readers that "the memories of the brave defenders of the Union should be cherished with respect and affection—and their families cared for and protected."

Fortunately, there would be more to this story. The *Argus* reported on November 3 that Private Anderson was alive. His wife received a letter that morning dated October 5 and written in Richmond, Virginia. "MY DEAR WIFE:—I embrace the first opportunity possible of letting you know that, although a prisoner, I am unhurt. I was taken, with five others, on Saturday the 19th of September, on the field of battle, at about 7 ½ o'clock P.M.—after dark. We were sent to this place—a long and hard journey. I feel very thankful that I was not hurt, for I had many narrow escapes."[57]

Writing a friend back in Amboy, Sergeant Warren O. Hawley told of the role played by Company I in the recent battle. "It was detailed to guard an ammunition train for one month, beginning with the 6th of September. We were with the train through the fight, not exposed to the fire only when there was a wagon sent on the field with ammunition." He acknowledge that "we lost one of our best men killed, [John H.] Johnson, (a Fireman between Wapella and Centralia, the boys will all remember him), and one of the Malugin boys wounded in the leg. His name is Dewitt Marsh." Hawley had a little something else to say. "You will please to show this to the boys and tell them that I would like to be with them, but not till my time is out or every d—d rebel is dead or in hell alive."[58]

---

[57]   *Rock Island Argus*, October 14, 1863 and November 3, 1863.
[58]   *Amboy Times*, October 22, 1863.

CHAPTER 11

"'FORWARD AND VICTORY!'"

Having fled the Chickamauga battlefield to the safety of Chattanooga, the Army of the Cumberland found itself in a precarious position. With their back to the Tennessee River and his troops controlling the high ground in front, Confederate General Bragg expected Rosecrans' Union force to retreat. But, fearing his army's destruction if he left Chattanooga, Rosecrans elected to fortify the city and wait for relief. With no movement on the Yankees' part, Bragg set out on October 1 to lay siege and starve the stubborn Federals into surrendering. The Confederates cut access to the city from all sources but one horrible mountain road. With food supplies slowed to a trickle, conditions for the 35,000 Union soldiers at Chattanooga shortly became desperate. All food and forage came by rail from Nashville to Stevenson, Alabama and then over to Bridgeport, some 27 miles west of Chattanooga, but no further since the route into Chattanooga lay under Rebel guns. The distance to Chattanooga on the remaining road was sixty circuitous miles, taking from eight to twenty days, depending on the weather. Besides broken and empty wagons, the route was soon lined with the carcasses of mules—dead from exhaustion and hunger. The plight of the trapped soldiers worsened when Wheeler's Rebel cavalry attacked the supply route, destroying the trains bound for Chattanooga. All the while, a stunned and overwhelmed Rosecrans barely functioned and did little to relieve the army's plight.

Kept abreast of the situation in Tennessee by Assistant Secretary of War Charles A. Dana, the Lincoln Administration wasted no time and responded to the crisis, by dispatching on September 25, Major General Joseph Hooker and 20,000 men from the Army of the Potomac. Five days later, on September 30, Hooker's advance elements arrived at Bridgeport. Further assistance came when General-in-Chief Halleck ordered 17,000 men from Sherman's Army of the Tennessee to Chattanooga. Still, the gravity of the situation warranted additional action. Lincoln and Stanton on October 16 created the Military Division of the Mississippi and named Major General Ulysses S. Grant commander. They left Rosecrans' future to Grant, who without hesitation relieved him and appointed Thomas to head the Army of the Cumberland. Grant personally arrived at Chattanooga on October 23.[1]

*   *   *

Using the first opportunity available to write his mother, William J. Tomlinson, the Hancock County, Illinois section hand, said this: "I am yet alive and well . . . I have had some hard times since I wrote you last. Our regiment lost eight commisshened officers and 100 men. We wer in the fight all Day Sunday. We lay on our faces seven hours that Day, the most of the time in a field supporting our battery. About sundown they began to shell us . . . . The shells were bursting all around and over us. Ther was not much artillery used before but sutch musketry I never heard before and I hope never shall again." He had become aware that "the rebels had reinforecements from Richmond. We did not have eny. We expected some but they did not get here in time." Tomlinson, though, was up front about the fight. "They whip[p]ed us but it been all they culd do to. At that, we left Dead unburied and them that was not able to be brought away . . . ." At the present, "we are fortifying as fast as we can. They may attack us but they cant whipe us here." He then turned to the

---

[1]   Boatner, *The Civil War Dictionary*, 142-142; Faust, ed., *Historical Times Illustrated Encyclopedia of the Civil War*, 133-134; Miles, *Paths to Victory, A History and Tour Guide of the Stone's River, Chickamauga, Chattanooga, Knoxville, and Nashville Campaigns*, 79-83.

local men from Augusta and mentioned: "There is four of us here from Augusta all right. Tom Sharp was taken prisoner I think. You must go and see Mrs. Austin and tell her that Ugene is well and come through the battle without a scratch." In an afterthought he jotted that "'we ar Dirty and rag[g]ed . . . ."[2]

October 2, Thomas Berry penned a second letter to his sister-in-law informing her that he had "not heard a word about brother George" since he last wrote. Thomas did feel confident that George "with the rest of [the] boys of our Company was taken prisoners." Having been a captive, Thomas knew what to expect and told Harriet: "If he is [a prisoner], it may be a long time before you will hear from him." He then added: "As I have learned to day that they are all sent to Richmond, with the exception of those that are wounded so bad they could not stand the trip. Those are brought through the lines here. Rosecrans got the privilege of going after them and bring[ing] our wounded back . . . ." He went on. "I understand that most them are brought in here now. I have made inquiry but cannot find George amongst the wounded. Some of the wounded have had a hard time of it. They have lain on the battle field one week without any care." Thomas became even more serious. "O that I could inform you of his fate. It's hard to be kept in suspense so long, but we must nerve ourselves up for the worst, putting trust in the Lord's will. May we look to him for support that we may be enabled to bear up under the worst that may have befallen him." More to himself than to Harriet, Thomas commented. "It makes it very hard to have a battle and to be driven from the field as we cannot tell to a certainty what has become of the missing." For Harriet and anyone back in Knox County who may not have heard yet, he provided a list of the local men still unaccounted for. "The following are the missing at the present time George, Capt. Whiting, T. Whitney, Rosy Rosenleaf, Stroyan, Goddard, Newton, and Stoddard." The men eventually learned that Thomas Whiting, Winslow B. Newton, Hiram J. Rosenleaf, and Elliott M. Stoddard were all killed September 19. And, for those who came through unhurt, Thomas stated that "we have had a pretty hard time since the battle, expecting an attack here every day. We have been kept pretty busy working on the fortifications."[3]

---

[2]   Tomlinson, *In Good Courage: The Civil War Letters of William James Tomlinson*, 12.

[3]   Thomas Berry, letter, October 2, 1863.

On October 12, three days after receiving a letter from Mary, Joseph Buckley wrote a long, newsy response. Concerning his and the regiment's present circumstances, he explained: "I am enjoying good health with the exception of a cold, and there are very few of us without colds. The nights are cold and very chilly, and we have no blankets to cover us with. We have ordered woolen blankets each but they have not yet arrived. So we will have to get along as well as we can til get them." Joe mentioned a former neighbor, now with the One Hundred Forth Illinois, came over for a visit and stayed for dinner. "I gave him the best I had which was nothing more or less than some fried Sowbelly and hard tack and a cup of coffee, but which he relished very much as we are on half rations and we get hungry sometimes. I would give a dollar for three good slices of your bread and butter if I could get it."[4]

He too passed along the status of the missing and wounded. "Nothing has been heard from Bill Hughes and Ed Hargraves since the battle. I have no doubt but they were taken prisoners. One of the boys who was wounded in the mouth is dead. His name is Benjamin Haigh." In a prior letter, Joe mentioned that those soldiers with minor wounds were furloughed home to recover. "O! I am so anxious to see you I actually wished I was slightly wounded so I could have gone when [Sam] Pletcher went." While touching on the company's losses, Buckley mentioned that "six new recruits come to our company last Saturday. I feel sorry for them for they know little what they have to go through." Buckley did, and he begged his wife: "Now Mary, if you can think of any way by which I can get out of this war and come home to you, I wish you would send me word what it is. Now you may possibly hit on some idea, which might be the means of my getting home, for I am tired of (Uncle Sam's) treatment. I have been shot at about as often as I want to be."[5]

With pen and paper in hand, William J. Tomlinson sent a few more words home to his mother. The date was October 4, and he quickly pointed out that nothing had changed. "The rebels are in front of us yet. We can see their campfires evry night." The exchange of newspapers brought information bolstering the besieged Yankees

---

[4]   Buckley, letter, October 12, 1863.

[5]   Buckley, letter, October 5 and 12, 1863.

spirit. William summarized: "The rebel papers say that if they cannot drive us out of here that the Battle of CHICKAMAUGA might as well not bin fought, for they have lost so meny of their brave men for nuthing." While on the other hand, the Federal situation and conditions in Chattanooga were dire—there was hope. The scuttlebutt filtering through the ranks, which Tomlinson sent on, was that the Army of the Cumberland would get "reinforcements from Grant's Army and Meade's Army and Burnside's entire Army." However, foremost on every soldier's mind was survival. To secure shelter and fuel, Tomlinson wrote that the trapped Union troops were tearing "down houses that is werth from $100 to $3000 . . . ." The lumber was used to build shanties and also as firewood for both warmth and cooking. Trying not to raise too much concern, he casually remarked that "we ar rather short of rations."[6]

A week passed and Private Tomlinson found time to again write his mother. To neighbors and friends back home, he was pleased to say that "the rest of the boys from Augusta ar well and in good courage yet." The front had quieted down. For the well-being both sides, an accord of sort was worked out. As evidence, he wrote: "The pickets has quit fireing at each other and change papers evry day." This was for the best since the Eighty-ninth's picket line was within a stone's throw of the enemy. Tomlinson put it this way: "I was posted so near the rebels that I could here them spit." He continued, reiterating a story circulating through the army. It went that "Longstreet's men threw it to Bragg's men that they had to come down here and fight ther battles for them," which made "Bragg's men mad and they went to fighting among themselves." And as a consequence, "they commenced to shell us to Drown the sound of ther fighting so that we could not hear enything of it."[7]

With time on their hands resulted, the men put more effort and detail in their letters. Joseph Buckley spelled out to his wife what a soldier experienced in a trench-like environment. "We came off picket duty Saturday morning [October 10] after being on for four days. Picket duty has been very dangerous. When we first did picket duty, we used to shoot at the Rebels, and they used to shoot at us,"

---

[6]   Tomlinson, *In Good Courage: The Civil War Letters of William James Tomlinson*, 12.

[7]   *Ibid.*

Buckley explained. "It was dangerous for us to show our heads above the breastworks, for if we did, the next moment a bullet would come so near a fellow's head that there was no fun in it. And if they showed their heads, we served them in the same way for we made loop holes to shoot through." He noted that the Eighty-ninth's "picket line is only about a hundred yards from the Rebel's picket line. Some of our men got shot on the picket line and some of the Rebels got shot on their line." For the welfare of both armies, Buckley wrote: "Our General and the Rebel General have given orders that there must not be any more shooting on the picket line of either party unless one party attacked the other in force." Buckley was relieved and "glad they made that arrangement, for there used to be so much shooting on the picket line that it disturbed the camp so much that we had to get up almost every night and fall into line of battle and sometimes march out to the front." When not on the picket line, Buckley told Mary that "we are still fortifying this place stronger.[8]

And indeed, to save the army and maintain their hold on Chattanooga, the Army of the Cumberland dug in, creating an impregnable arc of trenches and rifle pits that extended from river bank to river bank. The men in blue would not think of relinquishing Chattanooga without a fight. They realized that too much hard campaigning had gone into the capture of the city to just give it back over to the Rebels. The Army of the Cumberland may have been beaten at Chickamauga, but it had survived to fight another day, and fight it would. There was no doubt, even amongst the ordinary soldiers, that this was a perilous time, especially when rations were cut to three-quarters, then to a half, and finally to a quarter. Private Buckley summed the situation up as it stood. "The result of the battle is as follows. Their object was to take possession of Chattanooga, and our objective was to keep possession of it. They got possession of the battlefield and that is a victory to them. So far as possession of Chattanooga, the victory is ours for we have possession of it and calculate to keep it." He emphasized: "The Rebels don't brag about this battle for they own up that they lost more men than we did and also, they failed in their objective."[9]

---

8   Buckley, letter, October 12, 1863.
9   Hicken, *Illinois in the Civil War*, 216-219; Buckley, letter, October 12, 1863.

With the cease-fire between the pickets in place and holding, commerce bloomed. "The last time we were on picket," Buckley wrote, "the Rebel pickets changed newspapers with us." The two sides reached an agreement for their trades. Buckley described the process: "There is a creek between their picket and ours and it had to be done in the presence of a commissioned officer from our side and a commissioned officer on their side. That is done to prevent giving information with regard to the position of either Army." As Buckley observed, this was "quite a contrast from trying to shoot one another's heads off." Fraternization, however, was strictly prohibited. "We drink water out of the same creek, but are not allowed to have conversation across the creek with them."[10]

While the wounded and sick were sent North to convalesce, replacements and veterans returned to replenish the ranks of the Eighty-ninth. Back with the regiment after his imprisonment, Curtis Knox remembered the nightmarish march into Chattanooga where he witnessed "one of the most awful and saddest sights of his life—mules dropped of starvation one after another, and for a long distance they tramped over a corduroy road of living skeletons." After enlisting on August 19 at Brooklyn, Illinois, eighteen-year-old John D. Holdren arrived as a recruit in Company I. He came to replace his father, William, who had enlisted the previous August in Company I and was killed on December 31 at Stone's River. Company B received a thirty-five-year-old private from Milwaukee by the name of Frank Sumter. Nineteen-year-old Thomas Wheeler enlisted on August 20 in Chicago. Without delay he had been shipped to the front and assigned to Company K. Right off on September 19, he received an ankle wound and was later discharged with a disability. Adjutant Edward F. Bishop, who had been wounded and cited for gallantry at Stone's River, was wounded again on September 20. Captain Farquhar reported Bishop lost "three or four fingers of his left hand," resulting in his "being disabled from service and in the winter of 1864 was discharged with pension." Captain John M. Farquhar, himself, still recovering from being "struck in the throat by a piece of shell," came down with typhoid fever followed by pneumonia.

---

10   Buckley, letter, October 12, 1863.

He applied for and received a leave of absence to go home and recover. Quartermaster Frederick L. Fake, with the death of his brother-in-law, Lieutenant Colonel Hall, resigned his commission effective October 6, 1863 and returned to Chicago. Still others, like Alexander Patterson of Company H, soldiered on. At Stone's River he had been "struck in the head by a minie-ball, destroying the sight in his right eye."[11]

Stunned from defeat and unable to render decisions to lift the siege, Rosecrans nevertheless found the time and energy to reorganize the Army of the Cumberland. On October 10, he issued an order relieving McCook and Crittenden from their respective commands, dissolving the Twentieth and Twenty-first Army Corps, and consolidating the divisions into the new Fourth Army Corps, with Major General Gordon Granger as commander. A bitter William Sumner Dodge angrily wrote that "it was the misfortune of the SECOND DIVISION to be included in this humiliating order." The first and third brigades were transferred to the third division of the Fourth Army Corps commanded by General Thomas J. Wood. General Willich continued to command his brigade, but with additional regiments. The third brigade was turned over to General W. B. Hazen, "a tried and skillful officer." The second brigade was broken up and its regiments scattered throughout the army. "Such was the fate of the SECOND DIVISION. Its unity, its past glorious associations and its illustrious services merited a more noble termination," Dodge lamented. Private Joseph Buckley saw it more or less as a change of address and told his wife: "When you direct your letters you can leave out the words (20th Army Corps) as there is quite a change going on just now in organizing the different

---

[11]   *Soldiers' and Patriots' Album*, 631; Notes for William B. Holdren. [Internet website] http://www.duprel.com/holddes.html; *Adjutant General's Report*, V: 261, 268; Thomas Wheeler Civil War (Reprint West Chicago Newspaper-not dated) [Internet website] http://members.tripod.com/~simonfamily/wheelercivilwar.html; William N. Byers, *Encyclopedia of Biography of Colorado, History of Colorado* (Chicago: The Century Publishing and Engraving Company, 1901), I: 351; *Chicago Evening Journal*, October 6, 1863; Farquhar pension file; Bateman and Selby, ed., *Historical Encyclopedia of Illinois and History of Kendall County*, II: 1031.

Regiments, Brigades and Divisions. So I will send word in my next how you must direct them."[12]

Twenty-nine-year-old Walter S. Huff and his younger twenty-year-old brother, John B., on August 4, 1862 enlisted in William D. Williams' Company. Prior to answering Lincoln's call for more volunteers, the brothers farmed near Hampton, Illinois in Rock Island County. At Stone's River, Walter was captured and did not return to the regiment until May 20, 1863. While at Chattanooga, Walter acquired a pocket diary and began making short, entries. The first was dated October 15, 1863. He noted: "It is still raining and has been for two days. It rained very hard last night and [came] very near drowning the regt out. We draw rations today."[13]

Three weeks into the siege, news, gossip, and food became centerpiece in the Railroaders routine and thought. Huff made the following disjointed entry to his journal, reflecting his day and what was being said and heard about the camp. "On picket this morning at 4 o'clock. Had to move our bunks this morning to keep them dry. Ohio, Pennsylvania and Iowa have went with a heavy majority for the Union. We are making vegetable soup dinner today. It has nearly cleared off though the sun has shone some today. Continuing, Huff noted that "Goodspeed's battery leaves us today to go about 40 miles to guard a Fort. Nothing transpired today. Wrote a letter to Levi Dudley. No mail yet. Report today that Hooker had a fight with the rebs and took several prisoners. Not credited."[14]

Huff's jottings for October 16 began with the weather. "It has the appearance of clearing up today. Inspection this evening at three o'clock. The rebs are quiet." Due to the recent rains, he noted the river was rising; and consequently, "the bridges have to be taken up to keep the driftwood from taking them off." Also, he entered

---

[12] Dodge, *History of the Old Second Division, Army of the Cumberland*, 576-579; Buckley, letter, October 12, 1863.

[13] Walter Scott Huff diary entry for October 15, 1863. The original is in the possession of Roddy A. Burwell, Casper, Wyoming. Mr. Burwell provided the author a typed transcription and will hereafter be cited as Huff diary. The Civil War diary of Walter Scott Huff [Internet Website] http://www.geocities.com/HeartlandPointe/3497/.

[14] Huff, diary, October [no exact date shown 1863].

the latest rumor held that Bragg was getting siege guns to drive the Federals out. The next day began with another series of eclectic postings. "Heavy fog this morning. Details for carpentry. Received a letter from home dated the 4th. Answered it the same day. There has been some cannonading but the result is not known. The Regt goes on picket in the morning. Sent on two letters to John [his brother] who is at Bridgeport yet and two that have been here some time." On October 19, he recorded that a rebel raft "sent down to tare the pontoon bridge away" was caught and "no damage done." Other than that, the day on the whole was "very dull" with "nothing going on." But, he found the latest camp rumor worthy of a couple of lines. "Bragg intended to take dinner in Chattanooga today but he did not come. I expect he will postpone it for an indefinite period."[15]

Lieutenant Harkness said in a letter to his brother: "The only way there is of crossing the Tennessee river here is on a long pontoon bridge which the Rebels have injured quite often by sending down large rafts loaded with stone and railroad iron." To prevent the bridge's destruction, he noted that "our men keep a steamboat there all the time ready to catch the rafts and push them ashore. When the stone and iron is thrown off, the logs [are] taken to a steam sawmill [and] and made into plank and lumber for the use of the army. They have built a lots on new pontoon boats from the lumber so obtained." Harkness explained that "the raft that did the most damage came down in the night and was loaded down level with the water with R.R. iron and our lookouts did not see it till it struck the bridge."[16]

Arriving in Cairo on October 17, General Grant received instructions to proceed immediately to Louisville. There he was to meet an officer from the War Department with more instructions. Grant traveled by rail to Indianapolis. But as his car was pulling away from the depot, a messenger caught the engineer's attention and halted the train. A special train with Secretary of War Stanton was coming into the station, and he was there to confer with Grant. Stanton now accompanied Grant on to Louisville. Once settled in and on their way, Stanton handed Grant two orders, saying he could

15 Huff, diary, October 16, 17 and 19, 1863.
16 Harkness, letter, undated, but probably written very early November 1863.

take his choice of which to follow. Both created the Military Division of the Mississippi with Grant in charge of the Departments of the Ohio, the Cumberland and the Tennessee. One order made no change in the army commanders while the other replaced Rosecrans with Major General George H. Thomas. Dazed by the defeat at Chickamauga, Rosecrans had accomplished little in resolving the army's supply problem. Grant was also cognizant of Washington's deep concern that Rosecrans would retreat, abandoning the Gateway City. With Rosecrans temporarily ineffective and now considered untrustworthy, Grant recognized new leadership was necessary and quickly replaced him with Thomas.[17]

On arriving in Louisville, Grant telegraphed Rosecrans of the order from Washington that removed him and assigned the command of the Army of the Cumberland to Thomas. General Thomas was informed that "he must hold Chattanooga at all hazards" and that Grant would be "at the front as soon as possible." Stanton, having concluded his business, returned to the nation's capital while Grant started the morning of October 20 for Nashville. By the evening of the 21st, Grant was in Stevenson, Alabama, where he briefly spoke with Rosecrans who had stopped there on his way north. Grant moved on to Bridgeport where he stayed the night. The next day he traveled by horseback to Chattanooga, arriving at nightfall on October 23.[18]

On October 22, Private Huff jotted: "The report now is that Rosecrans has gone to take command of the Potomac Army and that Grant is going to take command of the department." Two days later the Company F soldier noted in his journal that General Grant was on his way Chattanooga. Followed by, Grant had arrived, and "says he must have possession of Lookout Mt." Grant may have taken charge, but Huff was pessimistic of any immediate change. "Time to draw rations today but do not expect to get them." While Grant was en route to Chattanooga, the Eighty-ninth was ordered to a new location. The Railroaders hurriedly dismantled their shebangs and "got our things packed [and] ready to move

---

[17]   Ulysses S. Grant, *Personal Memoirs of U. S. Grant* (New York: Charles L. Webster & Company, 1886), II: 17-19; Long, *The Civil War Day By Day*, 423-424.

[18]   Grant, *Personal Memoirs of U. S. Grant*, 19, 26-29.

camp." Huff related that the men moved about a mile, but they had not got fixed up yet, having not gotten all their boards up. The following day rain set in, making life very disagreeable. Huff added, "Haven't got our tent done yet on account of not getting the boards moved."[19]

*   *   *

In the Railroad Regiment ranks were a number of skilled artisans. Aware of their talent, the army called upon them, when needed, for special projects. With General William Farrar "Baldy" Smith's engineering staff combing the Army of the Cumberland in search of carpenters, one of the soldiers picked was Company E Corporal S. K McCullough. In civilian life Samuel Kirk McCullough had worked as a carpenter in the Chicago, Burlington, & Quincy car shops. With the need to bridge the Tennessee River, Corporal McCullough was detailed to the engineers where his carpentry skills were used in constructing pontoon bridges. Unbeknownst to the construction crew, the pontoons would be instrumental in breaking the siege.[20]

"Baldy" Smith struck out on the morning, of October 19, with Rosecrans and his staff searching for a way to cross the Tennessee River with enough force to drive away the Rebels, and therefore open the river to steamboat traffic. Frustrated with the dawdling Rosecrans, Smith ventured off on his own toward Brown's Ferry. After studying the terrain and the river for several hours, he came up with a plan for the army's relief. Returning to headquarters, he learned that Thomas had replaced Rosecrans. Undeterred, he now took his idea to open the river to General Thomas. Thomas listened and authorized Smith to proceed with the details. Grant arrived on October 23 and the next day he and Smith rode over to Brown's Ferry. On the way, Smith outlined the proposal, already approved by Thomas, for opening a "line of communication and relieving the army." Grant, too, endorsed the project and ordered Smith to implement it immediately.

---

[19]   Huff, diary, October 20 through 22, 24 and 25, 1863.

[20]   Ephemera File M (Newspaper Obituary I-59), Galesburg Public Library, Galesburg, Illinois.

It was pitch dark and foggy at 3:00 A.M.. on October 27 when two flatboats and fifty pontoons with nearly 1,500 handpicked men from Hazen's Brigade cast loose at Chattanooga and drifted slowly and silently downstream past Rebel pickets to Brown's Ferry. By 4:30 A.M.. the lead flatboat sighted the signal fire—the alert to head for the opposite bank and unload. The flotilla headed for the other side of the river and one by one the boats pulled ashore. The first troops ashore secured the landing area, while those that followed set off to their assigned tasks. The remainder of Hazen's Brigade, 700 men, and Turchin's entire brigade crossed the Tennessee River at Brown's Ford. With the heights overlooking the crossing secured, a pontoon bridge was put over. On October 28, Hooker's column arrived from Bridgeport, and the following day his troops were in possession of Lookout Valley.[21]

In a note home to his mother dated October 26, Private William Tomlinson said that he had been "unwell for the last few days—a cold—not bin to the sick camp . . . less than half rashuns." Food, however, was in foremost on his mind. He had "dremped" that his mother and an aunt came to see him "and set a table full of good things" to eat. The army's situation being as it was, he was quick to pass along the latest camp gossip and wrote: "I herd this morning that General Grant said he would have the rebels out of the way in three days . . . ." Whether Grant made the statement or not, the Rebel hold on the Federal army was broken, and on October 30, a steamboat loaded with rations and forage was unloaded at Chattanooga. It had been five days since Grant's arrival, and what the soldiers referred to as the Cracker Line was open and running. And, in less than a week after his dream of a home cooked meal, Tomlinson informed his mother that "we are to Draw full rashens of crackers and meat." He was also happy to write that the regiment "got some clothing yesterday. I shall draw a new overcoat." Tomlinson commented that "ther has been some fighting on the right for several days past."[22]

---

[21] Boatner, *The Civil War Dictionary*, 141-143; Peter Cozzens, *The Shipwreck of Their Hopes, The Battles for Chattanooga* (Urbana and Chicago: University of Illinois Press, 1994), 39-65; Faust, ed., *Historical Times Illustrated Encyclopedia of the Civil War*, 133-134; Long, *The Civil War Day By Day*, 426-428; Clarence Edward McCartney, *Grant and His Generals* (New York: The McBride Company, 1953), 196-200;

[22] Tomlinson, *In Good Courage: The Civil War Letters of William James Tomlinson*, 13; Boatner, *The Civil War Dictionary*, 143.

October 30, Charles Capron started a letter to his parents. He began: "There has been some pretty heavy fighting done the last two days." His comment, however, was based on hearsay rather than actual observation. Pointing out the Federals' dilemma, he wrote: "The rebels occupy Lookout Mountain and have got a battery planted on top of it so that we cannot run the cars in yet on account of their shelling there, but they will have to get off there if it takes all the forces in Chattanooga to do it as we cannot get supplies into the town." With that thought, Capron was forced to quit writing as it was raining "so hard that it beat through the tent and wet" his stationary. It was November 1 when he resumed his correspondence. Immediately, he opened with source of the army's problem. "One of the boys has brought in a shell that has been throwed in here by the rebs. It weighs 34 pounds. It did not burst. You had better believe it is a pretty good chunk of iron." News that the Rebel grip on Chattanooga had been broken, and with it the arrival of the first steamboat loaded with rations and forage, still had not reached Capron, or if it had, he felt it was a rumor and not worth repeating. In fact he revealed the severity of the army's situation to his mother and father. "We get 2 crackers a day now and quarter a pound of meat; coffee three times a day. Today we got 2 spoonful of sugar. Think we will draw full rations today. If we cannot get rations we will certainly have to evacuate the place."[23]

"Dear Wife," began Joseph Buckley on November 3. "It is now a little over six weeks since the Battle and we have been on very short rations ever since. I will give you some idea of how we have lived for the last six weeks. We are allowed two crackers per day and sometimes a very small portion of beef or pork. Sometimes we get some weak coffee and sometimes we don't. That is all we get . . . ." Continuing, he wrote: "I expect that we shall get more rations soon, at least I hope so. I have been offered 50 cents for a cracker but I would not taken a dollar for it. One ear of corn will fetch from 15 cents to 25 cents. Yesterday the Boys were picking kernels of corn off the ground, which the mules could not pick up themselves. And I could tell you of a great many worse cases that that, but that is sufficient to give an idea of what a soldier's living is

---

23   Capron, letter, October 30, 1863.

at present in Chattanooga." The condition of the army was critical, and Buckley told Mary that "the Boys all complain of being weak, and that is what is the matter with me. It is hard to go hungry for six weeks, but I would rather go hungry six weeks more, than to give up Chattanooga to the Rebs." Caught between hope and reality, Buckley ensured his wife that his morale was holding up. "I have no doubt but our commanders will get rations to us as soon as possible." Food was not the only shortage, Buckley revealed that most of the men had "no blankets except an oilcloth 3 feet wide and about 5 ½ feet long to cover" themselves with at night. "I lay down at night on a piece of board and throw my oilcloth (which is full of holes) over me, and sleep the best way I can. I am not complaining but I thought I would just give you some idea of how we are situated. I have faith in the Government, and my Faith in God is strong. I know he will watch over us and bring things around all right, so do not fret or make yourself uneasy about me . . . ."[24]

From these few letters it is apparent that the opening of the Cracker Line did not immediately affect the lives of those on the front line. Even though an avenue of relief was secured, the gloom that had settled over the Army of the Cumberland after Chickamauga and throughout the siege of Chattanooga remained. Until the specter of starvation and the possibility of retreat had been extinguished, the Army of the Cumberland would not be ready for another fight.

For a number of weeks Buckley's frustration with Mary began appearing in his correspondence. Long separation from family and friends, deprived of food, clothing and shelter could leave a soldier angry and depressed. On October 12, he responded to her question of his fidelity. "You say you suppose I am getting used to staying at my (Uncles). I am used to staying at my (Uncles). That you mean, I have no desires whatever for (coitus) with any Female but the one I married and the only one I love. So you may rest yourself content in that respect. The handsomest Female in Tennessee could not lead me astray in that respect under any circumstances whatsoever. For my love for you grows stronger every day of my life."

On November 15, Buckley wrote chastising Mary for her seeming lack of concern for his well-being. "With regard to sending me things

---

[24] Buckley, letter, November 2, 1863.

from home safely, all I can say is that the rest of the boys in the company get along safely. I believe I am the only one in the company that has not had clothing and all kinds of luxuries sent to them. You know I asked you to send me a small box once, but you thought it was too much trouble, so I made up my mind that I would not ask you again to send me anything unless it was a few postage stamps." Mary's thoughtlessness touched a nerve when she failed to put a stamp on a letter to Joseph. He explained: "A week ago last Thursday I received a notice from the Post Master at Nashville that there was a letter addressed to me which was detained there for no payment of postage and by enclosing six cents and returning the notice my letter would be forwarded to me." Buckley continued: "I did so right off and did not get the letter until day before yesterday. The letter cost me ten cents to get it—six cents enclosed; three cents to send it back; and one cent for the envelope. So you see it will be cheaper to pay the postage before you send letters." He alerted Mary that his clothing bill had run over his allowance "to the amount of twelve dollars and thirty-seven cents. That amount will be deducted from my pay next pay day." November 20, Buckley wrote a few hasty lines informing Mary that he had received four month's pay, totaling $39.60. The army kept $12.40 for clothing. He sent his wife $20 by express.

As a faithful husband and father, Buckley tried to keep his negative thoughts to himself and under control. But, the effect of the siege, the possibility of another battle, the lack of support from home all came to a head and he let his emotions pour forth. "Well Mary, if I should be killed, I hope you won't fret but take things as patient as you can for I don't see but you will get along just as well without me as you would with me. I am not well. My head aches awful today. I am not under the Doctor's care but I ought to be. I am very weak, but if there is any fighting to be done, I am bound to be in it. I feel desolate and lonely and I feel as though I would just a leave be killed as not. I have felt just so since I heard of Johnnie's death yesterday." Taking a fatalistic approach, he wrote: "But I will leave myself in the care of the Lord. If he sees fit to take me away it will be for the best. And if he sees fit to bring me through all right, it will be for the best."[25]

---

[25] Buckley, letters, October 12, November 2, 15, and 20, 1863.

*   *   *

The month-long siege may have been broken with the opening of communications and the "Cracker Line" on October 30, but Bragg's Rebels still peered down on Chattanooga from Lookout Mountain and Missionary Ridge. The besieging Rebel army, however, was not much better off than their counterparts holed-up in Chattanooga. Many in Bragg's ranks were sick, while all were hungry and lacked proper shelter. To make matters worse, the rebels were short on ammunition. Both President Davis and Longstreet urged Bragg to pullback to a better position in Georgia, but he rejected the idea. Rather than withdraw, Bragg weakened his force by dispatching Longstreet and his veterans to Knoxville on November 4. By shifting to Knoxville and Burnside, Bragg hoped to turn Grant's attention away from Chattanooga and his men on the heights. Grant did not take the bait and stayed focused on the situation before him. He reasoned that the best way to help Burnside was to drive the Confederate army away from Chattanooga, and do it as quickly as possible.[26]

A man of action Grant wasted no time in formulating a plan to clear the Confederates from the heights. Sherman and the leading elements of the Army of the Tennessee reached Bridgeport on November 15. Anxious to get things started, Grant hurried to Sherman and briefed him on his role in the coming battle. They agreed to commence the campaign on November 21. But, heavy rains and mud delayed Sherman's column, pushing back the offensive until November 24.[27]

Grant's plan was obviously not a tightly held secret, for the *Chicago Evening Journal's* Special War Correspondent, Benjamin F. Taylor, laid it out in print. He wrote that Sherman's men were to take "a position upon our extreme left, five miles to the northeast,

---

[26] Boatner, *The Civil War Dictionary*, 143; Faust, ed., *Historical Times Illustrated Encyclopedia of the Civil War*, 133; Hicken, *Illinois in the Civil War*, 223.

[27] Boatner, *The Civil War Dictionary*, 143-144; Faust, ed., *Historical Times Illustrated Encyclopedia of the Civil War*, 133-134; Miles, *Paths to Victory, A History and Tour Guide of Stone's River, Chickamauga, Chattanooga, Knoxville, and Nashville Campaigns*, 87-88.

were to attain Mission Ridge and roll the rebel army before them." At the same moment, Hooker, over on the extreme right, was to make a demonstration upon Lookout Mountain. General Gordon Granger's mission was to swing around towards Rossville. All the while Johnson and Howard's commands were to hold Chattanooga and act as reserves. Taylor reported that the plan was to go into motion Friday morning, November 20, at daylight, but a heavy rain set in and the roads became impassable. As a consequence, Sherman's ponderous trains of artillery bogged down, and Friday, Saturday, and Sunday and Monday came and went.[28]

While Sherman maneuvered in preparation for the main attack, Rebel deserters reported that Bragg had weakened his lines on Missionary Ridge. Some even hinted at a Confederate withdrawal. The *Journal's* correspondent commented that "field glasses were everywhere sweeping the mountains" and noted that "the rebel lines were restless; trains were moving, brigades passing and repassing . . . ." From his own observation, the reporter concluded: "It was apparent that the enemy apprehended danger, for on Sunday morning [November 22], two divisions moved northward along Mission Ridge and took position on" the extreme right. The reality was that Bragg was in the process of forwarding two divisions to reinforce Longstreet. Taylor wrote: "Deserters, officers and men, came into our picket lines that night; the rebels were astir; rations had been issued; their baggage sent to the rear, they were making ready for business." Having seen the rebel activity and digested the prisoner's interrogations, Grant could no longer be restrained. It was time to act.[29]

Between the Federal lines and Missionary Ridge was a small hill, known as Orchard Knob, where the Confederates had located an outpost. Before any advance on Missionary Ridge, Grant recognized this position would have to be cleared. He reasoned that it was time to make a move and ordered a reconnaissance in force toward Missionary Ridge for the afternoon of November 23. At 11:00 A. M., General Willich received orders to form his brigade in front of Fort

---

28 *Chicago Evening Journal*, December 5, 1863.

29 Cozzens, *The Shipwreck of Their Hopes, The Battles for Chattanooga*, 127; *Chicago Evening Journal*, December 5, 1863.

Wood. After having formed his brigade, Willich received amended orders. His men were to now take Orchard Knob, which was a mile and quarter in front of Fort Wood, and hold it until further orders.[30]

Taylor gave this detailed description of the ground to be covered by the Federal regiments. "From the Fort [Wood] the smooth ground descends rapidly to a little plain . . . then a fringe of oak woods, then an acclivity, sinking down to a second fringe of woods, until full in front of you and three-fourths of a mile distant rises Orchard Knob, a conical mound, perhaps a hundred feet high, once wooded now bald." The Federal line lay along the slope to the right and left of Fort Wood while the rebel advance held Orchard Knob in force. "Breastworks and rifle-pits seamed the landscape" that was the rebel outpost.[31]

The restructuring of the Army of the Cumberland resulted in undersized regiments being shuffled about to strengthen depleted brigades. Attached to Willich's old brigade were the Eighth Kansas, Sixty-eighth Indiana, Fifteenth Wisconsin, and Twenty-fifth and Thirty-fifth Illinois. With the newly arrived Eighth Kansas out in front as skirmishers, Willich deployed the Fifteenth and Forty-ninth Ohio, Twenty-fifth and Thirty-fifth Illinois in a line of battle. The second line was made up of the Thirty-second and Sixty-eighth Indiana, Eighty-ninth Illinois, and Fifteenth Wisconsin. The regiments were formed in "double column on the center, closed *en masse*." Once all the Federal troops were drawn up there were nearly 25,000 standing at attention in the open valley between the lines. The rebels, having no idea what was taking place, stared on, concluding the display before them was a grand review and settled in to watch. The Federals were not putting on a show. Willich's orders were to take the knob, while General William B. Hazen's brigade captured the entrenchments on the right. With the troops formed up, Lieutenant Colonel William D. Williams stated that at 1:00 P.M. the signal to move out was given. The Railroaders stepped off and steadily followed the skirmish line of the Forty-ninth Ohio Infantry. The Buckeyes drove before them the enemy's pickets and reserves.

---

[30]   Boatner, *The Civil War Dictionary*, 144; Cozzens, *The Shipwreck of Their Hopes, The Battles for Chattanooga*, 127; *OR*, Vol. 31, Pt. 2, 263.

[31]   *Chicago Evening Journal*, December 5, 1863.

Showing little desire to put up a fight, the rebels abandoned their entrenchments and fled. After taking the rebel positions at Orchard Knob, the Eighty-ninth, according to orders halted and lay upon their arms.[32]

Writing in the style of the period, Brigadier General Thomas J. Wood recounted the charge in his official report. "So as soon as the skirmishers moved forward the enemy opened fire. Across the open field and through the woods the skirmishers kept up a sharp rattling fire, steadily and rapidly driving in the enemy. As the knob and intrenchments were neared the fire became hotter, the resistance of the rebels more determined; but the majestic advance of our lines was not for a moment stayed." He continued: "Finally, Willich's brigade, which had met with less opposition than Hazen's, having arrived quite near the knob, 'by a bold burst' ascended its steep acclivity, crowned its summit, and it was ours." General Willich summarized the consolidation of the knob. On the crest of Orchard Knob, the men erected an epaulement, basically a mound of earth heaped up, to afford cover from the flanking fire, and breastworks in front and on both sides of it. The effort was done under heavy artillery fire from the enemy's guns, "which was little heeded by the men and with all its terrific appearance did very little damage."[33]

"On Monday the 23rd of November just after dinner," Joseph Buckley wrote, "we were ordered to fall in with 100 rounds of cartridges each. We were then ordered in front where we formed in line of Battle, and at two o'clock the word 'Forward' was given. We all started simultaneously, and it was one of the most splendid sights I ever saw." Buckley continued: "We advanced steadily but quickly and drove the REBS one mile before we stopped and took possession of their first line of Breastwork, and also a large knoll which went by the name of Orchard Knobb, but we call it Willicks Knobb now." The brigade consolidated the position. Private Buckley explained: "We went to work after dark and planted 6 cannons on the knoll and threw up a breastworks in front. It took most of the

---

32   *OR*, Vol. 31, Pt. 2, 255, 263, 269; Cozzens, *The Shipwreck of Their Hopes, the Battles for Chattanooga*, 129-130.

33   *OR*, Vol. 31, Pt., 255, 263.

night. The next day the Rebs threw some shells amongst us, but did no damage."[34]

The Rock Island County farm hand, Charles Capron, spoke of the hours leading to the capture of Orchard Knob. "We got marching orders last night [November 22] every man to have a hundred rounds of cartridges and full rations and be ready to go by four o'clock in the morning but from some cause or other the order was postponed for a while and I snatch this opportunity of writing to you." He spelled out that "yesterday they throwed about 30 shells over into the rebels camp from our fort [Wood] but could not get any reply. Tomorrow or [the] next day we will have some hot work with them for they have got to git out of there." But I must give you some more of the particulars . . . . It was this way, I was writing in the tent when the bugle sounded fall in. The officers gave orders for every man to have 60 rounds of cartridges." Capron later recalled how the action that day unfolded. "About noon the different regiments marched out and took their respective positions and soon we had 2 lines of battle formed stretching as far as the eye could reach both to the right and the left. It looked more like [a] grand review." The eighteen-year-old penned his description of the Federal charge. "Everything being ready the bugle sounded for the skirmishers to advance. Instantly there was a line of blue thin smoke arose, and then the sharp reports of the skirmishers' rifles told us plainly that the dance had opened. Then followed the lines of battle advancing about a mile and a half. We gained an important position where we built a line of works and remained there for the night subjected to a severe shelling from Mission Ridge."[35]

Observing the spectacle from a distance was correspondent Benjamin Taylor. A skilled wordsmith, he drew this written picture.

At ten minutes before two, 25,000 Federal troops were in a line of battle. The line of skirmishers moved lightly out, and swept true as a sword blade into the edge of the field. You should have seen that splendid line, two miles long, as straight and unwavering as a ray of light. On they went, driving in the

---

[34]   Buckley, letter, December 10, 1863.
[35]   Capron, letters, November 23-27, 1863 and January 24, 1865.

pickets before them; shots of musketry, like the first great drops of summer rain upon a roof, pattered along the line. One fell here, another there, but still . . . the skirmishers passed on. From wood and rifle-pit, from rocky ledge and mountain top, sixty-five thousand rebels watched . . . . The bugle sounded from Fort Wood and the divisions of Wood and Sheridan began to move . . . . Black rifle-pits were tipped with fire; sheets of flame flashed out of the woods; the spatter of musketry deepened into volleys and rolled like muffled drums; rebel batteries opened from the ledges; the 'Rodmans' joined in from Fort Wood; bursting shell and gusts of shrapnel filled the air; the echoes roused up and growled back from the mountains, the rattle was a roar and yet those gallant fellows moved steadily on; down the slope, through the wood, up the hills, straight for Orchard Knob . . . moved the glorious wall of blue. And our prairie boys were there—the 25th, 35th, 89th Illinois—for are they not *everywhere* where death is dealt and victory won![36]

Commanding Company F that afternoon, Lieutenant Laertes F. Dimick wrote this about the attack on Orchard Knob for the *Rock Island Union*. "The battle commenced on the 23d inst., at one o'clock. It was one of the most beautiful sights I ever witnessed. Our lines of battle formed on a ridge, and over two miles and a half in length. Very soon we were in readiness and the grand army moved off. The enemy thought we were on review, and was not quite prepared for us.

"We advanced some half mile or more and took the enemy's rifle pits—a very important position. That night we worked all night preparing breastworks and positions for our artillery. Hooker did most of the fighting on the 24th, taking Lookout Mountain. He had a very hard fight and continued until ten o'clock at night."[37]

The original order called for the reconnaissance brigades to be withdrawn, but the success was such that Thomas signaled General Wood that too much had been gained to withdraw. The position was to be held and supported. Thomas quickly ordered Blair's Division

---

[36] *Chicago Evening Journal*, December 5, 1863.
[37] *Rock Island Union*, December 16, 1863.

and Howard's XI Corps forward, securing the gain and allowing the entire Army of the Cumberland to come up. "This movement secured to us a line fully a mile in advance of the one we occupied in the morning and the one which the enemy had occupied up to this time. The fortifications were rapidly turned the other way. During the following night they were made strong," wrote Grant in his *Memoirs*. Grant noted Federal casualties were about 1,100 killed and wounded. General Willich reported four killed and 10 wounded in his brigade, and credited "the small loss" to "impetuosity of the advance, which did not permit the enemy to reform after being once broken by our skirmishers." Wood's Division lost 29 killed, 161 wounded, and none captured, while they took 174 prisoners.[38]

The next day, November 24, the Railroaders rested in line. All eyes and ears watched and listened to Hooker's "fight above the clouds" for Lookout Mountain. Capron recalled the day. "The 11 and 12 Corps attack Lookout Mountain and there was where the battle raged the fiercest. The very earth trembled under the fire of heavy guns [and] the air was full of shells bursting in every direction and soon the smoke was so thick and the top of old Lookout was no longer visible." That night the Eighty-ninth went on picket duty. With his colleagues Capron continued to be glued to action on Lookout Mountain. "But long after dark we could see the flash of their rifles like so many fireflies and it did not cease till after midnight. When it quieted down and nothing could be heard except an occasional report of a picket rifle."[39]

*　　*　　*

At 1:00 P.M. on November 24, Sherman's men crossed the Tennessee River on a 1,350-foot-long bridge built of 116 pontoon boats, kicking off the offensive to roll up Missionary Ridge. By 4:00

---

[38] W. H. Chamberlin, ed., *Sketches of War History, 1890-1896* (Cincinnati: The Robert Clark Co., 1896), IV: 28-29; Cozzens, *The Shipwreck of Their Hopes, The Battles for Chattanooga*, 132-133; Faust, ed., *Historical Times Illustrated Encyclopedia of the Civil War*, 547; Grant, *The Personal Memoirs of U. S. Grant*, 374; *OR*, Vol. 31, Pt. 2, 251, 263.

[39] Capron, letter, January 24, 1865.

P.M. and after sporadic fighting, Sherman, whose maps proved to be incorrect, found that he had unfortunately captured an isolated hill. Missionary Ridge lay ahead and across a small valley, and since 2:30 P.M., had been occupied by Cleburne's Division. Sherman ordered his divisions to dig in, and with reinforcements, he would assault the rebels in the morning. With daylight on November 25, the Federals found the Stars and Stripes floating from the summit of Lookout Mountain. Over on the left, Sherman began a daylong struggle to dislodge Cleburne. To Grant's chagrin, the Rebel veterans put up a stiff fight and by mid-afternoon Sherman was bogged down.[40]

Since the afternoon of November 23, General Wood had made his headquarters on Orchard Knob. On the morning of the November 25, Generals Grant, Thomas, Granger and their staffs also took-up a position there. Assistant Secretary of War Dana, Quartermaster-General Meigs, and General David Hunter joined them. "Sherman's attack was in full view, so that every movement was easily and plainly discernible," recalled General Wood. By 2:30 P.M., Wood remembered that "it was plainly and painfully evident to every beholder on Orchard Knob that Sherman's attack . . . had been hopelessly defeated, and was an irretrievable failure."

Roommates at West Point, Generals Grant and Wood discussed the situation, with Grant commenting that "General Sherman seems to be having a hard time." Wood concurred, and Grant stated, "I think we ought to try to do something to help him." Wood again agreed. Grant continued, "I think if you and Sheridan were to advance your divisions and carry the rifle pits at the base of the Ridge, it would so threaten Bragg's center that he would draw enough troops from the right, to secure his center, to insure the success of General Sherman's attack." Wood states General Grant walked over and had a short conversation with Thomas. When finished, Thomas in turn spoke with Granger, who came to Wood with the order to take the entrenchment at the base of Missionary Ridge and to halt there.

---

[40]   Boatner, *The Civil War Dictionary*, 144-146; Faust, ed., *Historical Times Illustrated Encyclopedia of the Civil War*, 133-135; Miles, *Paths to Victory, A History and Tour Guide of the Stone's River, Chickamauga, Chattanooga, Knoxville, and Nashville Campaigns*, 89-93.

Wood sent for his brigade commanders Hazen, Willich, and Beatty and repeated the order.[41]

In his *Personal Memoirs* Grant wrote, "Sherman's condition was getting so critical that the assault for his relief could not be delayed any longer." Grant also noted that "Sheridan's and Wood's divisions had been lying under arms from early morning, ready to move the instant the signal was given. I now directed Thomas to order the charge at once." Time passed with "no indication of any charge being made." Grant sought out Thomas to find out what was causing the delay and found him talking with General Wood. Grant stated: "I spoke to General Wood, asking him why he did not charge as ordered an hour before. He replied very promptly that this was the first he had heard of it, but that he had been ready all day to move at a moment's notice. I told him to make the charge at once."[42]

General Willich's account seems to support Grant's version of the day's events. "At 9 A.M.. on the 25th, under orders, our pickets drove the enemy back to their rifle-pits at the foot of Missionary Ridge. At 11 A.M. I received an order to prepare for an advance, and to advance toward Missionary Ridge at the signal of six rapid cannon shots," General Willich wrote afterward. He further emphasized. "I understand since that the order was given to take only the rifle-pits at the foot of the ridge; by what accident, I am unable to say, I did not understand it so; I only understood the order to advance."[43]

Additional support for Grant's recollection can be found in Lieutenant Colonel William D. Williams' official report. "The next morning [November 25] at 10 o'clock the Eighty-ninth was ordered forward to relieve the Forty-ninth Ohio Infantry in the first line, with orders to throw two companies to the front as skirmishers." Williams continued that around 11:00 A.M. "our skirmishing companies, under the command of Lieut. Erastus O. Young, were ordered forward to dislodge the enemy's skirmishers on their front. This was quickly and gallantly done on the double-quick. They advanced about 1,000 yards, and were then ordered to halt." Williams thankfully wrote that

[41] Chamberlin, ed., *Sketches of War History, 1890-1896*, 33-35; Cozzens, *The Shipwreck of Their Hopes, The Battles for Chattanooga*, 246-247.

[42] Grant, *The Personal Memoirs of U. S. Grant*, 383.

[43] *OR*, Vol. 31, Pt. 2, 264.

while carrying out the order no skirmishers were killed or wounded, although the men "were vigorously shelled by the enemy's batteries planted on Missionary Ridge and resisted with considerable vigor by the enemy's skirmish line." At 2:00 P.M. the Forty-ninth Ohio came up relieving the Railroaders, who returned to the foot of Orchard Knob, staying in this position until ordered forward at 4:00 P.M.[44]

The night of the November 24 Joseph Buckley spent on the picket line. "In the morning which was the 25th," he later told his wife, "our company and two other companies out of our Regiment, and a corresponding number out of each Regiment in the Brigade were ordered to make a reconnaissance, and find out what force there was in front of us. We advanced and drove the Rebs picket line into their second line of breastworks, when we were ordered to halt."[45]

Adding to Lieutenant Colonel Williams' and Private Buckley's words was Charles Capron's description of the Eighty-ninth's brush with the Rebels during the late morning and early afternoon of November 25. The night before Capron had "slept about 2 hours" and was still out on the picket line when "the bugle sounded to advance the lines." Capron proceeded to give a graphic account of the fighting that followed. "Every man of us took his arms at a trail and then went creeping through the bushes as though he was hunting deer. Well we went on about [a] half a mile that way when bang, bang came all along the rebels picket lines. However we routed them and drove them into camp when we was ordered to halt and hold our position which we did." After accomplishing the objective, Capron wrote: "We was then relieved and went back to a the reserve lines, rested about two hours, had our cartridge boxes replenished . . . ."[46]

When told of the plan to assault the seemly impregnable Missionary Ridge, General Willich was overheard to say, "Vell, I makes my vill." But, being the professional soldier he was, the Old Prussian formed his brigade for the attack. He deployed his regiments in two lines: "The first line, Fifteenth Ohio, Forty-ninth Ohio, Twenty-fifth Illinois, Thirty-fifth Illinois; second line, Thirty-second Indiana,

---

44   *OR*, Vol. 31, Pt. 2, 269.

45   Buckley, letter, December 10, 1863.

46   Capron, letter, November 23-27, 1863.

Eighty-ninth Illinois, Eighth Kansas, Sixty-eighth Indiana; last reserve, Fifteenth Wisconsin." On the given signal Willich's brigade advanced at a trot and quickly came under a heavy shelling. On their own the regiments picked up the pace, double-timing until they reached the rebel rifle-pits and camps at the foot of the ridge. At the thought of being overrun by the charging bluecoats, the enemy infantry abandoned their lines and fled up the ridge. Having accomplished the task at hand, the Federals were caught under fire from rebel artillery on the crest of the ridge. "It was evident to every one that to stay in this position would be certain destruction and final defeat; every soldier felt the necessity of saving the day and the campaign . . . and every one saw instinctively that the only place of safety was in the enemy's works on the crest of the ridge," Willich wrote in his official account.

Sending aids along to the different regiments, while he and a lieutenant went to the Eighth Kansas, Willich gave the command, and soon the cry "forward" was heard all along the line. He would later write that he believed—"even without any command the regiments would have stormed, as a great number of skirmishers were already climbing the ridge before the command was given."[47]

Major John McClenahan of the Fifteenth Ohio commanded the division skirmishers that afternoon and conferred with General Willich regarding any last minute instructions. "I asked General Willich where we should stop. He replied 'I don't know, at H—Hades, I expect.'" McClenahan stated, "The skirmish line pushed across the valley to the foot of the ridge. We found we could not stop there but were forced to mount the ridge half way, where we halted to await the line of battle then approaching the valley." In a letter to the *Louisville Anzeiger*, a soldier in the Thirty-second Indiana wrote: "'after we had rested some at the first fortifications the voice of our old Blucher [General Willich] resounded: 'Second line forward.' We rose as one man [and] stormed toward the mountain . . . .'"[48]

---

[47] Cope, *The 15th Ohio Volunteers and Its Campaigns 1861-1865*, 358; *OR*, Vol. 31, Pt. 2, 264.

[48] Cope, *The 15th Ohio Volunteers and Its Campaigns 1861-1865*, 381; Reinhart, *August Willich's Gallant Dutchman, Civil War Letters from the 32nd Indiana Infantry*, 162.

"Our bugle sounded attention and we was again on the move and then came the struggle. We advanced to the first line of works but it would not do to stop there for they had 60 pieces of artillery playing on us and was getting good range on us," wrote Private Charles Capron. Nearly forty-three years later Captain Hobbs of Company H recalled the charge up Missionary Ridge. "The position of the 89th when the signal was given to advance was right in the rear of 'Orchard Knob'. As we started forward we passed around to the left of the Knob & then right straight for the Ridge." He remembered his orders were "to go to the foot of the ridge & halt there, but when there, the cannonading was so heavy from the guns to the right & to the left of us at the top of the Ridge that we could not stay there & was compelled to go on without orders & not much of an alignment or order about it & every one for himself." To get away from the devastating rebel fire, Capron and his fellow Railroaders climbed out of the works "and started across the flat." He wrote that "the whole army moved forward to take Mission Ridge. Well we advanced through the timber without any difficulty but when we emerged into the open field no pen can describe with what swiftness they poured in their shot, shell, grape, canister, and every deadly missile you could think. Still we advanced right up the hill," Capron informed his parents back in Rock Island County. The enemy, he wrote, "aimed their guns directly at us, but by the time the shells would reach us we would be so far advanced that they would go over us and drop behind us and they did not damage us much." He noted that as the men moved upward, the enemy "could not longer depress their pieces to bear on us and then came the struggle to see who should be to the top first." However, the rebels still poured rifle fire into the climbing blue-coated infantry. "It was when we got about 2 thirds of the way up the hill," Capron wrote, that his "pardner was shot through the thigh and the lieutenant [Erastus O. Young] was shot in the breast killing him instantly." Lieutenant Colonel Williams stated that Young was "shot dead while shouting, 'Forward and victory!'" Capron noted: "Although our regiment was in the rear line, yet in their impetuosity, they ran over the 1st line and was the first to plant their colors on the hill. The bugle then sounded the rally and cheer after cheer was sent after the flying fugitives." Captain Hobbs later said, "When we reached the top we managed to get enough together in line to make quite a co."[49]

Writing his wife afterward, Private Buckley said that it was "about half past three in the afternoon, when "we were ordered to advance and drive the Rebs out of their second line of breastwork, and take possession of them. We did so nobly under a very heavy fire of artillery from the Rebs, and I tell you it was fun to see the Rebs throw away their guns, cartridge boxes, knapsacks, etc. and take to their heels." He pointed out that "we did not stay long behind the breastworks. We all rushed forward up the mountain as fast as we could, but it was so steep, we could not get along very fast. When we got out of breath, we rested behind a stump or anything which came handiest, and then took good aim and shot as many Rebs as we could. As soon as we got our breath, we started again until we found some protection, when we laid down and served them in the same way again, and kept doing so until we got to the top of the mountain." He added, "We took a great many prisoners when we were part way up the mountain."

The race to the top was not without its hazards. Buckley had a close call on the way up. He wrote: "The Rebs had a very heavy cross fire on us and that was where we lost most of our men." It was here, he told Mary, that he came very near losing his life. A number of his company had bunched together in a spot offering very little protection. Suddenly, the bullets were coming at them like hail. Buckley saw a stump about a foot high and got behind it. At the same time, four men in close proximity "were shot down and a piece of stump shot away." He jumped up "left that stump and advanced still further," picking up a rebel knapsack. He no sooner picked it up then a shell came over his head and burst a little behind, forcing him to lay down. He had no sooner done so, then another shell came and fell within three feet and burst, covering him with dirt and debris. He joked and wrote: "As the Irishman said, 'I didn't know whether I was kilt or not until I felt all over me.'" He soon left that spot and kept going up the mountain, staying hunched over and getting flat when necessary all the rest of the way until he got to the ridge. Once there, Buckley

---

49   Franklin M. Hobbs, letter to E. A. Carman, January 22, 1906; Capron, letters, November 23-27, 1863, January 24, 1865; *OR*, Vol. 31, Pt. 2, 270.

stated: "We took possession of what cannon we could and drove the Rebs down the other side of mountain." He concluded by telling Mary that "we had a hard time of climbing that mountain, but I think it was all the will of the Lord that we were permitted to gain the summit."[50]

Lieutenant Dimick, the faithful correspondent for Company F, ensured that Rock Island County was kept abreast of its men with the Eighty-ninth. Two days after the capture of Missionary Ridge he posted an update to the Republican newspaper, *The Union*. "On the morning of the 25th," he began, "our part of the army was in readiness to move forward again, but here came the trying point—breastworks to storm and take by the point of the bayonet. We succeeded in taking them without very heavy loss, but the trying point was *then* left to be taken—Missionary Ridge, a very hard position to take—but soon the command forward was given, and our brave men bounded over the breastworks at the command." Continuing, he wrote: "No sooner had we passed over the breastworks than the enemy opened upon us with their artillery and infantry in their breastworks at the summit of the hill. Eighteen pieces of artillery were used to check our brigade besides the infantry, but thank God they did not stop the old First of Gen. Willich." Dimick added: "If the enemy could have used canister and grape they might have checked our advance, but they could not depress the artillery enough. They fired principally shells. Six guns were in our immediate front, six on our right and six on our left." The young lieutenant noted that "as we came within one hundred yards of their works, which were not very formidable, their men run back; their officers tried to check them, but they could not. Quite a number remained in their breastworks and were glad to be captured."

"The forces on our left stood their ground and fought with great bravery," Dimick wrote. "Our men had to use their bayonets before they could get into the fort. Our flag and theirs would almost touch each other as they fluttered in the breeze." He concluded, "our men would have been repulsed there . . . if our regiment and the Forty-ninth Ohio had not moved to their assistance." But, "as soon as we gained the top of the hill we fired upon their flank and they

---

50   Buckley, letter, December 10, 1863

were obliged to fall back. They tried to haul off their artillery, but we shot down their horses and they were obliged to abandon it."[51]

Capron too was watching as the Forty-ninth Ohio moved within a stone's throw of the Rebel fort when they stopped and fixed bayonets before charging the works. The rebels furiously fought to hold their fort. The color guards "even shook their flags in each others faces but it was our brigade," Capron wrote that "captured 1000 prisoners, 18 pieces of artillery, and 1000 stand small arms."[52]

Summarizing the day, the Railroader Regiment's Lieutenant Colonel William D. Williams wrote:

> At 4 P.M. the Eighty-ninth moved steadily forward as a support to the Forty-ninth Ohio to assail the enemy's second line of intrenchments. The Eighty-ninth moved steadily forward in double column until within 500 yards of the enemy's works, and then deployed into line of battle; moved forward, under a heavy fire of musketry and artillery, over the enemy's second line of intrenchments up the steep sides of Missionary Ridge to crest, assailed meanwhile by the enemy's batteries on the right and left and a heavy infantry fire on the right, left, and front. We carried the top of Missionary Ridge, driving the enemy before us. After pursuing them and taking many prisoners, we halted about 1,000 yards beyond the crest. I halted the regiment, closed them up, and awaited further orders. At dark General Willich ordered us to stack arms and bivouac for the night.[53]

Following his regiments up Missionary Ridge, Willich caught up with them at the top. The Old Dutchman was in time to see the last of the fleeing Rebels and to join in the victory celebration. He would write in the brigade's after action report that "many men fell down exhausted in climbing up under the enemy's fire, some fainted, but irresistible a motivational encounter he had had with a lagging soldier. Laughing, the general said, "Look! As I was coming up the hill I saw a son-of-a-gun stopped behind a stump, and jumped on

---

51 *Rock Island Union*, December 16, 1863.
52 Capron, letter, November 23-27, 1863.
53 *OR*, Vol. 31, Pt. 2, 269.

him and kicked him, and see, I broke all my spurs." Surrounded by men from his brigade the old general, hat in hand, ecstatically proclaimed to everyone, "'My poys,you kills me mit joy, you kills me mit joy.'"[54]

William J. Tomlinson of Company A could not wait to inform his mother and all of Augusta, Illinois what had been accomplished. "I think this is one of the greatest victories of the war . . . . It made the hills and valleys ring all the Day yesterday with Cheers . . . ." Flushed with pride, Private Tomlinson told his mother that the Union soldiers "drove them out of the rifle pits at the foot of Mishon Ridge and took the most of them. Then we marched up the ridge under a heavy fire of artilery and musketry, but we wer bound to have the top of the ridge or get whipped, but we did the whipping part. We gained the top at last and threw them before us Down the other side . . . ." For a perspective, he explained that "if Mishen Ridge was in Illinois, you would think it a mountain and wonder how we ever got up ther under such heavy fire." Still excited, he told his mother that "General Wood gave us great prais . . . says we could take the moon by storm . . . ." And if victory was not enough, he wrote: "I got Mr. Turners nepsack with his blanket, 2 pair of drawers, 1 pair of socks and paper and envelopes to last me three months and all his trinkets—Testament and hymn book. He belonged to the 19th South Carolina Regiment. I am very thankful to him for his things, being he had to throw them away to give his feet more speed . . . ."[55]

"I think this is one of the most successful battles of the war," confided Lieutenant Dimick to the *Rock Island Union* readers. And for evidence of his conclusion, he noted: "We have captured almost all of Bragg's artillery, from seventy-five to one hundred pieces, and thousands of small arms." Willich's Brigade was credited with taking "5 pieces of artillery, 8 caissons, 1,200 stand of small-arms, 2 battle-flags, and between 300 and 400 prisoners." To a man, the

---

[54] OR, Vol. 31, Pt. 2, 264; Cope, *The 15th Ohio Volunteers and It Campaigns 1861-1863*, 381- 383; Karen Kloss, "Union General August Willich, The Eccentric Prussian Socialist," *America's Civil War* (September 2003), 52.

[55] Kammerer, *Hancock County, Illinois in the Civil War*, 78; Tomlinson, *In Good Courage: The Civil War Letters of William James Tomlinson*, 14.

Union soldiers saw Bragg's army as being badly demoralized, and like Dimick, didn't think these men could be "organized to fight with any success again."[56]

General Willich listed 337 casualties of whom 53 were killed and 284 were wounded. The *Chicago Evening Journal* reported that "the 89th bore a conspicuous part in the recent great victory. Charging upon the rebel rifle-pits at Missionary Ridge it lost four killed and had thirty-one wounded." But sadly, the article noted that Captain Henry L. Rowell of Company C and the Chicago and Milwaukee Railroad was mortally wounded. He succumbed on December 3 in a Chattanooga hospital. Officially the Union suffered 5,824 casualties at Chattanooga from November 23-25. In the same period the Confederates losses were 6,667 with 4,146 shown as missing.[57]

*   *   *

From Grand Army of the Republic encampments to the pages of the *National Tribune* old soldiers passionately argued whether their division, brigade, or regiment was the first on top of Missionary Ridge. Time and egos, however, managed to convolute what was obvious to many present that afternoon. General Wood took offense when both Grant and Sheridan asserted in their memoirs that Sheridan's Division was the first to reach the crest. In his words, Grant and Sheridan set out to "utterly pervert the truth of history." Clearly, the German-American soldier who wrote the *Louisville Anzeiger* on November 27 was certain. "Willich's Brigade was the first to climb up to the crest of the ridge and it was the flags of the 32nd Indiana and 15th Ohio that first floated on the fortifications." Keeping an eye on his command as he moved up the ridge General Willich, wrote after the battle: "The Thirty-second Indiana and Sixth Ohio claim the honor of being the first to plant their colors on the crest; but a few minutes [elapsed] and all the colors of the brigade were in the enemy's works." In the *History of the Army of the Cumberland* Thomas Van Horne drew his conclusion from General

---

56   *Rock Island Union*, December 16, 1863; *OR*, Vol. 31, Pt. 2, 265.

57   *OR*, Vol. 31, Pt. 2, 265; *Chicago Evening Journal*, December 5, 1863; *Adjutant General's Report*, 268; Boatner, *The Civil War Dictionary*, 147.

Bragg's statement that his line was first broken on his right and to the north of his headquarters, leaving no question that General Wood's division was the first to reach the summit. Historian Peter Cozzens, author of The *Shipwreck of Their Hopes, The Battles for Chattanooga* touched on the matter and wrote: "My guess—and it is only that—is that the honor should go to the Sixth Kentucky, Sixth Ohio, or Thirty-second Indiana." Both Sixth Kentucky and Sixth Ohio were from Hazen' Brigade and Wood's Division. Colonel Emerson Opdycke of the One Hundred Twenty-fifth Ohio (Harker's Brigade, Sheridan's Division) wrote the following to General Wood: "When the leading brigade [Sheridan's Division] had advanced about half way up the Ridge, perhaps slightly more, I looked to the left, and saw the troops of your division just crowning the crest of the Ridge."[58]

[58] *OR*, Vol. 31, Pt. 2, 264, 271; Chamberlin, *Sketches of War History, 1890-1896*, IV:41-47; Cozzens, *The Shipwreck of Their Hopes, The Battles for Chattanooga*, 460; Reinhart, *Gallant Dutchman, Civil War Letters from the 32nd Indiana Infantry*, 163; Van Horne, *History of the Army of the Cumberland*, I:431.

CHAPTER 12

"WE DID A GREAT DEAL
OF MARCHING
BACK AND FORTH . . ."

After the Battle of Chickamauga, Longstreet and Bragg engaged in an ongoing quarrel, forcing Confederate President Davis to separate the two generals like a father disciplining squabbling brothers. Longsreet's Corps was detached from Bragg's army and sent off to East Tennessee to deal with Burnside's force at Knoxville. Davis' decision, however, weakened the Army of Tennessee and thus factored into its disastrous defeat at Missionary Ridge. Nevertheless, what was eventually judged an overly ambitious attempt to destroy two Union armies resulted in a period of grave anxiety for the Lincoln Administration. But no sooner had the Federal armies broken the siege at Chattanooga than President Lincoln reminded Grant not to forget Burnside. Feeling pressured by Washington not only to rescue Burnside's army but to also save East Tennessee from Longstreet's rebels, Grant issued orders on November 27 to effect the relief.

For Grant the situation in Eastern Tennessee had been festering since Longstreet departed Chattanooga on November 4. By November 19, Longstreet was outside of Knoxville, but his force of 10,000 infantry and 5,000 cavalry lacked the means for a full-fledged siege. Having driven the Federals inside the city's defenses,

Longstreet carefully observed and surveyed the Union lines and finally concluded to attempt an assault on the Yankee works. But to ensure victory, he decided to delay the attack, and then waited for over a week for the arrival of reinforcements.

The situation in Knoxville had suddenly become critical on the morning of November 27, when Burnside reported rations enough to last ten or twelve days, and thereafter, he would have to retreat or surrender. Grant did not hesitate, but took immediate action, directing Major General Gordon Granger to take both Wood's and Sheridan's divisions and march to Knoxville. The next day Grant found Granger had not executed the order, but was still dilly-dallying about Chattanooga. He quickly put Sherman in charge of the expedition and added the 15th Corps to the force. Meanwhile, on November 29, Longstreet finally launched the long awaited attack on part of the Union works known as Fort Sanders. The assault was repulsed with the Confederates suffering heavy losses. In the midst of the fight, a courier rode up bringing Longstreet word of Bragg's defeat at Chattanooga and retreat into northern Georgia. The message included orders to end the siege and come to Bragg's support. While Longstreet was mulling over Bragg's message and orders, Rebel cavalry reported a large Federal force moving toward Knoxville. Longstreet made no effort to rejoin Bragg, but sought safety and retreated eastward.[1]

*   *   *

Three days after arriving in Knoxville, Joseph Buckley wrote his wife telling her, "as far as I can learn, we came here to support Burnside in case Longstreet was too much for him, but those things you will read about in the papers." He explained that after the battle the Eighty-ninth stayed on Missionary Ridge all night,

---

[1] Boatner, *The Civil War Dictionary*, 466-468; Cozzens, *The Shipwreck of Their Hopes, The Battles for Chattanooga*, 386-387; Daniel, *Days of Glory, The Army of the Cumberland, 1861-1865*, 378; Faust, ed., *Historical Times Illustrated Encyclopedia of the Civil War*, 420-421; Wiley Sword, *Mountains Touched with Fire, Chattanooga Besieged, 1863* (New York: St. Martin's Press, 1997), 348-349; Van Horne, *History of the Army of the Cumberland*, II: 1-4.

and the evening of the next day the regiment returned to their camp at Chattanooga, where they stayed two nights, leaving November 28 for Knoxville. Similarly, Charles Capron recalled that after the Battle of Missionary Ridge the Railroaders "camped on the hill that night and the next day . . . returned to our old quarters in Chattanooga and rested quietly that night. The next day we had orders to march and about 3 o'clock that day we started to Knoxville." The first day, Private Buckley wrote the column covered about five miles and then went into camp. He then proceeded to set forth a detailed summary of the Railroaders movement. November 29, he noted that the regiment camped outside the town of Harrison and wrote, "I suffered more from the cold that day and night than I have since been in the service. It froze very hard." The next day the Railroaders passed through Georgetown. While on Tuesday the first of December, they crossed the Hiawassee River on a steamboat. Wednesday the second, they passed through the town of Decatur. On Thursday the third, the men marched through the town of Sweetwater and camped on the other side. Buckley commented that it was "a nice town and right by the Railroad." Friday the fourth, camp was near Johnson's Hills. Saturday the fifth, the brigade crossed the Little Tennessee River and passed through Morgantown. Sunday the sixth, they went through Maryville. Monday the seventh, the column passed through Rockford and arrived outside Knoxville.[2]

The early winter march was a grueling ordeal for the Railroaders. "Suffice it to say," Private Capron recalled, "we suffered severely having half enough to eat and barefooted too. We reached Knoxville nearly exhausted stopping there a short time to rest and recruit." Buckley estimated that it was "about 160 miles from here [Knoxville] to Chattanooga the way we came." Having been ordered to leave immediately, the expedition left Chattanooga with insufficient rations to carry them through; and consequently, the regiments resorted, as Buckley pointed out, "to live on the country and are doing so now. We get very little meal or flour, but fresh pork, we get plenty of."[3]

---

[2] Buckley, letter, December 10, 1863.

[3] Capron, letter, January 24, 1865; Buckley, letter, December 10, 1865.

Clothed in tattered uniforms they had worn for months, wearing shoes that were more holes than leather, and marching over bad roads in numbing cold, the men in the relief column were relentlessly driven by Sherman. By December 5, the column was fifteen miles outside of Knoxville when a courier found Sherman and handed him a dispatch from Burnside. Reading the communication, Sherman was dumbfounded to find that his help was no longer necessary. Pushing on to Knoxville, Sherman found that Longstreet had broken off the siege and had withdrawn on December 4. That evening, while treating Sherman and Granger to a sumptuous meal, Burnside admitted that his army was never completely invested and had been supplied with foodstuff by the region's friendly Unionists. Miffed with Burnside, Sherman soon returned to Chattanooga with the Fifteenth Corps, leaving Granger's divisions at Knoxville to help keep Longstreet's rebels in check.[4]

Regimental records for the winter of 1863-1864 are vague, but those of Company G provide a basic chronology of the whereabouts of the Railroaders for this period. The Eighty-ninth "marched from Chattanooga to Knoxville, East Tennessee; thence to Strawberry Plains," having left Chattanooga on November 28 and arriving at Knoxville December 8. They came to Strawberry Plains on December 28 and remained in the vicinity all January through February 1864. March and April were spent at McDonald Station.[5]

"Camped near Blain's Cross Roads about 11 miles northeast of Knoxville," Private Joseph Buckley stated the regiment's orders to return to Chattanooga were countermanded, "and we got orders to come out here as it was reported that Longstreet was reinforced and was driving our men back." He wrote his wife on December 22 that "we certainly expected a fight out here, but as far as I can learn Longstreet moved back. I expect that if things work out in our favor that we shall go back to Chattanooga in the course of 4 or 5 days when I shall have a good chance to

4 Cozzens, *The Shipwreck of Their Hopes*, 387-388; Boatner, *The Civil War Dictionary*, 468.
5 Janet Hewett, ed., *Supplement to the Official Records of the Union and Confederate Armies*, Part II-Record of Events, Volume 13, Serial No. 25 (Wilmington, NC: Broadfoot Publishing Company, 1995), 401.

enjoy the good things you sent me." With only military supplies being shipped from Chattanooga, the box of goodies Mary finally sent Joseph was being held in a warehouse there. "We live chiefly on corn meal and beef, pork and mutton," Buckley wrote. "We have to forage in the country for our living. So much corn meal gives me the heartburn. I shall be glad when we can draw our full rations of crackers." And he continued, stating that she "never knew what it was to starve and suffer for want of clothing as I have done since the Battle of Chickamauga. One man in Company D in our regiment actually ate a dog. That is but one instance of what I could tell you but I hope it is sufficient to convince you that we used to go hungry every day while we were in Chattanooga."

Not everyone had such bad luck. "We fared first-rate on the march," Charles Capron informed his family. "We got all the flour, meal, molasses, honey, butter, mutton, beef, also chickens, turkeys, geese, dried fruit of all kinds. The way we get such things is by going out of a night to some rich secesh house and make him haul out or else the bayonet or revolver happen to get out in sight and then he has plenty of such as we want. We then fill our haversacks and make our way back to camp satisfied with our exploit." Back in camp "we then go to work and cook us a good supper then for bed. Up in the morning at five o'clock [and] get breakfast ready by daylight; [and] then if we are not a going to march, hurrah for another foraging expedition. We generally come into camp at night with as much as we can pack."[6]

By living off the land, the Eighty-ninth's ration situation had improved over what it had been in Chattanooga, but the army quartermasters were unable to replace the men's worn-out clothing and footwear or missing equipment. Joseph Buckley informed Mary: "The shirt I got on Mission Ridge I gave to Chauncy Talmadge as he did not have any and the drawers I gave to Ike Merritt as his pants were a great deal worse than mine. My shirt had got so rotten that I durst not wash it. I sewed it together until it would not hang together any longer. My socks were worn out." With part of his clothing consisting of rags, Buckley managed to get a pair of socks

---

[6]   Capron, letter, December 22, 1863.

and a shirt, but lamented to Mary that "it is a very thin one. I shall be very glad when I get the clothes you have sent."[7]

Writing his parents in late December, Second Lieutenant William Harkness remarked: "I suppose you have learned from the letters I have sent from time to time and also from the papers where we are and have been. We are now within about three miles of Strawberry Plains, a station on the R.R., northeast from Knoxville. We have been here a little over a week in a very good place for a camp. Plenty of wood and water." Continuing, he explained: "We live almost entirely on what we forage, corn meal and flour which we bake ourselves the best we can, plenty of fresh meat; we draw coffee and sugar from the government. So we manage to live very well for soldiers." Whether the regiment would spend the winter at its current location, he conjectured: "How long we will remain here I cannot tell. The cars run from here to Louden, on the Tennessee River and then steam boats from there to Chattanooga. So we will soon have our regular communication for provisions if we stay here which I doubt however."[8]

Lieutenant Harkness temporarily commanded Company B, while his permanent company, H, had been first sent off to a town known as Blaines Cross Roads. But, as Private Buckley wrote: "We left Blaines Cross Roads on the 30th or 31st of December and went to Strawberry Plaines Station to build a bridge across the river Holston." The sixteen-hundred-foot East Tennessee and Virginia Railroad Bridge over the Holston River had been destroyed by Union cavalry back on June 20, 1863. In early January 1864, Willich's brigade set out to rebuild the bridge.[9]

On January 1, 1864, Corporal Wallace McCloud of Company H was promoted to sergeant. However, the increased rank was not on his mind when he made the first entry in his newly acquired diary. The twenty-two year old former farmer from Kendall County penciled in that the new year blew in cold, and he with the rest of men had "done nothing but plant [themselves] around the fire," adding that "we're camped at Strawberry Plaines" and that

---

7   Buckley, letter, December 22 and 24, 1863.

8   Harkness, letter, December 29, 1863.

9   Buckley, letter, January 20 and 22, 1864.

"everything was quiet at the front." The next day, still focused on the temperature, he wrote, "Weather still very cold. Last night was said by [the] citizens to have bin the coldest night for seven years." The following day, Sunday the third, found McCloud and Company H up early and detailed to work on the railroad bridge. Relieved at noon, the men hustled back to camp where they huddled around the fires to keep warm.[10]

For the next ten days work continued on the bridge, and the weather stayed cold. While out working on the bridge, Private James B. David noted that the "boys teeth [were] chattering with the cold. They crack their jokes in double quick today for it is cold enough to freeze a dog." That same day, Wednesday, January 13, Sergeant McCloud stated we were up at the usual hour followed by roll call. The weather remained damp and unpleasant. The morning was spent in camp. In the afternoon Co. H was split up and went with B, I, F, and G to work on the bridge. The men threw stone down to shore up the levy. Later they received orders that they were to march tomorrow at 8:00 A.M.. Later they drew two days rations of hardtack and meal.[11]

"We had just about finished the bridge when our corps was ordered to the front which was about the 13th of the month. It took us two days to go there. We got there [Dandridge] about noon the second day when Colonel Williams told us to make ourselves as comfortable as possible," Joe Buckley commented in a letter to his wife. Buckley and his colleagues took the colonel at his word and "pulled down old buildings and made new ones of them that were comfortable. We had our house door boarded and a canopy roof, a boarded floor, a bedstead of boards with about a foot and a half of straw in depth." On the night of January 15, Sergeant McCloud recorded in his journal that the Eighty-ninth went into camp at Dandridge. McCloud and Francis Pomeroy grabbed enough boards

---

10   Wallace McCloud, diary entries for January 1 through 3, 1864, original diary at the Abraham Lincoln Presidential Library, Springfield, Illinois, hereafter cited as McCloud diary.

11   James B. David, diary entry for January 13, 1864, original diary at the University of Tennessee Hoskins Library, Knoxville, Tennessee, hereafter cited as David diary.

to build a shebang. Private James B. David "went in together" with Joseph Haigh and Richard Fields. Early the next morning, the trio found boards enough to build a house.[12]

Even though, with Sherman's approach, Longstreet abandoned the siege of Knoxville, his army still lurked in the vicinity, posing a threat to East Tennessee. On January 15, with Brigadier General Willich commanding, Wood's division advanced on Dandridge, driving Longstreet's cavalry from the town. Sheridan's division and McCook's cavalry linked up with Willich's men. Over the next two days, Federal cavalry skirmished with the rebel horsemen, eventually confronting Longstreet's infantry. Realizing Longstreet was present in force, the Union commanders opted not to bring on a general engagement. However, late on the afternoon of the 18th, McCook's cavalry became heavily engaged with Longstreet's advance. McCook was able to clear the field, capturing over a hundred prisoners and two field pieces. This action allowed the Union troops to fall back to Strawberry Plains. After crossing the Holston River, the railroad trestle bridge was once more destroyed. Willich's Brigade passed back through Knoxville on January 21 and was ordered south to Maryville, arriving on the 24th.[13]

Surviving letters and diary entries provide a first hand account of the Railroaders role in the two-day engagement that took place near Dandridge, Tennessee. Private James David of Company H wrote in his journal for January 16 that it was around 4:00 P.M., and he and his messmates were still on camp guard when the cavalry had a skirmish with the rebels. The second brigade was quickly called out and formed in a line of battle. He noted: "We were all ready to go out." But instead, "we fell in and stacked arms in camp quarters. The fighting stopped at dark." Sergeant McCloud briefly noted that there was a "general engagement [with] heavy artillery

---

12   Buckley, letter, January 20 and 22, 1864; David, diary, January 16, 1864.

13   Jacob Dolson Cox, *Military Reminiscences of the Civil War November 1863—June 1865* (New York: Charles Scribner's Sons, 1900), II: 113-121; Long, *The Civil War Day by Day*, 455; OR, Vol. 32, Pt. 1, 78-79; Reinhart, *August Willich's Gallant Dutchman, Civil War Letters from the 32nd Indiana Infantry*, 168; Van Horne, *History of the Army of the Cumberland Its Organization, Campaigns and Battles*, II: 15.

firing in the afternoon." He added, what appeared to be a rumor, that 200 prisoners, including a brigadier general, were captured. While Private Charles Capron gave this description: "We heard heavy cannonading all day. Just at dark the bugle blowed attention and then orders came to be ready to go at a minute warning with our guns and cartridge boxes." Around midnight the men were allowed to sleep, but were ordered to keep their equipment on and rifle in hand. The bugle sounded "fall in" at 5:00 A.M.., with orders following to keep all equipment on until 8:00 A.M.. Capron said that when "morning dawned at last without our being disturbed but still that ominous sound [of artillery] reached our ears accompanied with heavy volleys of musketry which increased so toward night as to be quite terrific. Just at dusk the bugle blowed attention." He stated that "again things appeared to look rather suspicious. About this time we formed in solid column, closed in mass, and then each company filed out four deep. We went about a quarter of a mile where we formed in line of battle. We was then ordered to load at will and then we stood there awaiting the enemy. [We] stayed there about a half an hour when we was ordered to our quarters." The Company A private continued: "When we got there the officers assembly was blown. They soon came back with orders to pack up everything as we had to leave town."[14]

Buckley explained: "The second night we were called out to be ready at a moments notice, but we finally went to bed and were not disturbed until the next day [January 17]. [It was] about 4 o'clock when we were ordered out again and formed a line of battle. There was some firing at the picket line. We stayed out about an hour. When the firing ceased, we went back to our quarters and packed up our traps. In fact our forces were falling back all the afternoon. Our Brigade was the rear guard and our Regiment was the rear guard of the Brigade. So we did not leave until about three o'clock in the morning."

When the regiment finally moved out, Buckley observed that "we had a small squad of cavalry with us. The rebs followed us with cavalry and if there were any stragglers they would be sure to be

---

[14] David, diary, January 16, 1864; McCloud, diary, January 16, 1864; Capron, letter, January 28, 1864.

picked up. They came up with us about two o'clock . . . when they fired on our cavalry. Our cavalry formed a line of Battle, what few them there was of them, and returned their fire. Our Regiment then formed a line of Battle to protect the cavalry in case they was overpowered, but the moment the Rebel cavalry saw us form in a line of Battle, they stopped short, and we were not trouble much after that." The 18-year-old Private Capron added that the Eighty-ninth had traveled "about three miles by daylight. But we was to have a little fuss with the rebs as yet, for we had not got more than six miles and was sitting down to rest when we was startled by the rebel cavalry giving us a salute of three or four guns." The regiment was up in an instant and "in 2 minutes we was in a line of battle waiting for them. Our cavalry shooting as fast as they could load. They did not charge us so we throwed out skirmishers and started again. They followed us a while longer but finding they could do us no damage they went back."[15]

Walter Huff's diary annotations are brief and to the point, but also summarize what took place. Saturday, the January 16, he penciled: "Wagons came up today about 10 o'clock. Heavy skirmishing in front. Pretty hot in front this evening. Brigade ordered to fall in and go to front. Order countermanded but men are ready to march at moments notice." Sunday, he commented: "Built a house today. Drawed 1 pair of shoes. Skirmishing in front. Ordered out, but did not get into action. Orders to be ready to fall back." He noted on Monday: "Commenced to retreat. [The brigade] marched very slow on account of the roads. 89th rear guard at 8 [o'clock] the rebel cavalry are reported in our rear with our cavalry. Our Brigade formed in line of battle but the rebs did not come up. They did not molest us any more through the day."[16]

Two days passed before Joe Buckley resumed the letter to his wife he had begun on January 20. He wrote the Eighty-ninth was now camped two-miles from Knoxville, and then explained, "I had not had time to finish my letter as we were ordered to march right off. We are now on the east side of the [Holston] river and we are going to move up this side of the river. Longstreet retreated the

---

[15] Buckley, letter, January 20 and 22, 1864; Capron, letter, January 28, 1864.

[16] Huff, diary, January 16, 17, 18, 1864.

same time as we did. I expect we shall come up with him in the course of a few days when I think there will be a chance for a fight. We may start from here in an hour or any moment. They are getting a supply of ammunition now, and I think we shall move as soon as they get it ready. We arrived here last night."[17]

He proceeded to go over with Mary the trial he had undergone during the past week. "I have had a rather tough march as my boots were worn out on the bottom and sides, so that my feet were on the ground. My socks were worn out also and there has been snow on the ground for two weeks. It is anything but pleasant marching in the snow barefooted almost, but I got a new pair of shoes and socks, which I put on last night. And, I tell you they feel comfortable, but after all my suffering I feel thankful to the Lord for sparing my life thus far."[18]

After returning to Knoxville, Willich's brigade was once more ordered south of the city, this time to Maryville, or Marysville as most of the Railroaders referred to it. Starting off on January 23, the regiment arrived the next day and stayed in the area about three weeks. While at Maryville, Buckley wrote Mary. "We are about 15 miles southwest of Knoxville. I don't know the reason of us falling back to this place unless it is so we will have a better chance to get forage. We left Knoxville last Saturday and we arrived here Sunday morning. We were detained some on Saturday as we had to cross a river on some planks and we could only cross in single file."[19]

* * *

In a letter to his brother George back in Rock Island, Lieutenant Copp reported that new recruits were coming in nearly every day and that most of the other companies were now full. So far, Copp's Company F had received nine men to date, but hoped there turn for additional troops would come next. At this point, Copp reported the Rock Island Company had 71 men on the roll, but it needed 13 more or a total of 84 to have a full complement of officers. With the

---

[17]   Buckley, letter, January 20 and 22, 1864.
[18]   *Ibid.*
[19]   Buckley, letter, January 29, 1864.

daily influx of men, he commented that "the regiment is again quite large." He further said, "There is no prospect of our being mounted, as it is impossible to keep the cavalry upon horses, on account of the scarcity of forage." But if the men were not to be mounted, the latest rumor was more to their liking. It was being bandied about the Eighty-ninth would "be detailed upon some railroad soon, to run it and keep it in repair," Copp wrote his brother. And, on February 21, Private David noted in his diary: "Colonel Williams had went to Knoxville to get the regiment detailed to go on the railroad. Hope he will succeed in it."[20]

One of the new arrivals in February was Joel R. Chambers, a cousin of William J. Tomlinson. He later recalled: "On the 4th day of January, 1864 . . . I enlisted in Company A, 89th Ill. Infantry Vols. This command, known as the 'Railroad Regiment,' had been in the service at the front about seventeen months when I enlisted in it." Chambers pointed out: "With that characteristic restlessness of a hot blooded young American, I preferred going into a regiment already in the field in order to 'get down to business' at once. Thus I became a new recruit or 'new root,' as the old vets called us—a thing not the most desirable as I afterwards learned. Yet it had its advantages, and altogether I never regretted it."

After signing up in Quincy, Illinois, Chambers left for Springfield on January 9 and spent the next 16 days between Camps Yates and Butler. On the January 25, he boarded a train for the front, first traveling to Indianapolis, then south to Louisville, on to Nashville, and finally arriving at Chattanooga on February 1. In the morning of February 4, Chambers later remembered, after being temporarily quartered at a convalescent camp, the new men, now armed with Enfield rifles, "started on the march to join our several regiments in upper East Tennessee." It was a motley group. Chambers recalled: "There were recruits for various commands: and men who had been sick and wounded, and now recovered, and returning to the front. There was two or three hundred of us, and quite a large supply train, all commanded by Col. Crain, of the 6th Ky." For the next nine days, the column trudged along until the afternoon of the February12 when it arrived at the camp of the Railroaders at Marysville, eighteen

---

20 *Rock Island Argus*, March 5, 1864; David Diary, February 21, 1864.

miles southwest of Knoxville. Chambers soon found a few familiar faces, but the larger number was strangers to him.[21]

Private Chambers recollected back to those first few days with the Railroaders: "The camp was pleasant and comfortable, but we only remained two days, when we were ordered, at 10 o'clock P.M., to be ready to march at a moments notice. At midnight we started. It had been raining during the day, the roads were muddy, it was dark, [and] altogether I thought it was a rough introduction to a soldier's life."[22]

The date was February 15 when the command abruptly abandoned its position at Maryville. The rain was ending when the diarist James B. David had gone on picket at 11:00 P.M., and with in an hour orders were received to march. He jotted: "It was rumored that a heavy cavalry force were about to attack us." In a letter home Lieutenant James B. Copp of Company F spelled out that the regiment left Maryville at midnight. "It had rained all the previous day, and it was very dark and muddy walking. We walked all night, coming to the Little Tennessee River at daylight," wrote Copp. In recalling the march, Private Capron wrote the mud was "knee deep and [the night] darker than pitch beside all the officers being drunk. However at daylight we brought up to the Little [Tennessee] River where we was obliged to stop and build a bridge and a worse looking set of chaps you never see for we was mud clear to the tops of our heads." On reaching the river, Lieutenant Copp wrote that first, "We breakfasted, and then, rigged a boom on which we crossed the river, and resumed our march, the weather being very cold. We could see snow on the high mountain tops, for miles around."[23]

The forced march ended when the brigade reached the safety of Knoxville, but the Eighty-ninth's ordeal was not over. "Near nightfall

---

[21] *Chanute Vidette*, "Campaigning in Tennessee and Georgia in 1864, No. 1," Series of six articles written by Joel R. Chambers and published from December 1889 through January 1890; Cheryl H. Beneke and Carol D. Summer, eds., *War Fever Cured, The Civil War Diary of Private Joel R. Chambers, 1864-1865* (Memphis, Tennessee: Crittenden Publishing Company, 1980), 15-18.

[22] *Chanute Vidette*, "Campaigning in Tennessee and Georgia in 1864, No. 1," December 1889.

[23] *Rock Island Argus*, March 5, 1864; David, diary, February 15, 1864.

we put into camp at the summit of one of the lofty hills across the river from Knoxville. A cold windy night, it was terrible for us all, but also for poor young [William P.] Chase, a noble young man, just out of Knox College, [Galesburg,] Ills., and who was now sick with pneumonia. Efforts were made to get him to the hospital that night, but in vain. Extra blankets were furnished by the boys, and all done for him that could be, but that cold night, on that bleak hill, was too much," recalled Joel R. Chambers. The eighteen-year-old new recruit from Macomb, McDonough County, was taken the next day to a hospital, but died soon afterward. "It was understood by us at the time, that whiskey among the officers had something to do with our suffering and our comrade's death," Chambers later wrote. Private Capron remembered that the Eighty-ninth arrived near Knoxville about 3:00 P.M. on February 19. He similarly remembered: "They then took us on to the top [of] a high hill and told us we would remain there for the night. It was cold enough to freeze the devil himself. Indeed I never suffered so in my life. I laid so close to the fire to keep warm that my blankets catched afire and burnt up and liked to burn me with them." That evening he wrote a short letter to his sister and noted: "It is cold that I have to crawl out of my tent every few minutes and go to the fire to warm my fingers, and I must close."[24]

After the cold snap and his close call with the fire, Private Capron reported the Eighty-ninth was off again, moving "to a more comfortable position where they remained a week and then started for the Plains again." The stay was short, after one day, the men got orders to leave everything they could get along without, as they were going on another forced march. Starting the next morning, they ended up in a small town called New Market and camped there for the night. This was not the final destination, however, as the next morning Capron stated the regiment "was on the move before daylight and marched all day [with] mud knee deep; till we came to Morristown where we went into camp. Our regiment went on picket and a wetter night I never saw. I was completely drenched

---

24 Capron, letter, January 24, 1865; *Chanute Vidette*, "Campaigning in Tennessee and Georgia in 1864, No. 1," December 1889; *Rock Island Argus*, March 5, 1864.

to the hide. And to top off with, it turned round and froze." Fed up with fighting the elements, Capron decided he "could not stand it in camp and put off for town" where he paid 50 cents for supper. Looking for shelter he headed for an "old rebel hospital" where he came across "3 or 4 more of the boys." The group "smashed up a couple of bunks and built a fire in the fire place." Capron then "hauled up another bunk to the fire and layed down and slept till morning."[25]

Private Chambers also remembered that Longstreet and his army had been at Morristown, but "all were gone now." After spending a rainy night on picket, the regiment had a muddy march back the way they came. Charles Capron wrote that we had "orders to march again, and where should we go to, but back to New Market and camped in our old quarters that night." Here the Eighty-ninth remained a few days and "then fell back to the Plains" where they staid three weeks. James David said this about the latter part of the odyssey. Even though the regiment was able to go part way on the railroad right away, the march to Strawberry Plains was very hard. On arrival, the men camped in a line of battle along the Holston River. Once more the higher-ups had sent Eighty-ninth marching and counter marching along the route of the East Tennessee and Virginia Railroad, which ran northeast out of Knoxville.[26]

While at Maryville, Private Capron told of being detailed back to Knoxville as a drover. After spending the night in the East Tennessee city, the men arose at daylight and went across town to pick up a herd of cattle to be driven back to the brigade. Capron sized up the beef. "Irascible cattle they was too." They were "nothing but skin and bones; not fit for a dog to eat much more a human being." But, orders are orders, so the boys headed the cattle out of the yard and got them about 60 yards and three of them keeled over unable to get up again. From Knoxville to Maryville, a two day trip and a distance of about sixteen miles, they lost 15 head. He continued: "Well our rations run out as we was expected to be gone 2 days

---

[25] Capron, letter, January 24, 1865
[26] *Chanute Vidette*, "Campaigning in Tennessee and Georgia in 1864, No. 1," December 1889; Capron, letter, January 24, 1865; David, diary, February 24, 1864.

only. The second night we see that we was not going to make camp and the boys seeing shoats [young pigs]. They up with their rifles and shot" them all." Needless-to-say, Private William Tomlinson wrote about the rations: "Our beef is so tuff that a Dog could not eat it without putting his foot on it . . . . I have spent all my money for tobacco, papers, and something to eat." In addition to the poor beef, Private Tomlinson was not too keen on the tobacco chewing habit of the local women. "The only fault I have to the girls, they will ask the soldiers for tobacco. They will take a chew as much as a man."[27]

But the Eighty-ninth's real problem still remained with Longstreet's army, and the rebels were never far off. On February 6, while the regiment was at Maryville, Capron remarked in a letter to his mother, "there was 75 prisoners brought in that was captured in the mountains." Over a month passed before Capron again found time to again write home. "Absent but not forgotten parents, brothers, and sisters. You must excuse my long neglect in not writing to you before. I know you would if you knew how it is here with us. I write these few lines in very poor health . . . ." He went on to explain that the Eighty-ninth had been stationed at Morristown 18 miles from Bull's Gap, but for the last eight days the regiment was at New Market about 10 miles from Strawberry Plains. He noted he Railroaders had recently fought a small skirmish with the Rebels at Lost Creek four miles north of town, and a local Rebel, Major Golforth, "was brought in pierced by 4 balls." He pointed out that the Eighty-ninth was no longer "in the Cumberland army . . . but in the Army of the Ohio. Do not know whether we will ever get back to the Cumberland army or not."[28]

When what was eventually designated Company F was formed in 1862, the muster roll included five men over age 40. A year later two remained—William D. Williams and Azron W. Copeland. Of the three others, two had died of illness and one was granted a disability discharge. Copeland, the company's teamster, took ill and was sent to the General Hospital at Murfreesboro on May 19,

---

[27] Capron, letter, February 7, 1864; Kammerer, *Hancock County, Illinois in the Civil War*, 78.

[28] Capron, letters, February 7, March 8 and 9, 1864.

1863 and was away for eight months. But, on Monday, February 22, 1864, Musician Walter S. Huff recorded in his pocket diary that a number of "convalescents and new recruits arrived [with] Copeland of F among them." Married with children of his own, some the age of his fellow soldiers, the forty-three-year-old Copeland was seen as a father figure. Acquainted with Copeland from back home, Charles Capron included him in many of his letters and asked his mother to "write about Mr. Copeland's folks every time you write for you do not know how anxious he it to hear from them." Being illiterate, Azron Copeland visited the eighteen-year-old Capron regularly to have him read his mail and write his family. Charles tactfully put it this way, "Mr. Copeland came over where I was and we concluded we would chatter up a letter together."[29]

*   *   *

   Since leaving Murfreesboro in June, the Eighty-ninth had lost six officers killed in action with two others dying of wounds. Five more vacancies occurred when two were medically discharged, two more resigned their commissions, and one other was cashiered. While still on recruiting service in Chicago, Colonel Hotchkiss wrote a letter to Illinois Adjutant General Fuller dated November 6 regarding the regiment's vacant officer slots and listed the men he considered worthy of promotion. In reviewing the list it is evident that many, like Major Williams, were filling the opening above them, whether it was a staff position or company officer, while a few came from the enlisted ranks. In recommending a private to the rank of second lieutenant in Company D, Colonel Hotchkiss wrote: "After the fall of Capt Spink on the 19th and in the absence of [any] non-com[missioned] officer, Private [Alexander] Beecher took & continued in the command of his company the subsequent days of the Battle of Chickamauga, with good conduct to himself & company." He asked that Private A. Galbraith Miller be made a first lieutenant in Company F. As for Private Miller's qualifications, Hotchkiss noted: "Miller was educated

---

29   Muster and Descriptive Roll of Company F, Record Group 301 Illinois State Archives; *Adjutant General's Report*, 274-275; Huff, diary, February 22, 1864; Capron, letters, April 10 and 24, 1864.

at West Point and resigned his Commission in the Regular Army in 1857. He enlisted with us as a Private and went forward to the Regiment with no promise of promotion, giving <u>sufficient</u> reasons for such a course, which I have since verified by diligent inquiry." Hotchkiss made it a point to add that Miller was "a man of character and respectability, and is vouched for by men of well known loyalty & respectability, and officers (classmates) in the Regular Army."[30]

The position of regimental major was a sensitive issue, and Hotchkiss advised Adjutant General Fuller to take a wait and see approach.

> Respecting the appointment of a Major <u>vice</u> [in the place of] Williams, I would state, that, there are three Captains of equal mark & experience and in the sense, equally capable & worthy of promotion, and equally urged by their friends, in & out of the Regiment, and as each one numbers among his friends a Railroad company. I am of the opinion that the appointment of either of the three or any other officer, at this time, would be injudicious, and an act I would not recommend, until the parties can arrange some scheme (which will take but a few weeks) by which all parties held responsible, would be relieved, by all concerned, from the onus of making an unjust and arbitrary appointment.

The thorny situation was resolved when Captain Bruce H. Kidder of Company E, the former machinist with the Chicago, Burlington, and Quincy Railroad, was mustered in on January 1, 1864 as the Eighty-ninth's new major.[31]

However, almost five months passed, and some, but not all of the recommendations had been acted upon by the Adjutant General and the Governor. Written at Strawberry Plains and dated March 29, Colonel Hotchkiss, now back with the regiment, sent a second letter. Once again, Hotchkiss forwarded a list of men to be promoted. He

---

[30]   Colonel Charles T. Hotchkiss, letter to Adjutant General Fuller, November 6, 1863, Record Group 301 Illinois State Archives.

[31]   Colonel Charles T. Hotchkiss, letter to Adjutant General Fuller, November 6, 1863, Record Group 301 Illinois State Archives; *Adjutant General's Report*, 261.

backed up the urgency of his request by citing specific companies and the dilemma they faced. Since its original organization, he pointed out Company A had gone through eight officers. Three of whom, he wrote, Lieutenant Colonel Hall, Captain Rice, and Lieutenant Young had been killed in action; Adjutant Bishop had been mustered out due to wounds; three others, Captain Smith, Lieutenant Hopper, and Quartermaster Fake, resigned; leaving First Lieutenant Walker, who was a recent promotion and had not yet the experience and ability to justify promotion to Captain. He further explained that the company had its first and two other sergeants killed at Chickamauga "so that there is not material in the company, developed as yet, out of which to make commissioned officers . . . ." Continuing, he pointed out that "Lieut Harkness has held a Commission ever since the organization of the Regt. and for the past year has proved himself to be a most valuable officer. At the Battles of Chickamauga & Mission Ridge he was conspicuous for his good conduct & gallantry. Particularly at the storming of Mission Ridge when he had command of, and led a company & by his gallantry (he being one of the first men on the ridge) he won the admiration of his Regt. and special compliment & mention by Genl Willich . . . ." Hotchkiss emphasized that Lieutenant Harkness had "proved himself a most efficient company commander and his appointment as Captain of Co "A" (in which he is very popular) would be for the good of the company & service, and not prejudice the rights of any person caring of and having claims to a promotion in the same. The 2 Lieutenancy is left open for any man in the company who may earn it." He added "two thirds of the company present for duty are recruits enlisted in the state at large."

Company C was in a similar strait. Captain Henry Rowell had died December 3 of wounds received at Missionary Ridge, while First Lieutenant John Darcy resigned as a consequence of wounds he received at Chickamauga. For over a year the company had been without a second lieutenant. Colonel Hotchkiss explained: "This company has no commissioned officers. Its first Srgt was killed & 2 other Srgts badly wounded at Liberty Gap (since discharged) & at the Battles of Chickamauga & Mission Ridge lost nearly all of its non-commissioned officers." The men remaining in the company, he stated were "of such material that proper men cannot be found as yet to fill all the vacancies in its non-commissioned officers," and he added, "aside from Srgt Rigney, there is no man in the company, who has proved himself as yet a proper person to receive a Commission in the 89th." As in Company A, the second lieutenancy was being "left open for some man in the company to earn the Commission." Whereas the company had initially been made up of men from the Milwaukee Railroad, Hotchkiss now wrote, "over one half of the aggregate of the company are recruits enlisted at large in the state." Placed in command of Company C back on December 3, Sergeant James M. Rigney would have to wait until June 28, 1864 to be officially mustered. The thirty-three-year-old former Cook County farmer had risen from the ranks—originally a private, then promoted to sergeant, and finally appointed company captain. Also, coming through the ranks was William H. Kinney. At age twemty-four, Kinney, a pre-war baggage man for the railroad, had earned a series of promotions, beginning with corporal, followed by sergeant, and ultimately a first lieutenant's commission. But, both promotions were delayed while the unusual circumstance of Sergeant Miller played out.[32]

In his November letter to Adjutant General Fuller, Hotchkiss laid the foundation for Sergeant Miller's promotion. Miller's situation, which was quite unusual and a bit awkward, was the fact that on enlistment with the Eighty-ninth he used the alias, Frank Sumter. Consequently, before again taking up the issue with Adjutant General Fuller, Colonel Hotchkiss requested, in writing, the opinion of his second in command. Lieutenant Colonel Williams replied that since arriving in October, Sergeant Frank Sumter had proven "himself a brave—prompt and obedient soldier, and in my judgement, possesses peculiar qualifications for a commissioned officer." At Missionary Ridge, Williams wrote "his gallantry was conspicuous and won universal praise." He concluded by stating that "his capacity and fitness for command," had, since joining the regiment, "been abundantly tested and he has not been found wanting."[33]

---

[32] Colonel Charles T. Hotchkiss, letter to Adjutant General Fuller, March 29, 1864, Record Group 301, Illinois State Archives.

[33] Lt. Colonel William D. Williams, letter to Colonel Charles T. Hotchkiss, March 29, 1864, Record Group 301, Illinois State Archives.

With Williams's endorsement, Colonel Hotchkiss set out Sergeant Miller's qualifications for Adjutant General Fuller. He then urged Fuller to commission Miller a captain, so he could be appointed to the command of Company C. Hotchkiss must have thought it necessary to state that "Srgt Miller is a man of good habits, character, and ability, and a graduate of West Point." He followed by saying out that Miller had been a captain in the First U. S. Infantry until his resigning his commission in 1857. He then noted that Miller had been the Colonel of the First Maryland Cavalry, but had resigned in June 1862. "In both cases he was honorably discharged [from] the service," he emphasized. Hotchkiss explained that Miller enlisted in the Eighty-ninth last September in Chicago "under the assumed name of "Frank Sumter, Jr." giving me at the time sufficient reasons (in which there was nothing dishonorable to him as a man) for such a course on his part. All of which, together with the facts of his former position[s] in the Army, I have since verified." On reaching the regiment he "was appointed a Srgt., carried a musket and conducted himself like a soldier & a gentleman ever since. And at the storming of Mission Ridge was conspicuous for gallantry. I earnestly recommend his appointment, on the merits of the man, for the good of the company & the service, fortunately it can be done without prejudice to the merits or rights of a man in the company." Hotchkiss enclosed Lieutenant Colonel Williams' statement on Miller's conduct along with an endorsement from Governor Yates.[34]

With Colonel Hotchkiss's supporting his promotion, Sergeant Miller wrote his wife on March 30, 1864. "My Dear Wife," he began. "Since I wrote you yesterday, I have had a long conversation with Col. Hotchkiss. He showed me what he had written to the Gov. recommending me for the Captaincy of Co. C. He states that I behaved with 'distinguished gallantry' at the storming of Mission Ridge, that the universal opinion of me in the Regt. is that I have always acted among them as a Gentleman and a soldier, that there are no Commissioned officers in Co. C & no Sergeants capable of filling the place, & that there is no one in the Regt. more suitable for the appointment than myself, etc. etc." To support his case for

---

[34] Hotchkiss, letter, March 29, 1864.

promotion, he asked that she "take from the tin box containing my commissions & other private papers, accepting my resignation in 1857 & granting me a leave of absence at the same time; also the order from Gen. Dix at Baltimore, accepting my resignation & honorably discharging me from the service, and send them to Dr. McVickar [Miller's cousin] in Chicago, since he has been kind enough to interest himself in the matter with the request that they be sent to Adjt Gen. Fuller. The papers must not however be lost. Probably it would do as well to send this note to Dr. McVickar with the papers. He will then understand all about it."

On Saturday, April 9, Caroline A. Miller sent a note to "Cousin Brock" asking him to forward Miller's paper to the Illinois Adjutant General. The next day Brock McVickar, a Chicago physician, composed a one-page letter to Adjutant General Fuller. In it he stated that he had met with Governor Yates in Chicago some weeks ago, and the governor had given him a letter on behalf of his "cousin A. G. Miller a private in said Regt., saying that if he [Hotchkiss] should recommend him for promotion, [that] he [Yates] would cheerfully comply. Mrs. Miller has just forwarded me the enclosed from her husband; the order discharging him honorably from the service . . . but I do not deem it necessary to forward them. I give you my assurance that he is a gentleman & a soldier. If Col Hotchkiss has forwarded you such statements in his I letter . . . I hope you will consider them favorably. A line from you containing such assurance will give me much satisfaction. Yours very truly, B. McVickar."[35]

In correspondence dated April 14, 1864, Governor Richard Yates wrote Colonel Hotchkiss in regard to Sergeant Miller. Yates appeared unaware of Hotchkiss' or Dr. McVickar's communications with Adjutant General Fuller, but did state that his friend B. McVickar had inquired about a promotion on behalf of Sergeant Galbraith Miller. The Governor's then proceeded to muddy the water. "The matter being entirely out of my control. I have declined to act, but will say that if you can find anything in that line for Mr. Miller [and

35 Andrew G. Miller, letter to Caroline A. Miller, March 30, 1864 and Caroline A. Miller, letter, to Brock McVickar, April 9, 1864, Record Group 301, Illinois State Archives Dr. Brock McVicar, letter to Adjutant General Fuller, April 10, 1864, Record Group 301, Illinois State Archives.

based] on your recommendation it will give me reason to act in his behalf."[36]

The curious case of Andrew Galbraith Miller, Jr. began in Chicago on October 21, 1863, when using the alias Frank Sumter; he enlisted as a private in the Eighty-ninth. On that day, when he signed up with First Lieutenant George F. Robinson of Company D, he stated his age as thirty-six and his occupation as soldier. Whether the recruiting officer suspected anything is unclear. But, in going from the command of the First Maryland Cavalry to the ranks of the Eighty-ninth Illinois Infantry, Andrew Galbraith Miller, Jr.'s Civil War service was very unusual. The abrupt about-face is a mystery with few clues; especially, since Miller's pre-war career is the material from which successful Civil War generals were produced. However for Miller, the War left a checkered and disappointing record.[37]

Miller was born in Gettysburg, Pennsylvania, the son of a noted lawyer. His father achieved prominence in Pennsylvania and served as attorney general of the state until being appointed by President Van Buren to the Supreme Court of the Wisconsin Territory in 1838. With solid Democratic connections, Judge Miller obtained an appointment to West Point for his eldest son, Andrew, Jr. Entering the military academy on July 1, 1843, Miller was age fifteen and six months. Graduating in 1848, he ranked twenty-eighth in a class of thirty-eight, which included several future Union and Confederate generals, most notable being John Buford, Jr.[38]

Assigned to the infantry, Lieutenant Miller spent his entire regular army career at various posts in Texas, of which he said, "My term of service, except when on Recruiting service, was mostly spent on the Texas frontier. I can state nothing worthy of <u>particular</u> note, having performed no duty except scouting & other service incident

[36] Governor Richard Yates, letter to Colonel Charles T. Hotchkiss, A[pril] 14, 1864, Record Group 301, Illinois State Archives.

[37] Muster and Descriptive Roll of Co. B, Record Group 301, Illinois State Archives.

[38] *State Bar Association Proceedings 1878, 1881, 1885* (Madison, Wisconsin: M.J. Cantwell Book and Job Printer, 1883), 1881:52-54; *Official Register of the Officers and Cadets of the U. S. Military Academy* (New York: J. P. Wright, Printer, 1848), 7;

to an Indian frontier, which is similar in the case of every officer so situated." Before resigning on October 31, 1857, Miller had risen to the rank of captain in the First U. S. Infantry. Returning to Wisconsin, he was employed as auditor for the Milwaukee and Mississippi Railroad. On December 20, 1861, Miller was appointment by then Secretary of War Simon Cameron to the Lieutenant Colonelcy of the First Maryland Cavalry. Promoted to colonel on May 4, 1862, he resigned May 22.[39]

On returning to the service as an enlisted man with the Railroaders, Miller was immediately sent to the depleted regiment at Chattanooga. It was here, on November 25, that he "won universal praise" and displayed "conspicuous gallantry" in the assault and capturing of Missionary Ridge. At some time in early 1864, Miller's true identity was revealed and subsequently verified. In dire need of qualified officers, Colonel Hotchkiss undertook to promote Miller to Company C's vacant captaincy. But in the end, the only obtainable position for Sergeant Miller was that of second lieutenant in that company.[40]

More conventional were the changes that occurred in Company F. "It is rumored that Capt. Wells is Ass't Adg't Gen'l on Gen. Johnson's staff," wrote Second Lieutenant James F. Copp to his brother. "If this is true it will give him the rank and pay of a Major, and permanently detach him from our regiment, and of course, cause some promotions in our company, provided we have the necessary number of men to give a full complement of officers." Copp's letter to his brother dated February 23 was in turn published by the *Rock Island Argus*. Since April 1863, Captain E. T. Wells had been detached to the Second Division, Twentieth Army Corps as a judge advocate general. A year later he was permanently commissioned by the President of the United States as Assistant Adjutant General of Volunteers with the First Division, Fourteenth Army Corps. With

---

39 A. G. Miller, Jr. letter to unknown, March 16, 1860, Alumni File U. S. Military Academy; Bvt. Maj.-Gen. George W. Cullum, *Biographical Register on the Officers and Graduates of the U. S. Military Academy West Point, N. Y.* (Boston: Houghton, Mifflin and Company, 1891) II: 361.
40 Hotckiss, letters, November 6, 1863 and March 29, 1864; Muster and Descriptive Roll of Co. C, Record Group 301, Illinois State Archives.

Captain Wells' promotion, First Lieutenant Laertes F. Dimik was mustered as the new Company F captain on April 19, 1864. Copp took over as first lieutenant, and Sergeant Charles J. Arenshield was promoted to second lieutenant.[41]

Born in Hanover, Germany on February 11, 1827, Arenshield's family came to the United States in 1835, settling in Ohio. It was at Urbana, Ohio, on January 21, 1847, that Charles enlisted in Company I, Regiment of Mounted Riflemen of the U. S. Army. Originally organized to guard immigrant wagon trains traveling westward, the mission changed with the outbreak of the Mexican War. The regiment was assigned to General Scott's army and marched from Vera Cruz to Mexico City. Discharged after 18 months service, Arenshield returned to Ohio where he worked as a farm hand for the next four year. Marrying in 1852, Charles left Ohio with his wife and newborn child for Illinois and eventually took up residence near Hampton, Rock Island County. Now in possession of his own land, Arenshield engaged in farming until August 1862 when he enlisted in Company F.[42]

Taking command of Company D was George Franklin Robinson, a former freight agent with the Illinois Central Railroad. Born in New York State, he came west to Milwaukee in 1850. In 1854, he crossed the plains and mountains to the gold fields of California. In 1858, he returned to New York City via the Isthmus of Panama and eventually to Chicago where he enlisted in August 1862 in the Eighty-ninth. Elected first lieutenant when the company was organized, he took command on the death of Captain Spink at Chickamauga and remained in that position until mustered out in June 1865.

Named to replace Captain Thomas Whiting of Company G, killed in action at Chickamauga, was William H. Howell. Originally mustered in as the company's second lieutenant, Howell became the first lieutenant with the resignation of Isaac Copley. Before his enlistment, Howell had been a well-liked Knox County merchant.[43]

---

[41] *Rock Island Argus*, March 5, 1863; *Adjutant General's Report*, 274-275.

[42] *The Biographical Record of Rock Island County, Illinois Illustrated* (Chicago: The S. J. Clarke Publishing Company, 1897), 342-345.

[43] *Adjutant General's Report*, 277; Muster and Descriptive Roll Co. G, Record Group 301, Illinois State Archives.

Company H Private Joseph Buckley began a lengthy letter to his wife on April 2. "I will now give you an account of what we have been doing and what we are doing at the present," he wrote. With only sketchy and incomplete regimental and company records surviving, Buckley's summary of the whereabouts and movement of the Eighty-ninth from late February through the month of March fills the void. The regiment departed Knoxville on February 24 and arrived at Strawberry Plains that the evening. After four days the Railroaders left "the Plains at noon and were ordered to leave our blankets, etc. behind" as they were off on another forced march, arriving at New Market in the evening. The following day, February 29, they set out for Morristown where they stayed for two, returning to New Market around 3:00 P.M. on March 2. The Eighty-ninth again left New Market on March 12 and marched to Panther Springs, which was only 5 miles from Morristown. March 18 they picked up and returned to New Market. The next morning they were again off for Strawberry Plains, crossing the Holston River and went into camp about 2 miles up river. "Sunday March 20th," Buckley wrote, "We left camp and recrossed the Holston at Strawberry Plains, where our Company and Company F were detailed to come to Thorn Grove to guard a grist and saw mill which goes by the name of Derwin's Mill." While guarding the mills, Buckley wrote that on March 22 "we had a snowstorm, which lasted all day. Snow fell to the depth of 8 inches." Two days later, a second snowstorm struck, which Buckley noted was "not so heavy as the one on the 22nd." "Saturday March 26th," he penned, "Ten of us with Sergeant Boomer went out to French Broad on a scout a short time before sundown and stopped at the house of a rebel by the name of Bowman (who is in the Rebel Army). The women folks gave us all a good supper and did not charge us anything for it. We had a pretty good time of it. We staid until nine o'clock when we left for camp but got lost in the woods for about 15 minutes (as it was so dark we could not see our hands before us), when we found the track and got to camp about eleven o'clock."[44]

[44] Buckley, letter, April 2, 1864.

"We did a great deal of marching back and forth . . ."

"Co. F and H is out about five miles guarding a mill. Co. K is train guards. You see our regiment is cut up," Charles Capron mentioned in a letter to his mother written on the last day of March. The rest of the regiment was still at Strawberry Plains where they continued to protect the railroad bridge. He then explained that he was part of a fifty-man detail assigned "to cut down timber from around the fort so as to give range for the cannons." Keeping his mother abreast of his current situation, Charles informed her that "the sutlers have come up so that I can get most of anything I want now." He quickly added. "You spoke in one of your letters asking whether I had drawn any pay. I have received pay once but it was at the time when we could get neither rations nor clothing and I was obliged to lay out a good deal, both for both clothing and rations to make myself comfortable." He followed with a subtle reminder that the regiment had "been on the move all winter more or less and obliged to lay on the ground. But we are getting full rations now and therefore have plenty to eat, and more than that, I think that we will be part of [The Army of the Cumberland] again before long." He added, "If I get 2 months [pay] than I shall send you ten dollars. If 4 months, than you will see 25 dollars."[45]

Joseph Buckley was happy to report to his wife that "we have received full rations from the government ever since the 18th of March so that we now get all we want to eat." Without regular rations and clothing the men had been resourceful in making do. Buckley then stated that "we go into the woods and chop wood for the women whose husbands are in our Army and in return they bake our flour into biscuits or bake us a cracker pudding or sew for us." However, not every interaction with the local population was civil. The new recruit, Joel R. Chambers, recalled two such instances. "While crossing the [Holston] river a Co. E man swapped hats with a fellow sitting in the end of the pontoon boat bailing out the water. A little out of the city another one of the boys did the same thing with a man coming into town with a load of wood. In neither case was the consent of the party of the second part asked for, or received; but the exchange was done all the same . . . ."[46]

---

45   Capron, letter, March 31, 1864.

46   Buckley, letter, April 2, 1864; *Chanute Vidette*, "Campaigning in Tennessee and Georgia in 1864,   No. 1," December 1889.

From near starvation in Chattanooga to living off the land in East Tennessee, the thought of food was a preoccupation with the men of the Eighty-ninth. Boxes from home, packed with delicacies that had become memories and lived only in dreams, were received, shared, and celebrated until gone. Having earlier chided Mary for failing to forward a package of goodies from home, Buckley informed his wife on January 20 that he had not received the box she sent, and it was now impossible to have it forwarded to him in East Tennessee. All he could say is that he had hoped that the regiment would have returned to Chattanooga by now and that there was no sign of any movement that way. Showing a bit of petulance, Buckley wrote: "I am sorry you sent the box without asking me whether it was best to send one or not, because you can't always tell when we are going to move. I am afraid the currant loaf and cheese will spoil and be apt to spoil the rest of the things in the box." He went on, "I will send you word next time when I want you to send me anything. The Government has more than they can do to supply us with rations and clothing to say nothing about supplying us with ammunition."

A month passed and Joseph updated Mary on the box. He still had not received the box she sent but he had spoken with Myron Scoville, another Company H soldier, who saw "it in Chattanooga and tried to get it on one of the wagons, but the wagons were loaded so heavy that they would not allow him to put it on." Not finished and still irritated, Buckley wrote: "I think I shall get it after a while but I am afraid that the contents will be spoiled. Don't send any more unless I send for them. You can send the socks you have knitted for me. You can send for two or four cents per ounce, I forgot which, by a new law that is passed for the benefit of soldiers. You can find out at the Post Office."

Another six weeks went by before Buckley mentioned the box. "There was a man belonging to our company who arrived from Chattanooga who says there is a box for me." Another soldier from Buckley's company, Nimrod Young, convalescing from wounds received at Chickamauga, agreed to forward the box. "I am going to write to him and tell him to forward it to Knoxville as I can get it from there easy enough."

Finally, on April 11, 1864, Buckley wrote: "Dear Wife: I received the long looked for but unexpected box which you sent to me last year and I found it in much better condition than I expected to find it." He did note that "the currant loaf was moldy in the middle but the outside was good. The can of preserved currants lost some of the syrup out and some of the syrup got onto my vest and a little on the gloves owing to the sealing wax coming off. The rest of the things are all in good condition." He was "very much pleased" with the shirt she sent, saying that "it is quite fancy and fashionable in the Army." But failing to quit when he was ahead, he wrote: "The gloves and cap you sent I think I will have to send home as the weather is getting too warm for such articles of wearing apparel. Besides a soldier in active campaignings always wants to wear hats because they stop the rain from running down a person's neck and the sun from burning his face and neck. If you have not sent my hat by the time you get this letter, I wish you would send the hat I bought in Chicago or if you have not got that one by you, get me another one and send it by mail."

Being a man of detail and a little controlling, he continued: "I also wish you would send me a case knife to eat my meals with as I have lost mine or somebody has borrowed it and not brought it back yet. They cost 50 cents each here. I also want you to send me a paper of round-headed boot tacks or nails. I want them to drive into the soles of my boots to stop them from wearing out so quick. Get them at some boot and shoe establishment and then you will get the right kind. I also want you to send me a pocket comb not more than three inches wide and one inch in width and fine teeth in it but not fine as a fine tooth comb. Send them by mail. The postage will be about three cents on the last three named articles. The best way to send them is to sew them up tight in a cloth, write the directions on the cloth."

Fortunately, he was kinder to his son: "Tell Georgie I found the candy in my vest pocket which he sent me and it was first rate. Give him a kiss for me. Tell him I am very pleased with him for sending the candy."

Eventually, he thanked his wife. "I am very much obliged to you for the things you sent to me. We had some of the preserved currants for breakfast and they went first rate. The dried cherries are beautiful." And, in an afterthought, he wrote, "I received the socks you sent me by mail last Monday, a week ago today. I received the box last night."[47]

With April the veteran regiments began returning from their thirty-day re-enlistment furlough home. Private Buckley noted that "the 15th Ohio have got back to our Brigade again. The 49th Ohio are going to meet us at Cleveland, [Tennessee]." William J. Tomlinson explained the importance of proven soldiers staying in the army to his mother. "'You need not be uneasy about my re-enlisting, but at the same time, I think it a great help to the government to have veteran soldiers then to fill the Army up with green troops. The old soldiers, you can depend upon them doing good fighting. The green troops will fight well until their ranks are broken. Then they are not worth their salt.'"[48]

By April 11, the Eighty-ninth was at Loudon, Tennessee west of Knoxville and heading toward Chattanooga. Buckley wrote that the regiment was on its "way to Cleveland 28 miles from Chattanooga. So you see we are going to our own department at last." He passed along too that "General Howard is now in command of our corps. I think he relieved General Granger yesterday. General Howard commanded Eleventh Corps at the Battle of Mission Ridge. He has only one arm." Regarding the Eighty-ninth's movement westward, Buckley commented: "I will continue to send an account of our march." The Railroaders left Thorn Grove on April 6 and returned to Strawberry Plains for the night. Up at half past five on the seventh, the regiment "passed through Knoxville and marched three miles southwest and camped for the night." Seeing he was in for a long march, Buckley bought a pair of boots from Chauncy D.Talmadge on April 8. The men left camp a 1:00 P.M. that day, marching six miles through rain and mud and then camped for the night. April 9, the men were on the road by "six o'clock A.M . . . and marched through mud and rain to Lenoir" where they spent the night. Buckley wrote that it "rained considerable in the night. Lenoir's is about 22 miles from Knoxville." They left Lenoir the next morning at 6:00 A.M . . . and were in Louden by mid-morning. It was here

---

47 Buckley, letters, January 20, February, 19, April 2 and 11, 1864.

48 Buckley, letter, April 11, 1864; Kammerer, *Hancock County, Illinois in the Civil War*, 78.

that Buckley's peripatetic box caught up with him. Monday, April 11, the regiment left Loudon and "crossed the river on a steamboat at half past two. Marched two miles and went into camp. Rained in the night. April 12th—Laid in camp all day weather squally," noted Buckley. April 13 brought better weather and the men were back on the road passing by a town named Philadelphia, through the town of Sweetwater, and went into camp. From Sweetwater the regiment moved to Athens, arriving around 11:00 A.M . . . on the April 14. The next stop was "the town of Charleston and crossed the river Hiawassee and went into camp about 5 o'clock. It is about 15 miles from Athens to Charleston" wrote Buckley. At 5:00 A.M . . . on April 16, the men left Charleston and marched 11 miles to Cleveland and on another seven miles on the Chattanooga road before making camp. After all this, Joseph Buckley informed Mary that he was "a little tired of marching . . . ." Constantly on the march for nearly two weeks, Buckley picked up a cold and a cough, but stated "with the exception of that I am first rate and in good spirits."[49]

Failure to drive Longstreet's Rebels from East Tennessee forced a large number of Union troops to remain there until April. Then, only after Longstreet was ordered in March to re-join the Army of Northern Virginian, could the Federal divisions leave the area. That winter Colonel Francis T. Sherman, Colonel of the Eighty-eighth Illinois, known as the "Second Board-of-Trade Regiment" and part of Sheridan's division spoke out and wrote: "On half rations; no shoes, hats, shirts, socks, pants, or coats; without tents or blankets; the earth frozen six inches deep and covered with snow—that sums up in brief the comforts of the men who were at Chickamauga and Missionary Ridge, and no prospect of relief. Is loyal East Tennessee worth the sacrifice? I say No, and the prayer of every man and officer of the Fourth Corps is that we may be ordered back to Chattanooga." In March 1865, still dumbfounded by the time spent in East Tennessee, Sergeant Isaac K. Young recalled. "We marched and counter-marched from Marysville to Morristown, many times in want, almost in perfect destitution, and all this in the heart of winter; constructing a railroad bridge across the Holston at Strawberry Plains, which was subsequently destroyed by our own hands upon

---

49   Buckley, letters, April 11 and 18, 1864.

our retreat . . . from Dandridge."He wrote: "We felt sore ashamed of that dastardly retreat, under the cover of night, half clothed, half fed, and through rivers of mud, we ran from '*seeming*' death and destruction. We fled while no one pursued us." Twenty-five years passed when Private Joel R. Chambers wondered: "I would just like to ask someone that knows, if anybody does, what good, after the relieving of Burnside at Knoxville, was accomplished by that hard winter campaign in East Tennessee?" He proceeded to answer his own question. "We did a great deal of marching back and forth over the same country; we suffered much from cold, was short on rations all winter . . . but there was nothing, absolutely nothing to show for all this sacrifice." Major General Jacob D. Cox drew a similar conclusion when he wrote: "The military operations in East Tennessee during the winter were unimportant."[50]

---

[50] Boatner, *The Civil War Dictionary*, 468; C. Knight Aldrich, ed., *Quest for a Star: The Civil War Letters and Diaries of Colonel Francis T. Sherman of the 88th Illinois* (Knoxville: University of Tennessee Press, 1999), 98; *Kendall County Record*, April 6, 1865; *Chanute Vidette*. "Campaigning in Tennessee and Georgia in 1864, No. 2," December 1889; Jacob D. Cox, *Atlanta* (New York: Charles Scribner's Sons, 1882), 16-17; Faust, ed., *Historical Times Illustrated Encyclopedia of the Civil War*, 421.

CHAPTER 13

"THEY HAVE PROVED THEMSELVES PATRIOTS AND SOLDIERS . . . ."

Having been driven from Missionary Ridge, Bragg's Army of Tennessee fell back south 25 miles to Dalton, Georgia and dug-in. Grant halted further pursuit of the fleeing Rebels and turned his attention to the besieged Burnside at Knoxville. With Burnside rescued and the onset of winter, the front in northern Georgia settled into a period of relative inactivity. Behind the scenes, however, both armies were undergoing a significant change. First, in mid-December, when the public outcry against Braxton Bragg rose to a level that Confederate President Jefferson Davis could no longer ignore, Bragg voluntarily asked to be relieved and was replaced by General Joseph E. Johnston. In Washington, the Lincoln Administration decided that Ulysses S. Grant should take charge of the Union army. On February 29, 1864, Lincoln signed the bill restoring the grade of lieutenant general of the army. The Senate confirmed Grant's appointment on March 2, and President Lincoln personally presented the commission to him at the White House on March 9. Within a week, Grant returned to Nashville to consult with and to turn command of the western theater over to Sherman. While together, Grant and Sherman developed a coordinated plan to defeat the rebel Confederacy. When the spring campaigns began, the Federal armies were to advance simultaneously, keeping pressure on both Lee and Johnston, preventing one from reinforcing the other. In his *Personal Memoirs* Grant explained: "The plan therefore was for Sherman to attack Johnston and destroy his army if possible, to capture Atlanta and hold it, and with his troops and those of Banks to hold a line through Mobile, or at least to hold Atlanta and command the railroad running east and west . . . . This would cut the Confederacy in two again, as our gaining possession of the Mississippi River had done before."[1]

Placed in charge of the Military Division of the Mississippi, with the Army Departments of the Ohio, Cumberland, Tennessee, and Arkansas under his command, Sherman immediately began to organize and prepare for the coming campaign. About March 25, Sherman set forth on an inspection tour of the separate armies, conferring with McPherson, Thomas, and Schofield. Discussion was held with each about the upcoming movement against Johnston's rebel army entrenched at Dalton. Additionally high priority was given to the build up and the equal distribution of supplies between the three Union armies. It was agreed to consolidate the Eleventh and Twelfth Corps under Hooker, and designate it the Twentieth Corps. Command of the Fourth Corps went to Oliver O. Howard when the ever-complaining Granger was granted a leave of absence.[2]

Grant originally set April 30 as the day for the simultaneous advance, but it was subsequently changed to May 5. Sherman wrote, "On the 5th I rode out to Ringgold, and on the very day appointed by General Grant . . . the great campaign was begun." On May 6, Schofield and McPherson were in position, "and on the 7th General Thomas moved in force against Tunnel Hill, driving off a mere picket-guard of the enemy . . . ." Sherman stated: "From Tunnel Hill I could look into the gorge by which the railroad passed through a straight and well-defined range of mountains, presenting

---

[1] Albert Castel, *Decision in the West: The Atlanta Campaign of 1864* (Lawrence, Kansas: University Press of Kansas, 1992), 56-57, 62-68; Grant, *The Personal Memoirs of U. S. Grant*, 403-406; W. T. Sherman, *Memoirs of Gen. W. T. Sherman* (New York: Charles L. Webster & Co., 1891), II: 25-26.

[2] Sherman, *Memoirs of Gen. W. T. Sherman*, II: 7-9.

sharp palisade faces, and known as 'Rock Face.' The gorge itself was called the 'Buzzard Roost.'" Sherman had no intention of attacking this strongly held position, but to hold the enemy in place, while McPherson swung to the west, turning the Rebel position.[3]

* * *

It was April 16, and while bivouacked near Loudon, Tennessee, that a Company H soldier took the time to write the editor of the *Kendall County Record*. He began by asking no one in particular: "Will the First Brigade never be allowed to rest from the arduous duties attendant upon the active campaigns? Ever since we left Murfreesboro we have been on a protracted march. It seems as though . . . the machinery destined to crush the unholy rebellion, could not be continued without the Herculean strength of Willich's 'Iron Brigade.'" The writer explained that the Railroaders "left Strawberry Plains on the 7th inst., passed through Knoxville, Lenoir, and after a disagreeable march through mud and rain, arrived at this place—only waiting our turn to cross the Tennessee River, in flat boats, to reach Loudon." And as far he was concerned, the most significant news he had to pass along was: "We are on our way to join the victorious 'Army of the Cumberland,' from which, may we never again be parted till the war is brought an honorable close. In order to fill our 'cup of happiness' quite to overflowing, return unto us 'Rosy.'" He went on to mention that "General Howard now commands the Corps (4th) *vice* General Granger removed. Rations Plenty."

For the folks at home, he wrote: "Capt. Hobbs is the same good natured 'Frank' of old, and is much respected by all with whom he comes in contact. Lieut. [John A.] Beeman is Acting Brigade Quartermaster. Lt. Billy Harkness, everybody's favorite, is at home on a leave of absence—and that he may have a glorious time is the wish of all. Orderly 'Aaron' [Boomer] is as *solid* both mentally, and *physically* as ever."[4]

---

[3]   *Ibid.*
[4]   *Kendall County Record*, May 7, 1864.

Three days later and with the Eighty-ninth halted outside of Cleveland, Tennessee, the anonymous writer posted a second letter to the *Record*. "It is very probable that we will, at last, be allowed a little rest; and it is right that we should," he commented. The regiment, he wrote, was camped near the railroad, and the men were excited by sight "of three trains of cars" which were going up to Cleveland and down to Chattanooga daily. The Eighty-ninth was located six miles from Cleveland and twenty from Chattanooga. With the regiment camped close to the railroad, the Eighty-ninth's new sutler arrived with "two and a half tons of goods." The writer stated that "the manner in which the boys are 'going in' on the canned fruit, cheese, tobacco, etc. is terrible to mention; but this is not to be wondered at, as we have not had a delicacy pass our lips for eleven months." He also informed the paper's readers that two of his company's men, Alex Patterson and Josiah Coleman had come down with smallpox, and appeared to be in no danger. The rest of his company was healthy and well. None of this was the consequence of rations provided by the quartermasters as our writer pointed out. "Could not the Sanitary Commission send vegetables to the front? I think so. Could the men have vegetables more and salt pork a *little* less, they would be healthier. It is encouraging to know that the Commission is doing do much good. The men in 'pest hospitals' have everything that is desirable for a sick soldier." He noted that only occasionally were "the well men supplied with vegetables for a few weeks."[5]

Joseph Buckley, who had worked in his father's apothecary in England, was assigned to look after Alexander Patterson. He remarked to Mary that the regimental surgeon requested that he be detailed to care for a fellow who had "taken sick with the Small Pox . . . ." To prevent a further outbreak of the dreaded disease, Buckley, Patterson, and the other sick were quarantined away from camp. Buckley told his wife that he was not allowed in the regimental camp for fear he might carry the disease in his clothes. "So everything is sent to the hospital tent that comes for Patterson or me and I get them there," he explained. Ten days passed and Joseph wrote that his "man is getting along first rate and will soon be well.

[5]   *Ibid.*

I have taken good care of him so far. It has been very lonesome up here all alone with a sick man. This is the first time I have been away from company since we left Chicago."

In the midst of a letter home, Joseph and his charge quickly abandoned their isolated camp. He explained: "I had to quit writing here as the 32nd are target shooting and the bullets came very thick. We had to move the sick out of the tent and move into a ravine where the bullets cannot reach us.""Aggravated, he wrote, "it is a wonder some of us were not hurt. It is perfectly ridiculous as the Lieut. Col. of the 32nd came and saw us before they commenced shooting." If this was not bad enough, two days later, and before he finished another letter, he had to evacuate once more. "We have just been shelled out of our tents by the artillerists who commenced shooting at a target just below and a little to the right of us. We had to leave in a hurry as the pieces of shells came right among us . . . . They stopped shooting as soon as they found out that we were in danger." Two weeks elapsed before Buckley was allowed to return to his company. Before reporting, he bathed and washed his clothes. Back in camp, he was issued "a new pair of pants, a shelter tent, and a blanket" by Captain Hobbs and ordered "to burn the old ones."[6]

"I will try to finish my letter. I had to quit rather sudden as they blowed the fall in call and then the order came that we would move camp about three quarters of a mile," wrote Charles Capron to his mother. When he returned to his letter, he said: "We may stay here [Cleveland] some time and we may not. There is no telling. We have plenty of rations now as we are camped near the railroad and the cars run regular." He too considered it worthwhile to mention the sutler was up with the regiment for the first time since the Eighty-ninth left Chattanooga. He pointed out that this was a two-sided. "We can get such articles as we need, although they come very high."

Two weeks passed and again with Sunday afternoon off, Private Capron found time to write his family. He concluded that the regiment was "stationed here for the purpose of drilling. We have company drill at 7, Battalion at 9 and brigade at 3, and then dress parade at 5, therefore keeping us pretty busy." Having lived for months on limited supplies, the quartermasters now provided

---

6   Buckley, letters, April 18 and 27, 1864, May 5, 1864.

the Railroaders with sorely needed clothing and equipment. Capron wrote: "They are bringing on large quantities of clothing consisting of pants, coats, socks, shoes, shirts, drawers, hats, canteens, and haversacks. In fact everything that a soldier needs."[7]

A quarter of century had passed, but Joel Chambers recalled like yesterday those days of April of 1864. "We were only *loaned* to the Department of the Ohio; and now we are back home again, with the other divisions of the 4th corps; and with the Army of the Cumberland where we belong." Sherman's command, however, was all hustle and bustle as he prepared his troops for the upcoming campaign. "But how busy they do keeps us! Camp is all cleaned up in apple pie order, and now it is drill, drill, battalion drill, and brigade drill, with now and then the awkward squad drill. Drill every day in the week, except Saturday which is wash day, and Sunday, which is rest day." Besides drilling, all were "refitted with clothing; and those of us recruits who have been carrying the clumsy Enfield rifle [were] pleased to receive orders to 'turn them over' and get new Springfield rifles."[8]

On April 29, Private David B. James recorded in his pocket diary that General Howard had conducted "a grand review" and had been accompanied by "a lady Lieutenant Colonel." After a lengthy absence, General Willich returned on April 30. Joel Chambers said that he "was received with continued and prolong cheers from all the boys under his command." Surrounded by "his poys," as he referred to them, the venerated Dutchman made a short speech, saying that he was happy to be back in time to lead the men in the upcoming advance on the Rebels. Also returning that day was the likable Company H lieutenant, William Harkness.[9]

Private Joel Chambers, the evening of May 2, was on guard duty at the regimental headquarters. "About ten o'clock," he recalled, "An orderly rode up to the colonel's tent and delivered orders which I learned was to march, and that we were to start the next day at

[7] Capron, letters, April 10 and 24, 1864.

[8] *Chanute Vidette*, "Campaigning in Tennessee and Georgia in 1864," December 1889.

[9] James, diary, April 29, 1864; Chambers, *War Fever Cured*, 31; Cope, *The 15th Ohio Volunteers*, 424.

noon." As ordered, the Eighty-ninth moved from McDonald's Station on the East Tennessee Railroad at noon on the third, "and thus was commenced one of the greatest campaigns of modern times." The Railroaders, in company with their brigade, division, and corps, marched seven or eight miles toward Ringgold just across the state line between Tennessee and Georgia. Chambers later wrote that "our corps, the 4th, was commanded by Gen. O. O. Howard, our division, the 2d, by Gen. T. J. Wood, and our brigade, the 1st, by Gen. August Willich. Our brigade, known as the Dutch or horn brigade, was composed of the 15th and 49th Ohio, the 32d Ind., the 15th Wis., the 8th Kansas, the 25th, 35th and 89th Ill."[10]

Several of Willich's innovations had come to him while he was being held in Richmond's Libby Prison. It was here that Willich developed his system of "advance firing," which he introduced on returning to the brigade and successfully used at Liberty Gap and at Chickamauga. Troubled by the chaotic communications of the battlefield, where verbal orders were sometimes misunderstood and written messages never received, Willich came up with his own unique method to deliver orders in the field. To overcome the confusion created by smoke, noise, and casualties, he worked out a system of bugle calls to direct his brigade, hence, the moniker of *Bugle* or *Horn Brigade*. One soldier later explained that "the order for every movement was made by the bugle." And, "as all calls were Prussian calls, the enemy could not understand them."[11]

Dalton, Georgia, located on the Western and Atlantic Railroad, was the terminus of Johnston's lifeline back to Atlanta. This is also where Bragg stopped after the debacle at Missionary Ridge. When Johnston took command, the Rebel Army of Tennessee remained here—secure behind the fortified Rocky Face Ridge. In the coming campaign Sherman planned for the Army of the Cumberland to hold

[10] *Chanute Vidette*, "Campaigning in Tennessee and Georgia in 1864," December 1889; Chambers, *War Fever Cured*, 31; *OR*, Vol. 38, Pt. 401.

[11] Barnett, "Willich's Thirty-Second Indiana Volunteers," 63; Newton Bateman and Paul Selby, eds., 2 vols., *Historical Encyclopedia of Illinois and History of Rock Island County* (Chicago: Munsell Publishing Co., 1914), II: 884; Burton, *Melting Pot Soldiers: The Union's Ethnic Regiments*, 82; Cope, *The 15th Ohio Volunteers*, 278-279, 290.

the rebels in place at Rocky Face Ridge while McPherson's Army of the Tennessee outflanked the Rebels. McPherson's men made a wide sweep, passing through Snake Creek Gap and emerging behind Johnston and across the railroad, trapping the rebels.[12]

Up early on May 4, the Railroaders formed up and hit the road at 5:30 A.M . . ., marching about eight miles and going into camp about 11:00 A.M . . . at Catoosa Springs. For the next few days the regiment marked time while awaiting further orders. Joel R. Chambers noted in his diary, "A dull monotony pervades the entire camp, which with the Enemy directly in our front makes it seem a little ominous." May 7, the regiment finally resumed the march, moving to Tunnel Hill. Off and on throughout the day, light skirmishing could be heard. The next day the Eighty-ninth was ordered forward and lay in line of battle behind a line of skirmishers. By May 9, the Railroaders were at Rocky Face Ridge where all but one of its companies was on the skirmish line. Chambers remembered that Rocky Face Ridge itself was "swarming with rebels."[13]

Specifically, Willich's Brigade faced the Rebels at a cut in the ridge called Mill Creek Gap. Here the rail and wagon roads ran connecting Atlanta and Chattanooga. The steep cliffs on either side of the gap were known locally as Buzzard's Roost. On the morning of the May 9, the Railroaders were ordered to pile their knapsacks. Stripped for action, with skirmishers deployed in advance, the regiment advanced up the steep heavily wooded side of Rocky Face Ridge. "And now . . . I am, for the first time, actually under fire," wrote Joel R. Chambers. The line temporarily halted and Chambers ears picked up "a strange whizzing sound," which suddenly whacked "against a dry elm limb, a few feet above and in front" of him. Nearby, his cousin, Jim Tomlinson, "coolly cast his eye up, and said 'How are you?'" The firing lasted all day. Joseph Buckley wrote: "The Rebs shoot almost straight down and we had to shoot almost straight up at them. Considerable firing between the Rebs and us and considerable fun . . . ." Years afterward, William E. Ward of Company G wrote a description of his part in the

---

[12]   Daniel, *Days of Glory*, 394-397; Van Horne, *History of the Army of the Cumberland*, II: 47.

[13]   Buckley, letter, May 5, 1864; Chambers, *War Fever Cured*, 33; *Chanute Vidette*, "Campaigning in Tennessee and Georgia in 1864," December 1889.

fight for the Galesburg, Illinois Grand Army of the Republic Post. "The rebels were encountered on the top of a mountain," so Ward "with two comrades took a position behind a rock" giving them "the best place to fire from." He convinced "his comrades [to] load the guns and he would do the shooting." With the Rebels well hidden, he blazed away "where the smoke of a gun showed the presence of an enemy. This continued [for] sometime without visible results, when . . . with [his] gun cocked and ready to fire," Ward remarked about a Minie ball "that had just passed above him, 'They cannot come as close as that again.' Just at that instant a bullet struck him and passing through his arm and was stopped by the stock of his gun." That ended Private Ward's tenure with the Eighty-ninth. After the campaign Lieutenant Colonel Williams reported the Railroader's lost 2 killed and 15 wounded in the fighting at Rocky Face Ridge. Listed as killed in action on May 9 was Private Jacob F. Craig, while James C. Lewis succumbed from a wound, dying at Chattanooga on July 23.[14]

*　　*　　*

Relieved as skirmishers on May10, the Eighty-ninth was held in reserve, but returned to the front line the next day. Chambers recorded in his diary for May 12 that the division "changed front to the Northward and hastily erected a line of breastworks expecting an attack, which however did not take place." The next day he scribbled: "We discovered that the demonstration on our left was only a feint of the enemy to cover his retreat which he effected during the night falling back beyond Dalton with our forces in hot pursuit. We rested for the night 8 miles south of Dalton." While Thomas confronted the Confederates at Rocky Face Ridge, McPherson, with Kilpatrick's cavalry division leading, first marched westward and then swung south ending up in Johnson's rear, threatening the rebels' line of

---

14   *Chanute Vidette*, "Campaigning in Tennessee and Georgia in 1864," December 1889; Buckley, letter, May 18, 1864; Knox County Roll of Honor, Knox County Recorder's Office, Galesburg, Illinois, "Grand Army of the Republic Personal War Sketch of Comrade William E. Ward," 79; *Adjutant General's Report*, 277; *History of Lee County* (Chicago: H. H. Hill and Company, Publishers, 1881), 386.

communication. To escape the trap, Johnson abandoned Dalton on May 12 and fell back to Resaca.[15]

"On the 13th, early in the morning the Rebs evacuated their 'Roost' and we followed close in their rear," a soldier using the *nom de plume* of "R" wrote the editor of the *Kendall County Record*. By April 14, the enemy was located in force and entrenched at Resaca where they were covering the railroad crossing of the Oostenaula River. That morning, Private Buckley wrote the Eighty-ninth "left camp and marched within about 2 ½ miles of [the Oostenaula] River where the Rebs made a stand." Coming upon the Confederates pickets, the brigade prepared for action with the Forty-ninth and Fifteenth Ohio forming the front line; the Thirty-second Indiana and the Eighty-ninth forming the second line; and Thirty-fifth Illinois and the Fifteenth Wisconsin rounding out the third line. Buckley continued: "We commenced skirmishing about 10 o'clock and drove the enemy into their Rifle Pits and strongholds. Fought the rest of the day and took their first line of Rifle Pits. At night our Regiment built a fresh line of Rifle Pits." While the infantry pushed the Rebels back, "R" pointed out that "our batteries kept up a steady fire on the enemies fortifications all day."[16]

In 1889, Private Chambers recalled a personal incident from the first day at Resaca. "While supporting the front line during the afternoon, with shells screaming over us and bullets whizzing carelessly around among us," Chambers wrote that he heard someone say, "'Be quiet there those shells will not hurt you.'" He looked "around to see from whence the voice came," and saw Colonel Hotchkiss "peeping out from behind a little forked limbed tree, with his eyes looking somewhat like two burned holes in a red blanket. I think the Colonel thought the shells *might* hurt somebody, after all." With all of the terrifying noise of battle, including the whizzing bullets and screaming shrapnel, soldier "R" noted that remarkably only "three men of the Eighty-ninth were wounded."[17]

---

[15]   Chambers, *War Fever Cured*, 34.

[16]   *OR*, Vol. 38, Pt. 1, 390; *Kendall County Record*, June 2, 1864; Buckley, letter, May 1864.

[17]   *Chanute Vidette*, "Campaigning in Tennessee and Georgia in 1864," December 1889; *Kendall County Record*, June 2, 1864.

As the rest of Union units moved into position on the May 15, orders came for Willich's brigade to shift to the right. Once his regiments had filed into place, Willich went forward to inspect his front and to observe the enemy. While peering over the parapet at the enemy's position, the old Prussian general was the victim of a rebel sharpshooter. Hit in the right shoulder, General Willich crumpled to the ground. Hurriedly a stretcher was found, and he was soon being carried to the rear. As he passed through the men, and obviously in severe pain, Willich was overheard exhorting "his poys" to do their duty the same as if he were with them.[18]

About 4:00 P.M. on the May 15, the Eighty-ninth relieved a portion of the front line and held this position until darkness settled in, when the left of the regiment cautiously moved forward straightening the line. Around 11:00 P.M., the rebels attacked the Railroaders' position, which, Colonel Hotchkiss reported "was repulsed with great loss to him and but trifling damage to us." Chambers jotted in his diary that "the enemy made an attempt to break our lines about 11 o'clock at night but was handsomely repulsed by the 89th Ills and 15th Ohio." With the river at his back, Bragg realized a successful flanking move could turn his position at Resaca into a trap; consequently, later that "same night the entire rebel army evacuated its position, crossing the Oostenaula River and retreating toward Kingston." Looking back through the years, Chambers reflected: "Thus we passed through the great battle of Resaca. Our regiment and brigade did not suffer severely in this battle, except that our brave old brigadier was wounded Sunday afternoon. Our brigade was now commanded by Col. Gibson of the 49th Ohio." A year would pass and the war end before Willich returned. The sniper's bullet left the Old Warrior's right arm partially paralyzed.[19]

"There was considerable hard fighting on the 14th and 15th at the battle of Resaca," Joseph Buckley informed his wife in a letter dated May 20. He told of a gruesome sight that only a soldier in

---

[18] OR, Vol. 38, Pt. 1, 391; Cope, *The 15th Ohio Volunteers and its Campaigns 1861-1865*, 435-436.

[19] OR, Vol. 38, Pt. 1, 391; Chambers, *War Fever Cured*, 35; *Chanute Vidette*, "Campaigning in Tennessee and Georgia in 1864," December 1889; James Barnett, "August Willich, Soldier Extraordinary," 73.

combat witnesses. "One of our Batteries got a cross fire on them and I tell you it was awful to see the destruction they caused among the Rebel troops. It literally cut them to pieces, but I will not try to describe to you how that scene of blood looked after the fight was over." In this action, Buckley commented that the Eighty-ninth boys "were shooting at a very short range." But so far, he reported: "Our Regiment has lost fewer men in this campaign than any other we have been in for which I feel very thankful." He could gratefully say that "we have none killed or wounded in our company so far." But he was also a realist, telling Mary: "I have no doubt we shall have some very hard fighting to do before long, and I am confident we shall conquer the Rebs in this department."[20]

Sherman wasted no time, and by the May 16 he had his blue-coated columns hot on the heels of the retreating Confederates. As the Eighty-ninth passed through the rebel lines, a wide-eyed Chambers saw sights that soon became too familiar, and they would never leave him. He later recalled the ghastly scene the Railroaders gazed on as they marched by.

Monday morning it was found that the Johnnies had decamped during the night. We were soon in motion, in pursuit. Ah! Here is some of the fruits of yesterday's work. Yes, there are six in a row,and there are some more over there; yes all around, I have not time to count them. Their blankets are spread over them, and soon they will rest in their lonely soldier's grave. But we, now pass on to the ground occupied by the rebs. Oh! What terrible work has been done here. Capt. Goodspeed evidently did not waste his ammunition, for here the very earth has been torn up, and all around, there are indications of death and destruction. We pass the rebel field hospital, Where there are arms, legs, hands and feet left to tell the ghastly story. A few of the wounded have been left, and an assistant surgeon left with them.[21]

---

[20]   Buckley, letter, May 20, 1864.

[21]   *Chanute Vidette*, "Campaigning In Tennessee and Georgia in 1864," December 1889.

Unable to crack the Rebel defenses at Resaca, Sherman opted again to send McPherson's army around the Confederate left to threaten Johnston's line of communications. Aware that he was in a poor strategic position, Johnston soon received word that Union troops were moving against his rear, forcing an abrupt break in contact and a hasty withdrawal from Resaca. Soldier "R" too described the end of the fighting at Resaca and the ensuing pursuit of the Rebels. "On the night of the 15th, about twelve o'clock, the enemy made a charge and were repulsed; the next morning the enemy were missing, leaving their dead only partially buried—a number of their wounded were left near the railroad track, and a surgeon had been left to care for them. Ever since we have followed them close giving them a 'power' of trouble to keep their wagon train out of our hands. We skirmish with them every day."[22]

May 17 saw the Eighty-ninth advancing seven more miles with skirmishing continuing throughout the day. In his daily diary notation Chambers' entered that the brigade came upon the enemy at dusk, resulting in considerable cannonading. The boys immediately went to work throwing up a barricade of rails and logs and slept in a line of battle, but during the night the rebels again fell back. The next two days the Railroaders moved further south, passing through Adairsville and Kingston. Five miles southeast of the latter, Johnston attempted to make a stand, having drawn his army up across the path of the Western & Atlantic Railroad. Facing the rebels, Howard's Fourth Army Corps held the right of Sherman's line. Wood's Division held the extreme right with Gibson's Brigade in reserve. Chambers remarked that "the enemy seemed to be a little stubborn in regard to going any farther." And, at dusk, the firing picked up and became quite heavy, but it ceased shortly after dark. Having concentrated his army near Cassville, Johnston intended to strike one of Sherman's advancing corps. But, dissension among his subordinates resulted in no counterattack, and the Confederates retired beyond the Etowah River to Allatoona Pass. Chambers later wrote that during the night the enemy again fell back. The next day, though, the Eighty-ninth remained in camp and stayed put for over three days, enjoying a much needed rest.[23]

---

[22] *Kendall County Record*, June 2, 1864.

[23] Chambers, *War Fever Cured*, 35-36; *Chanute Vidette*, "Campaigning in Tennessee and Georgia in 1864," December 1889; Boatner, *Civil War Dictionary*, 31-32;

"In a pretty little grove, taking it easy," Soldier "R" noted as he sat composing a letter to the editor of the *Kendall County Record*. He proceeded to explain that "our army is now about four miles south of Kingston making for Atlanta, a distance on the railroad of fifty-five miles. The towns we have passed through are all deserted; General Johnston takes all [the] citizens with him. Where he will make a stand is unknown . . . ." Bringing special delight was the success that the Union force had experienced so far. "R" even crowed a bit. "There are seven or eight corps of troops here . . . . Such a heap of 'Yanks,' Georgia has never seen. No wonder the 'Rebs' retreat; they know what is for their own good. The Yankee bullets are too many for them." Probably the best news he conveyed to the folk back home was that the local men in Company H were "all right, no one hurt, and the boys do their duty—hard as it is."[24]

*   *   *

When Sherman temporarily halted his force, he set about preparing for his next move, which called for the abandonment of his supply line, the Western & Atlantic Railroad. So while the men rested, the Yankee wagons were loaded with three weeks of rations and ammunition. Sherman once more planned to swing his troops around the entrenched Confederates and show up in their rear. Twenty years earlier, as a young lieutenant, Sherman had been assigned to this part of North Georgia and was still familiar with the terrain the rebels now occupied. In his memoirs, he confided: "I therefore knew that the Allatoona Pass was very strong, would be hard to force, and resolved not even to attempt it, but to turn the position, by moving from Kingston to Marietta *via* Dallas; accordingly, I made orders on the 20th to get ready for the march to begin the 23d." Sherman was also aware of the difficulties that lay before his men. The route was densely wooded, with few roads, and would be slow going; consequently, leaving the railroad would not be easy. Almost immediately the maneuver began to unravel as

---

Long, *The Civil War Day by Day*, 504-506; William R. Scaife, *The Campaign for Atlanta* (Saline, Michigan: McNaughton & Gunn, Inc., 1993), 39-48.

[24] *Kendall County Record*, June 2, 1864.

rebel scouts quickly discovered what was happening. The Federal columns had no sooner crossed the Etowah River on May 23, than Wheeler's horsemen reported the movement to Johnston. The wily Confederate general promptly countered Sherman's move by sending Hardee's Corps toward Dallas and shifting Polk's Corps west to the vicinity of Lost Mountain. While Sherman's troops groped along through the Georgia wilderness, the rebels effectively took up positions to block their way.[25]

With the enemy having fallen back on the night of the May 19, the brigade remained in camp, resting and receiving necessary supplies. On the afternoon of the May 23, with twenty day's rations in the supply train, Willich's regiments "moved with the division and the entire army to the right, with a view of turning the enemy's position in the Allatoona Mountains, where he was strongly fortified," Colonel Hotchkiss later wrote. Lieutenant Colonel Williams officially noted that from May 20 through the 22 the Eighty-ninth remained near Cassville, and "replenished our stores of rations, reduced baggage, and prepared to follow the enemy across the Etowah River to his stronghold at Atlanta." In his pocket diary for May 23, Joel Chambers recorded: "Received orders to march; started at one o'clock; marched 12 miles; crossed the Etowah river & camped on some creek name unknown." The next day he entered: "Marched 15 miles on a very dim road across hills, valleys and through the woods . . . it was very disagreeable marching on account of the dust which raised in great clouds." According to Colonel Hotchkiss, the Eighty-ninth headed "nearly due west about seven miles, crossing the Etowah River at Gillem's Bridge, thence moving on blind roads and over broken country in a southerly direction toward Dallas, Ga., crossing Euharlee Creek on the 23d and Pumpkin Vine Creek on the 25th, where heavy firing at the front was heard . . . ."[26]

Out in front of Thomas' Army of the Cumberland and in search of a road leading west to Dallas, Hooker's infantry plodded forward. With each mile it became evident, as Colonel Hotchkiss put it, that

---

[25]   Rheinhart, *August's Willlich's Gallant Dutchman, Civil War Letters from the 32nd Indiana Infantry*, 171; Scaife, *The Campaign for Atlanta*, 49; Sherman, *Memoirs of Gen. W. T. Sherman*, II: 43.

[26]   *OR*, Vol. 38, Pt. 1, 391, 402; Chambers, *War Fever Cured*, 37.

the enemy had "hastily abandoned his position at Allatoona Pass and by hurried march thrown himself near Dallas," placing the Rebels squarely across Sherman's path. The initial contact took place sometime after mid-morning on May 25 at a crossroads near New Hope Church. In mid-afternoon, Hooker's men attempted to overrun the main Confederate breastworks. But after heavy fighting, the blue-clad troops were stopped in their tracks, suffering 1,600 casualties. Overcome by darkness, the Yankees grabbed their shovels and dug in. While Sherman spent the May 26 contemplating his next move, Private Chambers noted in his diary: "A member of our Co accidentally shot himself through the left hand. Reg't went to the front and lay in line of battle to the rear of the skirmish line all day & night, had 2 men wounded."[27]

Hung-up at New Hope Church crossroads, Sherman weighed his options and concluded late on May 26 to have another go at turning the Rebel right flank. He placed General O. O. Howard in overall command of the next day's operation. For the task at hand, Howard was given 14,000 men comprised of Thomas J. Wood's Division from his own Fourth Corps, Richard W. Johnson's Division of the Fourteenth Corps, and Nathaniel C. McLean's brigade from the Twenty-third Corps. Additionally, Sherman ordered all the armies' batteries that could be brought to bear to bombard the rebels from early morning until 9:00 A.M. Around 10:00 A.M. on May 27, Wood's division was pulled from the center of the Union line and moved to a field out of sight of the enemy, where its three brigades (Hazen, Gibson, and Knefler) formed in a column to spearhead the movement to the left. After all were in place, the march kicked-off about 11:00 A.M.[28]

Sometime before noon on Friday, Company H Private Wallace McCloud hurriedly scratched in his pocket diary that earlier there

---

[27] Boatner, *The Civil War Dictionary*, 219; Scaife, *The Campaign for Atlanta*, 50-51; Chambers, *War Fever Cured*, 38.

[28] Castel, *Decision in the West: The Atlanta Campaign of 1864*, 229-230; James Dean, "The Battle of Pickett's Mill," *Blue & Gray Magazine* VI (July 1989), 28-29; Richard M. McMurry, *Atlanta 1864, Last Chance for the Confederacy* (Lincoln, Nebraska: University of Nebraska Press, 2000), 90; Phil Noblitt, "The 'Crime' at Pickett's Mill," *America's Civil War* (January 1996), 39-40.

had been brisk firing at the front and that Companies H, I, G, and B went out on the skirmish line at 5:00 A.M . . . As the morning progressed, he reported there had been "very little musketry," but there had been "heavy cannonading firing by volley." Relieved about 9:00 A.M . . . by first division, the regiments moved back to their former camp. However, after a half-hour the brigade moved over to the left of Twenty-third Corps. That same morning fellow Company H private, James B. David, too entered a few quick lines in his diary: "In the Field 5 miles from Mary Ethe [Marietta]. It is clear and hot to day. We staid on the line for support of the skirmish line. We are [now] on the skirmish line to day. We relieved the 15ᵗʰ Ohio. There is heavy cannonading this morning. We were relieved by Stanley's Division."[29]

Joel Chambers would later recall that it was close to noon when Wood's division began moving to the left. Hoping to get to or beyond the Rebel flank, the column moved east following no road worthy of name or description through a dense wood, cut by steep ravines and small streams. Hazen's scouts, armed with a pocket compass to maintain their bearing, pushed through the tangled underbrush marking the route. Trudging along behind, the sweating blue column struggled through a maze of briars and poison ivy. But making matters worse was the fact that any attempt to hide their intentions from the enemy was soon lost when Colonel Gibson, in keeping with Willich's method of communication, continued to give all brigade orders by bugle call. Soon grumbling voices were heard from officers and men alike protesting: "'If we are expected to surprise the enemy, why don't they stop those d___d bugles?'" As unnerving as the blaring bugles were to those headed for combat, they alone had not given away Sherman's plan. Of no consolation to the men in blue was the fact that Joe Johnston had already anticipated Sherman's latest move and on May 26, had reinforced and lengthened the right of the Confederate line with one of his best divisions, Patrick Cleburne's.[30]

---

[29] McCloud, diary, May 27, 1864; David, diary, May 27, 1864.

[30] *Chanute Vidette*, "Campaigning in Tennessee and Georgia in 1864, No. 3," December 1889; Cope, *The 15ᵗʰ Ohio Volunteers and Its Campaigns 1861-1865*, 450-451; Noblitt, "The 'Crime' at Pickett's Mill," 42;

Howard's detachment got underway about 11:00 A.M . . ., and according to Charles Capron, "We had been marching around in the timber till nearly noon when we stopped to rest awhile, but about 1 o'clock we started again marching to the left . . . ." The column had been on the move about an hour and a half and had covered approximately a mile and a half when the one-armed general concluded that his command was beyond the rebel flank. But first, scouts probed forward and found occupied Confederate works. Having guessed wrong, Howard ordered his weary column to continue on to the left another mile or two. Eventually, by mid-afternoon the Union troops had moved eastward to the vicinity of Pickett's Mill. Again, reconnaissance revealed butternut-clad troops off to the right hurriedly putting up works, but the area to the front appeared to be uncovered. Having reached what he thought was the end of the rebel line; Howard took no action, but rested his troops, giving the enemy valuable time to prepare for the coming assault.[31]

It was not exactly the open enemy flank that Howard had been searching for; however, with time running out to fulfill his orders, it would have to do. Wood's division swung into position and was soon ready to move on the rebels, but Johnson's division and McLean's brigade were slow to deploy. Meanwhile, Howard sent a staff officer off to Thomas with a note that in essence stated he thought he was turning the enemy's flank. A half-hour passed before a messenger returned with an order to proceed with the turning movement and attack. Shells were now falling among Wood's men. And while Howard mulled over the situation, a rebel sharpshooter fired into the group, wounding one of Howard's aides; ominous evidence that the rebels had not been fooled. It was now nearing 4:30 P.M., and Sherman's orders could no longer be put off.

It was General William Hazen's understanding that the plan called for Wood's three brigades to attack by column, hitting

---

[31] Capron, letter, May 30, 1864; Castel, *Decision in the West: The Atlanta Campaign of 1864*, 230-235; Dean, "The Battle of Pickett's Mill,", 29; Howard, Oliver Otis, *Autobiography of Oliver Otis Howard, Major General United States Army*, 2 vols. (Freeport, New York: Books for Libraries Press, 1971), I: 550-551; Noblitt, "The 'Crime' at Pickett's Mill," 40-41

the rebels in rapid succession, thus taking advantage of the gain made by those who went before. This formation was designed to concentrate overwhelming manpower against a small area of the enemy's line. Ideally the attacking brigades would follow each other at five-minute intervals, leaving the enemy little or no time to recover from the initial onslaught. While waiting for last minute instructions, Hazen overheard Wood tell General Howard, "We will put in Hazen, and see what success he has." Howard approved. Hazen was shocked when he heard that there would be no attack by column. About this time and unbeknownst to Howard, Sherman notified Thomas to have the detachment halt where they were and take up a defensive position. Unfortunately, Sherman's decision to call off the attack came too late for the assaulting brigades.[32]

At precisely 4:30 P.M., Hazen with his eight veteran regiments numbering 1,500 men, set off. His topographical engineer, Ambrose Bierce, had earlier made "a hasty examination of the ground in the front," which he "duly reported" to the general. Bierce had "pushed far enough forward through the forest to hear distinctly the murmur" of the awaiting rebels, but from the Federal lines "nothing could be heard but the wind among the trees and the songs of birds." Having had plenty of notice and time to prepare breastworks and artillery emplacements, the butternut-clad soldiers of Granbury and Govan's brigades of Cleburne's division lay in wait for the unseen bluecoats, who were a quarter-mile away and formed in two lines when they moved forward. Between the two sides lay an almost impassable wood crossed by steep ravines filled with tangles of undergrowth, which made quick work of the trim blue lines.[33]

As the Federal troops struggled to climb the last ravine, the waiting rebels suddenly unleashed a perfect storm of fire instantly toppling dozens of Hazen's men. Concealed to enfilade the advancing Federals, butternut artillery firing grape and canister

---

[32] Ambrose, Bierce. *The Collected Works of Ambrose Bierce*, 12 vols. (New York: Gordia Press Inc., 1966), I: 281-287; Castel, *Decision in the West: The Atlanta Campaign of 1864*, 233-236; Dean, "The Battle of Pickett's Mill," 30; William B Hazen, *A Narrative of Military Service* (Boston: Ticknor & Co., 1885), 257.

[33] Bierce, *The Collected Works of Ambrose Bierce*, I: 285-286; Castel, *Decision in the West: The Atlanta Campaign of 1864*, 235-236.

opened, hammering the blue ranks. Seeking any available cover from the murderous crossfire, the survivors began returning fire, while others sought shelter further back. At the right of the Union line, Bierce had an unobstructed view of the fight. He wrote: "It was dim with smoke, but not greatly obscured: the smoke rose and spread in sheets among the branches of the trees. Most of our men fought kneeling as they fired, many behind trees, stones, and whatever cover they could get, but there were considerable groups that stood." Soon there were hundreds of corpses within fifteen to twenty paces of the Confederate line. In forty-five minutes Hazen's brigade sustained 500 casualties or one-third of its number. By 5:45 P.M. and without orders, the survivors began falling back, "sifting through the trees into the cover of the ravines."[34]

Stripped for battle and in two lines, Gibson's men watched the remnants of Hazen's brigade clear their front. From left to right, the first line was made up of Thirty-second Indiana, Fifteenth Wisconsin, and Eighty-ninth Illinois. Forming the second line were the Forty-fifth Ohio, Thirty-fifth Illinois, and the Fifteenth Ohio. At the front, firing had slowed when the order to advance was sounded. A check of watches revealed it was closing on 6:00 P.M. when the brigade set forth to take the enemy's works. The six regiments "commenced the charge in fine order and good spirits," Lieutenant Colonel Williams reported after the campaign. His men "had no idea of it being so hot a place, but we soon found it out. For it was not many minutes as we advanced before the bullets came pattering around us [and that] told us the enemy was near," Private Charles Capron wrote. Capron stated that "we then charged across a little ravine and up another hill to within three rods of their breastworks when we could go no farther. We was then reinforced by the 15th Ohio who came up and tried to storm their works but was compelled to fall back. We had already lost 3 killed and 9 wounded in our company by dark."[35]

Joseph Buckley described the inferno of lead and iron that came at the Eighty-ninth that late May afternoon. "They had their cannon so fixed that they could rake the hill we went down; the ravine

---

[34] Bierce, *The Collected Works of Ambrose Bierce,*" 291-292;Hazen, *A Narrative of Military Service,* 257-258; Noblitt, "The 'Crime' at Pickett's Mill," 40-41.

[35] *OR,* Vol. 38, Pt. 1, 402; Capron, letter, May 30, 1864.

we crossed; and the hill we charged up close to their works with grape and canister, and I tell you they used it freely. [And] besides shells they threw amongst us very fast from another battery." He told his wife, Mary, "One thing you must bear in mind and that is the battle ground is very hilly and very heavily timbered with large white and black oak trees, and a very thick growth of underbrush (all the way close up to the Rebels' works)." As a consequence, he explained: "We could not see their works and did not know they had works there until twenty yards of them, when they opened a heavy volley of musketry, grape and canister amongst us, which killed and wounded a great many of our boys." But once in contact, "we laid down with 20 yards of their breastworks behind rotten logs, rocks, stumps, and trees or anything to protect us from their grape and canister. We gave them fits. They got so they dared not show their heads above their breastworks." Buckley said the Rebels "would lay their guns on top of their breastworks and fire at random, and if had not been for their grape and canister and shells, we could have taken their works and all their men in them [as] prisoners."[36]

"The second brigade took the advance, and when it became hotly engaged, the first,—our brigade,—was ordered forward. We went down a hill, crossed a deep hollow, and advanced up the other hillside; but all this in a perfect storm of lead and iron," remembered Joel Chambers. As he trotted along, he heard a close by zip and felt the swoosh of a Minie ball and thought, "Surely, that bullet could not have missed my ear more than an inch; but it crashed through the shoulder of Comrade Nash, just behind me, leaving him terribly wounded." No time to stop. "On up the hill, in the face of this carnival of death, we go. Here is brave Serg't Urle urging the men on to their work of death. There is our own Lieut. Walker, with Lieut. Beecher, of Co. D to aid him, both doing their duty." The Eighty-ninth, Chambers recalled, was now "within less than fifty feet of the rebel line" when the Railroaders saw "a white flag, and an officer waving his sword from the works, and saying, 'Don't shoot, we surrender!'" Automatically, "there is a lull in our firing for a moment, only a moment, for then a deadly volley is poured into our ranks from the treacherous Texas rebels in our front, who played surrender to stop our firing and draw

---

[36] Buckley, letter, June 8, 1864.

us up close to them." In an instant we "took cover the best we could behind trees and logs, but all the time giving the Johnnies Yankee lead as rapidly as possible, but our men were going down fast." Off to the right, "in a little open field," a rebel battery "has an enfilading fire on us and is raking the very ground all along the hillside with shell and canister shot. We have not gun to reply."

"Amid the terrible rattle of musketry, the roar of cannon, the hideous shrieks, and terrible crash of flying, bursting shells, the piteous groans of the wounded and dying, the moments, aye hours roll slowly away." This is the hell in which Chambers and the rest of the Eighty-ninth found themselves. Looking about, Chambers saw the two men nearest on his left go down, "both the same instant, shot through the left arm both of them." Peering up through "the murky smoke of battle," the Railroaders prayed for the sun to go down. Just as it is setting Chambers felt a sudden twinge in his right hand, and at the same time on the left side of his head, followed by blood trickling out from under his cap. Samuel Smith, a fellow Company A private, looked at Chambers and exclaimed, "'the top of your head is knocked off, Joe!'" Checking his head, Chambers found a hole in the top of his cap, but none in his head. He quickly surmised what happened. A wounded soldier had left his rifle leaning against a log behind which Chambers and Smith were shielding themselves, and a bullet struck the gun. Since the lead of the ball was the softer metal, it fragmented, and a number of those pieces struck Chambers in the hand and head. Unable to use his hand and with his left eye swollen shut, Chambers left the fight. On the way back he gave his cartridges to a captain of the Forty-ninth Ohio, but kept his rifle. Once out of range of the enemy missiles of death, Chambers got some water to wash the blood off his hand and face. After eating some raw salt pork and hardtack," he "laid down with a dutchman, of the 32d Ind., whose hand was all shot to pieces" and "fell into a troubled sleep, to dream of HOME and MOTHER."[37]

It was near sundown and the Umbaugh brothers of Company G, Jacob and Elias, had become separated a little when the fighting commenced, but Jacob still managed to keep an eye on his younger

[37] *Chanute Vidette*, "Campaigning in Tennessee and Georgia in 1864, No. 3," December 1889.

brother. Jacob recalled that he was no more than twenty feet from Elias when a bursting shell brought part of tree down on his brother. "I ran to him and helped take the tree off him, and helped carry him off the field." On reaching safety, Jacob examined the still stunned Elias and "found him very much bruised about the face, breast, and arms, and his right leg broken above the knee . . . ." There was also "a piece of shell sticking in his left leg on the outside near the knee joint which I picked out, and I tied my silk handkerchief around his leg." Jacob moved his brother to the rear, remaining by his side, and the next day assisted the surgeon in setting Elias' leg.[38]

Lieutenant Colonel Williams officially reported the Eighty-ninth "advanced to within about twenty-five yards of the enemy's works up a steep hill; here the fire was so murderous that the column paused, wavered, and sought shelter as they could find. After sustaining this terrific fire for about an hour they were recalled, but did not withdraw until after dark, then withdrew beyond range . . . ." While Joseph Buckley concurred about the heavy rebel fire, he pointed out: "We had no cannon in position to play against their cannon and no troops in connection with ours on our right, so that we were at the mercy of the Rebel's grape and canister and shell. We never hated to give up a position so bad as we did that. When so near gaining the victory and after losing so many noble men." But, "just about dusk, we got orders to retreat, which we did, to the next hill, which was about 60 or 80 rods [back]." The next day Company F Lieutenant James Copp wrote his brother back in Rock Island and summed up what had taken place. "We were brought into the engagement about 2 P.M. and remained in until after dark, leaving a strong skirmish line out. We fell back and built breastworks all night. We were under very heavy fire of the enemy's cannon. Grape and canister were thrown thick and fast at our lines. Heavy musketry on both sides. We had no cannon in position."[39]

---

[38]   Affidavits of Jacob Umbagh and William E. Ward respectively dated October 9, 1877 and March 7, 1878; Original Invalid Pension, February 21, 1876, all in Records of the Record of Pension Office of the War Department, Record Group 94.12, Nationals Archives, Washington, D.C.

[39]   *OR*, Vol. 38, Pt. 1, 402; Buckley, letter, June 8, 1864; *Rock Island Argus*, June 6, 1864.

More than one Railroader spoke of Confederate trickery at Pickett's Mill. In a letter to his mother, Hancock County and Company A Private Jim Tomlinson provided testimony to the Rebels' deceitfulness. "They tride ther old game on us, pretending to surrender, thinking when we came to take them to give us a volley then charge and take all of us, but they could not play it on us . . . . I was in four feet of ther brest works. I herd them saying cease firing, so I thought it was our men, untill I got wher I could see them." Having been held back with the First brigade pioneers, Isaac K. Young, Company H Second Sergeant, heard the survivors tell the same story and recounted it in a letter to the editor of the *Aurora Beacon*. "When the 32d Ind. and 89th Ills., our advance line came near the enemy's lines, they exhibited white flags over their works and shouted to our boys not to shoot, they would surrender. Our men advanced without firing to within a short distance of their fortifications, when they sprang to their guns, and let volley after volley of musketry, and burst after burst of grape and canister into our ranks, literally mowing down our men by scores."[40]

Eight months later Charles Capron took up his pen and again wrote of the slaughter he had witnessed at Pickett's Mill. "We advanced slowly till we got nearly to them and went for them. But when we got close to [their works] half the regiment was killed and wounded and we was obliged to lie down for if we attempt to gone back the balance of us would [have] been shot down." With the Eighty-ninth pinned down, the second line "consisting of the 15 and 49 Ohio . . . came up to where we was laying. I was lying behind a log when they came up. The officers urged them to go on. The line stepped up onto the log to get over when six of them was shot down, falling onto me literally covering me with blood and gore."

In a letter home written three days after the battle, Charles Capron revealed some of the sheer terror that he and his fellow Railroaders endured that night. "At dark the regiments all withdrew but ours. We then put out sentinels when their whole line arose about 3 rods from us doubtless thinking that we was a going to charge them," he wrote. Dark as it was he focused on the rebel line

40 Tomlinson, *In Good Courage: The Civil War Letters of William James Tomlinson*, 18; *Aurora Beacon*, June 16, 1864.

to see what, if anything was going to happen. "They remained in that position about five minutes when their bugle sounded. No one knowing what it meant, as we are unused to their call, but they soon advanced within bayonet reach when our men halted them." Still taking in the situation, Capron explained what soon followed. "They halted when a rebel officer stepped out of the ranks and fired a revolver twice. They then set up a yell and fired a volley into us. A good many of our men had no ammunition and then came on the massacre and all our men could do was to get out of their way." Continuing the vivid account, Capron wrote: "I immediately fired my gun knocking a rebel endways and commenced the race. They firing a volley after me, but I got out all right." Looking back, he worded that moment this way. "I was watching them and had my gun to my shoulder and when they rose up I fired into their ranks. The bullet opened a hole in their ranks and I waited no more, turning round I started pell-mell with 5 thousand bullets whistling round my ears but they only knocked my tin cup away. And I got off without a scratch."[41]

Joe Buckley provided another view of that fateful evening. "I shall never forget that night when we went to pick up our dead and wounded. Just as we commenced looking for them, the Rebs got up in their works and made a yell which sounded like so many demons and poured a volley of musketry among us, which brought us to the conclusion that it was no use to stay there to be butchered." Also out searching for the wounded was Company C Private Wesley Willson. He was carrying a wounded comrade to safety when the charging rebels captured him. Knocked unconscious by a bursting shell, John H. Decker of Company A was discovered by the enemy the next day and taken prisoner.[42]

With daylight Joel Chambers started for the division field hospital. Reflecting back on that morning he wrote: "I had gone but

---

[41]   Capron, letters, May 30, 1864 and February 12, 1865.

[42]   Buckley, letter, June 8, 1864; *Illinois in the Civil War*, [Internet website] *THE USGENWEB Project*, (Accessed April 29, 2005), http:\\www.rootsweb. com/~ilcivilw/photos/willsonwesleyhtml; *Kansas Genealogy Projects*, [Internet website], *Washington Co., KS Obituaries*, (Accessed January 5, 2005), http:// www.karensgen.com/lowe/otherobits.php.

a little distance when I found Sprouse of Co. G. He was bare-headed and walked like an old foundered horse. In getting away from the rebs the night before, he had fallen down the hill in the brush and, as he expressed it 'jammed himself up all over.'" Commenting on yesterday's fight, Sprouse told Chambers, "'I thought it was bad enough at Chickamauga, but it was nowhere by the side of that *slaughter pen.*'" Moving on, Chambers came upon his cousin Jim Tomlinson, who was "limping along using his gun for a cane with a buckshot in his thigh." The two soon found Pete Sanford, who Chambers referred to as, "our Swede man, with a bullet through his right breast, or rather, it had been through,—for the doctor had cut it out under his shoulder blade, and Pete had it in his pocket." The group reached the hospital about noon on Saturday. "The fight was Friday afternoon, and the doctors did not get through dressing the wounds the first time till late Sunday evening. While at this place I saw seven arms and two legs lying in a pile by the side of the amputating tent and still they were cutting off more," Chambers wrote.

"The hospital tents were, of course, all full, but there were three of us—Jim, with two sound hands and one leg, Pete, with hands and legs all right, but in poor condition to breathe, because of the bullet hole through the corner of his right lung; while I had two good feet (good size), one hand and one eye, the other swelled shut," Chambers humorously recounted years later. The trio went about seeing what they had between them for shelter. Chambers explained. He had "a half of a shelter tent," and Jim had one too; they would" make our own house. But alas! When Jim took his half-tent from the top of his knapsack, where it had been rolled up and on his back in the battle, we found the *tent* part all right, but the *shelter* was forever gone, there were no less than *thirty-two* bullet holes through it." They concluded, "One ball had done it all. The tent had been *folded* and then rolled, hence there were many thicknesses."[43]

Since a brother, Joel, had been killed in action in Arkansas in December 1862, Jim Tomlinson put off telling his mother that he had been wounded. "I would have wrote sooner but I wanted to hear from the Company. Our Division was badly cutup on the 27th.

---

43 *Chanute Vidette*, "Campaigning in Georgia in 1864, No. 4," December 1889.

It lost 1,653, but some has returned since. Ther was three killed and eight wounded and 17 capture" in Company A. "Don't let my being wounded truble you for it is slight. Our brigade lost 630. The men are in good courage still. We are bound to whip them. We have the largest army that I ever saw . . . ."[44]

The *Kendall County Record* received a letter from Soldier R bearing sad news. "It is a painful duty to be obliged to record the deaths of Color corporal Isaac Chittenden, Edgar Wood, Richard Fields and James Hopkins." He could report that "Capt. Hobbs and Lieut. Harkness although in the heat of the fray came off . . . unscathed. These two officers have been in *every fight* in which the 1st Brigade has taken part, and have done their duty *as men*, they must be 'bullet proof.'" Lieutenant Copp, likewise, sent home a detailed casualty list and put his company's losses in perspective. "Our division's loss was heavy, and that of our brigade very heavy, it being 670. Our regiment lost fifteen killed, sixty-two wounded, and seventy missing. Company F lost comparatively few—eight wounded, including the Captain; two of this number are present doing duty, and one man missing. Of those wounded, Captain Dimick was one of the more severely injured. Lieutenant Copp personally wrote Dimick's father spelling out his son's injuries. "He was wounded in three places, one severe, the other two slight. A small ball entered just back of his left side and came out a little below the right shoulder. It seemed to have passed just under the spine of the back; the second was by a piece of something (a shell I think) that raked his right side while lying down, cutting the skin about four inches in length; and the third a slight wound by a musket ball in the right wrist." During the fight, Lieutenant Copp saw to it that Dimick was taken to the rear and his wounds dressed. When the fighting subsided, he procured an ambulance and had the captain moved to the brigade hospital.[45]

On July 4, Captain Laertes F. Dimick was back in Rock Island and the following day he paid a visit to the *Rock Island Argus*. Though still weak, Dimick took time to give Colonel Danforth his account of the fight at Pickett's Mill. Having no reason to discount the captain's words, Colonel Danforth printed what he had been told. And the

44   Kammerer, *Hancock County, Illinois in the Civil War*, 77-79.
45   *Rock Island Argus*, June 6 and 22, 1864.

story was that Captain Dimick had been "shot by a sharpshooter, while standing on the breastworks at Dallas Georgia, leading his company in battle. He was a little distance in advance of his company when he was cut down by a bullet in the side, breaking one rib and passing through his lungs." Danforth pointed out that "he was twice wounded after he fell, and received several bullets through his hat and clothes." The editor continued, "When nearly exhausted from the loss of blood he made several desperate efforts to raise up by the aid of his sword, and at last succeeded in doing so enough to be discovered by his men and carried from the field. It was fortunate for him, for in a few moments the rebs came charging over the field and he would have had to go to Libby, if he had not died."

After reading the *Argus'* version of Captain Dimick's wounding, Private Curtis B. Knox sent a letter to the editor: "Col. Danforth—Sir: Allow me, as a member of Co. F, 89th Ill. Vol., to correct a few mistakes in your issue of July 6, in reference to Capt. Dimick getting wounded. In the first place Capt. Dimick was not wounded within 10 miles of Dallas, Ga. He was wounded at New Hope Church." Knox continued stating that "in the next place he was not in the advance of his company for this reason: It was not his place. He stood behind a tree, in his place, about 20 feet of his company. Allow me to say, also that he was on no breastwork. At the time he received his wound he stepped a little to the right of his tree and gave the command in these words, without orders from the colonel, 'forward 89th,' and he had hardly got it out of his mouth when the leaden messenger called for him." Private Knox made it perfectly clear that he did "not wish to make it appear that Capt. D is a coward,—and the members of Co. F do not like to have such a slur thrown at them, giving the public to understand that Capt. D went where the company dare not go, and therefore we wish you to correct those mistakes if you please." Colonel Danforth added: "The notice we gave of Capt. Dimick we thought was correct when we published it. Certainly there was no intention to cast any slur on the company. We have never spoken of the company except in complimentary terms.[46]

In a letter dated May 31, Lieutenant Copp mentioned that "Maj. Kidder now commands our regiment, Col. Hotchkiss having sprained

---

[46]   *Rock Island Argus*, July 6 and 26, 1864.

his ankle badly on the day of the fight I alluded to." Even though twenty-five years had passed, Joel R. Chambers still held his own opinion regarding the colonel's untimely twisted ankle. "Our Reg't in this battle was commanded by Maj. Kidder; the Lieut. Col. absent on furlough, and Col. C. F. Hotchkiss, just as we were going into the fight happened to trip himself on his sword-scabbard and sprained his ankle so he had to go to the rear." He sarcastically added: "I really think the Col. was afraid a bullet might hit him, and his fears were well grounded, for the balls flew very thick, and, as he was a large man, there might not always have been room between them for his body."[47]

After falling back about 600 yards, the Eighty-ninth spent the night constructing breastworks. For the next two days the only activity was an occasional enemy patrol checking out the Union line. On the night of May 30, the Railroaders advanced their line forward and to the right 500 yards and immediately went to work building new breastworks. For the next six days there was no substantial movement. Charles Capron related to his mother: "We had a pretty hard time of it as there was ten days that we was not allowed to take off our cartridge boxes night or days, and but one night that we did not have to git out and stand to arms." "Sunday morning June 5th—Our skirmish line found out that the Rebs LEFT during the night of the 4th. Three from each company were detailed to go on the part of the battlefield where we charged the Rebels' breastworks," Joseph Buckley confided to his wife. "I was very anxious to go for I wanted to find out for certain whether [Chauncy] Tallmadge was killed or wounded and taken prisoner. When we got there, our men were very decently buried," leaving Buckley still in the dark whether his friend was taken prisoner or among the dead. "One thing is certain," Buckley pointed out, "he was wounded through the arm and through the body. One of Company C's men said he saw him when he was wounded." The final brigade report noted that "on account of the constant heavy and effective firing of the enemy we were unable to bury our dead or bring off all of our wounded, consequently the dead and part of our wounded fell into his hands, together with a considerable number of prisoners, who were endeavoring during the

47 *Rock Island Argus*, June 13, 1864; *Chanute Vidette*, "Campaigning in Tennessee and Georgia in 1864,   No. 4," December 1889.

darkness of the night to remove our wounded." Lieutenant Colonel Williams wrote afterwards, "Our casualties were large, and attest [to] the terrible character of the assault." From the fight on May 27, the Eighty-ninth officially listed 16 killed, 71 wounded, and 67 missing for a total of 154 casualties. The Illinois *Adjutant General's Report* revealed 18 men killed in action with 7 more eventually dying of wounds. Another source, William F. Fox's *Regimental Losses in the American Civil War, 1861-1865*, calculated the Eighty-ninth lost 37 killed and mortally wounded in the bloody assault at Pickett's Mill. On May 27, Fox stated the Eighty-ninth "sustained a loss of 24 killed, 102 wounded, and 28 missing; total, 154." Since the enemy possessed the ground where those who were killed fell, where many of the critically wounded remained, and where those who were unhurt were capture, the exact breakdown of casualties will probably never be known. As for Chauncy Tallmadge, he was taken prisoner and died January 6, 1865 at Andersonville.[48]

After spending a week back at the division hospital, Private Chambers said goodbye to his wounded companions and his cousin Jim Tomlinson and started for the front. About the reunion he recalled: "A few miles walk brought me to the Reg't., but where is my company? Only *one third* of it left. And now call me what you may or will, but in spite of a hard soldier's heart my eyes *would get moist* when I shook hands with the few that were left. One thing I soon learned, after getting back to the company, was, that the terms 'New root'—'Lapeared recruit,' &c were no longer in use. That ordeal of fire and death through which we had passed burned out all such epithets. We were now *comrades* in deed and truth."[49]

*　*　*

Sherman's failed attempt to turn the rebel line had quickly settled into a stalemate of trench warfare; consequently, on June 1,

---

[48]   *OR*, Vol. 38, Pt. 1, 402; Capron, letter, June 6, 1864; Buckley, June 8, 1864; *Adjutant General's Report*, 261-287; Fox, *Regimental Losses in the American Civil War, 1861-1865*, 373, 448.

[49]   *Chanute Vidette*, "Campaigning in Tennessee and Georgia in 1864, No. 4," December 1889.

he began moving back eastward to the Western & Atlantic Railroad. By late afternoon on the first, Major General George Stoneman's cavalry division rode into a deserted and undefended Allatoona Pass. Now able to secure control of the railroad between Acworth and the Etowah River, Sherman over the next few days concentrated his force between Acworth and Big Shanty. Johnston reacted by evacuating his position, known as the "Dallas-New Hope Line," on the night of June 4 and occupied the heights around Marietta, dubbed the "Lost Mountain Line". On June 6, the Eighty-ninth along with the rest of the Fourth Corps set off on a nine-mile march to finish Sherman's concentration.[50]

"It is cloudy and still looks like rain this morning. It rained all night. We were aroused once in the night [and] had to stay in the pits for about 15 minutes. It is reported that the rebs have left," James B. David hurriedly jotted in his diary early Sunday, June 5. "This morning we discovered that the Rebs had played their old game and evacuated their works in front of us. Today I visited the field where our Div was engaged the 27th. To look at the position it seems a miracle to me that as many of us escaped as what did," Joel R. Chambers noted in his journal. The following day he recorded: "Received marching orders started early went 6 miles on a very crooked road over hills and through the woods. Camped 6 miles form Ackworth Station." June 6, Joseph Buckley wrote his wife that "we left our works and moved to the left of our line to within a distance of about two miles from the Railroad and 3 miles from Acworth Station where our cars run up to with rations. Our wounded are moved to Acworth Station."[51]

Back on the railroad, Sherman halted, waiting for the bridges and trestles to be repaired or in some instances rebuilt. Until the armies were re-supplied there was no movement. By June 9, these efforts were nearing completion, and therefore Sherman ordered Thomas, McPherson, and Schofield to move forward the next day.

---

[50] Castel, *Decision in the West, The Atlanta Campaign 1864*, 255-261; Daniel, *Days of Glory, The Army of the Cumberland, 1861-1865*, 404; Scaife, *The Campaign for Atlanta*, 59.

[51] David, diary, June 5, 1864; Chambers, *War Fever Cured*, 46-47; Buckley, letter, June 8, 1864.

"June 10th. Received marching orders [and] started at 8 o'clock but made very slow progress. Went about 3 miles and camped in front of the 20th Corps. Had some cannonading in front in the evening," Private Chambers wrote in his journal. The next day, he noted the Railroaders "moved about a mile and camped in line of battle. A few artillery shots in front now and then is all that is going on. Weather warm and showery." After remaining in place for two days, the regiment "advanced ¾ of a mile." That evening he recorded "considerable musket and artillery firing took place . . . without much effect that anyone knows of." The regiment woke on June 15 to find the enemy had again fallen back. "June 16th. Our Brig[ade] is laying still today. I went up on top of Pine Knob and enjoyed a fine view of the surrounding country." Chambers added, "This Knob is the place where the rebel Gen. Polk was killed by one of our shells." The following day he penned, "The rebs left another line of works in our front last night. We advanced on them today our Reg't in front. Had 8 men wounded. Heavy fighting on our left and heavy cannonading in our front in the evening."[52]

Often during the campaign General Sherman would pass along the line, and when he did, his presence was announced by shouts of "Hello, Uncle Billy!" Company D Private Nathan Salsbury remembered one mid-June afternoon, while up on an old cedar stump entertaining a group of Railroaders with a rollicking song and dance, Sherman momentarily stopped to watch. Years later, Salsbury, now famous as Buffalo Bill Cody's partner in the Wild West Show, met Sherman at a veterans' dinner and recounted his impromptu performance that June day in 1864. According to Salsbury, the general recalled the song he was singing, and shaking his hand said, "That was the class of man that made the best soldier." For a brief time, the general too had escaped the business at hand.[53]

The fighting continued, and Colonel Hotchkiss reported the brigade's action on the June 17. The Eighty-ninth Illinois was deployed as skirmishers covering the brigade front. The men moved

---

[52] Chambers, *War Fever Cured*, 42-43.

[53] *Reminiscences of Nate Salsbury* (unpublished), original at The Beinecke Rare Book and Manuscript Library, Yale University, New Haven, Connecticut. *OR*, Vol. 38, Pt. 1, 393-394, 402-403.

slowly and cautiously forward, and soon engaged the enemy. The Railroaders steadily drove the rebels back for about a mile until they came upon their infantry. What appeared to be large number of rebels were on the opposite side of an open field protected by rifle-pits. With Pickett's Mill still fresh in everyone's mind, the men hesitated and the advance turned into a long-range skirmish. But unlike Pickett's Mill, Thomas brought his artillery forward, which "vigorously shelled their position for about half an hour . . . ." Having softened up the rebels, the Eighty-ninth Illinois charged 200 yards across the open field, capturing the enemy rifle-pits, along with some prisoners, and pressed them back to their main line of works. The Railroaders reported seven wounded of which two later died.

Beginning June 17, the fighting became pretty much non-stop with the regiment advancing a short distance, constructing breastworks, and the next morning finding the enemy had once again fallen back to a new line. Chambers recalled one incident while out with the advance. He was on the skirmish line, firing as rapidly as possible, and even though it was raining, and had been all day, his rifle was so hot that he could not hold his hand on barrel, making it unsafe to put powder in it. His cover was an oak tree about eighteen inches in diameter. He pressed himself as close to the tree as possible while waiting for his rifle to cool. While in this position he began to hum the popular song, "Do they miss me at home, do they miss me?" When a rebel Minnie ball went whizzing past his legs, Chambers thought, "it came very near not missing me, whether they did at home or not." He wrote the bullet struck his "gun in front of the trigger guard, knocked off some of the stock and cut the string half in two; but at the same time 'raised my dutch,' so that I at once resumed the issuing of 'Yankee pills' to the rebs." He kept firing until his "whole stock—60 rounds—was exhausted," and then called for relief. His messmate came up to relieve him, taking a position a little further back and behind a much smaller tree.[54]

On leaving the skirmishing line, Chambers zigzagged back to the main line, found an ax, and went to "chopping timber for breastworks." He remembered how unpleasant the task was; trying

---

[54] *Chanute Vidette*, "Campaigning in Tennessee and Georgia in 1864, No. 4," December 1889.

"to chop with a dull ax, on a hot rainy day with a knapsack on and a rubber blanket on over it, and the bullets flying uncomfortably thick." He had no more than started working than his messmate, Charley Darans, showed up "with his arm all shattered at the wrist and elbow. I told him that tree was too small to protect him. He went to the rear, and died of gangrene two weeks afterwards [July 4]."[55]

"We have gained the ground from Dallas to where we now are [near Marietta, Georgia] by advancing our skirmish line, which, in several instances, were severe struggles," wrote Sergeant Isaac K. Young in a dispatch to the editor of the *Aurora Beacon*. "On the 21st," Young reported, "Gen. Wood gave the order for the 1st brigade to advance their lines, as they were so drawn that the enemy had a cross fire on them. Accordingly, in the afternoon of the 21st, we advanced over an open field under a terrific fire from the enemy's skirmishers and artillery." With the Forty-ninth and Fifteenth Ohio, deployed as skirmishers, the Railroaders under Lieutenant Colonel Williams moved out in support. The Buckeye regiments "drove the enemy from a position known as Bald Knob." The Eighty-ninth soon relieved the Forty-ninth Ohio from its "advanced position in the wood to the right of the knob." Charles Capron wrote: "We charged on the enemy . . . and gained our present position and throwed up works under a heavy fire. I was on the skirmish line at the time and fired one hundred and thirty rounds. My gun got so hot that I could scarcely hold my hand on it." Williams stated that the enemy continued to obstinately contest the ground now held by the Eighty-ninth. In this storm of lead, Lieutenant Harkness of Company H, while "supervising the erection of barricades," was hit in the abdomen by a rebel bullet. Casualties for the men from Kendall County quickly mounted as William Platt was wounded in the hand, which was later amputated. Charles Hayden was shot through the hip. Frank Estergreen's hipbone was shattered by a Minie ball. Thomas Morely was left with a shredded finger; later amputated. Charles Sprague and Leander Leach were both slightly wounded. Williams reported the regiment's losses as 2 killed and 14 wounded.

---

55   *Chanute Vidette*, "Campaigning in Tennessee and Georgia in 1864, No. 4," December 1889; *Adjutant General's Report*, 264.

However, both Privates Hayden and Estergreen succumbed from their wounds.[56]

The grim details of Harkness' death came to the *Beacon's* readers through the words of Sergeant Isaac K. Young. He wrote that the lieutenant fell, "pierced through by a Minnie ball; he was brought back to the rear to the Division Hospital, and was conscious of the fatality of his wound, and set to work to write a letter to his wife at Plattville, Illinois." Being among those watching over the mortally wounded officer, Young wrote, "kind hands fanned the brave Lieutenant, and he accomplished the feat while in the agonies of death." With his life ebbing away, Harkness could only write a few short lines. "'My dear Maggie. I am badly wounded; I shall soon be with our dear little Herbie. May God bless you my dear wife.—William.'" Young told the hometown newspaperman that "I assisted in consigning him to the earth at 10 o'clock at night, on a little lone knoll, which had been shorn of trees by solid shot from rebel guns during the day; a fit place to bury a hero, where the enemy's guns fired the martial burial salute." On his death Williams said that Lieutenant Harkness was "an energetic and brave officer, a sincere Christian, and urbane gentleman."[57]

One of the other casualties that afternoon was Joseph Buckley. Writing from a field hospital on June 24, he began: "My Dear Wife, You will probably have heard before this reaches you that we have had some hard fighting to do since I last wrote. Also, that quite a number of us have been severely wounded." Taking a moment to apologize, he continued. "I should have written to you sooner but I could not as my arm pained me too much. I was wounded soon after we got into an engagement with the enemy by a musket ball passing through my shoulder and through my left arm and came out just above my elbow. The ball broke my left arm, but Doctor Tuttle says he can save my arm."[58]

---

56 *Aurora Beacon*, June 21, 1864; *OR*, Vol. 38, Pt. 1, 403; Buckley, letter, June 24, 1864.

57 *Aurora Beacon*, July 7, 1864; *Letters Written by Captain William Harkness*, [Internet website], *The USGENWEB Project*, (Accessed April 30, 2004), http://www.rootsweb.com/~ilkendal/Military/CivilWar/INF089th/WmHarnesssLtrs.htm; *OR*, Vol. 38, Pt. 1 403.

58 Buckley, letter, June 24, 1864.

A fellow Company H soldier writing under the nom de plume of "Corporal" told the *Kendall County Record* that "Joseph Buckley was severely wounded in the shoulder and arm at the same time, and by the same bullet [as had struck Harkness]." Visiting with Buckley the next day in the hospital, he offered to write for him to his friends, but Joe "was unwilling to cause them unnecessary anxiety" and "proposed waiting a few days to have the extent of his injuries known." "Corporal" noted Buckley was "shot in the left arm and the bone broken." He added that "it was supposed by his companions that he would lose his arm, and some of them may have written home to that effect, he may pardon my adding the assurance the surgeons give him—that it can be saved." The writer pointed out that Buckley "was bearing his misfortune like a soldier, and patiently waiting for the bone to re-unite in his arm."[59]

In a quick letter to his mother dated June 27, Charles Capron explained that he had to temporarily suspend his writing "on account of a fierce artillery duel," which "we came out best as we silenced the rebel battery." Continuing, he wrote: "Yesterday [June26] our men and the rebels agreed not to fire on one another so we had a pretty quiet day, but we was ordered to commence hostilities again this morning [and] had one man killed [John B. Cummings, Co. K]." This same day, June 27, Sherman ordered a head-on assault. The entrenched rebels at Kennesaw Mountain repulsed the attack, leaving Sherman with 3,000 killed and wounded for the effort. The Eighty-ninth was spared, having been held in reserve. But as Capron described, their part of the line was still a pretty hot spot. "You should see the timber that we have been skirmishing in for the last few days. There is scarcely a tree but what has from 50 to a hundred bullets in it. Trees a foot and a half thick has been cut down by our cannon. The rebels know how to use their artillery for they put a solid shot into one of our portholes. It struck the end of our cannon glanced and struck one of the wheels smashing it up in general."[60]

Even as a nearby battery dueled with a rebel counterpart, Sergeant Isaac K. Young wrote the *Aurora Beacon* three days before Sherman's attack. He stated that "in all probability the great battle

---

[59] *Kendall County Record*, July 7, 1864.
[60] Capron, letter, June 27, 1864.

between the armies of Sherman and Johnston will be fought upon this ground." Maybe this was Sherman's thinking when he ordered the frontal assault on the rebels at Kennesaw Mountain, but what resulted was an utter and complete disaster. Despite the setback, morale and confidence remained high throughout the bluecoated ranks. Sergeant Young, who was detailed back with the pioneers, penned: "Surely the campaign is a rough one, slow and hotly contested by both armies; but with Sherman, Thomas and Hooker to lead, we must conquer, and glory will ere long crown the noble old army of the Cumberland." The frontline soldier, Private Capron, was more realistic. "Most of the boys think the war will close this summer," he told his mother, but "if I should get killed remember the government owes me 75 dollars bounty besides six months pay . . . ."[61]

From June 22 to July 2, the Railroaders alternated occupying the first and second lines of the breastworks with the Fifteenth Ohio. Joel R. Chambers remembered: "This siege . . . was terribly hard service. While in the front lines we were not allowed to sleep more than two or three hours in the night and that with our equipment on. In the second line we could sleep tolerably well—for soldier—but were not allowed to take our shoes off, and as the weather was very warm and rainy, it was hard on our feet." Both sides Chambers explained reached an accord. "The pickets had agreed that if ordered to fire . . . they would first yell and thus give notice, and then fire the first shot high." During this 10-day period, Lieutenant Colonel Williams recorded that the Eighty-ninth had 5 killed and 13 wounded.[62]

*　　*　　*

Unable to crack the rebel line, Sherman resorted once more to the flanking maneuver. McPherson's Army of the Tennessee, with ten days' supplies, moved from the left to the right, swinging around the rebel line, forcing Johnston to fall back, and by early July, driving the enemy across the Chattahoochee. On July 3, Joel R. Chambers

---

[61] *Aurora Beacon*, July 7, 1864; Capron, letter, June 27, 1864.

[62] *Chanute Vidette*, "Campaigning in Tennessee and Georgia in 1864, No. 5," January 1890; *OR*, Vol. 38, Pt. 1, 403.

recorded in his diary that "last night the rebs evacuated their position on and around Kenesaw mountain and fell back beyond Marietta." That evening there had been only "light skirmishing in the extreme front . . . ." The Railroaders celebrated Independence Day with a one mile advance while listening to the sound of "cannonading going on all day." Chambers observed that the Union cavalry had taken a considerable number of prisoners. During the night of July 4 and 5, "the rebs fell back again." Dawn arrived and Sherman continued the pursuit. Around noon sharp skirmishing broke out, but the Union force pushed on to the Chattahoochee River and camped for the night. The Eighty-ninth did not move on July 6. Chambers wrote, "Some picket firing going on across the river the rebs being on the other side." The following day he ascended "a knob near camp and had a fine view of the surrounding Country." The elevation was such that Chambers commented he "could see Atlanta plain it being about 11 miles distant." Overlooking the Federal line, he counted 36 pieces of artillery in front of the Fourth Corps, which at 8:00 P.M. opened on the enemy. There was no further movement until July 10 when the regiment marched "8 miles to the left up the river" and went into camp. Finally, on July 12, Chambers entered, "We crossed the river and went about a mile on the other side. Co A with 6 others of the reg't went on picket."[63]

Writing on July 20, Charles Capron updated his mother on his regiment's movement over the past two weeks. He began by saying the Eighty-ninth was "within 4 miles of Atlanta," having left Kennesaw Mountain around 11:00 A.M . . . on July 3 for Marietta. By July 4, the regiment was four miles beyond Marietta when they came upon the rebels. Having made contact with the enemy Capron explained, "We was busy getting into position the next morning [when] we found they had left our front and [we] started in pursuit. We came on to them again just this side of the [Chattahoochee] river. But getting one of our batteries into position we give them such a shelling that many of them swam the river." Johnston's force took up their position on the opposite bank, and began taunting the bluecoats by calling, "How are you Yankee?" No man's land was now the Chattahoochee River. In the past, Capron pointed out "the way

---

63   Chambers, *War Fever Cured*, 47-49.

our men generally cross is to shell them and swing a pontoon but the rebels has learned the trick." This time, he wrote: "Old Sherman quietly send a corps up the river and then let into them where we was and they thought we was trying to cross and while we was keeping them in our front the corps up the river quietly crossed. Now the whole army is all across and within 4 miles of the doomed city."[64]

On July 7, Chambers later recollected, "We moved down the river, opposite where we first came to it, to cover the crossing of the 14th corps. Once the maneuver was accomplished "we returned to camp, tired but otherwise none the worse for our Sunday tramp." The next morning, July 18, "we moved out about five miles mostly in the direction of Atlanta. The 19th, our division was in the advance and drove the enemy back about a mile and a half. After sharp fighting in the evening, we drove him across Peachtree creek. Here just after dark that fatal bullet struck Lieut. Street, of Co. D. He was only a few feet from me at the time. It ended his life in a few days." Lieutenant Nathan Street actually died in Nashville on August 6. A writer from the *Nashville Dispatch* was invited to witness his embalming which took place the next day, and pronounced the new process a success, stating that it preserved the body's "natural appearance, so that the coffin may be opened on arrival at its destination . . . ."[65]

Outnumbered nearly two to one, Johnston had chosen a defensive strategy, content to trade space for time, hoping Sherman would use up his army in frontal assaults or make a substantial blunder. But as time passed and Sherman cautiously advanced, it appeared Johnston's only hope of saving Atlanta would be that somehow either Forrest 's or Wheeler's horsemen could break Sherman's overextended and tenuous supply line, forcing the Yankees to fall back. Convinced Johnston was unwilling to change and exasperated with the endless retreat, Jefferson Davis on July 18 formally removed the veteran commander and replaced him with John Bell Hood, a more aggressive and impetuous general.[66]

---

[64]   Capron, letter, July 20, 1864.
[65]   *Chanute Vidette*, "Campaigning in Tennessee and Georgia in 1864, No. 5," January 1890; *Nashville Dispatch*, August 9, 1864.
[66]   Castel, *Decision in the West: The Atlanta Campaign of 1864*, 358-365.

Having turned the Confederate line on the Chattahoochee River, Sherman moved on Atlanta from the north and east. By early evening of July 19, Howard's Fourth Corps of the Army of the Cumberland had gained a series of bridgeheads across the stream. Seeing an opportunity, Hood hurriedly pulled together his troops and issued orders to attack the Federals as they crossed Peachtree Creek. The Rebel attack scheduled for 1:00 P.M. did not materialize until three hours later. But by this time Thomas had three corps across the creek and in defensive positions when the assault began. Hood's attack was beaten back with heavy losses.[67]

In a detailed letter published by *Aurora Beacon*, former locomotive engineer, now Company E captain, John Warren described the Eighty-ninth's role, along with the overall fighting leading to the siege of Atlanta. On July 20, the Eighty-ninth as part of the Third division moved to the left and went into position along side of Major General John Newton's Second division. When Wood's Third division moved into line, Captain Warren noted they connected with Newton's by a stretching a skirmish line "on our right by half a mile . . . ." The Battle of Peachtree Creek fought that day, Warren wrote, "Is where Newton's division of [the] fourth corps and all of the 20th corps repulsed the rebels with a loss to them of 6000 in killed, wounded and captured, our loss being about 1800."

Captain Warren continued his account. "On the 21st the Johnnies were gone again, leaving a strong line of works. We advanced about a mile and a half and built works again, the works of the rebels being in plain sight." That evening Warren commanded the pickets, "and as soon as it got dark the rebs commenced firing on us by guess; they could not see our picket line, and kept it up to our disgust until 12 P.M. When it ceased all at once, and we concluded that they had again left; and to be sure, myself, Sugar Hamilton, Salsbury, Ed. Weed and Mckenzie, went out at 3 A.M . . . and found the Johnnies *had* gone." At 5:00 A.M . . . Eighty-ninth with the brigade moved out, "and by 8 A.M . . . had started them again. They left another strong works. By 6 P.M. we had got another position, our works up and our skirmishers out 50 or 60 rods in front of us . . . ." Warren stated that during Railroaders advance on the July 22, "We heard heavy

---

[67] Boatner, *The Civil War Dictionary*, 32,625-627.

cannonading and terrific musketry on our left; it was McPherson's corps that were engaged, and they did more than whip the rebels." What was named the Battle of Atlanta, Warren noted: "Our loss, according to Gen. Thomas, was 3500, 12 pieces of artillery, and the gallant McPherson. The rebels lost in killed 3000; our forces buried 2,700, and in front of the 15th corps where we (the 15th A.C.) repulsed 5 lines of battle, the estimated killed is 300 more, making the 3000. We (the 15th, 16th and 17th corps) captured 3,200 prisoners, 17 stand of colors, 5,000 small arms, &c., making a heavy defeat for the enemy."

Accepted casualty figures on July 20 give Hood's losses at 2,500 killed and wounded with 246 prisoners while the Union figure totaled 1,600. On July 22, the Rebels suffered about 8,000 casualties with the Federals losing 3,722. Looking at the Rebel losses at Peachtree Creek and the Battle of Atlanta, Captain Warren wrote: "Well, I rather like the way we are thinning them out much better than following them through the wood and underbrush."

"From the 23d of July to this date [August 13]," Warren spelled out that "our division has been laying in the trenches, strengthening our works, picketing, &c., having advanced skirmish line, driving the rebs out and occupying their old line for our skirmish line. We are now about 1500 yards (our main works) from the rebel main works." In this 21-day period, "we have made three or four demonstrations on the enemy's lines, but have not succeeded in affecting much in our front. We (the Eighty-ninth) have lost about 15 men since we came here . . . . The stray bullets fall into our camp every few minutes, also some shell; but no shell for the last four or five days. We have had four wounded in the regiment with shell . . . ." To emphasize the danger, he remarked: "I think there has been 50 rebel bullets whistle over my tent since I commenced this letter . . . . They come with force enough to do considerable damage if they struck any one."

The Union hold on Atlanta was tightening. This was demonstrated, as Warren pointed out, that "we are about a mile and a quarter from the center of Atlanta; by climbing a tree in [the] camp of [the] 49th Ohio, we can see the city streets, and the graybacks in the streets. I don't know when we will get possession of the fated city, it being only a question of time. I think we will have a regular siege of it."

He noted that "the cars run across the river up to our lines, and everything looks favorable for a successful close of the campaign, and our victorious occupation of the rebel Gate[way] City."[68]

"I now seat my self amidst flying shot and shell for the purpose of answering your kind letter which I just received." Charles Capron began. "We are working toward Atlanta slowly. This morning we advanced within 3 hundred yards of this fort when zip zip come the bullets which makes us git down rather low till they got done firing when we up and give them a volley that makes them hunt their holes in a hurry." After this brief firefight the front settled down, and Capron wrote: "We was then relieved from the skirmish line and came back to camp where they commenced shelling us. One burst in the quarters. The pieces flying in every direction. One piece hit one of company G men tearing the skin off from his foot and bruising him considerable. In fact there is not a day goes round but what we have some one hurt."[69]

"I suppose you heard before this time that Mr. Copeland was wounded slightly in the knee. I think he will get home, and if he does, I want him to write me," Capron wrote his parents. During the siege, the Railroaders letters frequently mention the number of spent balls continually whizzing through their camp. On August 7, one found the fatherly Azron W. Copeland, the Company F wagoner, hitting him in the left knee. Shipped to a hospital in Nashville, the forty-four-year-old Copeland was eventually transferred to the Veteran Reserve Corps for the remainder of his service. While one Railroader was in the process of heading to the rear, another returned to the front. August 8, found Joel Chambers' cousin, Corporal Jim Tomlinson, back with the regiment "after an absence of a little more than two months caused by his wound received the 27th of May."[70]

Having lost one son killed in battle and another discharged disabled, Emily Tomlinson had written her eldest son, William

68 *Aurora Beacon*, August 25, 1864; Boatner, *The Civil War Dictionary*, 30, 626.

69 Capron, letter, July 29, 1864.

70 Capron, letter, August 20, 1864; Company Muster Roll, 89th Regiment Illinois Infantry, all in Records of the Record of Pension Office of the War Department, Record Group 94.12, National Archives, Washington, D.C.; Chambers, *War Fever Cured*, 55.

James, encouraging him to remain in the hospital indefinitely and, if possible, to seek a medical discharge. In mid-July he replied, stating that his knee was "somewhat weak, but it is getting beter fast. But then, I shant go to the regiment while they ar on the march. You must not be uneasy about me. I have bin in the Army long enuff to know how to take care of myself . . . ." Returning to the issue at hand, he penned, "but ther is no fear of me being sent away unless I want to be. The doctor don't want to send eny away if he can help it, for fear of geting worse instid of beter. Mother, Uncle Sam don't discharge men here of late like he did when Uriah got his. As for my officers getting my Discharge, they cant do enything with it. That is not all. They don't want me to get it while I am able for duty." He then pointed out. "It is the men that can stand hard marching and the hardship they want, not them that playing off all the time. Because I have don my Duty for the last 23 months that is no reason why I should not return to the regiment and do my Duty again when I get able."

Back with the regiment, Tomlinson immediately posted a letter to his mother giving his current military address. Regarding his wound, he mentioned that his leg was "somewhat weak yet," but he was able to complete the 20 mile march from Marietta and felt that he had "got along better than expected. I left Chattanooga last Saturday [August 1] and got here yesterday [August 8] and found Joel [Chambers] all right." The officers and men all welcomed him back, while he was "glad to see them and find them well . . . ." No doubt his next lines would have been troubling to his mother. "We are laying within three miles of town. Our battery has been shelling the town for the last three hours. The rebels has replied five times to it. The pickets exchange shells evry bit. Ther is no harm done." Tomlinson may have had second thoughts since he added: "I will take as good care of myself as I can. I have but one year to serve. That will pass away fast. This is my birthday. It is a rather grim place to pass a birthday. I hope I may pass the next at home."[71]

After July 22, the Railroaders found themselves in their "final position for the siege of Atlanta." Immediately the men set about

[71] Tomlinson, Sally Ryan, *In Good Courage: The Civil War Letters of William James Tomlinson*, 20.

building works even though they were under heavy fire. Reminiscing decades later, Chambers described the defenses the men built. "First there were logs piled up about three feet high, held in position by stakes driven firmly in the ground, then dirt, taken from our side and banked against the logs from two to four feet thick. On top of this was a 'head log' about a foot in diameter, with a space of two or three inches under it, to shoot through." Once the firing line was completed and a few feet in front was erected "a palisade,—split sticks, two to three inches square, the lower end placed in a ditch, held there by a log and all covered with dirt resting at an angle of 45 degrees, the upper end just breast high to a man; and made sharp. A few feet more was another line just like the one described. For twenty yards or more in front of these was 'abatis,' that is, brush with branches cut off from the size of the thumb to that of the wrist made sharp. This was laid all over the ground with points toward the enemy just leaving paths here and there so we could get out to our rifle pits."

During the siege, each brigade's regiments rotated in and out of the front line. While in the trenches, Chambers explained: "One half of us in the rifle pits all the time, and one third of those back in the works must keep awake all night." Unfortunately, the Eighty-ninth's section of the Union line was an exposed position; and as a consequence, casualties mounted daily. Private Chambers vividly remembered a couple of incidents. "One man of Co. G while sitting with his feet down in the ditch, had part of his foot knocked off by a piece of shell. Another day while I was in my tent writing a letter, a shell came screaming over, passed on into a tent in Co. B, and almost tore a man in two across the hips. The poor fellow lived an hour or two. I did not go to see him but oh his heart rending groans."[72]

As the days and weeks wore on, the Railroaders remained in the same position, following a daily routine the siege had established. A man went on picket every third day. Periodically, orders were given changing things up. "In the afternoon yesterday," Private Capron wrote on August 20, that he "noticed boxes of ammunition coming

---

[72] *Chanute Vidette*, "Campaigning in Tennessee and Georgia in 1864, No. 5," January 1890.

out on the skirmish line." He commented that there "would be fun before long and sure enough at five o'clock we was ordered onto the line and then the order was given to open on the Johnnies. Instantly a stream of fire issued from the rifle pits accompanied by the reports of our rifles, which sounded like the heaviest clap of thunder. The object was to draw the enemy's attention while another division charged on the left. We had one man killed and one wounded." Sherman called for demonstrations along the along the line from August 19 through the 21, masking Kilpatrick's cavalry's thrust to make a lasting break in the Macon and Western Railroad.[73]

Having suffered fearful losses in Hood's attacks and the daily shelling of Sherman's artillery, small numbers of Confederate soldiers who had had enough left their trenches and surrendered to the Yankee pickets. Capron related one such incident to his family. "Last night we took 7 prisoners with their guns and everything else they had. The prisoners we took to headquarters and the guns I took and fired at the rebels and then broke them over a stump." While the morale of some rebels flagged, others continued to fight on, inflicting a daily toll on the besiegers. On August 18, Private James David recorded in his diary that "Andrew Bigley [of Company I] was killed this P.M. He was shot in the rifle pit. Also one of Co. G boys was wounded . . . ."[74]

"Some of the time each of our batteries on certain parts of the line had orders to throw a shot into the city every five minutes. Some of these shots were hot. One night there was a great fire over in town, started as we supposed by these hot shots," Joel Chambers recalled. He further reminisced. "We were from 50 to 75 yards from the reb pickets, and when I saw the fire I said, 'Hallo Johnny!' 'Hallo! Came back in reply. Are you asleep? No. Your town is on fire, go put it out, and I will not shoot while you are gone. Thug came a bullet in the dirt of my pit. That was the reply. But I gave him as good as he sent; and thus there was a constant exchange of 'commodities' kept up between us."

---

[73] Capron, letter, August 20, 1864; Cox, *Campaigns of the Civil War: Atlanta*, 195-196.

[74] Capron, letter, July 29, 1864; David, diary, August 18, 1864.

As the siege went on, and more likely out of boredom than anything else, individual soldiers rigged their rifles to fire on Atlanta. Chambers gave this account. "My bunk mate Al Buckman would sometimes—as he said—'Shell Atlanta.' He would melt several bullets into one, thus making a slug three or four inches long, and then with two or three charges of powder would place it on top of the rifle pit, and by means of a string tied to the trigger, he would discharge it." Continuing his remembrance, Chambers wrote: "Sometimes we would yell and fire more rapidly than common, to draw the enemy to our part of the line, while a move was made on some other part of the line. This was done because we could not advance our part of the line . . . ." The result was that "the heavy guns in the rebel works would open out on us. Oh my! What a noise! Those shells sounded like a threshing machine going through the air over our heads." Still clear in Chambers' mind was the moment when "one of the smaller shells bursted a few feet" away, taking "the large part of the foot off one man" while striking "another in the back knocking him down." Taken to the rear, "the assistant surgeon examined the wound and said there was no metal in it, but at the hospital next day, they took a piece of iron from the wound weighing four ounces. So much for the *surgical skill* we sometimes had practiced on us." When he penned the following, Chambers spoke for many of the bluecoated soldiers entrenched before Atlanta: "We have now been pounding away here for a month, not a bit discouraged, not a shadow of doubt but we will at last take the city."[75]

*   *   *

Private Chambers, along with many of his comrades in arms, may have felt it was only a matter of time before Atlanta fell, but those in command had reached a different conclusion. By the third week in August, Sherman determined the struggle was a stalemate. Never able to completely invest the city, Sherman had turned to his cavalry to destroy the railroads supplying it. The effort proved unsuccessful. The daily pounding by the Federal heavy

---

[75] *Chanute Vidette*, "Campaigning in Tennessee and Georgia in 1864, No. 6," January 1890.

siege artillery created much noise and endless piles of rubble, but little else. Sherman, too restless to remain bogged down for long, had had enough and elected to abandon his own supply line and strike Hood's. On August 25, the bombardment suddenly ceased and most of the Union infantry disappeared from their investing trenches. The troops were quickly organized in the rear and sent off on another of Sherman's flanking marches—their objective, the Macon & Western Railroad at Jonesboro, southeast of Atlanta.

Mistakenly, Hood, along with many of Atlanta's citizens, celebrated the disappearance of Sherman and his hated Yankees, assuming they had given up the siege and were falling back to Chattanooga. But exuberant spirits were soon dampened when the bluecoats suddenly popped up south of Atlanta at work destroying the West Point Railroad. Still unsure what Sherman was up to, Hood sent Hardee's and Lee's corps to Jonesboro to dispatch what he considered a reinforced raid. What they found was Howard's Army of the Tennessee dug-in on the high ground. By mid-afternoon on August 31, Hardee was prepared and advanced on the Federals, who were ready and waiting behind fieldworks. The rebel attack was quickly repulsed; making matters worse, Sherman's Seventeenth and Fourth Corps reached the Macon & Western Railroad north of Jonesboro and now was between Atlanta and the two Confederate corps. A befuddled Hood ordered Lee back to Atlanta while Hardee, sensing a trap, slipped away from Jonesboro late on the afternoon of September 1. With all of Atlanta's railroads in Sherman's hands, Hood was forced to evacuate the "Gate City of the South." By noon on September 2, the Stars and Stripes were seen flying from Atlanta's city hall. After nearly a three-month campaign, Sherman could telegraph Washington with the message that "Atlanta is ours and fairly won. I shall not push much farther on this raid, but in a day or so will march to Atlanta and give my men some rest."[76]

---

[76]   Boatner, *The Civil War Distionary*, 33-34; Castel, *Decision in the West: The Atlanta Campaign of 1864,*485-506; Dennis, Kelly, *Kennesaw Mountain and the Atlanta Campaign: A Tour Guide* (Atlanta, Georgia: Kennesaw Mountain Historical Association, Inc., 1990), 51-52; Scaife, *The Campaign for Atlanta,* 131-135.

With his term of service expiring, Colonel Gibson of the Forty-ninth Ohio turned over command of the brigade to the Eighty-ninth's Colonel Hotchkiss on August 24. Respect is earned, and the Railroaders respected Colonel William H. Gibson. In a letter to the *Kendall County Record* a Company H corporal said this about the Ohio colonel: "When 'off duty' he was the genial kind-hearted gentleman, courteous to all, and accessible at all times to correct abuses or give friendly advice." Another soldier commented: "Col. Gibson, who in Gen. Willich's absence commanded our brigade, has gone home, and we are sorry to lose him as he was such an excellent officer and so good a man." While Colonel Gibson was taking his leave and saying goodbye, Chambers noted in his diary that the brigade "received orders to be ready to march at dark. Started at half past ten and went about 2 ½ miles to the right and stopped in the rear of the right of the 20 A.C. where we remained till daylight."[77]

"August 26th. We started early this morning and marched about 14 miles to the right and stopped for the night in the rear of the 23rd A.C. A great many men were overcome today by the heat. Some of whom I fear will never get over it," Chambers entered in his diary. Looking back through the years, Chambers gave a more detailed and vivid account of that day's march: "We . . . marched hard all day along a kind of dividing ridge between the head of [the] Flint River and the Chattahoochee." Cooped up in a trench for over a month, the men soon found they were out of marching shape and having a difficult time. Tack on to the fact that it was a hot day was also the lack of water, and "one by one the men were overcome by the heat." Chambers wrote: "Just before sundown as we were leaving the main road to go into camp, Lieut. Walker said to Serg't Holt, 'Sergeant I can't go any farther.' So saying, he dropped down in the shade of a little bush. He was no 'band-box' soldier, but a brave, true man and a good officer; but humanity can only bear just so much, and the heat was too much for him." He added that night "when we stacked arms in camp, our company consisted of Serg't Holt, Corporal Tomlinson and Private Chambers. We were not a whit better or truer than the

---

[77] Chambers, *War Fever Cured*, 58-59; *Kendall County Record*, September 15 and 29, 1864.

others; but had more power to resist the heat, that was all. The men all came in before 'taps.'"[78]

Reporting on the same subject and period, a Company H soldier known only as "R" wrote his local newspaper the following: "We left our position two miles northeast of Atlanta where we had remained in *status quo* a little over a month on the 25th inst., about 11 o'clock at night, and after two days rapid marching reached this point—about eleven miles southwest of Atlanta." He went on, "The Army of the Tennessee is in possession of the Eastpoint and Montgomery Railroad. The troops are still on the go, and we will start very soon." But he pointedly added: "The weather is remarkably warm, and several of the soldiers in our brigade died the day before yesterday from the effects.... The boys were very glad to leave those tiresome old breastworks and get out into the fresh country air; but as to being pushed through at a 2.40 rate, with the thermometer at a hundred—well they don't 'hanker arter' such exercise. However, it is a very good remedy for obesity, as it takes off the superfluous."

"August 29th.—I did not have time to finish my letter on the 28th .... We are now going for the Macon and Atlanta Railroad, which, if we capture, will compel the enemy to evacuate the 'Gate City,' or give us battle in open field—a problem yet to be solved," "R" explained. Continuing, he wrote: "It is reported that our forces will endeavor to strike the railroad thirty six miles south of the city. The boys are all in fine spirits and have great confidence in Gen. Sherman."[79]

After resting for a day, the Eighty-ninth picked up the march again on August 30, heading eastward, crossing the Atlanta and West Point Railroad near Red Oak Station and moving toward Rough and Ready and the Macon and Western Railroad. August 31, the regiment assisted "the pioneers of the brigade, under charge of Major Kidder, of the Eighty-ninth," in tearing up and destroyed two miles of the Macon Railroad. The first day of September the Eighty-ninth struck out marching south, following the railroad, toward Jonesboro, arriving too late to play a role in the battle.

---

[78] Chambers, *War Fever Cured*, 59; *Chanute Vidette*, "Campaigning in Tennessee and Georgia in 1864, No. 6," January 1890.

[79] *Kendall County Record*, September 29, 1864.

Held in reserve, the brigade observed the fight. Private Chambers recorded the following in his diary. "Parts of the 4th and 14th Corps (the latter mostly) had heavy fighting in front of Jonesboro for an hour before dark. Routing the rebs at all points with great slaughter and taking a large number of prisoners together with ten pieces of Artillery."[80]

"During the night we had heard terrible explosions in the direction of Atlanta. We half suspected that the rebs were evacuating the city and blowing up their magazines," remembered Joel Chambers. The next morning, September 2, Chambers entered in his diary: "This morning we discovered that the rebs fell back during the night leaving their dead in our hands." Nineteen-year-old, Charles Capron, gave this graphic description of the battle's aftermath. "The next day I was over the battlefield and it was sickening sight. Men laying around wherever you would look most them was dead. Some few was breathing their last. There was the most men shot in the head at that place ever I see before but suffice it to say that they got the worst whipping at Jonesborough that they have had on the campaign." Later that morning, Private Chambers penned in his journal, "Our forces started in pursuit . . . . We found the enemy near Lovejoy Station where sharp fighting took place . . . ."[81]

"Our regiment has been lucky so far. We have not been engaged yet," Corporal Tomlinson informed his mother in a letter dated September 3. According to Tomlinson the Eighty-ninth was "3 miles SE of Jonesboro." He explained, "We are on the railroad leading to Macon. We have torn up and burnt it for several miles. I think when the enemy leaves here we will get back to Atlanta and rest for awhile . . . ." That same day his cousin, Joel R. Chambers, noted in his diary: "We received the news of the capture of Atlanta today with loud and prolonged cheers." Though a common private and a youngster to boot, Private Charles Capron summed up the fall of Atlanta in a letter to his mother: "Old Hood the rebel commander stayed in Atlanta with part of his force till after we had got every railroad cut running into town and then he could not get his stuff away so he destroyed 84 car loads of ammunition, 5 locomotives

---

80   *OR*, Vol. 38, Pt. 1, 389, 404; Chambers, *War Fever Cured*, 61.
81   Chambers, *War Fever Cured*, 61; Capron, letter, September 9, 1864.

and 3 hundred cars besides several thousand stands of small arms and all the principle machine shops and left 28 large siege guns. [He] blew up his magazines in fact he destroyed several million dollars worth of property."[82]

"Today we received orders to be ready to march at 8 o'clock and started accordingly . . . . We all have no doubt but the intention of our Gen's in making this move is to take the army to the vicinity of Atlanta to rest the men," Private Chambers wrote in his daily journal on September 5. About noon on the September 8 Railroaders passed through the city, camping four miles east of town. Writing the *Kendall County Record* shortly afterward, a Company H soldier said, "The 'Gate City' is, at last, in our possession the 'Starry Banner of the United States' floats proudly over every fort. We made a 'triumphal march' through the town the day before yesterday."[83]

Five days after the Railroaders marched through Atlanta, "colors flying and drums beating," Lieutenant Colonel William D. Williams completed his report, detailing the Railroaders roll in the campaign. After the dates, places, and casualty numbers, Williams wrote from his heart:

I take the opportunity as the commanding officer of the Eighty-ninth to express my grateful acknowledgements to the rank and file of this regiment for their uncomplaining endurance and devoted bravery during this long, laborious, and eventful campaign. They have proved themselves patriots and soldiers of the highest type.

Of the commissioned officers . . . I can speak with pride and pleasure. Not one of them faltered in his duty. Ever foremost in the charge, the record of the . . . dead and wounded tells the story more eloquently then tongue and pen.[84]

---

[82] Tomlinson, Sally Ryan, *In Good Courage: The Civil War Letters of William James Tomlinson*, 20; Chambers, *War Fever Cured*, 61; Capron, letter, September 9, 1864.

[83] Chamber, *War Fever Cured*, 62; *Kendall County Record*, September 29, 1864.

[84] *OR*, Vol. 38, Pt. 1, 404.

CHAPTER 14

"HIS AGONIZED COMRADES . . . STOOD THERE AND SAW THE NOBLE LIFE FADE OUT . . . ."

Early on the morning of the September 2, Union pickets warily moved forward probing the abandoned Rebel lines, which had been evacuated during the night. On leaving, Hood's rear guard put the torch to the supply warehouses and munitions depots. Flames quickly lit the night sky while explosions soon resonated for miles, both signaling that the Battle for Atlanta was over. With the Confederate army gone, and to prevent further damage, the mayor and council held a hurried meeting and agreed to surrender the city. Carrying a white flag, the delegation rode out toward the Federal lines and, meeting an advancing Union column, formally surrendered Atlanta.

Saturday morning, September 3, a courier arrived at Sherman's headquarters bearing a dispatch that the Gateway City of the South was in Union hands. Soon after notifying Washington that Union troops were in control of Atlanta, Sherman concluded to halt further military operations. In his wire to Lincoln, he said: "I shall not push much further on this raid, but in a day or so will move back to Atlanta and give my men some rest. Since May 5, we have been in one constant battle or skirmish, and need rest." Having failed to

413

destroy the Army of Tennessee, Sherman was left with a symbolic victory rather than one of great military significance. Disgruntled he confided to Halleck, "I ought to have reaped larger fruits of victory." Sherman held Atlanta, but the former Rebel defenders had escaped destruction, surviving to fight another day. So after four months of marching and fighting, Sherman paused to regroup his armies and to plan the next campaign.

A few days after setting up headquarters in Atlanta, Sherman informed the civilian authorities that the city was to become a military garrison and that all the inhabitants were to be expelled. Once the citizenry were gone all future railroad traffic was restricted to military use only. The general told the local population to go either North or South. When the mayor protested, Sherman pointed out, "War is cruelty and you can not refine it." Those who still remained began leaving on September 11 and by September 21, a total of 446 families amounting to 1,600 people, mainly women and children, had left.

When news of Atlanta's fall reached Richmond, Confederate president Jefferson Davis hurried to Georgia where he set about using his personal influence to bolster both the public's and the Army of Tennessee's morale. While visiting the army, Davis together with Hood, developed a strategy to defeat Sherman and recover Atlanta. They agreed the point of emphasis in the coming campaign was Sherman's lifeline, the railroad coming down from Chattanooga. If the Western and Atlantic Railroad could be severed and held, Sherman would be without food or forage and would have to abandon Atlanta and retreat. Sherman too was aware that the railroad was his Achilles' heal. And consequently, he was seriously considering cutting loose from his link with the north and moving southeast, where he would eventually establish a supply base on the Georgia coast.

Looking to the future, Sherman sent General Thomas north to prepare for whatever strategy Davis and Hood put in motion. The same day Thomas left Chattanooga, September 29, Hood crossed the Chattahoochee heading north to cut the railroad. Having anticipated Hood's falling on his line of communication, Sherman had already dispatched three divisions to shore up the defenses at Chattanooga and key points along the railroad. However, by October

3, Hood's men had reached the railroad, forcing Sherman to take all but one corps and head back after the Confederates. Nine days later the Rebel army had advanced beyond Resaca. But Hood soon tired of the cat-and-mouse maneuvering along the rail link and on the October 17 moved off to the west, hoping Sherman would follow. Sherman, however, was unwilling to follow Hood and returned to the plan of a "marching to the sea." He now turned the Fourth Corps along with the garrisons in Tennessee and Alabama over to General Thomas. Finally, on November 12, Sherman severed all contact with the North. Fours days later, leaving Atlanta a smoldering ruins, General Sherman rode out beginning the campaign through Georgia to the coast. Monday, November 21, Hood led the Army of Tennessee north for Nashville, and, he hoped, on to the Ohio River.[1]

*　　*　　*

A Company H soldier, probably Sergeant Reuben W. Willett, wrote of an incredible incident in a letter to the *Kendall County Record*. "A private in our regiment run the picket, while the rebs were leaving Atlanta, to meet Sherman. This man, Ed. Stevens by name, was shot through the breast on the 27th of May, and had nearly recovered in a rebel hospital." He went on, telling the editor that after making his escape, Stevens "went to Gen. Slocum [Twentieth Corps] and told him that there were only 2000 militia in the town. General S. advanced his Corps, and the enemy retreated having first blown up eighty car loads of ammunition. We heard the explosions beyond Jonesboro, thirty miles south of the city." It had been little over a week since Jim Tomlinson wrote his mother back home in Augusta, Hancock County. So on Friday, September 12, he brought his mother up-to-date. "We

---

[1]　Anne J. Bailey, *The Chessboard of War: Sherman and Hood in the Autumn Campaigns of 1864* (Lincoln, Nebraska: University of Nebraska Press, 2000), 9-50; Boatner, *The Civil War Dictionary*, 305-306; Castel, *Decision in the West: The Atlanta Campaign of1864*, 539-555; Wiley Sword, *Embrace an Angry Wind, The Confederacy' Last Hurrah: Spring Hill, Franklin, and Nashville* (New York: Harper Collins Publishers, 1992), 62; Van Horne, *History of the Army of the Cumberland Its Organization, Campaigns, and Battles*, II:155-168.

went out as far as Lovejoy Station and stopped there three days, but I did not fight much. General Sherman was drawing the Army off—to start back to Atlanta, wher we ar at present. We came her[e] on the 8th . . . ." Continuing his letter, he gave an opinion of the city and a description of the damage. "Atlanta, you read what a fine city it was. I don't consider it a city at all. It is nothing more than a Southern town. Even that has been well shelled and torn to pieces. Nearly every family has holes dug for to stay when we was shelling the town." Tomlinson noted "the ruins of 80 cars that was burnt. They was loaded with ammunition and small arms. Ther was four engines somewhat damage, but our men had them on the track and will have them repaired. I saw some tremendous large shells." Private Charles Capron recalled that "on the 8th of September we marched triumphantly through Atlanta with drums beating and colors flying." Reflecting on the preceding four months, he wrote: "Many was the brave youth that started with us [who] never lived to see the town" and who is now "resting peacefully in a soldier's grave having gave their life freely for their country." When the Railroaders marched through Atlanta, Willett, like Jim Tomlinson, observed: "The place has a very desolate appearance, and the citizens look despondent on account, mostly, of Gen. Sherman's late order, which reads to this effect: 'All citizens having friends or relations in the Southern army are to go South, and all loyalist are to go North.'" He noted, maybe to his own surprise, that "there are a great number of really loyal people in the city, and to-morrow they start North. The secesh have nearly all gone." Sergeant Willett ended by stating that "the campaign has closed, we will be paid, the army re-organized, and then a winter campaign I think." While Corporal Tomlinson noted that "the Army started on this campaign on the 7th of May and went into camp on the 8th of this month."[2]

By September 9, the 89th "went into permanent camp" and "put up tents bunks etc." The next day Joel Chambers jotted in his journal that "we cleaned up camp in order to make ourselves more comfortable during our stay here." Though the Railroaders

---

[2] *Kendall County Record*, September 10, 1864; Capron, letter, February 12, 1865; Tomlinson, Sally Ryan, *In Good Courage: The Civil War Letters of William James Tomlinson*, 21.

were no longer in the trenches or on the field of battle, the enemy still lurked about. Any time the men went on picket or left camp, they faced a degree of peril. Chambers' entry for the 11th revealed what could happen. "Part of the reg't was on picket and part on a foraging expedition which was driven in by the rebs. There is four or five missing and one Negro cook probably killed." In a note to the *Kendall County Record*, Sergeant Willett added a bit more detail and the names of those taken prison. "Company H last Sunday met with quite a loss, a squad of men form the 89th were ordered on a foraging expedition; among the party were Corporal Solon Boomer, William Walker and privates Joseph Haigh, John Buffham, Albert Cooper and Robert Bentley, the foragers were attacked by rebel cavalry, and the above mentioned soldiers of Co. H were captured."

Ten weeks passed before word was received from the men captured back in September. Sergeant Willett dutifully informed the *Record's* editor, "This morning Corp Samuel Odell gave me a letter which was opened and addressed to Captain F. M. Hobbs, and it was desired that I should send a copy of this letter to you for publication." The letter written from Macon, Georgia and dated September 25, 1864, began: *"Dear Capt:*—As there is an opportunity of sending you a few lines, I thought that I would inform you that your stray boys are still in the land of the living. I wrote you from Lovejoy, but I do not think that the letter was sent. I am disposed to think that foraging is not my *forte,* as I was taken prisoner the very first time that I went out last summer; but there is no use crying over 'spilled milk.'" He continued: "If I am so fortunate as to get out of this, it will be late before I shall try foraging again. The boys gave me such glowing accounts of 'sweet potatoes" I thought I would try my luck, and only thought of being gone two or three hours; but fate seemed to have another course marked out for us." Somewhat chagrinned, he wrote: "We were picked up within hearing distance of our own camps. We could hear the musicians practicing. At the time Maj. Kidder was out beyond us with the train [when] some Texas scouts had crawled in close to our lines, and laid in wait for us, and took us out by a circuitous route on double quick; they more than made us travel for the first four hours. You no doubt, feel bad about our absence, but no worse than we. I can assure you we have got the worst of the bargain." He added: "'Joe' was left at Lovejoy.

Our quarters are comfortable. How long we shall stay in this place is unknown. With kind regards to the boys I am, sir, Yours truly, S. Boomer. W. Ward, J. Haigh, J. Buffham, Al. Cooper, A. Bentley."[3]

The sound of distant skirmishing could occasionally be heard, but on the whole the men enjoyed a respite from the daily sounds of cannon and rifle fire. The diarist, Joel Chambers, welcomed change. "Worked for a little while this morning on the breastworks. All quiet and pleasant in camp," he entered for September 13. The next day, he wrote: "We are now enjoying ourselves first-rate with no duty except picket and company inspection once a day . . . ." In response to his mother's most recent letter, a contented Charles Capron wrote: "This still finds me right side up with forked end down and enjoying life as good as a soldier can expect. We get plenty to eat and wear. The weather is quite moderate here at the present."[4]

September 29, Private Curtis B. Knox of Company F found time to compose and post a letter to the anti-Lincoln Administration *Rock Island Argus*. He began his letter to the newspaper's editor, Colonel J. B. Danforth, with the following: "We are camped in a splendid pine grove 4 miles east of Atlanta, only half a mile from Gen. McPherson's battle ground in which he lost his life. Small grave yards are all around us and it makes one feel sad and when he reflects upon the past and see his brother soldiers laying around him, killed in a useless war." After two years of misery, destruction, and death, Knox had soured on the conflict and expressed his current feelings to the pro-Democratic editor: "We still live in hopes that we will never have to go forth to meet the enemy excepting as brother and friends."

"There is considerable dissatisfaction prevailing among the soldiers at this place in regard to money." Knox further pointed out to Danforth: "It only lacks one day of being 9 months since we received any pay, and a great many soldiers' families are suffering for the want of money to support them[selves]. I don't think they are treated right." Not finished, his following words were perhaps a comfort to the Democratic editor. "We are all looking forward to

---

3   Chambers, *War Fever Cured*, 63; *Kendall County Record*, September 29 and December 1, 1864.

4   Chambers, *War Fever Cured*, 64; Capron, letter, September 18, 1864.

the day when little Mac will be elected, thinking that he may do our suffering country justice."[5]

To a neighbor from home, Captain George W. Reynolds of the 83rd Illinois, Company G, Second Lieutenant John W. Swickard wrote both a newsy and informative letter. "Inspection is just over. The jingle of the rammer as it glided down the bright Springfield has died away. And wherever the sun's rays pierce the boughs of the pines there you will see the boys in groups. Some writing—others discussing the merits of the two candidates for the next Presidency . . . ."

Casting about for something of interest to his old friend, Swickard turned to the situation in Atlanta. "The city . . . shows the ravages of war. Many of the buildings are badly demolished from our shell. The citizens have nearly all been sent South or North. The appeal in behalf of women and children has no effect on Gen. Sherman. He tells them to go and build in a more secluded spot until the passions and pride of men in arms against us cease to exist."

He continued conveying General Sherman's thoughts on this subject. "He tells them that he intends to prosecute this war in such a manner as to ensure victory and peace at the earliest moment possible. He tells them they are not the only ones interested in this matter, but millions throughout the North who he is laboring to please. Never since the war commenced has there been a letter written by any General that exhibits such a determination to put down this war by force of arms."

Swickard expressed both his opinion and observation on the upcoming canvas for the presidency. "I think the election of Lincoln is certain. There are McClellan men here but not many."[6]

The upcoming election elicited comments from men of both political parties. While hospitalized in Chattanooga, Sergeant Isaac K. Young co-authored a letter with a fellow Republican from the 96th Illinois. The two men presented the following perception to the editor of *The Waukegan Weekly Gazette*. "Lincoln enthusiasm rules high, and McClellan stock is greatly below par." They shared the opinion of their colleagues in U. S. Hospital No. 3. "The soldiers

---

[5]   *Rock Island Argus*, October 12, 1864.

[6]   John W. Swickard, letter to George W. Reynolds, September 25, 1864, original in possession of Don Hamerstrand, Victoria, Illinois.

know that Lincoln has piloted the old Ship of State with a steady arm through the maelstrom of rebellion thus far, in a masterly manner, they say let him still stand at the helm, and if the ship goes down, let it go with her colors flying." "But under Lincoln," the two held, "she will cut ride the storms, while under McClellan we fear, we dreadfully fear, she will make unholy concessions to the insolent, for and to Jeff Davis. Stand firm then for Lincoln and Johnson, and all will be well."[7]

Sergeant Young continued his personal effort to re-elect President Lincoln with a letter to the *Aurora Beacon*. He began by saying: "The contest is fairly upon us. The Republican Party has thrust its platform before the gaze of the army and of the world. The Democratic Party also has stuck under our noses their platform, and raised their banner, with its names of McClellan and Pendleton as their standard bearers." The ardent Republican and former Kendall County farmer presented what he interpreted as the difference in the candidates: "One goes in of a rigid prosecution of the war, the other cries out peace, peace on any terms. The one goes in on a determined prosecution of this war for the suppression and demolition of the rebellion; the other condemns such a course, and plainly teaches a cessation of hostilities on any terms . . . ." Further on in the letter, he challenged the readers to "let every inch of ground be fully examined, and every argument and every pledge and promise be weighed, as becomes him who is truly local to the government and the old flag, before casting his ballot at the November election." He continued: "We soldiers in the army of our country have a choice; our minds are made up; we know whom we have trusted, and know full well his purposes and designs as far as this accursed rebellion is called into question. We endorse the sentiments set forth in the Baltimore platform, and give our undivided suffrage to Honest Old Abe and Andy in the coming contest."[8]

William Sadler and his brother, Samuel, hailed from Camp Point in Adams County. Before enlisting, both worked as brakemen on the Chicago, Burlington & Quincy line. On July 30, 1864, William transfer to the Engineer Corps. The October 8, 1864 edition of *The*

---

[7]   *The Waukegan Weekly Gazette*, October 1, 1864.

[8]   *Aurora Beacon*, October 13, 1864.

Quincy Whig Republican prefaced a correspondence from William with the following: "We have been furnished with a letter from one who enlisted in the 89th Illinois regiment . . . . When he enlisted he was a Democrat, believing not only in the principles of the party, but in the *men* composing it. His present political sentiments are expressed in the extracts we make, as well as his opinion of some of his old political associates."

Replying to a friend back home, he wrote: "You ask for my opinion on some points, I will give it in my blundering way. I am still, and always shall be Old Bill. In the first place, I never for one moment doubted the result of this war, but I must confess it has been prolonged beyond my expectations." He continued, "I hold that slavery is, and was, the sole cause of the war; and it was begun by the Southern wing of the Democratic Party. Their aim was power and the extension of slavery. Slavery is dead, and the rebel slaveholders killed it." In a stronger tone he said: "I have seen enough of the accursed institution to satisfy me that it is of the devil; and when the black man is freed many of the poor white men will be freed also. You can believe this or not; it is the fact." He then made the point that his political principles were unchanged, but foremost, he favored putting down the rebellion. "I will support Lincoln, or any other man, who will do this. I like Old Abe's plan, and I think it will eventually win," he wrote. He then made it clear, "I have no sympathy for traitors, North or South, nor for those who sympathize with them. I am in favor of subjugation, confiscation, emancipation; and if necessary hell and damnation to punish traitors; I think there is no hell hot enough to do some of them justice." Not finished, he wrote: "And those poor, miserable, cowardly, white livered copperhead scoundrels at home, who blowing about the administration, I wish the last wretch of them was drafted and had to face their Southern brethren on the battle field. Then they could see what Southern chivalry is. I think a Southern traitor, who will fight for what he calls his rights, has more honor than a peace copperhead at home." Private Sadler unequivocally professed: "Lincoln and Johnson are my choice, and I believe they will be elected." It was his opinion that at two-thirds of the soldiers would vote for Lincoln. The soldiers, he explained, "favored settling the difficulty by fighting, as they can see no other way to obtain a permanent peace. They hate to hear a compromise spoken of.

421

The editor noted that "there is more of the same sort in the letter, only a "little more so;" but this will answer to define the position of this old Democrat, who speaks the sentiments of thousands, who like him, have had their eyes opened to the close affinity between "Democracy" and slavery."[9]

With the upcoming election on his mind and writing his mother on October 30, Jim Tomlinson requested that she "tell Uriah [his younger brother] to vote for Old Abe." And finally after weeks of debate, the Railroaders on Sunday morning November 8 cast their ballots. Writing home soon afterwards, Tomlinson passed along the results: "Ther was 213 votes cast, 158 for Father Abraham and 55 for Little Mack. I hope this will end the war." That same day Tomlinson's cousin, Joel Chambers, entered in his pocket diary. "An Election for president was held today simply to test the relative strength of the reg't. The vote stood: For Lincoln 192; For McClellan 64." The differing figures may be attributed to any number of reasons e.g. picket duty in the morning, and the men voting later in the day.[10]

*   *   *

After a little more than three weeks, the Railroaders period of rest abruptly ended. Private Chambers briefly commented in his diary for October 2. "All quiet to day. Received orders about midnight to be ready to march at daylight." That night, he penned the following account: "We started early this morning marched through Atlanta, Thence to the Chattahoochee river which we crossed about noon then moved on and camped 4 miles South of Marietta., marching in all [a] full 20 miles." October 4 found the Eighty-ninth breaking camp at 10:00 A.M . . ., passing through Marietta and ending the day at the base of Kennesaw Mountain. "We marched slowly all day," Chambers' recorded for the October 5, "and camped near Pine Knob. The enemy reported to be in the vicinity of lost M't'n." With no movement on the sixth, Chambers climbed to the top of Pine Knob where he looked down on "the smoke from the camp

---

9   *The Quincy Whig Republican*, October 8, 1864.

10 Tomlinson, Sally Ryan, *In Good Courage: The Civil War Letters of William James Tomlinson*, 21; Chambers, *War Fever Cured*, 75.

fires of both the Rebel and the Union Army." October 7 was more of the same, with the exception that Chambers mentioned hearing "a few cannon shots and a little musketry in the direction of Lost M't'n."

"Our reg't left the Brigade and went to Big Shanty where we worked all day clearing off the Railroad where the rebs destroyed it as they passed up [the line] in their late movement," Chambers explained in his journal entry for October 8. The next day the veteran railroad men set to work clearing "the track of burned ties and rails as far as Ackworth . . . ." By the eleventh, the Railroaders were "engaged in laying track," and did so through October 13. On the fourteenth, Chambers noted: "A train of cars came in today from Altoona bringing a Div of Bridge Builders to repair the road and thus relieved our reg't." With the arrival of the construction battalion, the Eighty-ninth was assigned to guard "the Bridge builders while they repaired the road." On October 16, the work was complete and "three trains ran back and forth during the day." With the repairs to the railroad finished, the regiment divided their time during the next two weeks between patrolling the track and working on nearby fortifications.[11]

It had been over a month since Charles Capron had had time "to pen a few lines" to his mother. "The reason of my long silence," he wrote "can be explained in a few words. The old rebel general Hood got into our rear and destroying about 30 miles of track and we have to start on the war path again and I have had no chance to send letters home or any where else." He then excitedly explained: "But I must tell you of our good luck. One morning we was ordered to pull out by ourselves. No one could imagine where we was a going to but come to find out we was detailed to repair the road while the army went to fight the Jonnies." Still ecstatic about the regiment's good fortune, he continued: "And the road is finished and we are not doing much of any thing now. Think we will be detached for train guards. If we do we will not have to go into any more big fights." As for the time being, Capron explained that "we have to patrol a mile and a half every two hours. I saw a bushwhacker this morning but could not get close enough to try my rifle on him." As

---

[11]   Chambers, *War Fever Cured*, 67-72.

an after thought, he added: "They [the Rebels] intended to cut the road and starve us out of Atlanta, but they did not make out."[12]

Jim Tomlinson also accounted to his mother for the month-long delay in writing and noted that "we left Atlanta on the 1st. The rebels have moved back to near Chattanooga. They tore up 15 miles of railroad but they have got the worst of it so far. We have the road nearly repaired . . . . We have not bin in eny fight yet." On October 30, while still near Ackworth, Georgia, Tomlinson again found time to write home and told his mother that "cars came through from Chattanooga yesterday for the first time since we've been here . . . ."[13]

The occasional alarm of an approaching Rebel column brought the camp to arms, but the enemy kept their distance and no fighting took place. Cousins Joel Chambers and Jim Tomlinson managed to put up a shebang that they found to be a "comfortable little dwelling." However, the pleasing routine of labor and the semblance of permanent camp was not to last. "Work on the breastworks is suspended to day and some preparation is being made to move," Chambers wrote in his journal for October 29. "We got on board the cars this afternoon [October 30] bound for Chattanooga and after a slow and tedious ride we arrived at Dalton about Midnight where we learned that the road was obstructed between that place and Chattanooga. Consequently our only chance of getting through Alabama [was] to take the branch road and go by way of Cleveland at which place we arrive early the following morning," Chambers recorded. "We left Cleveland this morning [October 31] soon after arriving and after a pleasant ride reached Chattanooga in safety about one oclock and went into camp before night."[14]

After remaining in camp all day, the Eighty-ninth boarded the railroad cars at dark and were soon bound for Stevenson, Alabama, arriving the next morning after an overnight ride in the rain. Joel Chambers reported the train stopped long enough at Stevenson for breakfast, "and again pushed on," passing through Huntsville in the

---

[12] Capron, letter, October, 25, 1864.

[13] Tomlinson, Sally Ryan, *In Good Courage: The Civil War Letters of William James Tomlinson*, 21.

[14] Chamber, *War Fever Cured*, 70-73.

evening and arriving at Athens around midnight. This leg had taken about 30 hours, and as Chambers wearily expressed, "This has been a toilsome ride on top of the cars in the cold and rain." But, this was the end of the line as the train could run no further. At noon the regiment took up the march for Pulaski, Tennessee. After a 10 mile march, the Railroaders camped near the Alabama and Tennessee State line. The following morning, November 3, Chambers began: "We marched early this morning, crossed the state line, and arrived at Elk river about eleven oclock and to our chagrin found no way of crossing but to wade it, which was a bitter pill. It being a cold day, the river about one hundred yards wide and 2 to 3 feet deep." Afterward, Jim Tomlinson had this to say about the incident. "I said that I would not [wade] the river, when I herd that we had to cross it, but when it came to the pinch, I stripped and went across just the same as if I had not said enything." Jokingly he told her, "It was the best bath that I ever got . . . ." Posted November 14, Pulaski, Tennessee, Charles Capron hurriedly scratched a short note home detailing the Railroaders recent move north. And like Tomlinson, he had a few words for the crossing of the Elk River. "And lo there was no bridge and we had to strip and ford it. Cold was no name for it. I thought I should freeze. It was breast deep. It used me up so that I could scarcely move the next day but I am getting over it now."[15]

On reaching Chattanooga, Thomas directed the Fourth Corps to Pulaski, where it was concentrated by November 3. Arriving at Pulaski on November 5, the Railroaders were reunited with their brigade after a four-week absence. Pulaski, located on the Central Alabama Railroad, lay about one third of the way between Decatur, Alabama and Nashville, Tennessee. Further south in Alabama, Hood faced Union resistance at Decatur and consequently pushed the Army of Tennessee on west toward Tuscumbia where it began arriving on October 30. Temporarily, Hood stopped to rest and re-supply. Nine days earlier, Sherman had given up his pursuit of Hood and headed back to Atlanta, leaving Thomas to deal with the impulsive Rebel general. And, by now, General Thomas expected

---

[15] Chambers, *War Fever Cured*, 72-74; Tomlinson, Sally Ryan, *In Good Courage: The Civil War Letters of William James Tomlinson*, 21; Capron, letter, November 14, 1864.

Hood's movement into Tennessee and forwarded the Twenty-third Corps to Pulaski, reinforcing the Federal troops there. On Monday, November 21, Hood's army set forth from Florence, Alabama, headed for Tennessee, with the initial objective of getting between the two Union corps at Pulaski and Thomas' gathering force at Nashville.[16]

"It is 70 miles from here [Pulaski] to Nashville," and "ther is a railroad from here [to] ther," noted Corporal Jim Tomlinson in a November 8 letter home. Pulaski, Tennessee had been a supply depot for the Union troops operating in that region. But now, it was the site Thomas selected to concentrate an army to confront Hood's expected advance into Tennessee. Major General John M. Schofield arrived on November 14 and assumed the in-field command over what would come to be a combined force made up the Fourth and Twenty-third Corps. For the men in the ranks, however, the current military picture was confusing, leading Tomlinson write: "We are throwing up breastworks, what for I don't know—unless it is to keep the men to work. Ther is no rebels here. Our Corps is here all alone. The others is going thru the Confederacy like a does of salts. I herd that they was 100 miles south of Atlanta." Having completed the fortifications, the Railroaders set about "putting up quarters for cold weather." "Jim Tomlinson and myself put up a shanty and [a] fireplace," Joel Chambers entered in his diary on November 12. While the Union high-command debated what might take place, the soldiers made themselves at home.[17]

The regiment quickly settled into a routine of picketing, foraging, and policing the camp. With no marching or fighting, the officers used the lull to catch up on a number of odds and ends—one item being the necessary paperwork needed for the men to be paid. Back on the October 13, payrolls were signed allowing the Eighty-ninth to get eight months pay. But without a paymaster, no greenbacks were received. "The 51st Indiana joined our Brig today and Col Straight of that reg't assumed command of the Brigade in place of Col Martin of the 8th Kansas," Chambers noted in his diary for the November 16. Two days later, he excitedly annotated, "We

---

16   Long, *The Civil War Day By Day*, 587-598, Chambers, *War Fever Cured*, 74-75.

17   Tomlinson, Sally Ryan, *In Good Courage: The Civil War Letters of William James Tomlinson*, 21; Chambers, *War Fever Cured*, 76.

received quite a treat today in shape of a lot of onions and Kraut from the U.S. Sanitary Commission." For the next few days all was "very quiet and dull in camp" with the first snow of the season falling on the November 21. Shortly after dark on the twenty-second, the Eighty-ninth was detailed to the depot where they "remained all night loading quartermaster's stores on the cars," returning to "camp about sunrise." Around 11:00 A.M. marching orders were received, and the regiment started out at 1:00 P.M., going 12 miles and bivouacking near Lynnville. November 24, the men were up and on the road at 4:00 A.M . . . Chambers remarked that "after a forced march of 21 miles we reached Columbia about eleven." The sound of light skirmishing could be heard off to the left of the pike as they arrived. Given a short rest, the remainder of the afternoon was spent putting up breastworks. Of all the unexpected occurrences, Chambers recorded in his diary: "The paymaster commenced paying our reg't about eleven oclock tonight which he accomplished during the night. I received $101.70 wages and $80 bounty."[18]

Beginning in mid-November, Brigadier General Edward Hatch's cavalry, acting as a screen for the Union troops at Pulaski, managed to pick up a mix of prisoners and deserters who all reported Hood's men were on the march for Tennessee. But unfortunately, both Generals Schofield and Thomas were slow to grasp the fact that Hood was moving north with the intent of interposing his army between the Federal soldiers at Pulaski and those gathering at Nashville. On the November 22, Hatch sent additional intelligence advising that Hood was at Lawrenceburg west of Pulaski and heading for the railroad. The day before, November 21, Thomas finally ordered Schofield to fall back and concentrate at Columbia. At this point Schofield realized that Hood was closer to Columbia than he was. And as a result, his troops set off on a day-and-night forced march, arriving barely ahead of Hood. [19]

On November 25, Chambers jotted in his journal: "We threw up a line of works on the right of the pike south of town. Light skirmishing

---

[18] Chambers, *War Fever Cured*, 76-78.

[19] Cope, *The 15th Ohio Volunteers*, 591-595; Winston Groom, *Shrouds of Glory: Atlanta to Nashville, the Last Great Campaign of the Civil War* (New York: The Atlantic Monthly Press, 1995), 128-129.

going on in front at times all day. With an occasional artillery shot." For November 26, he recorded that the enemy drove in the pickets leaving four wounded and capturing four others, while mortally wounding the brigade's inspector general. "Subsequently our boys rallied and drove the rebs back again. Skirmishing kept up all day." Skirmishing continued on the twenty-seventh, with the Eighty-ninth leaving their works at dark and falling back through Columbia, crossing the Duck River and camping about a mile-and-half north of the stream. "We marched four or five miles this morning in a very roundabout way and went back in sight of town near the river," Chambers noted on the November 28. Once in place the brigade commenced forming a new line and building light works. At times throughout the day the sound of skirmishing could be heard along with occasional artillery firing. The twenty-ninth found the two sides skirmishing most of the day where the Franklin-to-Columbia Pike crossed the Duck River. Chambers explained there was heavy artillery firing at the same point for awhile during the morning and again in the evening. During the latter the rebs tried to force, and succeeded in crossing the river, but they "were soon driven back by our boys." The Railroaders pulled out as darkness came on and marched toward Franklin, reaching Spring Hill shortly after midnight. Chambers noted that "the 2nd Div. of our Corps has been fighting the rebs near Spring Hill all day. Holding them in check without any definite result however." Their effort more than likely saved Schofield's army.[20]

Hood held to his plan of getting behind Schofield and cutting him off from Thomas at Nashville. While using Lee's Corps to hold the Federals in place at Columbia, Hood with Cheatham's and Stewart's Corps turned east and crossed the Duck River at the Davis' Ford Road and struck out for Spring Hill, a village on the turnpike connecting Columbia and Franklin. With the sun sinking in the autumn sky, Hood's men closed in on the Federal defenders holding the pike. Just as it looked like the bluecoats would be overrun and the trap sprung, reinforcements appeared and averted a disaster. With darkness, the day's fighting sputtered to a stop. Suddenly cognizant of the pending disaster, Schofield abandoned Columbia. Twenty

---

[20]   Chambers, *War Fever Cured*, 79-80.

thousand desperate Union soldiers trudged down the turnpike and quietly slipped past Hood's sleeping army, whose campfires were clearly visible in the darkness.[21]

Having escaped the trap, Schofield's army rushed off to Franklin and safety. Hood awoke to the news that his blue-coated quarry was gone and reacted by angrily setting off in hot pursuit. Danger was not only in the rear of the fleeing bluecoats but also on their flanks as Forrest's horsemen hovered about, looking for any opportunity to strike the Federal wagons. On that fateful last day of November, Company A Private Joel R. Chambers noted in his diary: "We left Spring Hill this morning at daylight. The rebs made a dash on our wagon train this morning at sunrise but our Brigade formed and soon drove them off." By 10:00 A.M . . ., the Eighty-ninth reached Franklin where they halted for breakfast, and afterward the brigade continued on, crossing the Little Harpeth River and camping north of town. Here, the Third division, which included the Eighty-ninth, was held in reserve and assigned to guard the army's supply trains. From this vantage point, the Railroaders observed the Battle of Franklin. Frustrated by the Yankees' narrow escape, Hood frontally attacked Schofield's barricaded troops, without artillery support, and suffered 6,252 casualties of which 1,750 were killed, including six generals. Chambers wrote one succinct sentence describing the destructive fight. "During the afternoon the rebs assaulted our works that were held by the 1st and 2nd Divisions of the 4th Corps and part of the 23d Corps but were repulsed with terrible slaughter." It was pitch dark when the fighting died out. Jim Tomlinson observed the rebel attack at Franklin and wrote that the enemy "charged our entire line several times. Some times they would take the works at different places," but "our men was the match for them." He noted the Union defenders "captured 1,500 men and 15 flags . . . ." He wrote the Rebel prisoners were quoted telling the Yankees that Hood said "that he was going to take Nashville and winter in Kentucky." The Eighty-ninth along with the First Brigade was ordered "back to the river in order . . . to

---

[21]   Bailey, *The Chessboard of War*, 80-90; Groom, *Shrouds of Glory*, 152; James Lee McDonough and, Thomas L. Connelly. *Five Tragic Hours: The Battle of Franklin* (Knoxville: The University of Tennessee Press, 1983), 36-57; Sword, *The Confederacy's Last Hurrah: Spring Hill, Franklin and Nashvilles*, 103-139.

cover the retreat of the army." Chambers recorded: "We left the river this morning [December 1] at four o'clock and after a forced march of 18 miles we reached Nashville. The rebs gave us no trouble on the march. We took up position before dark." He explained that on December 2 that "we threw up a line of works today and are now ready for the rebs when ever they want to call on us."[22]

The day after arriving in Nashville, Jim Tomlinson wrote a lengthy account of the Eight-ninth's travails to his mother back in Augusta, Illinois, but foremost he said that "[Joel and he were] both well but somewhat the worse of wear." Corporal Tomlinson, a veteran soldier who was not given to exaggeration, stated that the regiment had "had some of the hardest marching that I ever saw. The most of [which] was after night and that made it worse . . . ." He wrote that the men "had not slept eny for more than 48 hours . . . ." The Enemy was at our heels with a force," he added. Still feeling the effect of the gunshot wound suffered at Pickett's Mill, Tomlinson commented: "My leg has hurt me some since we marched . . . and nothing don't help it enuff . . . ." But on the positive side, Tomlinson told his mother that he was now well supplied with "fruit, salt, pork, hard bread, coffee and fresh beef." After last winter in East Tennessee, Tomlinson knew to prepare for cold weather and informed his mother that he had also "picked up an old overcoat," giving him "all the winter clothing" he wanted.[23]

*   *   *

Union troops on arriving in Nashville worked around the clock building defenses to ward off the Hood's Rebels. With his troops busy with picks, axes and spades, General Thomas simultaneously set about molding an army from the hodge-podge collection of units ordered to the Tennessee capital. On November 30, A. J. Smith's Sixteenth Corps arrived—9,000 tough veterans who had fought at

---

22   Chambers, *War Fever Cured*, 80-81; Tomlinson, Sally Ryan, *In Good Courage: The Civil War Letters of William James Tomlinson*, 21-22; Long, *Civil War Day by Day*, 603; Sword, *The Confederacy's Last Hurrah*, 151, 167, 250.

23   Tomlinson, Sally Ryan, *In Good Courage: The Civil War Letters of William James Tomlinson*, 21-22.

Vicksburg, on the Red River campaign, and throughout Missouri. Smith's command bolstered the 4,000 men who had garrisoned at Nashville. Coming from Chattanooga was Major General James B. Steedman's contingent of 8,500 troops, many of whom were black soldiers. By the morning of December 2, Wilson's badly depleted cavalry corps of 6,500 men rode in on jaded mounts. But by far the largest component of Thomas' command were the 24,000 men of the Fourth and Twenty-third Corps, who had beat back Hood's horde at Franklin. Thomas organized his force around his largest element of combat-tested troops, the Fourth Corps. On December 2, Hood's infantry showed up and, seeing Nashville's line of defenses, began digging its own entrenchments.[24]

General Thomas immediately notified Washington that he intended to remain in Nashville's fortifications while he refitted and remounted Wilson's cavalry. Having heard similar words from McClellan and Rosecrans, Lincoln was nonplussed with Thomas' plan and turned to Grant to spur him into action. Grant too was critical of Thomas for failing to finish Hood off after dealing him a staggering defeat at Franklin. Grant complained to Thomas that time only strengthened the Rebels, and that he should pounce on Hood before he recovered. Meanwhile, Hood, with no long range strategy and a force too small to besiege Nashville, was unwilling to retreat. Low on food and ammunition, he held to the twin delusions of receiving additional troops from the Trans-Mississippi Department and of Thomas faltering when he attacked. Bear in mind that Thomas' force would grow to more than twice the size of the ill-fed and poorly-clothed rebels facing them.

Prodded by both Lincoln at Washington and Grant at City Point, Thomas continued his deliberate preparations with the aim not only to defeat Hood but also to destroy his army in the process. Implementation of the attack was delayed by the sudden onset of a winter snowstorm that struck around noon on the December 7. By the morning of the eighth the snow gave way to biting cold. On the ninth, a second front hit Nashville. The cold further intensified with the temperature dropping below zero on December 11. The ground was covered with several inches of frozen sleet and snow—nothing

---

[24]   Sword, *The Confederacy's Last Hurrah*, 276-277.

moved and the soldiers huddled in their tents and shacks to stay warm. Thomas wired Washington on the thirteenth that he would attack with the first thaw that allowed his men to march. But by now a frustrated Grant had concluded to relieve Thomas of command and replace him with General John A. Logan. Grant ordered Logan to Nashville, but stipulated that if Thomas had attacked by the time Logan reached Louisville, he was to remain there and await further orders. By the morning of December 14, milder temperatures returned and the snow and ice rapidly melted. Thomas determined to move the following day.[25]

*   *   *

"Considerable firing done along the line today," Joel Chambers recorded in his diary for December 3. And as a consequence, the Eighty-ninth was ordered into the line that evening. Many in the ranks thought the enemy was preparing to attack. Nothing materialized, however, and the firing eventually slackened and quieted to an occasional shot. The following day the Railroaders provided four companies for the picket line, including Chambers' A Company. Throughout the day three Federal batteries kept up a continual fire on the enemy without getting a reply. When relieved from picket and back in camp, Chambers remarked that there was some picket firing during day "but not near so much shelling as there was yesterday." On December 8, Chambers and Tomlinson constructed a shebang complete with chimney. The effort was timely, for Chambers wrote that the next day "it rained and sleeted all forenoon and then tapered off with snow making it very disagreeable." He jotted on December 10 that it was "cold and dreary. Everything is very quiet. I have heard but a few shots during the day." On the eleventh, he reported: "Nothing now going on today. The weather is very cold. The sun has shone bright all day but has had but little effect the snow being dry and crusty even at noon." The following day he annotated, "We were ordered to draw

---

[25] Bailey, *The Chessboard of* War, 140-147; Foote, Shelby, *The Civil War, A Narrative, Red River to Appomattox* (New York: Vintage Books, 1986), 675-688; Sword, *The Confederacy's Last Hurrah*, 277-278, 301-312.

all the clothing we needed and to be ready to march at a moments notice." He noted for December 13 that "a rebel came in to our Brigade today and reported the rebs in strong force but on short rations." Everything was still quiet on the fourteenth.[26]

Wednesday, December 14, William James Tomlinson, or Jim, as his cousin Joel Chambers referred to him, was on duty in the trenches when he took time to write his widowed mother back in Hancock County, Illinois. "Well, we are laying in [a] line of battle behind a green line of breast works with the enemy in front of us yet but the longer they stop there the worse it will be for them." He wrote that recently he had not been very well and said that he been "bothered with [a] headache and [a] cold . . . ." Adding to his woes was the fact that "the weather has been very cold and disagreeable for several days." However, he was pleased that the commissary department was providing the regiment with "plenty to eat and plenty of good clothing;" but pointed out, "we will kneed all that we can get for I think we will be on the tramp all winter." Whether it was the thought of the upcoming battle or something else, Tomlinson reminded his mother that he had served 28 months and had only eight more remaining.[27]

Showing up at Nashville with money in their pockets, neither the thought of the impending battle nor a major winter storm prevented many of the Railroaders from taking advantage of what the city had to offer. Charles Capron expressed it this way: "We had just been paid before coming to Nashville and having been out of the world as you may say for a year and having nothing to eat but hardtack and bacon it is not to be wondered as if the boys did go in rather steep. I know I went in heavy. In fact it seemed [to] us if I never would be satisfied." Capron explained that the regiment "had full liberty to go to town. That is they would give us a pass whenever we asked for it, but I never took the trouble to ask them for a pass, but write one and approve it myself and go to town whenever I chose to. I was down three days and went to the theater 3 nights." Still others, like Jim Tomlinson, sent their money home. When Sergeant George

---

26   Chambers, *War Fever Cured*, 81-84.

27   Tomlinson, Sally Ryan, *In Good Courage: The Civil War Letters of William James Tomlinson*, 22.

W. Price of Company A was granted a furlough, Tomlinson gave him $100, most of his pay, to take to his mother back in Augusta, Illinois.[28]

No matter what an individual soldier did with his money, they each had an appointment with destiny. Hood had come north, laying it all on the line, and the final battle of the campaign was about to be fought. Odds against him or not, there would be no backing down; no withdrawal or admission of failure. His adversary, General Thomas, likewise, was determined that this fight would finish Hood and his army as an effective fighting force. With the clearing of the weather, the time had come for the end game to be played out.

During the evening of December 14, Colonel Abel D. Streight received instructions directly from General Beatty, commanding the Third division, to be ready to move at 6:30 A.M . . ., with sixty rounds of cartridges per man. Streight's men, the First brigade, were to form on the left of Post's Second brigade "in two lines, the first deployed in a line of battle, and the second in double column at half distance within supporting distance of the front line." At daylight four companies of the Eighty-ninth, B, F, D, and E, relieved four companies of the Fifty-first Indiana on the skirmish line forward of the breastworks. The rest of the Railroaders Joel Chambers explained had "received orders to march at daylight but did not go until eleven o'clock." In typical military fashion the hurry-up was followed by several hours of waiting. The delay was caused by a dense fog which hung over the two armies throughout the morning hours. But finally, around 11:00 A.M . . ., the fog lifted and the first brigade moved over the works and formed. The first line consisted of the Eighth Kansas on the right and the Fifty-first Indiana on the left while the second line, formed in double column, was composed of the Eighty-ninth Illinois on the right, the Fifteenth Ohio in the center, and the Forty-ninth Ohio on the left. More time passed until the final order was received around 1:00 P.M. "We then moved out and the skirmishers advanced followed by two lines of battle," wrote Joel Chambers. "Our advance was sharply contested at first, but the impetuosity of the men seemed almost uncontrollable, and soon

---

[28]   Capron, letter, February 12, 1865; Tomlinson, Sally Ryan, *In Good Courage: The Civil War Letters of William James Tomlinson*, 22-23.

all firing ceased on our side, and the only unsettled question . . . seemed to be . . . who among the officers and men should reach the works first," reported Colonel Streight. Speaking for those in the ranks, Chambers stated: "We routed the rebs pell mell and took their first line of works with many prisoners of whom our reg't took over one hundred." Private Capron later recalled that after "having got our lines formed and every thing ready at 12 o'clock, the word was given to charge them which we did up in style, taking the first line of works with a number of prisoners, losing but 2 or 3 men. We stopped there and built a line of works . . . ."[29]

Unfortunately, the exuberant attack had only taken the Confederates' skirmish line, with the main entrenchments lying beyond. So, unbeknownst to blue-clad infantry of the First brigade, another assault was ordered. Private Capron later related the chain of events as he remembered them. "We was lying around [and] the cook had just brought coffee when the batteries suddenly opened and the boys on the right set up a yell and we looked over to the second line of works and the rebels was ever lastingly skinning out, instantly the boys set up a yell threw their coffee, cups and all, and away we went after them." Colonel Streight in his official report explained that at about 3:00 P.M. he "received orders to advance upon the second line of the enemy's works." Streight stated that the "brigade was promptly put in motion" and conformed to movements of troops on their right, "and amid a most galling fire" from both the left flank and the front "carried the works in double-quick time, capturing a large number of prisoners and small arms." Deviating from Streight's after-action report, Private Capron claimed: "Our Colonel had the halt sounded but it was no use, he could not stop us and on we rushed through [a] shower of bullets right on to the works we went and all that would not surrender was shot down." For his own part, Capron wrote: "I saw a battle flag making off and off I started to capture it but I could not catch him so I concluded to shoot him and hauled up and blazed away but I was so tired I could not hold my gun steady and missed him and before I could load again he was out of my reach and the rally was sounded and I was obliged

29   OR, Vol. 45, Pt. 1, 294,297; Van Horne, History of the Army of the Cumberland, II-229; War Fever Cured, 84; Capron, letter, February 12, 1865.

to fall in to the ranks again." Lieutenant-Colonel Williams reported the Eighty-ninth captured 78 prisoners in the second charge. For the day, he wrote: "Our regimental loss in these two assaults was surprisingly small, which I attribute entirely to the celerity and vigor of the assaulting lines. Not an officer or man hesitated a moment, but rushed at the enemy on the double-quick, or rather run, and never stopped until the enemy's works were scaled and the victory won." For the fifteenth, Williams listed the Eighty-ninth's losses at 2 killed and 4 wounded.[30]

With the day's fighting over, the Eighty-ninth "was moved to the left about a half a mile, and after considerable marching and countermarching in the dark [the men] bivouacked in an open field." The next morning at sunrise, the Railroaders, with the brigade, moved down the Franklin Pike a number of miles until they encountered the enemy's works on Overton Hill. Here they halted and took a position in the rear of Post's Second brigade. The Fourth Corps commander, Brigadier General Thomas J. Wood, contemplated the situation. Overton Hill anchored the right of Hood's line. If it could be captured, the Rebel line would be turned and one of his two possible routes of retreat, the Franklin Pike, removed. Wood and Colonel Philip Sidney Post of the Fifty-ninth Illinois were both ambitious and viewed this as an opportunity of a lifetime. Post especially was eager for the recognition that could earn him a brigadier's star and offered to make a personal reconnaissance of the Rebel position. Back in forty-five minutes, Post confirmed it was a very strong position, but thought that a successful assault was possible and worth the try. Wood agreed to give it a go.[31]

Leading the assault would be Post's brigade supported by Streight's regiments and a brigade of colored troops from Steedman's division. With skirmishers scattered out in front, Post's brigade formed in two lines. When the bugle sounded, it was a little before 3:00 P.M., and the blue-clad lines headed forward. From Overton Hill the entrenched Rebels along with a four-gun battery looked down on the advancing blue infantry. Post's skirmishers made it safely to

---

30 *OR*, Vol. 45, Pt. 1, 295, 297; Capron, letter, February 12, 1865.

31 *OR*, Vol. 45, Pt. 1, 295, 298; Peter Cozzens, "Forgotten Hero: Philip Sidney Post," *Illinois Historical Journal*, Volume 84, Number 2 (Summer 1991) 87-88.

the base of the hill, but at this point the Rebel artillery opened up and soon volleys of fire erupted from butternut trenches. Caught in a maelstrom of lead and steel, the charging Federals were slowed by lines of abatis waiting to impale the unwary. With the air filled with the missiles of death, the bluecoats sought the shelter of mother earth and lay flat hugging the wet ground. The men were caught in an exposed position, and here occurred an incident, that would haunt William R. Hartpence of the Fifty-first Indiana as long as he lived. He observed First Lieutenant Peter G. Tait of the Eighty-ninth Illinois "standing a little in advance of his regiment," which had intermingled with the Fifty-first during the assault. With his eyes fixed on the young officer, Hartpence watched as Tait "was stuck by a cannon ball near the center of his body, tearing a great hole in the left side. As he fell, he threw his right arm around to his side, when his heart and left lung dropped out into it. The heart continued to throb for twenty minutes, its pulsations being distinctly seen by his agonized comrades, who stood there and saw the noble life fade out in heroic self-sacrifice."[32]

Private Charles Capron of Company A too recalled that afternoon and wrote: "About two o'clock the Ball opened in earnest. The earth fairly shook under the fire of [the] heavy guns and the heavens clouded with the smoke from the guns. They threw a solid shot at our batteries but it came over to our regiment striking an officer by the name of Tate cutting off both his arms and drove his heart out of him just as he was giving a command." Federal artillery now "opened a vigorous fire" on the Rebels, allowing the attackers, reinforced by the colored brigade, to resume the assault. Even with the artillery support, Private Capron explained that we were "advancing directly into the jaws of death. I was within a few feet of our captain [Edward P. Walker] when he was hit. [He] clapped his hand on his breast and said my God I am shot and immediately fell. I could not do anything for him and on I went. But it was no use for we could not get the works and we was obliged to fall back." Lieutenant-Colonel Williams wrote that in the "charge on the enemy's works; the troops behaved

---

32   Cousins, "Forgotten Hero: Philip Sidney Post," 88; Hartpence, William R., *History of the Fifty-first Indiana Veteran Volunteer Infantry*, (Cincinnati, Ohio: The Robert Clarke Co., 1894), 264-265.

gallantly, but on account of the murderous fire and stubborn resistance of the enemy, [we] were compelled to withdraw, which was done in good order and without confusion."[33]

Capron noted that "there was a brigade of colored troops charged on our left. They got cut up worse than we did. In front of one of the rebel's cannon there was about 100 of them lying in 2 rods square." "I have often herd men say that they would not fight beside a negro soldier, on the 16th the whites and blacks charged together and they fell just as well as we did," wrote Sergeant Jim Tomlinson of Company A. "The Cornels servant," Tomlinson told his mother, "picked up a gun and went in with us and fought within six feet of Joel [Chambers]." He fervently added, "When you here eney one say that negro soldiers wont fight just tell them that they ly for me."[34]

Jim Tomlinson had had a close call during the charge on Overton Hill, and by the time he was able to write his mother, a rumor had gone around back home that he had been wounded in the hip. His brother Uriah thought it best to say nothing to their mother until "he was shure of it." Tomlinson appreciated his brother's good judgment in not saying anything to their mother. In writing her, he touched on his good luck that afternoon. "I cant see how I missed getting wounded on the 16th. A ball cut my canteen strap where it crossed my brest."[35]

When the Union troops came off Overton Hill, they fell back to their original position to reform. While in the midst of reorganizing, they heard the cheers of thousands of voices raised in the sound of victory. Off to their right, they could see the enemy's line giving way, and shortly the Rebels on Overton Hill could also be seen fleeing. With this turn of events, "we were again ordered forward," Chambers wrote. Afterward he penned in his diary, "The rebs left their works in a perfect rout leaving their artillery, many small arms, and a large number of prisoners." He recorded that "our loss today was considerable heavier than yesterday. Our Brig had

33 Capron, letter, February 12, 1865; OR, Vol. 45, Pt. 1, 298.
34 Tomlinson, Sally Ryan, In Good Courage: The Civil War Letters of William James Tomlinson, 22-23.
35 Ibid.

about one hundred killed and wounded. Our reg't had two killed and seventeen wounded." But, overshadowing their losses was the sight of Hood's beaten army abandoning their lines. Chambers' cousin, Jim Tomlinson said that "we routed them and drove them like sheep," and "ther never was an army so badly demoralized as here." We "captured lots of them barfooted and hungry."[36]

The morning of December 17, the Eighty-ninth moved out early heading in the direction of Franklin. Joel R. Chambers hurriedly recorded in his diary, "Our Cavalry is skirmishing with the rear guard of the rebel army all the time. Capturing small squads of prisoners all along the road." That evening the Railroaders camped near Franklin on the north side of the Harpeth River. "We crossed the river this morning and pushed on after the flying rebs. Our Cavalry is still skirmishing with them and bringing in squads of prisoners," Chambers scratched on the eighteenth. That night the regiment camped three miles south of Spring Hill. On some days the Eighty-ninth marched further than others, but the chase never let up, continuing day-in and day-out with the Federal cavalry dogging and nipping at the Rebel's heels as they withdrew south. Captain James F. Copp of Company F sent his father a letter from near Columbia, Tennessee, dated December 20 in which he stated: "The enemy has retreated as fast as possible and would fight only when pressed. It is, indeed, the most demoralized army I ever saw." Five days later, Christmas, the Railroaders marched 15 miles and made camp near Pulaski. It was well after dark when the men settled in, and Chambers could hear the blue-clad horsemen having a sharp fight with the rebel rear guard. "The next day we went through Pulaski. There was several rebels laying around that our cavalry had stretched out while they was trying to burn bridge. They did not succeed however and we crossed anxious to capture their rear guard," but the enemy "succeeded in keeping out of our way till about 3 o'clock when our cavalry came on to them and a sharp fight took place which resulted in them drawing off" and we "taking a few prisoners," Capron later recalled. On December 28, the Eighty-ninth crossed into Alabama, camping that evening at Lexington. December 30, General Wood

---

[36] Chambers, *War Fever Cured*, 84-85; Tomlinson, Sally Ryan, *In Good Courage: The Civil War Letters of William James Tomlinson*, 22-23.

received a dispatch from General Thomas ending the campaign and directing the Fourth Corps to go into winter quarters in the vicinity of Huntsville, Alabama. Six days later, January 5, the Railroaders reached Huntsville and continued on south another four miles. The following day Chambers entered in his diary, "We received orders to put cabins and make ourselves comfortable." Once the work was complete, Tomlinson wrote his mother: "We have a hut 7 by 10 with a good fireplace, and every thing complete except seets. Ther is four of us together. We have one bunk over the other so we have plenty of room. This is called our winter quarters." Being somewhat permanent, Chambers wrote: "The camp is called Camp Green in honor of our late inspector general [Shepherd Green] who died of the wound he received at Columbia."[37]

On January 8, Lieutenant-Colonel William D. Williams completed his report of the campaign and in conclusion said:

> "Great praise and credit is due the officers and enlisted men of the Eighty-ninth . . . for their heroic conduct in the battles before Nashville, and their patient forbearance during all the hardships incident to such a glorious though tedious campaign; and . . . though depleted in numbers, yet ready at any and all times to battle for their country's flag and the Union."

The two-day Battle of Nashville effectively finished the Confederate Army of Tennessee, and with it, for all intents and purposes, the war in the west. The Eighty-ninth's losses during the campaign amounted to 4 killed and 16 wounded.[38]

---

[37] Chambers, *War Fever Cured*, 85-91; *Rock Island Argus*, December 31, 1864; Capron, letter, February 12, 1865; Cope, *The 15th Ohio Volunteers*, 675-676; Tomlinson, Sally Ryan, *In Good Courage: The Civil War Letters of William James Tomlinson*, 23.

[38] *OR*, Vol. 45, Pt. 1, 298.

CHAPTER 15

"OUR HISTORY IS WRITTEN ON THE HEAD-BOARDS OF RUDE MADE GRAVES . . ."

The remnants of Hood's army crossed the Tennessee River, escaped annihilation, and moved off to Tupelo, Mississippi to rest and reorganize. Hood's disastrous six-month stint as the commander of the Army of Tennessee ended with his resignation on January 13. P. G. T. Beauregard temporarily took command of the remaining men, who numbered around 17,700. But in a desperate need for troops to confront Sherman, President Jefferson Davis ordered the bulk of what remained of the Army of Tennessee east to the Carolinas. Seeing the war was lost, most of these men no longer had the stomach for more hardship or fighting and chose to melt away. Therefore, by the time this remnant succeeded in reaching Joe Johnston's force only around 5,000 men were left to rally around the Rebel colors.

Meanwhile the Railroaders settled into winter quarters, and with time to read, the men poured over every newspaper that arrived in camp. The articles reported that the Army of the Potomac's siege at Petersburg was slowly and methodically squeezing the life out of Lee's Army of Northern Virginia. The papers revealed that Sherman's army, after surfacing at Savannah, had crossed into South Carolina, the cradle of the rebellion, and on the first of February began burning its way north. And now, for the first time since enlisting in August 1862, the Railroaders could sense the war was nearing its end. They could see the figurative light at the end of the tunnel. But, even though the Eighty-ninth no longer confronted an organized enemy, the men on picket duty or forage detail had to be wary of the occasional bushwhacker or guerilla band that watched and waited for the opportunity to pick-off a lone Federal soldier or small group of bluecoats. It was in this environment of hope and survival that these weary soldiers lived one day at a time.

*   *   *

The army's subsistence rations still required supplementing and on January 11 Joel Chambers was sent out on a brigade foraging detail. That evening the men returned "with the wagons well loaded with corn." Wednesday, January 14, Private Joel R. Chambers no fan of Colonel Hotchkiss reported that he had "returned to the Reg't today having been sick and absent for a couple of months." Significantly more important to Chambers was the arrival of a comrade who had been missing in action since the fight at Pickett's Mill. Chambers noted in his diary that "a member of our Co returned today from prison having been captured near Dallas the 27th of May last. He gave us some information about our old friend Eugene Austin and a number of others that were captured at the same time." After visiting with the same returnee, Jim Tomlinson felt compelled to write his mother. "I should not have wrote so soon but one of the men that was taken prisoner on the 27 of May came back to the Company night before last. He was paroled on the 23 of November and exchanged on the 25. He was with Eugene [Austin] at Andersonville." Tomlinson learned that "Eugene was sick nearly all the time" and was sent to Charleston around September 1. He explained to his mother that in all likelihood Austin had been exchanged as "they ar exchangeing thare." He added: "It has been ther game to get rid of the sick first so I hope that he is in the land of freedom again if not home." Tomlinson continued: "When you get this take it or send it to his mother. I kno that she would give all that she has to here from him. Tell her to have courage. Ther is hope as long as ther is life. If they have herd from him, let me know wher and how he is getting along." While Tomlinson was finishing the letter to his mother, his company commander brought him information that Eugene Austin had been exchanged and was last in Annapolis, Maryland. Tomlinson passed on the good news and quipped that his friend was "in a Christian land where he will not starve . . ."[1]

Many of the captured Railroaders were not as fortunate as Eugene Austin. The Reverend Edmund W. Hicks in his *History of Kendall County Illinois* wrote: "Of the deaths in the Eighty-ninth, nearly one-forth must be credited to Andersonville. Fifty of its men were there first reduced to skeletons and then laid away in their hastily made graves." The only other Illinois regiment to exceed this number was the Sixteenth Cavalry, who left 80 men "in the soil outside the pine log stockade of that awful prison pen." William F. Fox in the work, *Regimental Losses in the American Civil War*, listed a total of 66 men from the Eighty-ninth died in Confederate prisons.[2]

Residing in a fixed camp, the Railroaders returned to regular drill and periodic inspections. Both measures are time honored methods used to maintain order and discipline, but probably did little to relieve the dullness and tedium of camp life that quickly overcame the men. Chambers diary entry for January 17 was as follows: "Our arms, ammunition, knapsacks, and quarters were inspected by Lieut Davis, Brigade inspector. He expressed himself very well pleased with the appearance of the Reg't." On January 21, Chambers penned, "We received orders to have Co and Battalion drill each day and Brig drill on Fridays." Sundays the men had regimental inspection and dress parade in the evening. As January wore on, Chambers penned, "All quiet and rather dull in camp." When not engaged in drill, policing the camp, or preparing for inspection, some of the men were always on picket or guard duty. On January 19, Chambers briefly remarked in his diary: "The Safeguards that have been out from our Div guarding citizens' property were ordered in today

---

[1]   Chambers, *War Fever Cured*, 92-93; Tomlinson, Sally R., *In Good Courage: The Civil War Letters of William James Tomlinson*, 24.

[2]   E. W. Hicks. *History of Kendall County Illinois* (Aurora, Illinois: Knickerbocker and Hodder Printers, 1877), 308; Fox, *Regimental Losses in the American Civil War*, 373.

owing to some of them having been murdered by bushwhackers within the last few days."[3]

Alcohol abuse, unfortunately, was the downfall of many a soldier, and the Eighty-ninth suffered its share. The officer with the unusual, maybe even checkered, past demonstrated how demon rum could be the ruin of a man. Having returned to the service under the alias "Frank Sumter," Andrew G. Miller, Jr. was acknowledged for bravery at Missionary Ridge, and in March 1864, was commissioned a second lieutenant by the Governor of Illinois. Still a troubled man, the West Point graduate, regular army captain, and Colonel of the First Maryland Cavalry was openly punished and humiliated for the abuse of spirits and a lapse in character. In his diary entry for January 29, 1865, Private Chambers recorded: "We had dress parade and had the sentence of a Court Martial read to us in the case of Lieut Miller Co C of our Reg't charged with drunkenness, neglect of duty, and absence without leave. He was found guilty and sentenced to forfeit four months pay allowance and to be publicly reprimanded by Gen Comn'd'g Div which was done in severe terms by Brig Gen Sam'l Beatty."[4]

More important to the rank and file than Lieutenant Miller's verbal flogging were the bits and pieces the men were hearing of peace negotiations. In a letter to his parents written January 31, Charles Capron saw fit to comment on the subject. He said: "There is pretty strong talk of peace now and God knows I hope they will make peace for I have seen blood enough spilled." In his diary entry for January 30, Private Chambers summarized his fellow soldiers' chatter. He wrote: "There has been considerable interest in camp for the last week on account of numerous peace rumors that have been afloat. Some credit is given them by some while others discredit them altogether." The rumor was, in fact, true. Francis Preston Blair, Sr., an aging Washington political leader, had, on his own, contacted Confederate President Davis to explore the possibilities of peace. By

---

[3]   Chambers, *War Fever Cured*, 93-94.

[4]   Cullum, *Biographical Register of Officers and Graduates of the U. S. Military Academy*, II-361, *History and Roster of Maryland Volunteers, War of 1861-5*, Vol. I (Baltimore: Press of Guggenheimer, Weil & Co., 1898), 704; Chambers, *War Fever Cured*, 95.

mid-January Blair had traveled to Richmond in hope of speeding along possible peace negotiations. Through Blair's effort, Davis and Lincoln exchanged letters. Both men affirmed their wish for peace, but the sticking point was Davis' desire for two separate countries, while with Lincoln, it was one country. On February 3, Lincoln and Seward sat down with Confederate envoys. Lincoln at once re-affirmed his stance that the authority of the Federal government over all the United States had to be agreed upon by the rebellious states. Having never recognized the Confederate States as a separate nation, the President would not agree to an armistice or entertain any sort of treaty with the Rebel government. Lincoln demanded an unconditional restoration of the Union. The peace effort subsequently ended, and the war continued. But as much as the men in blue wanted peace, to a man they would have concurred with Private Capron when he wrote, "They have trodden on the best government that ever was made and they are a set of high born fools."[5]

At noon on January 31, orders were given to the men to be ready to march the following morning. Maybe it was the thought of breaking camp, more than likely alcohol was involved, but whatever the reason, that night a number of the Railroaders became a bit rowdy. Corporal Tomlinson mischievously put it, "we had some sport the night before we left." It started out, Tomlinson wrote, when "some of the boys got to blasting stumps all threw the brigade and yelling so that no one could sleep." Soon the miscreants began verbally abusing the conscripts with the Fifty-first Indiana, who gave back as good as they got. Colonel Streight, temporarily commanding the brigade, had the bugler call the men to attention and then summoned the regimental officers to his tent where he proceeded, in no uncertain terms, to dress them down for their men's behavior. Not finished, Streight ordered the Hoosiers and the Railroaders to form in a line of battle and "to stand . . . under arms till midnight as punishment." Speaking on the discipline meted out, Joel Chambers said: "This was the first time I was ever on extra duty and the entire reg't Col and all was with me so I was not lonesome." Chambers

---

[5] Capron, letter, January 31, 1865; Chambers, *War Fever Cured*, 96; Long, *The Civil War Day By Day*, 616, 622, 625, 633.

continued that over the next few days "the boys of the 15th and 49th Ohio 8th Kansas and our Reg't have a great deal of fun over the dress parade at midnight."[6]

The brigade was up early, leaving camp at 5:00 A.M . . . and marching to Huntsville where at 10:00 A.M . . . they boarded a train for Stevenson, Alabama, arriving there around 1:00 P.M. "The weather being very fine we were allowed to ride in or on top of the cars whichever we choosed," Private Chambers wrote. Around 3:00 P.M. that afternoon they departed Stevenson for Nashville, arriving the following morning. After a breakfast near the depot, the brigade moved out to the place where they first drove the Rebels on December 15 and went into camp. Five days later and after innumerable rumors, the Eighty-ninth broke camp, marched back to depot, and around 3:00 P.M. climbed on or into the cars and set out for Huntsville, arriving a little before daylight at Stevenson. Herded back on the cars later that morning, the Railroaders rolled into Huntsville about three in the afternoon. Leaving the cars the men marched out to the old camp they abandoned seven days earlier. Chambers remarked, "We found the greater part of our cabins all right. Some had been destroyed by fire mostly I think by the carelessness of the boys in leaving them." Chambers' cousin, Jim Tomlinson noted their "shanty was all right. We stretched the tents over it, shook the snow out of our beds and started a fire, got supper and then took the best night's sleep that I got since we left here." The next day, February 8, Chambers wrote: "The men are repairing their cabins, those that were partly or all destroyed. Everything seems so much like home in our old camp that I hardly realize having been away at all."[7]

The day after returning to Camp Green, February 8, Jim Tomlinson sent his mother a letter advising her that the Eighty-ninth was no longer at Nashville but back in Alabama. Somewhere along the way or while at Nashville, Tomlinson had heard or read more on the peace discussions taking place back east. Optimistic as to the

---

[6] Tomlinson, Sally Ryan, *In Good Courage: The Civil War Letters of William James Tomlinson*, 24; Chambers, *War Fever Cured*, 96-97.

[7] Chambers, *War Fever Cured*, 96-99; Tomlinson, *Civil War Letters of William James Tomlinson*, 24.

outcome, he expressed his opinion when writing home: "Ther has been a great deal of talk about peace. I think it will be settle before long. It has went so far that the southern people and the rebel army wer rejoicing over the news when the peace commishoners was sent from Richmond to confer on terms of peace. They did not make a hitch the first time but I look for them to meet again soon . . . ." No further meetings took place.[8]

When Chambers updated his diary about the trip back to Alabama, he omitted mentioning the stop at Murfreesboro. But, by the tenth of February, he saw fit to address what had taken place that night. He was mindful that ever since a cloud hung over the Railroaders. Chambers noted: "There is quite a number of rumors in camp. Some say . . . our Reg't is going back to Louisville under arrest for misconduct at Murfreesboro." He then explained that "some of the boys . . . were engaged in cleaning out a Sutler at that place." His tent mate, Charles Capron, provided more details of the episode. He wrote that "when we got to Murfreesboro, the boys being short of money made up their minds to go through some of the storekeepers." The rowdies "went through 3 stores, took what they wanted, killed one nigger, knocked over two guards, and played smash in general." A black fellow working for a sutler tried to protect his employer's wares from the mob. In doing so a struggle ensued and his neck was broken. The scuffle and the ensuing murder aroused the provost guard, who came to quell the ruckus and arrest the culprits. But, Capron related, "We told them if they fired a shot we would tear them limb for limb." Outnumbered and seeing they had killed one man, the guards laid down their weapons and stood aside. "We took what we wanted and came away quietly." With each passing day, the regiment waited to hear what the authorities would do. Word spread that the incident was reported to Major General Thomas, and it was in his hands. "Do not know what he [Thomas] will do with us nor don't care. I do not think there is much danger of any harm," Capron told his mother. And, he was correct since no charges were ever brought.[9]

---

[8] Tomlinson, Sally Ryan, *In Good Courage: The Civil War Letters of William James Tomlinson*, 25.

[9] Chambers, *War Fever Cured*, 100; Capron, letter, February 12, 1865.

Discipline throughout the regiment and the brigade at this time was tightened with corresponding punishment meted out to serve as a deterrent. Take for example, Private John D. Holdren of Company I, who, on February 13, was out on his own foraging. On returning to camp, he was arrested and tried for leaving the regiment without permission and pillaging. Convicted on February 23, he was sentenced to three months in the military prison at Nashville, which he fortunately never served. The nineteen-year-old Holdren was recruited by Colonel Hotchkiss on August 19, 1863 and followed his father to the Eighty-ninth—the elder Holdren having been killed at Stones River. A week after Holdren was nabbed; Joel Chambers was detailed to guard a comrade doing extra duty carrying a rail. Chambers noted the man had a reputation for being "a bully and one of the hardest cases in the Reg't." But he was not without a friend, as a Company C comrade "commenced cutting off a piece of the rail" to lighten his load. Chambers grabbed the fellow with the saw and turned him over to the corporal of the guard, saving himself from being charged with neglect of duty. On March 13, Chambers entered in his diary: "There was a man belonging to the Forty-ninth Ohio drummed through the Brigade camp today with a board tied to his back and the word mutineer marked on it. His crime was refusing to carry a rail when he was on extra duty." He was sent to military prison for the remainder of his term of service . . . ." In recounting the episode, Charles Capron added that the poor fellow would be serving "out the rest of his time with a ball & chain to his leg." Not unexpectedly, those in the ranks denounced the whole affair "as outrageously severe and unnecessarily humiliating."[10]

As the war wound down, every parent's or spouse's nightmare was that their child or husband would be one of the last to be killed or maimed. Having already lost one son to the war and a second discharged due to injuries, Jim Tomlinson's mother fretted over his well being. Her fears led her to encourage William James to find any means possible to get out of the service. If that was not possible, she begged him to obtain a furlough and come home. In February,

---

[10] *Descendants of Matthias Holdren,* [Internet website] 9Accessed December 12, 20050, http://www.duprel.com/holddes.html; Chambers, *War Fever Cured,* 102, 106; Capron, letter, March 15, 1865; Cope, *The 15th Ohio Volunteers,* 696-697.

he told her emphatically, "Mother, don't give yourself trubble about my getting a furlow. My term of service is rather short for to get a furlow now." By early March, Tomlinson, at first, attempted to comfort his mother when he wrote: "Ther is a great meny that says they don't think that we will leave here until our time is out. I hope that may be true for I had just as live stay here as eny other plase." But on the other hand, he had had enough and said as much: "Mother for heavensake dont say anything more about my getting a furlow time. I hope that you don't think that I would say anything to a general about furlow time. Ther is a soft plase on the top of my head but it is not soft enuff for that. If I should speak of it, I would be called the regimental fool . . . ." Not finished, he continued: "You may be shure that I will not stay eny longer than I can help. Therefore let it drop." He then reminded his mother that "the cause in which I am engaged is the same today that it was the day I enlisted. I enlisted for three years unless sooner discharged and I expect to serve them if they see fit to keep me that long. If they do, I shall not murmer at it. I will remain true to my country if I die by it." In the follow-up correspondence with his mother, Tomlinson responded: "I am glad that you have consented to say no more about my getting furlow time for it only seems to prolong my term. If it laid in my power, I would return home soon but I have put myself where I cant get out until they see fit.[11]

*   *   *

"Huntsville, Ala., has been left 220 miles in the distant wake, and the 89th finds herself to-day at New Market, East Tenn., a small village situated 28 miles from Knoxville, on the East Tennessee and Virginia railroad, and nine miles from Strawberry Plains on the Holstein river," Corporal Isaac K. Young of Company H explained in a letter to the *Kendall County Record*. At three in the afternoon on March 15, the Railroaders left Camp Green, marching to Huntsville where they boarded an eastbound train. Here Lieutenant-Colonel Williams, who had been on leave, met the regiment and took command. Around

---

[11]   Tomlinson, Sally Ryan, *In Good Courage: The Civil War Letters of William James Tomlinson*, 25-26.

midnight they passed though Stevenson, Alabama, but at daylight, near the base of Lookout Mountain, everything came to a standstill when a landslide covered the track. A couple of hours passed until the debris was cleared and the cars could run on into Chattanooga where the men were allowed off to stretch. By noon all were back on the cars, and the brigade started for Knoxville, arriving there shortly after dark on March 17. After a brief stop the train moved on to New Market where the Eighty-ninth's journey ended on the eighteenth. In the chess game of war, the re-location of the Railroaders' and the Fourth Corps to East Tennessee was essential in establishing communications through to Virginia and in preventing any Rebel movement in that direction. It had been about a year since the Eighty-ninth had left this same area to join Sherman's campaign to capture Atlanta.[12]

The Eighty-ninth may have changed location, but the routine was still the same—drill, picket, inspection, and the occasional review. "I am getting tired of drill, but drill I must," Jim Tomlinson complained to his brother in a letter written in late March. But as March gave way to April, more important to Tomlinson and his fellow soldiers were the events unfolding in the east. On March 29, Grant launched his final effort to take Richmond. Aware that this could lead to the end of the war, the Railroaders anxiously awaited the outcome of the campaign. The night of April 3, Capron penned in his diary, "We received news of the fall of Petersburg and Richmond in the evening and a salute of one hundred guns was fired at corps Head Quarters in honor of the victory." That afternoon the Eighty-ninth played the Forty-ninth Ohio in "a match game of base ball," Chambers recorded. He commented that "the game was played by twenty on a side. It was played fairly and with the very best of feelings throughout the entire game." The Railroaders came out on top by a score of 50 to 23.[13]

Bright and early on the April 4, the regiment was up and on the march, covering 19 miles and camping near Greenville. As for the

---

[12] *Kendall County Record*, April 6, 1865; Chambers, *War Fever Cured*, 107-108; *Adjutant General's Report*, 288.

[13] Tomlinson, Sally Ryan, *In Good Courage: The Civil War Letters of William James Tomlinson*, 26; Chambers, *War Fever Cured*, 113-114.

regiment's current location, Charles Capron in a letter home told his mother that there was a high probability they would stay here two or three weeks. He quickly transitioned to the current information from the East. "I expect you have heard the news of the fall of Richmond. Our biggest General prophesy [is] that the war will be over before a month. It is my earnest prayer that it may come true. For God knows that there has been men enough slaughtered and homes made desolate by the loss of husbands, fathers, brothers, and lovers." Corporal Tomlinson took up the subject of the war's coming end when he too wrote his mother. "We received a dispatch the other day saying that old Jeff [Davis] had throwed up his hand to General Lee with the understanding that he was to make one more trial and if he failed in that, he was to give it up as lost for ever." A confident Tomlinson pointed out: "I have no doubt but he will make a hard strugle but Grant and Sherman will cut him to pieces." And as a result, "I don't think that the war will last til my time is out . . . ."[14]

The four-year conflict ended five days later, April 9, at Appomattox Court House. "We received the news of the surrender of Gen Lee and the army of Northern Virginia to Lieut Gen'l Grant, and soon after dark it was officially confirmed," Joel Chambers began his diary entry for April 10. A happy and relieved bunch turned in for the night. But, "about midnight considerable firing was heard in the direction of Blue Springs and we were all ordered out under arms, but it was soon after ascertained that it was only the troops of the 2nd Div of our Corps stationed at that place who having imbibed a little of the 'O-be-joyful' were rejoicing and firing their muskets in honor of our great victories," Chambers noted. Seeing no need to join the celebration, the Railroaders called it a "good joke and quietly went back to bed." Writing home on the eleventh, Chambers' cousin Jim noted that he and Joel were "feeling good over the surrender." To add to this feeling, Tomlinson reported that "ther was 40 dezerters came in today. They seame to think that the war is plaid out and that they had beter return to ther homes while ther is a chance."[15]

[14] Capron, letter, April 5, 1865; Tomlinson, Sally Ryan, *In Good Courage: The Civil War Letters of William James Tomlinson*, 26.

[15] Chambers, *War Fever Cured*, 115-116; Tomlinson, Sally Ryan, *In Good Courage: The Civil War Letters of William James Tomlinson*, 27.

Elated as they were over Lee's surrender, it was business as usual for the men. Pickets were posted; men detailed to guard a forage train; company areas policed; and drill conducted. But on the April 13, Chambers wrote: "We had dress parade and received notice that on tomorrow we would celebrate our late victories by abstaining from all duty." Major General David S. Stanley commanding the Fourth Corps requested that the each regimental chaplain hold services thanking the Almighty for the recent Union victories. In addition to the religious services, Sergeant Isaac Young reported the corps artillery fired one hundred gun salute at noon "in honor of 'United States' Grant's recent triumphant successes in the capture of Petersburg, Richmond, and Gen Robert E. Lee, together with the entire army of Northern Virginia."[16]

April 15 found five companies of Railroaders back on picket, and that afternoon, Joel Chambers wrote that we "received the rumor that President Lincoln and Secretary Seward were assassinated and although the report was doubted, it caused a great deal of uneasiness . . . ." The following day Chambers confided in his diary that "the news of the death of the president was confirmed this morning. It threw a deep gloom over all the soldiers." That afternoon Chambers made his way to church, where he gazed upon a pulpit "shrouded with the Stars and Stripes ornamented with a wreath of flowers all of which was draped in the deepest mourning. The countenance of every soldier in the congregation told plainly of the sorrow felt on account of the great National loss." Joining the men was Major General David S. Stanley, who Chambers remarked was quite "solemn and sorrow stricken."[17]

Not everyone was in a period of mourning. In a celebratory mood, Colonel Hotchkiss arranged for a ball to be held at brigade headquarters. In need of decorations, he commandeered each regiment's colors and hung them from the rafters where the officers and the local belles could dance under them. Word of the dance and the requisition spread to the camps, and "soon after dark the boys of the regiments collected around . . . Head Quarters and demanded their colors." Hotchkiss brushed the crowd off, telling

---

[16] Chambers, *War Fever Cured*, 116-117; *Kendall County Record*, April 27, 1865.

[17] Chambers, *War Fever Cured*, 117-118.

them it was "an honor to the colors to be there" and ordered the men back to their camps. The angry soldiers shouted "that there had been too many good boys killed and wounded under the old colors for them to be disgraced by having a lot of rebel women dancing under them." Closing in on Hotchkiss, the blue-coated mob threatened to "pull the house down over his head." Still trying to maintain control, Hotchkiss buckled when confronted with a number of "his dirty little tricks," prominent among which was his spraining an ankle and "skinning out of the battle of the 27th of last May." Seeing that his rank held no weight with the crowd, the colonel told the men they could have their colors back. More to the point, Joel Chambers wrote that it was "a disgrace to act in such a manner so soon after the country was shocked by the news of the murder of the president."[18]

"Again I seat myself in my pup tent to pen you a few lines," Charles Capron began in a letter to his "beloved mother" on April 21. As always, he informed her that he was "in good health," but added that he was "rejoicing with the rest of the brave and glorious army at the successful termination of the rebellion." With the rebels "coming in at the rate of 50 a day," he emphasized "they keep us busy on picket;" and as consequence, "we consider the war over." Two days prior, Joel Chambers indicated in his pocket journal: "About 60 rebels came in this morning under a flag of truce and gave themselves up. They were commanded by a Capt and formerly belonged to [Alfred Jefferson] Vaughan's command." In his next entry he commented the "Rebs continue to come in, in squads of from one to a dozen." And, on each passing day more rebels came in. Chambers wrote: "The boys send up a cheer occasionally when they see a squad of them coming in; thus verifying the passage of Scripture, There is joy in heaven over a sinner that repenteth etc." Writing his mother, Jim Tomlinson mentioned that he had "seen a great many of Lee's men that Grant paroled. They wer going home. The most of them said that they had enuff of war. Some of them had not been home in four years."[19]

---

[18]   *Ibid.*, 119.

[19]   Capron, letter, April 21, 1865; Chambers, *War Fever Cured*, 118, 120; Tomlinson, Sally Ryan, *In Good Courage: The Civil War Letters of William James Tomlinson*, 27.

With time to reflect, Corporal Tomlinson opined on the condition of freed slaves. His father, Daniel, a native of Tennessee, had been a slave-owning farmer. His mother came from North Carolina. The family lived in Tennessee, where William James was born, until 1852. He was age fifteen when they removed to Illinois. Now writing his mother, he spoke of what he had observed recently and how he felt on the issue of the Negro. But, in the end he realized the black man's ultimate fate was still in the hands of the politicians, not the blue-coated soldiers who had bore the brunt of the war. Hewrote: "The negroes ar free although some of them ar helt by ther former masters. I have seen some of them that would not leave ther old homes. Then I have seen some running from the advance of Hood's army last winter. Ther was women and children that took what they could cary and walked from Pulaski to Nashville, some 78 miles. Then I have seen a great meny fighting for our country. Then why should they not be free. I don't fear them going north. If they want to stay in the south I am willing they should. They are not equal to the white race, tho they are human beings and have souls to save. Well ther is no use of talking. I am not a politician, thare fore I will let the negro drop."[20]

*   *   *

The Railroaders were up early on April 27 and left camp by daylight, boarding the cars and pulling out of Bull's Gap at 8:00 A. M.. Their train arrived at Knoxville about the middle of the afternoon and after a short stop moved on, passing through Loudon and Cleveland. By 7:00 A.M . . ., the regiment was in Chattanooga, remaining at the depot until 10:00 A.M . . ., when they moved out for Nashville. At 6:00 A.M . . ., the following morning, April 29, the regiment was in Nashville. Jim Tomlinson gauged the current ride on the cars covered 317 miles. On the trip back to the Tennessee capital, newly promoted Sergeant Tomlinson told his mother: "The

---

[20]   Tomlinson, Sally Ryan, *In Good Courage: The Civil War Letters of William James Tomlinson, ix*, 26.

war is about plaid out and I hope this leter writing will play out all so for I would rather tell my story in a different way from this."[21]

With the capitulation of Johnston's army followed by Lieutenant General Richard Taylor's surrender of the remaining rebel troops east of the Mississippi, the Union soldiers' grapevine was rampant with rumors about if and when the Federal regiments would be discharged. In attempting to answer his mother's inquiry as to when he might be home, Charles Capron first responded by saying that she should not build her hopes too high. He then went on to explain what he had heard, "There is some talk of giving Mexico a call . . . ." Eight days went by and he again picked up his pen and wrote: "What are they going to do with us is more than I know. Rumor says we are going to Texas. Rumor says we are going to be mustered out. But it is more than I can tell what is going to be done with us. We would like to have them discharge us and let us go home." Writing his sister on May 4, Private Capron said: "We expect to start about the 20 of this month for Chicago. There to be mustered out and return to our homes." Jim Tomlinson too was anxious to get back to Illinois. In a letter to his mother dated May 28, he wrote: "Time still passes away slowly but we are having a good time and Camp rhumers without end in regard to going home. Ther is an order to muster out all '62 troops immeddatly. The veteran troops have orders to make out ther pay roles for 8 months pay. We have not had orders to make out ours yet. I think by that we will be mustered out soon."[22]

When Lincoln called for volunteers in the summer of 1862, those who came forth enlisted for three years or until the war ended. With the capitulation of the Rebel military leaders and with the capture and imprisonment of Confederate President Jefferson Davis, the War of the Rebellion, as it came to be known, was over. Meanwhile, the veteran Union troops patiently waited to be discharged. Sergeant Tomlinson told his mother that "time seams to pass away slo. Ther is no more campaigning for us or battles for us to fight. It seams so different from what it did three months ago. Ther is nothing for

---

21   Chambers, *War Fever Cured*, 122-123; Tomlinson, Sally Ryan, *In Good Courage: The Civil War Letters of William James Tomlinson*, 27.

22   Capron, letters, April 21, 29 and May 4, 1865; Tomlinson, Sally Ryan, *In Good Courage: The Civil War Letters of William James Tomlinson*, 27.

us to think or talk of but home . . . ." As these citizen soldiers bided their time, someone, probably a career officer, decided a parade was in order. "We had no drill on account of making preparation for a grand review," Joel Chambers quickly scratched in his diary while preparing for the Fourth Corps' review. "It is intended to be the grandest thing of the war. Every man is to be dressed his best in full uniform; officers to wear sashes and the corps to march through Nashville at a company abreast with fixed bayonets," Charles Capron excitedly wrote his sister. He wished she could be there "to see the old fourth corps that has seen so much hard service. They are so different from those band box soldiers that never smelt powder or ever had a hard day's march." The older Jim Tomlinson commented that "the less Duty a soldier has [to do] the less he wants [to do]." He was undoubtedly preparing for the big event. Afterward he wrote that "it was the best review that I have ever seen yet." His cousin, Joel Chambers, also concurred and penned a vivid account of the affair in his journal. "We left camp at seven oclock this morning for the grand review and to our great satisfaction had to carry nothing but our canteens, filled with water; and gun and equipments. The three Divs and the Brigade of Artillery was out together with the entire wagon train belonging to the Corps," he explained. "We were review by Maj Gen Thomas commanding the army of the Cumberland. The boys cheered long and loud when the old hero rode along the line. The troops were in splendid condition and the whole thing passed off in the best style and was by far the grandest scene I ever saw," he proudly conveyed. "What made it interesting," he pointed out, "was that it was not more than a half a mile from the place we first went for the rebs on the 15th of Dec last."[23]

The grand review provided a diversion, but on the whole, time continued to drag on. The men occupied their time by standing picket, performing periodic drill, going through inspection, and holding daily dress parade. But, the troops saw it for what it was, marking time. By May 26, the Eighty-ninth's camp was full of rumors regarding the regiments mustering out. Most of the men had "it

---

[23]   Tomlinson, Sally Ryan, *In Good Courage: The Civil War Letters of William James Tomlinson*, 27; Capron, letter, May 4, 1865; Chambers, *War Fever Cured*, 125-126.

that the '62 troops are to be mustered out as soon as possible." With no definite news of their fate and nothing to do but wait, the Railroaders camp remained quiet. Chambers found camp life was "quite dull and monotonous . . . ."[24]

"No excitement or amusement save company inspection at 9 o'clock in the morning; reading matter being scarce, and none to be had in the army, and the boys being too morally religious to play cards on a Sunday, something could be brought to bear on the mind to induce the boys to show anything like enjoyment, on this pleasant Sabbath day," Sergeant Isaac K. Young wrote. For most of the day, camp life went as Young expected. "We ate breakfast, lay down and take a nap; we dine, lay down for another nap; but supper over; and the rumor that General Willich is at Brigade Headquarters, is spread through the various regiments with lightning rapidity, and they gather in squads all along the lane to the right of company quarters, and their gaze is directed toward General Doolittle's tent; their faces brighten, their eyes twinkle, while with excited hearts and smiling faces, they watch for the venerable General." Intently watching for his appearance, the men soon "see his form, mounted on his favorite iron-gray charger; emerge from behind the green of trees . . . . He dashes toward the regimental headquarters of his favorite old Eighty-ninth, and the entire regiment move forward, down toward, and beyond the line of company commanders' tents; and with a remark addressed to Col. Hotchkiss, 'I must go and see my poys,' he dashes in among the boys, while hats fly in the air, and cheers, such as never were excelled in volume and loudness, rang upon the evening air . . . ."[25]

Entries in Joel Chambers' journal had become redundant. Since returning to Nashville, the daily routine for the Railroaders was one in the same. Life for the men of the Eighty-ninth revolved around the preparation for or inspection itself and followed by some sort of drill or a dress parade. As a consequence, Willich's return on the May 28 was as exciting for Private Chambers as it had been Sergeant Young. So Chambers too wrote extensively about the General's appearance at the Eighty-ninth's camp. "Our honored old

---

[24] Chambers, *War Fever Cured*, 130, 132.
[25] *Kendall County Record*, June 8, 1865.

Brigade commander Brigadier Gen. A. Willich gave us a visit this evening it being the first time we have seen the old hero since he was wounded at Resacca, Ga. on the 15th of May last," Chambers entered in his diary that evening. After spending the past year back in Cincinnati, Willich had recovered enough to return to the army and his beloved brigade. Chambers noted, "He came out to day to pay us a visit before taking command. He scarcely made any stop at H'd Q'r'ts but rushed up to . . . where he seen us flocking out to meet him. He was received with three rousing cheers." Typical of the old German's style, he quickly cracked a few jokes with the men, complimented them on their "good looks," and concluded by telling them that "he would come back in a few days and turn himself inside out," telling them "all Vat was in him." Bidding the Railroaders good evening, he "retired amid three loud deafening cheers." Reflecting on what had taken place, Chambers penned, "I am sure there is no other man living the sight of whom would cause the same amount of excitement, enthusiasm and real heartfelt joy as Gen. Willich . . . among the boys of this brigade."[26]

In keeping his mother up-to-date, Charles Capron wrote in a letter that General Willich had returned and took command of the brigade. He pointed out: "If you remember right he was wounded last summer in the Georgia campaign [and it was] given out to be mortal but he has returned and looks very well. On May 31, Chambers recorded in his diary that General Willich assumed command of the brigade that evening and commented that the men were "all very highly pleased at this . . . ." It had been felt at the time he was wounded that he "would never be able for field duty again." Chambers observed that "his right hand and arm is almost useless from the effect of his wound, but it is his desire to be with his old brigade."[27]

June 1 found Joel Chambers writing in his journal that "the boys of the Brigade are making great preparations for a grand torchlight procession . . . in honor of the return of General Willich." Captain Alexis Cope of the Fifteenth Ohio noted that the reception for General Willich "was conceived and carried out by the enlisted men

---

[26]   Chambers, *War Fever Cured*, 130-131.
[27]   Capron, letter, undated; Chambers, *War Fever Cured*, 132.

of the brigade,—the officers having nothing to do with it,—and was a most remarkable demonstration of their love for and confidence in their old brigade commander."[28]

"Dress parade came off at the usual hour and shortly afterward the lights began to start up as the procession began forming . . . ." Joel Chambers stated: "Each Reg't was commanded by the Serg't Maj assisted by the orderlies of Companies." Soon, the column began moving. It was headed by the Fifteenth Ohio and its band, while "two other bands were placed at intervals in the procession." A Lieutenant in the Fifteenth, Andrew J. Gleason, noted in his personal diary that his regiment had the most banners but "those of the Eighty-ninth Illinois were more artistic." One of the Eighty-ninth's banners "bore a fine picture of a railroad engine to symbolize the 'railroad regiment' as it was called, with an inscription of the general's own words at Chickamauga. 'Now boys one more charge,' and underneath them 'All right General we are on time.'" Captain Cope explained that the banners recalled incidents of Willich's command and nearly all gave some remark in the General's broken English. One of Cope's favorites was "Bugler blow fight."[29]

"The whole thing passed off in the very best of style and was by far the grandest thing of the kind that I ever saw in my life," confided Chambers in his diary. He further wrote: "There was a very large number of transparencies bearing almost every motto that could be conceived of that would convey the great idea of Patriotism and conspire to do honor to and show respect for Gen Willich. Such as Lafayette in '76—in '65 Willich. With Willich we defy the world. Willich we love as a father. We welcome back our old commander. He fell to rise again. Long may he live to drink Rhyne wine and Lager beer. etc." The parade was followed by a number of speeches, with Willich concluding the event by telling the men he had been "'received and honored here [United States] for what he was exiled for in his native home.'" Chambers noted "the Gen seemed to appreciate the respect shown him and I am told was moved to tears at the close of the welcome speech."[30]

---

28 Chambers, *War Fever Cured*, 132; Cope, *The 15th Ohio Volunteers*, 723.

29 Cope, *The 15th Ohio Volunteers*, 423-724; Chambers, *War Fever Cured*, 133.

30 Chambers, *War Fever Cured*, 133-134; Arnold D. Gates, ed., *The Rough Side of War: The Civil War Journal of Chesley A. Mosman 1st Lieutenant, Company D*

At the dress parade on June 2, Colonel Hotchkiss announced the arrival of the Eighty-ninth's muster-out rolls, and then told the assembled men that "the Reg't would start for home as soon as the rolls could be made out, probably in ten or twelve days," Joel Chambers recorded in his journal. The regiment's 196 recruits, Chambers noted, "Would not be mustered out but would be transferred to some other command." He concluded the entry by saying, "This of course includes me."[31]

Through backchannels, Hotchkiss had heard that some of his Railroaders were not to be mustered out, but dispatched to Texas. On May 31, he took immediate action, in the form of a letter to the Secretary of War seeking to preempt this order. Hotchkiss sought dispensation for 178 recruits and eight veteran volunteers on the regiment's rolls. He apprised the Secretary that on General Rosecrans' word, the Eighty-ninth enlisted recruits with the understanding that the regiment "would be mounted and equipped for service as 'mounted infantry.'" He pointed out that the Eighty-ninth had "never been mounted and the existing dissatisfaction of these men, in consequence, would be greatly incensed, by their transfer to another organization when this Regiment is mustered out of service." He emphasized the men had signed up based on "the arrangement and intension of Genl Rosecrans, as well as the promises of the recruiting officers," which "were made in good faith." Hotchkiss now adamantly argued that "these facts" were "sufficient and just grounds for their discharge . . . ." His request went up the chain of command where it fell on deaf ears and was subsequently returned.[32]

*   *   *

With the date for leaving Nashville fast approaching, Private Curtis B. Knox wrote a final letter for Company F to the *Rock Island Argus*. "Col. DANFORTH.—As we are to be mustered out of the

---

59th Illinois Infantry Regiment (Garden City, New York: The Basin Publishing Co., 1987), 360.

[31] Chambers, *War Fever Cured*, 133.

[32] Colonel Charles T. Hotchkiss, letter to Secretary of War, May 31, 1865, Record Group 301, Illinois State Archives.

United States service and start in route for Chicago in a day or two, I thought a line informing you would not be in appropriate," he started out. He then told the *Argus* that in August 1862, 98 men signed the muster rolls in Rock Island, but now only "36 of the original members" would go out together. Knox further explained: "Our recruits have been assigned to the 59th Illinois under the instructions of the war department," while a few others were still away on detached duty from the company and regiment. Knox noted one in particular. "Captain E. T. Wells will shortly leave the service. He is now assistant adjutant general for Maj. Gen. Johnson's command, the 6th division cavalry corps, at Pulaski, Tenn., and it is said he will resume the practice of law in Rock Island." He also reported that Wells had "recently been brevetted major and lieutenant colonel for gallant and meritorious service." He quickly added too, that "Lieut. Col. W. D. Williams has been recommended for brevet colonel by Brig. Gen. Willick and Maj. Gens. Wood and Stanley, for long, arduous and gallant service since the commencement of the war." Knox pointed out that Williams had "commanded, in the capacity of captain, major and lieutenant colonel, our regiment, two of the three years we have been in the service." Emphasizing that Williams had "led the 89th in every battle, skirmish, march; foraging, expedition or bivouac, in which we have been engaged . . . and it does seem as though a brevet was a mighty cheap and inadequate reward for such services." As he concluded his letter, Knox explained to Danforth that men would not be returning "to Rock Island as a company. I wish we could . . . but that is impossible. The majority of the survivors of our company live in the northern part of the county, Watertown, Hampton and Moline, and will stop off at the Junction and Moline; but some time in the future, God willing; we will get together in Rock Island . . . ."[33]

Joel Chambers wrote in his diary on June 5 that "the officers and all the clerks are very busy making out the muster out rolls." The following day he penned "our Regt was relieved from duty this morning and all the detailed men of the Reg't were relieved in order to be mustered out. There was Brigade drill in the evening but our Regt did not take part in it." He recorded on June 9 that "the old organization of the 89th was mustered out this evening. It would be

---

[33]   *Rock Island Argus*, June 14, 1865.

useless to say that the boys were very happy on thus being set free again." The following day, Friday, June 10, Chambers entered: "The 89th started for home at one oclock to day. The boys were of course very glad to get started home but they hated to leave the recruits behind."[34]

Fifty-six hours later the regiment detrained in the Windy City, and the next day's *Chicago Tribune* reported: "The 88th (Second Board of Trade) and 89th (Railroad Regiment) arrived in Chicago at 9 o'clock last evening [June 12] per the Michigan Central railroad, and took quarters for the night at Camp Douglas." The *Chicago Evening Journal's* June 13 edition announced that "several regiments, or parts of regiments, of Illinois troops reached Springfield yesterday, and the 74th, 78th, 86th, 88th, and 89th Illinois regiments have reached Chicago since yesterday morning." In writing about the regiments that had arrived or were expected shortly, the *Evening Journal* described the 89th—"'the Railroad regiment,' that always showed a head-light, never left the track, and never whistled down the 'brakes.'"[35]

As "the heroes of the war" poured into Chicago, a committee from the Board of Trade was joined by a number of prominent Railroad men at a hastily organized welcome for the brave and true men of the 88th (Second Board of Trade) and 89th Illinois (Railroad Regiment). Plans quickly took shape for a parade through town followed by a formal reception at the appropriately named Union Hall. Though the homecoming began with torrents of rain, "the boys took it all in good part—indeed it was a mere circumstance to what they have endured . . . ." It was around 10:00 A.M . . . when, with the Eighty-ninth leading and the Eighty-eighth following, the two regiments left camp with cartridge boxes and shouldered muskets, marching with "a swinging stride peculiar to Western soldiers." Out front of each regiment, their color guards marched carrying "the old tattered and torn and bullet riven flags, with the names of Perryville, Stone River, Chickamauga, Mission Ridge, Resaca, Franklin, Nashville" stitched for all to see. The column passed up Cottage Grove Avenue to Twenty-Second Avenue, turning right on Michigan Avenue, "followed on either side by hosts of small boys

---

[34] Chambers, *War Fever Cured*, 137-139.
[35] *Chicago Tribune*, June 13, 1865; *Chicago Evening Journal*, June 12, 1865.

and big men, all enthusiastic to do honor to the heroes blue . . . ."
"At Park Row the regiments were met by the committee . . . who
took a position immediately between the two regiments, and the
Great Western Light Guard Band fell in at the head of the column."
On "a given signal the regiments moved forward, and at the same
moment the Dearborn Light Artillery . . . opened a salute, firing
thirty-six guns as the regiments proudly marched on" to cheers all
along the avenue. On arriving at the Union Hall, arms were stacked,
and the troops forming by fours filed in.[36]

Once the men were in place Thomas B. Bryan stepped forward
from the gallery, saying it was his "pleasing duty to introduce to the
audience . . . the noble regiments, the 88th and 89th Illinois volunteers,
who have returned to us after breasting the storms of fifty battles."
Calling for the assembled to let their voices do what their hearts
dictated, he proposed "three cheers for the glorious 88th and 89th
regiments." Next, W. D. Manchester thanked the Board of Trade
committee, and "said a few words of welcome to the 89th . . . ." He
then introduced Colonel Hotchkiss who spoke briefly, saying: "The
89th left Chicago at the same time as the 88th, three years ago, 900
strong. It has been recruited up to 1,400; that is, that number have
been enrolled under its banners. It has lost by casualties very largely,
and return now with 300 men, 200 others being in the field. The
balance have been lost. Among the lost is one Lieutenant Colonel,
seven captains, four Lieutenants and over seven hundred men. Our
history is written on the head-boards of the rude made graves from
Stone River to Atlanta. Such a record we feel proud of." After Colonel
Hotchkiss' brief statement, Governor Richard Oglesby and former
Governor, now United States Senator, Richard Yates followed, each
making a short address to the gathered.[37]

While the gathered cheered and the speakers continued,
General Sherman could be seen passing through the ranks shaking
hands with the veteran soldiers. Calls were soon heard throughout
the hall for Sherman to come to the balcony and address the crowd.
Speaking with his "old soldier boys of the 4th corps," Sherman's
informal words were often interrupted with cheers and laughter.

---

[36] *Chicago Tribune*, June 13 and 14, 1865;

[37] *Chicago Tribune*, June 14, 1865; *Chicago Evening Journal*, June 13, 1865.

With heartfelt sincerity, he told the men in blue before him: "I believe there is no one more gratified to see you, and welcome you home to your wives, children and sweethearts than I am." And to let the soldiers know what he thought of them, he said: "I see before me men more capable of leading armies than the majority of the Major Generals appointed at the beginning of the war." Uncle Billy, as he was called by those in the ranks, closed by saying: "Once more, I say, go home and behave yourselves. I place myself hostage to Illinois for the good behavior of Sherman's army—and I know you will not betray me. Illinois is proud of you." With his final words, "the soldiers broke forth in loud cheers, the band struck up the 'Star Spangled Banner' and the boys filed" out, moving off "to the Soldiers' Rest, where an excellent dinner" was "provided, to which full justice was done."[38]

On Friday evening, June 16, the employees of the Car Department, Galena Division of the Chicago & Northwestern Railroad Company held a special reception for "the brave and noble heroes, comprising Co. K, 89th Illinois Volunteers (Galena Guards)." Captain William A. Sampson, a machinist with the railroad, First Lieutenant Horace G. Greenfield, a conductor on the line, and Major John M. Farquhar, who spoke on behalf of the soldiers, were greeted by a crowd of over 300 who had gathered to welcome their "old shopmates" back home. However, for the time being, the Railroaders were kept marking time at Camp Douglas until they were finally discharged on Saturday, June 24, making their total "term of service, 2 years, 9 months and 27 days." The regiment had traveled "2,253 miles on foot, and 1,127 by Railroad."[39]

When they enlisted back in August 1862, the men making up what became Company H called themselves the Kendall Guards. Arriving back in Kendall County, "the citizens at Bristol Station, and vicinity, received Company H . . . with a hearty welcome. The company was formed at the hotel and, preceded by the Yorkville Band, marched to the grounds prepared for the occasion just north of the Station." At the grove the boys found a hollow square of

---

[38] *Chicago Tribune*, June 14, 1865; *Chicago Evening Journal*, June 14, 1865.

[39] *Chicago Tribune*, June 20, 1865; *Geographic History of the Rail Road Regiment, 89th Regiment of Illinois vols. Infantry*, Lithograph: Chicago: Charles Shober.

tables set for dinner and a speaker's stand decorated with the Stars and Stripes. After the men were seated, the festivities kicked off with music from the Aurora Band, a welcoming address, and several orators. Dinner followed and when finished, a number of toasts were made. The first to be given: *"Soldiers of Co. H, 89th Ills. Vols.—*Whom we especially honor to-day—champions of Freedom—gallant warriors—veterans of nearly two score battles—we welcome you to our hearts and homes." Representing Co. H, Corporal John C. Sherwin spoke these words: *"Our Departed heroes—*Whose blood has nourished the tree of liberty. May their sacrifice be enshrined in the hearts of this people, and their names and deeds be cherished as a rich inheritance."[40]

The *Chicago Evening Journal* reported the Railroad Regiment returned "home with less than 400 men on the rolls, with but 367 reporting for duty." All told, according to the Illinois Adjutant General's Report 1,403 men were "borne on the rolls" of the 89th Illinois. While William F. Fox, in *Regimental Losses in the American Civil War*, states the Eighty-ninth's total enrollment to be 1,318, both sources agree that the Railroad Regiment lost 133 men killed and mortally wounded, of which 12 were officers. Only the Forty-second Illinois Infantry suffered a higher number of officers killed in action. Seven of the original captains died in battle. And, all but three of the officers present at discharge had been wounded. These two sources also concur that another 173 men did not return home, succumbing to disease, accidents, or dying in prison, bringing the total deaths to 306. Fox's statistics reveal another 334 men were wounded. Add in the men discharged on account of disability, and only 381 of the rank and file were on the rolls at the muster out. Of the 440 recruits added to the regiment, 202 were transferred to the Fifty-nine Illinois and eventually went to Texas. On December 8, 1865, at New Braunfels, Texas, the Fifty-ninth was officially mustered out. Shortly thereafter, the regiment returned to Springfield for final payment and discharge. With this last bit of paperwork, the remaining men who had served in the Eighty-ninth Illinois Volunteer Infantry were released from the service to return to their former occupations and families. And, in answering Lincoln's call to squash the Rebellion and

---

[40] *Kendall County Record*, July 6, 1865.

preserve the Union, the men of the Railroad Regiment had remained steadfast in battle and saw the fight through to finish. Battered, but never beaten, slowed but not stopped, the Railroaders maintained a head of steam in their regimental engine, lived up to their motto of "CLEAR THE TRACK," and in the end came on through.[41]

Meeting at the Kendall County Fair Grounds on September 4, 1884, 40 veterans of the Eighty-ninth Illinois Volunteer Infantry formed an association and began the tradition of holding an annual reunion. The first gathering took place January 22, 1885, nearly twenty years since the returned soldiers had gone their separate ways. One hundred former comrades met at the Palmer House, Chicago's finest hotel, where they "related army experiences, hardships, privations and temptations . . . ." After the first reunion the Eighty-ninth's association counted 272 members. At the March 1909 reunion held at Glenwood, Iowa, the association's roster totaled 337 members, and the secretary penned the following lines:

---

[41] *Chicago Evening Journal,* June 14, 1864; *Adjutant General's Report,* 168, 288; Fox, *Regimental Losses in the American Civil War, 1861-1864,* 373.

When Lincoln called on Illinois
For help upon the battle line,
She sent the 'Railroad' regiment—
Its number, eighty-nine.

A noble lot of loyal boys,
None better in the land;
They started for the seat of war
With Hotchkiss in command.

For three long years they faced the foe
Through winter's cold and summer's heat
They fought on many a battle field
But never did they meet defeat.

And Illinois need never blush
For th' record that they made,
The gallant 'Railroad' regiment
Of Willich's old brigade.

For in the thickest of the fight,
The starry flag they bore,
Till treason's cursed head was crushed
And sank, to rise no more.

Then to the north the boys returned,
The REMANT of that band;
They sought the quiet paths of peace,
And scattered through the land.

But four and forty years have passed
Since last they formed their line,
And of that gallant regiment
Here's all that I can find.[42]

---

[42] *Organization of the Eighty-Ninth Illinois Volunteer Infantry Reunion Association,*
Together with a Roster of Membership, original copy at the Chicago Historical
Society; *Roster of the "Railroad" Regiment, The 89th Illinois,* Glenwood, Iowa, March
1909, (Opinion Print, Glenwood, Iowa), original copy in possession of the author.

Bibliography

Official Publications

Annual Report of the Adjutant General of the State of Illinois. Springfield: Baker and Phillips, Printers, 1863.

Biographical Directory of the American Congress 1774-1971. Washington D.C.: U. S. Government Printing Office, 1971.

Indiana at Chickamauga, 1863-1900. A Report of the Indiana Commissioners, Chickamauga National Military Park. Indianapolis: Sentinel Printing Company, 1900.

Kreidberg, Marvin A. and Henry, Merton G. *History of Military Mobilization in the United States Army 1775-1945.* Washington D.C.: U. S. Government Printing Office, 1955.

Report of the Adjutant General of the State of Illinois, 1861-1865. 9 vols. Springfield, Illinois: Phillips Brothers, 1901.

Report of Indiana Commissioners: Chickamauga National Military Park. Indianapolis: William B. Buford Contractor for State Printing and Binding, 1901.

Turner, Ann. *Guide to Indiana Civil War Manuscripts*. Indianapolis: Indiana Civil War Centennial Commission, 1965.

The War of the Rebellion: A Compilation of the Official Records of the Union and Confederate Armies. 128 vols. Washington D.C.: Government Printing Office, 1880-1901.

Newspapers

Amboy Times
Aurora Beacon
Chanute Vidette
Chicago Evening Journal
Chicago Times
Chicago Tribune
The Elgin Advocate,
The Elgin Daily News
The Evening Argus
Galesburg Register-Mail
Galesburg Republican-Register
Nashville Dispatch
The Quincy Whig Republican
Rock Island Weekly Union
The National Tribune
Rock Island Argus
Rock Island Weekly Argus
Rock Island Register
The Waukegan Weekly Gazette

Diaries, Letters, and Manuscripts

Abraham Lincoln Presidential Library, Springfield, Illinois
    George G Sinclair Letters (transcriptions).
    Wallace McCloud, Diary.
Berry, George H. Diary in possession of Steve Stewart, Chicago, Illinois.

Berry, George H. Letters in possession of Steve Stewart, Chicago, Illinois.

Buckley, Joseph Letters in possession of Les Lipshutz, Flossmoor, Illinois.

Chicago Historical Society
 Robert Tarrant Diary
 Frederick L. Fake Manuscript
 Charles T. Hotchkiss Collection

Goddard, Fredrick W. Diary in possession of Karl Stark, Charlottesville, Virginia.

Huff, Walter Scott. Diary in possession of Roddy A. Burwell, Casper, Wyoming.

Illinois State Archives
 Adjutant General (Military and Naval Department). Record Group 301. Administrative Files on Civil War Companies and Regiments. 301.18.

Kendall County Historical Society

Franklin M. Hobbs Letter

Library of Congress

R. T. Lincoln Collection, Abraham Lincoln Papers

National Archives. Records of the Adjutant General's Office. RG 94. Records of the Record and Pension Office of the War Department 94.12.

Navarro College, Pearce Collections Museum, Pearce Civil War Collection
 Corsicana, Texas

Theodore F. Whitney Letters.

Old Court House Museum (Vicksburg, MS)
 Charles Capron Collection

Historical Society of Quincy and Adams County (Illinois)
 John Browning Letters

Stones River National Battlefield
 William E. Seaman Letter

Swickard, John W. Letter in possession of Don Hamerstrand, Victoria, Illinois.

University of Tennessee, Hoskins Library
 James B. David Diary

U. S. Pension Office

John M. Farquhar File
Yale University, The Beinecke Rare Book and Manuscript Library
Nate Salsbury Reminiscences

Articles, Books, Memoirs, and Pamphlets

Aldrich, C. Knight, ed. *Quest for a Star: The Civil War Letters and Diaries of Colonel Francis T. Sherman of the 88th Illinois.* Knoxville: University of Tennessee Press, 1999.

Andreas, Alfred T. *History of Chicago from the Earliest Period to the Present Time.* 3 vols. Chicago: The A. T. Andreas Company, Publishers, 1885.

Angle, Paul M. *"Here I Have Lived" A History of Lincoln's Springfield 1821-1865.* New Brunswick, New Jersey: Rutgers University Press, 1935.

Bailey, Anne J. *The Chessboard of War: Sherman and Hood in the Autumn Campaigns of 1864.* Lincoln, Nebraska: University of Nebraska Press, 2000.

Barnett, James. "August Willich, Soldier Extraordinary," *Historical and Philosophical Society of Ohio Bulletin* XX. January 1962.

Barnett, James. "The Vilification of August Willich," *Cincinnati Historical Society Bulletin* XXIV. January 1966.

Bateman, Newton and Selby, Paul, eds. *Historical Encyclopedia of Illinois and History of Kendall County.* 2 vols. Chicago: Munsell Publishing Company, 1914.

Bateman, Newton, McCulloch, David, and Selby, Paul. eds. *Historical Encyclopedia of Illinois and History of Peoria County,* 2 vols. Chicago and Peoria: Munsell Publishing Company, 1901.

Bauman, Ken. *Arming The Suckers, 1861-1865, A Compilation of Illinois Civil War Weapons.* Columbus, Ohio, 1989.

Belgians in the American Civil War, [Internet website] *Belgian Civil War Soldiers in Illinois.*

Beneke, Cheryl H. and Summer, Carol D. eds. *War Fever Cured, The Civil War Diary of Private Joel R. Chambers, 1864-1865.* Memphis, Tennessee: Crittenden Publishing Company, 1980.

Bierce, Ambrose, *The Collected Works of Ambrose Bierce,* 12 vols. New York: Gordia Press Inc., 1966.

The Biographical Record of Rock Island County, Illinois Illustrated. Chicago: The S. J. Clarke Publishing Company, 1897.

Boatner III, Mark M. *The Civil War Dictionary.* New York: David McKay Company, Inc., 1959.

Bowen, A. W. *Progressive Men of Western Colorado.* Chicago: A. W. Bowen & Co., 1905.

Burton, William L. *Melting Pot Soldiers: The Union's Ethnic Regiments.* Ames, Iowa: Iowa State University Press, 1988.

Byers, William N. *Encyclopedia of Biography of Colorado, History of Colorado.* Chicago: The Century Publishing and Engraving Company, 1901.

Carr, Edward H. *Karl Marx: A Study in Fanaticism.* London: J. M. Dent and Sons, Ltd., 1938.

Castel, Albert. *Decision in the West: The Atlanta Campaign of 1864.* Lawrence, Kansas: University Press of Kansas, 1992.

Chamberlin, W. H. ed., *Sketches of War History, 1890-1896.* Cincinnati: The Robert Clark Co., 1896.

Church, Charles A. *History of the Republican Party in Illinois, 1854-1912.* Rockford, Illinois: Press of Wilson Brothers Company Printers and Binders, 1912.

Cist, Henry M. *The Army of The Cumberland.* New York: Charles Scribner's Sons, 1882.

Cope, Alexis. *The 15th Ohio Volunteers and Its Campaigns, 1861-1865.* Columbus, OH: Edward T. Miller Company, 1916.

Cox, Jacob D. *Atlanta.* New York: Charles Scribner's Sons, 1882.

Cox, Jacob D. *Military Reminiscences of the Civil War November 1863-June 1865.* New York: Charles Scribner's Sons, 1900.

Cozzens, Peter. *No Better Place to Die: The Battle of Stones River.* Chicago: University of Illinois Press, 1991.

Cozzens, Peter. *This Terrible Sound: The Battle of Chickamauga.* Urbana and Chicago: University of Illinois Press, 1992.

Cozzens, Peter. *The Shipwreck of Their Hopes, The Battles for Chattanooga.* Urbana and Chicago: University of Illinois Press, 1994.

Cozzens, Peter, "Forgotten Hero: Philip Sidney Post," *Illinois Historical Journal,* Volume 84, Number 2. Summer 1991.

Cullum, Bvt. Maj.-Gen. George W. *Biographical Register on the Officers and Graduates of the U. S. Military Academy West Point, N. Y.* Boston: Houghton, Mifflin and Company, 1891.

Daniel, Larry J. *Days of Glory, The Army of the Cumberland, 1861-1865.* Baton Rouge, LA: Louisiana State University Press, 2004.

Dean, James. "The Battle of Pickett's Mill," *Blue & Gray Magazine* VI. July 1989.

Dewey, J. L. *Dewey's County Directory.* Galesburg, Illinois: Liberal Book and Job Office, 1868.

Dodge, William S. *History of the Old Second Division, Army of the Cumberland.* Chicago: Church & Goodman, 1864.

Duprel, Richard. [Internet website] Descendants of Matthias Holdren.

Eddy, Thomas M. 2 vols. *The Patriotism of Illinois: A Record of the Civil War and Military History of the State.* Chicago: Clarke, 1866.

Faust, Patricia L, ed., *Historical Times Illustrated Encyclopedia of the Civil War.* New York: Harper & Row Publishers, 1986.

Fisher, Horace C. *A Staff Officer's Story: The Personal Experiences of Colonel Horace Newton Fisher in the Civil War.* Boston: Thomas Todd Company, 1960.

Fisk, Franklin Woodbury. *The Chaplain's Memorial: A Sermon, Preached in Chicago, January 31, 1863, at the Funeral of Rev. James H. Dill, Chaplain of the Eighty-Ninth Regiment Illinois Volunteers, Called the "Railroad Regiment."* New York: John A. Gray and Green, 1863.

Fitch, John. *Annals of the Army of the Cumberland.* Philadelphia: J. B. Lippincott & Company, 1864.

Foote, Shelby. *The Civil War: A Narrative, Fredericksburg to Meridian.* New York: Vintage Books, 1986.

Foote, Shelby, *The Civil War, A Narrative, Red River to Appomattox.* New York: Vintage Books, 1986.

Fox, William F. *Regimental Losses in the American Civil War 1861-1865.* Albany, New York: Joseph McDonough, 1898.

Gates, Arnold D., ed. *The Rough Side of War: The Civil War Journal of Chesley A. Mosman 1st Lieutenant, Company D 59th Illinois Infantry Regiment.* Garden City, New York: The Basin Publishing Co., 1987.

Geographic History of the Rail Road Regiment, 89th Regiment of Illinois vols. Infantry, Lithograph: Chicago: Charles Shober.

George, Charles. *Forty Years on the Rail: Reminiscences of a Veteran Conductor*. Chicago: R. R. Donnelly & Sons, Publisher, 1887.

Goodwin, Doris Kearns. *Team of Rivals: The Political Genius of Abraham Lincoln*. New York: Simon & Schuster Paperbacks, 2006.

Grant, Ulysses S. *Personal Memoirs of U. S. Grant*. New York: Charles L. Webster & Company, 1886.

Groom, Winston, *Shrouds of Glory: Atlanta to Nashville, the Last Great Campaign of the Civil War*. New York: The Atlantic Monthly Press, 1995.

Grosh, Jere M. "His Last Contribution to Buffalo, Rochester & Pittsburgh Employees Magazine," *Railway Life: Employees Magazine, Buffalo, Rochester & Pittsburgh Railway Co*. February 1914.

Hafendorfer, Kenneth A. *Perryville: Battle for Kentucky*. Louisville, Kentucky: K H Press, 1991.

Hand-Book of Chicago Biography. Chicago: John J. Flinn, 1893.

Hartpence, William R. *History of the Fifty-first Indiana Veteran Volunteer Infantry*. Cincinnati, Ohio: The Robert Clarke Co., 1894.

Harkness, Captain William. Letters Written By. [Internet website].

Harper, Robert S. *Lincoln and the Press*. New York: McGraw-Hill Book Company, Inc., 1951.

Hazen, William B., *A Narrative of Military Service*. Boston: Ticknor & Co., 1885.

The Headlight, Regimental Newspaper.

Heitman, Francis B. *Historical Register and Dictionary of United States Army (1789-1903*. 2 vols. Urbana, Illinois: University of Illinois Press, 1903; rep., 1965.

Hewett, Janet, ed., *Supplement to the Official Records of the Union and Confederate Armies*, Part II-Record of Events, Volume 13, Serial No. 25. Wilmington, NC: Broadfoot Publishing Company, 1995.

Hicken, Victor *Illinois in the Civil War*. Urbana: University of Illinois Press, 1991.

Hicks, E. W. *History of Kendall County Illinois*. Aurora, Illinois: Knickerbocker and Hodder Printers, 1877.

Historical Encyclopedia of Illinois and History of Rock Island County. Chicago: Munsell Publishing Co., 1914.

History of Crawford and Richland Counties, Wisconsin. Springfield, Illinois: Union Publishing Company, 1884.

The History of Dubuque County, Iowa. Chicago: Western Historical Company, 1880.

History of Grundy County, Illinois Illustrated. Chicago: O. L. Baskin and Company, 1882.

History of Lee County. Chicago: H. H. Hill and Company, Publishers, 1881.

History and Roster of Maryland Volunteers, War of 1861-5, Vol. I. Baltimore: Press of Guggenheimer, Weil & Co., 1898.

Hofstadter, Jim. *Hard Dying Men: The story of General W.H.L. Wallace, General T.E.G. Ransom, and their "Old Eleventh" Illinois Infantry in the American Civil War*. Bowie, Maryland: Heritage Books, Inc., 1991.

Howard, Oliver Otis, *Autobiography of Oliver Otis Howard, Major General United States Army*, 2 vols. Freeport, New York: Books for Libraries Press, 1971.

Illinois in the Civil War, [Internet website] *Civil War Scrapbook-Alfred D. French Memoirs*.

Johannsen, Robert W. *Stephen A. Douglas*. New York: Oxford University Press, 1973.

Journal of Proceedings of the Methodist Episcopal Church of the Southern Illinois Conference, 1867.

Kammerer, Judith L. *"'Reflections" Hancock County, Illinois in the Civil War; includes accounts of Keokuk, Iowa, Adams Co., Ill. Northeast, Mo. Overview of war*. Carthage, Illinois: Journal Printing Company, 1988.

Karamanski, Theodore J. *Rally 'Round the Flag: Chicago and the Civil War*. Chicago: Nelson-Hall Publishers, 1993.

Kelly, Dennis, *Kennesaw Mountain and the Atlanta Campaign: A Tour Guide*. Atlanta, Georgia: Kennesaw Mountain Historical Association, Inc., 1990.

Knox County Roll of Honor, Knox County Recorder's Office, Galesburg, Illinois, "Grand Army of the Republic Personal War Sketch of Comrade William E. Ward."

Kloss, Karen. "Union General August Willich, The Eccentric Prussian Socialist,"

Law, R. I. compiler, *Knox County Roll of Honor, Department of Illinois Grand Army of the Republic, Jas. T. Shields Post No. 45, Personal War Sketch.*

Long, E. B. *The Civil War Day by Day: An Almanac 1861-1865.* Garden City, New York: Doubleday & Company, Inc., 1971.

Lonn, Ella. *Foreigners in the Union Army and Navy.* Baton Rouge: Louisiana State University Press, 1951.

Lowry, M.D., Thomas P. and Welsh, M.D., Jack D. *Tarnished Scalpels, The Court Martials of Fifty Union Surgeons.* Mechanicsburg, PA: Stackpole Books, 2000.

McCartney, Clarence Edward. *Grant and His Generals.* New York: The McBride Company, 1953.

Richard M. McMurry, *Atlanta 1864, Last Chance for the Confederacy.* Lincoln, Nebraska: University of Nebraska Press, 2000.

McDonough, James Lee and Connelly, Thomas L., *Five Tragic Hours: The Battle of Franklin.* Knoxville: The University of Tennessee Press, 1983.

McPherson, James M. *Battle Cry of Freedom: The Civil War Era.* New York: Oxford University Press, 1988.

Mehring, Franz. *Karl Marx: The Story of His Life.* London: George Allen & Unwin, 1951.

Memorials of Deceased Companions of the Commanderey of the State of Illinois, Military Order of the Loyal Legion of the United States From January 1, 1912 to December 31, 1922. Wilmington, NC: Broadfoot Publishing Company, 1993.

Miles, Jim. *Paths to Victory: A History and Tour Guide of the Stone's River, Chickamauga, Chattanooga, Knoxville, and Nashville Campaigns.* Nashville, Tennessee: Rutledge Hill Press, 1991.

Noblitt, Phil, "The 'Crime' at Pickett's Mill," *America's Civil War.* January 1996.

Official Register of the Officers and Cadets of the U. S. Military Academy. New York: J. P. Wright, Printer, 1848.

Organization of the Eighty-Ninth Illinois Volunteer Infantry Reunion Association, Together with a Roster of Membership.

Parker, H. M. *Proceedings of the First Reunion of the Eleventh Regiment Illinois Volunteer Infantry.* Ottawa, Illinois: Osman and Hareman, 1875.

The Past and Present of Rock Island County, Illinois. Chicago: H. F. Kett and Company, 1877.

Paul, Eden and Cedar. trans., Otto Ruhle, *Karl Marx: His Life and Work.* Garden City, New York: Garden City Publishing Co., Inc., 1928.

Payne, Robert. *Marx.* New York: Simon and Schuster, 1968.

Pearson, Tom. [Internet website] The 89th Illinois Infantry Regiment: Roll of Honor-Chronological.

Portrait and Biographical Album of Knox County, Illinois. Chicago: Biographical Publishing Company, 1886.

Reid, Whitelow. 2 vols. *Ohio in the War: Her Statesmen, Her Generals, and Soldiers.* Cincinnati: Moore, Wilstach, and Baldwin, 1868.

Reinhart, Joseph R. trans. and ed. August *Willich's Gallant Dutchman: Civil War Letters from the 32nd Indiana Infantry.* Kent, Ohio: The Kent State University Press, 2006.

Roster of the "Railroad" Regiment, The 89th Illinois. Glenwood, Iowa: Opinion Print, 1909.

Scaife, William R., *The Campaign for Atlanta.* Saline, Michigan: McNaughton & Gunn, Inc., 1993.

Sifokis, Stewart. ed. *Who Was Who in the Civil War.* New York: Facts on File Publications, 1988.

Stewart, Charles D. "A Bachelor General," *Wisconsin Magazine of History* XVII. 1933.

Schurz, Carl. *The Reminiscences of Carl Schurz, 1829-1852.* 2 vols. New York: The McClure Company, 1907.

Sherman, W. T. *Memoirs of Gen. W. T. Sherman.* New York: Charles L. Webster & Co., 1891.

Soldiers' and Patriots Biographical Album Containing Biographies and Portraits of Soldiers and Loyal Citizens in the American Conflict. Chicago: Union Veteran Publishing Company, 1892.

State Bar Association Proceedings 1878, 1881, 1885. Madison, Wisconsin: M.J. Cantwell Book and Job Printer, 1883.

Sword, Wiley. *Mountains Touched with Fire, Chattanooga Besieged, 1863*. New York: St. Martin's Press, 1997.

Sword, Wiley *Embrace an Angry Wind, The Confederacy' Last Hurrah: Spring Hill, Franklin, and Nashville*. New York: HarperCollins Publishers, 1992.

Tomlinson, Sally Ryan. *In Good Courage: The Civil War Letters of William James Tomlinson*. San Francisco: 1982, Revised 1995).

Troiani, Don. [Internet website] *Don Troiani-The Collection*, (Accessed February 23, 2003), http://www.dontroiana.com/collectionducansword.htl., 1862.

Van Horne, Thomas B. *History of the Army of the Cumberland, Its Organization, Campaigns, and Battles*, 2 vols., 1875; rep., Wilmington, NC: Broadfoot Publishing Co., 1988.

Villard, Henry. *Memoirs of Henry Villard, Journalist and Financier, 1835-1900*. 2 vols. New York: Houghton, Mifflin and Company, 1904.

Wallace, Lew. *An Autobiography Illustrated*, 2 vols. New York: Harper & Brothers Publishers, 1906.

Walton, Clyde C. *Illinois and the Civil War*. Springfield, Illinois, 1961.

Warner, Ezera J. *Generals in Blue: Lives of the Union Commanders*. Baton Rouge, LA: Louisiana State University Press, 1992.

Wells, E. T. "The Campaign and Battle of Chickamauga," *United Service*. September 1896.

Williams, J. Fletcher. *History of Hennepin County and the City of Minneapolis*. Minneapolis: North Star Publishing Co., 1881.

Youlin. [Internet website] *Family History—Post, Master, and Youlin Ancestors*,

INDEX

Boomer, Aaron M., 355, 364

Boomer, Solon S, 417-18

Booth, Martin, 168

Bramble, Hamilton G., 200

Bresee, Henman, 54

Bristol, IL, 23-24, 41, 144, 195, 464

Britton, Tom, 195

Brooklyn, IL, 302

Browning, John, 53, 236, 242, 471

Buckley, Joseph, 24-25, 30-32, 36-41, 46-47, 53-55, 60, 62, 76, 78, 110-12, 122-23, 125-26, 138, 140, 142-45, 151-52, 156-58, 161-62, 168, 174-76, 185, 192, 195, 209-10, 214-15, 221- 226-29, 246, 250-51, 253, 262-64, 266-68, 271-72, 299-304, 309-11, 315-16, 321, 324-25, 331-40, 355-57, 359-60, 365-66, 369-73, 381-82 384, 386, 390-92, 397, 471

Buckman, Albion, 407

Buffham, John, 195, 417-18

Bunce, J.A., 13

Burneson, Nelson, 138, 150, 281

Cahill, Edward, 208

Camp Douglas, 17-19, 24, 30, 32, 38, 76, 92, 180, 183, 225, 269, 462, 464

Camp E.H. Williams, 23-24, 29, 32-33, 38, 46-47

Camp Fuller, 90

Camp Holt, 52

Camp Manchester, 47, 52

Camp Point, IL, 53

Capron, Charles, 209, 270, 286-88, 292, 309, 316, 318, 321, 323, 326, 372, 334, 338-39, 342-46, 366-67, 379, 381, 395-96, 390, 395, 397-400, 403, 405-06, 411-12, 416, 418, 433-40, 444-45, 447-48, 423-25, 450-51, 453, 455-56, 458

Chambers, Joel R., 168, 341-44, 356, 361, 367-74, 376-78, 382-83, 386-87, 390-94, 398-400, 403-07, 409-12, 416-18, 422-30, 432-35, 438-40, 442-48, 450-53, 455, 462, 472

Chase, William B., 343

Chicago & Milwaukee Railroad, 3, 8, 13, 29, 41, 100-01, 108, 138, 151, 199, 206, 252, 302, 328, 349

Chicago & North-Western Railroad, 10, 13, 149, 464

Chicago & Rock Island Railroad, 10, 24, 36

Chicago, Alton & St. Louis Railroad, 10, 13

Chicago, Burlington & Quincy Railroad, 8, 10-12, 18, 36, 150, 180-81, 220, 224, 281, 307, 347, 420

Chittenden, Isaac T., 388

Christopher, John, 15, 26-29, 38, 48, 50-51, 88, 100, 177-79, 203

Codding, Jasper, 283

Coleman, Josiah, 195, 365